PRODUCERS, CONSUMERS, AND PARTIAL EQUILIBRIUM

PRODUCERS, CONSUMERS, AND PARTIAL EQUILIBRIUM

DAVID M. MANDY
Department of Economics,
University of Missouri,
Columbia, Missouri

ELSEVIER

AMSTERDAM • BOSTON • HEIDELBERG • LONDON
NEW YORK • OXFORD • PARIS • SAN DIEGO
SAN FRANCISCO • SINGAPORE • SYDNEY • TOKYO
Academic Press is an imprint of Elsevier

Academic Press is an imprint of Elsevier
125 London Wall, London EC2Y 5AS, United Kingdom
525 B Street, Suite 1800, San Diego, CA 92101-4495, United States
50 Hampshire Street, 5th Floor, Cambridge, MA 02139, United States
The Boulevard, Langford Lane, Kidlington, Oxford OX5 1GB, United Kingdom

Library of Congress Cataloging-in-Publication Data
A catalog record for this book is available from the Library of Congress

British Library Cataloguing-in-Publication Data
A catalogue record for this book is available from the British Library

ISBN: 978-0-12-811023-2

For information on all Academic Press publications
visit our website at https://www.elsevier.com/

Publisher: Nikki Levy
Acquisition Editor: J. Scott Bentley
Editorial Project Manager: Susan Ikeda
Production Project Manager: Lisa Jones
Cover Designer: Mark Rogers

Typeset by SPi Global, India

CONTENTS

PREFACE

This book presents a first-semester Ph.D. course in microeconomic theory I have taught at the University of Missouri for over twenty years. The book covers the neoclassical theories of producer and consumer price-taking behavior, partial equilibrium among those economic actors, some standard theories of partial equilibrium when producers depart from price-taking behavior, and a selection of mathematics directly relevant to those theories. The book is tightly focused on these topics and pursues depth. It can serve as a main text or supplement for a first semester of microeconomics in most Ph.D. curricula, and more generally as a reference for the covered topics, but a more encyclopedic text is needed for the remainder of the curriculum. I use both Varian [1] and Mas-Colell et al. [2] for breadth and have provided a concordance with those texts.

Two distinguishing features are a decidedly positive approach and formal completeness. Each economic actor is *defined* by an optimization objective and constraint. The book is concerned exclusively with relationships between each behavioral postulate and its predictions; hence the properties of optima are the main methodological tools. Doubts about the positive approach are not addressed herein. Skeptics are referred to Pareto's [3, p. 8] account of the role for economic theory and Friedman's [4] famous defense of positive economics.

Pursuit of Friedman's "simplicity" and "fruitfulness" (less initial knowledge, greater precision, and wider applicability) requires that each economic actor be defined as parsimoniously as possible. The weakest workable assumptions are imposed on each objective and constraint, with particular attention to avoiding redundancy. Assumptions are then added as needed to pursue more restricted results. For example, differentiability is not important for many of the refutable hypotheses, so it is not assumed except when needed. Similarly, uniqueness (or even existence) of extrema is not assumed except when important for a prediction.

This parsimony requires more maturity with mathematics than is needed for calculus characterizations of extrema. The book assumes familiarity with advanced calculus and basic knowledge of matrix algebra. However, in the interest of formal completeness, the book begins with a unified and complete reference for the mathematics directly used to study optimization in the economic theories covered, especially results that are scattered and somewhat inaccessible. Part 1 of the book provides this coverage and introduces notation. Except for two relatively difficult theorems on duality of Marshallian demand and the theorem on existence of a Nash Equilibrium, everything in the book is fully proven.

Each optimization behavioral postulate has two outcomes. First is the set of points at which the optimum is attained. Second is the optimized value of the objective. The particular values of these outcomes are usually of little interest for the theory. Interest centers instead on the implications of the optimizing behavior. Both the optimizing choices and optimized value vary with the optimization environment. The refutable hypotheses of the theory are the properties of these relationships between environment and observable outcomes.

Two particularly important tools in deriving these relationships are Samuelson's [5, Chapters 2 and 3] Envelope Theorem, and the duality of particular collections of refutable hypotheses most closely associated with McFadden [6, especially pp. 66–76, 81], Shephard [7], and Uzawa [8]. The Envelope Theorem is presented in an unusually general form based on the concept of an "active" constraint that is an extensive generator of properties between an optimization environment and the optimization outcomes. Duality establishes that these properties are often sufficient as well as necessary for the optimum. The parsimony of assumptions enables more integrated formal duality analysis than is usually encountered.

I am grateful to generations of graduate students at the University of Missouri who endured multiple incomplete drafts of this book over many years and helped identify both outright errors and unclear writing. The errors spotted post-publication for this edition, will be posted here: http://store.elsevier.com/978012811023. The University of Missouri provided a hospitable research environment during those years and generously funded a leave that proved critical to completion of the manuscript. A debt of gratitude is also due to the University of Florida for magnanimously hosting the leave during this final stage. Special thanks are due to Jonathan Hamilton, David E. M. Sappington, and Steven Slutsky for fruitful discussions and serving as generous hosts, and to economics department chair Roger D. Blair for helping arrange the visit.

David M. Mandy
Gainesville, Florida
April, 2016

REFERENCES

[1] Varian HR. Microeconomic analysis. 3rd ed. New York: Norton; 1992.
[2] Mas-Colell A, Whintson MD, Green JR. Microeconomic theory. New York: Oxford University Press; 1995.
[3] Pareto V. Manuale d'economia politica (Manual of political economy) [Schwier AS, Trans.]. New York: Kelley; 1971 [First ed. 1905].
[4] Friedman M. The methodology of positive economics. In: Essays in positive economics. Chicago: University of Chicago Press; 1953. p. 3–43.
[5] Samuelson PA. Foundations of economic analysis. Cambridge, MA: Harvard University Press; 1947.
[6] McFadden D. Cost, revenue and profit functions. In: Fuss M, McFadden D, editors. Production economics: a dual approach to theory and applications I. Amsterdam: North-Holland; 1978. p. 3–109.
[7] Shephard RW. Cost and production functions. Princeton, NJ: Princeton University Press; 1953.
[8] Uzawa H. Duality principles in the theory of cost and production. Int Econ Rev 1964;5:216–20.

Part 1

Optimization

Part 1 provides comprehensive coverage of the mathematics directly used to study optimization in the economic theories of Parts 2–4. The goal is to provide a unified and complete reference for this branch of the mathematics, with particular attention to assembling somewhat inaccessible proofs in a standardized notation and style. Notation used throughout the text is also introduced in Part 1.

The implications of constrained optimizing behavior are the behaviors of parameterized optima as the parameter changes. Hence the effect of parameter variation on the optimization problem is central. The concept of an inactive constraint is an organizing principle introduced in Chapter 1. A constraint is *inactive* if a local change in the parameter does not affect feasibility of an optimal choice. In this circumstance there is a full envelope relationship over the parameter space between the optimal value function and the underlying objective functions. This envelope relationship describes many of the consequences of the behavioral postulate and is a rich source of refutable hypotheses in the neoclassical economic theories of producer and consumer choice. Standard necessary calculus conditions are another source of implications. Continuity and homogeneity imply further properties of optima.

Chapter 2 reconsiders these properties when the constraint is active and binding. The standard calculus conditions become stationarity of a Lagrangian function and semidefiniteness properties of its Hessian. It is no longer assured that a full envelope relationship exists, but the tangency part of that relationship is preserved. These properties provide the input to investigating how optimal choices vary with the parameter using classical comparative statics.

Chapter 3 establishes many properties of convex functions. It is not explicitly about optimization but convexity plays an important role in optimization environments and leads to many properties of optima in economic theory.

CHAPTER 1

Properties of a Maximum

Chapter Outline

This chapter develops general properties of an optimal choice correspondence and an optimal value function, both considered in terms of their dependence on a parameter. The following notation is used throughout:

- $X \subset \mathbb{R}^n$ is a nonempty space of *choice variables* (e.g., consumption quantities, production plans).
- $\Theta \subset \mathbb{R}^k$ is a nonempty space of *parameters* (e.g., prices, income).
- $f : X \times \Theta \to \mathbb{R}^1$ is the decision-maker's *objective* (e.g., utility, profit).
- $\Gamma : \Theta \to 2^X$ is the decision-maker's *constraint correspondence* that defines the values of x available to the decision-maker for each $\theta \in \Theta$ (2^X denotes the *power set* of X, the set of all subsets of X; as we are interested in meaningful optimization problems we shall generally assume without comment that $\Gamma(\theta)$ is nonempty for every $\theta \in \Theta$).
- $f^* : \theta \to \overline{\mathbb{R}}$ is the *optimal value function* (e.g., indirect utility, cost, or profit), formally defined as $f^*(\theta) = \sup\{f(x;\theta) : x \in \Gamma(\theta)\}$ ($\overline{\mathbb{R}}$ denotes the extended real numbers; $\overline{\mathbb{R}} = \mathbb{R}^1 \cup \{-\infty, +\infty\}$).
- $x^* : \Theta \to 2^X$ is the *optimal choice correspondence* (e.g., demands, supplies), formally defined as $x^*(\theta) = \{x \in \Gamma(\theta) : f(x;\theta) = f^*(\theta)\}$ (possibly empty).

A circumflex is used for convenience throughout the text to denote an arbitrary element of a correspondence when describing a property that applies to all elements. For example, $\hat{\Gamma}(\theta) \in \Gamma(\theta)$ denotes an arbitrary feasible value of x when the parameter is θ, and $\hat{x}(\theta) \in x^*(\theta)$ denotes an arbitrary optimal choice of x when the parameter is θ.

The behaviors of the set $x^*(\theta)$ and the function $f^*(\theta)$ as θ changes are the consequences of the behavioral postulate that a decision-making unit chooses x to maximize f within the limitations imposed by Γ. These properties are the refutable hypotheses of the positive theory. In the neoclassical theory of producer or consumer choice these are responses of quantities demanded or supplied; or profit, cost or utility levels; to changes in prices or endowments. Characterizing x^* and f^* is similar to, but a bit different from, solving a maximization problem. Often extreme value problems are solved using conditions that first derivatives equal zero and second derivatives take on particular signs. However, it is taken as a *maintained hypothesis* that the decision-making unit chooses x to maximize f. We want to know: *Given* that x is chosen to maximize, what properties are possessed by the chosen value(s) of x and the resulting optimized value of f? Solving the optimization problem is not the main concern, as the decision-making unit will solve that problem, by assumption. The concern, rather, is the *consequences* of that optimizing behavior.

1.1 CONTINUITY

Continuity is a basic attribute of how an optimum responds to changes in the parameters of the optimization problem. Consideration of continuity requires that we first define upper and lower semicontinuity of functions, and analogous continuity concepts applicable to correspondences.

Definition 1.1. Assume $S \subset \mathbb{R}^n$, $\phi : S \rightarrow \mathbb{R}^1$, and $x^0 \in S$.

1. ϕ is *upper semicontinuous* at x^0 if, for every sequence $x^i \in S$ and for every $\delta > 0$:

$$x^i \rightarrow x^0 \text{ implies } \phi(x^i) < \phi(x^0) + \delta \text{ for } i \text{ sufficiently large.}$$

2. ϕ is *lower semicontinuous* at x^0 if, for every sequence $x^i \in S$ and for every $\delta > 0$:

$$x^i \rightarrow x^0 \text{ implies } \phi(x^i) > \phi(x^0) - \delta \text{ for } i \text{ sufficiently large.}$$

3. ϕ is *continuous* at x^0 if ϕ is both upper and lower semicontinuous at x^0.

4. ϕ is upper semicontinuous, lower semicontinuous, or continuous *on* S if ϕ is upper semicontinuous, lower semicontinuous, or continuous at every $x \in S$, respectively.

Fig. 1.1 illustrates these concepts.

A useful property of semicontinuous functions is that an envelope of any collection of semicontinuous functions is itself semicontinuous.

Theorem 1.1. *Assume* $S \subset \mathbb{R}^n$ *and* G *is a set of functions from* S *to* $\mathbb{R}^1$. *Let* $\underline{\phi} : S \to \bar{\mathbb{R}}$ *be defined by* $\underline{\phi}(x) = \inf\{\phi(x) : \phi \in G\}$. *If every* $\phi \in G$ *is upper semicontinuous at* $x^0 \in S$ *and* $\underline{\phi}(x^0)$ *is finite then* $\underline{\phi}$ *is upper semicontinuous at* x^0.

Proof. Fix $\delta > 0$ and consider any sequence x^i in S that converges to x^0. By definition of the (finite) infimum, there exists $\phi \in G$ such that:

$$\phi(x^0) < \underline{\phi}(x^0) + \frac{\delta}{2}.$$

Using upper semicontinuity of ϕ, there exists a positive integer I (depending on ϕ) such that:

$$\phi(x^i) < \phi(x^0) + \frac{\delta}{2} \text{ for } i > I.$$

Hence:

$$\phi(x^i) < \underline{\phi}(x^0) + \delta \text{ for } i > I.$$

$\underline{\phi}(x^i) \leq \phi(x^i)$ by definition of the infimum, so:

$$\underline{\phi}(x^i) < \underline{\phi}(x^0) + \delta \text{ for } i > I.$$ □

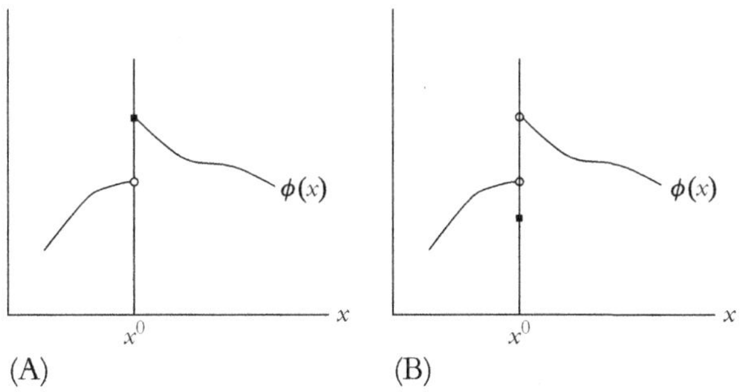

Fig. 1.1 Semicontinuous functions. In panel (A), ϕ is upper but not lower semicontinuous at x^0. In panel (B), ϕ is lower but not upper semicontinuous at x^0.

Note that an analogous result holds for any collection of functions that are lower semicontinuous at a point: The supremum of such a collection is lower semicontinuous at that point.

When postulating maximizing behavior, care must be exercised to think about whether a maximum exists (x^* nonempty) because, if not, then any properties established for the maximizing choice are vacuous. The following theorem establishes the standard sufficient conditions for existence of a maximum.

Theorem 1.2 (Existence of a Maximum). *Fix $\theta \in \Theta$. If $\Gamma(\theta)$ is nonempty, closed and bounded; and $f(x;\theta)$ is an upper semicontinuous function of x on $\Gamma(\theta)$; then $x^*(\theta)$ is nonempty.*

Proof. As $\Gamma(\theta)$ is nonempty, by definition of the supremum there exists a sequence $x^i \in \Gamma(\theta)$ such that $\lim_{i\to\infty} f(x^i;\theta) = f^*(\theta)$ (even when a supremum is infinite). As $\Gamma(\theta)$ is bounded, x^i has a convergent subsequence $x^{m_i} \to x^0$ [1, p. 205]. $x^0 \in \Gamma(\theta)$ because $\Gamma(\theta)$ is closed. Fix $\delta > 0$ and use upper semicontinuity of f at x^0 to obtain $f(x^{m_i};\theta) < f(x^0;\theta) + \delta$ for i large. Letting $i \to \infty$ therefore yields $f^*(\theta) \le f(x^0;\theta) + \delta$. As this holds for every $\delta > 0$, letting $\delta \downarrow 0$ yields $f^*(\theta) \le f(x^0;\theta)$. The opposite inequality holds by definition of the supremum, whence $f^*(\theta) = f(x^0;\theta)$. □

Note that this result implies $f^*(\theta)$ is finite. None of the conditions stated in the theorem are necessary except that the feasible set be nonempty (see Exercise 3). Concern also sometimes arises with whether a maximum is unique (x^* a singleton). The convexity concepts presented in Chapter 3 are needed to study uniqueness. Sufficient conditions for uniqueness are that f is a strictly concave function of x and Γ is a convex set (see Exercise 3.7 of Chapter 3).

Fig. 1.2 illustrates continuity concepts for correspondences.

Definition 1.2. Assume $S \subset \mathbb{R}^k$, $T \subset \mathbb{R}^n$, $\Phi : S \to 2^T$, and $x^0 \in S$.

1. Φ is *upper hemicontinuous* at x^0 if, for every pair of sequences $x^i \in S$ and $y^i \in T$:

$$x^i \to x^0, y^i \to y^0 \in T \text{ and } y^i \in \Phi(x^i) \text{ implies } y^0 \in \Phi(x^0).$$

2. Φ is *lower hemicontinuous* at x^0 if, for every sequence $x^i \in S$:

$$x^i \to x^0 \text{ and } y^0 \in \Phi(x^0) \text{ implies existence of a sequence}$$

$$y^i \in T \text{ such that } y^i \in \Phi(x^i) \text{ and } y^i \to y^0.$$

3. Φ is *continuous* at x^0 if Φ is both upper and lower hemicontinuous at x^0.

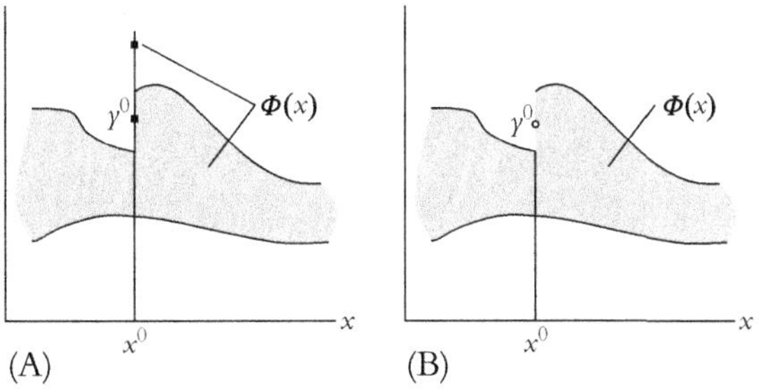

Fig. 1.2 Hemicontinuous correspondences. In panel (A), Φ is upper hemicontinuous at x^0 because any convergent sequence in the shaded area (i.e., in the graph of Φ) converges to a point in the shaded area (Φ includes the vertical boundary). But Φ is not lower hemicontinuous at x^0 because, for a sequence x^i converging to x^0 from the left, there is no corresponding sequence y^i in the shaded area such that y^i converges to y^0. In panel (B), the vertical boundary is omitted from Φ, and Φ is lower hemicontinuous at x^0 because y^0 is not in $\Phi(x^0)$. But Φ is not upper hemicontinuous at x^0 because there are sequences in the shaded area that converge to (x^0, y^0), which is not in the shaded area.

4. Φ is upper hemicontinuous, lower hemicontinuous, or continuous *on* S if Φ is upper hemicontinuous, lower hemicontinuous, or continuous at every $x \in S$, respectively.[1]

The following three results culminate in the Maximum Theorem, which gives sufficient conditions for an optimum to respond continuously to changes in the parameter.

Theorem 1.3. *Assume:*

1. *Γ is upper hemicontinuous at $\theta^0 \in \Theta$.*
2. *$\Gamma(\theta)$ is nonempty and uniformly bounded on an open ball $B_\epsilon(\theta^0) \cap \Theta$ for some $\epsilon > 0$.*
3. *f is upper semicontinuous at $(x; \theta^0)$ for every $x \in \Gamma(\theta^0)$.*

Then f^* is upper semicontinuous at θ^0.

Proof. Consider $x^i \in \Gamma(\theta^0)$ such that $x^i \to x^0$. Setting $\theta^i = \theta^0$ for every i and using upper hemicontinuity of Γ at θ^0 yields $x^0 \in \Gamma(\theta^0)$. That is, $\Gamma(\theta^0)$ is closed. This set is also bounded and nonempty, and $f(x; \theta^0)$ is upper semicontinuous on $\Gamma(\theta^0)$. Hence $f^*(\theta^0)$ is finite by Theorem 1.2.

[1] Extant definitions of continuity for correspondences on a set differ depending on whether they are based on a topology or a metric, whether they are local or global, and whether auxiliary properties such as boundedness or compactness are included in the definitions. The definitions here are restrictive in that they are stated for Euclidean spaces but omit all auxiliary properties, thereby allowing auxiliary properties to be imposed only as needed.

Now suppose f^* is not upper semicontinuous at θ^0. Then there exists $\delta > 0$ and $\theta^i \in B_{\epsilon/i}(\theta^0) \cap \theta$ such that:

$$f^*(\theta^i) \geq f^*(\theta^0) + \delta \text{ for } i = 1, 2, \ldots$$

If $f^*(\theta^i) = \infty$ then there exists $x^i \in \Gamma(\theta^i)$ such that $f(x^i; \theta^i) > f^*(\theta^0) + \frac{\delta}{2}$. If $f^*(\theta^i)$ is finite (it cannot be $-\infty$ because $\Gamma(\theta^i)$ is nonempty), there exists $x^i \in \Gamma(\theta^i)$ such that:

$$f(x^i; \theta^i) > f^*(\theta^i) - \frac{\delta}{2} \text{ for } i = 1, 2, \ldots$$

As $\Gamma(\theta^i)$ is uniformly bounded for $i = 1, 2, \ldots$, there is a convergent subsequence $x^{m_i} \to x^0$ [1, p. 205]. By upper hemicontinuity of Γ at θ^0, $x^0 \in \Gamma(\theta^0)$. Hence:

$$f(x^{m_i}; \theta^{m_i}) > f^*(\theta^{m_i}) - \frac{\delta}{2} \geq f^*(\theta^0) + \frac{\delta}{2} \geq f(x^0; \theta^0) + \frac{\delta}{2} \text{ for } i = 1, 2, \ldots$$

Thus:

$$f(x^{m_i}; \theta^{m_i}) > f(x^0; \theta^0) + \frac{\delta}{2} \text{ for } i = 1, 2, \ldots$$

irrespective of whether $f^*(\theta^{m_i})$ is finite. As $(x^{m_i}; \theta^{m_i}) \to (x^0, \theta^0)$, this violates upper semicontinuity of f at $(x^0; \theta^0)$. □

Theorem 1.4. *Assume:*

1. *Γ is lower hemicontinuous at $\theta^0 \in \theta$.*
2. *f is lower semicontinuous at $(x; \theta^0)$ for every $x \in \Gamma(\theta^0)$.*
3. *$f^*(\theta^0)$ is finite.*[2]

Then f^* is lower semicontinuous at θ^0.

Proof. Fix $\delta > 0$ and consider any sequence $\theta^i \in B_\epsilon(\theta^0) \cap \Theta$ that converges to θ^0. By definition of the (finite) supremum, there exists $x^0 \in \Gamma(\theta^0)$ such that:

$$f(x^0; \theta^0) > f^*(\theta^0) - \frac{\delta}{2}.$$

By lower hemicontinuity of Γ at θ^0, there exists $x^i \in \Gamma(\theta^i)$ such that $x^i \to x^0$. By lower semicontinuity of f at $(x^0; \theta^0)$, we have:

$$f(x^i; \theta^i) > f(x^0; \theta^0) - \frac{\delta}{2} \text{ for } i \text{ large.}$$

[2] $\Gamma(\theta^0)$ nonempty and f bounded above on $\Gamma(\theta^0) \times \{\theta^0\}$ are necessary and sufficient.

By definition of the supremum, $f^*(\theta^i) \geq f(x^i;\theta^i)$. Hence:

$$f^*(\theta^i) > f^*(\theta^0) - \delta \text{ for } i \text{ large.} \qquad \square$$

Theorem 1.5 (Maximum Theorem). *Assume:*

1. Γ *is continuous at* $\theta^0 \in \Theta$.
2. $\Gamma(\theta)$ *is nonempty and uniformly bounded on an open ball* $B_\epsilon(\theta^0) \cap \Theta$ *for some* $\epsilon > 0$.
3. f *is continuous at* $(x;\theta^0)$ *for every* $x \in \Gamma(\theta^0)$.

Then f^* *is continuous at* θ^0 *and* x^* *is upper hemicontinuous at* θ^0.

Proof. Continuity of f^* at θ^0 follows immediately from Theorems 1.3 and 1.4 (using the argument in Theorem 1.3 to establish that $f^*(\theta^0)$ is finite).

Consider any sequence $\theta^i \in B_\epsilon(\theta^0) \cap \theta$ that converges to θ^0 and a corresponding sequence $x^i \in x^*(\theta^i)$ that converges to some $x^0 \in \mathbb{R}^n$ (if any). Suppose x^* is not upper hemicontinuous at θ^0. That is, suppose $x^0 \notin x^*(\theta^0)$. As Γ is upper hemicontinuous at θ^0 and $x^*(\theta^i) \subset \Gamma(\theta^i)$, we have $x^0 \in \Gamma(\theta^0)$. Hence:

$$\delta = f^*(\theta^0) - f(x^0;\theta^0)$$

is strictly positive. As f^* is lower semicontinuous at θ^0:

$$f^*(\theta^0) < f^*(\theta^i) + \frac{\delta}{2} \text{ for } i \text{ large.}$$

That is, for i large:

$$f^*(\theta^0) + \frac{\delta}{2} < f^*(\theta^i) + [f^*(\theta^0) - f(x^0;\theta^0)]$$

$$f(x^0;\theta^0) + \frac{\delta}{2} < f^*(\theta^i).$$

As $x^i \in x^*(\theta^i)$, $f(x^i;\theta^i) = f^*(\theta^i)$. Hence:

$$f(x^0;\theta^0) + \frac{\delta}{2} < f(x^i;\theta^i) \text{ for } i \text{ large.}$$

This contradicts upper semicontinuity of f at $(x^0;\theta^0)$. $\square$

1.2 GRAPHS AND CONTINUITY

Associated with any correspondence $\Phi : S \rightarrow 2^T$ is the set of domain/range pairs that lie in the correspondence. This set is called the *graph* of Φ:

$$\text{gr}_\Phi = \{(x, y) : x \in S \text{ and } y \in \Phi(x)\}.$$

The shaded areas in Fig. 1.2 are the graphs of the illustrated correspondences. When a correspondence is singleton-valued (i.e., a function), the graph is the set of pairs in the domain/range space taken on by the function. As suggested by Fig. 1.2A, when the domain and range are subsets of Euclidean spaces upper hemicontinuity is equivalent to the graph being closed.

Theorem 1.6. *Assume $S \subset \mathbb{R}^k$, $T \subset \mathbb{R}^n$, and $\Phi : S \to 2^T$. Then Φ is upper hemicontinuous on S if and only if gr_Φ is closed (in $\mathbb{R}^{n+k}$).*

Proof. Consider a sequence $(x^i, y^i) \in S \times T$ that converges to $(x^0, y^0) \in S \times T$. Assume Φ is upper hemicontinuous. If $(x^i, y^i) \in \text{gr}_\Phi$ then $y^i \in \Phi(x^i)$, so $y^0 \in \Phi(x^0)$ by upper hemicontinuity. That is, $(x^0, y^0) \in \text{gr}_\Phi$, so gr_Φ is closed. Conversely, assume gr_Φ is closed. If $y^i \in \Phi(x^i)$ then $(x^i, y^i) \in \text{gr}_\Phi$, so $(x^0, y^0) \in \text{gr}_\Phi$ because gr_Φ is closed. That is, $y^0 \in \Phi(x^0)$, so Φ is upper hemicontinuous. □

When a function is real-valued there are two additional sets associated with the function that are sometimes useful in economic models. These are the *epigraph* of the function, consisting of the pairs in the domain/range space that lie on or above the function, and the *hypograph* of the function, consisting of the pairs in the domain/range space that lie on or below the function.

Definition 1.3. Assume $S \subset \mathbb{R}^k$ and $\phi : S \to \mathbb{R}^1$. The epigraph and hypograph of ϕ are, respectively:

$$\text{epi}_\phi = \{(x, y) \in S \times \mathbb{R}^1 : \phi(x) \leq y\}$$
$$\text{hyp}_\phi = \{(x, y) \in S \times \mathbb{R}^1 : \phi(x) \geq y\}.$$

Fig. 1.3 illustrates these concepts for the function in Fig. 1.1A. As suggested by the figure, upper (lower) semicontinuity of a function is equivalent to its hypograph (epigraph) being closed.

Theorem 1.7. *Assume $S \subset \mathbb{R}^n$ and $\phi : S \to \mathbb{R}^1$. ϕ is upper (lower) semicontinuous on S if and only if hyp_ϕ (epi_ϕ) is closed (in $\mathbb{R}^{n+1}$).*

Proof. Fix $x^0 \in S$ and assume first that ϕ is upper semicontinuous at x^0. Consider any $\delta > 0$ and any sequence $(x^i, y^i) \to (x^0, y^0)$ with $(x^i, y^i) \in \text{hyp}_\phi$. By upper semicontinuity:

$$\phi(x^i) < \phi(x^0) + \delta \text{ for } i \text{ large}.$$

And $y^i \leq \phi(x^i)$, so:

$$y^i < \phi(x^0) + \delta \text{ for } i \text{ large}.$$

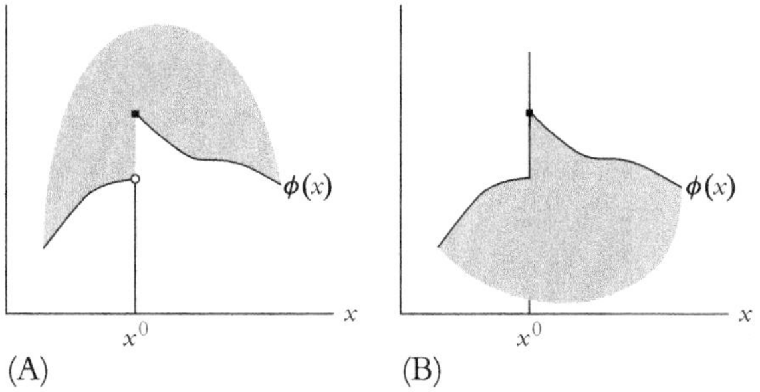

Fig. 1.3 Epigraph and hypograph. The shaded area in panel (A) is the epigraph of ϕ; the shaded area in panel (B) is the hypograph of ϕ. Note that the vertical boundary is part of the hypograph but not part of the epigraph.

Let $i \to \infty$ to obtain $y^0 \le \phi(x^0) + \delta$. Then let $\delta \downarrow 0$ to obtain $y^0 \le \phi(x^0)$. That is, $(x^0, y^0) \in \text{hyp}_\phi(y^0)$, so hyp_ϕ is closed.

Conversely, assume hyp_ϕ is closed. If ϕ is not upper semicontinuous at x^0 then there exists a sequence $x^i \to x^0$ in S and a $\delta > 0$ with the property: to each i there corresponds $k_i \ge i$ such that $\phi(x^{k_i}) \ge \phi(x^0) + \delta$. Therefore $(x^{k_i}, \phi(x^0) + \delta) \in \text{hyp}_\phi$ for every i. x^{k_i} is a subsequence of x^i, and therefore converges to x^0. hyp_ϕ closed therefore yields $(x^0, \phi(x^0) + \delta) \in \text{hyp}_\phi$. But this means $\phi(x^0) \ge \phi(x^0) + \delta$, a contradiction.

It is straightforward to mimic this proof to show that ϕ is lower semicontinuous if and only if epi_ϕ is closed. □

If y is fixed and a "slice" of the epigraph is taken consisting of the x-values for that fixed y, the result is the *lower contour set* of the function at y:

$$L_\phi(y) = \{x \in S : \phi(x) \le y\}.$$

Similarly, a "slice" of the hypograph for fixed y is called the *upper contour set* of ϕ at y:

$$V_\phi(y) = \{x \in S : \phi(x) \ge y\}.$$

The lower (upper) contour set at y is empty if ϕ is everywhere above (below) y; and is the entire domain S if ϕ is everywhere below (above) or equal to y. Varying y in these definitions yields correspondences that relate a value in the range of the function to the set of domain points at which the function is either below or above that value, respectively. We might aptly call these the *lower and upper contour correspondences* of the function, respectively. Their domain is $\mathbb{R}^1$ and their range is 2^S. It is plain from the definitions that the graph of V_ϕ is the hypograph of ϕ and the graph of L_ϕ is the epigraph of ϕ. Combining Theorems 1.6 and 1.7 therefore yields relationships between semicontinuity of a function and hemicontinuity of its contour correspondences.

Theorem 1.8. *Assume $S \subset \mathbb{R}^n$ and $\phi : S \to \mathbb{R}^1$. ϕ is upper (lower) semicontinuous on S if and only if V_ϕ (L_ϕ) is upper hemicontinuous on $\mathbb{R}^1$.*

If a correspondence with domain and range that are subsets of Euclidean spaces is singleton-valued then there are relationships between hemicontinuity of the correspondence and continuity of the implied function.

Theorem 1.9. *Assume $S \subset \mathbb{R}^k$, $T \subset \mathbb{R}^n$, and $\Phi : S \to 2^T$ is singleton-valued on S. Denote the unique value at $x \in S$ by $\phi(x)$ (i.e., $\Phi(x) = \{\phi(x)\}$). Let $x^0 \in S$.*

1. *If Φ is upper hemicontinuous at x^0 and uniformly bounded in a neighborhood of x^0 then ϕ is continuous at x^0.*
2. *If Φ is lower hemicontinuous at x^0 then ϕ is continuous at x^0.*
3. *If ϕ is continuous at x^0 then Φ is both upper and lower hemicontinuous at x^0.*

   Proof. Let x^i be an arbitrary sequence in S that converges to x^0.

1. Using boundedness, $\underline{y} = \liminf \phi(x^i)$ and $\bar{y} = \limsup \phi(x^i)$ are both finite. By definition of these limits, there exist subsequences x^{k_i} and x^{ℓ_i} such that $\phi(x^{k_i}) \to \underline{y}$ and $\phi(x^{\ell_i}) \to \bar{y}$. Hence $(x^{k_i}, \phi(x^{k_i})) \to (x^0, \underline{y})$ and $(x^{\ell_i}, \phi(x^{\ell_i})) \to (x^0, \bar{y})$. Both of these sequences are contained in gr_ϕ and, by Theorem 1.6, upper hemicontinuity implies gr_ϕ is closed. Hence $(x^0, \underline{y})$ and $(x^0, \bar{y})$ are both elements of gr_Φ. That is, $\underline{y} \in \Phi(x^0)$ and $\bar{y} \in \Phi(x^0)$. As $\phi(x^0)$ is the only element of $\Phi(x^0)$, we have $\underline{y} = \bar{y} = \phi(x^0)$. Hence $\phi(x^i) \to \phi(x^0)$.
2. $\phi(x^0) \in \Phi(x^0)$, so by lower hemicontinuity of Φ there exists $y^i \in \Phi(x^i)$ such that $y^i \to \phi(x^0)$. As $\phi(x^i)$ is the only element of $\Phi(x^i)$, $y^i = \phi(x^i)$. Therefore $\phi(x^i) \to \phi(x^0)$.
3. First consider lower hemicontinuity of Φ by selecting $y^0 \in \Phi(x^0)$. As $\phi(x^0)$ is the only element of $\Phi(x^0)$, $y^0 = \phi(x^0)$. The sequence $y^i = \phi(x^i)$ has the required properties: $y^i \in \Phi(x^i)$ and $y^i \to y^0$. Now consider upper hemicontinuity of Φ by selecting $y^i \in \Phi(x^i)$ such that $y^i \to y^0$. As $\phi(x^i)$ is the only element of $\Phi(x^i)$, $y^i = \phi(x^i)$. Therefore $y^0 = \phi(x^0)$ by uniqueness of limits. Hence $y^0 \in \Phi(x^0)$. $\qquad\square$

1.3 DEFINITE AND SEMIDEFINITE MATRICES

Necessary and sufficient calculus conditions for a maximum involve the matrix of second derivatives of the objective. Before stating these conditions in the next section we must first establish some properties of definite and semidefinite matrices.

Definition 1.4. A real symmetric $n \times n$ matrix A is called *negative (positive) definite* when $t^{\perp}At < (>)\ 0$ for every nonzero vector $t \in \mathbb{R}^n$.[3] If the defining inequality is weak then A is called *negative (positive) semidefinite.* Semidefiniteness or definiteness of a matrix has implications for its entries. For example, choosing t in Definition 1.4 to be the unit vector in direction i reveals that negative semidefiniteness implies the ith diagonal element of the matrix is nonpositive, for $i = 1, \ldots, n$. Similarly, the diagonal elements of a positive semidefinite matrix are nonnegative, and the diagonal elements of a negative (positive) definite matrix are negative (positive).

More generally, let $J \subset \{1, \ldots, n\}$ be an index set of the rows and columns of the matrix A in Definition 1.4 ($J \neq \emptyset$), and denote by $A^{(J)}$ the submatrix of A obtained by retaining the rows and columns indicated by J and discarding all other rows and columns. $A^{(J)}$ is called a *principal* submatrix of A, meaning that it is obtained from A be discarding the *same* rows and columns. We use $\#J$ to denote the number of elements in J (number of rows and columns in $A^{(J)}$), called the *order* of the principal submatrix. The determinant $|A^{(J)}|$ is called a *principal minor* of A. The n principal minors from the particular index sets $J = \{1\}, \{1,2\}, \ldots, \{1, \ldots, n\}$ are called the "leading" principal minors and are often denoted $A_1, A_2, \ldots, A_n$ (of course, $A_n = A$).

Theorem 1.10. *Assume A is an $n \times n$ real symmetric matrix. If A is negative (semi) definite then $(-1)^{\#J}|A^{(J)}|\ (\geq) > 0$ for every $J \subset \{1, \ldots, n\}$. If A is positive (semi) definite then $|A^{(J)}|\ (\geq) > 0$ for every $J \subset \{1, \ldots, n\}$.*

Proof. We prove the result for A negative semidefinite. The other cases are proven analogously.

Because A is real and symmetric, there exists an $n \times n$ real matrix U such that $U^{\perp}U = I_n$ and $A = U^{\perp}\Lambda U$, where Λ is a diagonal matrix with the eigenvalues $\lambda_1, \ldots, \lambda_n$ of A on the diagonal [2, p. 213]. Let t be column i of $U^{\perp}$. Then Ut is the unit vector in direction i, so:

[3] $t^{\perp}$ denotes the transpose of the matrix t.

$$t^{\perp}At = t^{\perp}U^{\perp}\Lambda Ut = \lambda_i.$$

This is nonpositive because A is negative semidefinite. That is, the eigenvalues of a symmetric real negative semidefinite matrix are nonpositive. Using standard properties of determinants:

$$|A| = |U^{\perp}\Lambda U| = |UU^{\perp}\Lambda| = |\Lambda| = \lambda_1 \cdots \lambda_n.$$

Therefore $|A|$ is either zero or has sign $(-1)^n$. That is, the determinant of a symmetric real negative semidefinite matrix is either zero, or is positive (negative) if the matrix has an even (odd) number of rows and columns. This proves the result for $J = \{1, \ldots, n\}$.

Now consider an arbitrary principal submatrix $A^{(J)}$, denote by $t^{(J)}$ the vector obtained from t by retaining the rows indicated by J and discarding all others, and consider a vector t consisting of zeros except for the $t^{(J)}$ part. Then $t^{\perp}At = t^{(J)\perp}A^{(J)}t^{(J)} \leq 0$ for every nonzero t (i.e., for every nonzero $t^{(J)}$). Hence $A^{(J)}$ is negative semidefinite. That is, every principal submatrix of a negative semidefinite matrix is negative semidefinite. And $A^{(J)}$ is real and symmetric. Applying the result above about determinants of symmetric real negative semidefinite matrices to $A^{(J)}$ yields $(-1)^{\#J}$ $|A^{(J)}| \geq 0$. □

Sometimes it is useful to have a converse to Theorem 1.10. For definite matrices, only the *leading* principal minors are needed.

Theorem 1.11. *Assume A is an $n \times n$ real symmetric matrix. If $(-1)^i|A_i| > 0$ for $i = 1, \ldots, n$ then A is negative definite. If $|A_i| > 0$ for $i = 1, \ldots, n$ then A is positive definite.*

Proof. Observe first that the pivots $d_1, \ldots, d_n$ of A are nonzero. $d_1 = a_{11} = |A_1|$, which is assumed to be either negative or positive, depending on which case we are studying. d_2 is in the $(2, 2)$ position following an elementary row operation, using the first row, that converts a_{21} to zero. Performing this same row operation on A_2 converts the second row of A_2 to $(0\ d_2)$. Elementary row operations do not change the determinant; whence $d_2 \neq 0$ because $|A_2| > 0$. Continuing in this manner shows that all n pivots are nonzero. This means Gaussian elimination factors A as $A = LDU$, where L is lower unit triangular, U is upper unit triangular, and D is diagonal with the pivots $d_1, \ldots, d_n$ on the diagonal [2, pp. 21–23]. Moreover, $U = L^{\perp}$ because A is symmetric [2, p. 38], so we have $A = LDL^{\perp}$. Therefore, for any nonzero vector t:

$$t^{\perp}At = t^{\perp}L^{\perp}DLt = \tilde{t}^{\perp}D\tilde{t} = \sum_{i=1}^{n}\tilde{t}_i^{\,2}d_i.$$

Hence we must show that the pivots of A are all negative (positive) when $(-1)^i|A_i| > 0$ ($|A_i| > 0$) for $i = 1, \ldots, n$.

The signs of the pivots are obtained from the factorization as follows. Partition A as:

$$A = \begin{bmatrix} A_i & \mathcal{B} \\ \mathcal{B}^\perp & \mathcal{C} \end{bmatrix}$$

and partition L and D conformably:

$$L = \begin{bmatrix} L_i & 0 \\ \mathcal{D} & \mathcal{E} \end{bmatrix} \quad D = \begin{bmatrix} D_i & 0 \\ 0 & \mathcal{F} \end{bmatrix}.$$

Then $A_i = L_i D_i L_i^\perp$, so standard properties of determinants yield:

$$|A_i| = |L_i||D_i||L_i^\perp| = |D_i| = d_1 \cdots d_i.$$

Therefore:

$$\frac{|A_{i+1}|}{|A_i|} = \frac{d_1 \cdots d_{i+1}}{d_1 \cdots d_i} = d_{i+1} \text{ for } i = 1, \ldots, n-1.$$

If the principal minors are assumed to alternate in sign, this shows every pivot of A is negative; if the principal minors are assumed to all be positive, this shows every pivot of A is positive. □

Combining Theorems 1.11 and 1.10 shows that, if the *leading* principal minors of a real symmetric matrix follow one of the sign patterns for definiteness, then *all* of the principal minors follow that sign pattern.

Unfortunately, semidefiniteness cannot be determined by examining only leading principal minors. For example, the leading principal minors of:

$$\begin{bmatrix} 0 & 0 \\ 0 & -1 \end{bmatrix}$$

are both nonnegative but this matrix is not positive semidefinite. In general, *all* of the principal minors must be examined to determine whether a matrix is semidefinite. We establish this by first proving a theorem with broader applicability that relies on existence of a definite submatrix. Sufficiency of a sign pattern on all principal minors for semidefiniteness is then an easy corollary.

Theorem 1.12. *Assume A is a real symmetric matrix with a principal submatrix $\tilde{A}$ satisfying:*

1. *$\tilde{A}$ is negative (positive) definite.*

2. *No higher order principal submatrix is negative (positive) definite.*

3. *Every principal submatrix $A^{(J)}$ that includes $\widetilde{A}$ satisfies $(-1)^{\#J}|A^{(J)}| \geq 0$ ($|A^{(J)}| \geq 0$).*

Then A is negative (positive) semidefinite.

Proof. We prove the result for A positive semidefinite first.

If $\widetilde{A} = A$ then A is trivially positive semidefinite, so assume $\widetilde{A}$ excludes some rows and (the same) columns. Let P be a permutation matrix that, when symmetrically applied to A, makes $\widetilde{A}$ a leading principal submatrix:

$$PAP^{\perp} = \begin{bmatrix} \widetilde{A} & B \\ B^{\perp} & C \end{bmatrix}.$$

Consider an arbitrary column b_i from B and the corresponding diagonal element c_{ii} from C. Using $|\widetilde{A}| > 0$ from item 1 (Theorem 1.10) and the standard formula for the determinant of a partitioned matrix ([3, pp. 137–138]) yields:

$$\begin{vmatrix} \widetilde{A} & b_i \\ b_i^{\perp} & c_{ii} \end{vmatrix} = |\widetilde{A}||c_{ii} - b_i^{\perp}\widetilde{A}^{-1}b_i| \overset{s}{=} c_{ii} - b_i^{\perp}\widetilde{A}^{-1}b_i \geq 0,$$

where the inequality is item 3 ($a \overset{s}{=} b$ means a and b have the same sign). If this is positive then the submatrix under consideration is positive definite (Theorem 1.11), contradicting item 2, so $c_{ii} - b_i^{\perp}\widetilde{A}^{-1}b_i = 0$. Now consider any two columns from B and the corresponding 2×2 submatrix from C:

$$\begin{aligned}
\begin{vmatrix} \widetilde{A} & b_i & b_j \\ b_i^{\perp} & c_{ii} & c_{ij} \\ b_j^{\perp} & c_{ji} & c_{jj} \end{vmatrix} &= |\widetilde{A}| \left| \begin{bmatrix} c_{ii} & c_{ij} \\ c_{ji} & c_{jj} \end{bmatrix} - \begin{bmatrix} b_i^{\perp} \\ b_j^{\perp} \end{bmatrix} \widetilde{A}^{-1} \begin{bmatrix} b_i & b_j \end{bmatrix} \right| \\
&\overset{s}{=} \begin{vmatrix} 0 & c_{ij} - b_i^{\perp}\widetilde{A}^{-1}b_j \\ c_{ji} - b_j^{\perp}\widetilde{A}^{-1}b_i & 0 \end{vmatrix} \\
&= -(c_{ij} - b_i^{\perp}\widetilde{A}^{-1}b_j)^2 \geq 0.
\end{aligned}$$

This implies $c_{ij} - b_i^{\perp}\widetilde{A}^{-1}b_j = 0$ for every i, j (including $i = j$). Therefore $C = B^{\perp}\widetilde{A}^{-1}B$.

$\widetilde{A}$ is real, symmetric and positive definite; therefore $\widetilde{A}^{1/2}$ exists as a unique positive definite square symmetric real matrix ([2, p. 241]). Let $F = [\widetilde{A}^{1/2}\ \widetilde{A}^{-1/2}B]$ and note that:

$$F^{\perp}F = \begin{bmatrix} \widetilde{A}^{1/2} \\ B^{\perp}\widetilde{A}^{-1/2} \end{bmatrix} \begin{bmatrix} \widetilde{A}^{1/2} & \widetilde{A}^{-1/2}B \end{bmatrix} = \begin{bmatrix} \widetilde{A} & B \\ B^{\perp} & B^{\perp}\widetilde{A}^{-1}B \end{bmatrix} = \begin{bmatrix} \widetilde{A} & B \\ B^{\perp} & C \end{bmatrix}.$$

Therefore, for any $t \neq 0$:

$$t^{\perp}At = t^{\perp}P^{\perp}F^{\perp}FPt = \tilde{t}^{\perp}\tilde{t} \geq 0,$$

where $\tilde{t} = FPt$.

For the negative semidefinite case, replace $\tilde{A}$ in the above argument by $-\tilde{A}$ and A by $-A$, noting that (1) $-\tilde{A}$ is positive definite, (2) no higher order principal submatrix of $-A$ is positive definite, and (3) $|-A^{(J)}| = (-1)^{\#J}|A^{(J)}| \geq 0$ for every principal submatrix of $-A$ that includes $-\tilde{A}$. The conclusion is $-A$ is positive semidefinite, or A is negative semidefinite. □

Corollary 1.1. *Assume A is an $n \times n$ real symmetric matrix. If $(-1)^{\#J}|A^{(J)}| \geq 0$ ($|A^{(J)}| \geq 0$) for every $J \subset \{1, \ldots, n\}$ then A is negative (positive) semidefinite.*

Proof. If every diagonal element of A is zero then:

$$\begin{vmatrix} a_{ii} & a_{ij} \\ a_{ji} & a_{jj} \end{vmatrix} = -a_{ij}^2 \geq 0 \text{ for every } i, j.$$

This implies $a_{ij} = 0$ for every i, j. That is, A is a matrix of zeros, and is therefore trivially negative (positive) semidefinite. So assume there is a nonzero diagonal element. That element is a negative (positive) definite principal submatrix, so A has a highest order negative (positive) definite principal submatrix $\tilde{A}$ satisfying the assumptions of Theorem 1.12. □

Corollary 1.2. *Assume A is an $n \times n$ singular real symmetric matrix. If A has an $(n-1)^{st}$ order negative (positive) definite principal submatrix $\tilde{A}$ then A is negative (positive) semidefinite.*

Proof. The only higher order principal submatrix is A, so the only principal minor that includes $\tilde{A}$ is $|A| = 0$. Apply Theorem 1.12. □

1.4 DERIVATIVES

Consider a set $S \subset \mathbb{R}^n$ and a function $\phi : S \to \mathbb{R}^m$. If all partial derivatives of ϕ exist at $x \in S$ then the *Jacobian Matrix* of ϕ at x [4, p. 351] is denoted by:

$$\mathbf{D}\phi(x) = \begin{bmatrix} \dfrac{\partial \phi_1(x)}{\partial x_1} & \cdots & \dfrac{\partial \phi_1(x)}{\partial x_n} \\ \vdots & & \vdots \\ \dfrac{\partial \phi_m(x)}{\partial x_1} & \cdots & \dfrac{\partial \phi_m(x)}{\partial x_n} \end{bmatrix}.$$

The argument x is often omitted when it is not needed. When $m = 1$, $\mathbf{D}\phi$ is a row vector, the gradient of ϕ, sometimes denoted $\nabla\phi$. When $m = n = 1$, $\mathbf{D}\phi$ is the ordinary derivative of ϕ, sometimes denoted ϕ'. The notation $\mathbf{D}_y\phi$ is used to denote the Jacobian of ϕ with respect to a subvector y of x. Note that the statement "$\frac{\partial\phi_i(x)}{\partial x_j}$ exists" implies ϕ is defined on an interval $(x_i - \delta, x_i + \delta)$ holding the other components of x constant (i.e., such points are in S).

Assume ϕ is differentiable at x (this implies $x \in \text{int } S$). If $Q \subset \mathbb{R}^m$, $g : Q \to \mathbb{R}^q$ and g is differentiable at $\phi(x)$ then the *Chain Rule* for the composite function $h(x) = (g \circ \phi)(x)$ is that $\mathbf{D}h(x)$ exists and is the matrix product [4, Theorem 12.7; Section 12.10]:

$$\mathbf{D}h(x) = \mathbf{D}g(\phi(x))\mathbf{D}\phi(x).$$

When used in matrix equations, $\phi(x)$ is regarded as an m-dimensional column vector. Assume all partial derivatives of ϕ exist at x. If $g : S \to \mathbb{R}^m$ and all partial derivatives of g exist at x it is straightforward to verify from the one-dimensional Product Rule [4, Theorem 5.4] that the *Product Rule* for the product $\phi(x)^{\perp}g(x)$ is that $\mathbf{D}(\phi^{\perp}g)$ exists at x and is:

$$\mathbf{D}(\phi^{\perp}g) = g^{\perp}\mathbf{D}\phi + \phi^{\perp}\mathbf{D}g.$$

If $m = 1$ and all partial derivatives of all components of $\mathbf{D}\phi$ exist then the *Hessian Matrix* of ϕ at x is denoted by:

$$\mathbf{D}^2\phi(x) = \mathbf{D}(\mathbf{D}\phi)^{\perp}(x) = \begin{bmatrix} \dfrac{\partial^2\phi(x)}{\partial x_1 \partial x_1} & \cdots & \dfrac{\partial^2\phi(x)}{\partial x_1 \partial x_n} \\ \vdots & & \vdots \\ \dfrac{\partial^2\phi(x)}{\partial x_n \partial x_1} & \cdots & \dfrac{\partial^2\phi(x)}{\partial x_n \partial x_n} \end{bmatrix}.$$

The notation $\mathbf{D}_y^2\phi$ is used to denote the Hessian of ϕ with respect to a subvector y of x.

Now we turn to a useful preliminary result.

Theorem 1.13. *Assume $S \subset \mathbb{R}^1$ and $\phi : S \to \mathbb{R}^1$ is differentiable at $x^0 \in S$. If $\phi'(x^0) > 0$ then there exists $\delta > 0$ such that $\phi(x) < \phi(x^0)$ for $x \in (x^0 - \delta, x^0)$ and $\phi(x) > \phi(x^0)$ for $x \in (x^0, x^0 + \delta)$.*

Proof. Let $\epsilon = \phi'(x^0) > 0$. By definition of the derivative, there exists $\delta > 0$ such that:

$$\phi'(x^0) - \epsilon < \frac{\phi(x) - \phi(x^0)}{x - x^0} < \phi'(x^0) + \epsilon \text{ for } x \in (x^0 - \delta, x^0 + \delta) - \{x^0\}.$$

Taking only the left side, we have:

$$0 < \frac{\phi(x) - \phi(x^0)}{x - x^0} \text{ for } x \in (x^0 - \delta, x^0 + \delta) - \{x^0\}.$$

For $x \in (x^0, x^0 + \delta)$, this is $0 < \phi(x) - \phi(x^0)$; for $x \in (x^0 - \delta, x^0)$, this is $0 > \phi(x) - \phi(x^0)$. □

Note that a similar result holds when $\phi'(x^0) < 0$, with $\phi(x)$ above $\phi(x^0)$ to the left of x^0 and below $\phi(x^0)$ to the right of x^0.

When attempting to establish that a particular point is a maximum, it is common to utilize zero first derivative and negative second derivative conditions that, jointly, are *sufficient* for a maximum. The task herein is to identify consequences of a postulate that an economic actor engages in maximizing behavior, so *necessary* conditions for a maximum are of primary interest.

Theorem 1.14 (First Order Necessary Condition). *Assume $S \subset \mathbb{R}^n$ and $\phi : S \to \mathbb{R}^1$. Assume $x^0 \in S$ is a local maximum of ϕ and that $\mathbf{D}\phi(x^0)$ exists. Then $\mathbf{D}\phi(x^0) = 0$.*

Proof. Consider ϕ exclusively as a function of x_i. By Theorem 1.13, if $\frac{\partial \phi(x^0)}{\partial x_i}$ is not zero then there exists x_i in a neighborhood of x_i^0 at which ϕ exceeds $\phi(x^0)$, contradicting that x^0 maximizes $\phi(x)$. Therefore $\frac{\partial \phi(x^0)}{\partial x_i} = 0$ for $i = 1, \ldots, n$. □

The standard strictly negative second derivative condition is sufficient (given the first order necessary condition) but not necessary for a maximum. However the same condition with a weak inequality *is* necessary for a maximum. Hence a weak inequality involving second derivatives is a consequence of postulated maximizing behavior. In the multivariate setting, these inequalities are negative (semi-) definiteness of the Hessian.

Theorem 1.15 (Second Order Necessary Condition). *Assume $S \subset \mathbb{R}^n$ and $\phi : S \to \mathbb{R}^1$. Assume $x^0 \in S$ is a local maximum of ϕ. Assume ϕ is differentiable at each point of the open ball $B_\epsilon(x^0)$ and that each partial derivative of ϕ is differentiable at x^0. Then the Hessian of ϕ at x^0 is negative semidefinite.*

Proof. Assume without loss of generality that $\phi(x) \leq \phi(x^0)$ for $x \in B_\epsilon(x^0)$. Suppose $\mathbf{D}^2\phi(x^0)$ is not negative semidefinite; that is, suppose there is a column vector $t \in \mathbb{R}^n$ such that:

$$t^{\perp}\mathbf{D}^2\phi(x^0)t > 0.$$

Define $h(y)$ by $h(y) = \phi(x^0 + yt)$ for real numbers y such that $x^0 + yt \in B_\epsilon(x^0)$. As ϕ is differentiable on $B_\epsilon(x^0)$, the Chain Rule yields:

$$h'(y) = \mathbf{D}\phi(x^0 + yt)t \text{ for values of } y \text{ such that } x^0 + yt \in B_\epsilon(x^0).$$

As each partial derivative of ϕ is differentiable at x^0, the Chain Rule again yields:

$$h''(0) = t^{\perp}\mathbf{D}^2\phi(x^0)t > 0.$$

By Theorem 1.13 there exists $\delta > 0$ such that:

$$h'(y) > h'(0) \text{ for } y \in (0, \delta)$$

(assume without loss of generality that δ is sufficiently small to ensure $x^0 + \delta t \in B_\epsilon(x^0)$). As x^0 is a local maximum of a function with partial derivatives at x^0, by Theorem 1.14 $\mathbf{D}\phi(x^0) = 0$; whence $h'(0) = 0$ and:

$$h'(y) > 0 \text{ for } y \in (0, \delta).$$

By the Mean-Value Theorem [4, Theorem 5.11], there exists $y^0 \in (0, \delta)$ such that:

$$h(\delta) - h(0) = h'(y^0)\delta > 0.$$

That is, $\phi(x^0 + \delta t) > \phi(x^0)$, which contradicts that x^0 is a local maximum of ϕ on $B_\epsilon(x^0)$. □

Combining Theorems 1.15 and 1.10 yields a necessary condition for a local maximum on the principal minors of the Hessian: Those for submatrices with an odd number of rows/columns are nonpositive and those for submatrices with an even number of rows/columns are nonnegative.

1.5 HOMOGENEITY

A function $\phi(x)$ is called *homogeneous of degree k* when $\phi(\alpha x) = \alpha^k\phi(x)$ for every positive scalar α. Optimization outcomes in economic models are sometimes homogeneous. Homogeneity requires that αx be an element of the domain of the function whenever x is an element of the domain. A set with this property is called a *cone*.

Definition 1.5. $S \subset \mathbb{R}^n$ is a *cone* if $x \in S$ and $\alpha \in \mathbb{R}^1_{++}$ imply $\alpha x \in S$.

Definition 1.6. Assume $S \subset \mathbb{R}^n$ is a cone and $\phi : S \to \mathbb{R}^m$. ϕ is *homogeneous of degree* $k \in \mathbb{R}^1$ if, for every $x \in S$ and $\alpha \in \mathbb{R}^1_{++}$:

$$\phi(\alpha x) = \alpha^k \phi(x).$$

Note that α is positive in these definitions. The definition of a cone sometimes permits $\alpha = 0$ but Euler's Theorem (below) requires $\alpha > 0$. Every ray emanating from the origin is a cone (irrespective of whether the origin is included). Hence every collection of rays emanating from the origin is a cone, and therefore $\mathbb{R}^n_{++}$, $\mathbb{R}^n_+ - \{0\}$, and $\mathbb{R}^n_+$ are all cones. The first two are not cones if zero is allowed in the definition but $\mathbb{R}^n_+$ is a cone with or without $\alpha = 0$, as is $\{0\}$. If ϕ is a correspondence (multi-valued) we say ϕ is homogeneous of degree k if, for every $x \in S$ and $\alpha \in \mathbb{R}^1_{++}$: $\phi(\alpha x) = \{\alpha^k y : y \in \phi(x)\}$.

Homogeneity of a function implies some properties of the derivatives when those derivatives exist. Note first that differentiation of $\phi(\alpha x) = \alpha^k \phi(x)$ with respect to x yields $\alpha \mathbf{D}\phi(\alpha x) = \alpha^k \mathbf{D}\phi(x)$, or $\mathbf{D}\phi(\alpha x) = \alpha^{k-1}\mathbf{D}\phi(x)$. That is, a homogeneous of degree k function has a homogeneous of degree $k-1$ Jacobian (when it exists). A second property relates the Jacobian to the original function.

Theorem 1.16 (Euler's Theorem). *Assume $S \subset \mathbb{R}^n$ is an open cone and $\phi : S \to \mathbb{R}^m$ is differentiable on S. Then ϕ is homogeneous of degree k if and only if $\mathbf{D}\phi(x)x = k\phi(x)$ for every $x \in S$.*

Proof. Define $g_x(\alpha) \equiv \phi(\alpha x)$ on $\mathbb{R}^1_{++}$ for arbitrary $x \in S$. By the Chain and Product Rules:

$$\begin{aligned}\mathbf{D}g_x(\alpha) &= \mathbf{D}\phi(\alpha x)x, \quad \text{and} \\ \mathbf{D}(\alpha^{-k} g_x(\alpha)) &= \alpha^{-k}\mathbf{D}g_x(\alpha) - k\alpha^{-k-1} g_x(\alpha) \\ &= \alpha^{-k-1}[\mathbf{D}\phi(\alpha x)(\alpha x) - k\phi(\alpha x)].\end{aligned}$$

If ϕ is homogeneous of degree k then $g_x(\alpha) = \alpha^k \phi(x)$ and therefore $\mathbf{D}g_x(\alpha) = k\alpha^{k-1}\phi(x)$. Setting the two expressions for $\mathbf{D}g_x(\alpha)$ equal and evaluating at $\alpha = 1$ yields $\mathbf{D}\phi(x)x = k\phi(x)$.

Conversely, if $\mathbf{D}\phi(x^0)x^0 = k\phi(x^0)\ \forall x^0 \in S$ then evaluating at $x^0 = \alpha x$ yields $\mathbf{D}\phi(\alpha x)(\alpha x) = k\phi(\alpha x)$. Therefore $\mathbf{D}(\alpha^{-k} g_x(\alpha)) = 0$ on $\alpha \in \mathbb{R}^1_{++}$. This means $\alpha^{-k} g_x(\alpha)$ is constant on $\mathbb{R}^1_{++}$; yielding:

$$\alpha^{-k} g_x(\alpha) = g_x(1) = \phi(x)\ \forall \alpha \in \mathbb{R}^1_{++}.$$

That is, $\phi(\alpha x) = \alpha^k \phi(x)\ \forall \alpha \in \mathbb{R}^1_{++}$. □

If ϕ is real-valued under the conditions of Theorem 1.16 ($m = 1$) and has a Hessian then differentiation of $\mathbf{D}\phi(x)x = k\phi(x)$ with respect to x yields:

$$(k-1)\mathbf{D}\phi(x) = x^{\perp}\mathbf{D}^2\phi(x). \tag{1.1}$$

This immediately gives a corollary.

Corollary 1.3. *Assume the conditions of Theorem 1.16 with ϕ real-valued ($m = 1$) and homogeneous of degree one ($k = 1$). If ϕ has a Hessian $\mathbf{D}^2\phi(x)$ at $x \in S$ ($x \neq 0$) then that Hessian is singular.*

Proof. Evaluate Eq. (1.1) at $k = 1$ to obtain $0 = x^{\perp}\mathbf{D}^2\phi(x)$. That is, $x^{\perp}$ forms a linear combination of the rows of $\mathbf{D}^2\phi(x)$. □

Combining Corollary 1.3 with Theorem 1.10 reveals that the Hessian of a homogeneous of degree one real-valued function cannot be definite because the principal minor from the submatrix with n rows and columns (i.e., the entire matrix) is zero. However, it is often useful to determine whether such a Hessian is semidefinite. Semidefiniteness cannot generally be determined by examining only leading principal minors; hence determining semidefiniteness can be tedious when n is large as there are $2^n - 1$ principal minors. Fortunately, the Hessian in economic applications often has a definite principal submatrix with $n - 1$ rows and columns. Verifying definiteness of such a submatrix is relatively easy because only the signs of the $n-1$ leading principal minors must be checked. Corollary 1.2 addresses this situation: If an n-dimensional symmetric real matrix is singular with a definite $n - 1$-dimensional principal submatrix the entire n-dimensional matrix is semidefinite.

In short, when a real-valued function on an appropriately-shaped domain in $\mathbb{R}^n$ is homogeneous of degree one and has a Hessian at a (nonzero) point that Hessian is singular. If it is symmetric, it is positive (negative) semidefinite if it has a positive (negative) definite $(n - 1)$-dimensional principal submatrix. The latter can be checked by examining signs of the $n - 1$ leading principal minors of the submatrix (if any of those principal minors are zero this shortcut does not determine whether the Hessian is semidefinite).

1.6 ENVELOPE PROPERTIES

Many properties of optima in economic models are fundamentally consequences of the following simple observation:

> *A maximal value cannot increase as constraints on the maximization become more restrictive.*

To formally explore the consequences of this observation, let $\widetilde{\Gamma}(\theta) \subset \Gamma(\theta)$ so that $\widetilde{\Gamma}$ is a more restrictive constraint correspondence than Γ, and define the outcomes from the more constrained optimization in the natural way:

$$\tilde{f}^*(\theta) = \sup\{f(x;\theta) : x \in \tilde{\Gamma}(\theta)\} \tag{1.2}$$

$$\tilde{x}^*(\theta) = \{x \in \tilde{\Gamma}(\theta) : f(x;\theta) = \tilde{f}^*(\theta)\}. \tag{1.3}$$

It is clear that $\tilde{f}^*(\theta)$ is no larger than $f^*(\theta)$. Moreover, if for some particular parameter value θ^0 there is a value of x that maximizes f subject to $\Gamma(\theta^0)$ that is also a feasible choice subject to $\tilde{\Gamma}(\theta^0)$, then $\tilde{f}^*(\theta^0)$ is equal to $f^*(\theta^0)$. It is less obvious, but nonetheless true, that these observations imply $\tilde{f}^*$ and f^* are "tangent" at θ^0 and that the second derivative of $\tilde{f}^*$ is "smaller" (in a sense made precise below) than the second derivative of f^* at θ^0 (under suitable differentiability conditions).

Theorem 1.17 (Generalized Envelope Theorem). *Assume $B(\theta^0) \subset \Theta$ is an open ball about θ^0 and that $\tilde{\Gamma} : B(\theta^0) \to 2^X$ is more restrictive than Γ: $\tilde{\Gamma}(\theta) \subset \Gamma(\theta)$ on $B(\theta^0)$. Define $\tilde{f}^*$ on $B(\theta^0)$ as in Eq. (1.2) and assume it is finite. Then:*

1. *$\tilde{f}^*(\theta) \leq f^*(\theta)$ for every $\theta \in B(\theta^0)$.*
2. *$\tilde{f}^*(\theta^0) = f^*(\theta^0)$ when $x^*(\theta^0) \cap \tilde{\Gamma}(\theta^0) \neq \emptyset$.*
3. *$\mathbf{D}\tilde{f}^*(\theta^0) = \mathbf{D}f^*(\theta^0)$ when (a) the condition of item 2 holds, and (b) each Jacobian exists.*
4. *$\mathbf{D}^2\tilde{f}^*(\theta^0) - \mathbf{D}^2f^*(\theta^0)$ is negative semidefinite when (a) the condition of item 2 holds, (b) $\tilde{f}^*$ and f^* are differentiable on an open ball about θ^0, and (c) each partial derivative of $\tilde{f}^*$ and f^* is differentiable at θ^0.*

Proof.

1. Definition of the supremum when $\tilde{\Gamma}(\theta) \subset \Gamma(\theta)$ ($\tilde{f}^*$ finite ensures we are not comparing infinities).
2. Definition of the maximum when $x^*(\theta^0) \cap \tilde{\Gamma}(\theta^0) \neq \emptyset$.
3. Items 1 and 2 establish that the difference $g(\theta) = \tilde{f}^*(\theta) - f^*(\theta)$ attains a maximum on $B(\theta^0)$ at θ^0. Item 3 is therefore the standard necessary condition that, if a function has a well-defined Jacobian at a local maximum, that matrix must be zero (Theorem 1.14).
4. Item 4 is the standard necessary condition that, if a function g satisfies the differentiability assumptions of Theorem 1.15 at a local maximum θ^0, then its Hessian must be negative semidefinite at that maximum. □

It is important to recognize that $\tilde{\Gamma}(\theta) \subset \Gamma(\theta)$ on an open ball about θ^0 can be a quite restrictive condition that makes Theorem 1.17 inapplicable in some settings. When this condition does not hold the methods developed in the next chapter must be utilized (see Theorem 2.2).

Theorem 1.17 is labeled the "Generalized" Envelope Theorem because it characterizes the relationship between more- and less-constrained maxima without explicitly specifying the more restrictive constraint. A special case of the more restrictive constraint, yielding the "standard" Envelope Theorem, can be constructed when an optimal choice of x for parameter value θ^0, say $\hat{x}(\theta^0)$, remains feasible as θ departs from θ^0. We call this a situation in which the constraint Γ is "inactive" at θ^0, in the sense that a small change in the parameter does not affect feasibility of an optimal choice.

Definition 1.7 (Active Constraint). Γ is called *inactive* at $\theta^0 \in \Theta$ if there exists an open ball $B(\theta^0)$ and an optimal choice $\hat{x}(\theta^0)$ (an element of $x^*(\theta^0)$) such that $\hat{x}(\theta^0) \in \Gamma(\theta)$ for every $\theta \in B(\theta^0) \cap \Theta$. Otherwise we say Γ is *active* at θ^0. Γ is inactive (active) on a subset of Θ if it is inactive (active) at every element of that subset.

Constraint "activity" concerns whether a change in the parameter changes the constraint in a way that affects the optimal choice. For example, if output increases in a standard cost minimization problem the former cost-minimizing input vector is (probably) no longer feasible, so the constraint is active in this case. Note that the concept of an "active constraint" is not the same as the concept of a "binding constraint." Constraint activity is concerned with whether local *changes* in parameters affect the constrained optimum whereas the concept of a binding constraint is concerned with whether the presence of the constraint affects the optimum at all. For example, the production constraint in a standard cost minimization problem is inactive when input prices change, even though it is usually binding, because input prices do not affect the constraint in that optimization problem (this lack of dependence is a particularly simple type of inactive constraint). Note from this example that it is sometimes useful to partition the parameter vector into parameters over which the constraint is active versus inactive at a point.

When the constraint is inactive a special case of the Generalized Envelope Theorem is obtained by *defining* $\widetilde{\Gamma}(\theta)$ to be the singleton $\{\hat{x}(\theta^0)\}$ for every θ in the open ball about θ^0. This more-constrained optimization problem satisfies the requirement in item 2 of the Generalized Envelope Theorem because the constraint is inactive.

Theorem 1.18 (Envelope Theorem). *Assume Γ is inactive at $\theta^0 \in \theta$. Then:*

1. $f(\hat{x}(\theta^0);\theta) \leq f^*(\theta)$ *for every* $\theta \in B(\theta^0) \cap \Theta$.
2. $f(\hat{x}(\theta^0);\theta^0) = f^*(\theta^0)$.
3. $\mathbf{D}_\theta f(\hat{x}(\theta^0);\theta^0) = \mathbf{D}f^*(\theta^0)$ *when each Jacobian exists (note that the left side holds x fixed at $\hat{x}(\theta^0)$ during the differentiation).*
4. $\mathbf{D}^2_\theta f(\hat{x}(\theta^0);\theta^0) - \mathbf{D}^2 f^*(\theta^0)$ *is negative semidefinite when (a)* $f(\hat{x}(\theta^0);\theta)$ *and* $f^*(\theta)$ *are differentiable (with respect to θ) on an open ball about θ^0, and (b) each* $\frac{\partial f(\hat{x}(\theta^0);\theta)}{\partial \theta_i}$ *and* $\frac{\partial f^*(\theta)}{\partial \theta_i}$ *is differentiable (with respect to θ) at θ^0, for* $i = 1, \ldots, k$.

Proof. In Theorem 1.17 let $\tilde{\Gamma}(\theta) = \{\hat{x}(\theta^0)\}$ on $B(\theta^0) \cap \theta$. Then $\tilde{\Gamma}(\theta) \subset \Gamma(\theta)$ because Γ is inactive at θ^0, $x^*(\theta^0) \cap \tilde{\Gamma}(\theta^0) = \{\hat{x}(\theta^0)\}$, and $\tilde{f}^*(\theta) = f(\hat{x}(\theta^0);\theta)$ (which is finite because f is real-valued). Items 1–4 are the corresponding items from Theorem 1.17 applied to this $\tilde{f}^*$ function. □

Item 3 of Theorem 1.18 states that an optimal value function is tangent to the underlying objective function considered as a function of the parameter, at the point of optimality, under suitable differentiability conditions when the constraint is inactive. This tangency, specifically, is the part of Theorem 1.18 usually referred to as the *envelope theorem*. It is a very useful property, as it allows us to quickly and easily differentiate optimal value functions without thinking about any implicit changes in the optimal choice that may occur in the background. It also has important implications in many economic models. Another way to see this is to realize that, at a well-behaved maximum, the partial derivatives of f with respect to x are all zero, so an infinitesimal change in $\hat{x}$ has no effect on f at this point; only the direct change in θ matters for f^*.

However, it is really more descriptive to call all four items in Theorem 1.18 the "envelope theorem," for the following reason. θ^0 is an arbitrary fixed value of θ in this discussion. Therefore these four relationships hold for every value of θ^0 in Θ, provided an optimal choice always exists and the constraint is globally inactive; and the differentiability conditions hold everywhere. Thus there is a collection of $f(\hat{x}(\theta^0);\theta)$ functions, one for each $\theta^0 \in \text{int}\,\Theta$, and $f^*(\theta)$ envelopes this collection (from above). Whence the term "envelope theorem." *When the constraint is globally inactive a maximal value function is an upper envelope over the parameter space of the individual objective functions, each evaluated at the optimum for the particular parameter.* This is illustrated in Fig. 1.4 when θ is a scalar.

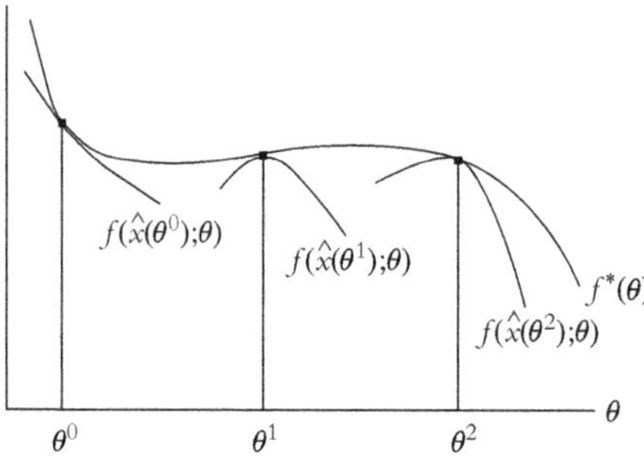

Fig. 1.4 The Envelope Theorem. When $\theta = \theta^0$, there is an optimal choice $\hat{x}(\theta^0)$. At θ^0, the objective evaluated at the optimal choice is, by definition, the optimal value f^*. As θ departs from θ^0, the objective f with x fixed drops below the optimal value f^* because the choice variable is not adjusting to remain optimal with the change in θ. The same phenomenon occurs at other values of θ, such as θ^1 and θ^2, with x held constant at the choice that is optimal for each of those θ values. The result is each $f(\hat{x}(\theta^i);\theta)$ curve is tangent to $f^*(\theta)$ at $\theta = \theta^i$ and below $f^*(\theta)$ at other θ values, making f^* an upper envelope of the individual $f(\hat{x}(\theta^i);\theta)$ curves.

1.7 NOTES ON PROPERTIES OF MINIMA

In some cases the behavioral postulate is to minimize an objective rather than maximize it. The problem of minimizing $g(x;\theta)$ subject to $x \in \Gamma(\theta)$ can be treated as a maximization problem by setting $f(x;\theta) = -g(x;\theta)$ and then maximizing $f(x;\theta)$ subject to $x \in \Gamma(\theta)$. Hence all of the results of this chapter hold for minima, with modifications needed only to keep track of the minus sign. For convenience, the results for minimizing g are listed here.

Let $g^*(\theta) = \inf\{g(x;\theta) : x \in \Gamma(\theta)\}$ and $x^*(\theta) = \{x \in \Gamma(\theta) : g(x;\theta) = g^*(\theta)\}$.

1. Theorem 1.2. Change the assumption to "$g(x;\theta)$ is a *lower* semicontinuous function of x on $\Gamma(\theta)$." The conclusion is then that a minimum exists (and the infimum is finite).
2. Theorem 1.3. Change assumption 3 to "g is *lower* semicontinuous ..." and assumption 4 to "$g^*(\theta)$ is finite ...." The conclusion is then "g^* is *lower* semicontinuous at θ^0."
3. Theorem 1.4. Change assumption 2 to "g is *upper* semicontinuous ..." and assumption 3 to "$g^*(\theta)$ is finite ...." The conclusion is then "g^* is *upper* semicontinuous at θ^0."

4. Theorem 1.5. Replace f with g in assumption 3 and f^* with g^* in assumption 4. The conclusion is then "g^* is continuous at θ^0 and x^* is upper hemicontinuous at θ^0."
5. Theorem 1.14. If x^0 is a local *minimum* of ϕ and all other conditions of the theorem hold then the conclusion is unchanged.
6. Theorem 1.15. If x^0 is a local *minimum* of ϕ and all other conditions of the theorem hold then $\mathbf{D}^2\phi(x^0)$ is *positive* semidefinite and therefore has nonnegative principal minors.
7. Theorem 1.17. Define $\widetilde{g}^*(\theta) = \inf\{g(x;\theta) : x \in \widetilde{\Gamma}(\theta)\}$. Replace f with g everywhere in the statement of the theorem. Conclusion 1 is then "$\widetilde{g}^*(\theta) \geq g^*(\theta)$ for every $\theta \in B(\theta^0)$" and conclusion 4 is "$\mathbf{D}^2\widetilde{g}^*(\theta^0) - \mathbf{D}^2 g^*(\theta^0)$ is *positive* semidefinite when ...." Conclusions 2 and 3 are unchanged.
8. Theorem 1.18. Replace f with g everywhere in the statement of the theorem. Conclusion 1 is then "$g(\hat{x}(\theta^0);\theta) \geq g^*(\theta)$ for every $\theta \in B(\theta^0) \cap \Theta$" and conclusion 4 is "$\mathbf{D}^2_{\theta} g(\hat{x}(\theta^0);\theta^0) - \mathbf{D}^2 g^*(\theta^0)$ is *positive* semidefinite when ...." Conclusions 2 and 3 are unchanged. Thus, in a minimization problem, the optimal value function is a *lower* envelope of the individual objective functions, each evaluated at the optimum.

1.8 NOTES

Much of the material in this chapter is sufficiently well-known that it belongs to the public domain of mathematical knowledge. Nonetheless, the presentation here relies heavily on a few references that should be mentioned.

Standard results from advanced calculus are mostly from Apostol [4]. Debreu [5, Chapter 1] and Takayama [6] also provide much background material.

Continuity of correspondences and the Maximum Theorem are from Berge [7, pp. 109–117]. All of Chapter 6 from Berge provides valuable discussion of correspondences, as do Debreu [5, Chapter 6 §3], Hildenbrand and Kirman [8, Appendix 3], and Stokey and Lucas [9, pp. 55–65].

The discussion of definite and semidefinite matrices relies heavily on Strang [2]. Gantmacher [10, pp. 306–307] is usually cited as the original source for these results. Debreu [11, Theorems 2 and 7] provides concise proofs that work directly with the quadratic forms. I am especially grateful to Jonathan Hamilton and J. Isaac Miller for helpful discussions on this material.

The proof of Euler's Theorem as an "if and only if" statement is mostly from Roberts and Schulze [12, pp. 140–141].

Samuelson [13, Chapters 2 and 3] brought the Envelope Theorem to the attention of economists. Silberberg [14] established the Generalized Envelope Theorem, although the version given herein is a bit more general than Silberberg's treatment (and also less general in that attention herein is confined to an "inactive" constraint—this is revisited in the next chapter).

1.9 EXERCISES

1. State $\Gamma(\theta)$ for a standard utility maximization problem and for a standard cost minimization problem.
2. Prove that the constraint correspondence for a standard utility maximization problem is continuous on the price/income space.
3. Consider Theorem 1.2. Give a graphical example demonstrating why none of the conditions are necessary for existence of a maximum except that the feasible set be nonempty.
4. Suppose $X = \Theta = \mathbb{R}^1$, $f(x;\theta) = 1 - \frac{1}{x^2+1}$ (i.e., f does not depend on θ), and:

$$\Gamma(\theta) = \begin{cases} \left\{0, \frac{1}{|\theta|}\right\} & \theta \neq 0 \\ \{0\} & \theta = 0 \end{cases}.$$

   a. Draw Γ. Is Γ upper hemicontinuous? Lower hemicontinuous?
   b. Is f continuous?
   c. Derive $x^*(\theta)$ and $f^*(\theta)$.
   d. Is x^* upper hemicontinuous? Is f^* continuous?
   e. Comment on how your results fit with the Maximum Theorem.
5. Assume $\Gamma : \mathbb{R}^1 \to 2^{\mathbb{R}^1}$ and $f : \mathbb{R}^2 \to \mathbb{R}^1$ are defined by:

$$\Gamma(\theta) = \begin{cases} \{0\} & \theta < 0 \\ \{0, 1\} & \theta \geq 0 \end{cases}$$

$$f(x;\theta) = -(x-\theta)(x-1).$$

   a. Discuss the hemicontinuity of Γ.
   b. Discuss the continuity of f.
   c. Find $f^*(\theta)$ and $x^*(\theta)$.

d. Compare your answers to the assumptions and conclusions of the Maximum Theorem; explain.

6. Here is a correspondence $\Phi : \mathbb{R}^1 \to 2^{\mathbb{R}^1}$ (x^0 is a real number):

$$\Phi(x) = \begin{cases} [1,2] & x < x^0 \\ [1,2] \cup [3,4] & x = x^0 \\ [3,4] & x > x^0 \end{cases}.$$

Discuss the hemicontinuity of Φ at x^0.

7. Suppose $f(x;\theta)$ is a nondecreasing function of θ on Θ for every $x \in X$ and $\Gamma(\theta) = X$ for all $\theta \in \Theta$ (i.e., the feasible set does not depend on θ). Show that $f^*(\theta)$ is nondecreasing.

8. Assume $X = \Theta = \mathbb{R}^1$, and:

$$f(x;\theta) = \theta - (x-\theta)^2$$

$$\Gamma(\theta) = \mathbb{R}^1 \text{ (i.e., no constraint)}$$

$$\widetilde{\Gamma}(\theta) = (-\infty, -\theta].$$

Find $x^*(\theta)$, $f^*(\theta)$, $\widetilde{x}^*(\theta)$, and $\widetilde{f}^*(\theta)$. Then carefully graph f^* and $\widetilde{f}^*$, and comment on how your graph compares to the Generalized Envelope Theorem.

9. Give a verbal statement of the Envelope Theorem.

10. Here is an optimization problem:

$$f^*(\theta) = \min_{\{x\}} f(x;\theta), \text{ where } f(x;\theta) = 2x^4 - \theta^3 x.$$

a. Find $\hat{x}(\theta)$, the optimal choice of x.

b. Graph f as a function of θ, with x fixed at an arbitrary positive value. Take care to label the intercepts and to correctly depict the slope and curvature.

c. Now suppose that the fixed value of x in part (b) is $\hat{x}(\theta^0)$ for some particular value θ^0 of θ. Add $f^*(\theta)$ to your graph in part (b) without actually deriving $f^*(\theta)$.

d. Based *only* on your graph in part (c), can you tell whether $f^*(\theta)$ is a concave function? Why/why not?

11. Here is an optimization problem:

$$f^*(\theta) = \max_{\{x_1,x_2,x_3,x_4,x_5\}} x_1x_2x_3x_4x_5 + x_1^{1/3}x_2^{1/9}x_4^5x_5 + x_3^{1/5}x_4x_5^{2/7} + \theta^2 x_3$$

$$\text{subject to } \sum_{i=1}^{5} p_i x_i = y \text{ and } x_i \geq 0,$$

where θ, p_i, and y are all positive numbers. Assume the solution is unique and has $\hat{x}_i > 0$ for $i = 1, \ldots, 5$.

a. What happens to f^* when θ changes? Why?

b. Give an explanation for why $f^{*\prime\prime}(\theta) \geq 2\hat{x}_3(\theta)$.

12. Here is an optimization problem ($\theta \in \mathbb{R}^1$):

$$f^*(\theta) = \max\{f(x;\theta) : x \in \mathbb{R}^1\} \text{ where } f(x;\theta) = -x^2 + xe^{\theta}.$$

a. Find $\hat{x}(\theta)$, the optimal choice of x.

b. Graph f as a function of θ, with x fixed at an arbitrary positive value. Take care to correctly depict the slope and curvature.

c. Now suppose that the fixed value of x in part (b) is $\hat{x}(\theta^0)$ for some particular value θ^0 of θ. Add $f^*(\theta)$ to your graph in part (b) without actually deriving $f^*(\theta)$.

d. Based *only* on your graph in part (c), can you tell whether $f^*(\theta)$ is a convex function? Why/why not?

13. Is the function $g(\theta)$ in Theorem 1.17 globally concave? Why or why not?

14. Consider a firm with production function $f(x_1, x_2) = \theta \ln(x_1 + 1) + (1 - \theta)\ln(x_2 + 1)$, where $\theta \in (0, 1)$. Take as given that the profit-maximizing demands for this firm are $\hat{x}_1 = \frac{p\theta}{w_1} - 1$ and $\hat{x}_2 = \frac{p(1-\theta)}{w_2} - 1$ (p is the price of output; w_i is the price of x_i). Use the tangency property of the Envelope Theorem to show that profit increases with a small increase in θ if and only if $\frac{w_2}{w_1} > \frac{1-\theta}{\theta}$ (Note: Do not grind it out; the point of the exercise is to apply the tangency property).

15. Consider a firm with average cost function $AC(y) = (\theta y - 1)^2 + 1$ for $y > 0$, where $\theta > 0$ is some parameter. Suppose this firm chooses its output level y to minimize average cost. Use the tangency property of the Envelope Theorem to show that this behavior yields total cost of $\frac{1}{\theta}$, no matter what the value of θ is.

16. Consider a duopolist facing demand function $q = \alpha - \beta p + \gamma p_r$ and constant marginal cost $c \geq 0$. Here, p is the firm's price, q is the firm's quantity, and p_r is the price charged by a rival firm who sells a substitute product. The demand parameters α, β, and γ are all strictly positive and $\gamma < \beta$. This firm's objective is to choose price to maximize profit $\pi = (p - c)q$ given the price charged by the rival. Assume throughout there is a unique interior solution. This question is about the effects of changes in the responsiveness of the firm's demand to the rival's price (i.e., changes in γ).

a. Write the firm's objective function π explicitly as a function of its choice variable.

b. Draw a graph with γ on the horizontal axis. Fix a value of γ, say γ_0, on that axis. Now draw the profit objective on your graph with the choice variable fixed at the value that is optimal when γ equals γ_0. Label important points and slopes.

c. Now add the optimal value function π^* to your graph. The placement and shape must be qualitatively correct to receive full credit. Explain why it appears as you illustrate. You are expected to do this without actually solving for π^*.

d. From your graph, what is the slope of π^* at γ_0? Also from your graph, what happens to the firm's optimal price choice as γ increases? Explain why.

REFERENCES

[1] Trench WF. Advanced calculus. New York: Harper and Row; 1978.
[2] Strang G. Linear algebra and its applications. New York: Academic Press; 1976.
[3] Johnston J. Econometric methods. 3rd ed. New York: McGraw-Hill; 1984.
[4] Apostol TM. Mathematical analysis. 2nd ed. Reading, MA: Addison-Wesley; 1974.
[5] Debreu G. Theory of value. Cowles Foundation for Research in Economics Monograph 17; 1959.
[6] Takayama A. Mathematical economics. Hinsdale, IL: The Dryden Press; 1974.
[7] Berge C. Topological spaces [Patterson EM, Trans.]. Edinburgh: Oliver & Boyd; 1959.
[8] Hildenbrand W, Kirman A. Equilibrium analysis. Amsterdam: North-Holland; 1988.
[9] Stokey N, Lucas R. Recursive methods in economic dynamics. Cambridge: Harvard University Press; 1989.
[10] Gantmacher FR, The theory of matrices, vol. 1. New York: Chelsea; 1959.
[11] Debreu G. Definite and semidefinite quadratic forms. Econometrica 1952;20:295–300.
[12] Roberts B, Schulze D. Modern mathematics & economic analysis. New York: Norton; 1973.
[13] Samuelson PA. Foundations of economic analysis. Cambridge, MA: Harvard University Press; 1947.
[14] Silberberg E. The Le Châtelier principle as a corollary to a Generalized Envelope Theorem. J Econ Theory 1971;3(l):146–55.

CHAPTER 2

Properties of a Maximum Under Active Constraint

Chapter Outline

The first and second order necessary conditions proven in Chapter 1 are for locally *unconstrained* maxima. Similarly, the Envelope Theorem in Chapter 1 is for an inactive constraint. Chapter 2 revisits these properties for actively constrained maxima. That is, for situations in which there is no optimal choice that remains feasible as the parameter changes (locally). The standard approach to this situation is to place more structure on the optimization by assuming the constraint can be written in terms of an inequality involving a function $h(x;\theta)$. Specifically, for a given parameter vector θ, the set of feasible choices is those values of x satisfying $h(x;\theta) \leq 0$. In all economic models we consider, the inequality can be expressed as an equality without loss of generality, and the equality case is considerably easier to characterize. Accordingly, the notation throughout this chapter is the same as introduced at the beginning of Chapter 1, with the addition that there is a function $h : X \times \Theta \to \mathbb{R}^m$ for $m \leq n$ such that $\Gamma(\theta) = \{x \in X : h(x;\theta) = 0\}$ for every $\theta \in \Theta$.

The last section of the chapter uses the first and second order conditions to develop the classical comparative statics methodology used in economic models to explore the direction of optimal choice response when the parameter changes.

2.1 LAGRANGE MULTIPLIER RULE

A necessary first order condition for a maximum can be stated in terms of the constraint function h under some assumptions.

Theorem 2.1 (Lagrange Multiplier Rule). *Assume f and h are continuously differentiable (as functions of x) on an open ball about $\hat{x}(\theta)$ (note that this assumes existence of a maximum on the interior of X) with $\mathbf{D}_{(x_{n-m+1},\ldots,x_n)}h(\hat{x}(\theta);\theta)$ nonsingular.*[1] *Then there exists a unique $\lambda \in \mathbb{R}^m$ such that:*

$$\mathbf{D}_x f(\hat{x}(\theta);\theta) = \lambda^{\perp}\mathbf{D}_x h(\hat{x}(\theta);\theta).$$

Proof. Suppress θ throughout the proof because it is a fixed vector. Let $x = (y, z)$ be a partition of x into the first $n-m$ and last m components. By the Implicit Function Theorem [1, Theorem 13.7], the assumptions of continuous differentiability, interiority, and nonsingularity are sufficient to ensure existence of an open ball $B_\epsilon(\hat{y}) \subset \mathbb{R}^{n-m}$ and a unique continuously differentiable function $\phi : B_\epsilon(\hat{y}) \to \mathbb{R}^m$ such that $(\hat{y}, \phi(\hat{y})) = \hat{x}$ and:

$$h(y, \phi(y)) = 0 \text{ for } y \in B_\epsilon(\hat{y}). \tag{2.1}$$

Therefore $\hat{y}$ maximizes the composite function $\tilde{f}(y) = f(y, \phi(y))$ over $y \in B_\epsilon(\hat{y})$. $\tilde{f}(y)$ is differentiable at $\hat{y}$ by the Chain Rule, so:

$$\mathbf{D}\tilde{f}(\hat{y}) = \mathbf{D}_y f(\hat{y}, \phi(\hat{y})) + \mathbf{D}_z f(\hat{y}, \phi(\hat{y}))\mathbf{D}\phi(\hat{y}) = 0, \tag{2.2}$$

also using Theorem 1.14. The Chain Rule ensures Eq. (2.1) can be differentiated at $\hat{x}$:

$$\mathbf{D}_y h(\hat{y}, \phi(\hat{y})) + \mathbf{D}_z h(\hat{y}, \phi(\hat{y}))\mathbf{D}\phi(\hat{y}) = 0. \tag{2.3}$$

As $\mathbf{D}_z h(\hat{y}, \phi(\hat{y}))$ is nonsingular by assumption, there exists a unique $\lambda \in \mathbb{R}^m$ satisfying:

$$\lambda^{\perp}\mathbf{D}_z h(\hat{y}, \phi(\hat{y})) = \mathbf{D}_z f(\hat{y}, \phi(\hat{y})). \tag{2.4}$$

Premultiplying Eq. (2.3) by $\lambda^{\perp}$ and substituting for $\lambda^{\perp}\mathbf{D}_z h$ in the resulting expression from Eq. (2.4) yields:

$$\lambda^{\perp}\mathbf{D}_y h(\hat{y}, \phi(\hat{y})) + \mathbf{D}_z f(\hat{y}, \phi(\hat{y}))\mathbf{D}\phi(\hat{y}) = 0.$$

Now using Eq. (2.2):

[1] Use of the last m x_i's is for notational convenience and is without loss of generality since the variable labels are arbitrary. The theorem requires only that there be *some* collection of m x_i's such that the Jacobian of h with respect to that collection is nonsingular at $\hat{x}$.

$$\lambda^{\perp}\mathbf{D}_y h(\hat{y}, \phi(\hat{y})) - \mathbf{D}_y f(\hat{y}, \phi(\hat{y})) = 0. \tag{2.5}$$

Horizontally stacking Eqs. (2.5) and (2.4) yields:

$$\lambda^{\perp}\mathbf{D}_x h(\hat{x}) - \mathbf{D}_x f(\hat{x}) = 0. \qquad \square$$

λ in Theorem 2.1 is the so-called "Lagrange multiplier." It is worth pausing to explore what this multiplier really is. For simplicity, suppose there is only one constraint ($m = 1$), and consider a change in x_i and a corresponding change in x_n that maintains the $h = 0$ requirement. As the conditions of the Implicit Function Theorem [1, Theorem 13.7] hold under the assumptions of Theorem 2.1 (specifically, the requirement that the Jacobian $\mathbf{D}_{x_n} h$ be nonsingular), $h = 0$ defines x_n as an implicit function of x_i with Jacobian satisfying:

$$\frac{\partial x_n}{\partial x_i} = -\frac{\frac{\partial h}{\partial x_i}}{\frac{\partial h}{\partial x_n}}. \tag{2.6}$$

Therefore the change in f caused by this coordinated change in x_i and x_n is:

$$\frac{\partial f}{\partial x_n}\left[-\frac{\frac{\partial h}{\partial x_i}}{\frac{\partial h}{\partial x_n}}\right] + \frac{\partial f}{\partial x_i}. \tag{2.7}$$

The same logic underlying the first order condition for an unconstrained maximum (Theorem 1.14) requires that, at a local maximum, any infinitesimal change in x that maintains $h = 0$ cannot change f. Setting Eq. (2.7) to zero and rearranging yields:

$$\frac{\partial f}{\partial x_i} = \left[\frac{\frac{\partial f}{\partial x_n}}{\frac{\partial h}{\partial x_n}}\right]\frac{\partial h}{\partial x_i}. \tag{2.8}$$

Note that the term in brackets does not depend on i. Hence Eq. (2.8) says, at a maximum, that $\mathbf{D}_x f$ is proportional to $\mathbf{D}_x h$. The proportion (the term in brackets) is the Lagrange multiplier λ (compare Eq. 2.8 to the statement of Theorem 2.1). Geometrically, Eq. (2.8) says the level curve $h = 0$, with slope given by Eq. (2.6), must be tangent to a level curve of f (which has slope $-\frac{\partial f}{\partial x_i}/\frac{\partial f}{\partial x_n}$) at a maximum; otherwise there would be a direction along the $h = 0$ curve in which f increases. Fig. 2.1 illustrates this.

Aside from an appropriate degree of differentiability, the main condition of the Lagrange Multiplier Rule is that $\mathbf{D}_x h$ has a nonsingular square

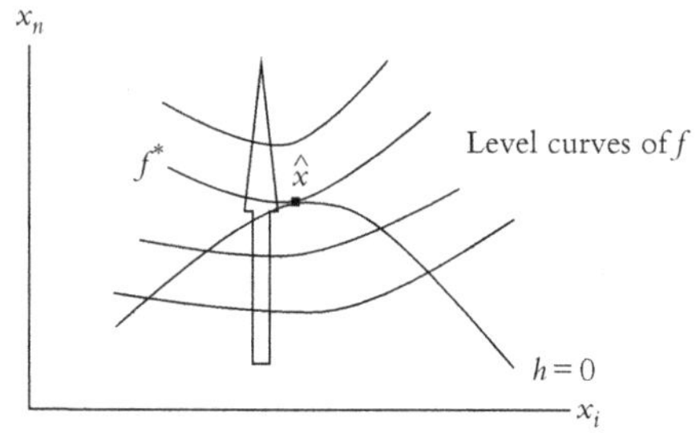

Fig. 2.1 The Lagrange Multiplier Rule. The level curve $h = 0$ is fixed. Four level curves of f are shown with f increasing in the direction of the arrow as we move across the level curves. Hence the highest constrained value of f is achieved where one of its level curves is just tangent to the $h = 0$ curve.

submatrix. This condition is called *constraint qualification*; without it, we could not divide by $\frac{\partial h}{\partial x_n}$ in deriving Eq. (2.6) or, more generally, could not be certain there is a unique vector λ that solves Eq. (2.4).[2]

2.2 THE "ENVELOPE THEOREM" WITH AN ACTIVE CONSTRAINT

Theorem 2.1 provides a zero Jacobian condition that, under some conditions, can be used to help solve for a constrained maximum, analogous to the way the zero Jacobian of an objective function in an unconstrained problem can often be used to solve for a maximum if the Jacobian exists at that point (Theorem 1.14). The Jacobian in Theorem 2.1 is usually derived in a convenient manner by defining a "Lagrangian function" $L : X \times \mathbb{R}^m \times \Theta \to \mathbb{R}$:

$$L(x, \lambda; \theta) = f(x; \theta) - \lambda^{\perp} h(x; \theta). \tag{2.9}$$

The Jacobians of this function with respect to x and λ are:

$$\begin{aligned} \mathbf{D}_x L(x, \lambda; \theta) &= \mathbf{D}_x f(x; \theta) - \lambda^{\perp} \mathbf{D}_x h(x; \theta) \\ \mathbf{D}_\lambda L(x, \lambda; \theta) &= -h(x; \theta)^{\perp}. \end{aligned}$$

[2]There are other forms of constraint qualification applicable to inequality-constrained optimization problems. Simon and Blume [2, Theorem 19.12] provide a summary. Exercise 1 at the end of this chapter shows what can go wrong when constraint qualification does not hold.

At a particular value of θ, say θ^0, any constrained maximum $\hat{x}(\theta^0)$ must satisfy the constraint $h(\hat{x}(\theta^0), \theta^0) = 0$. So the Lagrange Multiplier Rule gives conditions under which there exists λ^0 such that these two Jacobians are zero at the pair $(\hat{x}(\theta^0), \lambda^0)$:

$$\mathbf{D}_x f(\hat{x}(\theta^0); \theta^0) - (\lambda^0)^{\perp} \mathbf{D}_x h(\hat{x}(\theta^0); \theta^0) = 0 \tag{2.10}$$

$$-h(\hat{x}(\theta^0); \theta^0) = 0. \tag{2.11}$$

The system of Eqs. (2.10) and (2.11) has $n + m$ equations in the $n + m$ "unknowns" $(\hat{x}(\theta^0), \lambda^0)$. Hence, under some conditions, this system can be used to solve for value(s) of x that are candidates for a constrained maximum and the associated vector λ promised by the Lagrange Multiplier Rule.

As in the case of an inactive constraint, however, the economic actor is *assumed* to solve the optimization problem. Hence the immediate interest in the Lagrange Multiplier Rule is to explore what it conveys about the consequences of the behavioral postulate that an economic actor makes choices to maximize f while honoring the limitations imposed by Γ. The Lagrange Multiplier Rule might very well be useful in solving for $x^*(\theta)$ even when the constraint is binding but inactive, yet we did not make use of it in that setting because it is not needed there to derive the envelope relationship between $f^*(\theta)$ and the underlying objective functions $f(\hat{x}(\theta^0); \theta)$. The Rule is of interest now because it leads to refutable hypotheses when the constraint it active. One such property is an analog to the tangency property of Theorem 1.18 for the active constraint environment.

Theorem 2.2 ("Envelope Theorem"). *Assume the conditions of the Lagrange Multiplier Rule hold at* $\theta^0 \in \Theta$. *Denote by* λ^0 *the unique vector assured by Theorem 2.1 satisfying:*

$$\mathbf{D}_x f(\hat{x}(\theta^0); \theta^0) = (\lambda^0)^{\perp} \mathbf{D}_x h(\hat{x}(\theta^0); \theta^0).$$

Assume further that the conditions of the Implicit Function Theorem [1, Theorem 13.7] hold for the system of Eqs. (2.10) and (2.11) *at* $(\hat{x}(\theta^0), \lambda^0; \theta^0)$ *and let L be defined by Eq. (2.9). Then:*

$$\mathbf{D} f^*(\theta^0) = \mathbf{D}_\theta L(\hat{x}(\theta^0), \lambda^0; \theta^0).$$

Proof. Eq. (2.10) is evaluated at θ^0 and $\hat{x}(\theta^0)$; λ^0 therefore depends on θ^0. Since the conditions of the Implicit Function Theorem [1, Theorem 13.7] hold at θ^0 and the $(n + m)$-dimensional pair $(\hat{x}(\theta^0), \lambda^0)$ that satisfies the system of $(n + m)$ Eqs. (2.10) and (2.11), that system defines differentiable functions $\hat{x}(\theta)$ and $\hat{\lambda}(\theta)$ in a neighborhood of θ^0 such that $\hat{\lambda}(\theta^0) = \lambda^0$. $h(\hat{x}(\theta); \theta) = 0$ within that neighborhood, yielding:

$$L(\hat{x}(\theta), \hat{\lambda}(\theta); \theta) = f(\hat{x}(\theta); \theta) = f^*(\theta). \tag{2.12}$$

Under the conditions of the Lagrange Multiplier Rule, and those of the Implicit Function Theorem for Eqs. (2.10) and (2.11), the Chain Rule applies to Eq. (2.12) in the neighborhood of θ^0. Differentiating with respect to θ therefore yields:

$$\begin{aligned}\mathbf{D}f^*(\theta) &= \mathbf{D}_x L(\hat{x}(\theta), \hat{\lambda}(\theta); \theta)\mathbf{D}\hat{x}(\theta) + \mathbf{D}_\lambda L(\hat{x}(\theta), \hat{\lambda}(\theta); \theta)\mathbf{D}\hat{\lambda}(\theta) \\ &\quad + \mathbf{D}_\theta L(\hat{x}(\theta), \hat{\lambda}(\theta); \theta).\end{aligned}$$

Evaluating at θ^0 and using Eqs. (2.10) and (2.11) yields the result. □

In short, the Lagrange Multiplier Rule, plus the Implicit Function Theorem applied to Eqs. (2.10) and (2.11), are jointly sufficient for $f^*(\theta)$ and $L(\hat{x}(\theta^0), \hat{\lambda}(\theta^0); \theta)$ to have the same gradient with respect to θ at $\theta = \theta^0$. We may quickly and easily differentiate an optimal value function f^* at θ^0 without thinking about any implicit changes in the optimal choice, or the multiplier, that may occur in the background; even when the constraint is active; by differentiating the associated Lagrangian function L exclusively with respect to the parameter and evaluating that derivative at $(\hat{x}(\theta^0), \lambda^0; \theta^0)$.

Theorem 2.2 is usually called the "Envelope Theorem" because of the similarity between it and the tangency property of Theorem 1.18. Indeed, the former reduces to the latter when the constraint is inactive because $\mathbf{D}_\theta L = \mathbf{D}_\theta f - \lambda^\perp \mathbf{D}_\theta h$ and $\mathbf{D}_\theta h$ is zero at a point where the constraint is inactive. But labeling Theorem 2.2 an "Envelope Theorem" is a bit misleading for the reasons mentioned in Chapter 1: Theorem 2.2 is only a tangency property, not a result establishing an envelope relationship between f^* and L. Unlike the inactive constraint environment, there is no general envelope relationship between f^* and L even though they share the same gradient at the optimum. Exercise 2 at the end of this chapter provides an example.

Eqs. (2.10) and (2.11) may seem to suggest that unconstrained maximization of L is equivalent to constrained maximization of f. Although this is true in some cases (see Exercise 2 at the end of this chapter), Exercise 3 at the end of this chapter shows it is not true in general.

In many economic models component i of the constraint $h(x; \theta) = 0$ takes the special form $g_i(x; \theta_1, \ldots, \theta_{k-1}) - \theta_k = 0$ for some real-valued function g_i, and θ_k is absent from the objective and the other components of h. That is, there is one component of the parameter vector, denoted θ_k here, that appears exclusively as an additive constant in one constraint. This occurs when there is a limited amount of some resource available to the economic actor, such as money or wealth in a utility maximization problem, and g_i measures how much of that resource the actor uses as the choice vector x and other parameters $(\theta_1, \dots, \theta_{k-1})$ vary. An application of Theorem 2.2 to this situation yields:

$$\frac{\partial f^*(\theta^0)}{\partial \theta_k} = \lambda_i^0.$$

This equation states that the Lagrange multiplier for the constraint under study measures the marginal value of the resource to the economic actor: A small reduction in the resource endowment θ_k changes the optimum the actor can achieve by λ_i^0. Lagrange Multipliers are sometimes called *shadow prices* because they place prices, in units of the objective, on the scare resources the economic actor is optimally utilizing. They tell how much the resources are worth at the margin to the economic actor.

2.3 SECOND ORDER CONDITION

Theorem 1.15 gives the necessary second order condition for an unconstrained maximum. Just as a different first order condition is needed when there is a binding constraint (i.e., the Lagrange Multiplier Rule), a different second order condition applies when there is a binding constraint (irrespective of whether the constraint is active). The usual treatment derives a semidefiniteness condition on the Hessian of the objective function f for those directions around the constrained maximum in which the constraint h remains zero; and then derives new conditions on the principal minors of $\mathbf{D}^2L$ that are equivalent to this "semidefiniteness of $\mathbf{D}^2f$ subject to constraint." This second step is needlessly tedious, as the principal minor conditions on $\mathbf{D}^2L$ can be derived directly from the principal minor conditions for an unconstrained maximization (i.e., Theorem 1.10) by establishing the algebraic relationship between $\mathbf{D}^2L$ and the Hessian in an equivalent reduced-dimension unconstrained maximization problem. As in the proof of the Lagrange Multiplier Rule, θ is suppressed throughout this section because it plays no role.

Following the proof of the Lagrange Multiplier Rule let $x = (y, z)$ be a partition of x into the first $n - m$ and last m components and let $\tilde{f}(y) = f(y, \phi(y))$ for $y \in B_\epsilon(\hat{y})$. The following theorem provides the algebraic relationship between the Hessian of $\tilde{f}$ and the Hessian of L at a stationary point of L.

Theorem 2.3. *Assume* $\mathbf{D}^2 f$ *and* $\mathbf{D}^2 h$ *exist in a neighborhood of* $\hat{x} \in X$ *and are continuous at* $\hat{x}$*; and that* $\mathbf{D}_z h(\hat{x})$ *is nonsingular. Let* $\hat{\lambda} \in \mathbb{R}^m$ *be the vector promised by the Lagrange Multiplier Rule satisfying* $\mathbf{D}L(\hat{x}, \hat{\lambda}) = 0$. *Then:*

$$\mathbf{D}^2\tilde{f}(\hat{y}) = \mathbf{D}_y^2 L - (\mathbf{D}_y(\mathbf{D}_{(z,\lambda)}L)^\perp)^\perp (\mathbf{D}_{(z,\lambda)}^2 L)^{-1} \mathbf{D}_y(\mathbf{D}_{(z,\lambda)}L)^\perp. \quad (2.13)$$

Proof. From the definition of L:

$$\mathbf{D}_{(z,\lambda)}^2 L = \begin{bmatrix} \mathbf{D}_z^2 L & -(\mathbf{D}_z h)^\perp \\ -\mathbf{D}_z h & 0_m \end{bmatrix}. \quad (2.14)$$

Using nonsingularity of $\mathbf{D}_z h(\hat{x})$, it is straightforward to verify:

$$(\mathbf{D}_{(z,\lambda)}^2 L(\hat{x}, \hat{\lambda}))^{-1} = -\begin{bmatrix} 0_m & (\mathbf{D}_z h)^{-1} \\ ((\mathbf{D}_z h)^\perp)^{-1} & ((\mathbf{D}_z h)^\perp)^{-1} \mathbf{D}_z^2 L (\mathbf{D}_z h)^{-1} \end{bmatrix}.$$

Substitute this and $\mathbf{D}_y(\mathbf{D}_{(z,\lambda)}L)^\perp = [\mathbf{D}_z(\mathbf{D}_y L)^\perp \quad -(\mathbf{D}_y h)^\perp]^\perp$ into Eq. (2.13), and use symmetry of $\mathbf{D}_x^2 L$ (which is implied by continuity at $\hat{x}$), to obtain a restatement of Eq. (2.13) as:

$$\begin{aligned} \mathbf{D}^2\tilde{f}(\hat{y}) &= \mathbf{D}_y^2 L + [\mathbf{D}_z(\mathbf{D}_y L)^\perp \quad -(\mathbf{D}_y h)^\perp] \\ &\quad \times \begin{bmatrix} 0_m & (\mathbf{D}_z h)^{-1} \\ ((\mathbf{D}_z h)^\perp)^{-1} & ((\mathbf{D}_z h)^\perp)^{-1} \mathbf{D}_z^2 L (\mathbf{D}_z h)^{-1} \end{bmatrix} \begin{bmatrix} (\mathbf{D}_z(\mathbf{D}_y L)^\perp)^\perp \\ -\mathbf{D}_y h \end{bmatrix} \\ &= \mathbf{D}_y^2 L - (\mathbf{D}_y h)^\perp ((\mathbf{D}_z h)^\perp)^{-1} \mathbf{D}_y (\mathbf{D}_z L)^\perp - \mathbf{D}_z (\mathbf{D}_y L)^\perp (\mathbf{D}_z h)^{-1} \mathbf{D}_y h \\ &\quad + (\mathbf{D}_y h)^\perp ((\mathbf{D}_z h)^\perp)^{-1} \mathbf{D}_z^2 L (\mathbf{D}_z h)^{-1} \mathbf{D}_y h. \end{aligned} \quad (2.15)$$

Now pre-multiply Eq. (2.3) by $\hat{\lambda}^\perp$ and subtract the product from Eq. (2.2) to obtain:

$$\mathbf{D}\tilde{f}(y) = \mathbf{D}_y L(y, \phi(y), \hat{\lambda}) + \mathbf{D}_z L(y, \phi(y), \hat{\lambda}) \mathbf{D}\phi(y) \text{ for } y \in B_\epsilon(\hat{y}).$$

As this holds in an open ball about $\hat{y}$, we may differentiate again to obtain:

$$\begin{aligned} \mathbf{D}^2\tilde{f} = [\mathbf{D}_y^2 L + \mathbf{D}_y((\mathbf{D}\phi)^\perp (\mathbf{D}_z L)^\perp)] + [\mathbf{D}_z(\mathbf{D}_y L)^\perp \\ + \mathbf{D}_z((\mathbf{D}\phi)^\perp (\mathbf{D}_z L)^\perp)] \mathbf{D}\phi \end{aligned}$$

for $y \in B_\epsilon(\hat{y})$. $\mathbf{D}\phi$ is an $m \times (n - m)$ matrix; expanding in individual rows the first term where $\mathbf{D}\phi$ appears yields:

$$\mathbf{D}_y((\mathbf{D}\phi)^{\perp}(\mathbf{D}_zL)^{\perp}) = \mathbf{D}_y\left(\begin{bmatrix}(\mathbf{D}_{y_1}\phi)^{\perp}(\mathbf{D}_zL)^{\perp}\\ \vdots \\ (\mathbf{D}_{y_{n-m}}\phi)^{\perp}(\mathbf{D}_zL)^{\perp}\end{bmatrix}\right)$$
$$= \begin{bmatrix}\mathbf{D}_y((\mathbf{D}_{y_1}\phi)^{\perp}(\mathbf{D}_zL)^{\perp})\\ \vdots \\ \mathbf{D}_y((\mathbf{D}_{y_{n-m}}\phi)^{\perp}(\mathbf{D}_zL)^{\perp})\end{bmatrix}.$$

Apply the product rule to obtain:

$$\mathbf{D}_y((\mathbf{D}_{y_i}\phi)^{\perp}(\mathbf{D}_zL)^{\perp}) = (\mathbf{D}_zL)\mathbf{D}_y(\mathbf{D}_{y_i}\phi) + (\mathbf{D}_{y_i}\phi)^{\perp}\mathbf{D}_y(\mathbf{D}_zL)^{\perp} \text{ for}$$

$i = 1, \ldots, n - m$.

$\mathbf{D}_zL(\hat{y}, \phi(\hat{y}), \hat{\lambda}) = 0$ because $(\hat{x}, \hat{\lambda})$ is a stationary point of L, so evaluating at $\hat{y}$ yields:

$$\mathbf{D}_y((\mathbf{D}_{y_i}\phi)^{\perp}(\mathbf{D}_zL)^{\perp}) = (\mathbf{D}_{y_i}\phi)^{\perp}\mathbf{D}_y(\mathbf{D}_zL)^{\perp} \text{ for } i = 1, \ldots, n - m.$$

Therefore:

$$\mathbf{D}_y((\mathbf{D}\phi)^{\perp}(\mathbf{D}_zL)^{\perp}) = \begin{bmatrix}(\mathbf{D}_{y_1}\phi)^{\perp}\mathbf{D}_y(\mathbf{D}_zL)^{\perp}\\ \vdots \\ (\mathbf{D}_{y_{n-m}}\phi)^{\perp}\mathbf{D}_y(\mathbf{D}_zL)^{\perp}\end{bmatrix} = (\mathbf{D}\phi)^{\perp}\mathbf{D}_y(\mathbf{D}_zL)^{\perp}$$

at $(\hat{y}, \phi(\hat{y}), \hat{\lambda})$. This same derivation shows $\mathbf{D}_z((\mathbf{D}\phi)^{\perp}(\mathbf{D}_zL)^{\perp}) = (\mathbf{D}\phi)^{\perp}\mathbf{D}_z(\mathbf{D}_zL)^{\perp}$ at $(\hat{y}, \phi(\hat{y}), \hat{\lambda})$. Hence:

$$\mathbf{D}^2\tilde{f}(\hat{y}) = [\mathbf{D}_y^2L + (\mathbf{D}\phi)^{\perp}\mathbf{D}_y(\mathbf{D}_zL)^{\perp}] + [\mathbf{D}_z(\mathbf{D}_yL)^{\perp} + (\mathbf{D}\phi)^{\perp}\mathbf{D}_z^2L]\mathbf{D}\phi.$$

Substitute $\mathbf{D}\phi = -(\mathbf{D}_zh)^{-1}\mathbf{D}_yh$ from Eq. (2.3) to obtain Eq. (2.15). □

As noted in the proof of the Lagrange Multiplier Rule, $\tilde{f}(y)$ attains an unconstrained local maximum at $\hat{y}$, so $\mathbf{D}^2\tilde{f}(\hat{y})$ is negative semidefinite by Theorem 1.15. That is, the principal minors of $\mathbf{D}^2\tilde{f}(\hat{y})$ have the alternating sign pattern described in Theorem 1.10. Eq. (2.13), which is a purely algebraic relationship between the Hessians of the Lagrangian function L and the reduced-dimension objective function $\tilde{f}$ at a stationary point of L, provides a link between the principal minors of these two matrices.

Corollary 2.1. *Assume the conditions of Theorem 2.3. Using the notation of Theorem 1.10:*

$$\left|(\mathbf{D}^2L)^{(J+)}\right| = (-1)^m\,|\mathbf{D}_zh|^2\left|(\mathbf{D}^2\tilde{f})^{(J)}\right| \text{ for every } J \subset \{1, \ldots, n - m\},$$

where $J+ = J \cup \{n - m + 1, \ldots, n + m\}$ *and all derivatives are evaluated at* $(\hat{y}, \phi(\hat{y}), \hat{\lambda})$. *That is, at a stationary point of the Lagrangian function, each principal minor of the Hessian of the Lagrangian function formed from a subset of the first*

$n - m$ and all of the last $2m$ rows/columns is proportional to the corresponding principal minor of the Hessian of the reduced-dimension unconstrained objective function, with proportion $(-1)^m|\mathbf{D}_z h|^2$.[3]

Proof. Note that the Hessian of L can be partitioned as:

$$\mathbf{D}^2 L(y, z, \lambda) = \begin{bmatrix} \mathbf{D}_y^2 L & (\mathbf{D}_y(\mathbf{D}_{(z,\lambda)}L)^{\perp})^{\perp} \\ \mathbf{D}_y(\mathbf{D}_{(z,\lambda)}L)^{\perp} & \mathbf{D}_{(z,\lambda)}^2 L \end{bmatrix}.$$

Letting $(\mathbf{D}_y(\mathbf{D}_{(z,\lambda)}L)^{\perp})^{(J_c)}$ denote the submatrix formed from $\mathbf{D}_y(\mathbf{D}_{(z,\lambda)}L)^{\perp}$ by retaining the set J of columns (and retaining all rows), we have:

$$(\mathbf{D}^2 L)^{(J+)} = \begin{bmatrix} (\mathbf{D}_y^2 L)^{(J)} & ((\mathbf{D}_y(\mathbf{D}_{(z,\lambda)}L)^{\perp})^{(J_c)})^{\perp} \\ (\mathbf{D}_y(\mathbf{D}_{(z,\lambda)}L)^{\perp})^{(J_c)} & \mathbf{D}_{(z,\lambda)}^2 L \end{bmatrix}.$$

Applying the standard formula for determinants of partitioned matrices [3, pp. 137–138] yields:

$$\left|(\mathbf{D}^2 L)^{(J+)}\right| = \left|\mathbf{D}_{(z,\lambda)}^2 L\right| \Big|(\mathbf{D}_y^2 L)^{(J)} - ((\mathbf{D}_y(\mathbf{D}_{(z,\lambda)}L)^{\perp})^{(J_c)})^{\perp}(\mathbf{D}_{(z,\lambda)}^2 L)^{-1}(\mathbf{D}_y(\mathbf{D}_{(z,\lambda)}L)^{\perp})^{(J_c)}\Big|.$$

From Theorem 2.3:

$$(\mathbf{D}^2\tilde{f})^{(J)} = (\mathbf{D}_y^2 L)^{(J)} - ((\mathbf{D}_y(\mathbf{D}_{(z,\lambda)}L)^{\perp})^{(J_c)})^{\perp}(\mathbf{D}_{(z,\lambda)}^2 L)^{-1}(\mathbf{D}_y(\mathbf{D}_{(z,\lambda)}L)^{\perp})^{(J_c)}.$$

Therefore:

$$\left|(\mathbf{D}^2 L)^{(J+)}\right| = \left|\mathbf{D}_{(z,\lambda)}^2 L\right| \left|(\mathbf{D}^2\tilde{f})^{(J)}\right|.$$

From Eq. (2.14), and again using standard properties of determinants, we have:

$$\left|\mathbf{D}_{(z,\lambda)}^2 L\right| = (-1)^m \begin{vmatrix} -(\mathbf{D}_z h)^{\perp} & \mathbf{D}_z^2 L \\ 0_m & -\mathbf{D}_z h \end{vmatrix} = (-1)^m |\mathbf{D}_z h|^2.$$

Substituting yields the result. □

Using Corollary 2.1 and the necessary second order condition for unconstrained maximization of $\tilde{f}(y)$ (Theorems 1.15 and 1.10) yields the necessary second order condition when there is a binding constraint.

[3] The fact that the last $2m$ rows/columns are always included is a byproduct of the ordering (y, z, λ) used for the Hessian of L. If these subvectors are ordered differently (some authors use the ordering (λ, z, y)) then the set of rows/columns always retained changes accordingly.

Theorem 2.4 (Necessary Second Order Condition for a Binding Constraint). *Assume the conditions of Theorem 2.3. Then, in the notation of Corollary 2.1:*

$$(-1)^{\#J+m}\left|(\mathbf{D}^2L(\hat{x},\hat{\lambda}))^{(J^+)}\right| \geq 0 \textit{ for every } J \subset \{1,\ldots,n-m\}.$$

If there is no constraint then $m = 0$, $L = f = \tilde{f}$, and the condition in Theorem 2.4 reduces to that of Theorem 1.15.

Note also that the relationship between principal minors given in Corollary 2.1 is equally useful for translating the *sufficient* second order condition for an unconstrained maximum (i.e., *leading* principal minors of $\mathbf{D}^2f(\hat{x})$ have signs $(-1)^{\#J}$) into a *sufficient* second order condition for a constrained maximum (i.e., leading principal minors of $\mathbf{D}^2L(\hat{y},\hat{z},\hat{\lambda})$ have signs $(-1)^{\#J+m}$ for $J \subset \{1,\ldots,n-m\}$).

2.4 COMPARATIVE STATICS

When the Lagrange Multiplier Rule holds and the Implicit Function Theorem can be applied to the system (2.10) and (2.11), differentiating this system with respect to θ yields:

$$\begin{bmatrix} \mathbf{D}_x^2L(\hat{x}(\theta^0),\hat{\lambda}(\theta^0);\theta^0) & -(\mathbf{D}_xh(\hat{x}(\theta^0);\theta^0))^{\perp} \\ -\mathbf{D}_xh(\hat{x}(\theta^0);\theta^0) & 0_m \end{bmatrix} \begin{bmatrix} \mathbf{D}\hat{x}(\theta^0) \\ \mathbf{D}\hat{\lambda}(\theta^0) \end{bmatrix}$$
$$= -\begin{bmatrix} \mathbf{D}_\theta(\mathbf{D}_xL)^{\perp}(\hat{x}(\theta^0),\hat{\lambda}(\theta^0);\theta^0) \\ -\mathbf{D}_\theta h(\hat{x}(\theta^0);\theta^0) \end{bmatrix}. \quad (2.16)$$

The $(n+m)\times(n+m)$ coefficient matrix on the left side of Eq. (2.16) is the Jacobian of the system of Eqs. (2.10) and (2.11) with respect to (x,λ), nonsingularity of which is the main requirement of the Implicit Function Theorem. This Jacobian is also $\mathbf{D}^2_{(x,\lambda)}L$ (i.e., $\mathbf{D}^2L$ in Theorem 2.4) evaluated at $(\hat{x}(\theta^0),\hat{\lambda}(\theta^0))$. Letting $(\mathbf{D}^2_{(x,\lambda)}L)^{-(j,i)}$ denote this matrix with column j replaced by column i of the right side of Eq. (2.16) without the leading minus sign, Cramer's Rule can be applied to obtain:

$$\frac{\partial\hat{x}_j}{\partial\theta_i} = -\frac{\left|(\mathbf{D}^2_{(x,\lambda)}L)^{-(j,i)}\right|}{\left|\mathbf{D}^2_{(x,\lambda)}L\right|} \text{ for } j = 1,\ldots,n \quad (2.17)$$

$$\frac{\partial\hat{\lambda}_j}{\partial\theta_i} = -\frac{\left|(\mathbf{D}^2_{(x,\lambda)}L)^{-(n+j,i)}\right|}{\left|\mathbf{D}^2_{(x,\lambda)}L\right|} \text{ for } j = 1,\ldots,m; \quad (2.18)$$

for $i = 1, \ldots, k$. Once again, it is understood that these equations are evaluated at θ^0.

Eqs. (2.17) and (2.18) can yield explicit refutable hypotheses about the optimal choice $\hat{x}(\theta)$ and the shadow price $\hat{\lambda}(\theta)$. In principle, these equations can be evaluated directly for a particular objective function f and constraint function h, although doing so in a problem of any significant dimension might be impossible as a practical matter. However, even without fully specified objective and constraint functions, these equations often yield refutable hypotheses in economic models. From Theorem 2.4 the maximization behavioral postulate implies $(-1)^n \left|\mathbf{D}^2_{(x,\lambda)}L\right| \geq 0$ and, as this determinant cannot be zero when the Implicit Function Theorem is used, the denominators in Eqs. (2.17) and (2.18) cannot be zero and therefore have sign $(-1)^n$ (when the expressions exist). Only the number of choice variables must be known to evaluate this sign.

The numerators are more complicated but the signs can be determined for particular (j, i) pairs in some economic models. In particular, suppose the constraint is inactive with respect to θ_i so that $\mathbf{D}_{\theta_i}h = 0$. Suppose further that column i of $\mathbf{D}_\theta(\mathbf{D}_x L)^\perp$ is all zeros except for some number b in row i (a common occurrence in economic models). Then, for $i = j$, cofactor expansion of $\left|(\mathbf{D}^2_{(x,\lambda)}L)^{-(j,i)}\right|$ along column i yields $b\left|(\mathbf{D}^2L)^{(J^+)}\right|$ for $J = \{1, \ldots, i-1, i+1, \ldots, n-m\}$. Hence $\#J = n-m-1$ and by Theorem 2.4 the numerator in Eq. (2.17) has sign $b(-1)^{n-1}$ (or is zero). Combining this with the sign $(-1)^n$ of the denominator and with the leading (-1), $\frac{\partial \hat{x}_i}{\partial \theta_i}$ has the same sign as b (or is zero).

If there is no constraint then $m = 0$ and Eq. (2.16) reduces to:

$$\mathbf{D}^2_x f(\hat{x}(\theta^0); \theta^0)\mathbf{D}\hat{x}(\theta^0) = -\mathbf{D}_\theta(\mathbf{D}_x f)^\perp(\hat{x}(\theta^0)). \tag{2.19}$$

This is the basic comparative statics equation for an unconstrained optimization. It leads to an unconstrained version of Eq. (2.17):

$$\frac{\partial \hat{x}_j}{\partial \theta_i} = -\frac{\left|(\mathbf{D}^2_x f)^{-(j,i)}\right|}{\left|\mathbf{D}^2_x f\right|} \quad \text{for } j = 1, \ldots, n \text{ and } i = 1, \ldots, k. \tag{2.20}$$

The discussion above establishes that this expression has the same sign as b (or is zero) for $i = j$ when the only nonzero element in column i of $\mathbf{D}_\theta(\mathbf{D}_x f)^\perp$ is b in row i.

This result can be seen from the Envelope Theorem as well. When $\mathbf{D}_\theta h = 0$ in a neighborhood of $(\hat{x}; \theta)$, Theorem 1.18 holds, so $\mathbf{D}f^*(\theta) = \mathbf{D}_\theta f(\hat{x}(\theta); \theta)$ and $\mathbf{D}^2 f^* - \mathbf{D}^2_\theta f$ is positive semidefinite. Differentiating the former yields:

$$\mathbf{D}_x(\mathbf{D}_\theta f)^\perp \mathbf{D}\hat{x} = \mathbf{D}^2 f^* - \mathbf{D}^2_\theta f. \tag{2.21}$$

Thus, if the only nonzero entry in row i of $\mathbf{D}_x(\mathbf{D}_\theta f)^\perp$ is b in column i then $b\frac{\partial \hat{x}_i}{\partial \theta_i} \geq 0$.

The analysis here holds for any subvector $\tilde{\theta}$ of the parameter vector θ. Having no constraint is a special case of this situation, but the derivations go through even when there is a binding constraint provided the constraint is inactive with respect to $\tilde{\theta}$ in a neighborhood of $(\hat{x}; \tilde{\theta})$. With a binding but inactive constraint with respect to some $\tilde{\theta}$, Eq. (2.16) becomes:

$$\begin{bmatrix} \mathbf{D}^2_x L(\hat{x}(\theta^0), \hat{\lambda}(\theta^0); \theta^0) & -(\mathbf{D}_x h(\hat{x}(\theta^0); \theta^0))^\perp \\ -\mathbf{D}_x h(\hat{x}(\theta^0); \theta^0) & 0_m \end{bmatrix} \begin{bmatrix} \mathbf{D}_{\tilde{\theta}} \hat{x}(\theta^0) \\ \mathbf{D}_{\tilde{\theta}} \hat{\lambda}(\theta^0) \end{bmatrix}$$
$$= -\begin{bmatrix} \mathbf{D}_{\tilde{\theta}}(\mathbf{D}_x f)^\perp(\hat{x}(\theta^0); \theta^0) \\ 0 \end{bmatrix}, \tag{2.22}$$

from which analogues to Eqs. (2.17) and (2.18) can be derived.

2.5 NOTES ON PROPERTIES OF MINIMA

In some cases our behavioral postulate is to minimize an objective rather than maximize it. The problem of minimizing $v(x; \theta)$ subject to $x \in \Gamma(\theta)$ can be treated as a maximization problem by setting $f(x; \theta) = -v(x; \theta)$ and then maximizing $f(x; \theta)$ subject to $x \in \Gamma(\theta)$. Hence all of the results of this chapter hold for minima, with modifications needed only to keep track of the minus sign. For convenience, the results for minimizing v are listed here.

1. Theorem 2.1. Replace $\mathbf{D}_x f$ with $\mathbf{D}_x v$. The result is unchanged.
2. Theorem 2.2. Replace $\mathbf{D}_x f$ with $\mathbf{D}_x v$. The result is unchanged.
3. Theorem 2.4. The Hessian of $\tilde{f}$ must be positive semidefinite, which is equivalent to $\left|(\mathbf{D}^2\tilde{f})^{(J)}\right| \geq 0$ for every $J \subset \{1, \ldots, n-m\}$, so the necessary condition on $\mathbf{D}^2 L$ is that $(-1)^m \left|(\mathbf{D}^2 L)^{(J+)}\right| \geq 0$ for every $J \subset \{1, \ldots, n-m\}$.
4. Eq. (2.16). The principal minors $\left|(\mathbf{D}^2 L)^{(J+)}\right|$ do not alternate in sign, so $\frac{\partial x_i}{\partial \theta_i}$ has the opposite sign of b or is zero (under the specified conditions).

2.6 NOTES

Much of the material in this chapter is sufficiently well-known that it belongs to the public domain of mathematical knowledge. Nonetheless, the presentation here relies heavily on a few references that should be mentioned.

Standard results from advanced calculus are mostly from Apostol [1]. Debreu [4, Chapter 1] and Takayama [5] also provide much background material.

Samuelson [6, Chapters 2 and 3] brought the Envelope Theorem and the general methodology of comparative statics to the attention of economists. Silberberg [7], [8, Chapters 6 and 7] provide discussion. Pauwels [9] derives comparative statics results in a concise and elegant manner.

The proof of the Lagrange Multiplier Rule given in the text borrows heavily from Hadley [10, pp. 64–75]. Classic references are Courant [11, pp. 190–199] and Courant and Hilbert [12, pp. 231–233].

2.7 EXERCISES

1. Let $y = f(x_1, x_2) = -(x_1 - 1)^2 - x_2^2$ and $h_1(x_1, x_2) = x_1 + x_2$. f is a paraboloid with an unconstrained peak at $(1, 0)$ and the constraint $h_1 = 0$ requires that (x_1, x_2, y) lie in the vertical plane through the line $x_1 + x_2 = 0$.
   a. Use the Lagrange Multiplier Rule to derive a triple (x_1, x_2, λ_1) at which f reaches a constrained maximum.
   b. Verify that constraint qualification holds at the point derived in item (a).
   c. Now suppose the constraint were $h_1(x_1, x_2) = (x_1 + x_2)^2$. Try to use the Lagrange Multiplier Rule to derive a triple (x_1, x_2, λ_1) as in item (a).
   d. Note that the constraint in (c) effectively requires that (x_1, x_2, y) lie on the same plane as the original constraint. Therefore the solution to the problem in item (c) is the same as in item (a). Check constraint qualification for the constraint in item (c) at the point identified in item (a). What do you conclude?
2. Consider a price-taking firm that chooses two inputs $(x_1, x_2) \in \mathbb{R}_+^2$ to minimize cost $c(x_1, x_2) = w_1 x_1 + w_2 x_2$ subject to producing output level $y > 0$, where $y = (x_1 + 1)^\theta (x_2 + 1)^{1-\theta}$ is the firm's production function, $(w_1, w_2) \in \mathbb{R}_{++}^2$ are the input prices, and $\theta \in (0, 1)$ is a production parameter. Take as given that the cost-minimizing input choices for this firm are:

$$(\hat{x}_1, \hat{x}_2) = \left(y\left(\frac{w_2\theta}{w_1(1-\theta)}\right)^{1-\theta} - 1, y\left(\frac{w_1(1-\theta)}{w_2\theta}\right)^{\theta} - 1 \right).$$

Assume the prices, output level, and θ value are such that these input choices are both strictly positive. Use the tangency property of the envelope theorem to show that cost decreases with a small increase in θ if and only if $\frac{w_2}{w_1} > \frac{1-\theta}{\theta}$ (Note: Do not grind it out; the point of the question is to correctly apply the tangency property).

3. Let $X = \Theta = \mathbb{R}^1_{++}$; and $f(x;\theta) = (\theta+1)x^{1/2}$ with $h(x;\theta) = x - \theta$. This exercise provides an example showing that there may be no envelope relationship between f^* and L even when the unconstrained maximum of L is the same as the constrained maximum of f.
 a. By inspection, what is the constrained maximizing value $\hat{x}(\theta)$?
 b. Substitute $\hat{x}(\theta)$ into f to obtain $f^*(\theta)$. Derive $f^{*\prime}(\theta)$ and $f^{*\prime\prime}(\theta)$.
 c. Write $L(x,\lambda;\theta) = f(x;\theta) - \lambda h(x;\theta)$. Derive L_1 and L_{11}. Is L strictly concave in x?
 d. Use the Lagrange Multiplier Rule and the constraint to derive $\hat{\lambda}(\theta)$. Is $L(x,\hat{\lambda}(\theta);\theta)$ maximized over x at $\hat{x}(\theta)$? Why?
 e. Now consider a particular value of the parameter, θ^0, and fix λ at $\lambda^0 = \hat{\lambda}(\theta^0)$. Derive $L^*(\lambda^0;\theta)$. Derive $L^*_2(\lambda^0;\theta)$ and $L^*_{22}(\lambda^0;\theta)$.
 f. Fix x at $x^0 = \hat{x}(\theta^0)$ and write $L(x^0,\lambda^0;\theta)$. According to Theorem 1.18, $L^*(\lambda^0;\theta)$ is an upper envelope of the collection of $L(x^0,\lambda^0;\theta)$ functions (one for each θ^0). Verify that they are indeed tangent at $\theta = \theta^0$ and that $L_{33}(x^0,\lambda^0;\theta) - L^*_{22}(\lambda^0;\theta) < 0$ at $\theta = \theta^0$.
 g. Confirm from item (b) also that $f^{*\prime}(\theta)$ takes on this same value at $\theta = \theta^0$, as required by Theorem 2.2.
 h. Finally, compare $f^{*\prime\prime}(\theta)$ with $L_{33}(x^0,\lambda^0;\theta)$ at $\theta = \theta^0$. Is there an envelope relationship between $f^*(\theta)$ and the collection of $L(x^0,\lambda^0;\theta)$ functions?

4. This exercise provides an example showing that we cannot generally regard constrained maximization of f as equivalent to unconstrained maximization of L. Let $X = \mathbb{R}^1$; and $f(x) = x^2$ with $h(x) = x - 1$ (there are no parameters θ in this problem).
 a. By inspection, what is the constrained maximizing value $\hat{x}$?
 b. Substitute $\hat{x}$ into f to obtain f^*.
 c. Write $L(x,\lambda) = f(x) - \lambda h(x)$. What is the unconstrained maximum of L over $x \in \mathbb{R}^1$?

5. Suppose the parameter vector in a maximization problem has two parts: $\theta = (p, a)$, where $p \in \mathbb{R}^n_{++}$ and $a \in \mathbb{R}^1$. Consider the problem of maximizing $p^{\perp}x$ by choosing x from $\{x \in \mathbb{R}^n : h(x, a) = 0\}$. Assume h is real-valued and sufficiently well-behaved that the problem and the comparative statics of the solution can be studied using calculus techniques. If we know nothing more about h what, if anything, can be concluded about how the optimal choice of x changes as a changes? Fully explain your conclusion.
6. Consider the problem of maximizing $f(x;\theta)$ subject to $h(x;\theta) = 0$, where $x \in \mathbb{R}^n$ is the choice vector and $\theta \in \mathbb{R}^k$ is a vector of parameters. Assume f is real-valued, h is vector-valued of dimension m $(1 \leq m < n)$ and that f and h are sufficiently well-behaved that the problem and the comparative statics of the solution can be studied using calculus techniques. Suppose further that one component of θ, say θ_i, has two special properties:
   - Changes in θ_i do not affect the constraint vector h, and
   - θ_i is additively separable in f from all components of x except x_j (j is not necessarily equal to i).

   If we know nothing more about f and h what, if anything, can be concluded about how the optimal choice of x changes as θ_i changes? Fully explain your conclusion.
7. Consider the problem of maximizing the real-valued function $f(x_1, x_2; \theta_1, \theta_2)$ by choosing (x_1, x_2) subject to $h(x_1, x_2; \theta_1, \theta_2) = 0$. Here, (θ_1, θ_2) is a pair of parameters and h is real-valued. Assume throughout that f and h are both twice continuously differentiable on $\mathbb{R}^4$ and a unique maximum exists for every (θ_1, θ_2) pair. Denote that maximum by $(\hat{x}_1(\theta_1, \theta_2), \hat{x}_2(\theta_1, \theta_2))$. Denote the Lagrangian function by $L(x_1, x_2, \lambda; \theta_1, \theta_2) = f(x_1, x_2; \theta_1, \theta_2) - \lambda h(x_1, x_2; \theta_1, \theta_2)$.
   a. What additional assumption is needed to apply the Lagrange Multiplier Rule to this problem? Assume this for the remainder of the question and write the resulting necessary first order conditions in terms of partial derivatives of f and h. For brevity, use notation like $f_{x_1\theta_2}$ to denote $\frac{\partial^2 f}{\partial x_1 \partial \theta_2}$ and suppress arguments of functions.
   b. Write the necessary second order condition in terms of a matrix with entries that are partial derivatives of f and h.
   c. What additional assumption is needed to derive the comparative statics of $(\hat{x}_1, \hat{x}_2)$ from the necessary first order conditions? Assume this for the remainder of the question and write the basic

comparative statics matrix equation with entries that are composed from partial derivatives of f, h and $(\hat{x}_1, \hat{x}_2)$.

d. Use Cramer's Rule to write an equation for a typical comparative static derivative $\frac{\partial \hat{x}_i}{\partial \theta_j}$ in terms of determinants of matrices with entries that are composed from partial derivatives of f and h.

e. Describe the special features of some of the entries in your determinants that allow us to determine the signs of some of the comparative static derivatives in some economic models.

8. A firm in a Cournot duopoly is postulated to behave according to:

$$\pi^*(q_r) = \sup\{\pi(q; q_r) : q \in \mathbb{R}^1_+\},$$

where $\pi(q; q_r) = P(q + q_r)q - C(q)$. Here, P is an inverse demand function and C is a cost function (both real-valued); and $q_r \in \mathbb{R}^1_+$ is a rival's quantity. Assume there is a unique solution $\hat{q}(q_r)$.

a. Carefully draw $\pi(\hat{q}(q_r^0); q_r)$ and $\pi(\hat{q}(q_r^1); q_r)$ for two fixed values $q_r^0 < q_r^1$, assuming P is linear with slope $\beta < 0$. What can you say about $\hat{q}$ from this graph? Explain why. Include details.

b. Now redraw your graph and include $\pi^*(q_r)$ on the redrawn graph. What, if anything, can you say about the slope and curvature of π^* when P is linear? Explain why. Include details.

c. Assume the conditions of the implicit function theorem hold so that the basic comparative statics equation can be obtained. Derive that equation, still assuming P is linear. Explain what you know about $\hat{q}(q_r)$ from the equation. Compare your result to your graph.

d. Repeat the analysis of items a–c with the weaker assumption that P is convex rather than linear (still downward-sloping). How far can you get describing π^* and $\hat{q}$?

9. A firm in a (differentiated products) constant returns Bertrand duopoly is postulated to behave according to:

$$\pi^*(p_r) = \sup\{\pi(p; p_r) : p \in \mathbb{R}^1_+\},$$

where $\pi(p; p_r) = (p - c)Q(p; p_r)$. Here, c is the constant marginal cost and $p_r \in \mathbb{R}^1_+$ is a rival's price. Q is a (real-valued) demand function. The differentiated products are substitutes; hence Q is decreasing in p and increasing in p_r. Assume there is a unique solution $\hat{p}(p_r)$.

a. Carefully draw $\pi(\hat{p}(p_r^0); p_r)$ and $\pi(\hat{p}(p_r^1); p_r)$ for two fixed values $p_r^0 < p_r^1$, assuming Q is convex. Take care to accurately represent relative positions, slopes and curvatures. Can you say anything about $\hat{p}$ from this graph? Explain why. Include details.

b. Now redraw your graph and include $\pi^*(p_r)$ on the redrawn graph. What, if anything, can you say about the slope and curvature of π^* when Q is convex? Explain why. Include details.

c. Assume the conditions of the implicit function theorem hold so that the basic comparative statics equation can be obtained. Derive that equation, still assuming Q is convex. Explain what you know about $\hat{p}(p_r)$ from the equation. Compare your result to your graph.

d. Repeat the analysis of items a–c with the stronger assumption that Q is linear rather than convex. How far can you get describing π^* and $\hat{p}$?

10. Two symmetric firms engage in simultaneous noncooperative price competition. The demand for firm i at nonnegative prices and quantity is:

$$q_i = \alpha - p_i + \beta p_j \quad (i \neq j),$$

where $\beta \in [0, 1)$. Cost for firm i is $c(q_i)$, where $c' > 0$ and $c'' \geq 0$. Assume throughout this question we are studying a unique symmetric Nash equilibrium at positive prices and quantities.

a. Write the profit function and first and second order conditions for firm i.

b. Let p^e denote the equilibrium price. Use standard comparative statics methodology to place a sign on $\frac{\partial p^e}{\partial \beta}$.

c. Let π^e denote a firm's equilibrium profit. Use the envelope theorem to explore the effect of an increase in β on π^e.

REFERENCES

[1] Apostol TM. Mathematical analysis. 2nd ed. Reading, MA: Addison-Wesley; 1974.

[2] Simon CP, Blume L. Mathematics for economists. New York: Norton; 1994.

[3] Johnston J. Econometric methods. 3rd ed. New York: McGraw-Hill; 1984.

[4] Debreu G. Theory of value. Cowles Foundation for Research in Economics Monograph 17; 1959.

[5] Takayama A. Mathematical economics. Hinsdale, IL: The Dryden Press; 1974.

[6] Samuelson PA. Foundations of economic analysis. Cambridge, MA: Harvard University Press; 1947.

[7] Silberberg E. A revision of comparative statics methodology in economics, or, how to do comparative statics on the back of an envelope. J Econ Theory 1974;7:159–72.

[8] Silberberg E. The structure of economics: a mathematical analysis. 2nd ed. New York: McGraw-Hill; 1990.

[9] Pauwels W. On some results in comparative statics analysis. J Econ Theory 1979;21: 483–90.
[10] Hadley G. Nonlinear and dynamic programming. Reading, MA: Addison-Wesley; 1964.
[11] Courant R. Differential and integral calculus, vol. II. New York: Interscience; 1936.
[12] Courant R, Hilbert D. Methods of mathematical physics, vol. I. New York: Interscience; 1953.

CHAPTER 3

Convex Functions

Chapter Outline

Maxima in economic models are sometimes convex functions of parameters. We begin with definitions of convex sets and convex cones.

Definition 3.1. $S \subset \mathbb{R}^n$ is a *convex* set if, for every $x^0, x^1 \in S$ $(x^0 \neq x^1)$:

$$\alpha x^0 + (1 - \alpha)x^1 \in S \text{ for every } \alpha \in (0, 1).$$

The segment $\alpha x^0 + (1 - \alpha)x^1$ for $\alpha \in (0, 1)$ is called the *convex combination* of x^0 and x^1. Hence we say S is a convex set when the convex combination of every two elements in S lies entirely in S. S is a *strictly convex* set when the convex combination of every two (distinct) elements of S lies entirely in the interior of S.

These ideas are illustrated in Fig. 3.1.

Recall from Chapter 1 that S is called a *cone* when multiplication of its elements by positive scalars yields elements. Combining the concepts of cones and convex sets leads to the notion of a *convex cone*.

Definition 3.2. $S \subset \mathbb{R}^n$ is a *convex cone* if, for every $x^0, x^1 \in S$ $(x^0 \neq x^1)$ and $\alpha, \beta \in \mathbb{R}^1_{++}$:

$$\alpha x^0 + \beta x^1 \in S.$$

Every convex cone is a convex set. As with cones, α and β are sometimes permitted to be zero in the definition of convex cones. Every ray emanating

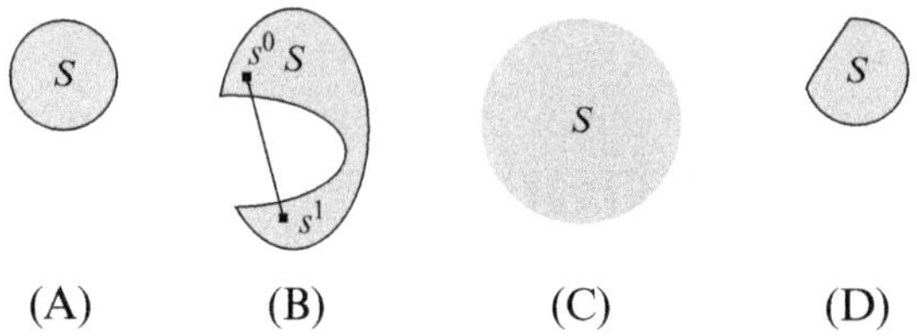

Fig. 3.1 Convex sets in $\mathbb{R}^2$. In (A), the set S is strictly convex. In (B), S is not convex because the convex combination of s^0 and s^1, both elements of S, passes outside of S. In (C), S is not closed but is strictly convex nonetheless. In (D), S is convex but, due to the linear boundary segment, is not strictly convex.

from the origin is a convex cone (irrespective of whether the origin is included). A collection of rays emanating from the origin is a cone but is not a convex cone unless every ray "between" any two rays in the set is also in the set. Therefore $\mathbb{R}^n_{++}$, $\mathbb{R}^n_+ - \{0\}$, and $\mathbb{R}^n_+$ are all convex cones. The first two are not even cones if zero scalars are allowed in the definition but $\mathbb{R}^n_+$ is a convex cone with or without zero scalars in the definition, as is $\{0\}$.

Definition 3.3. Assume $S \subset \mathbb{R}^n$ is a convex set and $\phi : S \to \mathbb{R}^1$. ϕ is a *convex* function if, for every $x^0, x^1 \in S$ $(x^0 \neq x^1)$:

$$\phi(\alpha x^0 + (1-\alpha)x^1) \leq \alpha\phi(x^0) + (1-\alpha)\phi(x^1) \text{ for every } \alpha \in (0,1).$$

ϕ is a *concave* function if $-\phi$ is convex. The convexity/concavity is *strict* if the inequality in the definition is strict.

Note the importance of S being convex in the definition. This ensures $\alpha x^0 + (1-\alpha)x^1 \in S$. The domains of convex functions in economic models are sometimes more restricted, being convex cones rather than merely convex sets. Fig. 3.2 displays a typical convex function. x^0 and x^1 are arbitrary points in the domain. For any such pair, the convex combination between the points $(x^0, \phi(x^0))$ and $(x^1, \phi(x^1))$ is traced out as α moves between 1 and 0. ϕ is a convex function if and only if that linear segment always lies on or above the function ϕ.

An often-used property of convex functions is *Jensen's Inequality*. The following theorem establishes that Jensen's Inequality is equivalent to the definition of a convex function (i.e., is an alternative way to define a convex function).

Theorem 3.1 (Jensen's Inequality). *Assume $S \subset \mathbb{R}^n$ is a convex set and $\phi : S \to \mathbb{R}^1$. Assume $x^i \in S$, $\alpha_i \geq 0$ for $i = 1, \ldots, m$, and $\sum_{i=1}^m \alpha_i = 1$. Then:*

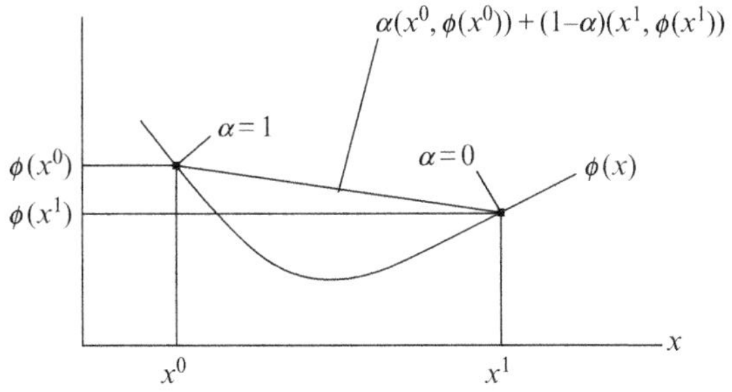

Fig. 3.2 A convex function. Every linear segment connecting two points on the function lies everywhere on or above the function.

$$\phi\left(\sum_{i=1}^{m} \alpha_i x^i\right) \leq \sum_{i=1}^{m} \alpha_i \phi(x^i)$$

for every such collection of x^i's and α_i's if and only if ϕ is a convex function.

Proof. The inequality obviously implies convexity by setting $m = 2$ and noting that $\alpha_2 = 1 - \alpha_1$. Conversely, assume ϕ is convex and, without loss of generality, assume $\alpha_i > 0$ for $i = 1, \ldots, m$. Then:

$$\begin{aligned}
\phi\left(\sum_{i=1}^{m} \alpha_i x^i\right) &= \phi\left(\alpha_1 x^1 + (1-\alpha_1)\sum_{i=2}^{m} \frac{\alpha_i}{1-\alpha_1} x^i\right) \\
&\leq \alpha_1 \phi(x^1) + (1-\alpha_1)\phi\left(\sum_{i=2}^{m} \frac{\alpha_i}{1-\alpha_1} x^i\right) \\
&= \alpha_1 \phi(x^1) + (1-\alpha_1)\phi\left(\frac{\alpha_2}{1-\alpha_1} x^2 + \frac{1-\alpha_2}{1-\alpha_1}\sum_{i=3}^{m} \frac{\alpha_i}{1-\alpha_2} x^i\right) \\
&\leq \alpha_1 \phi(x^1) + (1-\alpha_1)\left(\frac{\alpha_2}{1-\alpha_1}\phi(x^2) + \frac{1-\alpha_2}{1-\alpha_1}\phi\left(\sum_{i=3}^{m} \frac{\alpha_i}{1-\alpha_2} x^i\right)\right) \\
&= \alpha_1 \phi(x^1) + \alpha_2 \phi(x^2) + (1-\alpha_2)\phi\left(\sum_{i=3}^{m} \frac{\alpha_i}{1-\alpha_2} x^i\right).
\end{aligned}$$

Continuing in this manner yields $\sum_{i=1}^{m} \alpha_i \phi(x^i)$ on the right side. □

3.1 CONTINUITY AND DIFFERENTIABILITY

Convexity is a very strong property because it implies other properties, such as continuity on the interior of the domain and differentiability except on a set of measure zero. These properties follow from the behavior of the secant

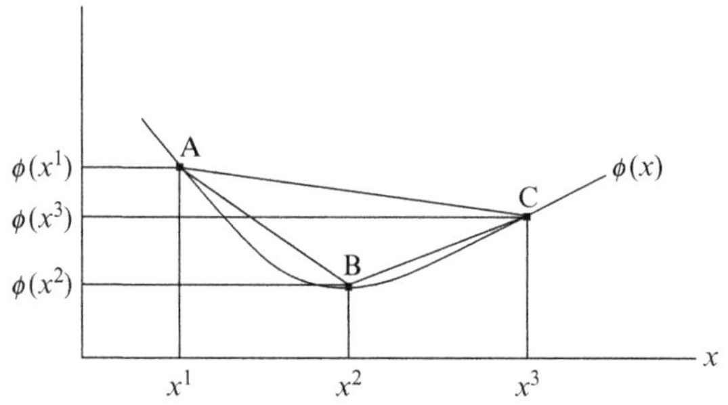

Fig. 3.3 Secant lines of a convex function. Notice that the slope of the segment AB is less than the slope of AC which in turn is less than the slope of BC.

line slopes which, as shown in Fig. 3.3, are increasing along any line in the domain.

Theorem 3.2. *Assume $S \subset \mathbb{R}^n$ is a convex set and $\phi : S \to \mathbb{R}^1$ is a convex function. Let x^1, x^2, x^3 lie on the same line in S with x^2 strictly between x^1 and x^3. Then:*

$$\frac{\phi(x^2) - \phi(x^1)}{\|x^2 - x^1\|} \leq \frac{\phi(x^3) - \phi(x^1)}{\|x^3 - x^1\|} \leq \frac{\phi(x^3) - \phi(x^2)}{\|x^3 - x^2\|}.$$

Proof. As x^2 is on the line between x^1 and x^3, there exists $\alpha \in (0, 1)$ such that $x^2 = (1 - \alpha)x^1 + \alpha x^3$. Rearranging and taking the norm of both sides reveals $\alpha = \frac{\|x^2 - x^1\|}{\|x^3 - x^1\|}$. By convexity of ϕ:

$$\begin{aligned}\phi(x^2) &\leq (1 - \alpha)\phi(x^1) + \alpha\phi(x^3) = \phi(x^1) + \alpha(\phi(x^3) - \phi(x^1)) \\ &= \phi(x^1) + \frac{\|x^2 - x^1\|}{\|x^3 - x^1\|}(\phi(x^3) - \phi(x^1)).\end{aligned} \tag{3.1}$$

This establishes the first inequality. Now select $\alpha \in (0, 1)$ such that $x^2 = \alpha x^1 + (1 - \alpha)x^3$, or $\alpha = \frac{\|x^3 - x^2\|}{\|x^3 - x^1\|}$. Again by convexity of ϕ:

$$\begin{aligned}\phi(x^2) &\leq \alpha\phi(x^1) + (1 - \alpha)\phi(x^3) = \phi(x^3) - \alpha(\phi(x^3) - \phi(x^1)) \\ &= \phi(x^3) - \frac{\|x^3 - x^2\|}{\|x^3 - x^1\|}(\phi(x^3) - \phi(x^1)),\end{aligned} \tag{3.2}$$

establishing the second inequality. □

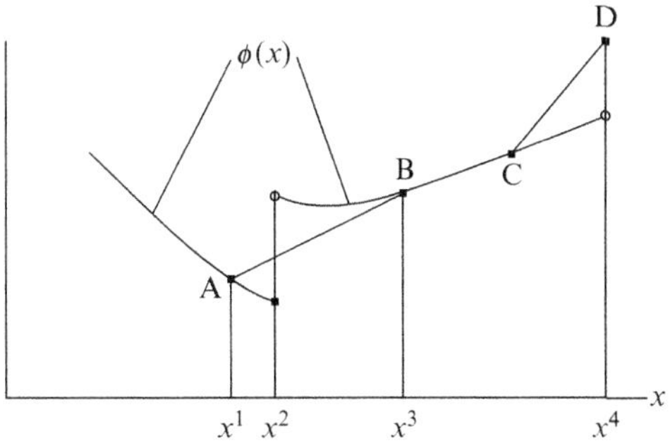

Fig. 3.4 Continuity of a convex function.

It is tedious to prove but geometrically obvious that a convex function is continuous on the interior of its domain. In Fig. 3.4, a "convex-looking" function has a discontinuity at the interior point x^2, which leads to existence of segments like AB that lie partly below the function (between x^2 and x^3 in this case). Formally, this violates the monotonicity of the secant slopes established in Theorem 3.2 because the slope of the segment AB is steeper than the slope of the segment between a point on ϕ just to the right of x^2 and B. Note, however, that it is possible for a convex function to have a discontinuity at the boundary of its domain. If the domain S were restricted to $(x^2, x^4]$ in Fig. 3.4 then ϕ is convex on S despite the discontinuity illustrated at x^4; all segments such as CD lie above the function.

Theorem 3.3. *Assume $S \subset \mathbb{R}^n$ is a convex set and $\phi : S \to \mathbb{R}^1$ is a convex function. Then ϕ is continuous at every interior point of S.*

Proof. Let $x^0 \in$ int S. We begin by showing that ϕ is bounded on an open ball about x^0. Select $\hat{\delta} \in (0, 1]$ such that $B_{\hat{\delta}}(x^0) \subset S$. Select $\delta \in (0, \hat{\delta})$ such that:

$$x \in B_\delta(x^0) \Rightarrow \sum_{i=1}^{n} |x_i - x_i^0| < \hat{\delta}.$$

Let u^i for $i = 1, \ldots, n$ be the unit vectors in $\mathbb{R}^n$ and $u^i = -u^{i-n}$ for $i = n+1, \ldots, 2n$. Then, for any $h \in \mathbb{R}^n - \{0\}$ we may let $\alpha_i = 0$ or $\alpha_i = |h_i|$ as needed to write:

$$h = \sum_{i=1}^{2n} \alpha_i u^i = \sum_{i=1}^{2n} \hat{\alpha}_i \hat{u}^i,$$

where $\hat{\alpha}_i = \frac{\alpha_i}{\sum_{j=1}^{2n} \alpha_j}$ and $\hat{u}^i = u^i \sum_{j=1}^{2n} \alpha_j$.

Now consider the function $\eta : B_{\hat{\delta}}(0) \to \mathbb{R}^1$ defined by $\eta(h) = \phi(x^0 + h)$. For $\alpha \in (0,1)$ and $h^0, h^1 \in B_{\hat{\delta}}(0)$:

$$\begin{aligned}\eta(\alpha h^0 + (1-\alpha)h^1) &= \phi(x^0 + \alpha h^0 + (1-\alpha)h^1) \\ &= \phi(\alpha(x^0 + h^0) + (1-\alpha)(x^0 + h^1)) \\ &\leq \alpha\phi(x^0 + h^0) + (1-\alpha)\phi(x^0 + h^1) \\ &= \alpha\eta(h^0) + (1-\alpha)\eta(h^1).\end{aligned}$$

That is, η is convex.

For any $h \in B_\delta(0) - \{0\}$, use the representation $h = \sum_{i=1}^{2n} \hat{\alpha}_i \hat{u}^i$ and note that:

$$\|\hat{u}^i\| = \|u^i\| \sum_{j=1}^{2n} \alpha_j = \sum_{j=1}^{2n} \alpha_j < \delta,$$

so $\hat{u}^i \in B_\delta(0)$. Therefore, Jensen's Inequality yields:

$$\eta(h) \leq \sum_{i=1}^{2n} \hat{\alpha}_i \eta(\hat{u}^i),$$

noting that $\hat{\alpha}_i \geq 0$ and $\sum_{i=1}^{2n} \hat{\alpha}_i = 1$. Note further that $\hat{u}^i = \alpha(\delta u^i) + (1-\alpha)0$, where $\alpha = \frac{1}{\delta} \sum_{j=1}^{2n} \alpha_j \in (0,1)$. Hence, convexity of η yields:

$$\eta(\hat{u}^i) \leq \alpha\eta(\delta u^i) + (1-\alpha)\eta(0),$$

where $\delta u^i \in B_{\hat{\delta}}(0)$ (i.e., in the domain of η). Let:

$$M = \max\{|\eta(0)|, |\eta(\delta u^1)|, \ldots, |\eta(\delta u^{2n})|\}.$$

Then:

$$|\phi(x^0 + h)| = |\eta(h)| \leq \sum_{i=1}^{2n} \hat{\alpha}_i M = M$$

for $h \in B_\delta(0)$. As any $x \in B_\delta(x^0) - \{x^0\}$ can be written $x = x^0 + h$ for $h = x - x^0 \in B_\delta(0) - \{0\}$, this establishes a bound for ϕ over $B_\delta(x^0)$.

Now consider $\beta \in (0,1)$ and $h \in B_\delta(0) - \{0\}$. The points:

$$x^0 - h, \quad x^0, \quad x^0 + \beta h, \quad x^0 + h$$

all lie on the same line in $B_\delta(x^0)$. In the notation of Theorem 3.2, let $x^1 = x^0 - h$, $x^2 = x^0$, and $x^3 = x^0 + \beta h$ to obtain:

$$\frac{\phi(x^0) - \phi(x^0 - h)}{\|h\|} \le \frac{\phi(x^0 + \beta h) - \phi(x^0)}{\beta\|h\|}.$$

Now let $x^1 = x^0$, $x^2 = x^0 + \beta h$, and $x^3 = x^0 + h$ in Theorem 3.2 to obtain:

$$\frac{\phi(x^0 + \beta h) - \phi(x^0)}{\beta\|h\|} \le \frac{\phi(x^0 + h) - \phi(x^0)}{\|h\|}.$$

Combining these inequalities and canceling $\|h\|$ yields:

$$\beta[\phi(x^0) - \phi(x^0 - h)] \le \phi(x^0 + \beta h) - \phi(x^0) \le \beta[\phi(x^0 + h) - \phi(x^0)],$$

or:

$$|\phi(x^0+\beta h)-\phi(x^0)| \le \beta \max\{|\phi(x^0)-\phi(x^0-h)|, |\phi(x^0+h)-\phi(x^0)|\} \le \beta 2M.$$

Letting $\beta \downarrow 0$ shows that ϕ is continuous at x^0. □

Because the slopes in Fig. 3.3 are monotone, those slopes have one-sided limits when, for example, x^1 approaches x^2 from the left or x^3 approaches x^2 from the right. These one-sided limits are the one-sided derivatives of the function at x^2, which exist at every interior point, and the monotonicity further implies that the left-derivative is never larger than the right-derivative.

Theorem 3.4. *Assume $S \subset \mathbb{R}^n$ is a convex set and $\phi : S \to \mathbb{R}^1$ is a convex function. Then the left- and right-partial derivatives of ϕ with respect to x_i, $\frac{\partial\phi_-(x^0)}{\partial x_i}$ and $\frac{\partial\phi_+(x^0)}{\partial x_i}$ respectively, both exist at every interior point x^0; and $\frac{\partial\phi_-(x^0)}{\partial x_i} \le \frac{\partial\phi_+(x^0)}{\partial x_i}$.*

Proof. Fix $x^0 \in \operatorname{int} S$, let u^i for $i = 1, \ldots, n$ be the unit vectors in $\mathbb{R}^n$, and define:

$$g_i(\beta; x^0) = \frac{\phi(x^0 + \beta u^i) - \phi(x^0)}{\beta}$$

for nonzero real numbers β of sufficiently small magnitude to ensure $x^0 + \beta u^i \in S$. When $\beta^0 < \beta^1 < 0$ or $0 < \beta^0 < \beta^1$, Theorem 3.2 yields:

$$g_i(\beta^0; x^0) \le g_i(\beta^1; x^0).$$

A slightly different application of Theorem 3.2 yields this same conclusion when $\beta^0 < 0 < \beta^1$. In short, g_i is increasing in β. Moreover, $g_i(\beta; x^0)$ for

$\beta < 0$ is bounded above by $g_i(\beta; x^0)$ evaluated at any $\beta > 0$, and $g_i(\beta; x^0)$ for $\beta > 0$ is bounded below by $g_i(\beta; x^0)$ evaluated at any $\beta < 0$. Hence:

$$\frac{\partial \phi_-(x^0)}{\partial x_i} = \sup\{g_i(\beta; x^0) : \beta < 0\} \text{ and}$$
$$\frac{\partial \phi_+(x^0)}{\partial x_i} = \inf\{g_i(\beta; x^0) : \beta > 0\}$$

are both finite, and $\frac{\partial \phi_-(x^0)}{\partial x_i} \leq \frac{\partial \phi_+(x^0)}{\partial x_i}$. □

As the one-sided partial derivatives of a convex function exist at every interior point x^0, the partial derivative $\frac{\partial \phi(x^0)}{\partial x_i}$ exists if and only if the two one-sided partial derivatives are equal. Whenever $\frac{\partial \phi_-(x^0)}{\partial x_i}$ is strictly less than $\frac{\partial \phi_+(x^0)}{\partial x_i}$ there is a rational number strictly between these two real numbers. Moreover, the secant slope monotonicity further implies that the rational number between these two real numbers is strictly less than every rational number between the two one-sided partial derivatives at an interior point x^1 that differs from x^0 only in the ith coordinate, with $x_i^0 < x_i^1$ (assuming the two one-sided partial derivatives are not equal at x^1). Hence, there exists a unique rational number corresponding to each interior point on any line in the domain of a convex function at which a partial derivative does not exist. This observation shows that the number of points on any line in the domain of a convex function at which a partial derivative does not exist is countable.

The vector of left-partial derivatives at x^0 is the left-gradient of ϕ at x^0, $\mathbf{D}\phi_-(x^0)$; the vector of right-partial derivatives at x^0 is the right-gradient of ϕ at x^0, $\mathbf{D}\phi_+(x^0)$. Theorem 3.4 shows that these one-sided gradients exist for a convex function ϕ at every interior point x^0, and $\mathbf{D}\phi_-(x^0) \leq \mathbf{D}\phi_+(x^0)$. The gradient of a function exists at a point when the one-sided gradients exist and are equal at that point. Because the number of points on any line in the domain at which these one-sided gradients are not equal is countable, the one-sided gradients of a convex function are equal at interior points except possibly on a set of Lebesgue n-measure zero.

Theorem 3.5. *Assume $S \subset \mathbb{R}^n$ is an open convex set and $\phi : S \to \mathbb{R}^1$ is a convex function. Then:*

$$N = \{x \in S : \mathbf{D}\phi(x) \textit{ does not exist}\}$$

has Lebesgue n-measure zero.

Proof. We will prove that:

$$N_1 = \left\{ x \in S : \frac{\partial \phi(x)}{\partial x_1} \text{ does not exist} \right\}$$

has Lebesgue n-measure zero. The same proof applies to the other partial derivatives, yielding the conclusion because $N = \bigcup_{i=1}^{n} N_i$.

Define $g_1(\beta; x)$ as in Theorem 3.4. $g_1(\beta; x)$ is a continuous function of x on S for every $\beta \neq 0$, due to continuity of ϕ (Theorem 3.3). Therefore $\frac{\partial \phi_+(x)}{\partial x_1}$ is an upper semicontinuous function of x and $\frac{\partial \phi_-(x)}{\partial x_1}$ is a lower semicontinuous function of x, due to Theorem 1.1. Hence:

$$h(x) = \frac{\partial \phi_+(x)}{\partial x_1} - \frac{\partial \phi_-(x)}{\partial x_1} \geq 0$$

is upper semicontinuous, implying h is a Lebesgue measurable function [1, p. 195, 259]. As the one-sided partial derivatives always exist, the partial derivative exists at x if and only if $h(x) = 0$. Thus:

$$N_1 = \{x \in S : h(x) > 0\},$$

and measurability of h implies this is a Lebesgue n-measurable set.

To derive the measure of N_1, partition the elements into the first coordinate x_1 and the other coordinates $y \in \mathbb{R}^{n-1}$, and consider the y-sections of N_1:

$$N_1^y = \{x_1 : (x_1, y) \in N_1\}.$$

Consider any two distinct elements $x_1^0, x_1^1 \in N_1^y$ and assume without loss of generality that $x_1^0 < x_1^1$. It is straightforward to apply Theorem 3.2 multiple times to conclude that, for $\beta^1 < 0$ and $0 < \beta^0 < x_1^1 - x_1^0 + \beta^1$:

$$g_1(\beta^0; (x_1^0, y)) \leq g_1(\beta^1; (x_1^1, y)).$$

Taking the infimum of the left side over $\beta^0 > 0$ and the supremum of the right side over $\beta^1 < 0$ therefore yields:

$$\frac{\partial \phi_+(x_1^0, y)}{\partial x_1} \leq \frac{\partial \phi_-(x_1^1, y)}{\partial x_1}.$$

As x_1^0 and x_1^1 are both elements of N_1^y:

$$\frac{\partial \phi_-(x_1^0, y)}{\partial x_1} < \frac{\partial \phi_+(x_1^0, y)}{\partial x_1} \leq \frac{\partial \phi_-(x_1^1, y)}{\partial x_1} < \frac{\partial \phi_+(x_1^1, y)}{\partial x_1}.$$

Therefore there exist rational numbers [2, Theorem 1.20]:

$$r(x_1^0) \in \left(\frac{\partial \phi_-(x_1^0, y)}{\partial x_1}, \frac{\partial \phi_+(x_1^0, y)}{\partial x_1}\right) \text{ and } r(x_1^1) \in \left(\frac{\partial \phi_-(x_1^1, y)}{\partial x_1}, \frac{\partial \phi_+(x_1^1, y)}{\partial x_1}\right),$$

so $r(x_1^0) < r(x_1^1)$. In short, to each element of N_1^y there corresponds a unique rational number. Therefore N_1^y is countable and has Lebesgue 1-measure zero [1, p. 22; Proposition 6; p. 58, Corollary 3 and Lemma 6; pp. 61–62]. That is, letting m_i be Lebesgue i-measure, we have $m_1(N_1^y) = 0$ for every $y \in \mathbb{R}^{n-1}$. Using the measurability of N_1, Tonelli's Theorem [1, p. 309] yields:

$$m_n(N_1) = \int_{\mathbb{R}^{n-1}} m_1(N_1^y)dm_{n-1} = 0. \qquad \square$$

3.2 TANGENT PLANES

One useful way to characterize a convex function is to look at the tangent planes of the function. When the gradient of a convex function exists at a point, a plane with slope vector given by that gradient and passing through the corresponding point on the function lies everywhere below the function. The geometry of this observation, illustrated in Fig. 3.5, suggests that existence of the gradient is not needed for the result. Theorem 3.4 establishes that the left-gradient $\mathbf{D}\phi_-(x^0)$ and right-gradient $\mathbf{D}\phi_+(x^0)$ of a convex function ϕ always exist at an interior point x^0, and $\mathbf{D}\phi_-(x^0) \leq \mathbf{D}\phi_+(x^0)$. A plane through the point on the convex function with a particular slope vector between these one-sided gradients lies everywhere below the function, and such a plane always exists at interior domain points. Equally clear from the geometry is the converse: When there is a tangent

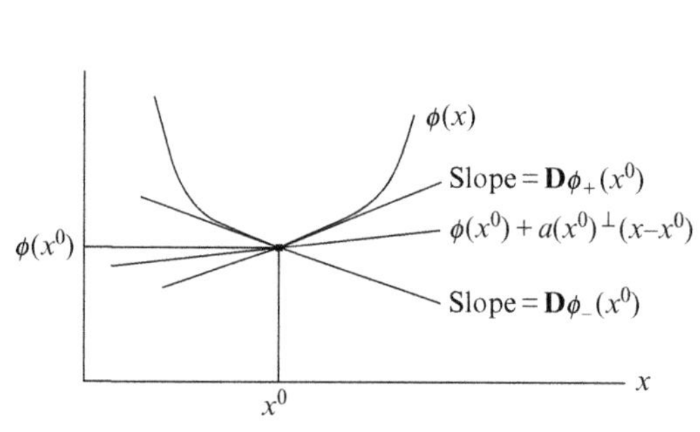

Fig. 3.5 Tangent to a convex function is a lower tangent plane.

plane at every interior point that lies everywhere below a function that function is convex. Hence the property of there being a tangent plane at every interior point that lies everywhere below a function is equivalent to convexity of the function on the interior of the domain. For reference, we give the property that tangent planes lie below the function a formal definition.

Definition 3.4. Assume $S \subset \mathbb{R}^n$ and $\phi : S \to \mathbb{R}^1$. ϕ has *lower tangent planes* on a subset $\tilde{S}$ of S when, to each $x^0 \in \tilde{S}$, there corresponds $a(x^0) \in \mathbb{R}^n$ such that:

$$\phi(x) \geq \phi(x^0) + a(x^0)^{\perp}(x - x^0) \text{ for every } x \in S.$$

Notice that the set of points on or above a convex function forms a convex set. That is, a function is convex if and only if its epigraph (see Definition 1.3) is convex.

Theorem 3.6. *Assume $S \subset \mathbb{R}^n$ is a convex set and $\phi : S \to \mathbb{R}^1$. ϕ is a convex function if and only if the epigraph of ϕ is a convex set (in $\mathbb{R}^{n+1}$).*

Proof. Assume ϕ is a convex function. Fix $(x^0, y^0) \in \text{epi}_\phi$ and $(x^1, y^1) \in \text{epi}_\phi$, and $\alpha \in (0, 1)$. Then:

$$\phi(\alpha x^0 + (1 - \alpha)x^1) \leq \alpha\phi(x^0) + (1 - \alpha)\phi(x^1).$$

As $\phi(x^0) \leq y^0$ and $\phi(x^1) \leq y^1$:

$$\phi(\alpha x^0 + (1 - \alpha)x^1) \leq \alpha y^0 + (1 - \alpha)y^1.$$

That is, $\alpha(x^0, y^0) + (1 - \alpha)(x^1, y^1) \in \text{epi}_\phi$.

Conversely, assume epi_ϕ is a convex set. Fix $x^0 \in S$ and $x^1 \in S$, and $\alpha \in (0, 1)$. Then $(x^0, \phi(x^0)) \in \text{epi}_\phi$ and $(x^1, \phi(x^1)) \in \text{epi}_\phi$. Hence $\alpha(x^0, \phi(x^0)) + (1 - \alpha)(x^1, \phi(x^1)) \in \text{epi}_\phi$. That is:

$$\phi(\alpha x^0 + (1 - \alpha)x^1) \leq \alpha\phi(x^0) + (1 - \alpha)\phi(x^1). \qquad \square$$

As convexity of a real-valued function on a convex domain is equivalent to convexity of its epigraph, the observation that the function has lower tangent planes could be stated in terms of the epigraph. In particular, there is a plane through any boundary point of a convex set such that the convex set lies entirely on one side of the plane (including the plane itself). This observation is known as the *supporting hyperplane theorem*. When the convex set under consideration is the epigraph of a convex function, this result proves existence of lower tangent planes on the interior of the domain of the convex function. We shall prove existence of such tangent planes in

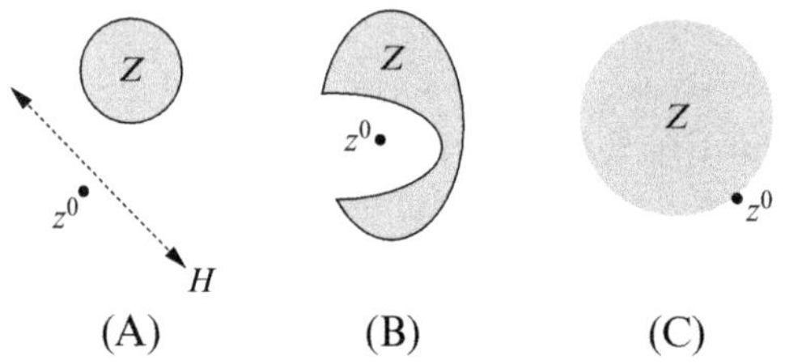

Fig. 3.6 Separating Hyperplanes in $\mathbb{R}^2$. In (A), the conditions of the theorem hold and a hyperplane H that separates z^0 and Z is illustrated. In (B), no hyperplane can be drawn between z^0 and Z because Z is not convex. In (C), no hyperplane can be drawn between z^0 and Z because Z is not closed (here, z^0 is on the boundary of Z). However, a supporting hyperplane can be drawn in (C) that passes through z^0 and is just tangent to Z.

two steps. First we prove a companion result, called the *separating hyperplane theorem*, that states existence of a plane that separates (lies between) a closed convex set and any point not in that set. The tangent plane (i.e., supporting hyperplane to the epigraph of the convex function) is then found by taking a limit of such separating hyperplanes. These ideas are illustrated in Fig. 3.6.

Theorem 3.7 (Separating Hyperplane Theorem). *Assume $Z \subset \mathbb{R}^k$ is a closed convex set; and $z^0 \in \mathbb{R}^k$ is not an element of Z. Then there exists a pair $(a, c) \in \mathbb{R}^{k+1}$ such that:*

$$a^{\perp} z^0 < c < a^{\perp} z \text{ for every } z \in Z.$$

Proof. Define:

$$d(z) = \left(z - z^0\right)^{\perp} \left(z - z^0\right)$$

(i.e., the squared Euclidean distance between z and z^0). Assume Z is nonempty (the theorem is vacuous if Z is empty) and let $d^* = \inf\{d(z) : z \in Z\}$, which is finite because $d(z)$ is bounded below by zero and Z is nonempty. So there exists a sequence $\{z^j\} \subset Z$ such that:

$$d^* \leq d(z^j) < d^* + \frac{1}{j} \text{ for } j = 1, 2, \ldots$$

Hence the sequence is bounded and therefore has a convergent subsequence in $\mathbb{R}^k$ [3, p. 205]; let z^* denote the limit point. $d(z)$ is a continuous function, so $d^* = d(z^*)$, and Z is closed, so $z^* \in Z$. Therefore $a \equiv z^* - z^0 \neq 0$, so $d^* = a^{\perp} a > 0$ and:

$$a^{\perp} z^0 = -a^{\perp} a + a^{\perp} z^* < a^{\perp} z^*. \tag{3.3}$$

Now consider any $z \in Z$. By convexity of Z:

$$\alpha z + (1-\alpha)z^* \in Z \text{ for every } \alpha \in (0,1).$$

So $d(\alpha z + (1-\alpha)z^*) \geq d^*$. Expanding this and canceling the common term d^* yields:

$$2a^{\perp}(z - z^*) + \alpha(z - z^*)^{\perp}(z - z^*) \geq 0.$$

Let $\alpha \downarrow 0$ to obtain:

$$a^{\perp}(z - z^*) \geq 0.$$

Combine with Eq. (3.3) to obtain:

$$a^{\perp}z^0 < a^{\perp}z^* \leq a^{\perp}z \text{ for every } z \in Z.$$

Set $c = a^{\perp}z^* - \epsilon$ for any $\epsilon \in (0, a^{\perp}z^* - a^{\perp}z^0)$ to obtain the result. □

Note that the direction of the inequalities in Theorem 3.7 is of no importance; once the theorem is established, multiplying the result by -1 yields a new pair $(-a, -c)$ such that the opposite inequalities hold.

The Separating Hyperplane Theorem is the tool needed to prove the relationship between a convex function and lower tangent planes.

Theorem 3.8. *Assume $S \subset \mathbb{R}^n$ is a convex set and $\phi : S \to \mathbb{R}^1$.*

1. *If ϕ is convex on S then ϕ has lower tangent planes on the interior of S.*
2. *If ϕ has lower tangent planes on S then ϕ is convex on S.*

Moreover, the slope vector $a(x^0)^{\perp}$ of the tangent plane of a convex function ϕ at a point $x^0 \in \text{int } S$ lies between $\mathbf{D}\phi_-(x^0)$ and $\mathbf{D}\phi_+(x^0)$.

Proof.

1. Let $x^0 \in \text{int } S$ and define Z as the closure in $\mathbb{R}^{n+1}$ of epi_{ϕ}.

   First we show Z is convex. Fix $z, \tilde{z} \in Z$. By definition of the closure, there exist sequences $z^i \to z$ and $\tilde{z}^i \to \tilde{z}$, both in epi_{ϕ}. By Theorem 3.6, epi_{ϕ} is convex, so $\alpha z^i + (1-\alpha)\tilde{z}^i \in Z$ for $i = 1, 2, \ldots$ and for every $\alpha \in (0,1)$. Letting $i \to \infty$ yields $\alpha z + (1-\alpha)\tilde{z} \in Z$ because Z is closed.

   Now note that $\left(x^0, \phi(x^0) - \frac{1}{i}\right) \notin Z$ for $i = 1, 2, \ldots$. Hence, by the Separating Hyperplane Theorem (Theorem 3.7), to each i there corresponds $a^i \in \mathbb{R}^{n+1}$ such that:

   $$(a^i)^{\perp}\left(x^0, \phi(x^0) - \frac{1}{i}\right) < (a^i)^{\perp}z \text{ for every } z \in Z.$$

   In particular:

   $$(a^i)^{\perp}\left(x^0, \phi(x^0) - \frac{1}{i}\right) < (a^i)^{\perp}(x, \phi(x)) \text{ for every } x \in S.$$

Evaluating at $x = x^0$ yields $a^i_{n+1} > 0$. $\frac{a^i}{\|a^i\|}$ is on the unit ball (bounded) in $\mathbb{R}^{n+1}$. Therefore there is a convergent subsequence on the unit ball [3, p. 205]; let a^0 denote the limit point. Taking the limit of the convergent subsequence yields:

$$(a^0)^{\perp}(x^0, \phi(x^0)) \leq (a^0)^{\perp}(x, \phi(x)) \text{ for every } x \in S.$$

Note that $a^0_{n+1} \neq 0$; if the last component were zero then the inequality would state $(a^0_1, \ldots, a^0_n)^{\perp}x^0 \leq (a^0_1, \ldots a^0_n)^{\perp}x$ for every $x \in S$. As $x^0 \in$ int S, there would then exist $x \in S$ near x^0 for which this inequality fails ($a^0 \neq 0$ because $\|a^0\| = 1$). Hence $a^0_{n+1} > 0$ (using $a^i_{n+1} > 0$), and we may therefore set $a(x^0) = \frac{-1}{a^0_{n+1}}(a^0_1, \ldots, a^0_n)$ to obtain:

$$-a(x^0)^{\perp}x^0 + \phi(x^0) \leq -a(x^0)^{\perp}x + \phi(x) \text{ for every } x \in S.$$

2. Fix $x^1, x^2 \in S$ and $\alpha \in (0, 1)$. Then:

$$\phi(x^1) \geq \phi(\alpha x^1 + (1-\alpha)x^2) + (1-\alpha)a(\alpha x^1 + (1-\alpha)x^2)^{\perp}(x^1 - x^2)$$
$$\phi(x^2) \geq \phi(\alpha x^1 + (1-\alpha)x^2) + \alpha a(\alpha x^1 + (1-\alpha)x^2)^{\perp}(x^2 - x^1).$$

Multiply the first inequality by α and the second by $(1-\alpha)$, and add, to obtain:

$$\alpha\phi(x^1) + (1-\alpha)\phi(x^2) \geq \phi(\alpha x^1 + (1-\alpha)x^2).$$

By Theorem 3.4, $\mathbf{D}\phi_-(x^0)$ and $\mathbf{D}\phi_+(x^0)$ both exist at $x^0 \in$ int S. As in the proof of that Theorem, define:

$$g_i(\beta; x^0) \equiv \frac{\phi(x^0 + \beta u^i) - \phi(x^0)}{\beta}$$

for nonzero real numbers β of sufficiently small magnitude to ensure $x^0 + \beta u^i \in S$ (u^i for $i = 1, \ldots, n$ are the unit vectors in $\mathbb{R}^n$). Now evaluate the definition of ϕ having lower tangent planes on the interior of S at $x = x^0 + \beta u^i$ to obtain:

$$g_i(\beta; x^0) \begin{cases} \geq a_i(x^0) & \text{when } \beta > 0 \\ \leq a_i(x^0) & \text{when } \beta < 0 \end{cases}.$$

Taking the supremum of $g_i(\beta; x^0)$ over $\beta < 0$ yields $\frac{\partial\phi_-(x^0)}{\partial x_i} \leq a_i(x^0)$; taking the infimum of $g_i(\beta; x^0)$ over $\beta > 0$ yields $a_i(x^0) \leq \frac{\partial\phi_+(x^0)}{\partial x_i}$. Hence $a(x^0)$ lies between the left- and right-gradients of ϕ at x^0. □

The result shows that convexity of a function is equivalent to having lower tangent planes when the domain is open (as well as convex), and that the slopes of those lower tangent planes always lie between the one-sided gradients (caution: The result does *not* state that *every* vector between the one-sided gradients is the slope of a lower tangent plane; see Exercises 4 and 5). When ϕ has a gradient $\mathbf{D}\phi(x^0)$ at every point of an open convex domain S, this result is that ϕ is convex if and only if:

$$\phi(x) \geq \phi(x^0) + \mathbf{D}\phi(x^0)(x - x^0) \text{ for every } x \in S \text{ and } x^0 \in S.$$

When the domain is not open x^0 can be a boundary point of S. Then the epigraph of a convex function ϕ still has a supporting hyperplane at $(x^0, \phi(x^0))$, but that supporting hyperplane may not be defined at all $x \in S$ and therefore may not be a lower tangent plane of ϕ (see Exercise 6).

Optimal value functions in economic models are sometimes both convex and homogeneous of degree one. In such a circumstance, the lower tangent planes have an additional property that is of particular economic relevance.

Theorem 3.9. *Assume $S \subset \mathbb{R}^n$ is a convex cone and $\phi : S \to \mathbb{R}^1$. Then:*

1. *If ϕ is convex and homogeneous of degree one on S then ϕ has lower tangent planes on the interior of S; and $\phi(x^0) = a(x^0)^{\perp}x^0$ when $a(x^0)$ is the slope of a lower tangent plane at $x^0 \in$ int S.*
2. *If ϕ has lower tangent planes at each $x^0 \in S$ with slopes $a(x^0)$ satisfying $\phi(x^0) = a(x^0)^{\perp}x^0$ then ϕ is convex and homogeneous of degree one on S.*

Proof.

1. Fix $x^0 \in$ int S. By Theorem 3.8 there exists $a(x^0) \in \mathbb{R}^n$ such that:

$$\phi(x) \geq \phi(x^0) + a(x^0)^{\perp}(x - x^0) \; \forall x \in S.$$

Note that $\alpha x^0 \in S$ for $\alpha > 0$ (α is a real number) because S is a cone. Evaluating the inequality at $x = \alpha x^0$ yields:

$$\phi(\alpha x^0) \geq \phi(x^0) + (\alpha - 1)a(x^0)^{\perp}x^0.$$

By homogeneity of ϕ:

$$(\alpha - 1)\phi(x^0) \geq (\alpha - 1)a(x^0)^{\perp}x^0.$$

This implies $\phi(x^0) \geq a(x^0)^{\perp}x^0$ when $\alpha > 1$, and $\phi(x^0) \leq a(x^0)^{\perp}x^0$ when $\alpha < 1$, so $\phi(x^0) = a(x^0)^{\perp}x^0$.

2. Theorem 3.8 ensures ϕ is convex.

Fix $x^0 \in S$ and $\alpha > 0$. From Definition 3.4, the lower tangent plane inequality at x^0 is $\phi(x) \geq a(x^0)^{\perp}x \; \forall x \in S$ when $\phi(x^0) = a(x^0)^{\perp}x^0$.

Evaluating the inequality at $x = \alpha x^0$ yields $\phi(\alpha x^0) \geq \alpha a(x^0)^{\perp} x^0$, which is $\phi(\alpha x^0) \geq \alpha\phi(x^0)$. The lower tangent plane inequality at αx^0 under the stated conditions is $\phi(x) \geq a(\alpha x^0)^{\perp} x \; \forall x \in S$. Evaluating at $x = x^0$ yields $\phi(x^0) \geq a(\alpha x^0)^{\perp} x^0$. Multiply by α to obtain $\alpha\phi(x^0) \geq \alpha a(\alpha x^0)^{\perp} x^0$, which is $\alpha\phi(x^0) \geq \phi(\alpha x^0)$. Combine inequalities to obtain $\alpha\phi(x^0) = \phi(\alpha x^0)$. □

Note that the Theorem shows the lower tangent plane inequality for a convex and homogenous of degree one function ϕ at an interior domain point x^0 is $\phi(x) \geq a(x^0)^{\perp} x$ for every $x \in S$. In other words, the tangent plane is $a(x^0)^{\perp} x$ for some $a(x^0) \in \mathbb{R}^n$.

3.3 HESSIAN MATRICES

Another useful way to characterize a convex function is to look at the second partial derivatives. When a function has differentiable partial derivatives everywhere on an open convex domain, convexity of the function is equivalent to global positive semidefiniteness of its Hessian.

Theorem 3.10. *Assume $S \subset \mathbb{R}^n$ is an open convex set and $\phi : S \rightarrow \mathbb{R}^1$ has differentiable partial derivatives everywhere on S. Then ϕ is convex if and only if $\mathbf{D}^2\phi(x)$ is a positive semidefinite matrix at every $x \in S$.*

Proof. Assume ϕ is convex. Suppose $\mathbf{D}^2\phi(x^0)$ is not positive semidefinite at $x^0 \in S$; that is, suppose there exists a column vector $t \in \mathbb{R}^n$ such that:

$$t^{\perp}\mathbf{D}^2\phi(x^0)t < 0.$$

Define $h(y)$ by $h(y) = \phi(x^0 + yt)$ for real numbers y such that $x^0 + yt \in S$. As ϕ is differentiable on S, the Chain Rule yields:

$$h'(y) = \mathbf{D}\phi(x^0 + yt)t \text{ for values of } y \text{ such that } x^0 + yt \in S.$$

As each partial derivative of ϕ is differentiable on S, the Chain Rule again yields:

$$h''(0) = t^{\perp}\mathbf{D}^2\phi(x^0)t < 0.$$

Therefore, for $y > 0$ but arbitrarily small, Theorem 1.13 yields $h'(y) < h'(0)$ (and $x^0 + ty \in S$ because S is open); that is, there exists $y > 0$ such that:

$$\mathbf{D}\phi(x^0 + yt)t < \mathbf{D}\phi(x^0)t.$$

By Theorem 3.8:

$$y\mathbf{D}\phi(x^0)t \leq \phi(x^0 + yt) - \phi(x^0).$$

Hence:

$$y\mathbf{D}\phi(x^0 + yt)t < \phi(x^0 + yt) - \phi(x^0).$$

On the other hand, Theorem 3.8 also yields:

$$-y\mathbf{D}\phi(x^0 + yt)t \leq \phi(x^0) - \phi(x^0 + yt),$$

a contradiction.

Conversely, assume $\mathbf{D}^2\phi(x)$ is positive semidefinite at every $x \in S$. Fix $x^0, x^1 \in S$ ($x^0 \neq x^1$) and $\alpha \in (0, 1)$. By Taylor's formula [2, Theorem 12.14], there exists $\hat{x}^0$ on the line between x^0 and $\alpha x^0 + (1-\alpha)x^1$ such that:

$$\phi(x^0) = \phi(\alpha x^0 + (1-\alpha)x^1) + (1-\alpha)(\mathbf{D}\phi(\alpha x^0 + (1-\alpha)x^1))(x^0 - x^1)$$
$$+ \frac{(1-\alpha)^2}{2}(x^0 - x^1)^{\perp}\mathbf{D}^2\phi(\hat{x}^0)(x^0 - x^1). \tag{3.4}$$

As $\mathbf{D}^2\phi(\hat{x}^0)$ is positive semidefinite:

$$\phi(x^0) \geq \phi(\alpha x^0 + (1-\alpha)x^1) + (1-\alpha)(\mathbf{D}\phi(\alpha x^0 + (1-\alpha)x^1))(x^0 - x^1).$$

Similarly:

$$\phi(x^1) \geq \phi(\alpha x^0 + (1-\alpha)x^1) + \alpha(\mathbf{D}\phi(\alpha x^0 + (1-\alpha)x^1))(x^1 - x^0).$$

Multiply the first inequality by α, the second by $(1-\alpha)$, and add to obtain:

$$\alpha\phi(x^0) + (1-\alpha)\phi(x^1) \geq \phi(\alpha x^0 + (1-\alpha)x^1). \qquad \square$$

It is common in economic models to explore whether a real-valued function on an open convex domain in $\mathbb{R}^n$ that has a symmetric Hessian everywhere on that domain is both convex and homogeneous of degree one. As convexity is equivalent to global positive semidefiniteness of the Hessian, one approach is to establish whether the function is homogeneous of degree one and, if so, use Corollary 1.3 and Corollary 1.2 to explore convexity by exploring whether the Hessian has a globally positive definite $(n-1)$-dimensional principal submatrix. The latter entails establishing that the $(n-1)$ leading principal minors of the submatrix are globally positive. Similarly, whether a homogeneous of degree one real-valued function with a globally symmetric Hessian on an open convex domain in $\mathbb{R}^n$ is concave can be explored by studying whether the Hessian has a globally negative definite $(n-1)$-dimensional principal submatrix. The latter entails establishing that the $(n-1)$ leading principal minors of the submatrix are globally negative when formed from a submatrix with an odd number of rows/columns; and globally positive when formed from an even number of rows/columns.

3.4 QUASICONVEX FUNCTIONS

Some functions that arise in economic models are not convex but possess a weaker property called *quasiconvexity*.

Definition 3.5. Assume $S \subset \mathbb{R}^n$ is a convex set and $\phi : S \to \mathbb{R}^1$. ϕ is a *quasiconvex* function if, for every $x^0, x^1 \in S$ $(x^0 \neq x^1)$:

$$\phi(\alpha x^0 + (1-\alpha)x^1) \leq \max\{\phi(x^0), \phi(x^1)\} \text{ for every } \alpha \in (0,1).$$

ϕ is a *quasiconcave* function if $-\phi$ is quasiconvex (or, equivalently, if:

$$\phi(\alpha x^0 + (1-\alpha)x^1) \geq \min\{\phi(x^0), \phi(x^1)\} \text{ for every } \alpha \in (0,1)).$$

The quasiconvexity/quasiconcavity is *strict* if the inequality in the definition is strict.

The definition differs from the definition of a convex function in that the right side is the larger of the values of the function at the two points under consideration, rather than the weighted average of these two values. Since the weighted average can be strictly less but cannot be larger than the larger of the two values, convex functions are necessarily quasiconvex but the converse does not hold. A particularly simple example is a monotone function on an interval in $\mathbb{R}^1$, which is quasiconvex irrespective of its curvature but is not convex if it has a downward-bending portion.

Quasiconvex functions are important in economic models because their lower contour correspondences are convex-valued.

Theorem 3.11. *Assume $S \subset \mathbb{R}^n$ is a convex set and $\phi : S \to \mathbb{R}^1$. ϕ is a quasiconvex (quasiconcave) function if and only if the lower (upper) contour set of ϕ at y is a convex set for every $y \in \mathbb{R}^1$.*

Proof. Assume ϕ is a quasiconvex function. Fix y and $x^0, x^1 \in L_\phi(y)$. Then:

$$\phi(\alpha x^0 + (1-\alpha)x^1) \leq \max\{\phi(x^0), \phi(x^1)\} \leq y \text{ for every } \alpha \in (0,1).$$

Hence $\alpha x^0 + (1-\alpha)x^1 \in L_\phi(y)$.

Conversely, assume $L_\phi(y)$ is a convex set for every $y \in \mathbb{R}^1$. Fix $x^0, x^1 \in S$ and note that:

$$x^0, x^1 \in L_\phi(\max\{\phi(x^0), \phi(x^1)\}).$$

Hence $\alpha x^0 + (1-\alpha)x^1 \in L_\phi(\max\{\phi(x^0), \phi(x^1)\})$ for every $\alpha \in (0, 1)$. That is:

$$\phi(\alpha x^0 + (1-\alpha)x^1) \leq \max\{\phi(x^0), \phi(x^1)\}.$$

It is straightforward to mimic this proof to show that quasiconcavity of ϕ is equivalent to convexity of its upper contour sets. □

Similar proofs show that ϕ is a strictly quasiconvex (quasiconcave) function if and only if the lower (upper) contour sets are strictly convex, provided ϕ is also continuous.

Another property of quasiconvex functions important in economic models is that the set of points at which a quasiconvex (quasiconcave) function attains a minimum (maximum) is convex (see Exercise 11).

3.5 NOTES ON CONCAVE FUNCTIONS

As ϕ is a concave function if and only if $-\phi$ is a convex function, all of the results of this chapter hold for concave functions. In particular:

1. Theorem 3.1. Jensen's Inequality is reversed for a concave function.
2. Theorem 3.3. A concave function is continuous at every interior point of its domain.
3. Theorem 3.4. A concave function ϕ has one-sided partial derivatives at every interior point x^0 of its domain; and $\mathbf{D}\phi_+(x^0) \leq \mathbf{D}\phi_-(x^0)$.
4. Theorem 3.5. A concave function of n variables has a gradient on the interior of its domain except possibly on a set of Lebesgue n-measure zero.
5. Theorem 3.8. A function on an open convex domain is concave if, and only if, at every point there is a plane tangent to the function that lies everywhere above the function, with slope vector between the right- and left-gradients at that point.
6. Theorem 3.10. A function on a convex domain with differentiable first partial derivatives at all interior points is concave on the interior of its domain if, and only if, its Hessian is negative semidefinite at every interior point.

3.6 NOTES

The results in this chapter are widely known but presented somewhat differently here. The presentation here relies on a few key references.

Apostol [2] is again relied upon for basic results from advanced calculus. The proof that convex functions are continuous (Theorem 3.3) relies partially on Courant [4, pp. 326–327]. The proof that convex functions have one-sided gradients (Theorem 3.4) is based partially on Fenchel [5, pp. 79–85]. The proof that convex functions have a gradient almost everywhere (Theorem 3.5) is based partially on Fenchel [5, pp. 86–87]. Rockafellar [6] is another classic reference on convex functions.

3.7 EXERCISES

1. Formally prove that there is at most one value of x that maximizes $\phi : X \to \mathbb{R}^1$ over $X \subset \mathbb{R}^n$ when ϕ is a strictly concave function and X is a convex set.
2. Assume $S \subset \mathbb{R}^n$ and $R \subset \mathbb{R}^1$ are convex sets; and $g : S \to R, f : R \to \mathbb{R}^1$, and $h = f \circ g$. Show:
   a. If f is nondecreasing and convex, and g is convex, then h is convex.
   b. If f is nonincreasing and convex, and g is concave, then h is convex.
3. Suppose the tangent plane of a function $\phi : \mathbb{R}^1 \to \mathbb{R}^1$ at the point x^0 is:

$$g(x) = 3(x^0)^2 x - 2(x^0)^3.$$

   Describe the concavity or convexity of ϕ.
4. Assume $\phi(x_1, x_2) = |x_2 - x_1|$, defined on all of $\mathbb{R}^2$.
   a. Is ϕ convex?
   b. Find $\mathbf{D}\phi_-(0)$ and $\mathbf{D}\phi_+(0)$. Does $\mathbf{D}\phi(0)$ exist?
   c. Does $\phi(x) \geq \phi(0) + a^\perp(x - 0)$ hold for every $a^\perp$ between $\mathbf{D}\phi_-(0)$ and $\mathbf{D}\phi_+(0)$? Why or why not? Explain.
5. Assume $\phi(x_1, x_2) = |x_2 - x_1 - 1|$, defined on all of $\mathbb{R}^2$.
   a. Is ϕ convex?
   b. Find $\mathbf{D}\phi_-(0, 1)$ and $\mathbf{D}\phi_+(0, 1)$. Does $\mathbf{D}\phi(0, 1)$ exist?
   c. Does $\phi(x) \geq \phi(0, 1) + a^\perp(x - (0, 1))$ hold for every $a^\perp$ between $\mathbf{D}\phi_-(0, 1)$ and $\mathbf{D}\phi_+(0, 1)$? Why or why not? Explain.
6. Notice that Theorem 3.8 establishes equivalence between convexity of a function and existence of lower tangent planes only when the domain of the convex function is open. Draw a graph of a continuous convex function ϕ on an interval $[x^0, x^1) \subset \mathbb{R}^1$ such that there is no (real) $a(x^0)$ satisfying the inequality in the definition of Lower Tangent

Planes at x^0. Is there a supporting hyperplane to the epigraph of your function through the point $(x^0, \phi(x^0))$?

7. Assume $S \subset \mathbb{R}^n$ is convex and $\phi : S \to \mathbb{R}^1$. Prove that ϕ is a concave function if and only if the hypograph of ϕ is a convex set in $\mathbb{R}^{n+1}$.

8. Assume $X \subset \mathbb{R}^n$, $\Theta \subset \mathbb{R}^m$ is an open convex set, and $f : X \times \Theta \to \mathbb{R}^1$. Let $f^*(\theta) = \sup\{f(x;\theta) : x \in X\}$ for $\theta \in \Theta$. Assume both f and f^* are twice continuously differentiable on the interior of their domains. Pick True or False, and explain why for each item:

   a. If f is a convex function of θ on Θ then f^* is a convex function. Provide both a calculus based and non-calculus based explanation.

   b. If f is a concave function of θ on Θ then f^* is a concave function.

9. Assume $S \subset \mathbb{R}^n$ is an open convex set and $\phi : S \to \mathbb{R}^1$ is a convex function. Fix $x^0 \in S$. Prove that, in the special case $n = 1$, *every* real number $a \in [\mathbf{D}\phi_-(x^0), \mathbf{D}\phi_+(x^0)]$ is the slope of a line through the point $(x_0, \phi(x_0))$ that is everywhere below the function ϕ.

10. Here is a Cobb-Douglas utility function for a consumer of two commodities: $u(x) = x_1^2 x_2^2$ for $x \in \mathbb{R}^2_+$.

   a. Describe the homogeneity of u. Verify that Euler's Theorem holds for u.

   b. Discuss the semidefiniteness of the Hessian. What can you conclude about concavity or convexity of u, and why?

   c. Consider an economic actor who takes price $p \in \mathbb{R}^2_{++}$ as given and chooses x to minimize $e(x;p) \equiv p^{\perp}x$ subject to $u(x) = 10$. Denote the optimal choice by $\hat{x}(p)$ and the minimal value of e by $e^*(p)$.

      i. Describe constraint "activity" with respect to p.

      ii. Taking account of the functional form of e, but without actually solving for the minimum, what does the Envelope Theorem say about $\hat{x}$ and e^* (assume the differentiability conditions hold)? Draw a graph that accurately depicts the Envelope Theorem for this problem.

      iii. Write the basic comparative statics equation for this problem without actually solving for the minimum.

11. Assume $X \subset \mathbb{R}^n$ is convex and $f : X \to \mathbb{R}^1$ is quasiconcave. Prove that the set of maximizers, $x^* = \{x \in X : f(x) \geq f(\tilde{x})\ \forall \tilde{x} \in X\}$, is convex.

REFERENCES

[1] Royden HL. Real analysis. 3rd ed. Englewood Cliffs, NJ: Prentice-Hall; 1988.
[2] Apostol TM. Mathematical analysis. 2nd ed. Reading, MA: Addison-Wesley; 1974.
[3] Trench WF. Advanced calculus. New York: Harper and Row; 1978.
[4] Courant R. Differential and integral calculus. New York: Interscience; 1961.
[5] Fenchel W. Convex cones, sets and functions. Monograph. Princeton University;1953.
[6] Rockafellar RT. Convex analysis. Princeton, NJ: Princeton University Press; 1970.

Part 2

Producers

Part 2 begins the study of price-taking behavior by individual economic actors. The actors in Part 2 use technical capabilities to convert quantities of some commodities (net inputs) into quantities of other commodities (net outputs). The actors who do so are called *firms*. In a circular flow diagram, firms are demanders in markets for inputs, or factors of production, and suppliers in markets where final products are traded. Throughout Part 2 the behavioral postulates are that firms choose quantities of inputs and/or outputs to optimize a monetary objective presuming those choices do not affect prices.

The first part of Chapter 4 defines the firm's production possibilities. These possibilities are conceived as a set of quantity vectors, or feasible production plans, called a *production set*. The set is a fixed constraint on the firm's behavior, although there is nothing in the assumed structure to interfere with an interpretation that some quantities could be chosen ("investment" or "research and development") for the purpose of enabling greater quantities of other commodities ("output"). However, any time element of the possibilities is implicit. The representation of production possibilities is fundamentally static and finite-dimensional. Standard axioms on production sets are nonempty, closed, free disposal, possibility of inaction, no free lunch, convexity, and that some commodities are always necessarily inputs. These axioms are defined and explained.

The profit maximization behavioral postulate and its refutable hypotheses are presented in the remainder of Chapter 4. Part 2 emphasizes the commonalities between this behavioral postulate and the price-taking cost minimization behavioral postulate developed in Chapter 6. The firm in both settings optimizes a monetary objective over a given set of feasible plans; thus the core implications of homogeneity, convexity/concavity, and monotonicity in prices differ only in interpretation between these two behavioral postulates. The cost context merely imposes more structure by presuming that production possibilities have some commodities predetermined to be inputs, and taking the output plan as exogenous to the firm. The property that input demands slope downward and output supplies slope upward is a consequence of price-taking optimization either way. The envelope theorem for a monetary value objective is an important relationship between the optimal monetary value and the quantity choices, and it applies equally to both objectives as well. Specifically, a profit-maximizing quantity vector is the gradient, or more generally a tangent slope, of the profit function, and its price Jacobian is positive semidefinite. A cost-minimizing quantity vector is a tangent slope of the cost function, and its price Jacobian is negative semidefinite. This tangency is known as *Hotelling's Lemma* in the profit context and *Shephard's Lemma* in the cost context. When the output plan is exogenous to the firm the behavior of optimal outcomes as the output plan changes are additional implications of the behavioral postulate, and mostly depend on whether the production set has properties such as free disposal, possibility of inaction, or convexity. In the special case when only one commodity is identified as output and the others as inputs, and a few minor technical assumptions hold, the profit and cost analyses are both restated in familiar terms using a production function and its isoquants.

Once the implications of these behavioral postulates are developed it is natural to inquire whether those properties are *all* that is implied by each behavioral postulate. This question is called *duality* in economic models. The duality inquiry asks whether the fundamental properties of an optimal value function or optimal choice correspondence are sufficient as well as necessary for the postulated behavior. Beginning with a homogeneous of degree one and convex real-valued function defined on an open convex cone in the price space, the central duality theorem shows that such a function is the profit function for a price-taking firm that maximizes profit over an implied "profit-relevant" production set. The profit-relevant production set is nonempty, closed, convex, and has free disposal. A second duality theorem establishes sufficiency of the fundamental properties of a profit-maximizing supply/demand function. A homogeneous of degree zero vector-valued function defined on an open convex cone in the price space, with a symmetric positive semidefinite Jacobian, is a supply/demand function for a price-taking firm that maximizes profit over the implied profit-relevant production set. This is the main content of Chapter 5. But the common structure of profit maximization and cost minimization makes these two theorems equally applicable, except for details of the context, to demonstrate that the properties of cost and input demand functions implied by the price-taking cost minimization behavioral postulate are sufficient as well as necessary for the postulated behavior. The last part of Chapter 6 fills in the details for cost minimization and relates them to profit maximization. For the single-output case, derivation of a cost-relevant production function is explained.

Part 2 concludes with a chapter on standard cost concepts including marginal, avoidable and various per-unit costs. The elasticity of scale is introduced as a local measure of returns to scale and the relationship between returns to scale and monotone average cost is carefully proven. Elasticity of substitution and cost subadditivity are also explained. Envelope relationships again generate refutable implications, in this context showing that short- and long-run marginal costs are equal at relevant output levels but short-run marginal cost increases faster. Price-taking behavior regarding output quantities leads to marginal cost as the supply relationship for prices at or above average avoidable cost.

CHAPTER 4

Profit Maximization

Chapter Outline

4.1 PRODUCTION SETS

The economic actors that supply final products are called *firms*. One behavioral postulate for these actors is that firms choose a production plan to maximize profit, subject to technical and environmental feasibility of the production plan. A production plan is represented by a vector $z \in \mathbb{R}^n$ that specifies a quantity for each of the n commodities the firm can manipulate. The convention is to measure outputs positively and inputs negatively. So, for example, the vector $(2, -1, -3)$ indicates that one unit of good 2 and three units of good 3 are used to produce two units of good 1. A firm's technical and environmental constraints limit the production plans it can choose to some subset Z of $\mathbb{R}^n$. The set Z represents the physical and societal limitations on the firm's ability to transform inputs into outputs, and is called the firm's *production set*. Vectors z that are elements of Z are *feasible* production plans.

A production set may reflect social rules imposed on the firm, for example requirements limiting pollutants or imposing particular safety standards. Of course in some circumstances such rules may be considered manipulable by the firm, perhaps at a cost. The same can be said of raw engineering capabilities, which can perhaps be improved through costly R&D. Hence the production set of the firm is a fixed concept *within some relevant time frame*; activities that are variable within that time frame (perhaps including some types of R&D or regulatory strategizing) can be considered parts of the firm's choices allowed by the production set.

Feasible production plans do not measure intermediate goods the firm produces and then uses internally to produce final outputs. It is only the *net* use of goods or production of goods that is represented by a vector z. That is, the amounts that are traded outside the firm. Some authors therefore label production plans "netput" vectors.

Often a production function is used to represent production capabilities. But this approach does not make clear exactly what is being assumed about production capabilities, and also does not easily accommodate multiple outputs. The production set is a more primitive concept from which a production function can be derived if doing so is convenient for some purpose.

Some examples of production sets are illustrated in Fig. 4.1.

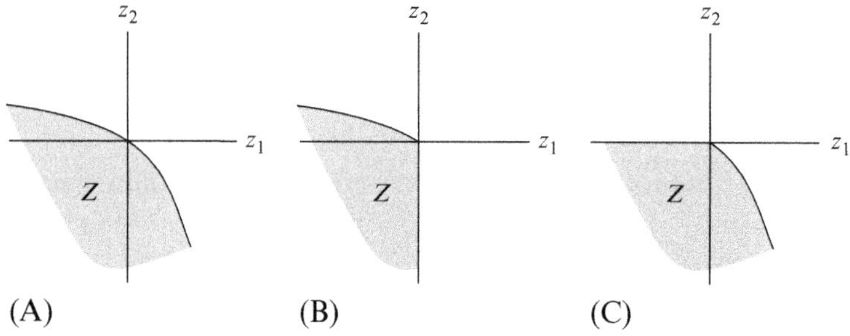

Fig. 4.1 Production sets. In (A), both z_1 and z_2 can be both inputs and outputs. In (B), z_1 can only be an input, while in (C) z_2 can only be an input.

The minimal assumptions usually placed on a production set Z are:

1. Z is nonempty: Something is feasible.
2. Z is closed: This assures existence of optima in some cases.

Sometimes we are interested in additional characteristics of the production set:

3. There is free disposal: Given a feasible production plan, every production plan that includes no less of each input and no more of each output is also feasible. In symbols: $z^0 \in Z \Rightarrow z^1 \in Z \; \forall z^1 \leq z^0$. This assumption has more content than the first two (think of radioactive material as an

input to electricity production—can it be disposed of freely within the societal rules imposed on the production set?). Free disposal may seem to imply infinite resources, but it does not. The assumptions here are only about technical ability, not about availability of resources. It is up to the market to ration potentially scarce inputs by placing positive prices on them.

4. Z is convex: Weighted averages of feasible production plans are feasible. This is quite a strong assumption and is often violated when, for example, there is increasing returns. However, as we will see, in an economic sense it is implied when maximal profit is well-defined.
5. There is no free lunch: Inputs must be used for outputs to be produced. In symbols: $Z \cap \mathbb{R}^n_+ \subset \{0\}$.
6. Inaction is always possible: $0 \in Z$. Note that this makes item 1 redundant and, in conjunction with item 5, implies $Z \cap \mathbb{R}^n_+ = \{0\}$. When this is violated, we say Z has one or more "sunk" inputs.
7. Z has natural inputs: Some of the commodities cannot be produced as outputs by the firm. In symbols: $(y, -x) \in Z \Rightarrow x \in \mathbb{R}^m_+$ for some $m < n$ (label the commodities so that the natural inputs are last in the production plan vector).

The examples in Fig. 4.1 all possess properties 1–6. Commodity 1 is a natural input in panel (B) of Fig. 4.1; commodity 2 is a natural input in panel (C). If the boundary of Z passes to the southwest of the origin then the possibility of inaction is violated and we have one or more sunk inputs. A variant of this is a "fixed" input, which means Z has a segment along an axis between zero and some amount of the input that must be utilized before any output can be produced. If the segment along the axis does not begin at zero then the fixed input is "partially" sunk.

When there are natural inputs a production set Z is sometimes described in other ways that are more convenient for some purposes.

- Feasible output set: $Y \equiv \{y \in \mathbb{R}^{n-m} : (y, -x) \in Z \text{ for some } x \in \mathbb{R}^m_+\}$. This is the set of output vectors that can be produced in some manner.
- Input requirement sets: $V(y) \equiv \{x \in \mathbb{R}^m_+ : (y, -x) \in Z\}$ for $y \in Y$ is the *input requirement set* for feasible output vector y. It is all input vectors capable of producing output vector y. V is a correspondence from Y to the collection of all subsets of natural input vectors.

Free disposal, and the presence or absence of fixed or sunk inputs, can be conveniently illustrated in terms of input requirement sets. This is pursued in Exercises 1 and 8.

4.2 BASIC OPTIMIZATION POSTULATE

Parts 2 and 3 of this text are about economic actors who are perfect competitors, meaning they regard prices as fixed when making choices. Let $p \in \mathbb{R}^n_+$ be a vector of prices, one price for each of the n goods. At price p the monetary value of production plan z is $\pi(z;p) \equiv p^{\perp}z$. This monetary value is the firm's *profit* from production plan z when price is p. A profit-maximizing firm that is a price-taker chooses a production plan z from its production set Z to maximize $\pi(z;p)$ while regarding p as unaffected by the choice of z. Note the role of the sign convention on inputs and outputs. Inputs are measured negatively, and thus contribute negatively to the profit expression, while outputs are measured positively and thus contribute positively to profit. The choice variable is z and the parameter is p. This leads to an optimal value function $\pi^*(p) \equiv \sup\{p^{\perp}z : z \in Z\}$ and an optimal choice correspondence $z^*(p) \equiv \{z \in Z : p^{\perp}z = \pi^*(p)\}$, which in this context are the *profit function* and *(net) supply/demand correspondence*, respectively, of the firm. Note that the constraint in this optimization problem is globally inactive because the firm's production set does not depend on prices.

As $\mathbf{D}_z\pi(z;p) = p^{\perp}$, a profit maximum is not characterized by a stationary point of the objective. None of the first derivatives can be zero unless there is a zero price, and if a price is zero the corresponding quantity has no effect on profit. Hence the production set constraint must bind for every commodity that has a positive price (and those with zero prices are irrelevant except to the extent they affect the feasible values of commodities with positive prices through the production constraint). In the two dimensional case, the maximization can be illustrated as in Fig. 4.2.

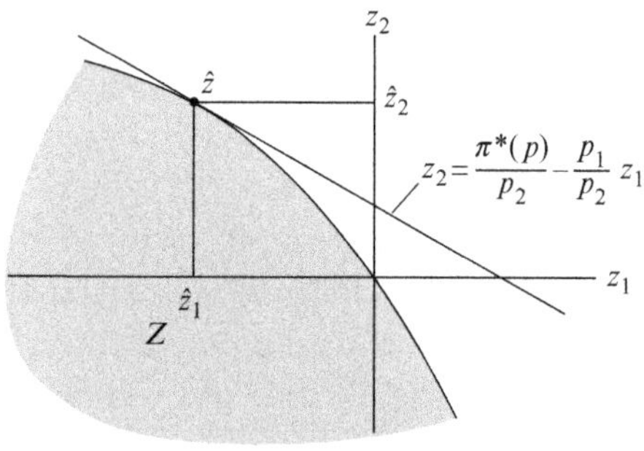

Fig. 4.2 Profit maximization. The intercept of the isoprofit line is optimal profit in units of good 2.

The firm's objective is to choose the value of z that places it on the highest isoprofit line while still staying in the production set Z.

Existence can be a real issue for profit maximization. With nondecreasing returns to scale it is possible for there to be no maximum due to unboundedness, depending on the prices, even when Z is nonempty and closed; so $z^*(p)$ can be empty in some cases. Uniqueness is also a real issue unless the production set is strictly convex (see Exercise 12); so $z^*(p)$ need not be a singleton in general. Fig. 4.3 illustrates these issues.

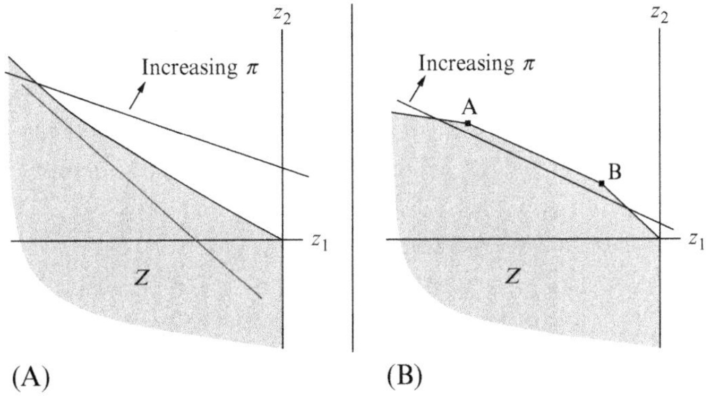

Fig. 4.3 Existence and uniqueness failures for a profit maximum. In panel (A) there is no maximum because profit can always be increased by moving further to the northwest along the boundary of the production set. Note, however, that if commodity 1 is relatively more expensive than illustrated so the slope of the isoprofits is steeper than the asymptote (dark gray line) then optimal profit is zero, with z^* being the origin. In panel (B) the maximum exists but is not unique because the isoprofits have the same slope as part of the production set boundary. At the illustrated price, z^* is the entire segment AB.

The behavioral postulate that a firm chooses a production plan within a fixed production set to maximize profit, while taking prices as given, immediately implies some refutable hypotheses.

Theorem 4.1 (Fundamental Properties of a Profit Maximum). *Assume the production set is nonempty and let P denote the set of relevant prices: $P \equiv \{p \in \mathbb{R}^n_+ : \pi^*(p)$ is finite$\}$.*

1. *The set $\{p \in \mathbb{R}^n_+ : z^*(p) \neq \emptyset\} \subset P$ is a cone and zero is an element. The supply/demand correspondence is homogeneous of degree zero on this cone (only relative prices matter for production decisions).*

2. *P is a convex cone. The profit function is homogeneous of degree one on P (a neutral inflation inflates profit by the same proportion).*
3. *The profit function is convex on P; on the interior of P this implies the profit function is continuous, has one-sided gradients, and has a gradient off a set of Lebesgue n-measure zero.*
4. $(p^1 - p^0)^\perp(\hat{z}(p^1) - \hat{z}(p^0)) \geq 0$ *on the cone where $z^*(p)$ is nonempty (positive semidefiniteness of supply/demand price responses).*
5. *Profit is nondecreasing in the prices of commodities that are outputs at an optimal production plan, and nonincreasing in the prices of commodities that are inputs at an optimal production plan.*

Proof. Fix $p^0, p^1 \in P$ and $\alpha > 0$.

1. $\pi(z;\alpha p^0) = (\alpha p^0)^\perp z = \alpha\pi(z;p^0)$. Thus $\pi(z;\alpha p^0)$ is a strictly increasing transformation of $\pi(z;p^0)$, so the former has the same set of maximizers as the latter: $z^*(\alpha p^0) = z^*(p^0)$ (also making use of the fact that Z is inactive). In particular, if $z^*(p^0)$ is nonempty then $z^*(\alpha p^0)$ is nonempty so the set of prices for which $z^*(p)$ is nonempty forms a cone. The profit function is identically zero at $p = 0$ so $z^*(0) = Z$, which is nonempty by assumption.
2. Fix $\beta > 0$. $\pi^*(\alpha p^0) = \sup\{(\alpha p^0)^\perp z : z \in Z\} = \alpha \sup\{(p^0)^\perp z : z \in Z\} = \alpha\pi^*(p^0)$ (again making use of Z inactive). In particular, if $\pi^*(p^0)$ and $\pi^*(p^1)$ are finite then $\pi^*(\alpha p^0) = \alpha\pi^*(p^0)$ and $\pi^*(\beta p^1) = \beta\pi^*(p^1)$ are both finite. By definition of the supremum, $\pi^*(\alpha p^0) \geq (\alpha p^0)^\perp z$ and $\pi^*(\beta p^1) \geq (\beta p^1)^\perp z$, both for every $z \in Z$. Add these two inequalities to obtain $\pi^*(\alpha p^0) + \pi^*(\beta p^1) \geq [\alpha p^0 + \beta p^1]^\perp z$ for every $z \in Z$. The left side is an upper bound of the right side over $z \in Z$. Therefore the left side exceeds the supremum of the right side: $\pi^*(\alpha p^0) + \pi^*(\beta p^1) \geq \pi^*(\alpha p^0 + \beta p^1)$. Hence the right side is finite, making P a convex cone.
3. Use the inequality just established with $\alpha < 1$ and $\beta = 1 - \alpha$, and homogeneity of π^*, to obtain $\alpha\pi^*(p^0) + (1-\alpha)\pi^*(p^1) \geq \pi^*(\alpha p^0 + (1-\alpha)p^1)$. Apply Theorems 3.3–3.5 for the supplemental statements about continuity and gradients.
4. By definition of the maximum, $(p^1)^\perp\hat{z}(p^1) \geq (p^1)^\perp\hat{z}(p^0)$ and $(p^0)^\perp\hat{z}(p^0) \geq (p^0)^\perp\hat{z}(p^1)$ (again making use of Z inactive). Add these two inequalities and rearrange to obtain $(p^1 - p^0)^\perp(\hat{z}(p^1) - \hat{z}(p^0)) \geq 0$.
5. Partition $\hat{z}(p^0)$ as $\hat{z}(p^0) = (\hat{z}(p^0)_+, \hat{z}(p^0)_-)$ where $\hat{z}(p^0)_+ \geq 0$ (outputs at p^0) and $\hat{z}(p^0)_- \leq 0$ (inputs at p^0) (label the commodities so the first subvector is those that are optimally non-negative at price p^0). Partition the price vectors in a corresponding manner, and consider

a price change from p^0 to p^1 when $p_+^1 \geq p_+^0$ and $p_-^1 \leq p_-^0$. By definition of the supremum, $\pi^*(p^1) \geq (p^1)^\perp \hat{z}(p^0)$. By construction of the price change, $(p^1)^\perp \hat{z}(p^0) \geq (p^0)^\perp \hat{z}(p^0) = \pi^*(p^0)$. Hence $\pi^*(p^1) \geq \pi^*(p^0)$. □

These five properties are "fundamental" in that they require no assumptions other than the behavioral postulate and that the firm be capable of doing *something* (i.e., Z is nonempty). Note that item 4 implies the *Law of Demand*: The supply/demand of each commodity is nondecreasing in its own price (recall that inputs are measured negatively, so when applied to an input "nondecreasing" means "no more negative" as price increases). The Law of Demand for firms is a refutable hypothesis stemming directly from the profit-maximization behavioral postulate. Note also that the domain of the supply/demand correspondence may not be convex (see Exercise 21).

4.3 ENVELOPE PROPERTIES

The production constraint is typically binding but always inactive at a profit maximum. Hence the Envelope Theorem (Theorem 1.18) applies: If a maximum exists on a subset S of the price space then $\pi^*(p)$ is an upper envelope on S of the collection of $\pi(\hat{z}(p^0); p) = p^\perp \hat{z}(p^0)$ functions, one such function for each p^0. The Envelope Theorem is a rich source of refutable hypotheses about the profit maximizing behavior of a price-taking firm.

The tangency conclusion of the Envelope Theorem takes the particularly simple form $\mathbf{D}\pi^*(p^0) = \hat{z}(p^0)^\perp$ for every p^0 where the Jacobian exists because $\hat{z}(p^0)$ is the Jacobian of the objective $p^\perp \hat{z}(p^0)$ with respect to p. In words, when the gradient of a profit function exists (and a maximum exists) that gradient is the corresponding supply/demand function, an observation known as *Hotelling's Lemma*.

As noted in Theorem 4.1, convexity of the profit function implies existence of the gradient at all interior prices where a maximum exists except possibly on a set of Lebesgue n-measure zero. Hence Hotelling's Lemma holds almost everywhere a maximum exists, without any explicit differentiability assumptions. Using the lower tangent planes of the convex function π^*, Hotelling's Lemma can be extended to include interior points where the gradient does not exist. Generally, the lower tangent plane slopes of the profit function are the elements of the supply/demand correspondence when those slopes are feasible production plans.

Theorem 4.2. *A feasible production plan maximizes profit if and only if it is the slope of a lower tangent plane of the profit function on the interior of P. Moreover, every such production plan lies between the one-sided gradients of the profit function at the tangency.*

Proof. Fix $p^0 \in \text{int } P$. If $z \in z^*(p^0)$ then $\pi^*(p^0) = z^\perp p^0$ and $\pi^*(p) \geq z^\perp p$ for every $p \in P$ (the latter using $z \in Z$). Adding yields:

$$\pi^*(p) \geq \pi^*(p^0) + z^\perp(p - p^0) \text{ for every } p \in P.$$

That is, z is the slope of a lower tangent plane of π^* on int P at p^0.

Conversely, assume $z \in Z$ is the slope of a lower tangent plane of π^* on int P at p^0. π^* is convex and homogeneous of degree one on P by Theorem 4.1. Therefore $\pi^*(p^0) = z^\perp p^0$ by Theorem 3.9. That is, $z \in z^*(p^0)$.

Either way, by Theorem 3.8 the slope of a lower tangent plane of the convex function π^* at p^0 lies between $\mathbf{D}\pi^*_-(p^0)$ and $\mathbf{D}\pi^*_+(p^0)$. □

The conclusion is: The set of production plans that maximize profit is exactly those elements of the production set that are slope vectors of planes tangent to the profit function (i.e., the tangency property of the Envelope Theorem), *even at a price for which the maximum is not unique and the profit function is not differentiable.* This is illustrated in Fig. 4.4. When there is only one such tangent plane at an interior price p^0, its slope vector is $\mathbf{D}\pi^*(p^0)$ and this slope vector is the unique optimal production plan.

The Envelope Theorem also has implications for the Hessian of the profit function. The Hessian of $\pi(\hat{z}(p^0); p) = p^\perp \hat{z}(p^0)$ with respect to p is

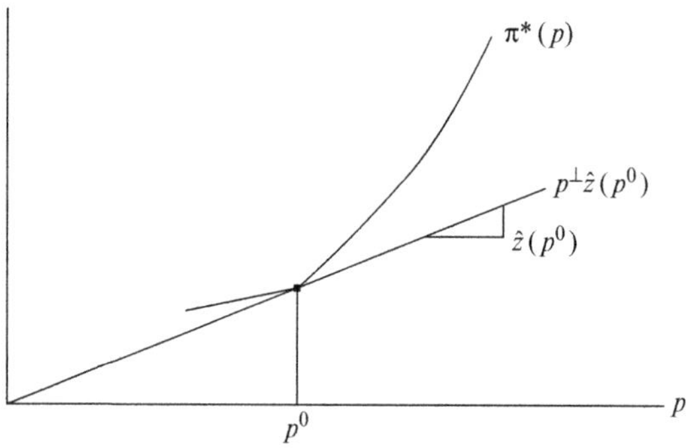

Fig. 4.4 The Envelope Theorem for a profit maximum. If π^* is not differentiable at p^0 then multiple slopes like $\hat{z}(p^0)$ between the left- and right-derivative can be optimal (the objective need not pass through the origin in one plane when $n > 1$).

a matrix of zeros (i.e., linearity in p for fixed $\hat{z}(p^0)$) so the semidefiniteness conclusion of the Envelope Theorem simplifies to $\mathbf{D}^2\pi^*(p^0)$ being a *positive* semidefinite matrix when the various differentiability conditions hold. Indeed, global positive semidefiniteness of the Hessian of π^* from the Envelope Theorem is the calculus version of the convexity property in Theorem 4.1 (see Theorem 3.10). Differentiating $\mathbf{D}\pi^*(p) = \hat{z}(p)^\perp$ (i.e., Hotelling's Lemma) and evaluating at p^0 reveals that this Hessian is $\mathbf{D}^2\pi^*(p^0) = \mathbf{D}\hat{z}(p^0)$, which is the matrix of supply/demand slopes with respect to changes in prices. Further, when the Hessian exists, Euler's Theorem (Corollary 1.3) for the homogeneous of degree one function $\pi^*(p)$ reveals that this matrix is singular. Finally, this Hessian is symmetric by Young's Theorem [1, Theorem 12.13] when the off-diagonal elements are continuous functions of p. Stated in terms of the supply/demand slopes, symmetry is $\frac{\partial \hat{z}_i}{\partial p_j} = \frac{\partial \hat{z}_j}{\partial p_i}$, an observation known as *reciprocity* of the supply/demand responses to price changes. In sum, when the profit function is differentiable in a neighborhood of a price p^0 and its partial derivatives are differentiable at p^0, *the Hessian is the matrix of supply/demand price slopes, which is positive semidefinite and singular; and those supply/demand slopes have reciprocity when they are continuous.* As the diagonal elements of a positive semidefinite matrix are non-negative, one implication is that the supply/demand of each commodity is non-decreasing in its own price, which is the calculus version of the Law of Demand.

A summary statement of the envelope properties of a profit maximum may be useful for future reference.

Theorem 4.3 (Envelope Properties of a Profit Maximum).

1. $\mathbf{D}\pi^*(p^0) = \hat{z}(p^0)^\perp$, *the unique maximum, at every* $p^0 \in P$ *where the gradient exists and is an element of the production set (Hotelling's Lemma). Even on the set of measure zero where the gradient does not exist, a feasible production plan* z *is profit-maximizing at a strictly positive price* $p^0 \in P$ *if and only if* $\pi^*(p) \geq \pi^*(p^0) + z^\perp(p - p^0)$ *for every* $p \in P$*; and every such production plan lies between* $\mathbf{D}\pi^*_-(p^0)$ *and* $\mathbf{D}\pi^*_+(p^0)$.
2. *The Hessian of* π^* *is singular and positive semidefinite at every* $p^0 \in P$ *where the partial derivatives of* π^* *are differentiable and where* π^* *is differentiable in a neighborhood. Together with Hotelling's Lemma, this implies the matrix of supply/demand price slopes is singular and positive semidefinite at all such prices. One implication of positive semidefiniteness is the comparative statics conclusion that each supply/demand is nondecreasing in its own price. If the off-diagonal*

elements are continuous then the matrix is symmetric, which is reciprocity of the supply/demand price responses: $\frac{\partial \hat{z}_i}{\partial p_j} = \frac{\partial \hat{z}_j}{\partial p_i}$.

Singularity and symmetry of the Hessian imply some relationships among the price elasticities of the profit-maximizing supplies and demands. Recall from the proof of Corollary 1.3 that $p^\perp$ forms a linear combination of the rows of $\mathbf{D}^2\pi^*(p)$ $(= \mathbf{D}\hat{z}(p))$. That is:

$$p^\perp \mathbf{D}\hat{z}(p) = 0. \tag{4.1}$$

Column i of this equation is $\sum_{j=1}^{n} \frac{\partial \hat{z}_j(p)}{\partial p_i} p_j = 0$. Multiplying term j by $\frac{\hat{z}_j(p)}{\hat{z}_j(p)}$ and the entire equation by $\frac{p_i}{\pi^*(p)}$ yields:

$$\sum_{j=1}^{n} \left(\frac{\partial \hat{z}_j(p)}{\partial p_i} \frac{p_i}{\hat{z}_j(p)} \right) \frac{p_j \hat{z}_j(p)}{\pi^*(p)} = 0.$$

That is, *the elasticities of all supplies/demands with respect to one price, each weighted by the monetary share of that commodity in total profit, sum to zero.* Similarly, transposing Eq. (4.1) and using symmetry yields $\mathbf{D}\hat{z}(p)p = 0$. Row i of this equation is $\sum_{j=1}^{n} \frac{\partial \hat{z}_i(p)}{\partial p_j} p_j = 0$. Multiplying the entire equation by $\frac{1}{\hat{z}_i(p)}$ yields:

$$\sum_{j=1}^{n} \frac{\partial \hat{z}_i(p)}{\partial p_j} \frac{p_j}{\hat{z}_i(p)} = 0.$$

That is, *the elasticities of a supply/demand with respect to all prices sum to zero.*

4.4 ADDITIONAL PROPERTIES

Additional refutable hypotheses emerge from the profit maximization behavioral postulate when the production set has additional properties.

Theorem 4.4 (Additional Properties of a Profit Maximum). *For* $p \in P$*:*

1. *If the production set is convex then* $z^*(p)$ *is a convex set.*
2. *If the production set is closed then* z^* *is upper hemicontinuous.*
3. *If the production set has the possibility of inaction property then* $\pi^*(p) \geq 0$.

Proof. Fix $p^0 \in S$.

1. Consider $z^0, z^1 \in z^*(p^0)$. By definition of the supremum, $(p^0)^\perp z^0 \geq (p^0)^\perp z$ and $(p^0)^\perp z^1 \geq (p^0)^\perp z$ for every $z \in Z$. Multiply the first inequality by $\alpha \in (0, 1)$, the second by $(1 - \alpha)$, and add to obtain

$(p^0)^\perp \left[\alpha z^0 + (1-\alpha)z^1\right] \geq (p^0)^\perp z$ for every $z \in Z$. We have $\alpha z^0 + (1-\alpha)z^1 \in Z$ because Z is convex; therefore $\alpha z^0 + (1-\alpha)z^1 \in z^*(p^0)$.

2. Consider a sequence $\{p^i\}_{i=1}^\infty \subset P$ that converges to p^0 and a corresponding sequence $z^i \in z^*(p^i)$ that converges to z^0. $z^i \in Z$ by definition of z^*, and Z is closed, so $z^0 \in Z$. Moreover, by definition of z^*:

$$(p^i)^\perp z^i \geq (p^i)^\perp z \text{ for every } z \in Z.$$

For a given $z \in Z$, letting $i \to \infty$ yields $(p^0)^\perp z^0 \geq (p^0)^\perp z$. As this holds for every $z \in Z$, and $z^0 \in Z$, we have $z^0 \in z^*(p^0)$.

3. $0 \in Z$, and $p^\perp 0 = 0$ for every $p \in P$, so the supremum must be at least zero when the zero vector is a feasible production plan. □

Due to convexity, the Maximum Theorem (Theorem 1.5) is not needed to establish continuity of π^*. The Maximum Theorem *could* be used to establish upper hemicontinuity of z^* if the production set were bounded, but boundedness is usually an undesirable assumption because it conflicts with free disposal (although it is sometimes possible to modify the production set in a way that bounds it without affecting the maximum). Item 2 above takes a more direct approach, relying on the special structure of the profit objective to show that the supply/demand correspondence is upper hemicontinuous whenever the production set is closed.

If a profit-relevant version of the production set can be stated in terms of an equality constraint $h(z) = 0$ then the Lagrangian function for profit maximization is:

$$L(z, \lambda; p) = p^\perp z - \lambda h(z)$$

(h is real-valued so λ is a scalar). Note that p is not shown as an argument of the constraint function h; this is because the production constraint is globally inactive. If h is continuously differentiable and $\mathbf{D}h$ is not a vector of zeros at an optimum then the Lagrange Multiplier Rule (Theorem 2.1) is:

$$p^\perp - \hat{\lambda}(p)\mathbf{D}h(\hat{z}(p)) = 0.$$

This equation can be used with $-h(\hat{z}(p)) = 0$ to identify candidate values for an optimal production plan and the corresponding Lagrange multiplier. If, in addition, the conditions of the Implicit Function Theorem [1, Theorem 13.7] hold for these two equations then the comparative statics equation (2.22) applies because the constraint is inactive. Moreover, the derivatives of L take special forms because of the simple functional form of the profit objective. Eq. (2.22) becomes:

$$\begin{bmatrix} -\hat{\lambda}\mathbf{D}^2 h(\hat{z}) & -(\mathbf{D}h(\hat{z}))^{\perp} \\ -\mathbf{D}h(\hat{z}) & 0 \end{bmatrix} \begin{bmatrix} \mathbf{D}\hat{z} \\ \mathbf{D}\hat{\lambda} \end{bmatrix} = -\begin{bmatrix} I_n \\ 0 \end{bmatrix}.$$

This equation can be used to derive supply/demand price slopes for a particular h function. One refutable hypothesis from this equation irrespective of h is that the own-price slopes are nonnegative. This conclusion follows because the profit objective indeed has the special structure that $\mathbf{D}_p(\mathbf{D}_z\pi)^{\perp}$ $(= I_n)$ has only one nonzero entry in column i and that entry is in row i, as described in the discussion of Eq. (2.20). Thus $\frac{\partial \hat{z}_i}{\partial p_i}$ has the same sign as that one nonzero entry, which is unity in the current model for $i = 1, \ldots, n$. This is another way to derive the Law of Demand for a price-taking firm that maximizes profit, although the conclusion derived in this manner depends on the profit-relevant production set being expressible in terms of a sufficiently "well-behaved" function h, whereas Theorem 4.1 shows that the Law of Demand does not depend on anything other than existence of a profit maximum.

4.5 SINGLE-OUTPUT PROFIT MAXIMIZATION

When all commodities except one are natural inputs we have the familiar single-output case. Then the *production function* for the production set Z can be defined. First define the *feasible output correspondence*, which relates the natural input vectors to the output levels each natural input vector can produce:

$$\Gamma(x) \equiv \{y : (y, -x) \in Z\} \text{ for } x \in \mathbb{R}_+^{n-1}.$$

The production function is the largest feasible output vector:

$$f(x) \equiv \sup \Gamma(x) \text{ for } x \in \mathbb{R}_+^{n-1}.$$

As usual, sufficient conditions for existence of this maximum at x^0 are that the set of feasible output levels $\Gamma(x^0)$ be nonempty, closed and bounded (Theorem 1.2). Nonempty is assured by the possibility of inaction and free disposal because then $(0, -x) \in Z \; \forall x \in \mathbb{R}_+^{n-1}$. Closed is assured by Z closed. Bounded is assured by, in addition, no free lunch and convexity of Z (see Exercise 11). By Theorem 1.3, if the feasible output correspondence Γ is upper hemicontinuous at x^0, and is nonempty and uniformly bounded on an open ball about x^0, then the production function is upper semicontinuous at x^0.

Note that $V(y) \subset \{x \in \mathbb{R}_+^{n-1} : f(x) \geq y\}$ for $y \in Y$ when the production function f exists, by definition. The converse requires free disposal: $x \in V(f(x))$ when f exists as a maximum (this is the meaning of f "existing"); and $V(f(x)) \subset V(y)$ for $f(x) \geq y$ when there is free disposal; hence $x \in V(y)$ when $f(x) \geq y$. When $V(y) = \{x \in \mathbb{R}_+^{n-1} : f(x) \geq y\}$ the input requirement set for output level y is the upper contour set of the production function at y. In this case the input requirement correspondence is upper hemicontinuous (each input requirement set is closed) if and only if the production function is upper semicontinuous (Theorem 1.8); and is convex if and only if the production function is quasiconcave (Theorem 3.11).

The *isoquant* for output level $y \in Y$ is:

$$I(y) \equiv \{x \in V(y) : y^0 > y \Rightarrow x \notin V(y^0)\}.$$

$I(y)$ is all input plans that are capable of producing output level y, but no more. Note that $I(y) = \{x \in \mathbb{R}_+^{n-1} : f(x) = y\}$ when the production function f exists as a maximum. If the conditions of the implicit function theorem apply to the equation $f(x) = y$ then the implicit function for the ith component of x, $x_i(x_{-i})$, has slope with respect to some other component x_j given by:

$$\frac{\partial x_i(x_{-i})}{\partial x_j} = -\frac{\partial f(x)/\partial x_j}{\partial f(x)/\partial x_i}.$$

The absolute value of this slope is called the *marginal rate of technical substitution* of input i for input j at point x ($\text{MRTS}_{ij}(x)$), since it gives the rate at which it is technically possible to substitute input i for input j while maintaining constant output. Free disposal implies a nonpositive slope, while convexity implies the MRTS is nonincreasing in x_{-i}. The implicit function theorem requires that $\partial f/\partial x_i$ be nonzero at the point in question. We sometimes utilize a non-calculus version of this assumption:

Definition 4.1. When the production function exists, production is called *locally non-exhaustible* if, for every $x \in \mathbb{R}_+^{n-1}$ and $\epsilon > 0$, there exists $x^0 \in \mathbb{R}_+^{n-1}$ such that $\|x - x^0\| < \epsilon$ and $f(x^0) > f(x)$.

When there are natural inputs it is common to partition the price vector as (p, w) corresponding to the partition $(y, -x)$ of the production plan (note that the role of p switches to the output price vector rather than the entire production plan price vector; w is called the input price or *wage* vector). Profit maximization is then equivalently written:

$$\pi^*(p, w) = \sup\{py - w^{\perp}x : (y, -x) \in Z\}.$$

Assume for the remainder of this section that the production function f exists as a maximum. If $p > 0$ profit maximization is then equivalent to:

$$\pi^*(p, w) = \sup\{\pi(x; p, w) = pf(x) - w^{\perp}x : x \in \mathbb{R}_+^{n-1}\}$$

because, for any given $x \in \mathbb{R}_+^{n-1}$, no choice of y that is less than $f(x)$ can be optimal. The optimal choices for the single-output case are $x^*(p, w) = \{x \in \mathbb{R}_+^{n-1} : \pi(x; p, w) = \pi^*(p, w)\}$ and $y^*(p, w) = f(x^*(p, w))$, both of which can be empty. We call $y^*(p, w)$ the output *supply* correspondence and $x^*(p, w)$ the factor or *input demand* correspondence.

If an interior maximum exists and f is differentiable then calculus can be used to describe the maximum. As the production constraint has been substituted into the objective, no Lagrangian function is needed. The necessary first order condition is:

$$p\mathbf{D}f(\hat{x}(p, w)) = w^{\perp}, \tag{4.2}$$

which says the marginal revenue product must equal the wage for every input. Dividing component i of Eq. (4.2) by component j yields:

$$\frac{\partial f(\hat{x}(p, w))/\partial x_i}{\partial f(\hat{x}(p, w))/\partial x_j} = \frac{w_i}{w_j},$$

which is the familiar condition that the MRTS between any two inputs must equal their price ratio (slope of the isocost line) at the firm's optimal choice. That is, the firm must choose its (interior) inputs so that its isoquant is tangent to its isocost.

It may be useful to restate for the single-output case some of the items from the general case, accounting particularly for the negative sign on the input vector. Positive semidefiniteness of supply/demand price responses is:

$$(p^1 - p^0)(\hat{y}(p^1, w^1) - \hat{y}(p^0, w^0)) - (w^1 - w^0)^{\perp}(\hat{x}(p^1, w^1) - \hat{x}(p^0, w^0)) \geq 0.$$

This version makes it more explicit that, if only the output price increases then the firm's output choice does not decrease and, if only one input price increases then the firm's use of that input does not increase. In other words, supply slopes upward and input demands slope downward in their own prices (again, the *Law of Demand*). The monotonicity in item 5 of

Theorem 4.1 takes the form $\pi^*(p^1, w^1) \geq \pi^*(p^0, w^0)$ when $p^1 \geq p^0$ and $w^1 \leq w^0$. That is, a higher output price and lower input prices cannot decrease profit.

Hotelling's Lemma is:

$$\frac{\partial \pi^*}{\partial p} = \hat{y}(p, w) \quad \text{and} \quad \frac{\partial \pi^*}{\partial w_i} = -\hat{x}_i(p, w) \text{ for } i = 1, \ldots, n-1$$

when these derivatives exist, which is almost everywhere on the interior of P where a maximum exists. At such a price where one of these derivatives does not exist, a feasible production plan $(y, -x)$ maximizes profit if and only if it is the slope vector of a lower tangent plane of the profit function at that price.

When the supply/demand vector is differentiable and its Jacobian is continuous (and the profit function is differentiable in a neighborhood), the matrix of supply/demand slopes:

$$\begin{bmatrix} \frac{\partial \hat{y}}{\partial p} & \frac{\partial \hat{y}}{\partial w_1} & \cdots & \frac{\partial \hat{y}}{\partial w_{n-1}} \\ -\frac{\partial \hat{x}_1}{\partial p} & -\frac{\partial \hat{x}_1}{\partial w_1} & \cdots & -\frac{\partial \hat{x}_1}{\partial w_{n-1}} \\ \vdots & \vdots & \ddots & \vdots \\ -\frac{\partial \hat{x}_{n-1}}{\partial p} & -\frac{\partial \hat{x}_{n-1}}{\partial w_1} & \cdots & -\frac{\partial \hat{x}_{n-1}}{\partial w_{n-1}} \end{bmatrix}$$

is singular, symmetric and positive semidefinite. Focusing on diagonal elements and using positive semidefiniteness again shows that supply does not slope downward as a function of the output price, and each input demand does not slope upward as a function of its own price. Focusing on off-diagonal elements and using symmetry shows that cross-price effects on supply/demand honor reciprocity. These off-diagonal elements can be either positive or negative. If $\hat{x}_j$ moves in the same direction as $\hat{x}_i$ when w_i changes (i.e., if $\frac{\partial \hat{x}_j}{\partial w_i} \leq 0$) then we say inputs i and j are *gross complements* in production. If the two inputs move in opposite directions (i.e., if $\frac{\partial \hat{x}_j}{\partial w_i} \geq 0$) then we say inputs i and j are *gross substitutes* in production. Similarly, if $\frac{\partial \hat{x}_i}{\partial p} \geq 0$ we say input i is *normal* in production (an increase in its price causes output to decrease), while if $\frac{\partial \hat{x}_i}{\partial p} < 0$ we say input i is *inferior* in production (an increase in its price causes output to increase!). These are local definitions; the signs can change at different points in the price space.

We have proceeded in these last few paragraphs as if there is a unique interior maximum characterized by calculus. Aside from the existence, uniqueness and differentiability issues already discussed, we must consider the requirement $x \geq 0$ (i.e., the single-output case). It is possible to have corner solutions of the form $x_i^* = \{0\}$, in which case the first derivative can be negative at the optimum: $pf_i(\hat{x}) < w_i$. If the minimum is unique x_i can be omitted from the production plan and everything holds as described here for the other components of x ($\hat{x}_i$ is fixed at zero for small changes in (p, w)). If it happens that a first derivative with respect to x_i is zero at $\hat{x}_i = 0$ then the comparative statics might be different for different changes in (p, w) ($\hat{x}_i$ remains zero for some changes but changes according to the first order conditions for other changes).

4.6 NOTES

Hotelling [2] first examined the profit function but did not fully establish its properties. A long line of development culminated in McFadden [3, especially pp. 66–76, 81]. Properties of the optimal choice correspondence are discussed by McFadden [3] as well, although Hotelling is of course responsible for the result $\mathbf{D}\pi^*(p) = \hat{z}(p)^{\perp}$ at a point of differentiability that has become known as Hotelling's Lemma. Hotelling [4] also derived reciprocity but this work is not presented in the broader context of the Envelope Theorem.

Koopmans [5] provides an early rigorous treatment of production. Debreu [6, section 3.3] provides properties of production sets. A nondifferentiable version of the tangency property in Theorem 4.2 was provided by Anderson and Takayama [7].

Lau [8] presents many properties of profit functions, especially involving differentiability, and also discusses functional forms.

4.7 EXERCISES

1. Determine whether each of these technologies satisfies: (i) closed (ii) no free lunch, (iii) possibility of inaction, (iv) free disposal, (v) convexity, and (vi) natural inputs (In (E) and (F) the figures show the typical shape of input requirement sets; assume $V(0) = \mathbb{R}^2_+$ in (E)):

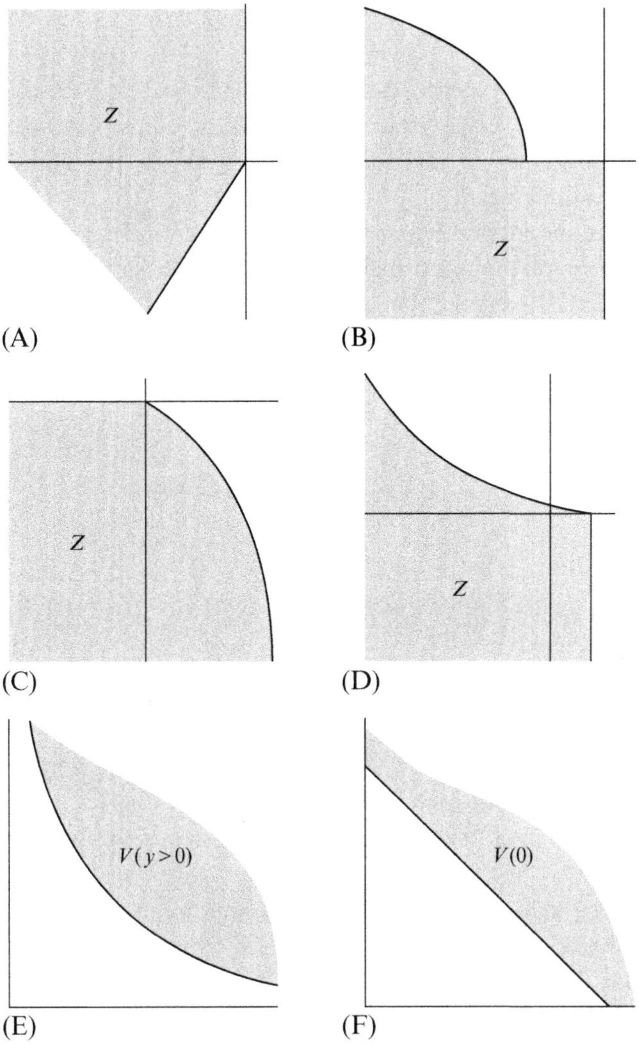

2. Consider the production set $Z = \{(z_1, z_2) \in \mathbb{R}^2 : z_2 \leq 1-(1+z_1)^2\}$.

a. Demonstrate geometrically whether Z has each of the following properties (Hint: Carefully plot the curve $z_2 = 1 - (1 + z_1)^2$): (i) nonempty, (ii) closed, (iii) no free lunch, (iv) possibility of inaction, (v) free disposal, (vi) convexity, and (vii) natural inputs.

b. Derive the supply/demand correspondence and the profit function.

c. For what price ratios is z_1 an input? For what price ratios is z_1 an output?

3. Consider the production set $Z = \{(z_1, z_2) \in \mathbb{R}^2 : z_1 \leq 0 \text{ and } z_2 \leq -z_1 + 2(-z_1)^{1/2}\}$.
   a. Demonstrate geometrically whether Z has each of the following properties: (i) nonempty, (ii) closed, (iii) no free lunch, (iv) possibility of inaction, (v) free disposal, (vi) convexity, and (vii) natural inputs.
   b. Derive the supply/demand correspondence and the profit function.
4. Draw a production set that satisfies no free lunch, possibility of inaction, and convexity; but violates free disposal.
5. Here is a production set $Z \subset \mathbb{R}^2$:

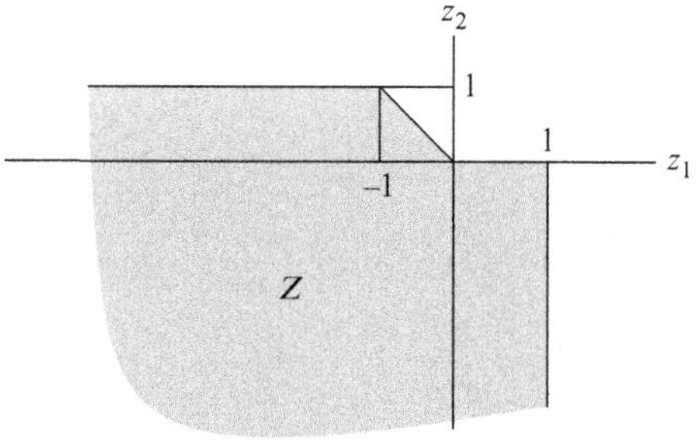

   a. Derive the profit maximizing choice correspondence $z^*(p)$ for a price-taking firm.
   b. Derive the profit function $\pi^*(p)$.
   c. Formally show that $\pi^*(p)$ is homogeneous of degree one and convex.
   d. Discuss zero profit and how it relates to the properties of this production set.
6. Suppose $Z = \{(z_1, z_2) \in \mathbb{R}^2 : z_1 \leq 0 \text{ and } z_2 \leq \ln(-z_1 + 1)\}$. Derive the profit function. What happens to $\pi^*(p)$ when $p_2 > 0$ and $p_1 \downarrow 0$? Comment on whether the domain P where π^* is finite is closed.
7. Some production sets Z have a global returns to scale property, defined as follows:
   a. Z has *nonincreasing returns to scale* if $z \in Z \Rightarrow \alpha z \in Z$ for every $\alpha \in (0, 1)$. That is, beginning from any feasible production plan, every linearly scaled-down version of that production plan is also feasible. If Z is closed and yet αz is always in the interior of Z when z has at least one positive component, we say Z has *decreasing returns to scale*.

b. Z has *nondecreasing returns to scale* if $z \in Z \Rightarrow \alpha z \in Z$ for every $\alpha \in (1, \infty)$. That is, beginning from any feasible production plan, every linearly scaled-up version of that production plan is also feasible. If Z is closed and yet αz is always in the interior of Z when z has at least one positive component, we say Z has *increasing returns to scale*.

c. Z has constant returns to scale if it has both nonincreasing and nondecreasing returns to scale.

Draw a production set that has decreasing returns to scale but that is not convex.

8. Decide whether each of the following technologies has each of the following properties: (i) nonempty, (ii) closed, (iii) no free lunch, (iv) possibility of inaction, (v) free disposal, (vi) convexity, and (vii) natural inputs. Also characterize the returns to scale of each.

a. $Z = \{(x, y) \in \mathbb{R}^2 : x < 1 \text{ and } y \leq \ln(-x + 1)\}$.

b. $Z = \{(x, y) \in \mathbb{R}^2 : x^2 + y^2 \leq 1\}$.

c. $V(y) = \{x \in \mathbb{R}^2_+ : x_1^2 + x_2^2 \geq y\}$ for $y \geq 0$.

d. $Z = \{(x, y) \in \mathbb{R}^2 : y \leq (-x)^3\}$.

e. $V(y) = \{x \in \mathbb{R}^2_+ : x_1 \geq \frac{y}{x_2}\}$ for $y \geq 0$.

f.

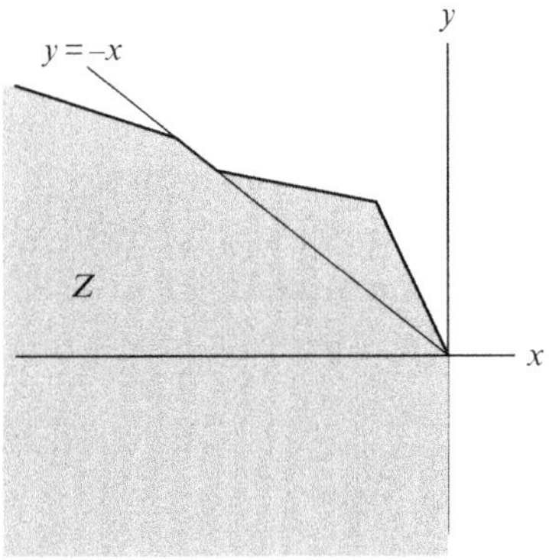

9. Assume a single-output production set Z is closed and satisfies no free lunch, free disposal, and possibility of inaction. Prove the following properties of the corresponding production function f (assume f exists as a maximum):

a. $f(0) = 0$.

b. f is upper semicontinuous.

c. f is nondecreasing.
d. For any $x \geq 0$:
i. $f(\alpha x) \geq \alpha f(x)\ \forall \alpha \in (0, 1)$ when Z has nonincreasing returns to scale; the inequality is strict when Z has decreasing returns to scale and $f(x) > 0$.
ii. $f(\alpha x) \geq \alpha f(x)\ \forall \alpha \in (1, \infty)$ when Z has nondecreasing returns to scale; the inequality is strict when Z has increasing returns to scale and $f(x) > 0$.
iii. $f(\alpha x) = \alpha f(x)\ \forall \alpha > 0$ when Z has constant returns to scale.
e. f is quasiconcave if and only if $V(y)$ is convex for every y.

10. Draw a single-output production set in $\mathbb{R}^2$ that is closed and satisfies no free lunch, free disposal, and possibility of inaction; but for which the corresponding production function is not continuous.

11. Give a geometric example of a single-output production set Z that is closed and satisfies no free lunch, free disposal, and possibility of inaction; yet the corresponding production function can take on infinite values. Prove that convexity solves this problem.

12. Formally prove that there is at most one production plan that maximizes profit when the production set is strictly convex (and the price vector is not zero).

13. Respond to the following statement: "Hotelling's Lemma is misleading because smoothness assumptions are not very plausible."

14. A price-taking firm's unique profit-maximizing choice is $(-4, 2)$ at prices $(1, 2)$. At these prices, the elasticity of the optimal choice of commodity 1 with respect to its own price is 3. What is the elasticity of the optimal choice of commodity 2 with respect to the price of commodity 1 (at these same prices)?

15. A price-taking firm has the following production set Z in $\mathbb{R}^2$:

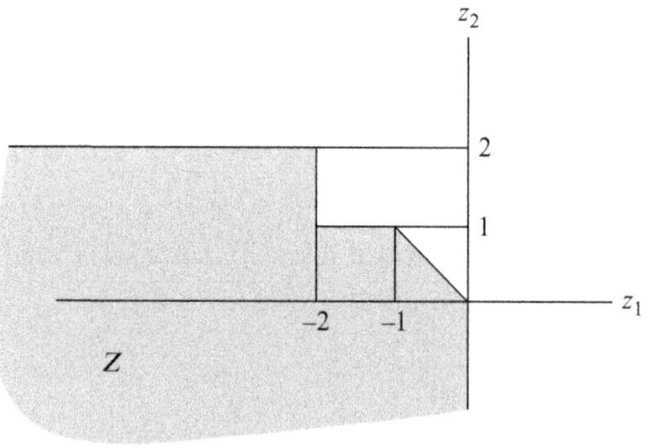

a. State which of the following properties this technology possesses, and say why for each: Closed, nonempty, no free lunch, possibility of inaction, free disposal, natural inputs, and convexity. Also characterize the returns to scale of this technology.

b. Derive the profit-maximizing supply/demand correspondence and profit function.

c. Is the profit-maximizing supply/demand correspondence a convex set for every positive price vector? Why/why not? Relate your answer to Theorem 4.4.

16. Consider the production function:

$$y = f(x) = \begin{cases} \frac{20}{20-x} - 1, & x \leq 15 \\ \theta x - 15\theta + 3, & x > 15 \end{cases},$$

where θ is a nonnegative constant. For what values of θ (if any) does the function display globally increasing returns to scale and for what values of θ (if any) does the function display globally decreasing returns to scale?

17. Consider a firm that produces output y using only one input, x, according to the production function:

$$y = f(x) = \begin{cases} x^{1/2}, & 0 \leq x \leq 1 \\ \theta x + 1 - \theta, & x > 1 \end{cases},$$

where θ is a nonnegative constant. For what values of θ does this production set display a global returns to scale?

18. Four common production functions for single-output technologies with two inputs are:

a. Cobb-Douglas: $f(x_1, x_2) = A x_1^{a_1} x_2^{a_2}$.

b. Leontief (fixed input proportions): $f(x_1, x_2) = (\min\{a_1 x_1, a_2 x_2\})^{\epsilon}$.

c. Perfect substitutes: $f(x_1, x_2) = (a_1 x_1 + a_2 x_2)^{\epsilon}$.

d. Constant Elasticity of Substitution (CES): $f(x_1, x_2) = [a_1 x_1^{\rho} + a_2 x_2^{\rho}]^{\epsilon/\rho}$.

Here, $A, a_1, a_2, \epsilon > 0$ are parameters; $\rho \leq 1$ $(\rho \neq 0)$ is a parameter in the CES. For each of these, give the corresponding production set Z, input requirement sets $V(y)$, isoquants, and MRTS. Sketch a typical isoquant for each production function.

For what values of a_1 and a_2 does the Cobb-Douglas form display decreasing returns? Increasing returns? Constant returns?

For what values of ϵ do the Leontief, perfect substitutes and CES forms display decreasing returns? Increasing returns? Constant returns?

What happens to the isoquants as ρ approaches 1 in the CES production function? What happens as ρ approaches 0? What happens as ρ approaches $-\infty$?

19. Here is a graph of a production set Z:

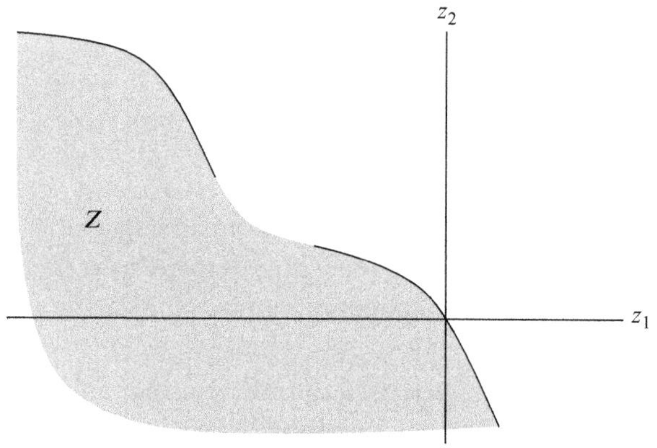

a. Does Z have each of the following properties: (i) nonempty, (ii) closed, (iii) no free lunch, (iv) possibility of inaction, (v) free disposal, (vi) convexity, and (vii) natural inputs?

b. Does the "abnormality" in Z affect the profit function of a price-taking firm with this production set? Why/why not?

20. Suppose a typical input requirement set is:

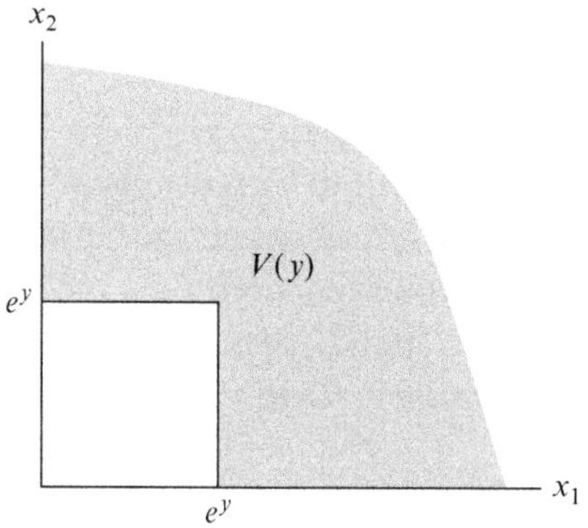

Comment on any unusual properties of this production set. Then find the profit function for a price-taking firm with this production set.

21. Suppose a firm has the production set $Z = \{(y, -x) \in \mathbb{R}^2 : x \geq 0 \;\&\; y \leq 2x \;\&\; y \leq 1 + x\}$.
   a. Carefully draw Z, labeling slopes and critical points.
   b. Does Z have each of the following properties: (i) nonempty, (ii) closed, (iii) no free lunch, (iv) possibility of inaction, (v) free disposal, (vi) convexity, and (vii) natural inputs?
   c. Characterize the returns to scale of Z.
   d. What are the input requirement sets $V(y)$ for $y \geq 0$?
   e. What is the feasible output set Y?
   f. Find the supply/demand correspondence and profit function for a price-taking firm with this production set.
   g. Verify that the profit function and supply/demand correspondence have the properties required by Theorem 4.1.

22. Consider the set $Z = \mathbb{R}^1_-$.
   a. Does Z have each of the following properties: (i) nonempty, (ii) closed, (iii) no free lunch, (iv) possibility of inaction, (v) free disposal, (vi) convexity, and (vii) natural inputs?
   b. What returns to scale does Z display? Why?
   c. Find the supply/demand correspondence and profit function for a price-taking firm with this production set.

23. Here is a production set: $Z = \{(0,0), (-1,2), (-3,3), (-4,5)\}$ (i.e., 4 points in $\mathbb{R}^2$).
   a. Carefully draw Z.
   b. Does Z have each of the following properties: (i) nonempty, (ii) closed, (iii) no free lunch, (iv) possibility of inaction, (v) free disposal, (vi) convexity, and (vii) natural inputs?
   c. Let p_1 be the price of the first commodity and p_2 be the price of the second commodity. Derive the profit function for a price-taking firm with this production set.
   d. Suppose the following points were added to Z:

$$\{(z_1, z_2) \in \mathbb{R}^2 : (z_1, z_2) < (0,0) \text{ or } (z_1, z_2) < (-1,2) \\ \text{or } (z_1, z_2) < (-3,3) \text{ or } (z_1, z_2) < (-4,5)\}.$$

   How would your answers to (a)–(c) change, if at all?

24. Suppose a firm has the production set as shown below.
   a. What are the input requirement sets $V(y)$ for $y \geq 0$?
   b. What is the feasible output set Y?

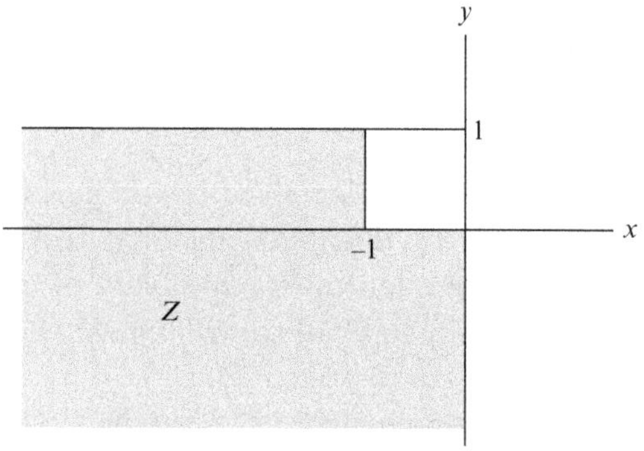

c. Find the supply/demand correspondence and the profit function for a price-taking firm with this production set.

25. Here is a production set in $\mathbb{R}^2$: $Z = \{(0, 0), (4, -10)\}$.

a. Explain why Z either has or does not have each of the following properties: nonempty, closed, no free lunch, possibility of inaction, free disposal, convex, and natural input(s).

b. Derive the profit-maximizing supply/demand relationship and the profit function.

c. Is there a "standard" production function for this technology? If so, derive it. If not, give a profit-relevant "standard" production function.

26. Suppose $p_x = 1$ and $p_y = 0$. Illustrate the profit maximizing point for a price-taking firm with the production set in Exercise 8(b). Does this firm earn positive profit?

27. A firm has the following production set Z:

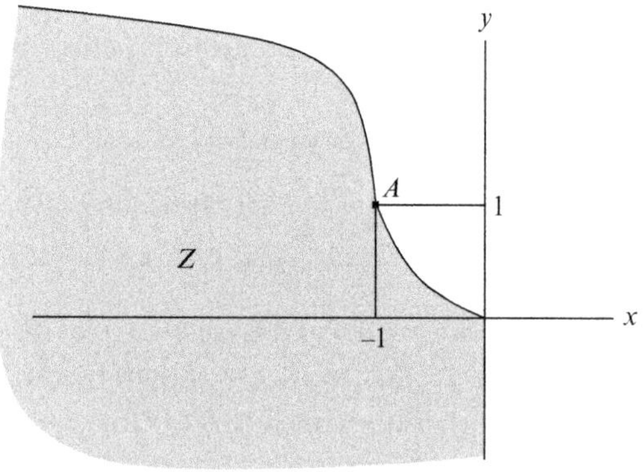

The equation of the boundary of Z above and to the left of point A on the graph is $y = 1 + \sqrt{-(x+1)}$. Let p denote the price of y and w denote the price of x. Find the demand/supply correspondence and profit function for this price-taking firm.

28. Suppose a firm produces one output y from one input x and the production set Z is:

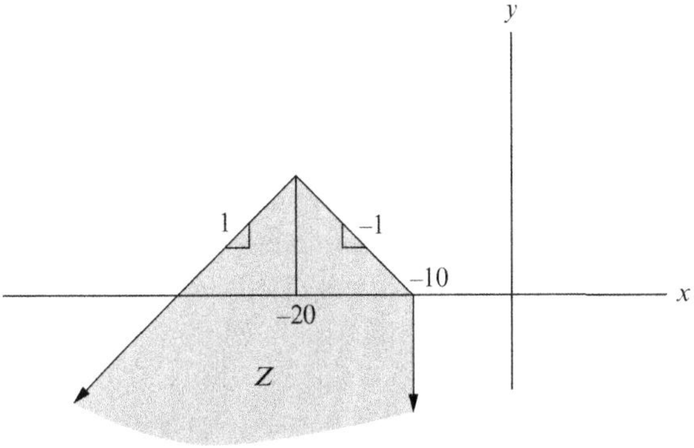

a. Let $w \geq 0$ represent the price of x and $p \geq 0$ represent the price of y. Find the profit function for a price-taking firm.

b. Which of the properties of a production set are violated by this firm's production set? Why? Which of the properties of a production set are satisfied by this firm's production set? Why?

29. Suppose the production function for a single-input and single-output production set is given by $f(x) = (50 - x)(2 + x)$.

a. Determine whether this production set has each of the following properties: (i) nonempty, (ii) closed, (iii) no free lunch, (iv) possibility of inaction, (v) free disposal, and (vi) convexity.

b. Based on your answer to part (a), what standard properties will the profit function for a price-taking firm possess? Which of the standard properties will not hold for the profit function? Answer this question by referring to the *reasons* that the profit function possesses certain properties, not by deriving the profit function and checking its properties.

30. Suppose $p_x = p_y$. Illustrate the profit maximizing point for a firm with the production set in Exercise 8(f). Does this firm earn positive profit?

31. Derive the supply/demand correspondence and the profit function for each of the production functions in Exercise 18. What condition must the parameters satisfy in each case? For the Cobb-Douglas, use the tangency property of the Envelope Theorem to explore the effect on optimal profit of a change in a_1.

32. Consider a price-taking firm with production function $f(x_1, x_2) = x_1 x_2$. Let p be the output price and (w_1, w_2) be the input price vector. Describe the input choices this firm makes.

33. Use the tangency property of the Envelope Theorem to construct an alternate proof that standard profit functions are homogeneous of degree one.

34. Consider a profit-maximizing firm that is not a perfect competitor in its output market. Instead, the firm faces an inverse demand curve $p(y; r)$, where p is its price, y is its output level, and r is the price charged by a rival firm whose product is regarded by consumers as a substitute product. Hence the revenue function is $R(y; r) = p(y; r)y$.

a. Use the tangency property of the Envelope Theorem to determine the effect on optimal profit of a change in the rival's price.

b. Use the traditional comparative statics methodology to show that the effect on optimal output of a change in the rival's price depends on how the change in the rival's price affects the *slope* of the inverse demand (with respect to output).

35. Here is a production set: $Z = \{(z_1, z_2) \in \mathbb{R}^2 : z_1 \leq 0 \text{ and } z_2 \leq (-z_1)^{1/2}\}$.

a. Carefully graph this production set.

b. Does this production set have each of the following properties: (i) nonempty, (ii) closed, (iii) no free lunch, (iv) possibility of inaction, (v) free disposal, (vi) convexity, (vii) natural inputs?

c. Consider a profit-maximizing firm that is a price-taker for z_1 at price p_1 but that believes the price of z_2 will vary with the quantity of z_2 chosen according to the following relationship: $p_2 = z_2^{-1/2}$ for $z_2 > 0$. Carefully graph an isoprofit curve for this firm on your graph from part (a), labeling the vertical intercept and any critical points. Indicate the direction of increasing profit on your graph. Use this information to illustrate the profit maximizing point on your graph.

d. Solve this problem for the profit maximizing values of z_1 and z_2 in terms of p_1.

e. Use your answer to part (d) to find the profit function.

36. A price-taking firm produces output y from two inputs: Labor (L) and raw material (M). Denote the prices by p_Y, p_L, and p_M. The government decides to impose a value-added tax (VAT), which taxes the difference between revenue and raw material cost at a rate of t.

a. Write the firm's profit maximization objective.

b. Assume labor and raw material are substitutes and normal in production. Show that the firm uses less labor as a result of the VAT.

37. Suppose the production set Z is the closed unit circle in $\mathbb{R}^2$ excluding the point $\left(\frac{1}{\sqrt{2}}, \frac{1}{\sqrt{2}}\right)$.

a. Find $z^*(p)$ for $p \gg 0$. Take care when $p_1 = p_2$.

b. Is z^* upper hemicontinuous at $p = (1, 1)$? Compare to item 2 of Theorem 4.4. Explain.

REFERENCES

[1] Apostol TM. Mathematical analysis. 2nd ed. Reading, MA: Addison-Wesley; 1974.

[2] Hotelling H. Edgeworth's taxation paradox and the nature of demand and supply functions. J Polit Econ 1932;40:577–616.

[3] McFadden D. Cost, revenue and profit functions. In: Fuss M, McFadden D, editors. Production economics: a dual approach to theory and applications I. Amsterdam: North-Holland; 1978. p. 3–109.

[4] Hotelling H. Demand functions with limited budgets. Econometrica 1935;3:66–78.

[5] Koopmans TC. Analysis of production as an efficient combination of activities. In: Activity analysis of production and allocation. Cowles Commission for Research in Economics Monograph 13 (University of Chicago). New York: Wiley; 1951.

[6] Debreu G. Theory of value. Cowles Foundation for Research in Economics Monograph 17 (Yale University). New York: Wiley; 1959.

[7] Anderson RK, Takayama A. Comparative statics with discrete jumps in shift parameters, or how to do economics on the saddle(-point). J Econ Theory 1979;21:491–509.

[8] Lau LJ. Applications of profit functions. In: Fuss M, McFadden D, editors. Production economics: a dual approach to theory and applications I. Amsterdam: North-Holland; 1978. p. 133–216.

CHAPTER 5

Duality of the Profit Maximum

Chapter Outline

The properties presented in Theorem 4.1 are *necessary conditions* for the postulated behavior of price-taking profit maximization subject to an inactive production constraint. A natural question is: What set of properties is *sufficient* for this maximizing behavior? That is, given some relationship between a convex cone $P \subset \mathbb{R}^n_+$ (price vectors) and either subsets of $\mathbb{R}^n$ (a candidate supply/demand correspondence) or points in $\mathbb{R}^1$ (a candidate profit function), that possesses the same properties as an outcome from profit maximization, is that relationship indeed an outcome from profit maximization? This question is in some ways more important for economic research than derivation of the necessary conditions because its affirmative answer enables us to use an outcome from profit maximization without regard for the details of the underlying production set. The sufficiency is called *duality* because it says the outcome is dual to the original problem, in the sense that for every maximization problem of this form there is an outcome with some fundamental properties, and vice-versa.

5.1 DUALITY OF THE PROFIT FUNCTION

Consider a function $\phi : P \to \mathbb{R}^1$ that is a possible profit function. We must attempt to construct an underlying production set over which ϕ is indeed the maximal profit function. To do so, for some price vector p^0 draw the isoprofit line for profit level $\phi(p^0)$ as illustrated in Fig. 5.1. The production set must lie everywhere below this isoprofit; otherwise profit larger than $\phi(p^0)$ would be possible. The boundary of the production set must also touch this isoprofit somewhere; otherwise a profit level as large as $\phi(p^0)$ would not be attainable. Repeat this argument for all different price vectors and then intersect the areas to obtain a proposed production set Z_ϕ from the original function ϕ. The result is a proposed "profit-relevant" production set:

$$Z_\phi = \{z \in \mathbb{R}^n : p^\perp z \leq \phi(p) \ \forall p \in P\}.$$

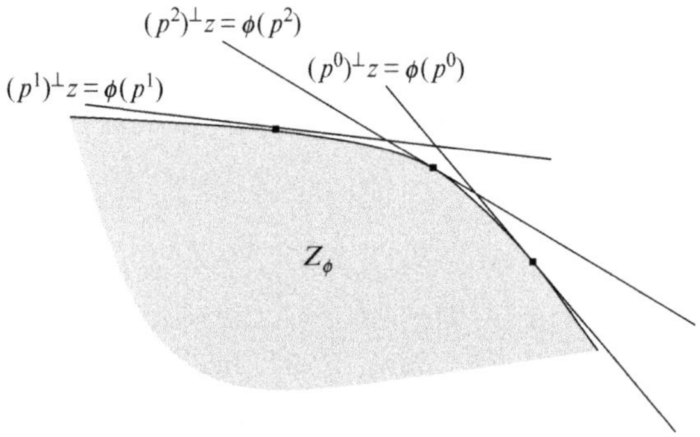

Fig. 5.1 Recovering the production set from the profit function. Isoprofit lines for three different price vectors p^0, p^1, and p^2 are shown. Z_ϕ is the set below and left of all such isoprofits.

There are two properties ϕ must possess to make this work. First, if one price vector is proportional to another, for example $p^3 = \alpha p^1$ for some $\alpha > 0$, then the isoprofit lines for those two price vectors have the same slopes. Hence those two isoprofit lines must coincide; otherwise the proposed production set will touch only the lower of the two. That is, $(p^1)^\perp z = \phi(p^1)$ and $(p^3)^\perp z = \phi(p^3)$ must be the same line. Multiplying the former by α and substituting for p^3 in the latter reveals that these are the same line if and only if $\alpha\phi(p^1) = \phi(\alpha p^1)$, which means ϕ must be homogeneous of degree one.

Second, if one price vector is a weighted average of two others, for example $p^2 = \alpha p^0 + (1 - \alpha)p^1$ for some $\alpha \in (0, 1)$, then the isoprofit line for p^2 has slope between the slopes of the isoprofit lines for p^0 and p^1. Again, the weighted average isoprofit line must simultaneously pass below both of the underlying isoprofit lines; otherwise the proposed production set will not touch the former. That is, there must be some z value, say z^0, at which the line $(\alpha p^0 + (1-\alpha)p^1)^{\perp} z = \phi(\alpha p^0 + (1-\alpha)p^1)$ is below both lines $(p^0)^{\perp} z = \phi(p^0)$ and $(p^1)^{\perp} z = \phi(p^1)$. Hence z^0 must satisfy three conditions: $(\alpha p^0 + (1-\alpha)p^1)^{\perp} z^0 = \phi(\alpha p^0 + (1-\alpha)p^1)$; but $(p^0)^{\perp} z^0 \leq \phi(p^0)$ and $(p^1)^{\perp} z^0 \leq \phi(p^1)$. Multiplying the first inequality by α, the second by $(1-\alpha)$, and adding yields $(\alpha p^0 + (1-\alpha)p^1)^{\perp} z^0 \leq \alpha\phi(p^0) + (1-\alpha)\phi(p^1)$. As the left side is $\phi(\alpha p^0 + (1-\alpha)p^1)$, this shows ϕ must be a convex function.

A third property of ϕ is required if some prices might be on the boundary of the domain. The main complication at boundary prices is the possibility of a discontinuity in ϕ. Recall from Fig. 3.4 that convexity of ϕ does not ensure continuity at the boundary of the domain. If ϕ is defined but discontinuous at a price vector on the boundary then ϕ can be strictly larger than the supremum of $p^{\perp} z$ (see Exercise 12). Accordingly, we must add the explicit requirement that ϕ is continuous to obtain a duality theorem that holds when some prices can be boundary points.

Theorem 5.1 (Duality of the Profit Function). *Assume $P \subset \mathbb{R}^n_+$ is a convex cone with a nonempty interior and $\phi : P \to \mathbb{R}^1$ is convex, homogeneous of degree one, and continuous (at boundary points of P that are in P). Define:*

$$Z_\phi \equiv \{z \in \mathbb{R}^n : p^{\perp} z \leq \phi(p)\ \forall p \in P\}.$$

Then:

1. *Z_ϕ is nonempty.*
2. *Z_ϕ is closed.*
3. *Z_ϕ has the free disposal property.*
4. *Z_ϕ is convex.*

Moreover, if $\pi^*_\phi : P \to \mathbb{R}^1$ and $z^*_\phi : P \to 2^{Z_\phi}$ are defined as:

$$\pi^*_\phi(p) \equiv \sup\{p^{\perp} z : z \in Z_\phi\} \text{ and}$$
$$z^*_\phi(p) \equiv \{z \in Z_\phi : p^{\perp} z = \pi^*_\phi(p)\},$$

then $\pi^*_\phi(p) = \phi(p)$ for every $p \in P$ and $z^*_\phi(p)$ is nonempty for every $p \in \text{int } P$.

Proof.

1. Select $p^0 \in \text{int } P$. As ϕ is convex and homogeneous of degree one, by Theorem 3.9 there exists $z \in \mathbb{R}^n$ such that:

$$\phi(p) \geq \phi(p^0) + z^{\perp}(p - p^0) \text{ for every } p \in P \quad \text{and} \quad \phi(p^0) = (p^0)^{\perp} z.$$

   Therefore $\phi(p) \geq z^{\perp} p$ for every $p \in P$.
2. Consider $z^i \in Z_\phi$ such that $z^i \to z^0$. Then, for each $p \in P$, $\phi(p) \geq p^{\perp} z^i$ and $p^{\perp} z^i \to p^{\perp} z^0$, so $\phi(p) \geq p^{\perp} z^0$.

3. Assume $z^0 \in Z_\phi$. For $z \leq z^0$, $\phi(p) \geq p^\perp z^0 \geq p^\perp z$ for every $p \in P$, so $z \in Z_\phi$.
4. Fix $z^0, z^1 \in Z_\phi$. Then $\phi(p) \geq p^\perp z^0$ and $\phi(p) \geq p^\perp z^1$, both for every $p \in P$. Select $\alpha \in (0, 1)$, multiply the first inequality by α, the second by $(1-\alpha)$, and add to obtain $\phi(p) \geq p^\perp[\alpha z^0 + (1-\alpha)z^1]$ for every $p \in P$. That is, $\alpha z^0 + (1-\alpha)z^1 \in Z_\phi$.

Now consider $\pi^*_\phi(p)$. As $\phi(p)$ is an upper bound for $\{p^\perp z : z \in Z_\phi\}$, we have $\phi(p) \geq \pi^*_\phi(p)$ by definition of the supremum. Conversely, if $p \in \text{int } P$ then by Theorem 3.9 there exists $z \in Z_\phi$ such that $p^\perp z = \phi(p)$. Therefore $\pi^*_\phi(p) \geq p^\perp z = \phi(p)$. Combining inequalities yields $\phi(p) = \pi^*_\phi(p)$ when $p \in \text{int } P$. Existence of $z \in Z_\phi$ such that $p^\perp z = \phi(p)$ then establishes that $z^*_\phi(p)$ is nonempty for $p \in \text{int } P$.

It remains to show $\pi^*_\phi(p) \geq \phi(p)$ when p is on the boundary of P (recall from Theorem 3.8 that there may not be a lower tangent plane at a boundary point of the domain of a convex function). Fix $\tilde{p} \in \text{int } P$ and define the convex combination:

$$p(\alpha) \equiv \alpha\tilde{p} + (1-\alpha)p \text{ for } \alpha \in (0, 1).$$

We first show $p(\alpha) \in \text{int } P$ for each α. By convexity, $p(\alpha) \in P$. Thus, if $p(\alpha)$ is not an interior point of P then it is a boundary point of P, in which case there exists a sequence $\{p^i\}_{i=1}^\infty \subset \mathbb{R}^n$ such that $p^i \notin P$ but $p^i \to p(\alpha)$. Define $\tilde{p}^i$ by:

$$p^i \equiv \alpha\tilde{p}^i + (1-\alpha)p.$$

Then $p^i \to p(\alpha)$ implies $\tilde{p}^i \to \tilde{p}$. As $\tilde{p} \in \text{int } P$, we have $\tilde{p}^i \in P$ for i large. By convexity, $p^i \in P$ for i large, a contradiction. Hence $p(\alpha)$ cannot be a boundary point, and thus is an interior point.

As noted above, there exists $z(\alpha) \in Z_\phi$ such that $p(\alpha)^\perp z(\alpha) = \phi(p(\alpha))$ because $p(\alpha) \in \text{int } P$. Therefore:

$$\begin{aligned}\pi^*_\phi(p) \geq p^\perp z(\alpha) = \frac{p(\alpha)^\perp z(\alpha) - \alpha\tilde{p}^\perp z(\alpha)}{1-\alpha} &= \frac{\phi(p(\alpha)) - \alpha\tilde{p}^\perp z(\alpha)}{1-\alpha} \\ \geq \frac{\phi(p(\alpha)) - \alpha\phi(\tilde{p})}{1-\alpha}.\end{aligned}$$

The first inequality is by definition of $\pi^*_\phi(p)$ as a supremum; the second is by definition of Z_ϕ. Letting $\alpha \to 0$ and using continuity of ϕ yields $\pi^*_\phi(p) \geq \phi(p)$. □

Hence ϕ is indeed the profit function at prices in P for the production set Z_ϕ derived from the homogeneous and convex real-valued function ϕ. That is, *the homogeneity and convexity properties (and continuity, if P is not open)* *are sufficient as well as necessary for a function $\phi : P \to \mathbb{R}^1$ to be the maximum of the profit expression over a well-behaved production set; and ϕ is a true maximum (a profit-maximizing production plan exists) on the interior of the price space. Thus we can interpret* **any** *function satisfying these properties as a profit function without actually deriving it from some underlying production set. This also shows Z_ϕ is a profit-relevant production set for a firm with profit function ϕ, and that profit-relevant production set* **always** *has the free disposal property and is convex.*

5.2 DERIVING A PROFIT-RELEVANT PRODUCTION SET

An equation for the boundary of Z_ϕ in Theorem 5.1 can usually be derived from a given ϕ. Homogeneity is used to arbitrarily declare one commodity, say commodity one, as the firm's *numéraire* by expressing all prices relative to p_1. Doing so requires that p_1 is never zero. A zero price can arise only on the boundary of P. The following lemma shows that the definition of Z_ϕ in Theorem 5.1 does not depend on whether boundary prices are considered in the definition. Indeed, the only insight from allowing boundary prices in Theorem 5.1 is the conclusion that π^*_ϕ and ϕ are the same function even on the boundary of P (provided ϕ is defined and continuous there).

Lemma 5.1. *Assume the conditions of Theorem 5.1. Then:*

$$Z_\phi = \{z \in \mathbb{R}^n : p^\perp z \le \phi(p) \ \forall p \in int\ P\}.$$

Proof. If $z \in Z_\phi$ then of course z satisfies the inequality $p^\perp z \le \phi(p)$ when p is an interior point of P. Conversely, suppose $z \in \mathbb{R}^n$ satisfies the defining inequality at all interior points of P and consider whether z then satisfies the inequality for $p \in P$ a boundary point of P. Select $\tilde{p} \in$ int P. It is shown in the proof of Theorem 5.1 that the convex combination:

$$p(\alpha) = \alpha\tilde{p} + (1-\alpha)p \text{ for } \alpha \in (0,1)$$

is an interior point of P. Therefore $p(\alpha)^\perp z \le \phi(p(\alpha))$. Letting $\alpha \to 0$ and using continuity of ϕ then yields $p^\perp z \le \phi(p)$. □

We may therefore assume P is open for the purpose of characterizing Z_ϕ, without loss of generality, which implies $p \gg 0$ for all $p \in P$.

Now partition the price vectors into the price of commodity one and the prices of all other commodities, $p = (p_1, p_{-1})$, and partition the production plans conformably. Using $\alpha = 1/p_1$ and the fact that P is a cone, we have $p \in P$ if and only if $(1, p_{-1}/p_1) \in P$. Therefore, using homogeneity, Z_ϕ may be written:

$$Z_\phi = \{(z_1, z_{-1}) \in \mathbb{R}^n : z_1 \le \phi(1, p_{-1}) - p_{-1}^\perp z_{-1} \ \forall (1, p_{-1}) \in P\}.$$

Define $g_\phi : \mathbb{R}^{n-1} \to \bar{\mathbb{R}}^1$ by:

$$g_\phi(z_{-1}) \equiv \inf\{\phi(1, p_{-1}) - p_{-1}^{\perp} z_{-1} : (1, p_{-1}) \in P\}. \tag{5.1}$$

It is immediate from this definition that $Z_\phi = \{(z_1, z_{-1}) \in \mathbb{R}^n : z_1 \leq g_\phi(z_{-1})\}$. That is, g_ϕ is the upper boundary of Z_ϕ (or Z_ϕ is the hypograph of g_ϕ) at z_{-1} points where g_ϕ is finite. When z_{-1} does not combine with any real number z_1 to form a feasible production plan (i.e., when there is no real number z_1 less than $\phi(1, p_{-1}) - p_{-1}^{\perp} z_{-1}$ for every $(1, p_{-1}) \in P$) then $g_\phi(z_{-1}) = -\infty$. When $g_\phi(z_{-1})$ is finite, the pair $(g_\phi(z_{-1}), z_{-1})$ is a feasible production plan (an element of Z_ϕ).

The equation $z_1 = g_\phi(z_{-1})$ might aptly be called the firm's profit-relevant production possibilities frontier. It is derived from ϕ by solving the minimization problem in Eq. (5.1). If a minimum exists there is a price $(1, \hat{p}_{-1}(z_{-1})) \in P$ satisfying:

$$g_\phi(z_{-1}) = \phi(1, \hat{p}_{-1}(z_{-1})) - \hat{p}_{-1}(z_{-1})^{\perp} z_{-1}.$$

This equation says the production plan $(g_\phi(z_{-1}), z_{-1})$ is profit-maximizing at price $(1, \hat{p}_{-1}(z_{-1}))$ for a firm with production set Z_ϕ (as ϕ is the profit function). By Theorem 4.3 $(g_\phi(z_{-1}), z_{-1})$ is therefore the slope of a lower tangent plane of ϕ at price $(1, \hat{p}_{-1}(z_{-1}))$. In particular, if the gradient of ϕ exists at $(1, \hat{p}_{-1}(z_{-1}))$ (the gradient exists almost everywhere due to convexity) then the price/quantity pair obeys Hotelling's Lemma:

$$\mathbf{D}\phi(1, \hat{p}_{-1}(z_{-1})) = (g_\phi(z_{-1}), z_{-1}^{\perp}).$$

These observations provide an algorithm for deriving the firm's profit-relevant production possibilities frontier when ϕ has a gradient everywhere on int P. Write the Hotelling's Lemma equation $\mathbf{D}\phi(p) = z^{\perp}$, set $p_1 = 1$ in that equation, and solve for p_{-1} from $n - 1$ of the columns. If there is a solution (along with $p_1 = 1$) interior to P then it is a value of p that solves Eq. (5.1) for the z in that equation (convexity of ϕ ensures it is a global minimum). Substitute the solution into the remaining column, thereby obtaining an equation that involves only z. The z_1 element is $g_\phi(z_{-1})$ for the remaining z_{-1} elements. Commodity 1, the *numéraire*, is arbitrary; convenience can be the criterion for choosing which commodity to label commodity 1.

Note that g_ϕ is nonincreasing and quasiconcave because Z_ϕ has the free disposal property and is convex (for each z_1, the "input requirement set" $\{z_{-1} \in \mathbb{R}^{n-1} : (z_1, z_{-1}) \in Z_\phi\}$ is convex; Theorem 3.11 then implies quasiconcavity). If the components of z_{-1} are natural inputs in Z_ϕ then the boundary $f_\phi(x) = g_\phi(-x)$ is the firm's production function for $-x$ in the domain where g_ϕ is finite.

5.3 ORIGINAL VERSUS DERIVED PRODUCTION SETS

Suppose the function ϕ in Theorem 5.1 were known *a priori* to be the profit function for the production set $Z \subset \mathbb{R}^n$. That is, $\phi(p) = \sup\{p^\perp z : z \in Z\}$ for $p \in P \subset \mathbb{R}^n_+$. As ϕ is necessarily homogeneous of degree one and convex we can derive a well-behaved feasible set Z_ϕ and the profit function π^*_ϕ as above, and Theorem 5.1 ensures $\pi^*_\phi(p) = \phi(p)$ at least on the interior of P. It is tempting to infer from this that $Z_\phi = Z$; that is, the "profit-relevant" production set derived from ϕ is the same as the original production set. Theorem 5.1 implicitly shows this cannot be true in general because Z_ϕ is closed, convex and has free disposal while there is no requirement that Z have these properties for existence of a profit function.

If $z \in Z$ then $p^\perp z \leq \phi(p)$ by definition of ϕ as a supremum. As this statement holds for every $p \in S$, we can conclude $z \in Z_\phi$ and, therefore, $Z \subset Z_\phi$. But the converse is not true in general, for three reasons, as illustrated in Fig. 5.2 for $n = 2$. The figure shows Z as the light shaded area, the resulting optimal isoprofit lines for three different prices, and the optimal choices z^* for each price. Given those lines with positions defined by the function ϕ, the set Z_ϕ includes all (z_1, z_2) points that are to the southwest of all such iso-ϕ lines. Z_ϕ includes the two dark shaded areas A and B that are not part of Z. Area A arises because Z is not convex whereas the intersection Z_ϕ of areas below all iso-ϕ lines is convex. Area B arises because Z does not have free disposal whereas Z_ϕ possess this property. The third potential difference between Z and Z_ϕ is closedness: If Z did not include part of the boundary shown, say, near $z^*(p^2)$ (in which case $z^*(p^2)$ would be empty), then those boundary points would be in Z_ϕ but not in Z.

The intersection of all the sets below the iso-ϕ lines cannot exclude choice vectors from Z_ϕ that are not in Z but would never be chosen as maxima even if they were. This is natural: The maximal value $\phi(p)$ cannot contain information about points that are not maximal. Z will exclude some such "irrelevant" points whenever Z is not convex or has an upward-sloping portion of its boundary, as illustrated by areas A and B respectively. Similarly, the intersection Z_ϕ cannot exclude "relevant" choice vectors that

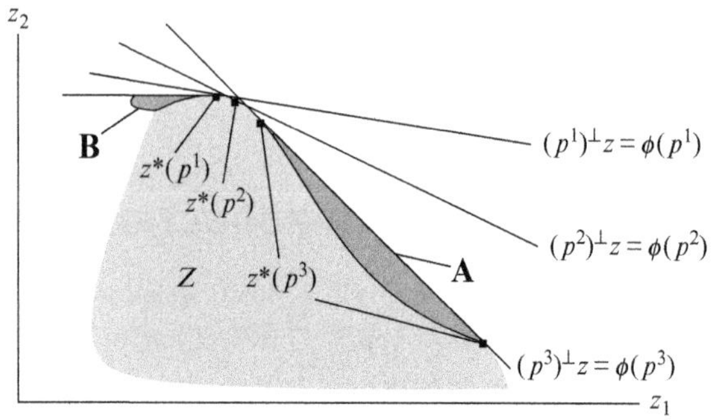

Fig. 5.2 Relationship between original and derived production sets. A production set Z can be a proper subset of the "profit-relevant" version recovered from the profit function when Z is not convex, or does not have free disposal, or is not closed.

would be chosen as maxima but for the fact that they are on an omitted part of the boundary of Z. This is also natural: The maximal value $\phi(p)$ *does* contain information about all points that are maximal, even if Z excludes some such points.

If Z is convex, has free disposal, and is closed the Separating Hyperplane Theorem can be used to show $Z_\phi \subset Z$, in which case the two sets are actually equal, provided the domain P permits consideration of *all* positive isoprofit slopes. Notice, for example, that the area B in Fig. 5.2 could extend above the illustrated horizontal upper boundary, thereby enlarging Z_ϕ, if isoprofit slopes approaching zero are not considered; while Z could exclude such points while still satisfying free disposal. In short, if the profit function is defined at all strictly positive prices and the original production set is convex, has free disposal, and is closed then Z_ϕ recovers the exact production set underlying ϕ, even if all one knows *a priori* is ϕ.

Theorem 5.2. *Assume the conditions of Theorem 5.1 with* $P \supset \mathbb{R}^n_{++}$. *Assume further that* $Z \subset \mathbb{R}^n$ *is convex, has free disposal, and is closed; and that* $\phi(p) = \sup\{p^{\perp}z : z \in Z\}$ *for* $p \in P$. *Then* $Z_\phi \subset Z$.

Proof. Suppose otherwise. Then there exists $\bar{z} \in Z_\phi$ with $\bar{z} \notin Z$. Then the Separating Hyperplane Theorem (Theorem 3.7) yields $\bar{p} \in \mathbb{R}^n$ and $\bar{\phi}$ such that:

$$\bar{p}^{\perp}z < \bar{\phi} < \bar{p}^{\perp}\bar{z} \; \forall z \in Z. \tag{5.2}$$

If there is any vector $\bar{p} \in P$ satisfying Eq. (5.2) then, for that $\bar{p}$, taking the supremum of the left side over $z \in Z$ yields $\phi(\bar{p}) \leq \bar{\phi} < \bar{p}^{\perp}\bar{z}$; but

$\bar{p}^{\perp}\bar{z} \leq \phi(\bar{p})$ because $\bar{z} \in Z_{\phi}$, a contradiction. Therefore $\bar{p} \notin P$, implying $\bar{p} \notin \mathbb{R}^n_{++}$.

Free disposal implies $\bar{p} \geq 0$. Otherwise there is a component of $\bar{p}$, say $\bar{p}_i$, that is strictly negative; but then selecting $z^0 \in Z$ and letting $z_i \to -\infty$ while holding all other components of z^0 fixed causes Eq. (5.2) to be violated. It is also plain that Eq. (5.2) cannot hold if $\bar{p} = 0$.

It remains to show, therefore, that there is a contradiction when every $\bar{p}$ satisfying Eq. (5.2) is positive (at least one positive component) but has a zero subvector. Consider one such $\bar{p}$ and partition it as $\bar{p} = (0, \bar{p}_+)$ to denote the part that is zero and the part that is strictly positive. Let **1** be a vector of ones that has the same dimension as the subvector of zeros in $\bar{p}$. As the zero subvector is required for Eq. (5.2), to each i there corresponds $z^i \in Z$ such that:

$$\left(\frac{1}{i}\mathbf{1}, \bar{p}_+\right)^{\perp} z^i \geq \left(\frac{1}{i}\mathbf{1}, \bar{p}_+\right)^{\perp} \bar{z}. \tag{5.3}$$

Partition production plans as (z_0, z_+) to conform with the partition of $\bar{p}$. For the z^i sequence, Eq. (5.2) is:

$$\bar{p}_+^{\perp} z_+^i < \bar{\phi} < (\bar{p}_+)^{\perp} \bar{z}_+.$$

Combining these two equations yields:

$$\left(\frac{1}{i}\mathbf{1}\right)^{\perp} z_0^i > \left(\frac{1}{i}\mathbf{1}\right)^{\perp} \bar{z}_0 + [\bar{p}_+^{\perp} \bar{z}_+ - \bar{\phi}].$$

As $\lim_{i\to\infty} \left(\frac{1}{i}\mathbf{1}\right)^{\perp} \bar{z}_0 = 0$, we know:

$$\left(\frac{1}{i}\mathbf{1}\right)^{\perp} \bar{z}_0 > -\frac{\bar{p}_+^{\perp}\bar{z}_+ - \bar{\phi}}{2} \text{ for } i \text{ large.}$$

Thus:

$$\left(\frac{1}{i}\mathbf{1}\right)^{\perp} z_0^i > \frac{\bar{p}_+^{\perp}\bar{z}_+ - \bar{\phi}}{2} \text{ for } i \text{ large.}$$

Hence $\lim_{i\to\infty} \mathbf{1}^{\perp} z_0^i = \infty$. One implication is $\mathbf{1}^{\perp} z_0^i > 0$ for i large.

Now consider $p^{\perp} z^i$ for $p = (\mathbf{1} + \mathbf{1}, \bar{p}_+) \in \mathbb{R}^n_{++}$. We have:

$$\begin{aligned} p^{\perp} z^i &= (\mathbf{1}, \bar{p}_+)^{\perp} z^i + \mathbf{1}^{\perp} z_0^i \\ &> \left(\frac{1}{i}\mathbf{1}, \bar{p}_+\right)^{\perp} z^i + \mathbf{1}^{\perp} z_0^i \text{ for } i \text{ large} \end{aligned}$$

$$\geq \left(\frac{1}{i}\mathbf{1}, \bar{p}_+\right)^\perp \bar{z} + \mathbf{1}^\perp z_0^i \text{ by Eq. (5.3).}$$

Hence:

$$\lim_{i\to\infty} p^\perp z^i \geq \bar{p}_+^\perp \bar{z}_+ + \lim_{i\to\infty} \mathbf{1}^\perp z_0^i = \infty.$$

Using $z^i \in Z$, we have $\sup\{p^\perp z : z \in Z\} = \infty$. But $p \in \mathbb{R}^n_{++}$, so $\sup\{p^\perp z : z \in Z\} = \phi(p) \in \mathbb{R}^1$, a contradiction. □

5.4 DUALITY OF THE SUPPLY/DEMAND CORRESPONDENCE

As with the profit function, it is valuable for economic research to know under what conditions a given correspondence is a supply/demand correspondence for a price-taking profit-maximizing firm. Knowing this enables use of any such correspondence as some firm's supply/demand behavior without specifying or deriving the production set. Theorem 4.1 shows any candidate must be homogeneous of degree zero and have positive semidefinite price responses. The question here is whether these properties are sufficient.

Consider a correspondence $\eta : P \to 2^{\mathbb{R}^n}$ for some convex cone $P \subset \mathbb{R}^n_+$. At the most basic level, if η is to be a supply/demand correspondence then, for a given $p \in P$, every element of $\eta(p)$ must maximize $p^\perp z$ over z values in some inactive feasible set and, conversely, there can be no elements of that feasible set that maximize $p^\perp z$ but are excluded from $\eta(p)$. As the feasible set is inactive it must include every element of $\eta(p)$ for every $p \in P$. Thus the smallest potential feasible set is the image $\eta(P)$. The feasible set could include other elements, but any other elements must be superfluous in the sense that they are not optimal for any p value.

Formally, η is a supply/demand correspondence for production set $\eta(P)$ if and only if, for every $p \in P$:

$$\hat{z} \in \eta(p) \Leftrightarrow p^\perp \hat{z} \geq p^\perp z \;\forall\; z \in \eta(P).$$

This criterion is merely the definition of the supply/demand correspondence for a profit-maximizing firm. Establishing that a given η actually satisfies this criterion can be difficult to do in practice.

If η is singleton-valued and the implied function $\hat{\eta}$ is differentiable on the interior of P (nonempty) then it becomes relatively easy to check whether η is a supply/demand correspondence on that interior.

Theorem 5.3. *Assume $P \subset \mathbb{R}^n_+$ is an open convex cone and $\hat{\eta} : P \to \mathbb{R}^n$ is homogeneous of degree zero and differentiable on P, with a symmetric positive semidefinite Jacobian everywhere. Then $\hat{\eta}(p)$ is the unique value of z that maximizes $p^\perp z$ subject to $z \in Z_{\phi_\eta}$, for every $p \in P$. Here, Z_{ϕ_η} is defined from $\phi_\eta(p) \equiv p^\perp \hat{\eta}(p)$ for $p \in P$ as in Theorem 5.1.*

Proof. Given $\hat{\eta}$, the implied candidate profit function is ϕ_η. Homogeneity of $\hat{\eta}$ immediately implies ϕ_η is homogeneous of degree one. The Jacobian of ϕ_η is:

$$\mathbf{D}\phi_\eta(p) = \hat{\eta}(p)^\perp + p^\perp \mathbf{D}\hat{\eta}(p).$$

Using symmetry, the transpose of the second term is $\mathbf{D}\hat{\eta}(p)^\perp p = \mathbf{D}\hat{\eta}(p)p$. This is zero by Euler's Theorem (Theorem 1.16). Hence $\mathbf{D}\phi_\eta(p) = \hat{\eta}(p)^\perp$. Differentiating again therefore yields $\mathbf{D}^2\phi_\eta(p) = \mathbf{D}\hat{\eta}(p)$. As this Jacobian, which is the Hessian of ϕ_η, is positive semidefinite on P Theorem 3.10 states ϕ_η is a convex function. As ϕ_η is homogeneous of degree one and convex on an open convex cone, Theorem 5.1 states ϕ_η is indeed a profit function. Hotelling's Lemma (Theorem 4.3) then states $\mathbf{D}\phi_\eta$ is the corresponding supply/demand function. But $\mathbf{D}\phi_\eta(p)$ is $\hat{\eta}(p)^\perp$. □

Note that $\hat{\eta}(P)$ will be a proper subset of Z_{ϕ_η} in most applications even when $\hat{\eta}$ satisfies the assumptions of Theorem 5.3, if for no other reason than the latter satisfies free disposal whereas the former is usually only (part of) the boundary of the latter. This may seem to open the possibility that the optimal choice correspondence from maximizing $p^\perp z$ over Z_{ϕ_η} is not singleton-valued, with $\hat{\eta}(p)$ being only one of many elements. However, ϕ_η is differentiable by assumption, so the optimal choice at each p is unique by Theorem 4.3.

It can be more difficult to recognize whether a given η that is not singleton-valued and differentiable is a supply/demand correspondence. As mentioned above, to be optimal any given $\eta : P \to 2^{\mathbb{R}^n}$ must be homogeneous of degree zero and have positive semidefinite price responses. Of course, it must also be the case that $p^\perp z$ is constant on $z \in \eta(p)$ (at any p for which $\eta(p)$ has more than one element). But these are merely necessary conditions. If they hold we can define an implied candidate profit function by $\phi_\eta(p) = p^\perp \hat{\eta}(p)$ and use Theorem 5.1 to determine whether ϕ_η is a profit function. Even so, as $\eta(P)$ is a proper subset of Z_{ϕ_η}, it is easily possible that $\eta(p)$ will be a proper subset of $z^*_{\phi_\eta}(p)$ at some values of p. For example, if $\eta(p)$ were the two endpoints of the shaded region A in Fig. 5.2 then $z^*_{\phi_\eta}(p)$ would be the entire convex combination of those two endpoints. Such an η is not a supply/demand correspondence for Z_{ϕ_η} but can be optimal for a feasible set that excludes the shaded area A.

In short, although every homogeneous of degree one and convex function ϕ on an open convex cone $P \subset \mathbb{R}^n_+$ is a profit function, there can be multiple valid supply/demand correspondences associated with each such function. Every valid optimal choice set is contained in the optimal choice set derived from the largest feasible set Z_ϕ consistent with the given ϕ, but optimal choice behavior can be quite different from that corresponding to that largest optimal choice set. In particular, optimal choice behavior need not be convex-valued or upper hemicontinuous.

5.5 NOTES

Shephard [1] is generally credited with the first rigorous duality theorems in production economics, although the results were anticipated in the consumer theory context and this early work generally relied on differentiability and is focused on duality of the cost function. Uzawa [2] provides the first duality theorem in production economics without differentiability. Shephard [3] generalizes and expands on the earlier work; Friedman [4] and Diewert [5] address some additional issues.

Duality between the profit function and the underlying production set was not well developed until McFadden [6, especially pp. 66–76, 81]; Lau [7, p. 133] labels a basic duality theorem like Theorem 5.1 the "McFadden Duality Theorem."

The direct approach to duality of the choice correspondence is based on Varian [8].

The duality literature is enormous and no attempt is made here to provide all appropriate citations. Diewert [9, 10] provides summaries of much of this work and extensive references.

5.6 EXERCISES

1. Consider the function $\phi(p, w) = p$ for $p \geq 0$ and $w \gg 0$.
   a. Verify that ϕ is a profit function.
   b. For simplicity, suppose w is a scalar (i.e., $w \in \mathbb{R}^1_{++}$). Use algebraic and geometric arguments to draw a production set Z_ϕ such that $\phi(p, w) = \max py - wx$ subject to $(y, -x) \in Z_\phi$. Does your production set satisfy no free lunch?

2. Is $\phi(p, w) = \frac{p^2}{4w}$ a profit function for a price-taking firm? Why/why not? If so, find the supply/demand correspondence.
3. Consider the following function:

$$\phi(p_1, p_2, p_3) = \begin{cases} \frac{p_1^3}{p_2 p_3} + \frac{p_2^3}{p_1 p_3} & \text{if } p_i > 0 \text{ for } i = 1, 2, 3 \\ 0 & \text{if } p_i = 0 \text{ for any } i = 1, 2, 3 \end{cases}.$$

Check each property of a profit function and report which properties hold and which are violated.
4. Suppose:

$$\phi(p, w) = \frac{p^\alpha}{Kw^\beta}.$$

If we interpret p as the price of an output and w as the price of a natural input:
   a. For what values of α, β and K, is ϕ a profit function?
   b. For those values of α and β, find the
      i. supply/demand correspondence.
      ii. production function.
      iii. production set.
      iv. input requirement set for output level $y \geq 0$.
5. Suppose:

$$\phi(p, w_1, w_2) = \frac{p^2}{4A},$$

where $A = w_1^{1-\alpha} w_2^\alpha + w_1^\beta w_2^{1-\beta}$, $p \geq 0$, and $w_1, w_2 > 0$.
   a. For what values of α and β is ϕ a profit function for a price-taking firm?
   b. For those values of α and β, find the
      i. supply/demand correspondence.
      ii. production function.
6. Consider the following function defined on $\mathbb{R}^3_{++}$:

$$\phi(p_1, p_2, p_3) = p_1 + p_2 + p_3 - 3(p_1 p_2 p_3)^{1/3}.$$

   a. Verify that ϕ satisfies the sufficient conditions to be a profit function.
   b. Derive the supply/demand function.
   c. Derive a profit relevant production set. Does the production set have the possibility of inaction and no free lunch properties?

7. Consider the function $\phi : \mathbb{R}^2_+ \to \mathbb{R}^1$ given by $\phi(p_1, p_2) = 2(p_1 + p_2 - \sqrt{2p_1 p_2})$.

a. Demonstrate that ϕ is a profit function for a price-taking firm.

b. Derive the demand/supply function.

c. Draw an accurate graph of a production set for which ϕ is the profit function.

8. Show that each of the following sets of relationships (for strictly positive prices (p, w_1, w_2)) are the profit-maximizing supply/demand correspondences of a price-taking firm, and derive the profit and production functions.

a.

$$(\hat{y}, -\hat{x}_1, -\hat{x}_2)(p, w_1, w_2) = \left(\frac{p}{2}\left(\frac{1}{w_1} + \frac{1}{w_2}\right), \left(\frac{p}{2w_1}\right)^2, \left(\frac{p}{2w_2}\right)^2\right).$$

b.

$$\hat{y}(p, w_1, w_2) = \frac{p}{2\min\{w_1, w_2\}}$$

$$-(x_1, x_2)^*(p, w_1, w_2) = \begin{cases} \left\{\left(0, \frac{p^2}{4w_2^2}\right)\right\}, & w_1 > w_2 \\ \left\{(x_1, x_2) \in \mathbb{R}^2_+ : x_1 + x_2 = \frac{p^2}{4w_1^2}\right\}, & w_1 = w_2 \\ \left\{\left(\frac{p^2}{4w_1^2}, 0\right)\right\}, & w_1 < w_2 \end{cases}.$$

9. A firm is observed to use production plans $(z_1, z_2) \in \mathbb{R}^2$ that obey the equations $z_1 = 1 - \left(\frac{2p_2}{p_1}\right)^{1/3}$ and $z_2 = 1 - \left(\frac{p_1}{2p_2}\right)^{2/3}$; for price vectors $(p_1, p_2) \in \mathbb{R}^2_{++}$. Determine whether this firm behaves as a price-taking profit maximizer. If not, explain why. If so, derive a profit function and production set that are consistent with this firm's observed behavior, and describe the properties of the production set.

10. Suppose we have the function $\phi(p, w) = \frac{p^2}{w}$ for $p, w > 0$ (both p and w are scalars).

a. Verify that ϕ is a profit function for a price-taking firm.

b. Find the underlying production function, $f_\phi(x)$.

c. Verify that $\phi(p, w) = \max pf_\phi(x) - wx$.

11. Here is a production set:

$$Z = \{(z_1, z_2) \in \mathbb{R}^2 : (z_1 + 2)^2 + z_2^2 \leq 1\}.$$

a. Carefully graph Z.

b. Let (p_1, p_2) denote the prices. Derive the profit maximizing choice function $\hat{z}(p_1, p_2)$ for a price-taking firm.

c. Verify that the profit-maximizing choice function satisfies the symmetry property.

d. Derive $\pi^*(p_1, p_2)$, the optimal profit function. What is $\pi^*(4, 3)$? Why?

e. Carefully graph the set:

$$Z_{\pi^*} = \{(z_1, z_2) \in \mathbb{R}^2 : p_1 z_1 + p_2 z_2 \leq \pi^*(p_1, p_2) \ \forall \ (p_1, p_2) \gg 0\}.$$

Is Z_{π^*} the same set as Z? Why/why not?

12. Let:

$$\phi(p_1, p_2) = \begin{cases} 2p_2 & \text{when } p_1 = 0 \\ p_1 & \text{when } p_1 > 0 \end{cases}$$

for $(p_1, p_2) \in \mathbb{R}^2_+$.

a. Show that ϕ is homogeneous of degree one and convex.

b. Draw the set Z_ϕ defined in Theorem 5.1.

c. Use your graph of Z_ϕ to geometrically derive π^*_ϕ. For what values of (p_1, p_2) is $\pi^*_\phi(p_1, p_2)$ equal to $\phi(p_1, p_2)$? Are there points in $\mathbb{R}^2_+$ where the two functions differ? Why?

13. Assume a production set Z is closed and nonempty. Here is a claim: "The refutable hypotheses about price-taking profit-maximizing behavior are the same when Z is convex as when Z is not convex. Therefore no generality of the theory is lost by assuming Z is convex." What do you think about this claim?

REFERENCES

[1] Shephard RW. Cost and production functions. Princeton, NJ: Princeton University Press; 1953.

[2] Uzawa H. Duality principles in the theory of cost and production. Int Econ Rev 1964;5:216–20.

[3] Shephard RW. Theory of cost and production functions. Princeton, NJ: Princeton University Press; 1970.

[4] Friedman JW. Duality principles in the theory of cost and production—revisited. Int Econ Rev 1972;13:167–70.

[5] Diewert WE. An application of the Shephard duality theorem: a generalized Leontief production function. J Polit Econ 1971;79:481–507.

[6] McFadden D. Cost, revenue and profit functions. In: Fuss M, McFadden D, editors. Production economics: a dual approach to theory and applications I. Amsterdam: North-Holland; 1978. p. 3–109.

[7] Lau LJ. Applications of profit functions. In: Fuss M, McFadden D, editors. Production economics: a dual approach to theory and applications I. Amsterdam: North-Holland; 1978. p. 133–216.

[8] Varian HR. The nonparametric approach to production analysis. Econometrica 1984;52:579–97.

[9] Diewert WE. Applications of duality theory. In: Intriligator MD, Kendrick DA, editors. Frontiers of quantitative economics II. Amsterdam: North-Holland; 1974. p. 106–71.
[10] Diewert WE. Duality approaches to microeconomic theory. In: Arrow KJ, Intriligator MD, editors. Handbook of mathematical economics II. Amsterdam: North-Holland; 1982. p. 535–99.

CHAPTER 6

Cost Minimization

Chapter Outline

6.1 BASIC OPTIMIZATION POSTULATE

Sometimes the price-taking profit maximization behavioral postulate is not useful. For example, if a firm has a production set with nondecreasing returns to scale and prices are such that positive profit is possible then a profit maximum does not exist and the profit function is infinite, suggesting that some aspect of the behavioral postulate is flawed for the setting under study. Alternatively, we may be interested in an explicit study of non-price taking behavior (imperfect competition) in output markets. Or we may wish to study a firm that is required by regulation to meet an output plan exogenous to the firm's objective. In these cases we can still study the implications of the *cost minimization* behavioral postulate when the production set has natural inputs.

We retain the same notation as in Chapter 4. $Z \subset \mathbb{R}^n$ is a nonempty production set whose elements z can be partitioned into a nonnegative vector of natural inputs $x \in \mathbb{R}^m_+$ $(1 \leq m < n)$ and a vector of remaining commodities $y \in \mathbb{R}^{n-m}$ (usually thought of as outputs at a profit maximum).

Y is the set of feasible outputs and $V(y)$ is the input requirement set for output $y \in Y$. $(p, w) \in \mathbb{R}^n_+$ is a price vector partitioned to conform with $z = (y, -x)$; and $\pi^*(p, w)$ and $z^*(p, w)$ are the profit function and net output supply/input demand correspondence, respectively.

The cost minimization behavioral postulate is that the firm chooses a feasible input plan x to produce a given output level y at minimal cost $c(x; w) = w^{\perp}x$, taking the input price w as given. The outcomes from this behavioral postulate are the *cost function* $c^*(w, y) \equiv \inf\{w^{\perp}x : x \in V(y)\}$ and *conditional input (or factor) demand correspondence* $x^*(w, y) \equiv \{x \in V(y) : w^{\perp}x = c^*(w, y)\}$. Note that this x^* differs from the profit-maximizing x^*, in that the former is conditional on y while the latter is not (the latter is sometimes called an *unconditional input demand*). The fact that y is a parameter is what distinguishes the cost minimization behavioral postulate from the profit maximization behavioral postulate.

The cost minimization behavioral postulate is worth studying for firms with natural inputs just as a way of better understanding profit maximization because, at profit-relevant output levels, the input choices are the same under the two behavioral postulates. A "profit-relevant" output is an output that is part of *some* profit-maximizing production plan. The correspondence of profit-relevant outputs is:

$$y^*(p, w) = \{y \in \mathbb{R}^{n-m} : (y, -x) \in z^*(p, w) \text{ for some } x \in \mathbb{R}^m_+\}. \tag{6.1}$$

Theorem 6.1. *An input plan minimizes the cost of a profit-relevant output plan if and only if the input/output combination maximizes profit. That is:*

$$z^*(p, w) = \{(y, -x) : y \in y^*(p, w) \text{ and } x \in x^*(w, y)\}.$$

Proof. Begin by assuming $(y, -x) \in z^*(p, w)$. Then $y \in y^*(p, w)$ trivially and $p^{\perp}y - w^{\perp}x \geq p^{\perp}y - w^{\perp}\tilde{x}$ for every $\tilde{x} \in V(y)$. Therefore $w^{\perp}x \leq w^{\perp}\tilde{x}$ for every $\tilde{x} \in V(y)$. Using $x \in V(y)$, this means $x \in x^*(w, y)$.

Conversely, assume $y \in y^*(p, w)$ and $x \in x^*(w, y)$. Then there exists $\hat{x}$ such that $(y, -\hat{x}) \in z^*(p, w)$. As $\hat{x} \in V(y)$, $w^{\perp}x \leq w^{\perp}\hat{x}$. Therefore $p^{\perp}y - w^{\perp}x \geq p^{\perp}y - w^{\perp}\hat{x}$. Using $x \in V(y)$, this means $(y, -x) \in z^*(p, w)$. □

If the profit-relevant output and conditional input demand correspondences are singleton valued, the theorem says $\hat{z}(p, w) = (\hat{y}(p, w), -\hat{x}(w, \hat{y}(p, w)))$.

As in the profit maximization problem, $\mathbf{D}_x c(x; w) = w^{\perp}$, so a cost minimum is not characterized by a stationary point of the objective. None of the first derivatives can be zero unless there is a zero price, and if a price

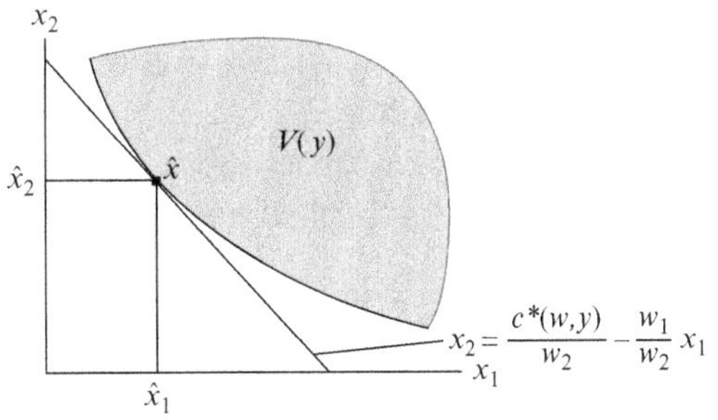

Fig. 6.1 Cost minimization.

is zero the corresponding quantity has no effect on cost. Hence the input requirement set constraint must bind for every input that has a positive price (and those with zero prices are irrelevant except to the extent they affect the feasible values of inputs with positive prices through the production constraint). With two inputs, the minimization can be illustrated as in Fig. 6.1. The firm's objective is to choose a value of x that places it on the lowest possible isocost line while still staying in the input requirement set $V(y)$.

Existence is not much of an issue for the cost minimization problem. Although $V(y)$ may be unbounded, $V(y)$ is nonempty for $y \in Y$, so if $V(y)$ is closed and $w \gg 0$ we can discard all elements of $V(y)$ above some (arbitrary) feasible isocost line without loss of generality, and thereby obtain an extremum problem with a continuous function on a closed, bounded and nonempty set. Even if $V(y)$ is not closed (note, however, that Z being closed implies $V(y)$ is closed) or w is not strictly positive the infimum is finite when $y \in Y$ since $w^{\perp}x \geq 0$ for $x \in V(y) \subset \mathbb{R}^m_+$. Uniqueness is a real issue, however, unless $V(y)$ is strictly convex (the proof that strict convexity implies uniqueness is the same as for profit maximization; see Exercise 12 in Chapter 4); so $x^*(w, y)$ need not be a singleton in general. The geometry of non-uniqueness is the same as for profit maximization, illustrated in Fig. 4.3. A linear boundary segment or nonconvexity of $V(y)$ will generate multiple optima for some prices.

The behavioral postulate that a firm chooses an input plan within a fixed input requirement set to minimize cost, while taking input prices as given, immediately implies some refutable hypotheses. These fundamental properties of a cost minimum are almost the same as the fundamental properties of a profit maximum and hold for the same reasons: The objectives in both problems are products of a fixed price vector with a chosen quantity vector subject to an inactive constraint on the quantity vector (holding the output level fixed).

Theorem 6.2 (Fundamental Properties of a Cost Minimum). *Assume the production set is nonempty and has natural inputs. Let y be a fixed feasible output vector ($y \in Y$) and $w \in \mathbb{R}^m_+$.*

1. *The set $W \equiv \{w \in \mathbb{R}^m_+ : x^*(w, y) \neq \emptyset\}$ is a cone and zero is an element. The conditional input demand correspondence is homogeneous of degree zero in w on this cone (only relative prices matter for production decisions). If the production set is closed then $W \supset \mathbb{R}^m_{++}$.*
2. *The cost function is finite and homogeneous of degree one in w (a neutral inflation inflates cost by the same proportion).*
3. *The cost function is concave in w; on the interior of $\mathbb{R}^m_+$ this implies the cost function is continuous, has one-sided gradients, and has a gradient off a set of Lebesgue m-measure zero (all as a function of w).*
4. *$(w^1 - w^0)^\perp(\hat{x}(w^1, y) - \hat{x}(w^0, y)) \leq 0$ for $w^0, w^1 \in W$ (negative semidefiniteness of conditional input demand price responses).*
5. *The cost function is nondecreasing in w (higher input prices increase cost).*
6. *$c^*(w, y) \geq 0$.*

Proof. With y fixed the structure of the cost minimization problem is identical to the profit maximization problem (except that the feasible set is known to contain only nonnegative vectors). Minimization of c is identical to maximization of $-c$, so aside from the implications of a nonnegative choice vector for existence and finiteness, Theorem 4.1 delivers items 1–5 (taking account of the minus sign) by relabeling $-c$ as π, x as z, w as p, and $V(y)$ as Z (constraint inactivity is important; properties that arise from changes in y require a different approach).

$W \supset \mathbb{R}^m_{++}$ in item 1 is established as follows. $V(y)$ is nonempty because $y \in Y$. Select $x^0 \in V(y)$ and define a set of relevant input plans by $R = \{x \in V(y) : w^\perp x \leq w^\perp x^0\}$. This set is closed (because Z closed implies $V(y)$ closed) and bounded (because $w \gg 0$ and $V(y) \subset \mathbb{R}^m_+$), and is nonempty because x^0 is an element. Also, any feasible input plan not in R costs more than x^0 and therefore is not optimal. Hence $c^*(w, y) = \inf\{w^\perp x : x \in R\}$. A minimum exists for this optimization problem by Theorem 1.2.

The infimum $c^*(w, y)$ is finite because $w^\perp x$, for $w \geq 0$ and $x \in V(y) \subset \mathbb{R}^m_+$ (natural inputs), has a lower bound of zero and the feasible set $V(y)$ is nonempty (because $y \in Y$). Hence, in the notation of Theorem 4.1, $P = \mathbb{R}^m_+$ and this is a convex cone. These observations also establish item 6. □

Again these properties are "fundamental" in that they require no assumptions other than the behavioral postulate and that the environment is sensible for cost minimization (natural inputs and a feasible output plan). Item 4 is the *Law of Demand* for conditional input demands. Item 5 is included for consistency with Theorem 4.1 but is actually a redundant property in the cost minimization context (see Exercise 16).

6.2 ENVELOPE PROPERTIES

The production constraint is inactive at a cost minimum with respect to changes in the input price (but usually not with respect to changes in output). Thus, as with profit maximization, the Envelope Theorem (Theorem 1.18) applies to changes in the input price. The envelope function c^* is, however, a *lower* envelope on $\mathbb{R}^m_+$ of the collection of $c(\hat{x}(w^0, y); w) = w^{\perp}\hat{x}(w^0, y)$ functions (one for each w^0) because c^* is a minimum rather than a maximum. This fact is a rich source of refutable hypotheses. The tangency conclusion, in particular, is $\mathbf{D}_w c^*(w^0, y) = \hat{x}(w^0, y)^{\perp}$ for every w^0 where the Jacobian exists, and in this context is known as *Shephard's Lemma.* It says the gradient of a cost function with respect to input prices, when it exists (and when a minimum exists), is the corresponding conditional input demand function. More generally, Theorems 4.2 and 4.3 apply to a cost minimum without modification provided due note is taken of the minus sign.

Theorem 6.3. *Assume the production set is nonempty and has natural inputs. Let y be a fixed feasible output vector ($y \in Y$). A feasible input plan minimizes cost if and only if it is the slope of an upper tangent plane of the cost function (considered as a function of w) on the interior of $\mathbb{R}^m_+$. Moreover, every such input plan lies between the one-sided gradients of the cost function at the tangency.*

Theorem 6.4 (Envelope Properties of a Cost Minimum). *Assume the production set is nonempty and has natural inputs. Let y be a fixed feasible output vector ($y \in Y$).*

1. $\mathbf{D}_w c^*(w^0, y) = \hat{x}(w^0, y)^{\perp}$, *the unique minimum, at every $w^0 \in \mathbb{R}^m_+$ where the gradient exists and is an element of the input requirement set (Shephard's Lemma). Even on the set of measure zero where the gradient does not exist, a feasible input plan x is cost-minimizing for producing output y at a strictly positive price w^0 if and only if $c^*(w, y) \leq c^*(w^0, y) + x^{\perp}(w - w^0)$ for every $w \in \mathbb{R}^m_+$; and every such input plan lies between $\mathbf{D}_w c^*_+(w^0, y)$ and $\mathbf{D}_w c^*_-(w^0, y)$.*
2. *The Hessian of c^* with respect to w is singular and negative semidefinite at every $w^0 \in \mathbb{R}^m_+$ where the partial derivatives of c^* are differentiable and*

where c^* is differentiable (with respect to w) in a neighborhood. Together with Shephard's Lemma, this implies the matrix of conditional input demand price slopes is singular and negative semidefinite at all such prices. One implication of negative semidefiniteness is the comparative statics conclusion that each conditional input demand is nonincreasing in its own price. If the off-diagonal elements are continuous in w then the matrix is symmetric, which is reciprocity of the conditional input demand price responses: $\frac{\partial \hat{x}_i}{\partial w_j} = \frac{\partial \hat{x}_j}{\partial w_i}$.

The elasticity properties of profit-maximizing supply/demand functions carry over to cost-minimizing input demand functions with equal ease because these properties rely only on singularity and symmetry of the Hessian with respect to prices. The key equation is Eq. (4.1): $w^{\perp}\mathbf{D}_w\hat{x}(w, y) = 0$. This implies the elasticities of all conditional input demands with respect to one input price, each weighted by the monetary share of that input in total cost, sum to zero:

$$\sum_{j=1}^{m}\left(\frac{\partial \hat{x}_j(w, y)}{\partial w_i}\frac{w_i}{\hat{x}_j(w, y)}\right)\frac{w_j\hat{x}_j(w, y)}{c^*(w, y)} = 0.$$

Similarly, the elasticities of a conditional input demand with respect to all input prices sum to zero:

$$\sum_{j=1}^{m}\frac{\partial \hat{x}_i(w, y)}{\partial w_j}\frac{w_j}{\hat{x}_i(w, y)} = 0.$$

6.3 ADDITIONAL PROPERTIES

Additional refutable hypotheses emerge from the cost minimization behavioral postulate when the production set has additional properties.

Theorem 6.5 (Additional Properties of a Cost Minimum). *Assume the production set is nonempty and has natural inputs. For $(w, y) \in \mathbb{R}^m_+ \times Y$:*

1. *If the input requirement set $V(y)$ is convex then $x^*(w, y)$ is a convex set.*
2. *If the input requirement set $V(y)$ is closed then $x^*(w, y)$ is upper hemicontinuous in w.*
3. *If the production set is convex then the cost function is convex in y; this implies the cost function is continuous, has one-sided gradients, and has a gradient off a set of Lebesgue $(n - m)$-measure zero, all as a function of y on the interior of Y.*
4. *If the production set has the possibility of inaction property then $c^*(w, 0) = 0$.*

5. *If the production set has free disposal then the cost function is nondecreasing in y (higher output increases cost).*

Proof. Items 1 and 2 are again direct from the profit maximization context; simply make the notational conversion stated in the proof of Theorem 6.2 and keep track of the minus sign.

For item 3, select $w \in \mathbb{R}^m_+$ and $y^0, y^1 \in Y$. By definition of the infimum, there exist sequences $\{x^{0,i}\}_{i=1}^{\infty} \subset V(y^0)$ and $\{x^{1,i}\}_{i=1}^{\infty} \subset V(y^1)$ such that $w^{\perp}x^{0,i} \rightarrow c^*(w, y^0)$ and $w^{\perp}x^{1,i} \rightarrow c^*(w, y^1)$. Multiply the first by $\alpha \in (0, 1)$, the second by $(1 - \alpha)$, and add to obtain:

$$w^{\perp}(\alpha x^{0,i} + (1 - \alpha)x^{1,i}) \rightarrow \alpha c^*(w, y^0) + (1 - \alpha)c^*(w, y^1).$$

By convexity of Z, $\alpha x^{0,i} + (1 - \alpha)x^{1,i} \in V(\alpha y^0 + (1 - \alpha)y^1)$. Hence:

$$c^*(w, \alpha y^0 + (1 - \alpha)y^1) \leq w^{\perp}(\alpha x^{0,i} + (1 - \alpha)x^{1,i}) \rightarrow \alpha c^*(w, y^0) + (1 - \alpha)c^*(w, y^1).$$

Item 4 uses nonnegativity of c^* (item 3 of Theorem 6.2) and the fact that $0 \in V(0)$ when the production set has the possibility of inaction (so $c^*(w, 0) \leq w^{\perp}0$).

Item 5 follows because $y^1 \geq y^0 \Rightarrow V(y^1) \subset V(y^0)$ when the production set has free disposal, so the minimization is over a smaller feasible set at y^1 and therefore the infimum is no smaller than at y^0. □

Item 3 states that the marginal cost gradient exists almost everywhere when the production set is convex.

6.4 SINGLE-OUTPUT COST MINIMIZATION

Assume now that $m = n - 1$, so all but one of the commodities are natural inputs. There are some additional properties of the cost minimum in the single-output case.

As noted in Section 4.5, if there is free disposal and the production function f exists as a maximum then the feasible set is the upper contour set of f: $V(y) = \{x \in \mathbb{R}^{n-1}_+ : f(x) \geq y\}$. Suppose, in addition, that the production function is continuous. Free disposal ensures f is nondecreasing and continuity ensures f takes on all intermediate values of y, whence the set of feasible output levels is the interval $Y = [f(0), \sup Y)$ (or $[f(0), \sup Y]$ if there is a maximal feasible output level). Often the left end of this interval is zero ($f(0) = 0$) due to the possibility of inaction and no free lunch, although this is not required for the current discussion.

Theorem 6.6. *Assume there is free disposal and the production function f exists as a maximum and is continuous on $\mathbb{R}_{+}^{n-1}$. Then:*

1. *$c^*(w, y)$ is strictly increasing in $y \in Y$ for every $w \in \mathbb{R}_{++}^{n-1}$.*
2. *When production has the local nonexhaustion property: $c^*(w, y)$ is continuous, and unbounded in $y \in Y$ for every $w \in \mathbb{R}_{++}^{n-1}$; and $x^*(w, y)$ is upper hemicontinuous in (w, y) on $\mathbb{R}_{++}^{n-1} \times Y$.*

Proof. The feasible set $V(y) = \{x \in \mathbb{R}_{+}^{n-1} : f(x) \geq y\}$ is closed due to continuity of f. Therefore, as previously discussed, a minimum $\hat{x}(w, y)$ exists for every $(w, y) \in \mathbb{R}_{++}^{n-1} \times Y$.

1. Assume $y^0 < y^1$ (both feasible). Then $f(\hat{x}(w, y^1)) \geq y^1 > y^0 \geq f(0)$, whence $\hat{x}(w, y^1) > 0$. Thus there exists $0 \leq x^0 < \hat{x}(w, y^1)$ with $f(x^0) > y^0$, by continuity. So $c^*(w, y^0) \leq w^{\perp}x^0 < w^{\perp}\hat{x}(w, y^1) = c^*(w, y^1)$.
2. First we show $c^*(w, y)$ is unbounded in y for fixed $w \in \mathbb{R}_{++}^{n-1}$. Consider any proposed bound $c \in \mathbb{R}_{+}^{1}$. By continuity, f has a maximum $\bar{x}$ on the nonempty, closed and bounded set $\{x \in \mathbb{R}_{+}^{n-1} : w^{\perp}x \leq c\}$. By local nonexhaustion, there exists $y^0 \in Y$ such that $y^0 > f(\bar{x})$. As $f(\hat{x}(w, y^0)) \geq y^0 > f(\bar{x})$, we have $c^*(w, y^0) = w^{\perp}\hat{x}(w, y^0) > c$.

   We shall apply the Maximum Theorem (Theorem 1.5) to prove continuity of c^* and upper hemicontinuity of x^*. The cost objective is trivially continuous. Although the constraint correspondence $V(y)$ may not be uniformly bounded, a *relevant* constraint correspondence that is uniformly bounded near $w^0 \in \mathbb{R}_{++}^{n-1}$ can be constructed by intersecting $V(y)$ with points below any arbitrary isocost line for w near w^0 (see Exercise 48). $V(y)$ is also upper hemicontinuous because f is continuous (Theorem 1.8). Hence the only difficulty in applying the Maximum Theorem is establishing lower hemicontinuity of $V(y)$.

   Given a sequence $y^i \to y^0$ and a point x^0 satisfying $f(x^0) \geq y^0$, we must show existence of a sequence $x^i \to x^0$ such that $f(x^i) \geq y^i \; \forall i$. By local non-exhaustion, there exists a sequence $\tilde{x}^j \to x^0$ such that $f(\tilde{x}^j) > f(x^0) \; \forall j$, and it can be assumed without loss of generality that $f(\tilde{x}^j) \geq f(\tilde{x}^{j+1})$ for $j = 1, 2, \ldots$. Consider any $\tilde{x}^j$. As $y^i \to y^0$, there exists k^j such that $f(\tilde{x}^j) \geq y^i \; \forall i \geq k^j$, and it can be assumed without loss of generality that $k^1 < k^2 < \cdots$. Now construct the x^i sequence as follows:

$$x^i = \begin{cases} \text{any } x \text{ satisfying } f(x) \geq y^i & \text{for } i = 1, \ldots, k^1 - 1 \\ & \text{(such } x \text{ exist because } y^i \in Y \; \forall i) \\ \tilde{x}^j & \text{for } i = k^j, \ldots, k^{j+1} - 1; \; j = 1, 2, \ldots \end{cases}$$

This x^i has the required properties. By construction, $f(x^i) = f(\tilde{x}^j) > y^i$ when $k^j \leq i < k^{j+1}$. Moreover, for any $\epsilon > 0$ there exists J such that $\left|\tilde{x}^j - x^0\right| < \epsilon$ for $j \geq J$. Letting $I = k^J$, we have $i \geq I \Rightarrow i \geq k^J \Rightarrow x^i = \tilde{x}^j$ for some $j \geq J$. So $i \geq I \Rightarrow \left|x^i - x^0\right| < \epsilon$. □

Under the conditions of free disposal and a continuous production function the constraint can be written without loss of generality as "$f(x) = y$ and $x \geq 0$" for $y \in Y$ provided attention is confined to strictly positive prices. This equality-constrained version of the optimization problem is equivalent to the original problem because an input plan x satisfying $f(x) > y$ cannot be optimal when f is continuous; corresponding to any such x is a feasible input plan x' that costs strictly less than x. To see this, use continuity to select $x' < x$ such that $f(x') > y$, and note that $x' > 0$ can be assured since $x > 0$ from $f(x) > y \geq f(0)$. Therefore x' is feasible. Using $w \gg 0$, we have $w^{\perp}x' < w^{\perp}x$, whence x does not minimize cost over $V(y)$. Therefore nothing is lost under these conditions by assuming the production constraint is the isoquant $I(y) = \{x \in \mathbb{R}_{+}^{n-1} : f(x) = y\}$, which is nonempty for relevant output levels $y \in Y$.

With an equality constraint $f(x) = y$ the Lagrangian function for cost minimization is:

$$L(x, \lambda; w, y) = w^{\perp}x - \lambda(f(x) - y). \tag{6.2}$$

If, in addition to free disposal, f is continuously differentiable and $\mathbf{D}f$ is not a vector of zeros at an optimum then the Lagrange Multiplier Rule (Theorem 2.1) is:

$$w^{\perp} - \hat{\lambda}(w, y)\mathbf{D}f(\hat{x}(w, y)) = 0. \tag{6.3}$$

Dividing component i of Eq. (6.3) by component j yields:

$$\frac{\partial f(\hat{x}(w, y))/\partial x_i}{\partial f(\hat{x}(w, y))/\partial x_j} = \frac{w_i}{w_j},$$

which again is the familiar tangency condition that the MRTS between any two inputs must equal their price ratio (slope of the isocost line) at the firm's optimal choice (note that Eq. 6.3 implies the denominator cannot be zero at an interior optimum with nonzero prices). That is, the firm must choose its (interior) inputs so that its isoquant is tangent to its isocost. Eq. (6.3) can be used with the constraint:

$$-\left[f(\hat{x}(w, y)) - y\right] = 0 \tag{6.4}$$

to identify candidate values for an optimal input plan and the corresponding Lagrange multiplier.

If the conditions of the Implicit Function Theorem [1, Theorem 13.7] hold for Eqs. (6.3) and (6.4) then the functional form of L yields the particular version of the comparative statics equation (2.16) for the single-output cost minimization problem:

$$\begin{bmatrix} -\hat{\lambda}\mathbf{D}^2 f(\hat{x}) & -(\mathbf{D}f(\hat{x}))^{\perp} \\ -\mathbf{D}f(\hat{x}) & 0_{n-1} \end{bmatrix} \begin{bmatrix} \mathbf{D}\hat{x} \\ \mathbf{D}\hat{\lambda} \end{bmatrix} = -I_n.$$

This equation can be used to derive the price and output slopes of the conditional input demands for a particular production function, as well as the price and output slopes of the Lagrange multiplier. One refutable hypothesis from this equation irrespective of f is that the own-price demand slopes are nonpositive. This conclusion follows because the Lagrangian function (6.2) indeed has the special structure that $\mathbf{D}_{(w,y)}(\mathbf{D}_{(x,\lambda)}L)^{\perp}$ $(= I_n)$ has only one nonzero entry in column i and that entry is in row i, as described in the discussion of Eq. (2.16). Thus $\frac{\partial \hat{x}_i}{\partial w_i}$ has sign opposite that of the one nonzero entry (see item 3 of Section 2.5), which is unity in the current model for $i = 1, \ldots, n-1$. This is another way to derive the Law of Demand for a price-taking firm that minimizes cost, although the conclusion derived in this manner depends on there being a sufficiently "well-behaved" production function f, whereas Theorem 6.2 shows that the Law of Demand does not depend on anything other than existence of a cost minimum.

The Implicit Function Theorem also makes the Envelope Theorem for an active constraint (Theorem 2.2) applicable, which yields:

$$\frac{\partial c^*(w,y)}{\partial y} = \hat{\lambda}(w,y). \tag{6.5}$$

This says the Lagrange Multiplier is marginal cost, which is a specific example of the interpretation discussed in Section 2.2 of Lagrange Multipliers as shadow prices. The "resource" here is an obligation (a required production level), and the economic actor is minimizing, so an additional unit of the resource inhibits the firm's ability to minimize and thereby increases the cost minimum by $\hat{\lambda}$. Eq. (6.3) then has the interpretation that cost is minimized when the price of each input equals the marginal cost of producing an increment of output using that input. Note that Shephard's Lemma (item 1 of Theorem 6.4) could also be obtained from the Envelope Theorem for an active constraint, similar to Eq. (6.5), but deriving Shephard's Lemma in this manner requires assumptions about existence and differentiability of the production function that are not needed in Theorem 6.4.

It may be useful to restate for the single-output case property 2 of Theorem 6.4, accounting for Eq. (6.5), which reveals that the Lagrange multiplier is a derivative of the cost function just as is the input demand. Hence the Hessian of the cost function taken with respect to both input prices *and* output includes derivatives of $\hat{\lambda}(w, y)$. The matrix of demand and Lagrange multiplier slopes that must be symmetric with singular and negative semidefinite lower-right $(n-1) \times (n-1)$ submatrix is:

$$\begin{bmatrix} \frac{\partial \hat{\lambda}}{\partial y} & \frac{\partial \hat{\lambda}}{\partial w_1} & \cdots & \frac{\partial \hat{\lambda}}{\partial w_{n-1}} \\ \frac{\partial \hat{x}_1}{\partial y} & \frac{\partial \hat{x}_1}{\partial w_1} & \cdots & \frac{\partial \hat{x}_1}{\partial w_{n-1}} \\ \vdots & \vdots & \ddots & \vdots \\ \frac{\partial \hat{x}_{n-1}}{\partial y} & \frac{\partial \hat{x}_{n-1}}{\partial w_1} & \cdots & \frac{\partial \hat{x}_{n-1}}{\partial w_{n-1}} \end{bmatrix}.$$

Focusing on the diagonal elements and using negative semidefiniteness of the lower-right $(n-1) \times (n-1)$ submatrix again shows that each conditional input demand does not slope upward as a function of its own price. Focusing on off-diagonal elements and using symmetry shows that cross-price effects on conditional input demands are symmetric and the effect of a price change on marginal cost (i.e., the Lagrange multiplier) equals the effect of a change in output on the corresponding input. These off-diagonal elements can be either positive or negative. If $\hat{x}_j$ moves in the same direction as $\hat{x}_i$ when w_i changes (i.e., if $\frac{\partial \hat{x}_j}{\partial w_i} \leq 0$) then we say inputs i and j are *(net) complements* in production. If the two inputs move in opposite directions (i.e., if $\frac{\partial \hat{x}_j}{\partial w_i} \geq 0$) then we say inputs i and j are *(net) substitutes* in production. These labels are "net" because the changes under study here are net of any changes in output, but usually the complement/substitute nature of conditional input demands is described without using the word "net" (as compared to the "gross" complements or substitutes characterization of profit maximizing demands, which are gross of changes in the optimal output level, and which are usually described by explicit use of the word "gross"). Similarly, if $\frac{\partial \hat{x}_i}{\partial y} \geq 0$ we say input i is *normal* in production (an increase in its price causes marginal cost to increase), while if $\frac{\partial \hat{x}_i}{\partial y} < 0$ we say input i is *inferior* in production (an increase in its price causes marginal cost to decrease!). These are local definitions; the signs can change at different points in the price/output space.

We have proceeded in these last few paragraphs as if we have an interior minimum characterized by calculus. Aside from the existence, uniqueness and differentiability issues already discussed for the cost minimization problem, the requirement $x \geq 0$ (i.e., the single-output case) must be considered. It is possible to have corner solutions of the form $x_i^* = \{0\}$, in which case the first derivative can be positive at the minimum: $w_i > \hat{\lambda} f_i(\hat{x})$. If the minimum is unique x_i can be omitted from the input vector and everything holds as described here for the other components of x ($\hat{x}_i$ is fixed at zero for small changes in (w, y)). If it happens that a first derivative with respect to x_i is zero at $\hat{x}_i = 0$ then the comparative statics might be different for different changes in (w, y) ($\hat{x}_i$ remains zero for some changes but changes according to the FOC's for other changes).

6.5 DUALITY OF THE COST MINIMUM

Theorem 6.2 established that a cost function *necessarily* has the basic properties of homogeneity and concavity. These basic properties rely only on finiteness of the infimum of the monetary-valued cost expression $w^{\perp}x$ over an input requirement set $V(y)$, which is assured for feasible y because $V(y)$ is bounded below, so aside from assuming there are natural inputs these properties are pure consequences of the price-taking cost minimization behavioral postulate.

As in our study of profit maximization, a natural question to ask now is whether these properties are *sufficient* for a cost function. That is, given an arbitrary function ϕ possessing these properties but that is not known *a priori* to be the infimum of $w^{\perp}x$ over some set $x \in V(y)$, is that function indeed a cost function for some price-taking firm? If so, any function with these properties can be used in an econometric or applied theory investigation with the knowledge that the function is a complete representation of cost-minimizing behavior.

Theorem 6.7 (Duality of the Cost Function). *Assume $Y \subset \mathbb{R}^{n-m}$ ($n > m$) is nonempty, P is a convex cone satisfying $\mathbb{R}^m_{++} \subset P \subset \mathbb{R}^m_+$, and $\phi : P \times Y \to \mathbb{R}^1_+$ is concave, homogeneous of degree one, and continuous (at boundary points of P that are in P) in the first m arguments. Let $V_\phi : Y \to 2^{\mathbb{R}^m_+}$ be defined by:*

$$V_\phi(y) = \{x \in \mathbb{R}^m_+ : w^{\perp}x \geq \phi(w, y) \; \forall w \in P\}.$$

Then, for $y \in Y$,

1. *$V_\phi(y)$ is nonempty.*

2. *$V_\phi(y)$ is closed.*

3. *$V_\phi(y)$ has the free disposal property (for inputs); if $\phi(w, y)$ is nondecreasing in y then V_ϕ has the free disposal property (for all commodities).*
4. *$V_\phi(y)$ is convex.*
5. *If $y > 0 \Rightarrow \phi(w, y) > 0$ for some $w \in P$ then V_ϕ has the no free lunch property.*
6. *If $\phi(w, 0) = 0\ \forall w \in P$ then V_ϕ has the possibility of inaction property.*

Moreover, if $c^*_\phi : P \times Y \to \mathbb{R}^1_+$ and $x^*_\phi : P \times Y \to 2^{\mathbb{R}^m_+}$ are defined as:

$$c^*_\phi(w, y) = \inf\{w^\perp x : x \in V_\phi(y)\}$$
$$x^*_\phi(w, y) = \{x \in V_\phi(y) : w^\perp x = c^*_\phi(w, y)\}$$

then $c^*_\phi(w, y) = \phi(w, y)$ for every $(w, y) \in P \times Y$ and $x^*_\phi(w, y)$ is nonempty for every $(w, y) \in int\ P \times Y$.

Proof. Let $\tilde{\phi} = -\phi$. Then $V_\phi = -\tilde{V}_\phi$, where:

$$\tilde{V}_\phi(y) = \{x \in \mathbb{R}^m_- : w^\perp x \leq \tilde{\phi}(w, y)\ \forall w \in P\};$$

and $c^*_\phi = -\tilde{c}^*_\phi$ and $x^*_\phi = -\tilde{x}^*_\phi$, where:

$$\tilde{c}^*_\phi(w, y) = \sup\{w^\perp x : x \in \tilde{V}_\phi(y)\}$$
$$\tilde{x}^*_\phi(w, y) = \{x \in \tilde{V}_\phi(y) : w^\perp x = \tilde{c}^*_\phi(w, y)\}.$$

Noting that y is fixed and therefore a nuisance parameter (except in the second part of item 3 and in item 5), Theorem 5.1 applies directly to $\tilde{\phi}$, $\tilde{V}_\phi$, $\tilde{c}^*_\phi$, and $\tilde{x}^*_\phi$ (x being restricted to nonpositive vectors in the definition of $\tilde{V}_\phi$ is of no consequence because $\tilde{\phi}$ is nonpositive and w is nonnegative). Items 1–4 (except the second part of item 3); and $\tilde{c}^*_\phi = \tilde{\phi}$ and $\tilde{x}^*_\phi$ nonempty; are then translated back to the original notation from the corresponding items of Theorem 5.1.

Although the first part of item 3 follows directly from item 3 of Theorem 5.1, the interpretation is that only inputs are known to be freely disposable since $V_\phi(y)$ is interpreted as a set of inputs for each y. If, however, $y^0 \leq y^1 \Rightarrow \phi(w, y^0) \leq \phi(w, y^1)$ then the definition of V_ϕ immediately gives $V_\phi(y^1) \subset V_\phi(y^0)$, in which case free disposal holds for the y vectors as well.

Items 5 and 6, that zero is not an element of $V_\phi(y)$ when y is positive, and zero is an element of $V_\phi(0)$, respectively, follow directly from the definition of V_ϕ (under the stated conditions). □

This theorem leaves open the possibility that the function ϕ is not specified at zero prices even though Theorem 6.2 shows cost functions are defined at all nonnegative prices. This slightly expands the applicability:

ϕ is a cost function on the prices where it is defined and, of course, no claim is made about whether ϕ coincides with c_{ϕ}^{*} at zero prices where ϕ is not defined.

Hence ϕ is indeed the cost function at positive prices for the natural inputs production set $Z_{\phi} = \{(y, -x) : y \in Y \text{ and } x \in V_{\phi}(y)\}$ derived from the homogeneous and concave nonnegative function ϕ. That is, *the homogeneity and concavity properties are sufficient as well as necessary for a function* $\phi : \mathbb{R}_{++}^{m} \times Y \to \mathbb{R}_{+}^{1}$, *for some nonempty set* $Y \subset \mathbb{R}^{n-m}$, *to be the minimum of the cost expression over a well-behaved input requirement set; and* ϕ *is a true minimum (a cost-minimizing input plan exists). Hence we can use* ***any*** *function satisfying these properties as a cost function without actually deriving it from some underlying technology. This extends to zero prices when the function is defined and continuous at zero prices but* ϕ *may not be a true minimum at such prices. This also shows* $Z_{\phi} = \{(y, -x) : x \in V_{\phi}(y)\}$ *is a cost-relevant technology for a firm with cost function* ϕ, *and the cost-relevant technology* **always** *has free disposal of inputs and convex input requirement sets.*

As discussed in Section 5.2, it is possible for ϕ to be the infimum over a set $V(y)$ that is a proper subset of $V_{\phi}(y)$ if $V(y)$ is either non-convex, does not satisfy free disposal of inputs, or is not closed. However, $V_{\phi}(y)$ is *always* a cost-relevant input requirement set for the cost function ϕ.

As discussed in Section 5.3, *any correspondence* $\eta : \mathbb{R}_{++}^{m} \times Y \to 2^{\mathbb{R}_{+}^{m}}$ *whose elements at each* $(w, y) \in \mathbb{R}_{++}^{m} \times Y$ *minimize* $w^{\perp}x$ *over* $x \in \eta(\mathbb{R}_{++}^{m}, y)$ *is a conditional input demand correspondence for a price-taking firm with input requirement set* $\eta(\mathbb{R}_{++}^{m}, y)$. *Hence we can use* **any** *correspondence satisfying this basic minimization property as a conditional input demand correspondence without actually deriving it from some underlying technology.* Homogeneity and negative semidefiniteness of the price responses are necessary but not sufficient for any such η. The corresponding cost function is derived from any such η via $\phi(w, y) = w^{\perp}\hat{\eta}(w, y)$. There are other conditional input demand correspondences that are consistent with this cost function; but all such conditional input demand correspondences are contained in x_{ϕ}^{*}, the conditional input demand correspondence for the input requirement correspondence V_{ϕ}. In the relatively simple case of a singleton-valued correspondence with implied function $\hat{\eta}(w, y)$ that is differentiable with respect to w, a sufficient condition for $\hat{\eta}$ to be a conditional input demand function is that its Jacobian with respect to w be symmetric and negative semidefinite (in addition to homogeneity of degree zero with respect to w).

6.6 RECOVERING THE PRODUCTION FROM THE COST FUNCTION

The input requirement sets V_ϕ in Theorem 6.7 are not directly operational for actually deriving the cost-relevant technology from a homogeneous and concave real-valued function ϕ defined on $\mathbb{R}^m_{++} \times Y$ for some nonempty subset Y of $\mathbb{R}^{n-m}$. As in the profit context, the definition of the technology involves an infinity of constraints $w^\perp x \geq \phi(w, y)$; one for each $w \in \mathbb{R}^m_{++}$. In the single-output case it would be most useful if a cost-relevant production function f_ϕ corresponding to V_ϕ could be derived directly. To do so we mimic the procedure used in the profit context: Fix the input vector $x \in \mathbb{R}^{n-1}_{+}$ and find the maximal output this vector can produce *conditional* on a given input price vector $w \in \mathbb{R}^{n-1}_{++}$:

$$g_\phi(w, x) = \sup\{y \in Y : w^\perp x \geq \phi(w, y)\}.$$

Under some conditions, a maximal output that is consistent with *every* input price vector is then the smallest of these conditional values:

$$g^*_\phi(x) = \inf\{g_\phi(w, x) : w \in \mathbb{R}^{n-1}_{++}\}.$$

Theorem 6.8. *Assume the conditions of Theorem 6.7 for $m = n - 1$ and that $\phi(w, y)$ is continuous (jointly in both w and y). Assume further that Y is an interval containing its infimum $\underline{y}$; and that $\phi(w, y)$ considered as a function of y is nondecreasing and unbounded on this interval for every $w \in \mathbb{R}^{n-1}_{++}$. Let:*

$$X_\phi = \cup_{y \in Y} V_\phi(y)$$

be the set of feasible input vectors and define g_ϕ and g^*_ϕ as above for $x \in X_\phi$. Then $g^*_\phi(x) = f_\phi(x)$ for every $x \in X_\phi$, where $f_\phi(x) = \max\{y \in Y : x \in V_\phi(y)\}$. That is, g^*_ϕ is a cost-relevant production function corresponding to the technology V_ϕ. Moreover, g^*_ϕ is continuous, nondecreasing, and quasiconcave.

Proof. Fix $x \in X_\phi$. Consider first the set:

$$G(w, x) = \{y \in Y : w^\perp x \geq \phi(w, y)\}$$

for $w \in \mathbb{R}^{n-1}_{++}$. $G(w, x)$ is nonempty, bounded and closed: Nonempty is due to the definition of X_ϕ; bounded is due to unboundedness and monotonicity of $\phi(w, y)$ on $y \in Y$; and closed is due to continuity of $\phi(w, y)$ on $y \in Y$, noting also that $G(w, x) \subset [\underline{y}, g_\phi(w, x)] \subset Y$ because the upper bound is in Y (i.e., all accumulation points are in Y).

Therefore $g_\phi(w, x) \in G(w, x)$. Indeed, $G(w, x) = [\underline{y}, g_\phi(w, x)]$.

Now consider the set:

$$\Gamma(x) = \bigcap_{w\in\mathbb{R}^{n-1}_{++}} G(w,x).$$

As $f_\phi(x) = \sup \Gamma(x)$ and $\Gamma(x) \subset G(w,x)$ for every $w \in \mathbb{R}^{n-1}_{++}$, we have:

$$f_\phi(x) \leq g_\phi(w,x)\ \forall w \in \mathbb{R}^{n-1}_{++}.$$

Thus $f_\phi(x) \leq g^*_\phi(x)$. On the other hand, $g^*_\phi(x) \in G(w,x)$ for every $w \in \mathbb{R}^{n-1}_{++}$, so $g^*_\phi(x) \in \Gamma(x)$, yielding $f_\phi(x) \geq g^*_\phi(x)$. Therefore $f_\phi(x) = g^*_\phi(x)$.

$\Gamma(x)$ is closed and bounded because it is an intersection of closed and bounded sets; $\Gamma(x)$ is also nonempty (it contains $\underline{y}$). This justifies use of "max" rather than "sup" in the definition of f_ϕ.

Continuity of $f = g^*_\phi$ is an application of the Maximum Theorem because $\Gamma(x)$ is uniformly bounded on an open ball about $x^0 \in X_\phi$ and is continuous at such x^0. To obtain a uniform bound, fix $w^0 \in \mathbb{R}^{n-1}_{++}$ and let $\bar{x}$ maximize $(w^0)^\perp x$ over the closure of the open ball ($\bar{x}$ exists because we are maximizing a continuous function on a nonempty, closed and bounded set; also $\bar{x} \geq x^0$, so $\bar{x} \in X_\phi$ due to free disposal). Now note:

$$\Gamma(x) \subset G(w^0,x) \subset G(w^0,\bar{x}) = [\underline{y}, g_\phi(w^0,\bar{x})]$$

for every x in the open ball. This interval provides the uniform bound. Continuity of Γ is due to continuity of $w^\perp x - \phi(w,y)$ as a function of (x,y) (i.e., continuity of $\phi(w,y)$ on $y \in Y$) for each $w \in \mathbb{R}^{n-1}_{++}$, noting again that all accumulation points of y values are in Y because $[\underline{y}, g_\phi(w^0,\bar{x})] \subset Y$.

g^*_ϕ is nondecreasing and quasiconcave because $V_\phi(y)$ is the input requirement set (upper contour set of g^*_ϕ) and has the free disposal and convexity properties. □

In applications of this theorem $\phi(w,y)$ is usually *strictly* increasing in y for every relevant price vector w, rather than being merely nondecreasing. Then $g_\phi(w,x)$ is found by setting:

$$w^\perp x = \phi(w,y) \tag{6.6}$$

and inverting to solve for y. The first order condition that might be used to find the minimum of $g_\phi(w,x)$ over $w \in \mathbb{R}^{n-1}_{++}$ is $\mathbf{D}_w g_\phi = 0$. Implicitly differentiating Eq. (6.6) yields:

$$x^\perp = \mathbf{D}_w\phi + \mathbf{D}_y\phi\mathbf{D}_w g_\phi.$$

Therefore the first order condition is $x^\perp = \mathbf{D}_w\ \phi(w,y)\big|_{y=g^*_\phi(x)}$, which is Shephard's Lemma applied to the function ϕ. This equation defines $\hat{w}$, a minimizing choice of w (the necessary second order condition holds automatically due to concavity of ϕ). However, this first order condition is homogeneous of degree zero in w so effectively there are n equations here (the first order condition and the homogeneity condition) with only $n-1$ "unknowns" w. In principle, this means we can solve for w and still have one unused equation leftover (usually by using homogeneity to divide by one of the prices thereby expressing all prices relative to that price). The leftover equation relates the cost-minimizing value of x (because the first order condition is Shephard's Lemma) to the optimal output level $y = g_\phi^*(x)$, and is therefore the cost-relevant production function.

6.7 DUALITY BETWEEN COST AND PROFIT FUNCTIONS

Given a function ϕ as described in Theorem 6.7, there is a cost-relevant production set Z_ϕ from which a profit function could be derived. Conversely, given a function ϕ as described in Theorem 5.1, there is a profit-relevant production set Z_ϕ from which a cost function could be derived if Z_ϕ has natural inputs. Thus, in principle, we can derive the profit function corresponding to any given cost function and vice-versa. Doing so through the production set would be quite tedious, however, especially with functions ϕ for which there is no closed form representation of the corresponding production set (such as when ϕ has a translog functional form). It would be much better to have a direct way of moving between cost and profit functions.

Moving directly from a cost function to a profit function is straightforward. We simply choose output levels to maximize the difference between revenue and the given cost function. Note that this result holds even if some components of the "output" vector y are, in fact, natural inputs and/or if an optimal output level for one or more outputs is nonpositive.

Theorem 6.9. *Assume the conditions of Theorem 6.7 and let:*

$$Z_\phi = \{(y, -x) : y \in Y \text{ and } x \in V_\phi(y)\}.$$

Then $\pi_\phi^* : \mathbb{R}_+^{n-m} \times P \to \bar{\mathbb{R}}^1$ defined by:

$$\pi_\phi^*(p, w) = \sup\{p^\perp y - \phi(w, y) : y \in Y\}$$

is the profit function for the production set Z_ϕ.

Proof. Let:

$$\tilde{\pi}_\phi^*(p, w) = \sup\{p^\perp y - w^\perp x : (y, -x) \in Z_\phi\}$$

be the profit function for Z_ϕ. By definition of π_ϕ^*:

$$\pi_\phi^*(p, w) \geq p^\perp y - \phi(w, y) \text{ for every } y \in Y.$$

As ϕ is the cost function for Z_ϕ (Theorem 6.7):

$$\phi(w, y) \leq w^\perp x \text{ for every } (y, -x) \in Z_\phi.$$

Hence:

$$\pi_\phi^*(p, w) \geq p^\perp y - w^\perp x \text{ for every } (y, -x) \in Z_\phi.$$

So $\pi_\phi^*(p, w) \geq \tilde{\pi}_\phi^*(p, w)$. In particular, if $\tilde{\pi}_\phi^*(p, w) = \infty$ then $\pi_\phi^*(p, w) = \infty$, establishing the result, so assume for the remainder of the proof that $\tilde{\pi}_\phi^*(p, w)$ is finite.

Conversely, as $\tilde{\pi}_\phi^*$ is the profit function:

$$\tilde{\pi}_\phi^*(p, w) \geq p^\perp y - w^\perp x \text{ for every } (y, -x) \in Z_\phi.$$

That is:

$$w^\perp x \geq p^\perp y - \tilde{\pi}_\phi^*(p, w) \text{ for every } (y, -x) \in Z_\phi.$$

As ϕ is the cost function for Z_ϕ (Theorem 6.7):

$$\phi(w, y) = \inf\{w^\perp x : (y, -x) \in Z_\phi\}.$$

Hence:

$$\phi(w, y) \geq p^\perp y - \tilde{\pi}_\phi^*(p, w) \text{ for every } y \in Y.$$

That is:

$$\tilde{\pi}_\phi^*(p, w) \geq p^\perp y - \phi(w, y) \text{ for every } y \in Y.$$

Hence $\tilde{\pi}_\phi^*(p, w) \geq \pi_\phi^*(p, w)$.

Combining inequalities yields $\pi_\phi^*(p, w) = \tilde{\pi}_\phi^*(p, w)$. □

The function π^* in this theorem is the supremum of the profit expression over Z_ϕ irrespective of whether that supremum is finite. Once this is established, attention can be restricted to the convex cone in $\mathbb{R}_+^n$ where π^* is finite.

In applications of this result interest sometimes centers on profit-maximizing supply and demand choices rather than the profit function. Starting from a cost function $\phi(w, y)$, typically calculus is used to find the values of y that maximize $p^\perp y - \phi(w, y)$. Once $y_\phi^*(p, w)$ is derived, one route to deriving all of $z_\phi^*(p, w)$ is to substitute optimal values of y into the objective to obtain $\pi_\phi^*(p, w)$ and then apply Hotelling's

Lemma. However there is another option that avoids a full derivation of $\pi_\phi^*(p, w)$. Shephard's Lemma can be applied to $\phi(w, y)$ to obtain $x_\phi^*(w, y)$ and then Theorem 6.1 gives $z_\phi^*(p, w)$. In many applications $y_\phi^*(p, w)$ and $x_\phi^*(w, y)$ are singleton-valued, in which case Theorem 6.1 is $\hat{z}_\phi(p, w) = (\hat{y}_\phi(p, w), -\hat{x}_\phi(w, \hat{y}(p, w)))$.

Moving directly from a profit function to a cost function is a bit more delicate. Start with a given function ϕ with profit-relevant production set Z_ϕ as in Theorem 5.1, and suppose this production set has natural inputs. Fix the input price vector $w \in \mathbb{R}^m_{++}$ and consider a feasible output vector $y \in Y_\phi$. We seek the cost of producing y when input prices are w. If the output vector y is profit-maximizing at prices (p, w) then we can calculate cost as the difference between revenue $p^\perp y$ and profit $\phi(p, w)$. Hence we must find an output price vector $p \in \mathbb{R}^{n-m}_+$ for which y is profit-maximizing when the input price vector is w. Suppose p^0 is such a vector, implying cost is $c_\phi^*(w, y) = (p^0)^\perp y - \phi(p^0, w)$. If there were another output price $p \in \mathbb{R}^{n-m}_+$ such that $(p^0)^\perp y - \phi(p^0, w) < p^\perp y - \phi(p, w)$ then we would have $\phi(p, w) < p^\perp y - c_\phi^*(w, y)$, contradicting that $\phi(p, w)$ is maximal profit. Hence an output price vector for which y is profit-maximizing when the input price is w must maximize $p^\perp y - \phi(p, w)$ over $p \in \mathbb{R}^{n-m}_+$. In the differentiable case an interior maximum satisfies $y^\perp - \mathbf{D}_p\phi(p, w) = 0$, which is just Hotelling's Lemma (and convexity of ϕ ensures that $p \gg 0$ satisfying this condition is indeed a maximum).

Theorem 6.10. *Assume the conditions of Theorem 5.1 with Z_ϕ having natural inputs and with $P = \mathbb{R}^{n-m}_+ \times \mathbb{R}^m_{++}$. Let:*

$$Y_\phi = \{y \in \mathbb{R}^{n-m} : (y, -x) \in Z_\phi \text{ for some } x \in \mathbb{R}^m_+\}.$$

Then $c_\phi^* : \mathbb{R}^m_{++} \times \text{ int } Y_\phi \rightarrow \mathbb{R}^1_+$ defined by:

$$c_\phi^*(w, y) = \sup\{p^\perp y - \phi(p, w) : p \in \mathbb{R}^{n-m}_+\}$$

is the cost function for the production set Z_ϕ (on the interior of the feasible output set).

Proof. Let:

$$V_\phi(y) = \{x \in \mathbb{R}^m_+ : (y, -x) \in Z_\phi\} \text{ for } y \in Y_\phi \tag{6.7}$$

$$\tilde{c}_\phi^*(w, y) = \inf\{w^\perp x : x \in V_\phi(y)\} \tag{6.8}$$

be the input requirement correspondence and cost function for Z_ϕ, respectively. Fix $(w, y^0) \in \mathbb{R}^m_{++} \times \text{int } Y_\phi$. From the definition of Z_ϕ (Theorem 5.1):

$$w^{\perp}x \geq p^{\perp}y^0 - \phi(p, w) \text{ for every } x \in V_\phi(y^0); \text{ for every } p \in \mathbb{R}_+^{n-m}$$

(note that ϕ is assumed to be finite in Theorem 5.1). From the definition of c_ϕ^*:

$$w^{\perp}x \geq c_\phi^*(w, y^0) \text{ for every } x \in V_\phi(y^0).$$

From the definition of $\tilde{c}_\phi^*$, $\tilde{c}_\phi^*(w, y^0) \geq c_\phi^*(w, y^0)$.

Conversely, Theorem 5.1 ensures Z_ϕ is nonempty, closed, and convex; therefore $\tilde{c}_\phi^*(w, y)$ is convex in y by item 3 of Theorem 6.5. Use Theorem 3.8 (and the subsequent note) to obtain $p \in \mathbb{R}^{n-m}$ such that:

$$\tilde{c}_\phi^*(w, y) \geq \tilde{c}_\phi^*(w, y^0) + p^{\perp}(y - y^0) \text{ for every } y \in Y_\phi.$$

That is:

$$p^{\perp}y^0 - \tilde{c}_\phi^*(w, y^0) \geq p^{\perp}y - \tilde{c}_\phi^*(w, y) \text{ for every } y \in Y_\phi.$$

Theorem 5.1 also ensures Z_ϕ has the free disposal property. This implies $p \geq 0$ because, if some p_i were negative, the right side of this inequality could be made arbitrarily large by letting $y_i \to -\infty$ while the left side is fixed, a contradiction. By Theorem 6.9, the profit function is the supremum of the right side. Hence:

$$\phi(p, w) = p^{\perp}y^0 - \tilde{c}_\phi^*(w, y^0). \tag{6.9}$$

From the definition of c_ϕ^*:

$$c_\phi^*(w, y^0) \geq p^{\perp}y^0 - \phi(p, w) = \tilde{c}_\phi^*(w, y^0).$$

Combining inequalities yields $c_\phi^*(w, y^0) = \tilde{c}_\phi^*(w, y^0)$ when $y^0 \in \text{int } Y_\phi$. □

Note that the theorem is proven only at output levels y^0 that are in the interior of the set of feasible output levels. The proof of $\tilde{c}_\phi^*(w, y^0) \geq c_\phi^*(w, y^0)$ does not depend on y^0 being interior. However the proof of the converse is not valid when y^0 is a boundary point, because Theorem 3.8 does not hold at a boundary point of the domain of a convex function (see also Exercise 6 of Chapter 3). Y_ϕ is open in most applications, rendering this point moot. As Z_ϕ has free disposal, the issue arises only when there are one or more outputs that have a globally maximal feasible level (i.e., production can be exhausted for these outputs).

Note also that $p \gg 0$ cannot be assured in the proof of $\tilde{c}_\phi^*(w, y^0) \leq c_\phi^*(w, y^0)$, so the conclusion relies on ϕ being defined and continuous when output prices are zero (note the construction of P in the statement of the theorem). See Exercise 12 of Chapter 3. In contrast, the theorem explicitly assumes $w \gg 0$. This ensures global continuity of $\tilde{c}_\phi^*$ (by convexity) so Theorem 6.9 can be called upon. Hence the theorem is restrictive in that it enables derivation of a cost function only from profit functions that are finite on all nonnegative output prices and all positive input prices. Although restrictive, this is intuitive: Cost is finite at every feasible output plan, including output plans that are not profit-maximizing at any price. If profit is infinite, all that can be inferred about cost is that it is the difference between infinite revenue and infinite profit. Such a comparison does not reveal the finite value of the difference. An alternate approach would be to consider a profit function ϕ that is finite on some convex cone $P \subset \mathbb{R}_+^{n-m} \times \mathbb{R}_{++}^m$ but restrict attention to output plans y^0 that are profit-maximizing for *some* output price at every input price. Then, by assumption, for the fixed w there exists p such that $(p, w) \in P$ satisfies Eq. (6.9). This approach enables derivation of a cost function from a profit function that is finite on only a subset of the price space, but only on a set of profit-relevant output plans, even though cost is always finite at all feasible output plans. The point here is that a profit function cannot reveal the cost of output plans that are irrelevant for profit maximization.

In applications of Theorem 6.10, often the profit-relevant output correspondence $y_\phi^*(p, w)$ is singleton-valued so we may think of it as a function $\hat{y}_\phi(p, w)$. If this function is one-to-one for each fixed w then there is an inverse function $\hat{p}_\phi(y, w)$ satisfying $y = \hat{y}_\phi(\hat{p}_\phi(y, w), w)$. Theorem 6.1 then says:

$$z_\phi^*(\hat{p}_\phi(y, w), w) = \{y\} \times (-x_\phi^*(w, y)) \text{ for } y \in y_\phi^*(\mathbb{R}_+^{n-m}, w).$$

That is, a profit-relevant conditional input demand $x_\phi^*(w, y)$ can be obtained directly from the unconditional input demand by inverting the supply function and evaluating the unconditional input demand at the implied output price. The profit-relevant cost function is then $c_\phi^*(w, y) = w^\perp \hat{x}_\phi(w, y)$. Indeed, Hotelling's Lemma always gives:

$$\mathbf{D}\phi(p, w) = \hat{z}_\phi(p, w) = (\hat{y}_\phi(p, w), -\hat{\hat{x}}_\phi(p, w))$$

almost everywhere (the double circumflex distinguishes the profit-maximizing input choice relationship from the cost-minimizing one). When this Jacobian exists everywhere and $\hat{y}_\phi(p, w)$ is one-to-one in p we obtain a profit-relevant conditional input demand quite easily. Simply apply Hotelling's Lemma to ϕ, invert the supply relationship, and substitute the result into the unconditional demand relationship: $\hat{x}_\phi(w, y) = \hat{\hat{x}}_\phi(\hat{p}_\phi(y, w), w)$.

6.8 NOTES

See the references for Chapters 4 and 5. Key contributors to duality of cost are Shephard [2, 3], Uzawa [4], Friedman [5], and Diewert [6–8].

The observation that many properties of the cost minimum are implied directly by the behavioral postulate, and the notion of an "economically relevant" technology, are due to McFadden [9].

Properties of the conditional factor demand when the minimum is unique can be found in Samuelson [10, pp. 63–69]. Symmetry and the observation that the Lagrange multiplier is marginal cost are in this section of Samuelson.

6.9 EXERCISES

1. Assume a price-taking firm has natural inputs and its conditional input demand and unconditional demand/supply choices are unique and differentiable. Denote the unconditional input demand with a double circumflex. Use the identity:

$$\hat{\hat{x}}(p, w) = \hat{x}(w, \hat{y}(p, w))$$

from Theorem 6.1 to show that net complements that are either both normal or both inferior in production are gross complements, but the converse need not hold (Hint: Use symmetry of the demand/supply derivatives). Similarly, show that net substitutes, when one is normal and the other is inferior, are gross substitutes, but the converse need not hold. Can you begin with a gross characterization and infer a net characterization if particular normal/inferior combinations hold?

2. Assume the single-output case. Use the comparative statics methodology to derive expressions (in terms of minors of the Hessian of the Lagrangian function) for the slope of a conditional input demand with respect to an input price and also with respect to output; and the slope of the optimal Lagrange multiplier with respect to an input price and also with respect to output. Verify that the only slopes with known signs are each input demand with respect to the own-price.

3. Find the conditional input demand correspondence and cost function for a price-taking firm with each of the four standard production functions introduced in Exercise 18 of Chapter 4.

4. Find the conditional input demand correspondence and cost function for a price-taking firm with production function $f(x_1, x_2) = x_1 x_2$. Compare to Exercise 32 of Chapter 4.

5. Derive the conditional input demand for z_1 and the cost function for the production set in Exercise 3 of Chapter 4.

6. Here is a production function: $y = x_1(1 + x_2)$ (all three variables are nonnegative real numbers). Derive the conditional input demand correspondence, the cost function and the profit function for a price-taking firm with this production function.

7. For a firm with each of the following production functions on $\mathbb{R}^2_+$:

a. Give an expression for the MRTS and the second derivative of the isoquant.

b. Use the equation for f and the first and second derivatives of the isoquant to carefully draw a typical isoquant. Pay particular attention to the MRTS, concavity, and intercepts; all along the isoquant; and the value of y.

c. Let w_1 and w_2 be the prices of x_1 and x_2, respectively. Find the conditional input demand correspondence, and the cost function, for feasible output levels.

i. $y = f(x_1, x_2) = x_1 + 1 - \frac{1}{x_2+1}$.

ii. $y = f(x_1, x_2) = e^{x_1+x_2} - 1$.

iii. $y = f(x_1, x_2) = 1 - e^{-x_1} + x_2$.

iv. $y = f(x_1, x_2) = 2 - [(x_1 - 1)^2 + (x_2 - 1)^2]$.

8. Assume standard cost minimization with two inputs. Draw two graphs of the input space that show the effect on minimum cost when the level of output is doubled. Draw the first graph so that the technology has increasing returns to scale and the second graph so that the technology has decreasing returns to scale. Compare the effect on minimum cost in the two cases.

9. A price-taking firm produces output y from inputs x_1 and x_2 according to the production function:

$$y = \begin{cases} \ln(6x_1 + 6x_2 + 1), & \text{if } x_2 \leq 4x_1 \\ \ln(10x_1 + 5x_2 + 1), & \text{if } x_2 \geq 4x_1 \end{cases}.$$

a. Derive the conditional factor demand functions for x_1 and x_2.

b. Derive the cost function.

c. Derive the supply function.
d. Derive the profit function.
e. Write an expression for the production set Z.
f. Does this firm's technology possess the 5 basic properties of technologies? Why?

10. Here is a production set Z with a piecewise linear boundary:

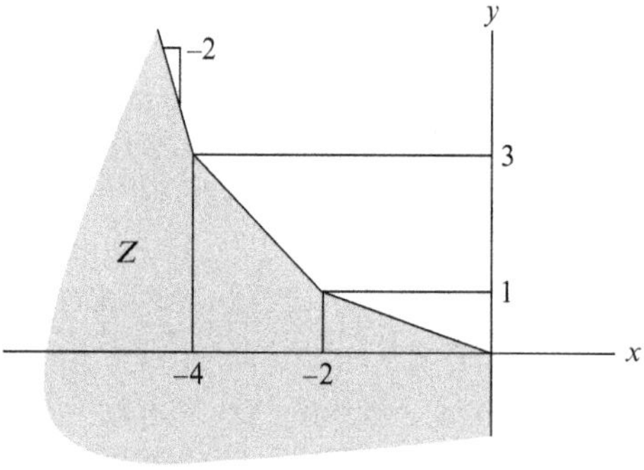

a. Find the cost function $c^*(w, y)$ for a price-taking firm, where w is the price of x.
b. Check whether the cost function you found in part (a) has the fundamental properties of a cost function. If not, explain why.

11. Consider a price-taking firm that chooses two natural inputs $(x_1, x_2) \in \mathbb{R}^2_+$ to minimize the cost of producing one output $y \in \mathbb{R}^1_+$. This firm's isoquant for output level y is the piecewise linear dark line:

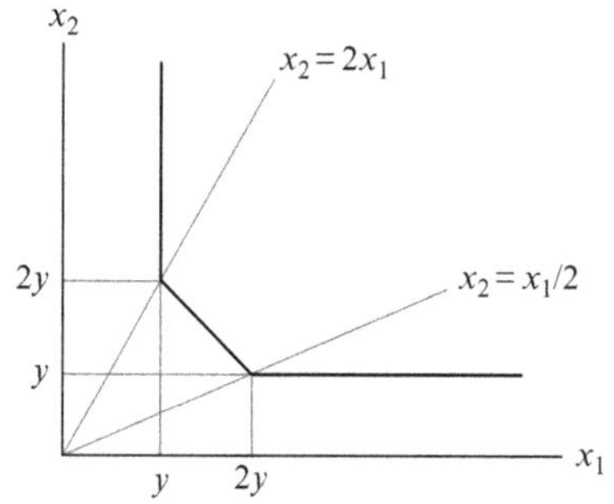

a. Derive the conditional input demand correspondence $x^*(w, y)$.
b. Derive the cost function $c^*(w, y)$.

c. Derive the one-sided gradients $\mathbf{D}_w c_+^*(w^0, y)$ and $\mathbf{D}_w c_-^*(w^0, y)$ at a price vector w^0 where prices are equal ($w_1^0 = w_2^0$). Shade the area on the above graph where x is between these one-sided gradients. Compare the shaded area to your answer to part (a); comment on this comparison.

12. Here is a cost function for a price-taking firm:

$$c^*(w_1, w_2, w_3, y) = \left(w_1 + \sqrt{w_2 w_3}\right)\left(e^y - 1\right).$$

a. Find the conditional input demand correspondence.

b. Verify that the matrix of demand slopes with respect to prices is symmetric and negative semidefinite. Also verify that the change in marginal cost when a price changes equals the change in the corresponding input when output changes.

13. Here is a Hessian with respect to (w_1, w_2, w_3) of a function that depends on (w_1, w_2, w_3) and y, evaluated at a particular point where (w_1, w_2, w_3) and y are all positive:

$$\begin{bmatrix} -1 & 1 & 0 \\ 1 & -3 & 0 \\ 0 & 0 & -1 \end{bmatrix}.$$

If we interpret (w_1, w_2, w_3) as input prices, can the function be a cost function for a price-taking cost-minimizing producer? Explain why or why not.

14. Suppose $\phi(w_1, w_2, y) = 2\sqrt{y w_1 w_2}$ and $\hat{\eta}(w_1, w_2, y)^\perp = \left(\sqrt{y\frac{w_2}{w_1}}, \sqrt{y\frac{w_1}{w_2}}\right)$. Verify that ϕ has the properties of a cost function for a price-taking firm and that Shephard's Lemma holds. Then derive an economically relevant production function for ϕ.

15. Might $\phi(w, y) = y e^{\frac{1}{2}\ln(w_1) + \frac{1}{2}\ln(w_2)}$ be a cost function for a price-taking firm? Why/why not? If so, find the conditional input demand correspondence.

16. Item 5 of Theorem 6.2 is that cost functions are nondecreasing in input prices. Theorem 6.7 establishes that a nonnegative function on $\mathbb{R}_{++}^m$ that is homogeneous and concave is indeed a cost function (we are ignoring the role of output because output is held fixed in this exercise). These two observations are mutually consistent if and only if homogeneity and concavity of a nonnegative function on $\mathbb{R}_{++}^m$ together imply that the function is nondecreasing. Prove that this is, indeed, the case. In other words, monotonicity of cost in input prices is a redundant property.

17. Assume $\phi(w_1, w_2, y) = (w_1 + w_2)\ln(y + 2)$ for $w_1, w_2, y \geq 0$. Check whether ϕ satisfies sufficient conditions for a cost function. If not, identify which of the standard properties the underlying technology does not possess.
18. Suppose $\phi(w_1, w_2, y) = (y + y^2)(w_1 + (w_1 w_2)^{1/2} + w_2)$. Is ϕ a cost function for a price-taking firm? Why?
19. Consider the function $\phi(w_1, w_2, y) = 2\sqrt{y w_1 w_2}$ defined for $y \geq 0$, $w_1 > 0$ and $w_2 > 0$.
    a. List the necessary and sufficient properties for a cost function and explicitly verify that ϕ has each property.
    b. Derive an economically relevant production function for ϕ.
20. Consider the function $\phi(w_1, w_2, y) = y w_1^{\alpha} w_2^{\beta}$ for $(w_1, w_2, y) \geq 0$.
    a. For what value(s) of α and β is ϕ a cost function for a price-taking firm? Why?
    b. For these value(s) of α and β, find the conditional input demand correspondence.
    c. For these value(s) of α and β, derive the production function for this firm.
21. Consider the function:

$$\phi(w_1, w_2, y) = \begin{cases} 3y^2(w_1 + w_2) + \left(4 - \frac{5}{2}y\right) y 2\sqrt{w_1 w_2} & y \leq 1 \\ (6y - 3)(w_1 + w_2) + \left(\frac{1}{2} + \frac{1}{y}\right) 2\sqrt{w_1 w_2} & y > 1 \end{cases},$$

defined for $(w_1, w_2, y) \in \mathbb{R}^3_+$.
    a. Confirm that ϕ is a cost function for a price-taking firm that uses two natural inputs with prices (w_1, w_2) to produce output y.
    b. Does the cost-relevant production set have free disposal, possibility of inaction, and no free lunch?
    c. Confirm that ϕ is a convex function of y. What do you expect about the cost-relevant production set?
    d. Derive the profit-maximizing supply set when the input price vector is $(1, 0)$ or $(0, 1)$ and the output price is $p = 6$.
    e. Derive the profit-maximizing supply set when the input price vector is $\frac{1}{2}(1, 0) + \frac{1}{2}(0, 1) = \left(\frac{1}{2}, \frac{1}{2}\right)$ and the output price is $p = 6$. What do you conclude about convexity of the set of prices where the profit-maximizing choices exist?

22. Here is a production set:

$$Z = \{(y_1, y_2, -x) \in \mathbb{R}^3 : x \geq 0 \text{ and at least one of the following holds:}$$
$$(1)\ y_1 y_2 \in [0, x^{1/2}],\ \text{or}$$
$$(2)\ y_1 \text{ and } y_2 \text{ are both negative}\}.$$

a. Explain whether this production set has each of the following properties: Closed, free disposal, possibility of inaction, no free lunch, and convex.

b. Derive the conditional input demand and cost functions. Is the cost function convex in (y_1, y_2)? Relate your answer to the answer you gave in item (a).

c. Use your cost function to derive the profit function.

23. Suppose a price-taking firm has production set:

$$Z = \{(y, -x_1, -x_2) \in \mathbb{R}^3 : y \leq x_1 + (x_2 + 1)^{1/2}\ \&\ x_1 \geq 0\ \&\ x_2 \geq 0\}.$$

a. Carefully draw a typical isoquant, labeling important slopes and intercepts.

b. Describe the properties of this firm's technology in terms of standard properties of technologies.

c. Derive the conditional input demands, using w_i to denote the price of x_i. Then write the cost function.

d. Derive the profit function, using p to denote the price of y.

24. Consider the function $\phi(p_1, p_2, w) = \frac{p_1^2 + p_2^2}{w}$ for $(p_1, p_2) \in \mathbb{R}^2_+$ and $w \in \mathbb{R}^1_{++}$.

a. Discuss whether ϕ can be interpreted as a profit function for a price-taking producer.

b. Now interpreting ϕ as such a profit function, does the implied production set Z_ϕ have any natural inputs? Explain.

c. Continuing to interpret ϕ as such a profit function, derive the cost function. What is the set of feasible outputs?

25. Consider the function $\phi(w, y_1, y_2) = w(y_1^2 + y_2^2)$ for $w \in \mathbb{R}^1_+$ and $(y_1, y_2) \in \mathbb{R}^2$.

a. Discuss whether ϕ can be interpreted as a cost function for a price-taking producer.

b. Now interpreting ϕ as such a cost function, what are the implied input requirement sets V_ϕ?

c. Continuing to interpret ϕ as such a cost function, derive the profit function.

d. Give a graphical representation of the production possibilities by drawing the set of outputs that can be produced for a given input level.

26. Suppose the real-valued function $\phi(\theta, y)$ is homogeneous of degree 1 and concave in θ. Here, $\theta \in \mathbb{R}^n_{++}$ and $y \in \mathbb{R}^1_+$. Define:

$$V_\phi(y) = \{x \in \mathbb{R}^+_n : \theta^\perp x \geq \phi(\theta, y)\ \forall \theta \gg 0\}.$$

Think of V_ϕ as a hypothetical production technology expressed in terms of input requirement sets.

a. Identify which standard properties of technologies this hypothetical technology necessarily has, and which properties might not hold. Explain why for each property.

b. Is $\phi(\theta, y)$ the minimum over x of $\theta^\perp x$ subject to $x \in V_\phi(y)$? Why/why not?

27. Here is an incompletely defined function that we suspect might be a cost function:

$$\phi(w_1, w_2, y) = \begin{cases} 3w_2 y & \text{when } \frac{w_1}{w_2} \geq 2 \\ 3w_1 y & \text{when } \frac{w_2}{w_1} \geq 2 \end{cases}.$$

We want to retrieve an implied input requirement set:

$$V_\phi(y) = \{(x_1, x_2) \in \mathbb{R}^2_+ : w_1 x_1 + w_2 x_2 \geq \phi(w_1, w_2, y)\ \forall (w_1, w_2) \gg 0\}$$

that would yield ϕ as a cost function.

a. First consider price pairs satisfying $\frac{w_2}{w_1} \geq 2$. Which among such pairs make $w_1 x_1 + w_2 x_2$ smallest for any given (x_1, x_2)? Infer from this a condition that every (x_1, x_2) pair in $V_\phi(y)$ must satisfy.

b. Now do the same thing for price pairs satisfying $\frac{w_1}{w_2} \geq 2$. Specifically, state a condition that every (x_1, x_2) pair in $V_\phi(y)$ must satisfy from the $\frac{w_1}{w_2} \geq 2$ scenario.

c. Combine your answers to parts (a) and (b) to give a proposed $V_\phi(y)$ set. Graph your proposed $V_\phi(y)$.

d. Using your proposed $V_\phi(y)$, define $\phi(w_1, w_2, y)$ when $\frac{1}{2} < \frac{w_1}{w_2} < 2$ so that ϕ really is the cost function associated with $V_\phi(y)$.

28. Suppose $\phi(w_1, w_2, y) = y w_1$.

a. Verify that ϕ could be the cost function of a price-taking firm that can use two inputs to produce output.

b. Draw the economically relevant input requirement set $V_\phi(y)$ in $\mathbb{R}^2_+$ for arbitrary $y > 0$.

c. Draw another input requirement set in $\mathbb{R}^2_+$ that is consistent with ϕ but that perhaps violates some of the standard assumptions on technologies. Which assumption(s) are violated by your input requirement set?

29. Give a technology and input price for which $AC(y) = y + \frac{1}{y}$ is the average cost function.

30. Suppose $\phi(w_1, w_2, w_3, y) = y\,(w_1(w_2 + w_3))^{1/2}$.

a. Verify that ϕ is a cost function for a price-taking firm.

b. Derive the conditional input demand correspondence and the Hessian $\mathbf{D}^2_w\phi$ with respect to prices.

c. Note that $\frac{\partial \hat{x}_2}{\partial w_3} = \frac{\partial \hat{x}_2}{\partial w_2} = \frac{\partial \hat{x}_3}{\partial w_3} < 0$. This shows that two inputs can be net complements *globally* (example due to Saku Aura).

31. Suppose we have the functions $\hat{x}_1(w_1, w_2, y) = \hat{x}_2(w_1, w_2, y) = \ln(y + 1)$. Check whether $\hat{x}_1$ and $\hat{x}_2$ are conditional input demands for a price-taking firm.

32. For what values of α and β is $\hat{x}$ a conditional input demand function?

$$\hat{x}(w_1, w_2, y)^{\perp} = [e^y - 1]\left(\left(\frac{w_2}{w_1}\right)^{\alpha}, \left(\frac{w_1}{w_2}\right)^{\beta}\right).$$

For those values of α and β, find the cost function, supply/demand function, profit function, and production function.

33. Let $y \in \mathbb{R}^1_+$ be an output level and $(w_1, w_2) \in \mathbb{R}^2_{++}$ be an input price vector. Suppose a cost-minimizing price-taking firm has the following conditional input demand:

$$\hat{x}(w_1, w_2, y)^{\perp} = \begin{cases} (\ln(y+1), 0), & \frac{w_1}{w_2} \leq 1 \\ (0, \ln(y+1)), & \frac{w_1}{w_2} \geq 1 \end{cases}.$$

a. Verify that this expression has the properties of a conditional input demand.

b. Derive the cost function and verify that the derived expression has the properties of a cost function.

c. Derive a production function for which the given conditional input demand is cost-minimizing.

34. For the profit function in Exercise 5 of Chapter 5, derive the conditional input demand correspondence and cost function.

35. For the supply/demand relationships in Exercise 8 of Chapter 5, derive the conditional input demand correspondence and cost function.

36. Consider a price-taking producer of output $y \geq 0$ using two natural inputs $(x_1, x_2) \in \mathbb{R}^2_+$. Denote the price of y by p and the price of x_i by w_i. Suppose the profit function is:

$$\pi^*(p, w_1, w_2) = \frac{p^2}{4}\begin{cases}(w_1 + 3w_2)^{-1} & \text{if } w_1 \geq w_2 \\ (3w_1 + w_2)^{-1} & \text{if } w_1 \leq w_2\end{cases}.$$

a. Derive an economically relevant cost function for this firm.

b. Derive an economically relevant production function for this firm with convex input requirement sets.

c. List standard properties of technology and describe whether this firm's economically relevant production set has each property.

37. Suppose a price-taking firm uses only one input with price w to produce output y, and has cost function $c^*(y, w) = \frac{w}{y}$. Discuss the properties of this firm's technology in terms of standard assumptions.

38. Is the following a conditional input demand for a production set that is closed and nonempty, and has possibility of inaction, free disposal and no free lunch? Why? If not, which of the basic assumption(s) are violated by the underlying production set? Why?

$$\hat{x}(w_1, w_2, y)^{\perp} = (y - 1)\begin{cases}\left(\sqrt{\frac{w_2}{w_1}}, \sqrt{\frac{w_1}{w_2}}\right) & \text{for } y \geq 1 \\ (0, 0) & \text{for } 0 \leq y < 1\end{cases}.$$

39. A firm has the following production function:

$$y = f(x_1, x_2) = \begin{cases}x_1 x_2 & x_2 \geq x_1 \\ \frac{1}{9}(2x_1 + x_2)^2 & x_2 \leq x_1\end{cases}.$$

a. Carefully draw a typical isoquant for this firm.

b. Find the cost function for this firm as a price-taker (use w_i to denote the price of input i).

c. Comment on the returns to scale of this firm's technology.

d. Describe the profit function for this firm.

40. Suppose a price-taking firm has conditional input demand, in standard notation:

$$\hat{x}^{\perp} = \ln(y + 1)\left(\left(\frac{w_2}{w_1}\right)^{1/2}, \left(\frac{w_1}{w_2}\right)^{1/2}\right).$$

What should this firm do to maximize profit?

41. Here is a cost-minimizing input demand ($y \in \mathbb{R}^1_+$ is output and $(w_1, w_2) \in \mathbb{R}^2_{++}$ are input prices):

$$(\hat{x}_1, \hat{x}_2) = \left(\left(\frac{y}{1 + 16\left(\frac{w_1}{w_2}\right)^{1/3}} \right)^4, \left(\frac{2y}{\left(\frac{w_1}{w_2}\right)^{-1/3} + 16} \right)^4 \right).$$

Derive a production function for which this is the conditional input demand.

42. Consider a price-taking firm that produces output y using two inputs, x_1 and x_2, whose prices are w_1 and w_2, respectively. Suppose the government imposes an *ad valorem* tax at a rate of t on purchases of x_2 (that is, if w_2 is the market price then the effective price to the purchaser is $(1 + t)w_2$). Show, *using the tangency property of the envelope theorem*, that the firm's cost function is increasing in the tax rate t. From this, characterize the concavity of the cost function in t.

43. **a.** Graph the set $Z_1 = \{(z_1, z_2) \in \mathbb{R}^2 : z_1 \leq -1 \text{ or } z_2 \leq -1\}$.

b. Graph the set $Z_2 = \{(z_1, z_2) \leq (2, 2) : (z_1 - 2)(z_2 - 2) \geq 3\}$. Pay particular attention to the points $(-1, 1)$ and $(1, -1)$.

c. Consider the intersection $Z = Z_1 \cap Z_2$ as a production set. Carefully graph this set, paying particular attention to the points $(-1, 1)$ and $(1, -1)$. State whether this technology has each of the following properties: Closed, no free lunch, possibility of inaction, free disposal, convexity. Explain why for each property.

d. Find the demand/supply correspondence and profit function for a price-taking firm with production set Z.

e. Now consider only the part of Z at which z_1 is nonpositive. Find the conditional input demand correspondence and cost function considering z_2 as the output and z_1 as the input.

44. Suppose $f(x_1, x_2)$ is a production function and w_1 and w_2 are the prices of one *logarithmic* unit of x_1 and x_2, respectively, so that the cost minimization problem is:

$$\min_{\{(x_1,x_2)\geq 0\}} \quad w_1 \ln x_1 + w_2 \ln x_2 \text{ subject to } f(x_1, x_2) \geq y.$$

Is the resulting cost function homogeneous and concave in (w_1, w_2)? Why or why not?

45. Assume a price-taking firm's production set is:

$$Z = \{(y_1, y_2, -x) \in \mathbb{R}^3 : x \geq 0 \;\&\; y_1 \leq x^{1/2} \;\&\; y_2 \leq x^{1/2}\}.$$

The notation is meant to indicate that this firm can produce two outputs, y_1 and y_2, using one input x. Let (p_1, p_2, w) denote the corresponding prices.

a. Show that the profit maximum is:

$$\hat{x} = \left(\frac{p_1 + p_2}{2w}\right)^2, \; \hat{y}_1 = \hat{y}_2 = \frac{p_1 + p_2}{2w}, \; \pi^*(p_1, p_2, w) = \frac{(p_1 + p_2)^2}{4w}.$$

Is the profit function defined and continuous when output price(s) are zero?

b. Show that the cost minimum is:

$$\hat{x} = \max\{y_1^2, y_2^2\}, \quad c^*(w, y_1, y_2) = \max\{y_1^2, y_2^2\}w.$$

c. Now consider the problem of deriving the cost function from the profit function. The procedure is to choose $(p_1, p_2) \in \mathbb{R}^2_+$ to maximize $p_1 y_1 + p_2 y_2 - \pi^*(p_1, p_2, w)$, where $y_1, y_2 \geq 0$. Derive this maximum. What is the maximum when the two output levels are unequal?

d. Compare your answer to item (c) with the discussion following Theorem 6.10. Discuss. Is the supremum in item (c) the correct cost function despite the "difficulty"?

46. Assume a price-taking firm's production set is:

$$Z = \{(y, -x) \in \mathbb{R}^2 : x \geq 1 \text{ and } y \leq 1 + (x - 1)^{1/2}\}.$$

The notation is meant to indicate that this firm can produce one output y using one input x. Let (p, w) denote the corresponding prices.

a. Carefully draw this production set.

b. Derive the profit function. Can profit be negative? Explain.

c. Derive the cost function.

d. Now consider the problem of deriving the cost function from the profit function. The procedure is to choose $p \in \mathbb{R}^1_+$ to maximize $py - \pi^*(p, w)$ for given $y \geq 0$ and $w > 0$. Derive this maximum.

e. Compare your answer to item (d) with the discussion following Theorem 6.10. Discuss. Is the supremum in item (d) the correct cost function despite the "difficulty"?

47. Assume a price-taking firm's production set is:

$$Z = \{(y, -x) \in \mathbb{R}^2 : x \geq 0 \text{ and } (1)\ y \leq \sqrt{x} \text{ when } x \notin (1, 4);\ (2)\ y \leq 1 \text{ when } x \in (1, 4)\}.$$

The notation is meant to indicate that this firm can produce one output y using one input x. Let (p, w) denote the corresponding prices.

a. Carefully draw this production set.

b. Show that the profit function is:

$$\pi^*(p, w) = \begin{cases} \frac{p^2}{4w} & \text{if } \frac{p}{w} \le 2 \text{ or } \frac{p}{w} \ge 4 \\ p - w & \text{if } 2 \le \frac{p}{w} \le 3 \\ 2p - 4w & \text{if } 3 \le \frac{p}{w} \le 4 \end{cases}.$$

c. Show that the cost function is:

$$c^*(w, y) = \begin{cases} wy^2 & \text{if } y \le 1 \text{ or } y \ge 2 \\ 4w & \text{if } 1 < y \le 2 \end{cases}.$$

d. Now consider the problem of deriving the cost function from the profit function. The procedure is to choose $p \in \mathbb{R}^1_+$ to maximize $py - \pi^*(p, w)$ for given $y \ge 0$ and $w > 0$. Derive this maximum.

e. Compare your answer to item (d) with the cost function derived in item (c). Are there values of y for which the functions are not equal? Discuss this in view of Theorem 6.10, paying particular attention to economic relevance of the production set.

48. Consider single-output cost minimization with free disposal. Construct a relevant constraint correspondence $\Gamma(y)$ that is uniformly bounded in a neighborhood of $(y^0, w^0) \in Y \times \mathbb{R}^{n-1}_{++}$.

REFERENCES

[1] Apostol TM. Mathematical analysis. 2nd ed. Reading, MA: Addison-Wesley; 1974.

[2] Shephard RW. Cost and production functions. Princeton, NJ: Princeton University Press; 1953.

[3] Shephard RW. Theory of cost and production functions. Princeton, NJ: Princeton University Press; 1970.

[4] Uzawa H. Duality principles in the theory of cost and production. Int Econ Rev 1964;5:216–20.

[5] Friedman JW. Duality principles in the theory of cost and production—revisited. Int Econ Rev 1972;13:167–70.

[6] Diewert WE. Applications of duality theory. In: Intriligator MD, Kendrick DA, editors. Frontiers of quantitative economics II. Amsterdam: North-Holland; 1974. p. 106–71.

[7] Diewert WE. Duality approaches to microeconomic theory. In: Arrow KJ, Intriligator MD, editors. Handbook of mathematical economics II. Amsterdam: North-Holland; 1982. p. 535–99.

[8] Diewert WE. An application of the Shephard duality theorem: a generalized Leontief production function. J Polit Econ 1971;79:481–507.
[9] McFadden D. Cost, revenue and profit functions. In: Fuss M, McFadden D, editors. Production economics: a dual approach to theory and applications I. Amsterdam: North-Holland; 1978. p. 3–109.
[10] Samuelson PA. Foundations of economic analysis. Cambridge, MA: Harvard University Press; 1947.

CHAPTER 7

Cost in Output Markets

Chapter Outline

7.1 BASIC COST CONCEPTS

The cost function is very useful for studying imperfectly competitive output markets. If the firm is not a price-taker in its output markets but still has output levels as choice variables and remains a price-taker in its input markets then the profit objective is:

$$\max_{\{(y,-x)\in Z\}} R(y) - w^{\perp}x$$

for some revenue function $R(y)$, where $R(y)$ may not take the fixed price form $R(y) = p^{\perp}y$ as in the perfectly competitive case. Although this is a new behavioral postulate, it is not necessary to start from first principles to analyze this problem because we know every profit maximizing firm also minimizes cost (Theorem 6.1—the same proof applies when $R(y)$ is not $p^{\perp}y$). Thus, in this problem the economically relevant aspects of the firm's technology can be summarized using its cost function, rather than by going all the way back to the production set. Then the objective becomes:

$$\max_{\{y\in Y\}} R(y) - c^{*}(w, y).$$

In imperfectly competitive output markets a central aspect of cost is its shape as a function of output. Hence we usually suppress the input price vector w (i.e., assume these prices are not changing) and write $c^*(y)$ or just $c(y)$. If there is possibility of inaction then $c^*(0) = 0$. This along with monotonicity (free disposal) implies $c^*(y)$ appears as in Fig. 7.1 for the single-output case. If, in addition, the production set is convex then the curve in Fig. 7.1 would be convex.

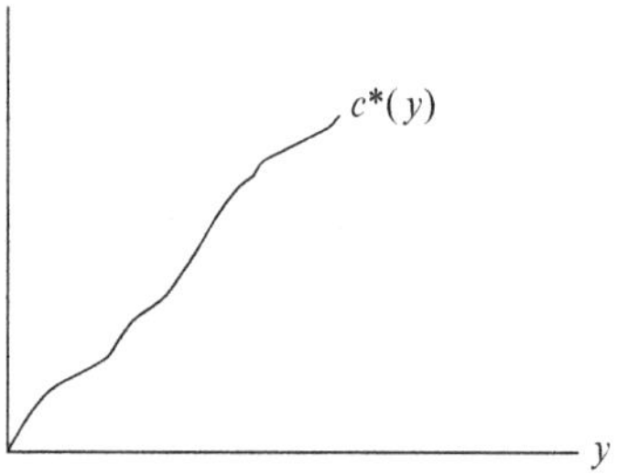

Fig. 7.1 Cost as a function of output.

There are several cost concepts useful for studying cost as a function of output in the single-output case:

- Marginal Cost: $MC(y) = \frac{\partial c^*}{\partial y}$ for $y > 0$ when the derivative exists (assumed whenever MC is written).
- Fixed Cost: FC is that part of $c^*(y)$ that does not vary with $y > 0$ (if any); fixed cost can be sunk, partially sunk, or not sunk.
- Variable Cost: $VC(y)$ is that part of $c^*(y)$ that varies with $y > 0$. So:

$$c^*(y) = FC + VC(y)$$
$$MC(y) = VC'(y).$$

- Avoidable Cost: $AvC(y)$ is $VC(y)$ plus that part of FC that is not sunk. So, if $\alpha \in [0, 1]$ is the proportion of FC that is not sunk:

$$AvC(y) = \alpha FC + VC(y)$$
$$MC(y) = AvC'(y).$$

- Average Cost: $AC(y) = c^*(y)/y$ for $y > 0$.
- Average Fixed Cost: $AFC(y) = FC/y$ for $y > 0$.
- Average Variable Cost: $AVC(y) = VC(y)/y$ for $y > 0$. So:

$$AC(y) = AFC(y) + AVC(y).$$

- Average Avoidable Cost: $AAvC(y) = AvC(y)/y$ for $y > 0$. So:

$$AAvC(y) = \alpha AFC(y) + AVC(y).$$

Fixed cost arises when there is a threshold amount of one or more input(s) that must be used before any positive output can be produced. For specificity, suppose $x_1^0 > 0$ is such a threshold amount of input 1. Writing $c^*(y) = w_1 x_1^0 + w_1(\hat{x}_1(y) - x_1^0) + w_{-1}^{\perp}\hat{x}_{-1}(y)$, we have $FC = w_1 x_1^0$ and $VC(y) = w_1(\hat{x}_1(y) - x_1^0) + w_{-1}^{\perp}\hat{x}_{-1}(y)$. This is illustrated in Fig. 7.2. If the fixed cost were sunk, then the production set would not include the horizontal segment and the cost function would take on the value $w_1 x_1^0$ at $y = 0$. Similarly, if the fixed cost were partially sunk then the production set would include only the left-most α share of the horizontal segment and the cost function would take on the value $(1 - \alpha)w_1 x_1^0$ at $y = 0$.

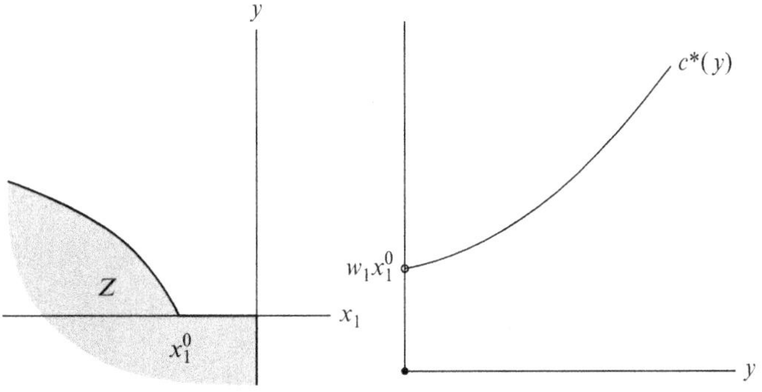

Fig. 7.2 Fixed cost.

If $FC > 0$ then AFC is everywhere strictly decreasing as a function of y. Thus, if in addition AVC is eventually rising then the relationship $AC = AFC + AVC$ shows that AC curves are roughly U-shaped. This is illustrated in Fig. 7.3. The smallest output at which AC reaches its minimum is called

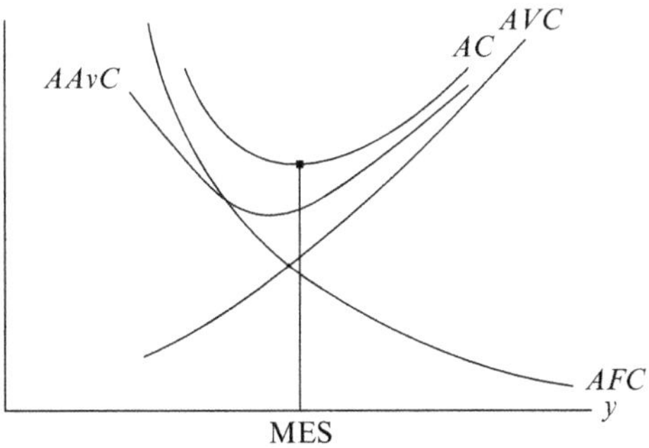

Fig. 7.3 U-shaped average cost and the MES.

the *Minimum Efficient Scale* (MES). There can be more than one output at which AC takes on its minimum value, and they are all *efficient scales*, but only the smallest such output is the MES.

The relationship between average and marginal cost is seen from:

$$AC'(y) = \frac{MC(y) - AC(y)}{y} \text{ for } y > 0,$$

as in Fig. 7.4. At a given output level y^0, $AC(y^0)$ is the slope of the ray from the origin through the point $(y^0, c^*(y^0))$ while $MC(y^0)$ is the slope of the tangent line at that point. When MC is below AC, as at y^0 in the figure, AC' is negative. Conversely, when MC is above AC, AC' is positive. Hence MC crosses AC at every local extremum of AC. Although it is often plausible to think of AC as being U-shaped, there is nothing in the theory that ensures this. If AC has multiple local extrema MC must cross AC at each such point. These same relationships hold between AVC and MC, and between $AAvC$ and MC, since MC is the derivative of VC.

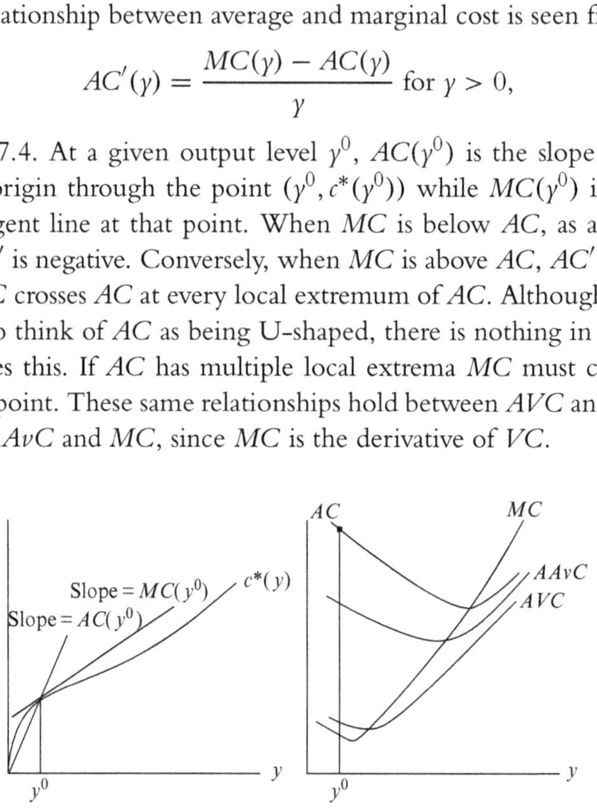

Fig. 7.4 Average and marginal cost.

7.2 RETURNS TO SCALE AND AVERAGE COST

The shape of the average cost curve is often of central importance in the study of imperfectly competitive industries. Average cost that decreases as output increases is sometimes described as a situation of increasing returns. It is true that an increasing returns single-output technology always has a decreasing average cost curve, but the converse does not always hold. We begin by showing the former.

Theorem 7.1. *Assume* $f : \mathbb{R}^n_+ \to \mathbb{R}^1$ *is a continuous production function. Let* $c^*(w, y)$ *be the cost function for the technology* f *and* $AC(w, y) = \frac{c^*(w,y)}{y}$ *be the* *average cost function for $y > 0$. If f has increasing returns to scale then $AC(w, y)$ is strictly decreasing in y for each $w \in \mathbb{R}^n_{++}$.*

Proof. Fix $w \in \mathbb{R}^n_{++}$ and $y^1 > y^0 > 0$ (note that continuity and $f(\alpha x) > \alpha f(x)$ for $\alpha > 1$ together imply $f(\mathbb{R}^n_+) = \mathbb{R}^1_+$, so $c^*(w, y)$ is defined for every $y \in \mathbb{R}^1_+$). From the discussion following Fig. 6.1 and the discussion preceding Theorem 6.6, there exists $x^0 \in \mathbb{R}^n_+$ such that $c^*(w, y^0) = w^\perp x^0$ and $f(x^0) = y^0$. Let $\alpha = \frac{y^1}{y^0} > 1$. By increasing returns:

$$y^1 = \alpha y^0 = \alpha f(x^0) < f(\alpha x^0).$$

Recalling that $f(x) > y$ cannot minimize cost at positive prices and output when f is continuous:

$$c^*(w, y^1) < w^\perp(\alpha x^0) = \alpha c^*(w, y^0) = \frac{y^1}{y^0} c^*(w, y^0).$$

Divide by y^1 to obtain $AC(w, y^1) < AC(w, y^0)$. □

Minor modification shows that average cost is nonincreasing when the production function has nondecreasing returns to scale; and average cost is strictly increasing (nondecreasing) when the production function has decreasing (nonincreasing) returns to scale.

Fig. 7.5 shows why decreasing average cost might not imply increasing returns. At the illustrated price w, x^0 is the cost-minimizing input vector for producing output level $y^0 = f(x^0)$. Hence $c^*(w, y^0) = w^\perp x^0$. Now consider any $\alpha > 1$ and let $y^1 = \alpha f(x^0) = \alpha y^0$. The isoquant for output level y^1 in the figure lies above the isoquant for output level $f(\alpha x^0)$, so $f(\alpha x^0) < \alpha f(x^0)$ and we therefore do not have increasing returns. However, the isocost line for producing y^1 at minimum cost lies below the isocost line through αx^0, yielding $c^*(w, y^1) < w^\perp(\alpha x^0) = \alpha c^*(w, y^0)$.

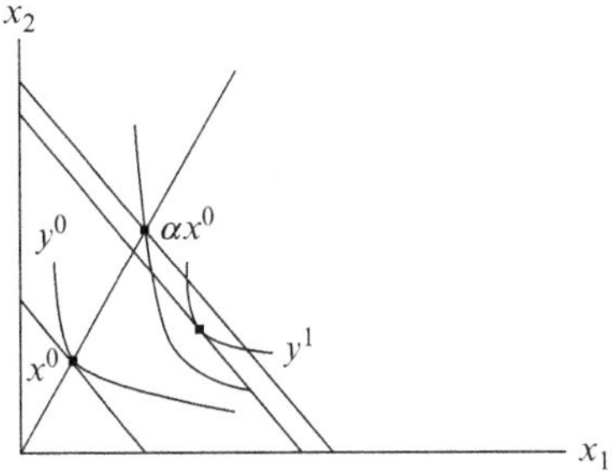

Fig. 7.5 Average cost, increasing returns, and homotheticity.

Substituting $\frac{y^1}{y^0}$ for α and rearranging yields $AC(w, y^1) < AC(w, y^0)$. That is, average cost decreases from y^0 to y^1 yet the technology does not display increasing returns over this range.

The complication in Fig. 7.5 is that the optimal input mix changes as output expands, due to the shift in the isoquants toward the x_1 axis. This suggests a converse to Theorem 7.1 can be proven under the assumption that the isoquants have a constant slope along input expansion lines; that is, when the technology is homothetic. As a first step toward this result we first prove the stronger result (under a stronger assumption) that homogeneity of the production function implies homogeneity of the cost function in output. Homotheticity is then a minor generalization.

Theorem 7.2. *Assume $f : \mathbb{R}^n_+ \to \mathbb{R}^1$ is a continuous production function and let $c^*(w, y)$ be the cost function for the technology f. If f is homogeneous of degree $k > 0$ then c^* is homogeneous of degree $(1/k)$ in y for every $w \in \mathbb{R}^n_{++}$.*

Proof. Fix $(w, y) \in \mathbb{R}^n_{++} \times \mathbb{R}^1_+$. As in the proof of Theorem 7.1, there exists $x \in \mathbb{R}^n_+$ such that $c^*(w, y) = w^\perp x$ and $f(x) = y$. Now fix $\alpha > 0$. By homogeneity, $\alpha^k y = f(\alpha x)$ and, by definition of the infimum:

$$c^*(w, \alpha^k y) \leq w^\perp(\alpha x) = \alpha(w^\perp x).$$

Therefore:

$$c^*(w, \alpha^k y) \leq \alpha c^*(w, y). \tag{7.1}$$

Eq. (7.1) holds for every $(w, y) \in \mathbb{R}^n_{++} \times \mathbb{R}^1_+$ and $\alpha > 0$. Given (w, y) and α, apply Eq. (7.1) to $\tilde{y} = \alpha^k y$ and $\tilde{\alpha} = 1/\alpha$ to obtain:

$$c^*(w, \tilde{\alpha}^k \tilde{y}) \leq \tilde{\alpha} c^*(w, \tilde{y}).$$

That is:

$$c^*(w, y) \leq \frac{1}{\alpha} c^*(w, \alpha^k y). \tag{7.2}$$

Combine Eqs. (7.1) and (7.2) to obtain:

$$c^*(w, \alpha^k y) \leq \alpha c^*(w, y) \leq c^*(w, \alpha^k y).$$

That is:

$$c^*(w, \alpha^k y) = \alpha c^*(w, y). \tag{7.3}$$

Now consider any $\beta > 0$. Define $\alpha = \beta^{1/k}$. Then Eq. (7.3) becomes:

$$c^*(w, \beta y) = \beta^{1/k} c^*(w, y).$$ □

Theorem 7.3. *Assume* $g : \mathbb{R}^n_+ \to \mathbb{R}^1_+$ *is a homothetic production function. That is,* $g = h \circ f$, *where* $f : \mathbb{R}^n_+ \to \mathbb{R}^1_+$ *is continuous and homogeneous of degree* $k > 0$; *and* $h : \mathbb{R}^1_+ \to \mathbb{R}^1_+$ *is strictly increasing and continuous with* $h(0) = 0$.[1] *Let* $c^*_g : \mathbb{R}^n_{++} \times g(\mathbb{R}^n_+) \to \mathbb{R}^1_+$ *be the cost function for the technology* g *and* $AC_g(w, y) = \frac{c^*_g(w,y)}{y}$ *for* $y > 0$ *be the average cost function for* g. *If* AC_g *is strictly decreasing in* y *(for arbitrary* $w \in \mathbb{R}^n_{++}$*) then* g *has increasing returns to scale.*

Proof. Let $c^*_f : \mathbb{R}^n_{++} \times \mathbb{R}^1_+ \to \mathbb{R}^1_+$ be the cost function for the technology f, which is defined for all $y \in \mathbb{R}^1_+$ as explained in the proof of Theorem 7.1. As $f(x) = y$ if and only if $g(x) = h(y)$, we have:

$$c^*_f(w, y) = c^*_g(w, h(y)) \text{ for every } (w, y) \in \mathbb{R}^n_{++} \times \mathbb{R}^1_+.$$

Suppress w for the remainder of the proof as it is fixed throughout.

Now fix $x \in \mathbb{R}^n_+$ ($x \neq 0$ because average cost is undefined at $g(0) = 0$) and $\beta > 0$. Let $y^0 = f(x)$ and $y^1 = f(\beta x) = \beta^k y^0$; and $\tilde{y}^0 = h(y^0) = g(x)$ and $\tilde{y}^1 = h(y^1) = g(\beta x)$. We have:

$$c^*_g(\tilde{y}^0) = c^*_f(y^0) \quad \text{and} \quad c^*_g(\tilde{y}^1) = c^*_f(y^1);$$

and, from Theorem 7.2 (using homogeneity of f):

$$c^*_f(y^1) = c^*_f\left(\left(\frac{y^1}{y^0}\right) y^0\right) = \left(\frac{y^1}{y^0}\right)^{1/k} c^*_f(y^0).$$

Therefore:

$$c^*_g(\tilde{y}^1) = \left(\frac{y^1}{y^0}\right)^{1/k} c^*_g(\tilde{y}^0).$$

If $\beta > 1$ then $\tilde{y}^1 > \tilde{y}^0$, in which case monotonicity of AC_g yields:

$$\frac{c^*_g(\tilde{y}^1)}{\tilde{y}^1} < \frac{c^*_g(\tilde{y}^0)}{\tilde{y}^0}.$$

[1] The condition $h(0) = 0$ is sometimes omitted from the definition of a homothetic production function. However, continuity and homogeneity of f imply $f(0) = 0$; so if $h(0) > 0$ the production set does not have the no free lunch property while if $h(0) < 0$ the production set does not have the possibility of inaction property. A production set that does not have no free lunch cannot have global increasing returns (unless infinite output is possible with no inputs), and a (closed) production set that does not have possibility of inaction cannot have global decreasing returns. Hence these anomalies must be ruled out if there is to be a relationship between returns to scale and monotonicity of average cost. These issues do not arise when studying homothetic utility because utility is ordinal.

Substituting for $c_g^*(\tilde{y}^1)$ yields $\left(\frac{y^1}{y^0}\right)^{1/k} < \frac{\tilde{y}^1}{\tilde{y}^0}$. That is:

$$\left(\frac{\beta^k y^0}{y^0}\right)^{1/k} < \frac{g(\beta x)}{g(x)}, \quad \text{or } \beta < \frac{g(\beta x)}{g(x)}.$$

Hence $\beta > 1 \Rightarrow \beta g(x) < g(\beta x)$ (increasing returns). □

Minor modification shows that a homothetic production function has nondecreasing returns to scale when average cost is nonincreasing; and a homothetic production function has decreasing (nonincreasing) returns to scale when average cost is strictly increasing (nondecreasing).

7.3 SUBADDITIVITY

If average cost of the most efficient available technology is downward-sloping between output levels zero and MES then any such output level is produced at lowest cost when it is all produced by one firm. That is, productive efficiency is achieved by one firm at any output level below which AC is decreasing. The converse, however, is not true. The general property of cost that determines whether productive efficiency of output y is achieved by one firm is *subadditivity*, meaning that it is not possible to attain cost lower than $c^*(y)$ by disaggregating production of y.

Definition 7.1. Assume $Y \subset \mathbb{R}^1_+$ is a feasible output set and $c^* : Y \rightarrow \mathbb{R}^1_+$ is a cost function. A *disaggregation* of output level $y \in Y$ is a set $\{y^1, \ldots, y^k\} \subset Y$ (all elements strictly positive), for any integer $k > 1$, with the property $\sum_{i=1}^k y^i = y$. c^* is *subadditive* at output level $y \in Y$ if $\sum_{i=1}^k c^*(y^i) \geq c^*(y)$ for every disaggregation $\{y^1, \ldots, y^k\}$ of y. If the defining inequality is strict then c^* is *strictly subadditive* at y. c^* is *subadditive on* $S \subset Y$ if c^* is subadditive at every $y \in S$.

It is straightforward to prove that a single-output cost function is (strictly) subadditive at y when average cost is (strictly decreasing) nonincreasing on $(0, y]$; it is also relatively easy to construct a counter-example showing that the converse is not true (see Exercise 7). Indeed, when average cost is U-shaped there is an interval of output levels above the MES on which the cost function is subadditive. At such output levels, productive efficiency requires that all production be conducted by one firm even though average cost begins increasing prior to the target output level.

An industry is called a *natural monopoly* when the cost function of the most efficient available technology is strictly subadditive on some "relevant" output set $S \subset Y$. The relevant output set is determined by the position of the demand curve relative to average cost, but the exact relative position is often left vague in discussions of natural monopoly. Certainly an industry in which a downward-sloping inverse demand is no greater than the minimum of a U-shaped average cost curve at the MES can be considered a natural monopoly, but this definition is overly restrictive because cost is subadditive at some larger output levels.

7.4 ELASTICITIES OF SUBSTITUTION AND SCALE

It is sometimes useful to measure locally the input substitution and returns to scale properties of a technology. Hicks [1] proposed the following measure of input substitution.

Definition 7.2. Let $f(x_1, \ldots, x_{n-1})$ be a production function and, for brevity, denote partial derivatives of f with subscripts. The (Hicks) *elasticity of substitution* of input i for input j at input vector x is:

$$\sigma_{ij}(x) \equiv \frac{d\left(\frac{x_i}{x_j}\right)}{\left(\frac{x_i}{x_j}\right)} \Bigg/ \frac{d\left(\frac{f_j(x)}{f_i(x)}\right)}{\left(\frac{f_j(x)}{f_i(x)}\right)}$$

$$= -\frac{f_{ij}(x)[f_i(x)x_i + f_j(x)x_j]}{x_i x_j [f_{jj}(x) f_i^2(x) - 2 f_{ij}(x) f_i(x) f_j(x) + f_{ii}(x) f_j^2(x)]}.$$

The (Hicks) elasticity of substitution is the percent change in an input mix that results from a percent change in the corresponding marginal rate of technical substitution, evaluated at input vector x and holding output constant. It measures the curvature of the isoquant at x. To see this, consider two possible isoquants at a point x, having the same MRTS at x, but one of which is more curved than the other. The slope of the line from the origin to x in Fig. 7.6 is the input ratio $\frac{x_2}{x_1}$ at x. If this input ratio changes to the steeper slope, and the isoquant is the curve through x^0, then the change in the MRTS (slope of the isoquant) for the given change in the input ratio is relatively small. On the other hand, if the isoquant is the curve through x^1, then the change in the MRTS for the given change in the input ratio is relatively large. Hence the elasticity of substitution at x for the isoquant through x^1 is smaller than the elasticity of substitution at x for the isoquant through x^0 (recall that the percent change in the MRTS is in the denominator of the elasticity of substitution). That is, the more curved isoquant is less elastic—a given percent change in the MRTS along the more curved isoquant yields a smaller percent change in the input ratio. Intuitively, it is "harder" to change the input ratio along the more curved isoquant (i.e., it would take a larger change in relative prices).

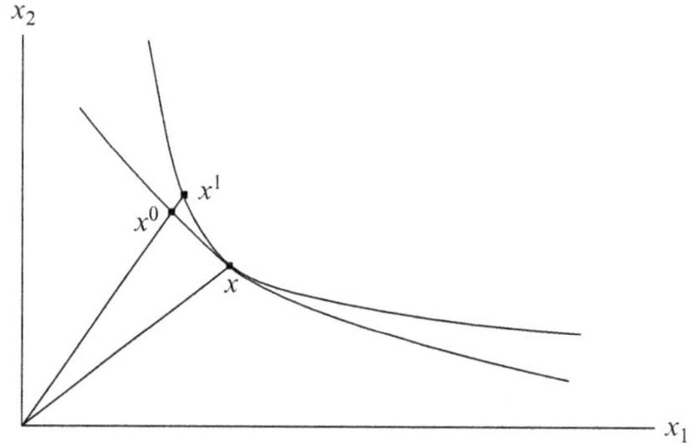

Fig. 7.6 The Hicks elasticity of substitution.

In the limit, if the elasticity of substitution approaches infinity at all x on an isoquant then the isoquant approaches a straight line. Conversely, if the elasticity of substitution approaches zero at some x while approaching infinity at all other x on the isoquant then the isoquant approaches an L-shaped Leontief form.

The Hicks elasticity of substitution measures the percent change in an input mix resulting from a percent change in a technical rate of substitution *along a two-dimensional isoquant.* Although this describes the curvature of the isoquant in the particular two-dimensional plane, it does not describe optimal input mix changes for a cost-minimizing firm because the Hicks elasticity does not permit all inputs to change at once, which is generally what happens to the cost-minimizing input bundle in response to a relative price change. Relating an input mix change to a change in a technical rate of substitution restricts the firm to a two-dimensional isoquant rather than the $n-1$-dimensional isoquant on which a cost-minimizing firm actually substitutes inputs. Thus, while the technical rate of substitution equals the price ratio in the (x_i, x_j) plane at an optimal input mix, this slope may not be the relevant direction for calculating a change in an optimal input mix. R.G.D. Allen proposed partial (also called Allen) elasticities of substitution for the case of $n-1$ inputs and it has been common practice in some empirical studies to report estimates of these partial elasticities. Partial elasticities of substitution acknowledge that all inputs may change in response to a relative price change but do not measure the input mix change as a response to a change in a *particular* price. For the Hicks elasticity, it is enough to simply examine the consequences of a change in an input price ratio (optimally, a technical rate of substitution) because the direction of change is presumed to be along the isoquant in a two-dimensional plane. This is not sufficient for a partial elasticity; all inputs are allowed to change hence there is no presumption of a direction of change. The change in an optimal input mix will generally depend on *which* price is changing. This led Morishima to propose the following measure of substitution.

Definition 7.3. The *Morishima elasticity of substitution* of input i for input j (in the direction w_i) at any relevant (w, y) is:

$$\hat{\sigma}_{ij}(w,y) \equiv \frac{d\left(\frac{\hat{x}_i(w,y)}{\hat{x}_j(w,y)}\right)}{\left(\frac{\hat{x}_i(w,y)}{\hat{x}_j(w,y)}\right)} \Bigg/ \frac{d\left(\frac{w_j}{w_i}\right)}{\left(\frac{w_j}{w_i}\right)} = \frac{\partial \hat{x}_j(w,y)}{\partial w_i}\frac{w_i}{\hat{x}_j(w,y)} - \frac{\partial \hat{x}_i(w,y)}{\partial w_i}\frac{w_i}{\hat{x}_i(w,y)},$$

where it is understood the differentiation is with respect to w_i.

Note that in general $\hat{\sigma}_{ij}(w,y) \neq \hat{\sigma}_{ji}(w,y)$ since the latter is in a different direction, w_j, than the former. It is straightforward to apply this definition to any particular conditional factor demand.

Now consider returns to scale. Frisch [2] proposed the following local measure.

Definition 7.4. Let $f(x_1, \ldots, x_{n-1})$ be a production function. The *elasticity of scale* at x is:

$$\left.\frac{\left(\frac{df(\alpha x)}{f(\alpha x)}\right)}{\left(\frac{d\alpha}{\alpha}\right)}\right|_{\alpha=1} = \left.\frac{df(\alpha x)}{d\alpha}\frac{\alpha}{f(\alpha x)}\right|_{\alpha=1} = \frac{\sum_{i=1}^{n-1} f_i(x)x_i}{f(x)}.$$

The elasticity of scale is the percent change in output that results from a percent change in the scale of all inputs, evaluated at input vector x. It is a local measure of returns to scale that can be used to describe a technology at a particular input vector even though the technology may not have any specific global returns to scale. It is clear from the definition that the elasticity of scale may change as x changes, so it can only be a measure of returns to scale for infinitesimal changes in scale at a particular input vector x. If the technology possesses global constant returns to scale then the production function is homogenous of degree one, so Euler's Theorem yields $\sum_{i=1}^{n-1} f_i(x)x_i = f(x)$. Hence, global constant returns to scale implies a unit elasticity of scale everywhere, and so a technology is said to possess constant returns to scale at input vector x if the elasticity of scale is 1 at x.

Similarly, a technology is said to possess decreasing returns to scale at input vector x if the elasticity of scale is less than 1 at x, and increasing returns to scale at input vector x if the elasticity of scale is greater than 1 at x.

The elasticity of scale of the underlying technology, at an input $\hat{x}(w, y)$ that minimizes cost for some relevant (w, y), can be calculated directly from the cost function as the ratio of average to marginal cost. At an optimal input vector $\hat{x}(w, y)$, $f_i(\hat{x}) = w_i/\hat{\lambda}$ can be substituted from the first order conditions for a cost minimum to obtain $\frac{w^{\perp}\hat{x}(w,y)}{\hat{\lambda}(w,y)f(\hat{x}(w,y))}$. Since $\hat{x}(w, y)$ is cost minimizing, $c^*(w, y) = w^{\perp}\hat{x}(w, y)$; and by the Envelope Theorem $\hat{\lambda}(w, y) = MC(y)$. Finally, we have $y = f(\hat{x}(w, y))$ due to continuity of f, so substituting yields the elasticity of scale at $\hat{x}(w, y)$ as $\frac{c^*(w,y)}{MC(y)y} = \frac{AC(y)}{MC(y)}$. This ratio is easily calculated for many standard functional forms.

The elasticity of scale and the Morishima elasticity of substitution can also be calculated directly from an estimated profit function by making use of the fact that profit maximizing firms also minimize cost. For clarity, denote cost minimizing choices with a single $\hat{}$ and profit maximizing choices with a double $\hat{\hat{}}$. We have $c^*(w, \hat{\hat{y}}(p, w)) = p\hat{\hat{y}}(p, w) - \pi^*(p, w)$. Using $p = MC(\hat{\hat{y}}(p, w))$, the elasticity of scale expressed in terms of profit-maximizing values is:

$$\frac{AC(\hat{\hat{y}}(p, w))}{MC(\hat{\hat{y}}(p, w))} = \frac{p\hat{\hat{y}}(p, w) - \pi^*(p, w)}{p\hat{\hat{y}}(p, w)}.$$

Similarly, for the elasticity of substitution we have $\hat{x}(w, \hat{\hat{y}}(p, w)) = \hat{\hat{x}}(p, w)$ for every (p, w). Differentiating the ith component with respect to w_j and with respect to p yields:

$$\frac{\partial \hat{x}_i(w, \hat{\hat{y}}(p, w))}{\partial w_j} = \frac{\partial \hat{\hat{x}}_i(p, w)}{\partial w_j} - \frac{\partial \hat{x}_i(w, \hat{\hat{y}}(p, w))}{\partial y}\frac{\partial \hat{\hat{y}}(p, w)}{\partial w_j}$$

$$\frac{\partial \hat{\hat{x}}_i(p, w)}{\partial p} = \frac{\partial \hat{x}_i(w, \hat{\hat{y}}(p, w))}{\partial y}\frac{\partial \hat{\hat{y}}(p, w)}{\partial p}.$$

Substituting the latter into the former yields:

$$\frac{\partial \hat{x}_i(w, \hat{\hat{y}}(p, w))}{\partial w_j} = \frac{\partial \hat{\hat{x}}_i(p, w)}{\partial w_j} - \frac{\frac{\partial \hat{\hat{x}}_i(p,w)}{\partial p}\frac{\partial \hat{\hat{y}}(p,w)}{\partial w_j}}{\frac{\partial \hat{\hat{y}}(p,w)}{\partial p}}.$$

This, and $\hat{\hat{x}}_i(p, w)$ for $\hat{x}_i(w, \hat{\hat{y}}(p, w))$, can be substituted into $\hat{\sigma}_{ij}$ to express the Morishima elasticity of substitution in terms profit-maximizing values.

7.5 SHORT-RUN AND LONG-RUN COSTS

Usually sunk cost is thought of as arising when the time available to adjust input levels is too short for all input levels to be freely varied. For example, it takes time to change the size of a factory or office building (even when leasing flex space), but the raw material and energy (and perhaps too labor) inputs required to run these facilities can be manipulated more quickly. Thus, short-run cost minimization is a more-constrained optimization problem compared to long-run cost minimization, when everything can be freely varied. This means there is a relationship between a short- and long-run cost minimum via the Generalized Envelope Theorem (Theorem 1.17).

Consider a "short-run" time period during which some subset of the inputs cannot be varied. Partition the input vector into those that are sunk and those that can be varied, respectively: $x = (x_s, x_v)$. Let x_s^0 be the particular level at which x_s is sunk. Partition the input price vector conformably. Then the short-run objective is:

$$\tilde{c}^*(y, x_s^0) = \inf\{w_s^\top x_s^0 + w_v^\top x_v : (x_s^0, x_v) \in V(y)\},$$

where it is understood that x_v is the choice variable in this optimization problem (x_s^0 is a parameter). Thus, the sunk cost is $w_s^\top x_s^0$, and since x_s is fixed the optimal choices of x_v:

$$\tilde{x}_v^*(y, x_s^0) = \{x_v : (x_s^0, x_v) \in V(y) \text{ and } w_s^\top x_s^0 + w_v^\top x_v = \tilde{c}^*(y, x_s^0)\},$$

will generally differ from $x_v^*(y)$. For example, with two inputs and x_1 fixed at x_1^0 the short-run choice of x_2 might appear as in Fig. 7.7, where x_1^0 is optimal for output level y^0 but not for output level y.

It is possible that $\tilde{x}_v^*(y, x_s^0)$ is empty and $\tilde{c}^*(y, x_s^0)$ is infinite. This will happen if x_s^0 is inconsistent with output vector y (i.e., it is not possible to

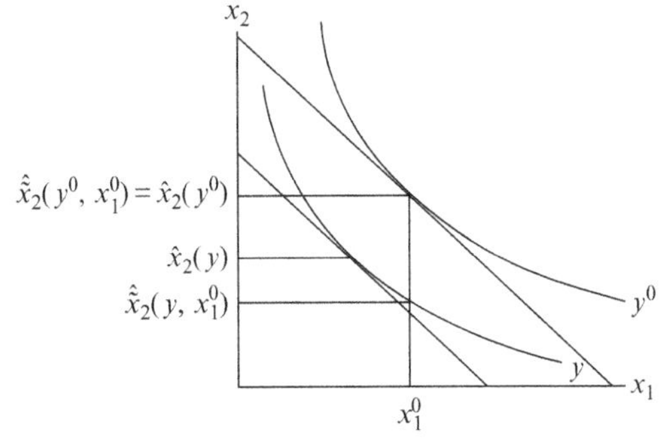

Fig. 7.7 Short-run cost minimization.

produce y with the given level of x_s, even though y is feasible at some other level of x_s).

Theorem 7.4. *Let $Y(x_s^0) \subset Y$ be the set of feasible output vectors for which $\tilde{c}^*(y, x_s^0)$ is finite. Then:*

1. $\tilde{c}^*(y, x_s^0) \geq c^*(y)$ *for every* $x_s^0 \geq 0$ *and* $y \in Y(x_s^0)$.

2. $\tilde{c}^*(y^0, x_s^0) = c^*(y^0)$ *when there exists* x_v *such that* $(x_s^0, x_v) \in x^*(y^0)$ *for some* $y^0 \in Y(x_s^0)$.

3. $\widetilde{MC}_i(y^0, x_s^0) = MC_i(y^0)$ *under the condition of item 2 when these derivatives exist at* y^0 *(MC_i denotes marginal cost with respect to output i).*

4. $\mathbf{D}_y^2\tilde{c}^*(y^0, x_s^0) - \mathbf{D}_y^2 c^*(y^0)$ *is a positive semidefinite matrix under the condition of item 2 when* $\tilde{c}^*$ *and* c^* *are both differentiable (with respect to y) on an open ball about* y^0 *and each marginal cost is differentiable at* y^0.

Proof. Apply Theorem 1.17 (Generalized Envelope Theorem). □

Item 1 states that the short-run cost function lies above the long-run cost function everywhere they both exist. Item 2 states that short- and long-run costs are equal at an output vector for which the sunk inputs are sunk at a level that is long-run optimal. Item 3 states that short- and long-run marginal costs are equal, when they exist, at such an output vector (the short-run and long-run cost functions are tangent at such points). One implication of item 4 is that the diagonal elements of the short-run Hessian are larger than the diagonal elements of the long-run Hessian, when they exist, at an output vector for which the sunk input levels are long-run optimal. That is, each short-run marginal cost is more steeply sloped than its long-run counterpart at such an output vector.

Theorem 7.4 reveals a lot about the relative positions of the two cost functions, as illustrated in Fig. 7.8 for the single-output case. From the definition of average cost, these same relationships must hold between the short- and long-run average cost curves, as in Fig. 7.9.

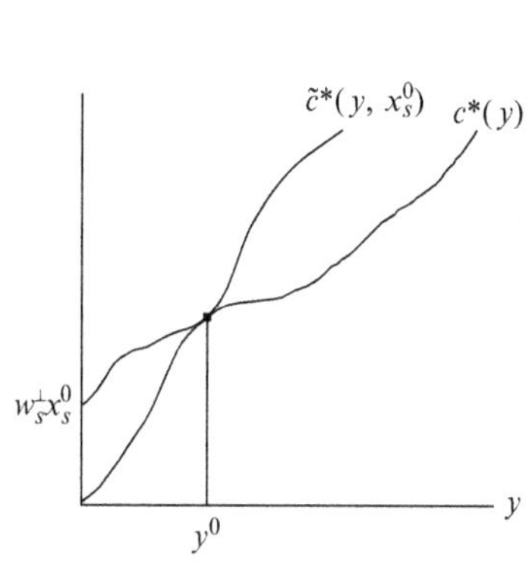

Fig. 7.8 The short- and long-run cost functions.

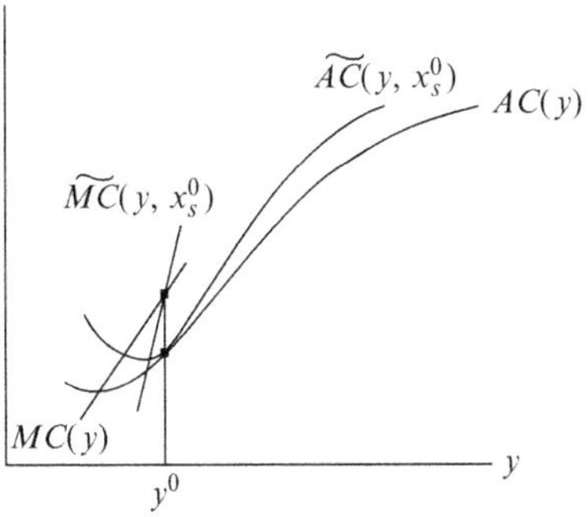

Fig. 7.9 The short- and long-run average and marginal cost functions.

7.6 SUPPLY

Return now to the firm's optimization problem stated in terms of the cost function:

$$\max_{\{y \in Y\}} R(y) - c^*(y).$$

The necessary first order condition is $\frac{\partial R(y)}{\partial y_i} = MC_i(y)$ for $i = 1, \ldots, n-m$. This condition defines the optimal output choice(s) y^* provided the solution is an interior maximum and both the revenue and cost functions are differentiable. $\frac{\partial R(y)}{\partial y_i}$ is the change in revenue resulting from a change in output i, and is therefore called the firm's *marginal revenue with respect to output i*, or MR_i. The first order condition thus states the familiar condition that a profit-maximizing firm chooses its output levels to equate marginal revenues with marginal costs. The necessary second order condition is that the Hessian be negative semidefinite, implying $\frac{\partial MR_i(y)}{\partial y_i} \leq \frac{\partial MC_i(y)}{\partial y_i}$ at $y \in y^*$. This says each marginal cost curve must cross the corresponding marginal revenue curve from below as y_i increases, at an optimal y.

If the firm is a price-taker in its output markets then $R(y) = p^{\perp}y$ for some fixed output price vector p. In this case marginal revenue is $MR_i(y) = p_i$, a constant for all y, and the Hessian matrix of $R(y)$ is zero. Thus the necessary first order condition is $p_i = MC_i(y)$ and the necessary second order condition includes $\frac{\partial MC_i(y)}{\partial y_i} \geq 0$. Again, the first order condition defines the optimal choice(s) y^* if we have an interior maximum. The y^* choice depends on p because the output price vector is a parameter for a price-taking firm, so $y^*(p)$ is the *supply correspondence*, implicitly defined by:

$$p^{\perp} \equiv (MC_1(\hat{y}(p)), \ldots, MC_{n-m}(\hat{y}(p))).$$

This shows that *a price-taking firm chooses output vectors that equate prices with marginal costs.* The comparative statics of price changes require that the firm adjust its supply choice to maintain the "price equals marginal cost" conditions as prices change.

Thus, geometrically, *the price-taking firm's supply curve is its marginal cost curve* when there is one output, as illustrated in Fig. 7.10. Algebraically, the single-output supply function is the inverse of the marginal cost function evaluated at the price:

$$\hat{y}(p) = MC^{-1}(p).$$

This statement presumes the inverse exists (i.e., that MC is strictly monotonic) and that the second order condition holds. Since marginal revenue is constant, the second order condition requires that MC be nondecreasing. At price p^0, the firm's optimal output choice is y^0 because MC equals p^0 at this output level. At a different price, say p^1, the firm's optimal output choice adjusts to y^1 so that the $p = MC$ condition is maintained. Thus, as p varies the MC curve traces out the optimal output choices.

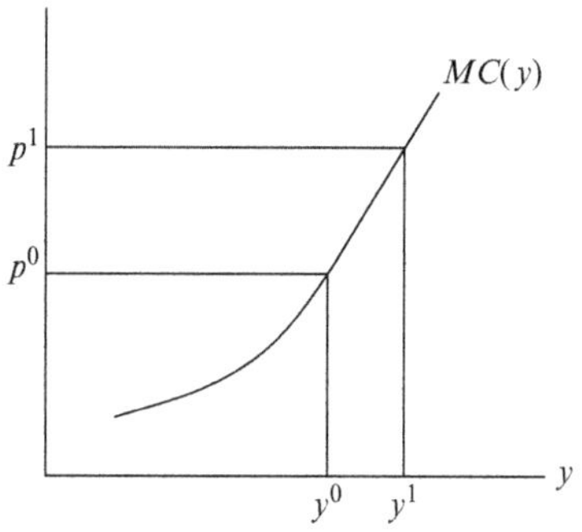

Fig. 7.10 Supply for a perfectly competitive firm.

A major exception to this depiction of a perfect competitor's supply relationship occurs if there is a non-sunk or partially sunk fixed cost. In that case, as illustrated in Fig. 7.2, the cost function has an upward discontinuity and thus it is not convex as a function of output. This means the profit objective is not concave, and therefore there is a chance the local first and second order conditions do not describe the global maximum. Fig. 7.11 illustrates this case for one output. Here, the AC and AVC curves are U-shaped because there is a fixed cost and increasing marginal cost. At prices below p^2, the local conditions indicate that the optimal supply choice is along the MC curve, for example at y^1 when price is p^1. But at this output choice revenue per unit is p^1, which is below cost per unit of $AC(y^1)$, and so the firm is earning negative profit. This negative profit is due to the fixed cost. As the fixed cost is not fully sunk, the firm might be better off choosing an output of zero and just incurring whatever part of the fixed cost is sunk.

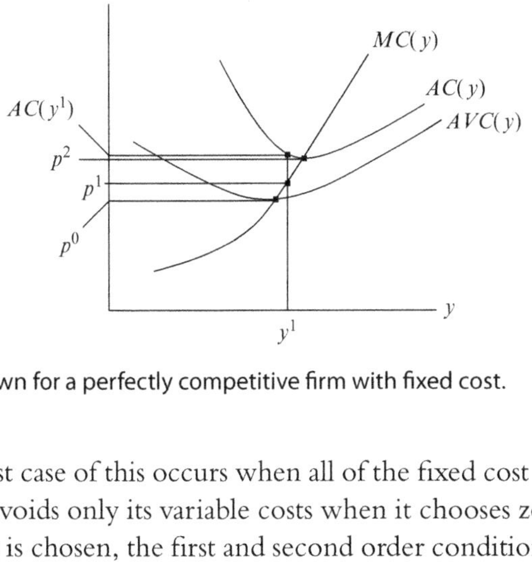

Fig. 7.11 Shutdown for a perfectly competitive firm with fixed cost.

The simplest case of this occurs when all of the fixed cost is sunk. In that case, the firm avoids only its variable costs when it chooses zero output. If a positive output is chosen, the first and second order conditions indicate that it must be along the MC curve. So the decision about whether to produce positive or zero output is based on whether the price line intersects the MC curve above the AVC curve. If so, then revenue is more than variable cost and so the firm can recoup at least some of its fixed cost by producing positive output. This is the situation at price p^1 in Fig. 7.11. However, if price is below p^0 then revenue is less than variable cost and so the firm is better off (incurs a smaller loss) choosing zero output. In this situation, price p^0 is called the *shutdown point* for the firm. Note that the AVC curve may lie below the MC curve at all output levels, because fixed cost is not included in AVC. If this is the case and all of the fixed cost is sunk, then the firm always chooses output to satisfy $p = MC$ (assuming this is possible and the second order condition holds).

The other polar extreme occurs when none of the fixed cost is sunk. Then the firm avoids both its variable and fixed costs when it chooses zero output. Hence, the firm chooses zero output whenever price is below p^2, and p^2 is the shutdown point.

If the fixed cost is partially sunk, then the firm avoids some but not all of it by choosing zero output. In this case there is a shutdown price between p^0 and p^2, depending on how much of the fixed cost is sunk. In general, the shutdown price is the minimum of the $AAvC$ curve, and marginal cost crosses $AAvC$ at this minimum. The case of totally sunk fixed cost is $\alpha = 0$ (then $AAvC = AVC$) and the case of no sunk cost is $\alpha = 1$ (then $AAvC = AC$).

In all cases, the optimal supply behavior of the firm is to choose y along the MC curve when price is above the shutdown price and $y = 0$ when price is below the shutdown price. When price is exactly equal to the shutdown price the firm is indifferent between $y = 0$ and the output level where $p = MC$, *but the intermediate output levels are not optimal because they generate less profit than the two extremes* (unless MC has a horizontal segment at the shutdown price). This is illustrated in Fig. 7.12.

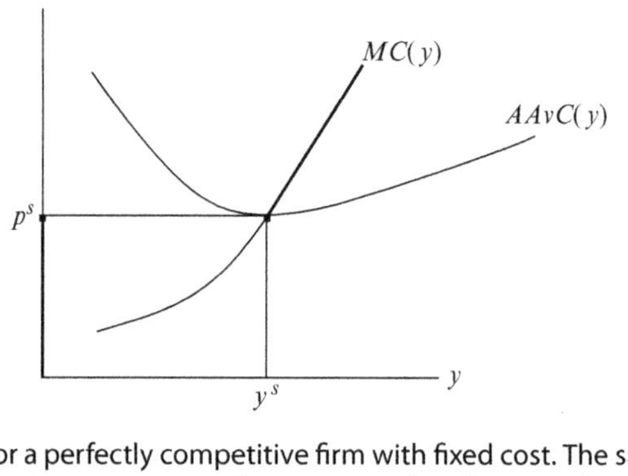

Fig. 7.12 Supply for a perfectly competitive firm with fixed cost. The supply curve is the dark line. It is discontinuous, jumping from zero to y^S at p^S. Output levels between 0 and y^S are not optimal at price p^S.

7.7 LE CHÂTELIER PRINCIPLE

During a time period sufficiently short to have sunk inputs, a price-taking firm's supply decisions are based on the short-run marginal cost curve. As shown in Theorem 7.4 and Fig. 7.9, this means short-run supply is less elastic than long-run supply at an output y^0 for which the sunk inputs x_s^0 are long-run optimal. This is natural: The firm cannot reorganize its input plan in response to a price change as flexibly in the short-run as it would in the long-run (this is the meaning of the "short-run"), and therefore does not change output as readily. This type of observation is sometimes called the Le Châtelier Principle.

The same Principle applies to input demands. We could have included the variable input price w_v along with y in the statement of Theorem 7.4. Item 4 would then include a statement that $\mathbf{D}^2_{w_v}\tilde{c}^*(y^0, w_v^0, x_s^0) - \mathbf{D}^2_{w_v}c^*(y^0, w_v^0)$ is a positive semidefinite matrix under appropriate differentiability assumptions, where (y^0, w_v^0) is an output/variable input price pair for which x_s^0 is long-run optimal. In particular, the diagonal elements of this matrix difference are nonnegative. Using Shephard's Lemma, each diagonal element is the own-price slope of a short-run input demand less the own-price slope of the corresponding long-run input demand. Hence the own-price slope of each short-run input demand exceeds the corresponding long-run input demand slope at a point where they cross (the fact that they are equal at (y^0, w_v^0, x_s^0) would be the addition to item 3 of Theorem 7.4 when w_v is included in the statement of the Theorem). That is, short-run input demands are less elastic than long-run input demands at a common point (keeping in mind that these slopes are nonpositive, so "exceeds" here means "is less negative than").

7.8 NOTES

Panzar [3] discusses cost subadditivity and natural monopoly. Hicks [1] and Hicks and Allen [4] present the Hicks elasticity of substitution. Allen [5, p. 504] defines the partial elasticity of substitution, while Blackorby and Russell [6, 7] popularized the Morishima elasticity of substitution (originally published in 1967 in Japanese). Frisch [2] presents the elasticity of scale.

7.9 EXERCISES

1. What, if anything, is wrong with this graph of a price-taking firm's cost curves?

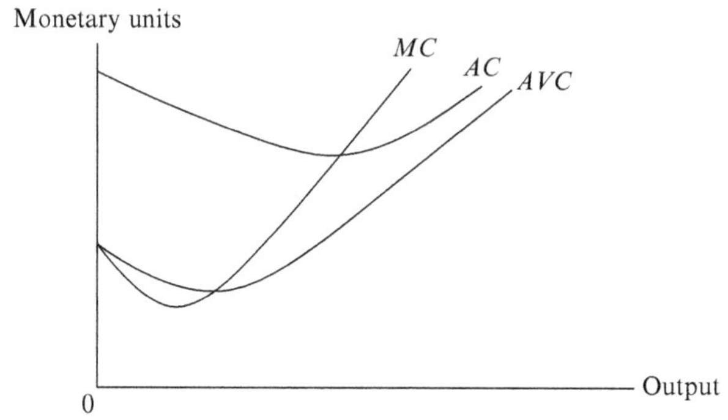

2. A price-taking firm has production function $f(x_1, x_2) = Ax_1x_2$, where $A > 0$ is a parameter that captures technical progress (a higher value of A means a more advanced technology). Use the tangency property of the envelope theorem to show that the effect of a technical advance on the cost of producing output level y is $-MC(y)y/A$.
3. Consider a firm that produces one output.
   a. Draw a production set, average cost/marginal cost graph, and total cost graph that all reflect global nondecreasing returns to scale. Now draw a production set and total cost graph indicating why marginal cost can increase even when there is global nondecreasing returns to scale.
   b. Redo part (a) for the case of global nonincreasing returns to scale.
   c. What do average and marginal cost look like when there is global constant returns to scale?
   d. Use the relationship between average and marginal cost to compare the characterization of local returns to scale given by the elasticity of scale with the global characterizations given in parts (a)–(c) above.
4. Consider the function $\phi(w_1, w_2, y) = (2w_1^\alpha + w_2)(e^y - 1)$ for $(w_1, w_2, y) \geq 0$.
   a. For what value(s) of α is ϕ a cost function for a price-taking firm? Why?
   b. For these value(s) of α, characterize the returns to scale of the technology underlying ϕ.
   c. For these value(s) of α, find the conditional factor demand correspondence.

5. Consider a price-taking single-output firm with cost function (input prices are fixed at some (unstated) values):

$$c^*(y) = \begin{cases} y^2 & 0 \le y \le 1 \\ 2y - 1 & y > 1 \end{cases}.$$

   a. Derive the marginal and average cost curves. Does marginal cost exist at $y = 1$?
   b. Carefully graph the MC and AC curves on a standard cost curve graph.
   c. Assume the underlying production function is homothetic (this is possible; all it imposes is that cost be multiplicatively separable in output and input prices). Describe the returns to scale of the technology.
   d. Derive the supply curve for this firm.
   e. Does decreasing returns imply either existence or uniqueness of a profit maximum?

6. Assume the production function for a free disposal technology is:

$$y = f(x_1, x_2) = (x_1 + x_2)^2 \text{ for } (x_1, x_2) \ge 0.$$

   a. Draw a typical isoquant.
   b. Find the cost function.
   c. Suppose input 1 is fixed at $x_1^0 = 10$. Find the short-run cost function $\tilde{c}^*(w_1, w_2, y, x_1^0)$.

7. a. Formally prove that a single-output cost function c defined on $[0, y]$ is (strictly) subadditive at y if $AC(y)$ is (strictly decreasing) nonincreasing on $(0, y]$.
   b. Suppose $c^*(y) = F + \frac{cy^2}{2}$ is a single-output cost function, where F and c are both strictly positive and $y \in \mathbb{R}^1_+$. Carefully graph the AC and MC curves. Show that $MES = \sqrt{\frac{2F}{c}}$. Then show that $c^*(y)$ is strictly subadditive on $y \in \left[0, MES\sqrt{2}\right]$.

8. Given a production function, conditional factor demand, and cost function (respectively):

$$f(x_1, x_2) = x_1 x_2, \quad \hat{x}_1(w, y) = \sqrt{y w_2 / w_1}, \quad c^*(w, y) = 2\sqrt{y w_1 w_2};$$

   a. Find short-run cost $\tilde{c}^*(w, y, x_1^0)$ for some fixed x_1^0.
   b. Verify $\tilde{c}^*(w, y^0, x_1^0) = c^*(w, y^0)$, where $x_1^0 \in x^*(w, y^0)$ (Hint: find y^0 first!).

9. Consider a firm that purchases inputs $x = (x_1, x_2, x_3)$ in competitive markets at prices $w = (w_1, w_2, w_3)$. The firm's production function is $y = x_1^{3/4} x_2^{1/2} x_3^{1/2}$.

a. This firm is facing (global): Constant, increasing, decreasing, or indeterminate returns to scale? Explain.

b. Derive the conditional factor demand equation for input x_2.

c. If in the time period considered, the amount of input x_3 is fixed at x_3^0, is the cost function $\tilde{c}^*(w, y, x_3^0)$ homogeneous in w?

10. Suppose a firm builds a production facility by investing $K > 0$ units of capital and that the amount of capital cannot be altered in the short-run. The cost of producing output level y in this production facility (including all capital costs) is:

$$\tilde{c}^*(y, K) = K + \frac{y}{K}.$$

a. Find the short-run average and marginal cost curves, and accurately draw them on a standard cost graph.

b. If the firm knows in advance that it wants to produce y units of output, what level of K should the firm invest? Use this to find the long-run cost function for this firm.

c. Find the long-run average and marginal cost curves and accurately add them to the graph you produced in part (a) of this question. Carefully label intercepts and points where curves meet.

11. Here is a cost function for a price-taking producer who uses two inputs, x_1 and x_2, to produce output y: $c^*(w_1, w_2, y) = 2(yw_1w_2)^{1/2}$. Find the short-run cost function when x_1 is fixed at the level that is optimal when prices are w_1^0 and w_2^0, and output is y^0.

12. Consider a price-taking firm with production function $y = f(x_1, x_2) = x_1x_2$ facing input prices $w_1 = w_2 = 1$.

a. Find the cost function, $c^*(y)$.

b. Suppose input x_1 is fixed in the short-run at $x_1 = 2$. Find the short-run cost function, $\tilde{c}^*(y, 2)$.

c. List four properties of the relationship between $c^*(y)$ and $\tilde{c}^*(y, 2)$.

d. Verify that the properties you listed in part (c) hold for the functions you derived in parts (a) and (b).

13. Suppose $\tilde{c}^*(w_1, w_2, y, x_1^0)$ is a short-run cost function with x_1 sunk at level x_1^0.

a. Illustrate the short-run optimal choice of x_2 on an isoquant/isocost graph.

b. Use your graph to argue geometrically that the value of x_1^0 that minimizes $\tilde{c}^*(w_1, w_2, y, x_1^0)$ is the long-run cost-minimizing choice of x_1, for the given w and y.

c. Use the result in part (b) to find the long-run cost function when

$$\tilde{c}^*(w_1, w_2, y, x_1^0) = w_1 x_1^0 + \frac{w_2 y}{x_1^0}.$$

14. A price-taking firm that uses natural inputs (x_1, x_2) to produce output y has cost function $c^*(w_1, w_2, y) = (w_1^{1/2} w_2^{1/2} + w_1)y$.

a. Derive and carefully graph the marginal and average cost curves when $w_1 = 1$ and $w_2 = 4$ (leave enough room on your graph for additions described below).

b. Derive the firm's cost-minimizing input demands.

c. Now suppose input 2 is fixed at $x_2 = 2$. Derive the firm's short-run cost function $\tilde{c}^*$ when $w_1 = 1$ and $w_2 = 4$.

d. Using the short-run cost function derived in part (c), derive the short-run marginal, average, and average avoidable cost curves. Add these curves to your graph in part (a), taking care to accurately represent their shapes and positions relative to each other, and labeling important points on the graph.

e. Comment on this firm's returns to scale in both the short and long run.

15. The following production function for transforming inputs x_1 and x_2 into output y is available to all potential producers: $y = x_1^{1/4} x_2^{1/4}$. Assume the input prices are fixed at $w_1 = 1$ and $w_2 = 3$. Also assume x_1 is an easily varied input in the short-run but x_2 can only be varied in the long-run.

a. Derive the long-run cost, average cost, and marginal cost curves for a typical firm.

b. Derive the short-run cost, average cost, and marginal cost curves for a typical firm when $x_2^0 = 100$.

c. Graph your short-run and long-run AC and MC curves from items (a) and (b) on one graph, taking care to correctly show their relative positions and labeling important points.

d. Suppose x_2 can only be varied in increments of 100. That is, firms must choose among $x_2 = 0$, $x_2 = 100$, $x_2 = 200, \ldots$. Suppose further that aggregate inverse demand for y is $p = 105 - y$ for $0 \leq y \leq 105$. Finally, suppose long-run competition among a large number of firms proceeds in the following two stages: (1) Firms simultaneously and noncooperatively choose x_2 values, correctly anticipating the equilibrium profits that will occur in stage 2; and (2) Firms supply as short-run price takers with price set to equate supply and demand. Find an equilibrium (subgame perfect).

16. Here is a production function for a price-taking firm that can use the inputs x_1 and x_2:

$$y = f(x_1, x_2) = \begin{cases} 0 & \text{if } x_1 \le 1 \\ \sqrt{\min\{x_1 - 1, x_2\}} & \text{if } x_1 > 1 \end{cases}.$$

a. Find the cost function $c^*(w_1, w_2, y)$, where w_i is the price of x_i and y is the output level.

b. Use the cost function to describe the optimal supply behavior of this seller.

17. Consider the function:

$$\phi(w_1, w_2, y) = \ln(y+1)\left[w_1^{1/4} w_2^{3/4} + w_1^{3/4} w_2^{1/4}\right].$$

a. Verify that this is a cost function for a price-taking firm (in input markets) with two inputs and one output y.

b. Find the conditional factor demand correspondence.

c. Suppose this firm behaves as a price taker in its output market. Describe its supply behavior.

18. Consider a firm with production function $y = \ln(x_1 + 1) + x_2$ for $(x_1, x_2) \ge 0$. Find the conditional factor demand correspondence. How much will this firm supply if it maximizes profit with prices satisfying $p = w_1 = w_2$? Answer the same questions for a firm with production function $y = e^{x_2} - 1 + x_1$ for $(x_1, x_2) \ge 0$.

19. Here is a production function:

$$f(x_1, x_2) = \begin{cases} 0, & \frac{1}{4} \le x_1 < 1 \\ \sqrt{x_2}, & x_1 \ge 1 \end{cases} \quad \left(x_1 < \frac{1}{4} \text{ is impossible}\right).$$

a. Find the cost function.

b. Suppose $w_1 = 12$ and $w_2 = 1$. Find the supply curve for a firm with this production function that is a price-taker in the output market. Carefully graph the supply curve.

20. Here is a production function for a firm that uses the two inputs $x_1 \geq 0$ and $x_2 \geq 0$ to produce output y:

$$y = \begin{cases} \min\{x_1, x_2\} & \text{when } 0 \leq y \leq 1 \\ \min\{2x_1 - 1, x_2\} & \text{when } 1 < y \end{cases}.$$

a. Draw enough isoquants to make clear the basic shape of the isoquant family.

b. Let w_1 denote the price of x_1 and w_2 denote the price of x_2. Find the cost function for a price-taking cost-minimizing producer.

c. Plot the average and marginal cost functions on one graph. Label important points on the graph.

d. Suppose $w_1 = 4$, $w_2 = 1$, and the price of output is $p = 4$. How much will a profit-maximizing price-taking seller produce?

21. Here is a possible cost function for a price-taking firm, in standard notation:

$$\phi(w_1, w_2, y) = 8y^2(w_1 w_2)^{1/2}.$$

a. Verify that this function is indeed a cost function.

b. Derive the conditional factor demands.

c. Assume the input prices are $w_1 = 2$ and $w_2 = 8$. Derive and graph the marginal and average cost curves as functions of output y.

d. Continue to assume the input prices are $w_1 = 2$ and $w_2 = 8$, and take as given that the production function for this cost function is $y = \frac{1}{2}(x_1 x_2)^{1/4}$. Find the short-run cost function when input x_1 is fixed at $x_1^0 = \hat{x}_1(2, 8, 1)$. Now find the corresponding short-run marginal and average cost curves, and graph them on the same graph with the long-run marginal and average cost curves. Be careful to draw the curves in the correct relative positions and to label ALL important points of intersection. How much will this firm supply in the short-run and long-run if the output price is $p = 8$? Give an economic explanation for the short-run supply decision, in particular compared to sunk cost and the long-run supply decision.

22. A price-taking firm has production function $Y = f(K, L) = KL^{1/2}$, where Y, K, and L are the quantities of output, capital input, and labor input, respectively. The prices are: output 20, capital 12, labor 100. The firm is operating in the short-run because the quantity of capital is fixed at $K^0 = 10$ during the time period under consideration.

a. Should this firm shut down? Explain.

b. Is this firm earning positive profit?

c. Does this production function exhibit increasing, decreasing, constant, or indeterminate (global) returns to scale?

23. Here is a production set: $Z = \{(y, -x) \in \mathbb{R}^2 : x \geq 0 \text{ and } y \leq x^2\}$. Find the cost function, average cost function, and marginal cost function. Graph the AC and MC curves on a standard graph.

24. Suppose a price-taking firm has the production set $Z = \{(y, -x) \in \mathbb{R}^2 : x \geq 0 \; \& \; y \leq 2x \; \& \; y \leq 1 + x\}$.

a. Find the conditional factor demand function and the cost function.

b. Verify that the cost function has the properties of a cost function.

c. Use the cost function to find average cost and marginal cost for some fixed value $w \gg 0$ of the input price. Graph these curves as a function of output y.

d. Where is the supply function on the graph? Reconcile this geometric derivation of the supply function with the supply function you found in Exercise 21 of Chapter 4.

25. Suppose a price-taking firm has the following production set:

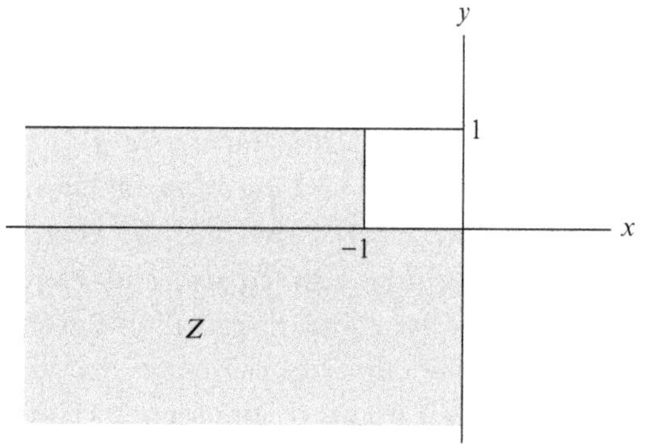

a. Find the conditional factor demand correspondence and the cost function.

b. Use the cost function to find average cost, average variable cost, and average fixed cost for some fixed value $w \gg 0$ of the input price. Graph these curves as a function of output y.

c. What is the *effective* "marginal cost curve" of this firm? Use this to illustrate the supply function on your graph.

26. Consider a price-taking firm with cost function:

$$c^*(y) = 1 + \begin{cases} y & \text{when } y \leq 1 \\ 2y^2 - 1 & \text{when } y > 1 \end{cases},$$

where $y \geq 0$ is the level of output and the input prices are constant and therefore suppressed. Assume α% of the fixed cost is avoidable.

a. Derive the avoidable, average, marginal, and average avoidable cost expressions. Carefully graph the latter three curves, labeling important points on the graph.

b. Derive the supply curve for this firm.

27. Suppose a single-output (y) price-taking firm has cost function:

$$c^*(y) = \begin{cases} F + y^2 & y > 0 \\ \alpha F & y = 0 \end{cases}.$$

Here, $F > 0$ is fixed cost and $\alpha \in [0, 1]$ is the proportion of fixed cost that is sunk.

a. Graph the average, average variable, average avoidable, and marginal cost curves for this firm.

b. Now find and graph the supply curve for this firm when

i. $\alpha = 1$.

ii. $0 < \alpha < 1$.

iii. $\alpha = 0$.

28. A price-taking firm has cost function:

$$c^*(y) = \begin{cases} F + \frac{y}{y+1} + \frac{y^2}{4}, & y > 0 \\ \alpha F, & y = 0 \end{cases},$$

where $\alpha \in [0, 1]$ is the proportion of fixed cost that is sunk.

a. Suppose $\alpha = 1$. Carefully graph the firm's supply function.

b. Illustrate in qualitative terms what happens to the supply function if $\alpha < 1$.

29. Consider a price-taking firm with cost function $c^*(y) = 36 + y^2$ for $y > 0$. If one-fourth of the fixed cost is avoidable, how high must the price of y be in order for this firm to supply positive output?

REFERENCES

[1] Hicks JR. Theory of wages. London: MacMillan; 1932.
[2] Frisch R. Theory of production. Chicago: Rand McNally; 1965.

[3] Panzer JC. Technological determinants of firm and industry structure. In: Schmallensee R, Willig R, editors. Handbook of industrial organization, vol. I. Amsterdam: Elsevier; 1989. p. 3–59.
[4] Hicks JR, Allen RGD. A reconsideration of the theory of value, Pt. II. Economica 1934;1:196–219.
[5] Allen RGD. Mathematical analysis for economists. London: MacMillan; 1938.
[6] Blackorby C, Russell RR. The Morishima elasticity of substitution: symmetry, constancy, separability, and its relationship to the Hicks and Allen elasticities. Rev Econ Stud 1981;48:147–58.
[7] Blackorby C, Russell RR. Will the real elasticity of substitution please stand up? (A comparison of the Allen/Uzawa and Morishima elasticities). Am Econ Rev 1989; 79:882–8.

Part 3

Consumers

Part 2 studies the supply side of product markets and the demand side of factor markets. The economic agent, or actor, is the firm.

Part 3 switches to the demand side of product markets and the supply side of factor markets, and studies *consumers*, which is the name we use for these final demanders and factor suppliers. The study of consumer supply behavior in factor markets is specialized and studied in courses on general equilibrium and labor economics. Thus the focus here is mostly on consumer demand behavior in product markets.

The behavioral postulates continue to presume price-taking. Each consumer is hypothesized to make quantity choices that optimize an objective without regard to potential effects on prices.

Chapter 8 defines the consumer's objective. This begins with an axiomatic presentation of a binary relation that expresses preference between two options. Preference axioms required for an optimization-based theory of choice are completeness, transitivity and continuity. A major theorem establishes equivalence between these axioms and existence of a continuous ordinal representation of preferences, or a *utility function*. Chapter 8 explains why these axioms are required and proves this theorem. The chapter ends with additional preference axioms that are sometimes useful, including monotonicity (more is better), convexity (averages are preferred to extremes), and local nonsatiation (improvement is always possible via a small change in choice).

The expenditure minimization behavioral postulate and its refutable hypotheses are presented in Chapter 9. A major role of this hypothesis is to reveal hidden refutable propositions about the important Marshallian demands that result from the utility maximizing behavior postulated in Chapter 10. Expenditure minimization is formally identical to single-output cost minimization except for a few minor details. This makes most of the refutable hypotheses in Chapter 9 reinterpretations of results from Chapter 6. The chapter ends with a restatement of the duality results from cost minimization—homogeneity, concavity, and monotonicity (and the existence of a "zero utility" level of expenditure) are sufficient as well as necessary for expenditure minimizing behavior, just as these properties are both necessary and sufficient for cost minimizing behavior. And a homogeneous of degree zero vector-valued function with a symmetric negative semidefinite Jacobian is a demand function for a price-taking consumer who minimizes expenditure over the implied expenditure-relevant preferred set. When these properties hold, an expenditure-relevant utility function can be derived just as a cost-relevant production function can be derived.

Chapters 10 and 11 explore the price-taking utility maximization behavioral postulate. This hypothesis is structurally different from other behavior studied in the book because the objective is not a monetary value function and the constraint is active with respect to prices. But utility-maximizing behavior is equivalent to expenditure minimizing behavior under the weak assumption that an increase in monetary resources benefits the consumer, and this equivalence is the source of the famous Hicks-Slutsky Decomposition of a price change into income and substitution effects on the Marshallian demand. The structural differences between utility maximization and other behavioral postulates make the duality results for utility maximization, presented in Chapter 11, less direct. But once again the equivalence between expenditure minimization and utility maximization proves useful, making it possible to restate questions about properties sufficient for a utility maximum in terms of expenditure. Chapter 11 also states the classical theorems about revealed preference and integrability as sufficient descriptions of utility-maximizing demand behavior.

Part 3 concludes with Chapter 12 on the compensating and equivalent variations, which provide monetary measures of consumer welfare and the deadweight loss from price changes. Marshallian surplus is usually not a valid welfare measure because of income effects. These monetary measures can be aggregated, however, and aggregate demand retains the properties of individual demands.

CHAPTER 8

Preferences

Chapter Outline

As with all economic agents, there are two basic pieces to consumer behavior: The objective and the constraints. For consumers the constraint is relatively straightforward, merely requiring that the consumer stay within a budget. But the objective requires some explanation; it has two parts:

- The consumption set X. This is the set of all possible bundles the consumer might consume. This set includes everything that exists or might conceivably exist, not merely those things that satisfy some individual or aggregate resource constraint. The description here is only about preferences, not about availability of resources. It is up to the market to ration potentially scarce commodities by placing positive prices on them.
- The preference ordering $\succsim$. This is known as a *binary relation* over X. It expresses the preference of the consumer between two bundles in X. $x \succsim y$ means "x is at least as desirable as y" for the consumer under study.

For convenience, we sometimes write $y \precsim x$ to denote $x \succsim y$.

8.1 RATIONALITY

Some assumptions must be made about $(X, \succsim)$ if this concept of preference is to serve as a useful foundation for a theory of consumer choice. The two main assumptions are:

1. Completeness: For every $x, y \in X$, either $x \succsim y$ or $y \succsim x$, or both. Note that this includes reflexivity as the special case of $x = y$.
2. Transitivity: For $x, y, z \in X$, if $x \succsim y$ and $y \succsim z$, then $x \succsim z$.

These may seem obvious, but are in fact assumptions of substance. For example, set containment is a binary relation that is not complete, and "defeated" among teams in a sports league is a binary relation that need not be transitive. Preferences that satisfy these two assumptions are called *rational*.

Note that the preference ordering is weak. Under completeness, strict preference and indifference can be defined from $\succsim$, rather than introducing them as new primitive concepts, as follows: For $x, y \in X$,

- $x \succ y$ means not($y \succsim x$) ("x is (strictly) preferred to y").
- $x \sim y$ means both $x \succsim y$ and $y \succsim x$ ("indifference" between x and y).

For convenience, we sometimes write $y \prec x$ to denote $x \succ y$. We also sometimes need to speak of the consumption bundles that are all at least as desirable as a given bundle, or the set of bundles that are equally desirable as a given bundle. Hence we define:

- Preferred set (to $y \in X$): $\{x \in X : x \succsim y\}$.
- Indifference set (to $y \in X$): $\{x \in X : x \sim y\}$.

The completeness and transitivity assumptions are primitive, having the advantage that they lay bare exactly what is being assumed, but they are cumbersome. It would be much more convenient if $(X, \succsim)$ could be replaced with a system of index numbers that expresses the same information. Such a system of index numbers is called a *utility function.* It is a real-valued function over X whose values give the same ordering as $\succsim$. If there is a utility function for any given preference relation then we can use all of our standard optimization tools on the utility function in order to describe consumer behavior, thereby avoiding direct consideration of the preference relation. Hence an important task is to determine what properties a preference relation must possess in order to assure that a utility function exists.

Definition 8.1. Let $(X, \succsim)$ be a preference ordering. We say a function $u : X \rightarrow \mathbb{R}^1$ *represents* $(X, \succsim)$ when, for every $x, y \in X$:

$$u(x) \geq u(y) \Leftrightarrow x \succsim y.$$

Theorem 8.1. *If u represents $(X, \succsim)$ then $(X, \succsim)$ is complete and transitive.*

Proof. Fix $x, y, z \in X$. Since $\geq$ is complete over $\mathbb{R}^1$, either $u(x) \geq u(y)$ or $u(y) \geq u(x)$. Hence, either $x \succsim y$ or $y \succsim x$ (completeness). Now assume

$x \succsim y$ and $y \succsim z$. Then $u(x) \geq u(y)$ and $u(y) \geq u(z)$, so $u(x) \geq u(z)$ since $\geq$ is transitive over $\mathbb{R}^1$. Hence $x \succsim z$ (transitivity). □

This theorem shows a bit more than may be immediately apparent. *Any* function $u : X \to \mathbb{R}^1$ represents *some* complete and transitive preference relation. Beginning with u, we simply define $\succsim$ by $x \succsim y \Leftrightarrow u(x) \geq u(y)$ for $x, y \in X$.

A utility representation cannot be unique. If u represents $(X, \succsim)$ and $h : \mathbb{R}^1 \to \mathbb{R}^1$ is a strictly increasing function then $h \circ u$ also represents $(X, \succsim)$. Hence there is a great profusion of representations that can be derived from a given representation. This is to be expected. $\succsim$ merely *orders* the points in X; it does not express a strength of preference. Hence the *magnitude* $u(x) - u(y)$ cannot be informative, for this would mean the utility representation of $(X, \succsim)$ conveys more information than the original preference ordering. Only the *ordering* that $u(x) \geq u(y)$ or $u(y) \geq u(x)$ is informative, whence we say that utility is an *ordinal*, not a *cardinal*, concept. A utility function can be thought of as technical tool that, when it exists, eases the task of deriving refutable hypotheses from a behavioral postulate regarding a consumer's objective, but the magnitudes of the numerical values have no meaning.

Some other properties of a utility representation are explored in the exercises. In particular, if u represents $(X, \succsim)$ then $x \succ y \Leftrightarrow u(x) > u(y)$ and $x \sim y \Leftrightarrow u(x) = u(y)$. Thus, when there is a utility representation, the preferred and indifference sets can be defined in terms of that utility function, as follows. Let $U = u(X)$ denote the set of feasible utility levels, which plays a role analogous to the set of feasible output levels Y from producer theory. Then we can define $V : U \to 2^X$ and $I : U \to 2^X$ by:

- Preferred set: $V(\bar{u}) = \{x \in X : u(x) \geq \bar{u}\}$, the set of bundles that are (weakly) preferred to those bundles that deliver feasible utility level $\bar{u}$. This set plays a role analogous to the input requirement set in producer theory; V is the upper contour correspondence of the utility function. It is straightforward from the definitions of U and $V(\bar{u})$ that $u(x) = \max\{\bar{u} \in U : x \in V(\bar{u})\}$ for $x \in \mathbb{R}^n_+$, just as the production function at a given input vector (when it exists as a maximum) is the maximal output level that is jointly feasible with that given input vector.
- Indifference set: $I(\bar{u}) = \{x \in X : u(x) = \bar{u}\}$, the set of bundles that all deliver feasible utility level $\bar{u}$. This set plays a role analogous to the isoquant in producer theory.

Note that an indifference set need not be a "curve." It is a level curve of u just as an isoquant is a level curve of a production function. But a level curve of u is a curve in some conventional sense only if the conditions of the implicit function theorem apply to the equation $u(x) = \bar{u}$ at every x in the indifference set. In that case the implicit function for the ith component of x, $x_i(x_{-i})$, has slope with respect to some other component x_j given by:

$$\frac{\partial x_i(x_{-i})}{\partial x_j} = -\frac{\partial u(x)/\partial x_j}{\partial u(x)/\partial x_i}.$$

The absolute value of this slope is called the *marginal rate of substitution of commodity i for commodity j* (MRS_{ij}), since it gives the rate at which the consumer can substitute commodity i for commodity j while maintaining a constant level of satisfaction. The implicit function theorem requires that $\frac{\partial u}{\partial x_i}$ be nonzero at the point in question. Note that the MRS is a basic property of the preference relation, in that the same MRS arises no matter which utility representation is utilized. In particular, MRS_{ij} at some point $x \in \mathbb{R}^n_{++}$ for the strictly increasing transformation $h o u$, by the chain rule, is:

$$\frac{\partial x_i(x_{-i})}{\partial x_j} = -\frac{h'(u(x))\partial u(x)/\partial x_j}{h'(u(x))\partial u(x)/\partial x_i} = -\frac{\partial u(x)/\partial x_j}{\partial u(x)/\partial x_i}.$$

The important question about utility representations is whether there is a converse to Theorem 8.1. That is, if we have a preference ordering that is complete and transitive, is there necessarily a utility function that represents it? The answer is "no," as established by the following famous counter-example.

Example 8.1 (Lexicographic Preference Relation). Let $X = \mathbb{R}^2_+$ and define $\succsim$ over X as follows: $(x_1, x_2) \succsim (y_1, y_2)$ if and only if either (1) $x_1 > y_1$ or (2) $x_1 = y_1$ and $x_2 \geq y_2$. The basic idea of the lexicographic relation is that it assigns a *unique* position to every point in $\mathbb{R}^2_+$, so that there is no indifference. The lexicographic ordering does this by proceeding hierarchically: If the first component is decisive, then the ordering is established. If not, proceed to the second component. Geometrically, it appears as shown in Fig. 8.1.

Now suppose there were a utility representation u of the lexicographic preference relation. Then, for any $x_1 \in \mathbb{R}^1_+$, we must have $u(x_1, 1) > u(x_1, 0)$ since not($(x_1, 0) \succsim (x_1, 1)$) according to the preference relation. Hence there exists a rational number $r(x_1)$ between $u(x_1, 0)$ and $u(x_1, 1)$. Moreover, $\tilde{x}_1 > x_1 \Rightarrow u(\tilde{x}_1, 0) > u(x_1, 1)$ according to the preference relation. Hence $r(\tilde{x}_1) > r(x_1)$. That is, to each $x_1 \in \mathbb{R}^1_+$ there corresponds a *unique* rational number $r(x_1)$. This contradicts countability of the rational numbers, since $\mathbb{R}^1_+$ is uncountable. Hence there cannot be

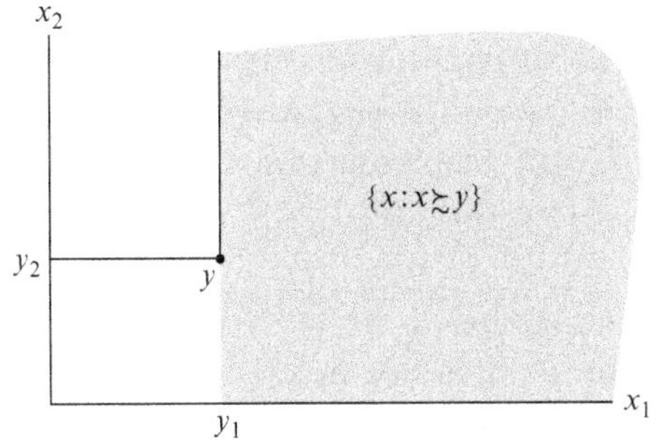

Fig. 8.1 Lexicographic preference relation.

such a function u. Note, however, that the lexicographic preference relation *is* complete and transitive. Thus, this example shows that some additional property must be imposed on a preference relation if we want to ensure existence of a utility representation.

8.2 CONTINUITY

For most applications it suffices to assume $X = \mathbb{R}^n_+$. Then each $x \in X$ is an n-dimensional vector, and we can think of each component as being the quantity of a commodity that is included in the bundle. Thus, there are n commodities. This notion of commodities is quite general. Each component can have a place and time stamp, so that spatial and dynamic problems can be encompassed. In some contexts it is necessary to consider continuous space and/or time, in which case an infinite-dimensional commodity space must be considered. This makes things more complicated. For our purposes, we will henceforth assume $X = \mathbb{R}^n_+$ for n finite.

With the assumption $X = \mathbb{R}^n_+$, the representation problem can be solved using a third assumption on $(X, \succsim)$:

3. Continuity: $\{x \in \mathbb{R}^n_+ : x \succsim y\}$ and $\{x \in \mathbb{R}^n_+ : x \precsim y\}$ are closed sets for every $y \in X$.

Note that the lexicographic preference relation violates this assumption. This assumption is called "continuity" because of the relationship between closed sets and continuous functions. When there is a utility representation, the two sets listed here are the upper and lower contour sets of the utility function, respectively. Recall from Theorem 1.7 that a function is continuous if and only if its hypograph and epigraph are both closed sets. The upper and lower contour sets are "slices" of the hypograph and epigraph, and therefore are closed sets as well.

Theorem 8.2 (Utility Representation Theorem). *There exists a* ***continuous*** *function u that represents* $(\mathbb{R}^n_+, \succsim)$ *if and only if* $(\mathbb{R}^n_+, \succsim)$ *is complete, transitive, and continuous.*

Proof. It is straightforward to show that existence of a continuous representation function u implies completeness, transitivity and continuity. Given u, Theorem 8.1 shows $(\mathbb{R}^n_+, \succsim)$ is complete and transitive. As u represents $(\mathbb{R}^n_+, \succsim)$, for $y \in \mathbb{R}^n_+$ we have:

$$\{x \in \mathbb{R}^n_+ : x \succsim y\} = \{x \in \mathbb{R}^n_+ : u(x) \geq u(y)\} \text{ and}$$
$$\{x \in \mathbb{R}^n_+ : x \precsim y\} = \{x \in \mathbb{R}^n_+ : u(x) \leq u(y)\}.$$

Continuity of u implies these contour sets of u are closed, by Theorem 1.7. Hence $(\mathbb{R}^n_+, \succsim)$ is continuous.

The converse is much more difficult. Assume $(\mathbb{R}^n_+, \succsim)$ is complete, transitive, and continuous. Note that we may assume existence of $x, y \in \mathbb{R}^n_+$ such that $x \prec y$; otherwise every consumption bundle is equally desirable and therefore $(\mathbb{R}^n_+, \succsim)$ is represented by any constant function, for example $u(x) = 0$ for every $x \in \mathbb{R}^n_+$.

Let $\mathbb{Q}^n$ denote the vectors in $\mathbb{R}^n$ with all rational components. The proof proceeds in four steps.

1. Define a function $\hat{u} : \mathbb{Q}^n_+ \to \mathbb{Q}^1$ that represents $(\mathbb{Q}^n_+, \succsim)$.

Any subset of the positive integers is closed and bounded below; and therefore has a minimum if it is nonempty. Select $r^1, r^2 \in \mathbb{Q}^1$ with $r^1 < r^2$. Let $R = \mathbb{Q}^1 \cap (r^1, r^2)$ denote the rationals between r^1 and r^2, and enumerate R as $R = \{r^3, r^4, r^5 \ldots\}$. Given $a \in [r^1, r^2)$ and $b \in (a, r^2]$, $\{q : r^q \in (a, b)\}$ is a set of positive integers and is nonempty because R enumerates all rationals between r^1 and r^2 and the rationals are dense in $\mathbb{R}^1$. Hence this set of indexes has a minimum, even though there is no minimal rational number in the interval (a, b). For $a \in [r^1, r^2)$ and $b \in (a, r^2]$, let:

$$\underline{q}(a, b) = \min\{q : r^q \in (a, b)\}$$

denote this minimal index.

Now let $q_1 = 1$ and $q_2 = 2$. If there exists $x^1 \in \mathbb{Q}^n_+$ such that $x^1 \precsim y$ for every $y \in \mathbb{Q}^n_+$, set $\hat{u}(x^1) = r^{q_1}$. If there exists $x^2 \in \mathbb{Q}^n_+$ such that $x^2 \succsim y$ for every $y \in \mathbb{Q}^n_+$, set $\hat{u}(x^2) = r^{q_2}$. Enumerate the remainder of $\mathbb{Q}_+^n$ as $\{x^3, x^4, x^5, \ldots\}$, and let $X^k = \{x^1, x^2, x^3, \ldots, x^k\}$ (omitting x^1 and/or x^2 if either or both do not exist).

The definition of $\hat{u}$ is given sequentially for $x^3, x^4, \ldots$. To begin, if $x^3 \sim x^i$ for $i = 1, 2$ then let $q_3 = q_i$. Otherwise let $q^3 = \underline{q}(r^{q_1}, r^{q_2})$. Either way, set $\hat{u}(x^3) = r^{q_3}$. Then $\hat{u}$ represents $(X^3, \succsim)$:

a. $x^1 \prec x^2$ (if they exist) because not every consumption bundle is equally desirable, by assumption; and $\hat{u}(x^1) = r^{q_1} = r^1 < r^2 = r^{q_2} = \hat{u}(x^2)$.

b. If $x^3 \sim x^1$ then $\hat{u}(x^3) = r^{q_3} = r^{q_1} = \hat{u}(x^1)$; likewise if $x^3 \sim x^2$.

c. Otherwise, $x^1 \prec x^3 \prec x^2$; while $r^{q_3} \in (r^{q_1}, r^{q_2})$, so $\hat{u}(x^1) = r^{q_1} < r^{q_3} = \hat{u}(x^3) < r^{q_2} = \hat{u}(x^2)$ (to the extent x^1 and/or x^2 exist; if one or both does not exist the definitions still give $r^{q_3} \in (r^{q_1}, r^{q_2})$).

At step $k > 3$, let $p_1, \ldots, p_{k-1}$ be an indexing of $q_1, \ldots, q_{k-1}$ such that:

$$r^{q_{p_m}} \leq r^{q_{p_{m+1}}} \text{ for } m = 1, \ldots, k-2.$$

The sequential definition of q_{p_i} at steps $i = 3, \ldots, k-1$ is:

$$q_{p_i} = \begin{cases} q_{p_m} & \text{if } x^{p_i} \sim x^{p_m} \text{ for some } m = 1, \ldots, i-1 \\ \underline{q}(r^{q_{p_m}}, r^{q_{p_{m+1}}}) & \text{if } x^{p_m} \prec x^{p_i} \prec x^{p_{m+1}} \text{ for some } m = 1, \ldots, i-2 \end{cases}.$$

This same definition is used for q_k at step k by letting $p_k = k$ (the set of q_{p_m} values is added to at each step; the entire p_m indexing is then reset at the next step to place the $r^{q_{p_m}}$ values in ascending order as $m = 1, \ldots, k$). With these q_{p_i} values, $\hat{u}(x^{p_i}) = r^{q_{p_i}}$ for $i = 1, \ldots, k$ represents $(X^k, \succsim)$:

a. $q_{p_i} = q_{p_m}$ is used when x^{p_i} is in the indifference set of some x^{p_m} that occurs earlier in the enumeration of $\mathbb{Q}_+^n$.

b. An index q_{p_i} on a rational strictly between two rationals already assigned is used when x^{p_i} is strictly between (in a preference sense) the two corresponding x^{p_m} values (or q_{p_i} is smaller (larger) than all previously assigned rationals if x^{p_i} is strictly worse (better) than all x^{p_m} that occur earlier in the enumeration of $\mathbb{Q}_+^n$).

c. Completeness ensures this definition assigns an index q to every x^i up to $i = k$ (the p_i indexing is merely a reordering of the integers $1, \ldots, k$).

d. Transitivity ensures this assignment is unique for each x^i and that comparisons between bundles in X^k that are not adjacent in a preference sense have the same ordering as the assigned $\hat{u}$ values.

Continuing for $k = 3, 4, \ldots$ yields $\hat{u}(x^p) = r^{q_p}$ for $p = 1, 2, \ldots$ that represents $(\mathbb{Q}^n_+, \succsim)$.

2. The particular $\hat{u}$ defined in step 1 is onto R.

We first show that for $x, y \in \mathbb{R}^n_+$, if $x \prec y$ then there exists $z \in \mathbb{Q}^n_+$ such that $x \prec z \prec y$. Let $z(\alpha) = (1-\alpha)x + \alpha y$ for $\alpha \in [0, 1]$. Note that:

$$\underline{\alpha} = \inf\{\alpha \in [0,1] : z(\alpha) \succsim y\}$$

is an element of this set because the set is nonempty ($\alpha = 1$ is an element), bounded below (by $\alpha = 0$), and closed (by continuity of $(\mathbb{R}^n_+, \succsim)$). Hence $z(\underline{\alpha}) \succsim y$, implying $\underline{\alpha} > 0$ because $z(0) = x$; and $z(\alpha) \prec y$ for every $\alpha \in [0, \underline{\alpha})$. Similarly:

$$\bar{\alpha} = \sup\{\alpha \in [0, \underline{\alpha}] : x \succsim z(\alpha)\}$$

is an element of this set because the set is nonempty ($\alpha = 0$ is an element), bounded above (by $\alpha = \underline{\alpha}$), and closed (by continuity of $(\mathbb{R}^n_+, \succsim)$). Hence $x \succsim z(\bar{\alpha})$, implying $\bar{\alpha} < \underline{\alpha}$; and $x \prec z(\alpha)$ for every $\alpha \in (\bar{\alpha}, \underline{\alpha}]$. We now have $x \prec z(\alpha) \prec y$ for every $\alpha \in (\bar{\alpha}, \underline{\alpha})$, a nonempty interval. By continuity, $\{z \in \mathbb{R}^n_+ : x \prec z \prec y\}$ is an open set (in $\mathbb{R}^n_+$). Select any α for which $z(\alpha)$ is an element, form a ball that is contained in the set about this $z(\alpha)$, and recall that every such ball contains elements of $\mathbb{Q}^n_+$ due to density of the rationals in $\mathbb{R}^n$.

Now consider the subset of R that is not in the image of $\hat{u}$: $S = R - \hat{u}(\mathbb{Q}^n_+)$. The task is to show S is empty. Continuing to use the enumeration of R introduced in step 1, if $\{q : r^q \in S\}$ is nonempty then it has a minimum q^*. r^q is an element of $\hat{u}(\mathbb{Q}^n_+)$ for every $q < q^*$, so there exists a step k in the sequential definition of $\hat{u}$ such that r^q is an element of $\hat{u}(X^k)$ for every $q < q^*$. Let $p_1, \ldots, p_k$ be the indexing of $q_1, \ldots, q_k$ such that $r^{q_{p_m}}$ is in ascending order as $m = 1, \ldots, k$. As $r^1 < r^{q^*} < r^2$, we have $r^{q_{p_m}} < r^{q^*} < r^{q_{p_{m+1}}}$ for some $m = 1, \ldots, k-1$. As there exists x^p such that $x^{p_m} \prec x^p \prec x^{p_{m+1}}$:

$$p^* = \min\{p : x^{p_m} \prec x^p \prec x^{p_{m+1}}\}$$

exists, and $p^* > k$ because $X^k = \{x^{p_1}, \ldots, x^{p_k}\}$ (if $m = 1$ ($m = k-1$) and x^1 (x^2) does not exist the set is modified to omit x^{p_m} ($x^{p_{m+1}}$); it is still nonempty because in this case $\mathbb{Q}^n_+$ has no worst (best) element). At step p^* in the sequential definition of $\hat{u}$, we set $\hat{u}(x^{p^*}) = r^{q_{p^*}}$, where:

$$q_{p^*} = \min\{q : r^q \in (r^{q_{p_m}}, r^{q_{p_{m+1}}})\} = q^*.$$

This contradicts that r^{q^*} is an element of S (i.e., that it is not an element of the image of $\hat{u}$).

3. Extend $\hat{u}$ to a function $u : \mathbb{R}^n_+ \to \mathbb{R}^1$ that represents $(\mathbb{R}^n_+, \succsim)$.

If there exists $x \in \mathbb{R}^n_+$ such that $x \precsim y$ for every $y \in \mathbb{R}^n_+$, set $u(x) = r^1$ (if x^1 exists then $x = x^1$; otherwise there would exist a rational bundle between x and x^1 (in a preference sense), contradicting existence of x^1). If there exists $x \in \mathbb{R}^n_+$ such that $x \succsim y$ for every $y \in \mathbb{R}^n_+$, set $u(x) = r^2$ (if x^2 exists then $x = x^2$).

For any other $x \in \mathbb{R}^n_+$, denote by $\underline{\hat{u}}(x) = \inf\{\hat{u}(y) : y \in \mathbb{Q}^n_+$ and $y \succsim x\}$ the utility from the worst rational consumption bundle that is at least as desirable as x; and by $\bar{\hat{u}}(x) = \sup\{\hat{u}(y) : y \in \mathbb{Q}^n_+$ and $y \precsim x\}$ the utility from the best rational consumption bundle that is no more desirable than x (both sets are contained in (r^1, r^2), and nonempty by the existence of intermediate consumption bundles and the assumption that not all bundles are equally desirable). We have $\bar{\hat{u}}(x) \leq \underline{\hat{u}}(x)$ because $y \precsim x \precsim y'$ implies $\hat{u}(y) \leq \hat{u}(y')$ (since $\hat{u}$ represents $(\mathbb{Q}^n_+, \succsim)$). Moreover, if $\bar{\hat{u}}(x) < \underline{\hat{u}}(x)$ then there exists a rational between these two real numbers, while for each $y \in \mathbb{Q}^n_+$ either $\hat{u}(y) \leq \bar{\hat{u}}(x)$ or $\underline{\hat{u}}(x) \leq \hat{u}(y)$, contradicting that $\hat{u}$ is onto R. Hence $\bar{\hat{u}}(x) = \underline{\hat{u}}(x)$. Set $u(x) = \bar{\hat{u}}(x) = \underline{\hat{u}}(x)$.

If $x \in \mathbb{Q}^n_+$ then $\hat{u}(x)$ is an element of each set of utility values, providing a lower bound to the first and an upper bound to the second. In this case, $u(x) = \hat{u}(x)$. Hence u is indeed an extension of $\hat{u}$. Moreover:

$$\begin{aligned} x \precsim x' \Leftrightarrow \quad & \{\hat{u}(y) : y \in \mathbb{Q}^n_+ \text{ and } y \precsim x\} \subset \{\hat{u}(y) : y \in \mathbb{Q}^n_+ \text{ and } y \precsim x'\} \\ \Leftrightarrow \quad & u(x) \leq u(x'), \end{aligned}$$

so u represents $(\mathbb{R}^n_+, \succsim)$.

4. The particular u defined in step 3 is continuous.

Using Theorem 1.7, we show that $\{x \in \mathbb{R}^n_+ : u(x) \geq \bar{u}\}$ is a closed set for arbitrary $\bar{u} \in \mathbb{R}^1$ (a similar argument shows $\{x \in \mathbb{R}^n_+ : u(x) \leq \bar{u}\}$ is closed). If $\bar{u} > r^2$ then the set in question is empty and therefore trivially closed, so assume henceforth that $\bar{u} \leq r^2$. Note that, for $r^q \leq \bar{u}$:

$$\{x \in \mathbb{R}^n_+ : u(x) \geq \bar{u}\} \subset \{x \in \mathbb{R}^n_+ : u(x) \geq r^q\}.$$

Conversely:

$$\{x \in \mathbb{R}^n_+ : u(x) \geq \bar{u}\} \supset \bigcap_{r^q \leq \bar{u}} \{x \in \mathbb{R}^n_+ : u(x) \geq r^q\}$$

because, if this were not true, there would exist $x \in \mathbb{R}^n_+$ satisfying $r^q \leq u(x) < \bar{u} \leq r^2$ for every rational $r^q \leq \bar{u}$, contradicting density of R in $[r^1, r^2]$. Hence:

$$\{x \in \mathbb{R}^n_+ : u(x) \geq \bar{u}\} = \bigcap_{r^q \leq \bar{u}} \{x \in \mathbb{R}^n_+ : u(x) \geq r^q\}.$$

From step 2, u is onto R. That is, to each q there corresponds $x^q \in \mathbb{R}^n_+$ such that $u(x^q) = r^q$. Hence:

$$\{x \in \mathbb{R}^n_+ : u(x) \geq \bar{u}\} = \bigcap_{u(x^q) \leq \bar{u}} \{x \in \mathbb{R}^n_+ : u(x) \geq u(x^q)\}.$$

As u represents $(\mathbb{R}^n_+, \succsim)$:

$$\{x \in \mathbb{R}^n_+ : u(x) \geq \bar{u}\} = \bigcap_{u(x^q) \leq \bar{u}} \{x \in \mathbb{R}^n_+ : x \succsim x^q\}.$$

By continuity of $(\mathbb{R}^n_+, \succsim)$, the right side is an intersection of closed sets and is therefore closed. □

The Utility Representation Theorem shows *there is an equivalence between complete, transitive, and continuous preference relations and continuous utility functions. One always implies existence of the other with the same hierarchy of desirability, so it makes no difference which is used as a starting point for analysis of consumer choice.* As the Theorem ensures existence of a *continuous* utility function, by the intermediate value theorem the set of feasible utility levels U is an interval in $\mathbb{R}^1$. Usually we confine attention to the set of *relevant* utility levels $[u(0), \sup U) \subset U$, which is analogous to the set $[f(0), \sup Y)$ of relevant single-output levels in producer theory. There may be feasible utility levels smaller than $u(0)$ but they are economically irrelevant since they cannot be optimal under the behavioral postulates we will consider (if there is global satiation, $\sup U$ is a feasible utility level, in which case we close the interval). Note also that it is sometimes possible to represent preferences that are complete and transitive, but not continuous, with a utility function. Theorem 8.1 shows that completeness and transitivity are necessary for a representation, but Theorem 8.2 shows that continuity of a preference relation is necessary only for existence of a *continuous* representation. Exercise 12 asks you to construct a counter-example to necessity of preference continuity; the utility function cannot be continuous in such cases.

8.3 FURTHER AXIOMS

Although completeness, transitivity, and continuity are the central properties for a utility representation of a preference ordering, we sometimes make use of additional properties. Let $x, x', y \in X = \mathbb{R}^n_+$. The most important additional properties are:

4. Free Disposal (or Weak Monotonicity): $x \geq y \Rightarrow x \succsim y$.
5. Local Nonsatiation: For every $x \in \mathbb{R}^n_+$ and $\epsilon > 0$, there exists $y \in \mathbb{R}^n_+$ such that $\|y - x\| \leq \epsilon$ and $y \succ x$.
6. Convexity: $x \succsim y$ and $x' \succsim y$ together imply $\alpha x + (1 - \alpha)x' \succsim y$ for every $\alpha \in (0, 1)$.
7. Strict Convexity: $x \succsim y$ and $x' \succsim y$ $(x \neq x')$ together imply $\alpha x + (1 - \alpha)x' \succ y$ for every $\alpha \in (0, 1)$.

These properties can be conveniently illustrated on a graph of preferred and indifference sets when $n = 2$.

Fig. 8.2 illustrates free disposal. Starting from any particular consumption bundle (y_1, y_2), preferences display free disposal if and only if the shaded area is contained in the preferred set to (y_1, y_2). As multiple particular consumption bundles are considered, it is clear that the boundary of each preferred set cannot slope upward when there is free disposal. Note, however, that the points in the shaded area need not be strictly preferred to (y_1, y_2). For example, the dark shaded area could be in the indifference set to (y_1, y_2). Free disposal implies MRS_{ij} is nonpositive (before taking the absolute value) when it exists.

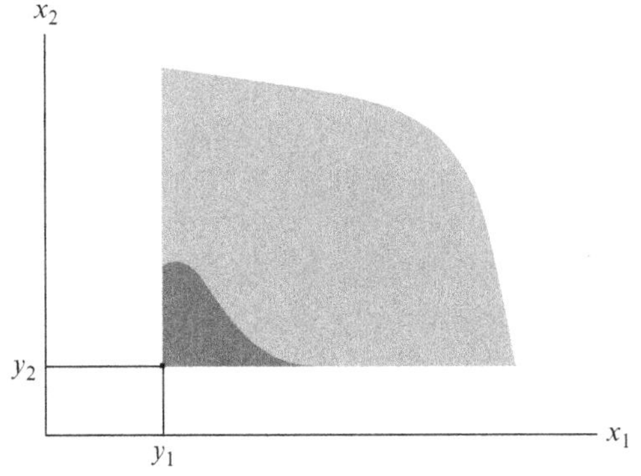

Fig. 8.2 Preferences with free disposal.

Local nonsatiation is illustrated in Fig. 8.3. At any bundle (x_1^0, x_2^0), a ball drawn about that point with any positive radius must contain a bundle y that is strictly preferred to (x_1^0, x_2^0). The bundle y need not include more of any commodity; it simply must be within an arbitrarily small radius of the original point. Note that the requirement is that the strictly preferred point be in the consumption set. Thus, at a point like x^1, the strictly preferred point must be in the illustrated semicircle. Local nonsatiation is a non-calculus version of the assumption that the Jacobian of u is nonzero at x, which is used in the implicit function theorem to derive the MRS at x.

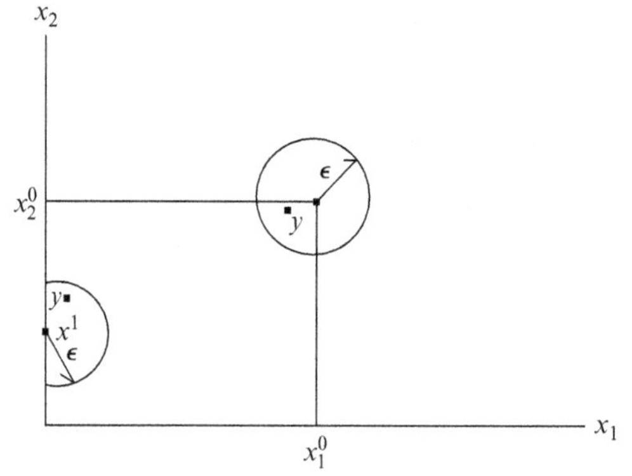

Fig. 8.3 Preferences with local nonsatiation.

Convexity and strict convexity refer to the shape of the preferred sets, with the usual interpretations for convex sets. Loosely speaking, convexity requires that the boundary of each preferred set not bend away from the interior but allows for linear segments on the boundary. Strict convexity rules out linear boundary segments. Note that convexity is equivalent to quasiconcavity of the utility function when there is a utility representation because the preferred sets are the upper contour sets of u (Theorem 3.11). Note also that strict convexity implies local nonsatiation; an indifference set cannot have an interior because, if it did, the convex combination of any point in that interior with an interior point within an $\epsilon-$ball of the first point would lie entirely in the interior. That is, all points on the convex combination would be equally desirable, contradicting the strict convexity property. Convexity implies MRS_{ij} is nonincreasing in x_j when it exists; strict convexity implies MRS is strictly decreasing.

Another property sometimes used is the "more is better" assumption, although it is not needed in most contexts and is a rather strong characteristic of preferences:

8. Strong Monotonicity: $x > y \Rightarrow x \succ y$.

This property is illustrated similarly to free disposal. In Fig. 8.2 the entire shaded area must be strictly preferred to (y_1, y_2), including the lines directly above and to the right of (y_1, y_2). The dark shaded area cannot be in the indifference set when there is strong monotonicity (strong monotonicity implies local nonsatiation). Strong monotonicity implies a negative MRS (before taking the absolute value).

8.4 NOTES

Debreu [1, ch. 4] defines the consumption set and discusses most of the properties of a preference relation. Completeness was first introduced by Pareto [2, 3], although the term completeness was not used. Transitivity and weak monotonicity were introduced by Wold [4, p. 222]. Wold [5, p. 95] also introduced strong monotonicity, at least in its current form. Wold [4, p. 223] is responsible for continuity as well, at least in the sense that there is a consumption bundle "between" $x \prec y$ and any continuous curve from x to y intersects all intermediate indifference sets. Local nonsatiation can be found in Koopmans [6, p. 47]. Schmeidler [7] shows that completeness is redundant when transitivity and local nonsatiation hold, provided $x \succ y$ is redefined as "not $(y \succsim x)$ *and* $x \succsim y$."

The first preference representation theorem by a continuous utility function appears in Wold [4, pp. 224–226, 259–262] and relies on monotonicity. The version in the text that gives an equivalence between a complete, transitive, and continuous preference relation and a continuous utility function is due to Debreu [8][1, §4.6(1)], although some of the details in the text differ from Debreu's original proof. Rader [9] weakens Debreu's continuity assumption by discarding the requirement that $\{x \in \mathbb{R}^n_+ : x \precsim y\}$ be closed, requiring only that $\{x \in \mathbb{R}^n_+ : x \succsim y\}$ be closed. Rader calls this "upper continuity" of preferences, which he characterizes as allowing for consumer "aspiration," and he shows equivalence between complete, transitive (Rader weakens the transitivity assumption as well) and upper continuous preferences and existence of an upper semicontinuous utility function that represents those preferences. Upper semicontinuity is adequate for existence of a utility maximum but not for the zero excess utility property of an expenditure minimum (i.e., that a Hicksian demand point yields exactly the target level of utility) which, in turn, is necessary for equivalence between a utility maximum and expenditure minimum and therefore plays a role in establishing the Hicks-Slutsky Decomposition. Debreu [1, pp. 72–73] presents the counterexample of the lexicographic preference relation. Both Debreu and Rader present their results in more abstract consumption sets than $\mathbb{R}^n_+$. Further consolidations and generalizations in this direction are presented in Debreu [10], Jaffray [11], and Beardon and Mehta [12]. Derivation of demand behavior through the use of a convexity assumption in lieu of transitivity is examined by Sonnenschein [13] and Chipman [14]. Some of these authors discuss representation of a preference relation that may not be complete or transitive. For this to be possible the utility function cannot be defined on the entire consumption set. This is why completeness and transitivity are necessary for the utility representations discussed herein. Part of the definition of a representation given herein is that the domain of the utility function is the entire consumption set.

Arrow and Hahn present a utility representation theorem that has a nice interpretation in terms of Euclidean distance [15, §4.2]. Glustoff [16] observes that there is some confusion in their presentation concerning the role of local nonsatiation, and tries to correct Arrow and Hahn. However, Mehta [17] notes an error in Glustoff and concludes that the Euclidean distance approach is untenable unless preferences are locally nonsatiable.

The debate about ordinal versus cardinal utility has a long history dating from the Marginalist Era. Pareto [3, pp. 159, 540–542] is the first to argue that only ordinality matters for consumer choice theory, but does not make use of this observation. The issue is resolved definitively by Slutsky [18] (see Stigler [19] for a discussion). Hicks and Allen [20, 21] construct a theory of consumer choice using the marginal rate of substitution as the primitive concept rather than the utility function, thereby avoiding cardinality.

The relationships between convex preferences and quasiconcave utility functions are discussed by Debreu [1, p. 73], where further notes and references may be found. Barten and Böhm [22] provide a more modern summary, while Wold [5, 23] and Stigler [19, 24] provide summaries of early work.

8.5 EXERCISES

1. Assume $(X, \succsim)$ is a complete and transitive preference ordering. Using *only* the completeness and transitivity assumptions, show for $x, y, z \in X$:

a. $x \succ y$ and $y \succ x$ cannot both hold.
b. $x \succ x$ cannot hold (i.e., $\succ$ is *irreflexive*).
c. $\succ$ is transitive.
d. $x \succsim y$ and $y \succ z$ together imply $x \succ z$.
e. $x \succ y$ and $y \succsim z$ together imply $x \succ z$.
f. $x \sim x$ (i.e., $\sim$ is *reflexive*).
g. $\sim$ is transitive.
h. If $x \sim y$ then $y \sim x$ (i.e., $\sim$ is *symmetric*).

2. Assume $u : \mathbb{R}^n_+ \to \mathbb{R}^1_+$ represents $(\mathbb{R}^n_+, \succsim)$ and is continuous. Prove the following:
a. $x \succ y$ if and only if $u(x) > u(y)$.
b. $x \sim y$ if and only if $u(x) = u(y)$.
c. If $(\mathbb{R}^n_+, \succsim)$ has the free disposal property then u is nondecreasing.
d. If $(\mathbb{R}^n_+, \succsim)$ has the strong monotonicity property then u is strictly increasing.
e. If $(\mathbb{R}^n_+, \succsim)$ has the local nonsatiation property then: For every $x \in X$ and $\epsilon > 0$ there exists $y \in X$ such that $\|y - x\| \leq \epsilon$ and $u(y) > u(x)$ (i.e., u is *locally non-maximal*).
f. If $(\mathbb{R}^n_+, \succsim)$ has the convexity property then u is a quasiconcave function.
g. If $(\mathbb{R}^n_+, \succsim)$ has the strict convexity property then u is a strictly quasiconcave function.

3. Show that the lexicographic preference relation is both strongly monotonic and strictly convex.

4. Are there optimal choice(s) for a price-taking consumer with standard lexicographic preferences despite the unusual nature of the preferences? If so, describe the optimal choice(s). If not, explain why not.

5. State whether each of the following preferences on $\mathbb{R}^2_+$ have each of the following properties, and explain why in each case: Complete, transitive, continuous, local nonsatiation, free disposal, convex. Also state whether there is a utility function that represents the preferences and, if so, give one such function; if not, explain why not.
a. $(x_1, x_2) \succsim (y_1, y_2)$ if and only if either $x_1 + x_2 \geq 1$ or $y_1 < 1$.
b. In the following graph, C and $B \cap C$ both include their boundaries, and B is all of $\mathbb{R}^2_+$ except the part labeled C. The preferences are defined by: $y \succsim x$ if and only if either 1) $x \in B$ and $y \in B$, or 2) $x \in C$.

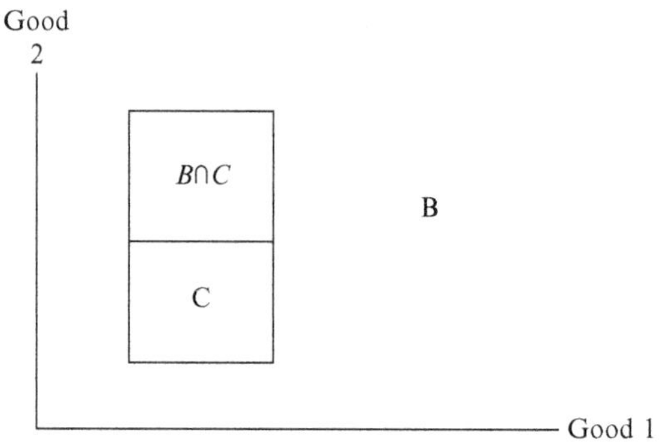

c. $(x_1, x_2) \succsim (y_1, y_2)$ if and only if $|x_1 - 10| + |x_2 - 10| \geq |y_1 - 10| + |y_2 - 10|$.

6. A consumer has the following preferences $(\mathbb{R}^2_+, \succsim)$: For $(x_1, x_2) \in \mathbb{R}^2_+$ and $(y_1, y_2) \in \mathbb{R}^2_+$, $(x_1, x_2) \succsim (y_1, y_2)$ if and only if one of the following holds:
   a. $x_1 = y_1 = 0$ and $x_2 \geq y_2$; or
   b. $x_1 = 0$ and $y_1 > 0$; or
   c. $x_1 x_2 \geq y_1 y_2$ and $y_1 > 0$.

   Explain whether these preferences have each of the following properties: Complete, transitive, continuous, and local nonsatiation. Provide a utility representation, if one exists. If a utility representation does not exist, explain why.
7. A consumer has the following preferences $(\mathbb{R}^2_+, \succsim)$: For $(x_1, x_2) \in \mathbb{R}^2_+$ and $(y_1, y_2) \in \mathbb{R}^2_+$, $(x_1, x_2) \succsim (y_1, y_2)$ if and only if one of the following holds:
   a. $x_1 \leq 1$ and $y_1 \leq 1$ and $x_1^{1/3} + x_2^{1/3} \geq y_1^{1/3} + y_2^{1/3}$.
   b. $x_1 > 1$ and $x_1 \geq y_1$.

   Explain whether these preferences have each of the following properties: Complete, transitive, continuous, and local nonsatiation. Provide a utility representation, if one exists. If a utility representation does not exist, explain why. Irrespective of whether a utility representation exists, derive the Marshallian demand.
8. Suppose the consumption set X is the set of nonnegative integers. Consider the following preferences: For $x \in X$ and $y \in X$, $x \succsim y$ if and only if x is an even number.
   a. Is $(X, \succsim)$ complete? Why?
   b. Is $(X, \succsim)$ transitive? Why?
   c. Does $(X, \succsim)$ satisfy free disposal? Why?

9. Suppose $X = \{\text{Tree}, \text{Grass}, \text{Iron}, \text{Flower}\}$ is a consumption set and $\succsim$ is a binary relation defined on X as follows: For $a \in X$ and $b \in X$, $a \succsim b$ if and only if a is a plant.
a. Is $(X, \succsim)$ complete? Why?
b. Is $(X, \succsim)$ transitive? Why?

10. The color of visible light is determined by the wave length of the light, which ranges continuously from red (longest visible wave length) to violet (shortest visible wave length). Three of the visible wave lengths are called red, blue, and yellow. Suppose my preferences concerning visible wave lengths are:

$x \succsim x$, for any visible wave length x
red $\succsim$ blue
yellow $\succsim$ blue
yellow $\succsim$ red
$y \succsim x$, where y is red, blue, or yellow and x is any other wave length.

a. Are these preferences complete, transitive and continuous on the set of visible wavelengths? Explain.
b. Suppose we augment these preferences with $y \succsim x$ when neither y nor x is red, blue, or yellow. Give a utility function that represents these augmented preferences, if it is possible to do so; otherwise, explain why a utility function does not exist.

11. Sound audible to humans has wave frequencies that vary continuously from 12 Hertz (very low bass sound) to 20,000 Hz (very high-pitched sound). Suppose my preferences concerning audible sound are fully described by:

not(10,000 Hz $\succsim y$), if y is any audible wave length other than 10,000 Hz
$x \succsim y$, if x and y are any audible wave lengths other than 10,000 Hz satisfying $x \leq y$.

Are these preferences complete, transitive and continuous on the set of audible wave lengths? Explain. Give a utility function that represents these preferences and discuss its properties.

12. Give an example of preferences that are complete and transitive, but not continuous, and for which a utility representation exists (provide the representation). Can you give an example of preferences that are complete and continuous, but not transitive, for which a utility function exists? Explain.

13. Consider the following preferences. The consumption set is the set of real numbers between zero and one, inclusive: $[0, 1]$. The ordering for x and y in this set is: $x \succsim y$ if and only if either: (1) x and y are both irrational, or (2) x is rational and y is irrational, or (3) x and y are both rational and $x_n \geq y_n$, where the subscript n denotes the integer numerator of the rational number when it is written in its most reduced form.

a. Are these preferences complete?

b. Are these preferences transitive?

c. Is there a utility function that represents these preferences? Is not, explain why. If so, give such a function and discuss whether it is continuous.

14. Carefully draw enough indifference curves for each of the following utility functions on $\mathbb{R}^2_+$ to get an accurate assessment of the shape of the indifference family. Label important points and slopes at important points. Then state whether the preferences represented by each utility function have each of the following properties, and explain why in each case: Complete, transitive, continuous, locally nonsatiable, free disposal, and convex.

a. $u(x_1, x_2) = \begin{cases} x_1^2, & x_1 \neq 10 \\ 200 + x_2, & x_1 = 10 \end{cases}.$

b. $u(x, y) = \sqrt{x^2 + (y - 10)^2}$.

c. $u(x_1, x_2) = x_2 - (x_1 - 1)^2$.

d. $u(x_1, x_2) = g(x_1 + x_2)$, where:

$$g(z) = \begin{cases} z & 0 \leq z \leq 1 \\ 2 - z & 1 \leq z \leq 2 \\ z - 2 & 2 \leq z \end{cases}.$$

e. $u(x_1, x_2) = x_1^2 + 2x_2$.

15. Assume $(\mathbb{R}^n_+, \succsim)$ is complete. Two properties that $\succsim$ might possess are:

- Nonsatiation: For every $y \in \mathbb{R}^n_+$, there exists $x \in \mathbb{R}^n_+$ such that $x \succ y$. Note: This is NOT local because there is no requirement that x be "close" to y.
- Semi-Strict Convexity: If $x \succ y$ and $x' \succsim y$ (x, y, x' all elements of $\mathbb{R}^n_+$) then $\alpha x + (1 - \alpha)x' \succ y$ for every $\alpha \in (0, 1)$.

a. Prove $(\mathbb{R}^n_+, \succsim)$ has the local nonsatiation property when it has the nonsatiation and semi-strict convexity properties.

b. Prove $(\mathbb{R}^n_+, \succsim)$ has the nonsatiation property when it has the local nonsatiation property.

c. Give an example of $(\mathbb{R}^n_+, \succsim)$ that has the nonsatiation property but not the local nonsatiation property (this shows that item (a) relies on semi-strict convexity).

d. Prove $(\mathbb{R}^n_+, \succsim)$ has the local nonsatiation property when it has the strong monotonicity property. Give an example showing that the converse can fail.

e. Give an example of $(\mathbb{R}^n_+, \succsim)$ that is transitive, continuous, and has the semi-strict convexity property but does not have the nonsatiation property (and therefore, by item (a), does not have the local nonsatiation property).

f. Prove that, if $n = 1$ and $\succsim$ is strongly monotonic, then there exists a continuous utility representation of $\succsim$ on X (do not rely on the utility representation theorem in the text).

16. Suppose there are three commodities in the world: Guns, Butter, and Mayonnaise. Ann, Beth, and Carol each have complete and transitive preferences over these three goods. Pop U. List is a politician elected by Ann, Beth, and Carol; who has the following preferences over these three goods:

> *"I think commodity 1 is at least as good as commodity 2 if and only if a majority of my constituents think commodity 1 is at least as good as commodity 2."*

Are Pop's preferences complete and transitive? Why or why not?

17. Suppose the consumption set is the collection of all cars in the world. Alice has no opinion about car 1 and car 2 unless car 1 is a BMW, in which case she thinks car 1 is at least as good as car 2. Is there a utility function that represents Alice's preferences? Why/why not?

18. **a.** Give an example of a preference relation that is complete but not transitive.

b. Give an example of a preference relation that is transitive but not complete.

c. For each example you gave, either give a utility function that represents the preferences or explain why you cannot construct such a function.

19. Assume the consumption set is $\mathbb{R}^3_+$. Here is a description of the preferences of two consumers on this consumption set:

Consumer 1: Utility increases by 1 unit when consumption of good 1 increases by 1 unit; utility increases by 1 unit when consumption of good 2 increases by 1 unit; utility decreases by 1 unit when consumption of good 3 increases by 1 unit. These utility increments do not vary with the total amounts consumed of the goods.

Consumer 2: Utility increases by 1 unit when consumption of good 1 increases by 1/2 unit; utility increases by 1 unit when consumption of good 2 increases by 1/2 unit; utility decreases by 1 unit when consumption of good 3 increases by 1/2 unit. These utility increments do not vary with the total amounts consumed of the goods.

a. Explain whether each consumer's preferences are complete, transitive, continuous, locally nonsatiable, convex, and monotonic.
b. In what way, if any, do the preferences of the two consumers differ?

20. Suppose a consumer's preferences are represented by a utility function that is not monotone. What standard properties must this consumer's preferences satisfy? Why? What standard properties are definitely not satisfied by this consumer's preferences? Why?

21. Assume the preferences $(\mathbb{R}^1, \succsim)$ are defined by: $x \succsim y$ if and only if either (a) $x > 1$ and $y < -1$, or (b) $x > 1$ and $y > 1$, or (c) $x < -1$ and $y < -1$. Are these preferences (i) complete? (ii) transitive? Why/why not?

22. Consider a consumer with utility function $u = x_1x_2 + x_1^2x_2^2 + \ln x_1 + \ln x_2$ for $(x_1, x_2) \in \mathbb{R}^2_{++}$. Does this consumer have Cobb-Douglas preferences? Carefully explain why or why not.

23. Bozo has preferences $(\mathbb{R}^2_+, \succsim)$ defined by:

$$(x_1, x_2) \succsim (y_1, y_2) \text{ if } x_1 \geq y_1 \text{ or } x_2 \geq y_2 \,.$$

Are Bozo's preferences:
a. complete?
b. transitive?
c. strongly monotonic?
d. convex?

24. A consumer has a utility function of the form $u(x_1, x_2) = x_1^a + x_2^b$ on $\mathbb{R}^2_+$, where both a and b are nonnegative. What additional restrictions on the values of the parameters a and b are imposed by each of the following assumptions?
a. Preferences are homogenous.
b. Preferences are homogenous and convex.
c. Goods x_1 and x_2 are perfect substitutes.

25. Mr. Aristotle's consumption set is $\mathbb{R}^2_+$ and his preferences are as follows:

> *"When comparing a bundle in which the quantities of the two items are the same to another bundle in which the quantities of the two items are the same, I strictly prefer the bundle with larger quantities and am indifferent if the two bundles are the same. All bundles with unequal quantities of the two items are identical to me, and are strictly worse than all bundles having equal quantities of the two items."*

a. Draw a graph of indifference curves for Mr. Aristotle that clearly shows the important features of his preferences.

b. Are these preferences: Complete, continuous, transitive, locally nonsatiable, monotonic (weak or strong), and convex? Explain why for each property.

c. Is there a utility representation of these preferences? If so, provide a utility function. If not, explain why not.

REFERENCES

[1] Debreu G. Theory of value. Cowles Foundation for Research in Economics Monograph 17; 1959.

[2] Pareto V. Cours d'économie Politique; 1896–1897. Lausanne.

[3] Pareto V. Manuale di Economia Politica; 1906. Milan.

[4] Wold H. A synthesis of pure demand analysis, Part II. Skandinavist Aktuarietidskrift 1943;26:220–63.

[5] Wold H. A synthesis of pure demand analysis, Part I. Skandinavist Aktuarietidskrift 1943;26:85–118.

[6] Koopmans TC. Three essays on the state of economic science. New York: McGraw-Hill; 1957.

[7] Schmeidler D. A condition for the completeness of partial preference relations. Econometrica 1971;39:403–4.

[8] Debreu G. Representation of a preference ordering by a numerical function. In: Thrall RM, Coombs CH, Davis RL, editors. Decision processes. New York: Wiley; 1954. p. 159–65.

[9] Rader T. The existence of a utility function to represent preferences. Rev Econ Stud 1963;30:229–32.

[10] Debreu G. Continuity properties of Paretian utility. Int Econ Rev 1964;5:285–93.

[11] Jaffray J-Y. Existence of a continuous utility function: an elementary proof. Econometrica 1975;43:981–3.

[12] Beardon AF, Mehta GB. The utility theorems of Wold, Debreu, and Arrow-Hahn. Econometrica 1994;62:181–6.

[13] Sonnenschein HF. Demand theory without transitive preferences, with applications to the theory of competitive equilibrium. In: Chipman JS, Hurwicz L, Richter MK, Sonnenschein HF, editors. Preferences, utility, and demand. New York: Harcourt Brace Jovanovich; 1971. p. 215–23.

[14] Chipman JS. Consumption theory without transitive indifference. In: Chipman JS, Hurwicz L, Richter MK, Sonnenschein HF, editors. Preferences, utility, and demand. New York: Harcourt Brace Jovanovich; 1971. p. 224–53.

[15] Arrow KJ, Hahn FH. General competitive analysis. San Francisco: Holden-Day; 1971.

[16] Glustoff E. On continuous utility: the Euclidean distance approach. Q J Econ 1975;89:512–7.

[17] Mehta GB. The Euclidean distance approach to continuous utility functions. Q J Econ 1991;106:975–7.

[18] Slutsky E. Sulla Teoria del Bilancio del Consumatore. Giornale degli Economistri e Rivista di Statistica 1915;51:1–26. English Translation: On the theory of the budget of the consumer. In: Boulding KE, Stigler GJ, editors. Readings in price theory. London: George Allen and Unwin; 1953. p. 27–56.

[19] Stigler GJ. The development of utility theory I. J Polit Econ 1950;58:307–27.

[20] Hicks JR, Allen RGD. A reconsideration of the theory of value, Part I. Economica 1934;1:52–76.

[21] Hicks JR, Allen RGD. A reconsideration of the theory of value, Part II. Economica 1934;1:196–219.

[22] Barten AP, Böhm V. Consumer theory. In: Arrow KJ, Intrilligator MD, editors. Handbook of mathematical economics; vol. II. Amsterdam: North-Holland; 1982. p. 381–429.

[23] Wold H. A synthesis of pure demand analysis, Part III. Skandinavist Aktuarietidskrift 1944;27:69–120.

[24] Stigler GJ. The development of utility theory II. J Polit Econ 1950;58:373–96.

CHAPTER 9

Expenditure Minimization

Chapter Outline

9.1 BASIC OPTIMIZATION POSTULATE

The last chapter described properties of a preference ordering over a consumption set X. Now we add an optimizing behavioral postulate and study the properties of the optimum. We continue to assume $X = \mathbb{R}^n_+$, so that a vector $x \in X$ is a *commodity bundle*. We also assume the preference ordering is complete, transitive, and continuous; so that we can proceed by using a continuous utility representation u of the preference ordering. The set of feasible utility levels is $U = u(\mathbb{R}^n_+)$ and depends on the utility representation. $V : U \to 2^{\mathbb{R}^n_+}$ is the upper contour correspondence of the utility function: $V(\bar{u}) = \{x \in \mathbb{R}^n_+ : u(x) \geq \bar{u}\}$.

Let $p \in \mathbb{R}^n_+$ be a nonnegative price vector, one price for each commodity. We begin with the behavioral postulate that a price-taking consumer chooses a commodity bundle x to minimize the expenditure $e(x; p) = p^{\perp}x$ required to achieve a given feasible level of utility $\bar{u} \in U$. The choice variable for the expenditure minimization behavioral postulate is x and the parameters are $(p, \bar{u})$. The expenditure minimization behavioral postulate leads to an optimal value function $e^*(p, \bar{u}) = \inf\{p^{\perp}x : x \in V(\bar{u})\}$ and optimal choice correspondence $h^*(p, \bar{u}) = \{x \in V(\bar{u}) : p^{\perp}x = e^*(p, \bar{u})\}$, which are the *expenditure function* and *Hicksian (or compensated) demand correspondence*, respectively, of the consumer.

With two commodities, the minimization can be illustrated as in Fig. 9.1. The consumer's objective is to choose a value of x that places it on the lowest isoexpenditure line while staying in the preferred set $V(\bar{u})$.

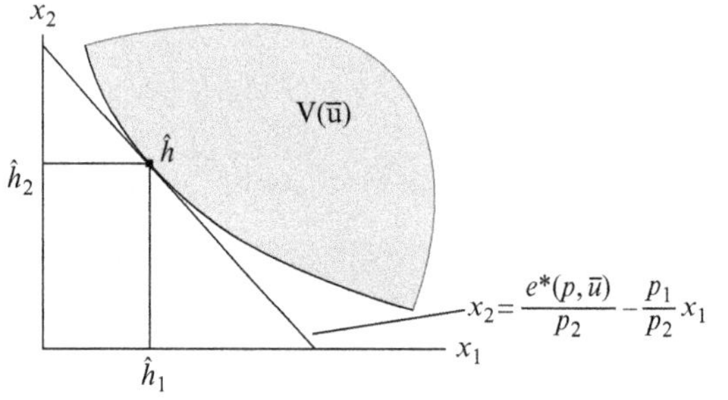

Fig. 9.1 Expenditure minimization. The indifference curve and the preferred set need not have the conventional shape.

The expenditure minimization problem is formally equivalent to single-output cost minimization in all important respects. Recall that the cost minimization behavioral postulate is $c^*(w, y) = \inf\{w^{\perp}x : x \in V(y)\}$ for a given input price $w \in \mathbb{R}^m_+$ and given input requirement correspondence $V : Y \to 2^{\mathbb{R}^m_+}$. Hence only the symbols and, perhaps, the properties of the feasible set are changed: We are now using p in place of w, $\bar{u}$ in place of y and a feasible set V that is the preferred set from a continuous utility function rather than the input requirement set from an underlying production set. Thus the fundamental properties of an expenditure minimum are mostly repeats of the fundamental properties of a cost minimum.

As we know from producer theory, the feasible set can be regarded as an isoquant when there is one output, the input requirement sets are upper contour sets of a continuous production function, and prices are strictly positive; and, in that case, the cost minimum has a few additional properties. Therefore any properties of a cost minimum, including the single-output properties that rely on continuity of the production function, are immediate for an expenditure minimum. In short, because utility is continuous, the feasible set can be regarded as the indifference set $I(\bar{u})$ without loss of generality when prices are strictly positive. The property that a Hicksian demand point $\hat{h}(p, \bar{u})$ always delivers exactly utility $\bar{u}$ (i.e., $u(\hat{h}(p, \bar{u})) = \bar{u}$) at positive prices is sometimes called "zero excess utility."

Furthermore, the properties of a cost minimum that rely on non-exhaustion or differentiability of the production function are immediate for an expenditure minimum when, respectively, there is local nonsatiation or the utility function is differentiable.

In particular, the expenditure function is finite for all nonnegative prices and a minimum exists when $p \gg 0$ because we are minimizing a continuous function on a closed (because u is continuous), nonempty (because $\bar{u}$ is feasible) and "effectively" bounded set. Uniqueness is not assured unless the preference relation is strictly convex so that each preferred set is strictly convex.

Theorem 9.1 (Fundamental Properties of an Expenditure Minimum). *Assume $u : \mathbb{R}^n_+ \to \mathbb{R}^1$ is a continuous function. Let $U = u(\mathbb{R}^n_+)$ be the set of feasible utility levels, and assume $(p, \bar{u}) \in \mathbb{R}^n_+ \times U$.*

1. *The set $W \equiv \{p \in \mathbb{R}^n_+ : h^*(p, \bar{u}) \neq \emptyset\}$ is a cone containing $\mathbb{R}^n_{++} \cup \{0\}$. The Hicksian demand correspondence is homogeneous of degree zero in p on this cone (only relative prices matter for consumption decisions).*
2. *The expenditure function is homogeneous of degree one in p (a neutral inflation inflates expenditure by the same proportion).*
3. *The expenditure function is concave in p; on the interior of $\mathbb{R}^n_+$ this implies the expenditure function is continuous, has one-sided gradients, and has a gradient off a set of Lebesgue n-measure zero (all as a function of p).*
4. *$(p^1 - p^0)^{\perp}(\hat{h}(p^1, \bar{u}) - \hat{h}(p^0, \bar{u})) \leq 0$ for $p^0, p^1 \in W$ (negative semidefiniteness of Hicksian demand price responses).*
5. *The expenditure function is nondecreasing in $(p, \bar{u})$ (higher prices and utility increase expenditure); the monotonicity in $\bar{u}$ is strict when $p \gg 0$.*
6. *$e^*(p, \bar{u}) \geq 0$ for every p; $e^*(p, u(0)) = 0$.*
7. *$h^*(p, \bar{u})$ is upper hemicontinuous in p.*

Proof. Except for the monotonicity in $\bar{u}$ of item 5 and the second part of item 6, items 1–6 are the corresponding properties of the cost minimum from Theorem 6.2 with nothing more than a change in notation (noting for item 1 that the preferred sets are automatically closed when preferences are continuous). Monotonicity in $\bar{u}$ is immediate from the definition of $V(\bar{u})$ as an upper contour set of the function u; the feasible set shrinks as $\bar{u}$ increases. Strict monotonicity in $\bar{u}$ when $p \gg 0$ is item 1 from Theorem 6.6 (the only role of free disposal there is to establish that the feasible set is the upper contour set of the production function; the analogous property for utility is automatic when preferences are continuous). The second part of item 6 is item 4 from Theorem 6.5, noting that $u(0)$ in the consumer context plays the role played by output level $y = 0$ in the producer context.

Item 7 is item 2 from Theorem 6.5 (noting again that $V(\bar{u})$ is automatically closed due to continuity of u). □

As with cost minimization, these properties are "fundamental" in that they require no assumptions other than the behavioral postulate (including preferences represented by a continuous utility function); and monotonicity in prices (first part of item 5) is included for consistency but is a redundant property (see Exercise 16 in Chapter 6). Item 4 is the *Law of Demand* for Hicksian demands.

9.2 ENVELOPE PROPERTIES

The envelope properties of a cost minimum carry over to an expenditure minimum without modification except that continuity of the utility function ensures a minimum exists at all strictly positive prices. The constraint is inactive with respect to changes in the price (but not with respect to changes in utility), thus e^* is a lower envelope on W of the collection of $e(\hat{h}(p^0); p) = p^{\perp}\hat{h}(p^0)$ functions. Most importantly, the gradient of an expenditure function with respect to prices, when it exists, is the corresponding Hicksian demand function.

Theorem 9.2 (Envelope Properties of an Expenditure Minimum). *Assume $u : \mathbb{R}^n_+ \to \mathbb{R}^1$ is a continuous function. Let $U = u(\mathbb{R}^n_+)$ be the set of feasible utility levels, and assume $\bar{u} \in U$.*

1. $\mathbf{D}_p e^*(p^0, \bar{u}) = \hat{h}(p^0, \bar{u})^{\perp}$, *the unique minimum, at every $p^0 \in \mathbb{R}^n_+$ where the gradient exists (Shephard's Lemma). Even on the set of measure zero where the gradient does not exist, a feasible consumption bundle x is expenditure-minimizing for delivering utility level $\bar{u}$ at a strictly positive price p^0 if and only if $e^*(p, \bar{u}) \leq e^*(p^0, \bar{u}) + x^{\perp}(p - p^0)$ for every $p \in \mathbb{R}^n_+$; and every such consumption bundle lies between $\mathbf{D}_p e^*_+(p^0, \bar{u})$ and $\mathbf{D}_p e^*_-(p^0, \bar{u})$.*
2. *The Hessian of e^* with respect to p is singular and negative semidefinite at every $p^0 \in \mathbb{R}^n_+$ where the partial derivatives of e^* are differentiable and where e^* is differentiable (with respect to p) in a neighborhood. Together with Shephard's Lemma, this implies the matrix of Hicksian demand price slopes is singular and negative semidefinite at all such prices. One implication of negative semidefiniteness is the comparative statics conclusion that each Hicksian demand is nonincreasing in its own price. If the off-diagonal elements are continuous in p then the matrix is symmetric, which is reciprocity of the Hicksian demand price responses:* $\frac{\partial \hat{h}_i}{\partial p_j} = \frac{\partial \hat{h}_j}{\partial p_i}$.

Singularity and symmetry of the Hessian with respect to prices imply the same elasticity identities for Hicksian demands as hold for conditional input demands:

$$\sum_{j=1}^{m}\left(\frac{\partial \hat{h}_j(p,\bar{u})}{\partial p_i}\frac{p_i}{\hat{h}_j(p,\bar{u})}\right)\frac{p_j\hat{h}_j(p,\bar{u})}{e^*(p,\bar{u})}=0.$$

$$\sum_{j=1}^{m}\frac{\partial \hat{h}_i(p,\bar{u})}{\partial p_j}\frac{p_j}{\hat{h}_i(p,\bar{u})}=0.$$

9.3 ADDITIONAL PROPERTIES

An expenditure minimum has the additional refutable hypotheses of a single-output cost minimum when the utility function has the analogous additional properties.

Theorem 9.3 (Additional Properties of an Expenditure Minimum). *Under the assumptions of Theorem 9.1:*

1. *If the preferred set $V(\bar{u})$ is convex (i.e., if u is quasiconcave) then $h^*(p,\bar{u})$ is a convex set for every p.*
2. *When preferences have the local nonsatiation property: $e^*(p,\bar{u})$ is continuous, and unbounded in $\bar{u}$ for every $p \in \mathbb{R}^n_{++}$; and $h^*(p,\bar{u})$ is upper hemicontinuous in $(p,\bar{u})$ on $\mathbb{R}^n_{++} \times U$.*

Proof. Item 1 is the corresponding item from Theorem 6.5. Item 2 is the corresponding item from Theorem 6.6; noting that local nonsatiation is the consumer version of locally non-exhaustible production. □

As in the production context, by continuity the constraint can be written as an equality, leading to the Lagrangian function:

$$L(x,\lambda;p,\bar{u}) = p^{\perp}x - \lambda(u(x)-\bar{u}). \tag{9.1}$$

If u is continuously differentiable and $\mathbf{D}u$ is not a vector of zeros at an optimum then the Lagrange Multiplier Rule (Theorem 2.1) is:

$$p^{\perp} - \hat{\lambda}(p,\bar{u})\mathbf{D}u(\hat{h}(p,\bar{u})) = 0. \tag{9.2}$$

Dividing component i of Eq. (9.2) by component j yields:

$$\frac{\partial u(\hat{h}(p,\bar{u}))/\partial x_i}{\partial u(\hat{h}(p,\bar{u}))/\partial x_j} = \frac{p_i}{p_j},$$

which is the familiar tangency condition that the MRS between any two commodities must equal their price ratio (slope of isoexpenditure line) at the consumer's optimal choice (note that Eq. 9.2 implies the denominator cannot be zero at an interior optimum with nonzero prices). That is, the consumer must choose an (interior) consumption bundle so that its indifference curve is tangent to its isoexpenditure line. Note that only the MRS is involved in this condition, not the individual utility derivatives. Hence, this description of the optimal choice is independent of the utility representation used. Eq. (9.2) can be used with the constraint:

$$-\left[u(\hat{h}(p,\bar{u}))-\bar{u}\right]=0, \tag{9.3}$$

to identify candidate values for an optimal consumption bundle and the corresponding Lagrange multiplier.

All of the comparative statics expressions from cost minimization apply in the expenditure minimization context, with nothing more than a change in symbols. If the conditions of the Implicit Function Theorem [1, Theorem 13.7] hold for Eqs. (9.2) and (9.3) then the basic comparative statics equation for expenditure minimization is:

$$\begin{bmatrix} -\hat{\lambda}\mathbf{D}^2u(\hat{h}) & -(\mathbf{D}u(\hat{h}))^{\perp} \\ -\mathbf{D}u(\hat{h}) & 0_n \end{bmatrix}\begin{bmatrix}\mathbf{D}\hat{h} \\ \mathbf{D}\hat{\lambda}\end{bmatrix}=-I_{n+1}.$$

This equation can be used to derive the price and utility slopes of the Hicksian demands for a particular utility function, as well as the price and utility slopes of the Lagrange multiplier. As with cost minimization, the special structure of the Lagrangian function (9.1) implies the refutable hypothesis that the own-price demand slopes are nonpositive, irrespective of u. Again, this is another way to derive the Law of Demand, under the extra assumptions that the utility function is sufficiently differentiable with an interior expenditure minimum described by Eqs. (9.2) and (9.3).

The Implicit Function Theorem also makes the Envelope Theorem for an active constraint (Theorem 2.2) applicable, which yields:

$$\frac{\partial e^*(p,\bar{u})}{\partial \bar{u}}=\hat{\lambda}(p,\bar{u}). \tag{9.4}$$

This says the Lagrange Multiplier is the marginal expenditure of an additional increment of utility; the shadow price of the obligation to meet the required utility level for an economic actor who is minimizing, for whom an additional unit of the utility "resource" inhibits the ability to minimize and thereby increases the expenditure minimum by $\hat{\lambda}$. Eq. (9.2) then has the interpretation that expenditure is minimized when the price of each commodity equals the marginal expenditure of generating an increment of utility using that commodity. Note that Shephard's Lemma (item 1 of Theorem 9.2) could also be obtained from the Envelope Theorem for an active constraint, similar to Eq. (9.4), but deriving Shephard's Lemma in this manner requires assumptions about differentiability of the utility function that are not needed in Theorem 9.2.

The matrix of demand and Lagrange multiplier slopes (Hessian of the expenditure function) that must be symmetric with singular and negative semidefinite lower-right $n \times n$ submatrix is:

$$\begin{bmatrix} \frac{\partial \hat{\lambda}}{\partial \bar{u}} & \frac{\partial \hat{\lambda}}{\partial p_1} & \cdots & \frac{\partial \hat{\lambda}}{\partial p_n} \\ \frac{\partial \hat{h}_1}{\partial \bar{u}} & \frac{\partial \hat{h}_1}{\partial p_1} & \cdots & \frac{\partial \hat{h}_1}{\partial p_n} \\ \vdots & \vdots & \ddots & \vdots \\ \frac{\partial \hat{h}_n}{\partial \bar{u}} & \frac{\partial \hat{h}_n}{\partial p_1} & \cdots & \frac{\partial \hat{h}_n}{\partial p_n} \end{bmatrix}.$$

In particular, own-price effects on Hicksian demands are nonpositive (the Law of Demand), cross price effects are symmetric, net substitutes (complements) are defined by positive (negative) cross-price effects, and the effect of a price change on the Lagrange multiplier equals the effect of a change in utility on the corresponding Hicksian demand, all as established elsewhere.

As with cost minimization, the requirement $x \geq 0$ can lead to corner solutions at which partial derivative(s) of L are positive. In this event the calculus properties of the expenditure minimum must be reconsidered especially when an incremental change in a parameter moves the minimum off of the $x \geq 0$ boundary.

9.4 DUALITY OF THE EXPENDITURE MINIMUM

As expenditure minimization is formally equivalent to cost minimization, an expenditure-relevant preferred set is recovered from a homogeneous of degree one, concave, and continuous function in the same manner used to recover a cost-relevant input requirement set. However, any candidate expenditure function must possess two properties not required for candidate cost functions. These are existence of a minimum relevant "utility" level at which the candidate expenditure is zero, and strictly increasing candidate expenditure in the "utility" argument (when the "price" argument is positive). These additional properties are required because existence of a continuous utility function was a maintained assumption when establishing the fundamental properties of an expenditure function, whereas the fundamental properties of a cost function were derived in a multiproduct setting without even assuming existence, and certainly not continuity, of a production function. The extra structure of the feasible set in the expenditure context imposes these two additional properties on expenditure functions, whence no function can be an expenditure function (for a consumer with complete, transitive, and continuous preferences) unless it possesses these properties.

Theorem 9.4 (Duality of the Expenditure Function). *Assume $U \subset \mathbb{R}^1$ is a nonempty interval containing its infimum $\underline{u}$; P is a convex cone satisfying $\mathbb{R}^n_{++} \subset P \subset \mathbb{R}^n_+$; and $\phi : P \times U \to \mathbb{R}^1_+$ is concave, homogeneous of degree one, and continuous (at boundary points of P that are in P) in the first n arguments; strictly increasing in the last argument when the first n arguments are strictly positive; and has the property $\phi(p, \underline{u}) = 0$ for every $p \in P$. Let $V_\phi : U \to 2^{\mathbb{R}^n_+}$ be defined by:*

$$V_\phi(\bar{u}) = \{x \in \mathbb{R}^n_+ : p^\perp x \geq \phi(p, \bar{u})\ \forall p \in P\}.$$

Then, for $\bar{u} \in U$:

1. *$V_\phi(\bar{u})$ is nonempty.*
2. *$V_\phi(\bar{u})$ is closed.*
3. *$V_\phi(\bar{u})$ has the free disposal property.*
4. *$V_\phi(\bar{u})$ is convex.*
5. *$0 \notin V_\phi(\bar{u})$ for $\bar{u} > \underline{u}$.*
6. *$V_\phi(\underline{u}) = \mathbb{R}^n_+$.*

Moreover, if $e^*_\phi : P \times U \to \mathbb{R}^1_+$ and $h^*_\phi : P \times U \to 2^{V_\phi(\bar{u})}$ are defined as:

$$e^*_\phi(p, \bar{u}) = \inf\{p^\perp x : x \in V_\phi(\bar{u})\}$$
$$h^*_\phi(p, \bar{u}) = \{x \in V_\phi(\bar{u}) : w^\perp x = e^*_\phi(p, \bar{u})\}$$

then $e^*_\phi(p, \bar{u}) = \phi(p, \bar{u})$ for every $(p, \bar{u}) \in P \times U$ and $h^*_\phi(p, \bar{u})$ is nonempty for every $(p, \bar{u}) \in \text{int}\, P \times U$.

Proof. Apply Theorem 6.7 (for item 5, use strict monotonicity of $\phi(p, \bar{u})$ in $\bar{u}$ and $\phi(p, \underline{u}) = 0$ to conclude $\bar{u} > \underline{u} \Rightarrow \phi(p, \bar{u}) > 0$ for any $p \gg 0$; for item 6, use $\phi(p, \underline{u}) = 0$ to conclude $0 \in V_\phi(\underline{u})$). □

In short, ϕ is indeed the expenditure function at positive prices for the preferred sets $V_\phi(\bar{u})$ derived from the function ϕ. *The homogeneity, concavity, monotonicity, and zero properties are sufficient as well as necessary for a function $\phi : \mathbb{R}^n_{++} \times U \to \mathbb{R}^1_+$, for some nonempty interval $U \subset \mathbb{R}^1$ containing its infimum, to be the minimum of the expenditure expression over a well-behaved preferred set; and ϕ is a true minimum (an expenditure-minimizing consumption bundle exists) on the interior of the price space. Hence we can use* **any** *function* *satisfying these properties as an expenditure function without actually deriving it from some underlying continuous utility function. This extends to zero prices when the function is defined and continuous at zero prices but ϕ may not be a true minimum at such prices. This also shows V_ϕ is the expenditure-relevant preferred set correspondence for a consumer with expenditure function ϕ, and the expenditure-relevant preferences* **always** *have the free disposal and convexity properties.*

As discussed in Section 5.2, it is possible for ϕ to be the infimum over a set $V(\bar{u})$ that is a proper subset of $V_\phi(\bar{u})$ if $V(\bar{u})$ is either non-convex or does not satisfy free disposal ($V(\bar{u})$ is always closed when it is the upper contour set of a continuous utility function). However, $V_\phi(\bar{u})$ is *always* an expenditure-relevant preferred set for the expenditure function ϕ.

As discussed in Section 5.3, *any correspondence $\eta : \mathbb{R}^n_{++} \times U \rightarrow 2^{\mathbb{R}^n_+}$ whose elements at each $(p, \bar{u}) \in \mathbb{R}^n_{++} \times U$ minimize $p^\perp x$ over $x \in \eta(\mathbb{R}^n_{++}, \bar{u})$ is a Hicksian demand correspondence for a price-taking consumer with preferred set $\eta(\mathbb{R}^n_{++}, \bar{u})$. Hence we can use* **any** *correspondence satisfying this basic minimization property as a Hicksian demand correspondence without actually deriving it from some underlying preference relation.* Homogeneity and negative semidefiniteness of the price responses, upper hemicontinuity in p, and the zero property that there exists $\underline{u}$ such that $\eta(p, \underline{u}) = \{0\}$ for every p; are necessary but not sufficient for any such η. The corresponding expenditure function is derived from any such η via $\phi(p, \bar{u}) = p^\perp \hat{\eta}(p, \bar{u})$, and another necessary condition on η is that this implied ϕ function be strictly increasing in $\bar{u}$ for every p. There are other Hicksian demand correspondences that are consistent with this expenditure function; but all such Hicksian demand correspondences are contained in h^*_ϕ, the Hicksian demand correspondence for the preferred set correspondence V_ϕ. In the relatively simple case of a singleton-valued correspondence with implied function $\hat{\eta}(p, \bar{u})$ that is differentiable with respect to p, a sufficient condition for $\hat{\eta}$ to be a Hicksian demand function is that its Jacobian with respect to p be symmetric and negative semidefinite (in addition to homogeneity of degree zero with respect to p, $\hat{\eta}(p, \underline{u}) = 0$ for every p, and strict monotonicity of $p^\perp \hat{\eta}(p, \bar{u})$ in $\bar{u}$ for every p).

Analogous to the cost minimization context; a continuous, nondecreasing and quasiconcave expenditure-relevant utility function $u_\phi : \mathbb{R}^n_+ \rightarrow U$ corresponding to V_ϕ can be derived under the conditions of Theorem 9.4 with the additional assumptions that $\phi(p, \bar{u})$ is jointly continuous in $(p, \bar{u})$ and unbounded on $\bar{u} \in U$ for every $p \in \mathbb{R}^n_{++}$. The proof is identical to Theorem 6.8, except that we automatically know from item 6 of

Theorem 9.4 that $X_\phi = \mathbb{R}^n_+$. The procedure is to fix x; use the Shephard's Lemma equation $x^\perp = \mathbf{D}_p\phi(p, \bar{u})$ to solve for p that minimizes the value of $\bar{u}$ satisfying $p^\perp x = \phi(p, \bar{u})$ (there is *always* a unique value of $\bar{u}$ corresponding to each (p, x) pair in the expenditure minimization context because ϕ is strictly increasing in $\bar{u}$), using only $n - 1$ of the equations to do so because of homogeneity; and then substitute that value of p into the remaining equation to obtain the expenditure-relevant relationship between a consumption bundle x and a utility level $\bar{u}$: $\bar{u} = u_\phi(x)$.

9.5 NOTES

Expenditure minimization lies behind the Hicks-Slutsky Decomposition and thus can be attributed to [2, 3]. The label "Hicksian demand" is essentially due to the careful distinction between substitution and income effects given in [2, Chapter II]. However the first formal statement of the expenditure minimization problem appears to be in Samuelson [4, p. 103]. Properties of the expenditure minimum appear in fairly complete form in [5]. Duality of the expenditure minimum is essentially a reinterpretation of the duality results for the cost function; see the references in Chapters 5 and 6.

9.6 EXERCISES

1. Find the Hicksian demand correspondence and the expenditure function for a price-taking consumer with each utility function in Exercise 14 of Chapter 8.
2. Reinterpret each of the standard functional forms in Exercise 18 of Chapter 4 as a utility function on $\mathbb{R}^2_+$ rather than a production function. Find the Hicksian demand correspondence and the expenditure function for each.
3. Find the Hicksian demand correspondence and the expenditure function for a price-taking consumer with each of the following utility functions on $\mathbb{R}^2_+$. In each case, begin by carefully drawing a typical indifference curve, labeling important points and slopes at important points.
   a. $u(x_1, x_2) = x_1^2 + x_2$.
   b. $u(x_1, x_2) = (x_1 + x_2)^2$.

c.

$$u(x_1, x_2) = \begin{cases} \min\{x_1, x_2\} & \text{when } 0 \le \min\{x_1, x_2\} \le 1 \\ \min\{2x_1 - 1, x_2\} & \text{otherwise} \end{cases}.$$

d.

$$u(x_1, x_2) = \begin{cases} \frac{1}{3}x_1 + \frac{2}{3}x_2, & \text{if } x_2 \ge x_1 \\ \frac{2}{3}x_1 + \frac{1}{3}x_2, & \text{if } x_2 \le x_1 \end{cases}.$$

4. Consider a price-taking consumer with utility function on $\mathbb{R}^2_+$ given by:

$$u(x_1, x_2) = \begin{cases} x_1 + x_2 & \text{when } x_1 \ne x_2 \\ x_1 + x_2 + 1 & \text{when } x_1 = x_2 \end{cases}.$$

   a. Carefully draw the indifference curve for utility level $\bar{u} > 1$, labeling intercepts and any other important points.
   b. Comment on the properties of this consumer's preferences.
   c. Derive the expenditure function for values of $\bar{u}$ exceeding 1.
5. Find the Hicksian demand correspondence and expenditure function for Mr. Aristotle, introduced in Exercise 25 of Chapter 8.
6. Assume $e^*(p, \bar{u}) = p\bar{u}$ is an expenditure function, where p is a scalar.
   a. Verify that e^* has the properties of an expenditure function.
   b. Find the Hicksian demand correspondence.
   c. Verify that the Hicksian demand correspondence has the properties of a Hicksian demand.
7. For each of the following functions defined on $\bar{u} \ge 0$ and $(p_1, p_2) \in \mathbb{R}^2_{++}$, state whether there is a complete, transitive, continuous, and locally nonsatiated preference relation $(\mathbb{R}^2_+, \succsim)$ for which ϕ is the expenditure function, and explain why. If so, derive a utility function for which ϕ is the expenditure function:

   a.

$$\phi(p_1, p_2, \bar{u}) = \frac{p_1 p_2 \bar{u}}{p_1 + p_2}.$$

   b. $\phi(p_1, p_2, \bar{u}) = \bar{u} p_1$.
8. Suppose a consumer receives utility u from consumption of only one good, $x \in \mathbb{R}^1_+$, whose price is p. Can $\hat{h} = \bar{u}$ be a Hicksian demand for x? Why or why not? If so, find the expenditure function and the (direct) utility function.

9. Suppose the matrix of price derivatives of a consumer's Hicksian demand is:

$$\begin{pmatrix} a & b \\ 2 & -\frac{1}{2} \end{pmatrix},$$

and the prices are $(8, p_2)$. Find a, b, and p_2.

10. Assume $(\hat{h}_1, \hat{h}_2, \hat{h}_3)$ is the Hicksian demand for a price-taking consumer. Suppose prices on the three goods are $p_1 = 1$, $p_2 = 2$, and $p_3 = 4$. At these prices, the following observations are made:

$$\frac{\partial \hat{h}_1}{\partial p_1} = -1 \quad \frac{\partial \hat{h}_1}{\partial p_2} = 1 \quad \frac{\partial \hat{h}_2}{\partial p_2} = -2.$$

Find the Hicksian substitution matrix among these three goods at the stated prices.

11. Is the following a Hicksian demand on prices $(p_1, p_2) \in \mathbb{R}^2_{++}$ for a consumer whose consumption set is $\mathbb{R}^2_+$:

$$\hat{\eta}(p_1, p_2, \bar{u})^\perp = (\bar{u} - 1)\left(\left(\frac{p_2}{p_1}\right)^{1/2}, \left(\frac{p_1}{p_2}\right)^{1/2}\right)?$$

Explain why. If $\hat{\eta}$ is a Hicksian demand, provide the expenditure function.

REFERENCES

[1] Apostol TM. Mathematical analysis. 2nd ed. Reading, MA: Addison-Wesley; 1974.
[2] Hicks JR. Value and capital. 2nd ed. Oxford: Oxford University Press; 1946.
[3] Slutsky E. Sulla Teoria del Bilancio del Consumatore. Giornale degli Economisti 1915; English reprint "On the theory of the budget of the consumer" by O. Ragusa. In: Stigler GJ, Boulding KE, editors. A.E.A. Readings in price theory VI. Homewood, IL: Irwin; 1952.
[4] Samuelson PA. Foundations of economic analysis. Cambridge, MA: Harvard University Press; 1947.
[5] McKenzie L. Demand theory without a utility index. Rev Econ Stud 1957; 24:185–9.

CHAPTER 10

Utility Maximization

Chapter Outline

10.1 BASIC OPTIMIZATION POSTULATE

The second standard behavioral postulate for consumers is that a price-taking consumer; with a given monetary resource and a complete, transitive, and continuous preference ordering over the consumption set $X = \mathbb{R}^n_+$; chooses a commodity bundle x within the consumer's monetary feasible set to maximize a utility representation $u(x)$. Let $m \in \mathbb{R}^1_+$ denote the monetary resource and $p \in \mathbb{R}^n_{++}$ denote the price. Then the postulate is that x is chosen from $B(p, m) \equiv \{x \in \mathbb{R}^n_+ : p^{\perp}x \leq m\}$, which is the *budget set* of the consumer for the given (p, m) pair, to maximize $u(x)$. The choice variable for the utility maximization behavioral postulate is x and the parameters are (p, m). The postulate leads to an optimal value function $u^*(p, m) = \sup\{u(x) : x \in B(p, m)\}$ and optimal choice correspondence $x^*(p, m) = \{x \in B(p, m) : u(x) = u^*(p, m)\}$, which are the *indirect utility function* and *Marshallian demand correspondence*, respectively, of the consumer.

Geometrically, the objective is to get in the highest possible indifference set while staying in the budget set. When there are two commodities the maximization can be illustrated as in Fig. 10.1.

Note that we have assumed $p \gg 0$. This is because the budget set is unbounded when a price is zero, in which case there is no assurance

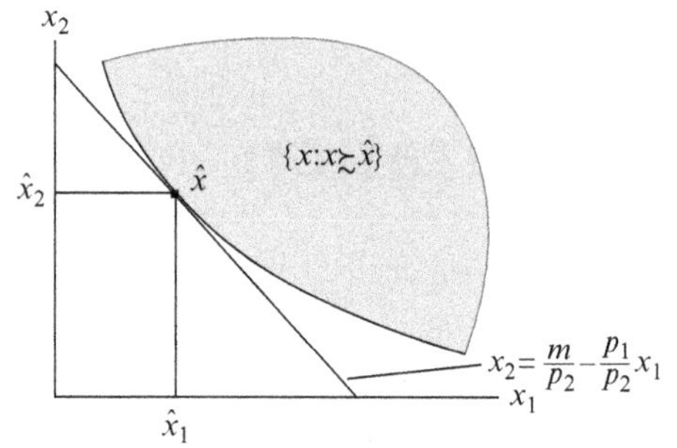

Fig. 10.1 Utility maximization. The budget set must appear as illustrated, but without additional assumptions the indifference and preferred sets could take almost any shape.

u^* is finite or x^* is nonempty. Given $p \gg 0$ and $m \geq 0$, the optimal choice set $x^*(p, m)$ is always nonempty and indirect utility $u^*(p, m)$ is always finite because the budget set is closed, bounded, and nonempty; and the utility function is continuous. As with other optimization problems studied herein, the optimal choice need not be unique. Uniqueness is guaranteed if preferences are strictly convex (this guarantees uniqueness of the expenditure minimum; Theorem 10.5 then implies uniqueness of the utility maximum because strict convexity implies local nonsatiation).

The utility maximization behavioral postulate is structurally different from the behavioral postulates studied in previous chapters because the objective is not a monetary value function and the constraint is active with respect to price. There is some specialized structure; as the constraint boundary is a monetary value function, the parameters do not enter the objective, and the objective is continuous. Still, the fundamental properties of a utility maximum are structurally different from those of a profit maximum or cost/expenditure minimum.

Theorem 10.1 (Fundamental Properties of a Utility Maximum). *Assume $(\mathbb{R}^n_+, \succsim)$ is complete, transitive and continuous; and let u be a continuous function that represents $(\mathbb{R}^n_+, \succsim)$. Let $p \in \mathbb{R}^n_{++}$ and $m \in \mathbb{R}^1_+$. Then:*

1. *$x^*(p, m)$ is nonempty and $u^*(p, m)$ is finite.*
2. *$x^*(p, m)$ and $u^*(p, m)$ are homogeneous of degree 0 (consumers do not have "money illusion:" Only **relative** prices and income matter for consumption decisions).*
3. *$u^*(p, m)$ is a quasiconvex function.*
4. *$u^*(p, m)$ is nondecreasing in m and nonincreasing in p (higher income and lower prices improve consumer welfare).*

5. *$u^*(p, m)$ is continuous and $x^*(p, m)$ is upper hemicontinuous.*
6. *$u^*(p, \mathbb{R}^1_+)$ is an interval of the form $[u(0), \sup U)$ or $[u(0), \sup U]$ for every p.*

Proof.

1. u is continuous and $B(p, m)$ is nonempty, closed and bounded. Apply Theorem 1.2.
2. u is unaffected by p and m. Moreover, $B(p, m) = B(\alpha p, \alpha m)$ for $\alpha > 0$. So the maximization problem is the same when the parameters are $(\alpha p, \alpha m)$ as when the parameters are (p, m), whence $x^*(p, m) = x^*(\alpha p, \alpha m)$ and $u^*(p, m) = u^*(\alpha p, \alpha m)$.
3. Fix $(p^0, m^0), (p^1, m^1) \geq 0$ and $\alpha \in (0, 1)$. By definition:
$$[\alpha p^0+(1-\alpha)p^1]^\perp \hat{x}(\alpha p^0+(1-\alpha)p^1, \alpha m^0+(1-\alpha)m^1) \leq \alpha m^0+(1-\alpha)m^1.$$
Hence, one or both of the following hold:
$$(p^0)^\perp \hat{x}(\alpha p^0 + (1-\alpha)p^1, \alpha m^0 + (1-\alpha)m^1) \leq m^0$$
$$(p^1)^\perp \hat{x}(\alpha p^0 + (1-\alpha)p^1, \alpha m^0 + (1-\alpha)m^1) \leq m^1.$$
That is, $\hat{x}(\alpha p^0 + (1-\alpha)p^1, \alpha m^0 + (1-\alpha)m^1)$ is feasible when prices and income are either (p^0, m^0) or (p^1, m^1). Hence, one or both of the following hold:
$$u^*(p^0, m^0) \geq u(\hat{x}(\alpha p^0 + (1-\alpha)p^1, \alpha m^0 + (1-\alpha)m^1))$$
$$u^*(p^1, m^1) \geq u(\hat{x}(\alpha p^0 + (1-\alpha)p^1, \alpha m^0 + (1-\alpha)m^1)).$$
Either way:
$$\begin{aligned} &u^*(\alpha p^0 + (1-\alpha)p^1, \alpha m^0 + (1-\alpha)m^1) \\ &\quad = u(\hat{x}(\alpha p^0 + (1-\alpha)p^1, \alpha m^0 + (1-\alpha)m^1)) \\ &\quad \leq \max\{u^*(p^0, m^0), u^*(p^1, m^1)\}. \end{aligned}$$
4. Let $m^1 \geq m^0$ and $p^1 \leq p^0$. Then $(p^1)^\perp \hat{x}(p^0, m^0) \leq (p^0)^\perp \hat{x}(p^0, m^0) \leq m^0 \leq m^1$. So $\hat{x}(p^0, m^0)$ is feasible when prices and income are (p^1, m^1), hence $u^*(p^1, m^1) \geq u(\hat{x}(p^0, m^0)) = u^*(p^0, m^0)$.
5. Continuity of u^* and upper hemicontinuity of x^* are a direct application of the Maximum Theorem. (Theorem 1.5; see also Exercise 2 of Chapter 1).
6. Fix $p \gg 0$. The utility maximum exists for every nonnegative income level, so $u^*(p, m) \in U$ for every $m \in \mathbb{R}^1_+$. Moreover, $0 \in B(p, m)$ for every such m, so $u^*(p, m) \geq u(0)$. Therefore $u^*(p, m) \in [u(0), \sup U)$ for every $m \in \mathbb{R}^1_+$ (if $\sup U \in U$ we close the interval and conclude

$u^*(p,m) \in [u(0), \sup U]$). Conversely, fix $\bar{u} \in [u(0), \sup U)$ (or $\bar{u} \in [u(0), \sup U]$). Then $\bar{u} \in U$ because U is an interval due to continuity of u. Hence, there exists $x' \in \mathbb{R}^n_+$ such that $u(x') = \bar{u}$. So for $m' = p^\perp x' \in \mathbb{R}^1_+$ we have $x' \in B(p,m')$, and therefore $u^*(p,m') \geq u(x') = \bar{u}$. Moreover, $\bar{u} \geq u(0) = u^*(p,0)$, so $\bar{u} \in [u^*(p,0), u^*(p,m')]$. By continuity of $u^*(p,m)$ in m (item 5 above), there exists $m \in [0,m']$ such that $u^*(p,m) = \bar{u}$ (from the intermediate value theorem; [1, Theorem 4.33]). Hence $\bar{u} \in u^*(p,\mathbb{R}^1_+)$. □

These properties are "fundamental" in that they require no assumptions other than the behavioral postulate (including the assumptions that the economic actor has complete, transitive, and continuous preferences on $\mathbb{R}^n_+$ and $p \gg 0$).

10.2 ADDITIONAL PROPERTIES

Additional refutable hypotheses emerge from the utility maximization behavioral postulate when the preference relation has additional properties.

Theorem 10.2 (Additional Properties of a Utility Maximum). *Assume the conditions of Theorem 10.1.*

1. *If the preference relation has the local nonsatiation property then:*
   - **a.** $p^\perp \hat{x}(p,m) = m$ *(Walras' Law).*
   - **b.** $u^*(p,m)$ *is strictly increasing in* m.
2. *If the preference relation is convex then* $x^*(p,m)$ *is a convex set for every* (p,m).

Proof.

1. **a.** By definition, $x^*(p,m) \subset B(p,m)$, so $p^\perp \hat{x}(p,m) \leq m$. If $p^\perp \hat{x}(p,m) < m$, then by local nonsatiation there exists $x \in \mathbb{R}^n_+$ such that $u(x) > u(\hat{x}(p,m))$ and $\|x - \hat{x}(p,m)\| < \epsilon$, where $\epsilon = \frac{m - p^\perp \hat{x}(p,m)}{\|p\|} > 0$. Hence, using the Cauchy-Schwarz inequality [1, Theorem 1.23]:

$$p^\perp (x - \hat{x}(p,m)) \leq \|p\| \, \|x - \hat{x}(p,m)\| < \|p\|\epsilon = m - p^\perp \hat{x}(p,m),$$

   or $p^\perp x < m$. That is, $x \in B(p,m)$, which contradicts that $\hat{x}(p,m)$ maximizes u over $B(p,m)$.

   b. If $m^1 > m^0$, then $\hat{x}(p,m^0)$ cannot maximize u when income is m^1, since $p^\perp \hat{x}(p,m^0) = m^0 < m^1$ while Walras' Law requires $p^\perp \hat{x}(p,m^1) = m^1$. Hence $u^*(p,m^1) > u(\hat{x}(p,m^0)) = u^*(p,m^0)$.
2. The preferred sets $V(\bar{u})$ are convex when $(\mathbb{R}^n_+, \succsim)$ is convex. The budget set $B(p,m)$ is trivially convex. Note that $x^*(p,m)$ is the intersection of $V(u^*(p,m))$ and $B(p,m)$, an intersection of two convex sets, which is convex. □

Nineteenth century French economist Léon Walras is credited with the observation that, under some conditions, *the value of aggregate excess demand in an economy must be zero*, an observation now known as *Walras' Law*. Walras' Law is a simple sum of individual demands and supplies provided that individuals exhaust their monetary resources. The notion that individuals do not leave any available resources unused is central to competitive equilibrium theory, so we have labeled here the important theorem establishing conditions under which individual consumer choice has this property "Walras' Law." Walras' Law establishes conditions under which we may, without loss of generality, regard the consumer's feasible set as the budget line $p^{\perp}x = m$ rather than the entire budget set $B(p, m)$. That is, conditions under which the constraint is effectively an equality rather than an inequality. The key condition is local nonsatiation.

Walras' Law implies the constraint is active with respect to all parameters so there are no true envelope properties of a utility maximum. However the "Envelope Theorem" for an active constraint (Theorem 2.2) applies under appropriate assumptions. As the constraint is an equality when preferences have the local nonsatiation property, the Lagrangian function for utility maximization is:

$$L(x, \lambda; p, m) = u(x) - \lambda(p^{\perp}x - m). \tag{10.1}$$

If, in addition, u is continuously differentiable on an open ball about $\hat{x}(p, m)$ then the Lagrange Multiplier Rule (Theorem 2.1) is[1]:

$$\mathbf{D}u(\hat{x}(p, m)) - \hat{\lambda}(p, m)p^{\perp} = 0. \tag{10.2}$$

Dividing component i of Eq. (10.2) by component j yields:

$$\frac{\partial u(\hat{x}(p, m))/\partial x_i}{\partial u(\hat{x}(p, m))/\partial x_j} = \frac{p_i}{p_j},$$

[1]Note that constraint qualification is automatic because the Jacobian of the constraint with respect to x is $p^{\perp} \gg 0$. As with our other calculus approaches to optimization, since we did not explicitly incorporate the constraint $x \geq 0$ the first order condition can fail at the maximum if the maximum occurs at a corner so that $x_i^* = \{0\}$ for some i, in which case $u_i(\hat{x}) - \hat{\lambda}p_i < 0$ is possible. In this case, if the maximum is unique x_i can be omitted from the consumption vector and everything holds as described here for the other components of x ($\hat{x}_i$ is fixed at zero for small changes in (p, m)). If it happens that the first order conditions hold at $\hat{x}_i = 0$ then the comparative statics might be different for different changes in (p, m).

which is the familiar tangency condition that the MRS between any two commodities must equal their price ratio (slope of the budget line) at a consumer's optimal choice (note that Eq. (10.2) implies the denominator cannot be zero at an interior optimum with nonzero prices unless the entire Jacobian of u is zero). That is, the consumer must choose an (interior) consumption bundle so that the indifference curve is tangent to the budget line. Only the MRS is involved in this condition, not the individual utility derivatives. Thus this description of the optimal choice is independent of the utility representation used. Another way of saying this is to recall that different utility representations are monotonic transformations of each other, so the maximal choice is independent of which representation is used. Eq. (10.2) can be used with the constraint:

$$-\left(p^{\perp}\hat{x}(p,m) - m\right) = 0, \tag{10.3}$$

to identify candidate values for an optimal consumption plan and the corresponding Lagrange multiplier.

If the conditions of the Implicit Function Theorem ([1, Theorem 13.7]) hold for Eqs. (10.2) and (10.3) then the "Envelope Theorem" for an active constraint (Theorem 2.2) yields:

$$\mathbf{D}u^{*}(p,m) = \left(-\hat{\lambda}(p,m)\hat{x}(p,m)^{\perp}, \hat{\lambda}(p,m)\right). \tag{10.4}$$

The first part of Eq. (10.4) is similar to Hotelling's and Shephard's Lemmas. It states that the price gradient of the optimal value function is (almost) the optimal demand vector, but differs from Hotelling's and Shephard's Lemmas due to the presence of the Lagrange multiplier. The second part of Eq. (10.4) is yet another shadow price statement. The Lagrange multiplier is the marginal utility of income: It measures the marginal value of an increment of the monetary resource to a utility maximizing consumer. If this shadow price is nonzero (which, from Eq. (10.2), it must be at an interior optimum with positive prices unless the entire utility Jacobian $\mathbf{D}u(\hat{x})$ is zero) then substitution yields the important relationship between the indirect utility function and the Marshallian demand known as *Roy's Identity*.

Theorem 10.3 (Roy's Identity). *Assume (1) the conditions of Theorem 10.1, (2) the preference relation has the local nonsatiation property, (3) the utility representation u is continuously differentiable in an open ball about $\hat{x}(p,m)$, (4) the conditions of the Implicit Function Theorem ([1, Theorem 13.7]) hold* *for Eqs. (10.2) and (10.3), and (5) the unique Lagrange multiplier* $\hat{\lambda}(p, m)$ *is nonzero. Then:*

$$\hat{x}(p, m)^{\perp} = \frac{-1}{\mathbf{D}_m u^*(p, m)} \mathbf{D}_p u^*(p, m).$$

In short, the Marshallian demand can be derived from the indirect utility function by differentiating with respect to price and dividing by the negative of the income derivative.

10.3 RELATIONSHIP TO EXPENDITURE MINIMIZATION

Although an expenditure minimum has the same basic properties as a cost minimum, an important difference is that expenditure minimizing behavior is not observable because it depends on unobservable utility. Thus the properties of Hicksian demand, taken alone, are not refutable propositions from the theory because we currently have no way to obtain data on utility levels that might be used to confirm whether observed demand behavior conforms to the properties of Hicksian demand. The same criticism applies to properties of the utility maximum derived above that involve indirect utility. However, some properties of Marshallian demand; which is observable in principle as Marshallian demand involves only on prices, income and quantities; are derived from relationships between the utility maximum and the corresponding expenditure minimum. In particular, a consumer who minimizes expenditure also maximizes the utility that can be attained from that minimal expenditure.

Theorem 10.4 (Expenditure Minimization Implies Utility Maximization). *Assume the conditions of Theorem 10.1 and* $\bar{u} \in [u(0), \sup U)$. *Then* $h^*(p, \bar{u}) \subset x^*(p, e^*(p, \bar{u}))$ *and* $\bar{u} = u^*(p, e^*(p, \bar{u}))$.

Proof. Consider $x \in \mathbb{R}^n_+$ satisfying $u(x) > \bar{u}$. Then $x \in V(\bar{u})$ and, by zero excess utility, $x \notin h^*(p, \bar{u})$, so $p^{\perp}x > e^*(p, \bar{u})$. Hence $\bar{u} = u^*(p, e^*(p, \bar{u}))$ (i.e., $\bar{u}$ is the maximal utility attainable with income $e^*(p, \bar{u})$ at prices p). As $u(\hat{h}(p, \bar{u})) = \bar{u}$ by zero excess utility and $p^{\perp}\hat{h}(p, \bar{u}) = e^*(p, \bar{u})$, we have $\hat{h}(p, \bar{u}) \in x^*(p, e^*(p, \bar{u}))$. □

The converse to this theorem holds when the indirect utility and expenditure functions have the properties implied by local nonsatiation. Without these properties, the utility function can have a "flat spot" that allows the minimal expenditure for achieving a given utility level to be strictly below an income level that delivers that same utility level. This is illustrated in Fig. 10.2.

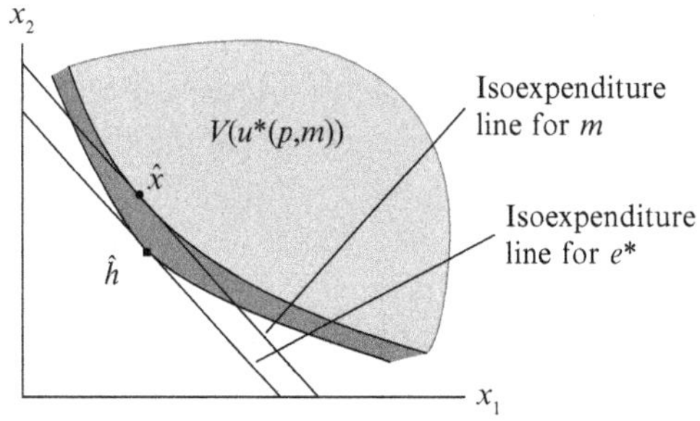

Fig. 10.2 Utility maximization implies expenditure minimization. $\hat{x}$ is the optimal choice for income m. If the light shading is the preferred set for $\hat{x}$ then we obtain the lowest possible isoexpenditure line subject to this preferred set by choosing $\hat{x}$ as the Hicksian demand point, in which case expenditure minimization coincides with utility maximization. Note, however, that if the indifference set for utility level $u^*(p,m)$ were "thick," for example the dark shaded area, then $\hat{x}$ still maximizes utility but expenditure minimization occurs at the illustrated $\hat{h}$. Thick indifference sets are inconsistent with local nonsatiation. Thus the graph shows that the properties implied by local nonsatiation are central to the coincidence of utility maximization and expenditure minimization.

Theorem 10.5 (Utility Maximization Implies Expenditure Minimization). *Assume the conditions of Theorem 10.1 and* $\bar{u} \in [u(0), \sup U)$. *For every* $p \gg 0$: $e^*(p,\bar{u})$ *is continuous and unbounded on* $\bar{u} \in U$ *if and only if* $u^*(p,m)$ *is strictly increasing in* $m \in \mathbb{R}^n_+$. *If these conditions hold then* $x^*(p,m) \subset h^*(p,u^*(p,m))$ *and* $m = e^*(p,u^*(p,m))$.

Proof. Fix $p \gg 0$.

Assume $e^*(p,\bar{u})$ is continuous and unbounded on $\bar{u} \in U$, and select $m^0 < m^1$. Using unboundedness, there exists $\bar{u} \in U$ such that $e^*(p,\bar{u}) \geq m^1$. And $m^0 \geq e^*(p,u^*(p,m^0))$ from the definition of e^*. Hence $e^*(p,\bar{u}) \geq m^1 > e^*(p,u^*(p,m^0))$. Continuity (intermediate value theorem) then implies existence of $\bar{u}^1 \in (u^*(p,m^0),\bar{u}]$ such that $e^*(p,\bar{u}^1) = m^1$. Strict monotonicity of e^* in $\bar{u}$ (Theorem 9.1) then yields $\bar{u}^1 > u^*(p,m^0)$, and $u^*(p,m^1) = \bar{u}^1$ from Theorem 10.4.

Conversely, assume $u^*(p,\bar{u})$ is strictly increasing in $m \in \mathbb{R}^n_+$. Then $p^\perp\hat{x}(p,m) = m$: Otherwise there exists $m^1 \in \mathbb{R}^n_+$ such that $p^\perp\hat{x}(p,m^1) < m^1$, but then $\hat{x}(p,m^1)$ is optimal for every $m^0 \in [p^\perp\hat{x}(p,m^1),m^1)$, yielding $u^*(p,m^0) = u^*(p,m^1)$, which contradicts strict monotonicity of u^*. Thus $e^*(p,u^*(p,m)) = m$ from the definition of e^*. Letting $m \to \infty$ establishes unboundedness. Now suppose $e^*(p, \bar{u})$ is not continuous at $\bar{u}^0 \in U$. Then there exists $\epsilon > 0$ and a sequence $\bar{u}^i \to \bar{u}^0$ (in the interval U) such that $|e^*(p, \bar{u}^i) - e^*(p, \bar{u}^0)| \geq \epsilon$ for every $i = 1, 2, \ldots$. That is, either $e^*(p, \bar{u}^i) \leq e^*(p, \bar{u}^0 - \epsilon)$ or $e^*(p, \bar{u}^i) \geq e^*(p, \bar{u}^0 + \epsilon)$. By strict monotonicity of u^*, either $u^*(p, e^*(p, \bar{u}^i)) \leq u^*(p, e^*(p, \bar{u}^0 - \epsilon))$ or $u^*(p, e^*(p, \bar{u}^i)) \geq u^*(p, e^*(p, \bar{u}^0 + \epsilon))$. Using $\bar{u} = u^*(p, e^*(p, \bar{u}))$ from Theorem 10.4, either $\bar{u}^i \leq \bar{u}^0 - \epsilon$ or $\bar{u}^i \geq \bar{u}^0 + \epsilon$. Letting $i \to \infty$, either $\bar{u}^0 \leq \bar{u}^0 - \epsilon$ or $\bar{u}^0 \geq \bar{u}^0 + \epsilon$. Both are contradictions.

Now consider $x \in \mathbb{R}^n_+$ satisfying $p^\perp x < m$. Then $x \in B(p, m)$ and, as x is feasible at an income level strictly less than m while u^* is strictly increasing in m, $u(x) < u^*(p, m)$. Hence $m = e^*(p, u^*(p, m))$ (i.e., m is the minimal expenditure required to achieve $u^*(p, m)$ at prices p). As $p^\perp \hat{x}(p, m) = m$ and $u(\hat{x}(p, m)) = u^*(p, m)$, we have $\hat{x}(p, m) \in h^*(p, u^*(p, m))$. □

Theorems 9.3 and 10.2 show that local nonsatiation implies the properties on the indirect utility and expenditure functions assumed in this theorem. Hence the last part of the theorem could have been stated as "utility maximization implies expenditure minimization whenever preferences have local nonsatiation." This statement has the advantage of placing the assumptions on the primitives of the consumer's choice problem but has the disadvantage of imposing more restrictive assumptions (it is easy to draw indifference curves that violate local nonsatiation but for which indirect utility is strictly increasing, at least when preferences are either not weakly monotonic or not convex).

Theorems 10.4 and 10.5 jointly imply $x^*(p, m) = h^*(p, u^*(p, m))$ and $h^*(p, \bar{u}) = x^*(p, e^*(p, \bar{u}))$ (i.e., the set of points that maximize utility is exactly the set of points that minimize expenditure). To see this, fix m and set $\bar{u} = u^*(p, m)$ in the expenditure minimization problem. Then $h^*(p, \bar{u}) \subset x^*(p, e^*(p, \bar{u}))$ is really $h^*(p, u^*(p, m)) \subset x^*(p, m)$, which is the converse of the result that utility maximization implies expenditure minimization. Similarly, fix $\bar{u}$ and set $m = e^*(p, \bar{u})$ in the utility maximization problem. Then $x^*(p, m) \subset h^*(p, u^*(p, m))$ is really $x^*(p, e^*(p, \bar{u})) \subset h^*(p, \bar{u})$, which is the converse of the result that expenditure minimization implies utility maximization.

10.4 HICKS-SLUTSKY DECOMPOSITION

The identities from Theorems 10.4 and 10.5 can be used to further investigate the properties of Marshallian demands. Suppose for this discussion that the indirect utility function is strictly increasing in income at all positive prices and the Hicksian and Marshallian demands are both differentiable functions so, in particular, $\hat{h}(p, \bar{u}) = \hat{x}(p, e^*(p, \bar{u}))$ is a differentiable identity. Differentiating this identity using the Chain Rule yields:

$$\mathbf{D}_p \hat{h}(p, \bar{u}) = \mathbf{D}_p \hat{x}(p, m)\big|_{m=e^*(p,\bar{u})} + \mathbf{D}_m \hat{x}(p, m)\big|_{m=e^*(p,\bar{u})} \mathbf{D}_p e^*(p, \bar{u}).$$

By Shephard's Lemma $\mathbf{D}_p e^*(p, \bar{u}) = \hat{h}(p, \bar{u})^{\perp}$, so:

$$\mathbf{D}_p \hat{x}(p, m)\big|_{m=e^*(p,\bar{u})} = \mathbf{D}_p \hat{h}(p, \bar{u}) - \mathbf{D}_m \hat{x}(p, m)\big|_{m=e^*(p,\bar{u})} \hat{h}(p, \bar{u})^{\perp}.$$

Now evaluate this equation at $\bar{u} = u^*(p, m)$ for some arbitrary income level $m \geq 0$, and substitute $m = e^*(p, u^*(p, m))$ and $\hat{x}(p, m) = \hat{h}(p, u^*(p, m))$, to obtain:

$$\mathbf{D}_p \hat{x}(p, m) = \mathbf{D}_p \hat{h}(p, \bar{u})\Big|_{\bar{u}=u^*(p,m)} - \mathbf{D}_m \hat{x}(p, m) \hat{x}(p, m)^{\perp}.$$

This equation, known as the *Hicks-Slutsky Decomposition,* expresses the price slopes of the Marshallian demand in two terms. The first term is the corresponding price slopes of the Hicksian demand, called the pure *substitution effect* of the price change, because it expresses how much demand would change if the consumer reacted only to the change in relative prices while ignoring the fact that the price change also changes how much can be purchased with the fixed level of money income. The second term is called the *income effect* of the price change because it tells how the Marshallian demand for good i changes when income changes by $\mathbf{D}m = -\hat{x}^{\perp}\mathbf{D}p$, which is the implicit change in monetary purchasing power experienced by the consumer from the price change $\mathbf{D}p$. The Hicks-Slutsky Decomposition is illustrated in Fig. 10.3.[2]

It is known from the properties of the expenditure minimum that the own-price slope of a Hicksian demand is nonpositive. However, as we will establish both formally and geometrically below, the income effect

[2]The Hicks and Slutsky decompositions differ for finite price changes and the version illustrated here is due to Hicks. Slutsky's decomposition holds consumption rather than utility constant when calculating the hypothetical intermediate income level, thereby rotating the budget line to the new slope but simultaneously changing income to $m' = (p_1'', p_2)^{\perp} \hat{x}(p_1', p_2, m)$ versus Hicks's income change to $e^*(p_1'', p_2, \bar{u})$. This makes Slutsky's intermediate budget line pass through the original consumption point instead of being tangent to the original indifference curve. Slutsky's substitution effect is from $\hat{x}(p_1', p_2, m)$ to an optimum $\hat{x}(p_1'', p_2, m')$ on this intermediate budget line (not illustrated), which entails a change in utility. Slutsky's income effect is then the change from $\hat{x}(p_1'', p_2, m')$ to $\hat{x}(p_1'', p_2, m)$. The two decompositions are the same for an infinitesimal price change.

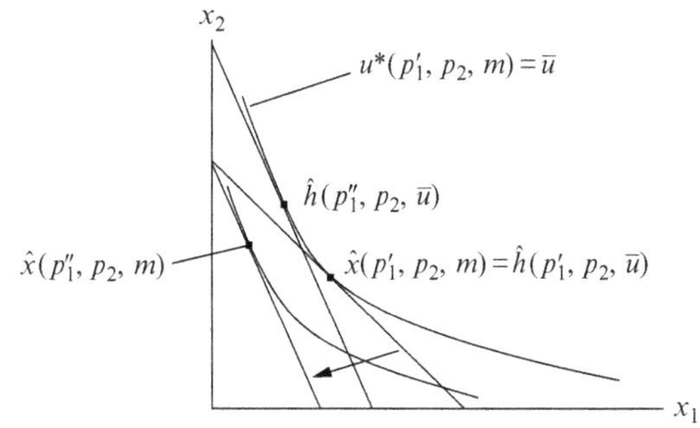

Fig. 10.3 The Hicks-Slutsky Decomposition. When p_1 increases from p_1' to p_1'' the budget line swings down, as indicated by the arrow. The new price ratio determines the slope of the new budget line. At this new price ratio, the consumer cannot afford any bundle that yields the original utility level $\bar{u}$. Rather, at the new price, income would have to be increased enough to make point $\hat{h}(p_1'', p_2, \bar{u})$ affordable in order for the consumer to maintain the original level of utility. Hence the price increase imposes an implicit income decrease corresponding to the distance between the two parallel budget lines, and the change in demand from point $\hat{h}(p_1'', p_2, \bar{u})$ to point $\hat{x}(p_1'', p_2, m)$ that would occur from such an income change is the *income effect* of the price change. The change in demand from $\hat{x}(p_1', p_2, m)$ to $\hat{h}(p_1'', p_2, \bar{u})$ that would occur if there were no implicit income change is the pure *substitution effect* of the price change, and it is always nonpositive on the good whose price is changing (note that x_1 decreases as we move from $\hat{x}(p_1', p_2, m)$ to $\hat{h}(p_1'', p_2, \bar{u})$). Point $\hat{h}(p_1'', p_2, \bar{u})$ is the Hicksian demand point for the original utility level $\bar{u}$ and the new higher price. Since the consumer would have to be compensated for the implicit income loss in order to buy point $\hat{h}(p_1'', p_2, \bar{u})$, the Hicksian demand is sometimes called the (income) *compensated* demand (and, likewise, the Marshallian demand is sometimes called the *uncompensated* demand).

term in the Hicks-Slutsky Decomposition has unknown sign in general. Hence Marshallian demand does not obey the law of demand in general (i.e., does not always slope downward as a function of the own-price). Still, rearranging the decomposition yields important properties of the Marshallian demand from the Hicksian demand.

Theorem 10.6 (Properties of the Hicks-Slutsky Substitution Matrix). *Assume the conditions of Theorem 10.1, the indirect utility function is strictly increasing in income, and the Hicksian and Marshallian demands are both differentiable functions at a price/income pair (p, m) (and the implied utility level $\bar{u} = u^*(p, m)$). Then:*

$$\mathbf{D}_p\hat{x}(p, m) + \mathbf{D}_m\hat{x}(p, m)\hat{x}(p, m)^{\perp}$$

is a singular and negative semidefinite matrix. If the off-diagonal entries are continuous in p then the matrix is symmetric: $\frac{\partial \hat{x}_j}{\partial p_i} + \frac{\partial \hat{x}_j}{\partial m}\hat{x}_i = \frac{\partial \hat{x}_i}{\partial p_j} + \frac{\partial \hat{x}_i}{\partial m}\hat{x}_j$.

Proof. From the Hicks-Slutsky Decomposition, this is the matrix of Hicksian price slopes at utility level $u^*(p, m)$, which is singular and negative semidefinite from Theorem 9.2; and symmetric when the off-diagonal elements are continuous. □

Singularity of the Hicks-Slutsky substitution matrix can be viewed as a consequence of homogeneity of Marshallian demand. Euler's Theorem applied to the homogeneous of degree zero Marshallian demand is:

$$\mathbf{D}_p\hat{x}(p, m)p + \mathbf{D}_m\hat{x}(p, m)m = 0.$$

That is, the (p, m) vector forms a linear combination of the columns of the Hicks-Slutsky matrix evaluated at that (p, m) vector.[3] As in the profit maximization and cost/expenditure minimization models, this linear dependence can be expressed in elasticity form. Dividing row i by $\hat{x}_i$ yields:

$$\sum_{j=1}^{n} \frac{p_j}{\hat{x}_i(p, m)} \frac{\partial \hat{x}_i(p, m)}{\partial p_j} + \frac{m}{\hat{x}_i(p, m)} \frac{\partial \hat{x}_i(p, m)}{\partial m} = 0, \tag{10.5}$$

showing that *the price and income elasticities of a Marshallian demand sum to zero.*

A second elasticity relationship arises from Walras' Law. Differentiating the identity $p^{\perp}\hat{x}(p, m) = m$ with respect to m yields $\sum_{j=1}^{n} p_j \frac{\partial \hat{x}_j}{\partial m} = 1$. Hence:

$$\sum_{j=1}^{n} \left(\frac{\partial \hat{x}_j}{\partial m} \frac{m}{\hat{x}_j} \right) \frac{p_j \hat{x}_j}{m} = 1.$$

That is, *the income elasticities of all Marshallian demands, each weighted by the share of income spent on that commodity, sum to unity.*

These two elasticity results can be combined to form a third elasticity identity. Recall from item 8 of Theorem 9.1 that, due to symmetry of Hicksian demand slopes, we have:

$$\sum_{j=1}^{n} p_j \frac{\partial \hat{h}_j}{\partial p_i} = 0.$$

[3] The slopes of the marginal utility of income $\hat{\lambda}(p, m)$ have the same linear dependence because $\hat{\lambda}(p, m)$ is also homogeneous of degree zero. Recall from the Lagrange Multiplier Rule that $\hat{\lambda}$ is unique, and that the homogeneity in Theorem 10.1 is due to the fact that the optimization problem is unchanged when (p, m) is rescaled to $(\alpha p, \alpha m)$.

Using the Hicks-Slutsky Decomposition, this can be expressed in terms of Marshallian demands:

$$\sum_{j=1}^{n} p_j \frac{\partial \hat{x}_j}{\partial p_i} + \hat{x}_i \sum_{j=1}^{n} p_j \frac{\partial \hat{x}_j}{\partial m} = 0.$$

This second term is $\hat{x}_i$ due to the income elasticity identity. Multiplying by $\frac{p_i}{m}$ and forming elasticities yields:

$$\sum_{j=1}^{n} \left(\frac{\partial \hat{x}_j}{\partial p_i} \frac{p_i}{\hat{x}_j} \right) \frac{p_j \hat{x}_j}{m} + \frac{p_i \hat{x}_i}{m} = 0.$$

That is, *the elasticities of all Marshallian demands with respect to one price, each weighted by the share of income spent on that commodity, plus the share of income spent on the commodity whose price is changing, sum to zero.*

10.5 COMPARATIVE STATICS

If u is continuously differentiable in a neighborhood of $\hat{x}$ and the Implicit Function Theorem applies to Eqs. (10.2) and (10.3) then the functional form of L yields a particular version of the comparative statics equation (2.16) for the utility maximization problem:

$$\begin{bmatrix} \mathbf{D}^2 u(\hat{x}) & -p \\ -p^{\perp} & 0 \end{bmatrix} \begin{bmatrix} \mathbf{D}\hat{x} \\ \mathbf{D}\hat{\lambda} \end{bmatrix} = - \begin{bmatrix} -\hat{\lambda} I_n & 0 \\ -\hat{x}^{\perp} & 1 \end{bmatrix}.$$

This equation can be used to derive the price and income slopes of the Marshallian demands for a particular utility function, as well as the price and income slopes of the Lagrange multiplier. Column $i = 1, \ldots, n$ of the (negative of the) right side $\mathbf{D}_{(p,m)}(\mathbf{D}_{(x,\lambda)}L)^{\perp}$ has nonzero entry $-\hat{\lambda}$ in row i and nonzero entry $-\hat{x}_i$ in row $n+1$. Although this is a simple form, it is not the special structure discussed for Eq. (2.16). When this column is substituted into column j of $\mathbf{D}^2_{(x,\lambda)}L$ on the left side for an application of Cramer's Rule, and cofactor expansion is performed, there are two nonzero terms:

$$\frac{\partial \hat{x}_j}{\partial p_i} = \frac{(-1)^{i+j}\hat{\lambda} M_{i,j} + (-1)^{n+1+j} \hat{x}_i M_{n+1,j}}{\left| \mathbf{D}^2_{(x,\lambda)} L \right|}, \tag{10.6}$$

where $M_{i,j}$ is the minor of the (i,j) entry in $\mathbf{D}^2_{(x,\lambda)}L$. Even when $i = j$, only the first term involves a *principal* minor. The necessary second order condition (Theorem 2.4) therefore does not establish a sign for $\frac{\partial \hat{x}_j}{\partial p_i}$ even when $i = j$: Marshallian demands do not necessarily have nonpositive own-price slopes. The last (i.e., $(n+1)^{\text{st}}$) column of $\mathbf{D}_{(p,m)}(\mathbf{D}_{(x,\lambda)}L)^{\perp}$ has only one nonzero entry, a 1 in the last position. Cramer's Rule therefore yields:

$$\frac{\partial \hat{x}_j}{\partial m} = \frac{(-1)^{n+1+j}(-1)M_{n+1,j}}{\left|\mathbf{D}^2_{(x,\lambda)}L\right|}. \tag{10.7}$$

Although there is only one term, it again involves a non-principal minor: Marshallian demands do not necessarily have nonnegative income slopes. Comparing Eqs. (10.6) and (10.7), we see they are related:

$$\frac{\partial \hat{x}_j}{\partial p_i} = \frac{(-1)^{i+j}\hat{\lambda}M_{i,j}}{\left|\mathbf{D}^2_{(x,\lambda)}L\right|} - \hat{x}_i\frac{\partial \hat{x}_j}{\partial m}.$$

This is another way to derive the Hicks-Slutsky Decomposition. The first term is the substitution effect of the change in p_i on the demand for x_j and the second term is the income effect. The first term is nonpositive when $j = i$ because the necessary second order condition requires that the numerator and denominator have opposite signs. The second term has ambiguous sign because the necessary second order condition provides no general information about the sign of $M_{n+1,j}$. Hence the signs of $\frac{\partial \hat{x}_j}{\partial p_i}$ and $\frac{\partial \hat{x}_j}{\partial m}$ are not implied by the utility maximization behavioral postulate, even when $j = i$.

Similarly, Eq. (2.18) can be applied to the particular comparative statics equation above for the utility maximization problem to find expressions for $\frac{\partial \hat{\lambda}}{\partial p_j}$ and $\frac{\partial \hat{\lambda}}{\partial m}$. This is pursued in Exercise 7. The necessary second order condition does not imply a sign for either expression. As $\hat{\lambda}$ is the marginal utility of income, this shows that diminishing marginal utility of income is *not* implied by the utility maximization behavioral postulate.

The Hicks-Slutsky Decomposition allows us to characterize situations in which Marshallian demand indeed obeys the law of demand:

- If $\frac{\partial \hat{x}_i}{\partial m} \geq 0$ we say x_i is a *normal good*, and we then know its Marshallian demand slopes downward as a function of p_i. The Hicksian demand curve is at least as steep as the Marshallian demand curve in this case (the Hicksian demand changes no more than the Marshallian demand when price changes, but since price is on the vertical axis in a conventional demand graph this means the Hicksian curve is at least as steep as the Marshallian curve). In Fig. 10.3, x_1 decreases as we move from $\hat{h}(p_1'', p_2, \bar{u})$ to $\hat{x}(p_1'', p_2, m)$, so x_1 is normal in that graph. The corresponding demand curves are illustrated in Fig. 10.4.

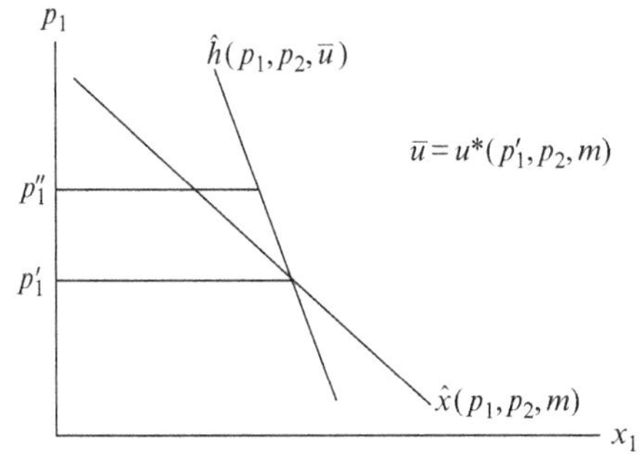

Fig. 10.4 Hicksian and Marshallian demands for a normal good.

- If $\frac{\partial \hat{x}_i}{\partial m} < 0$ we say x_i is an *inferior good*. If this income derivative, weighted by $\hat{x}_i$, is smaller in absolute value than $\frac{\partial \hat{h}_i}{\partial p_i}$ then the Marshallian demand still slopes downward but is now steeper than the Hicksian demand. This is illustrated in Fig. 10.5. If not, then the Marshallian

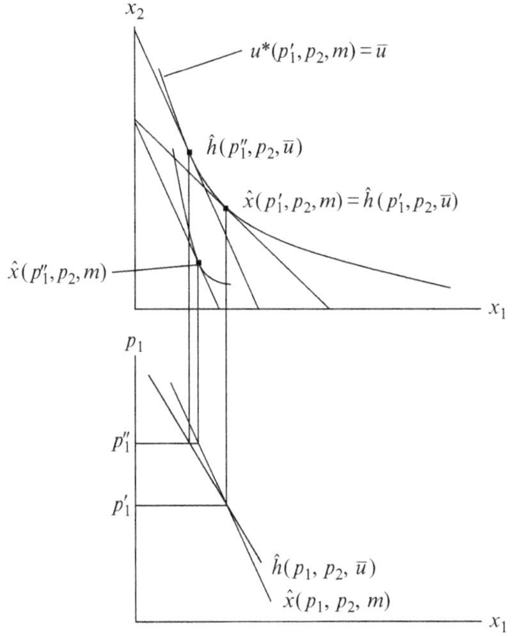

Fig. 10.5 Hicksian and Marshallian demands for an inferior (non-Giffen) good.

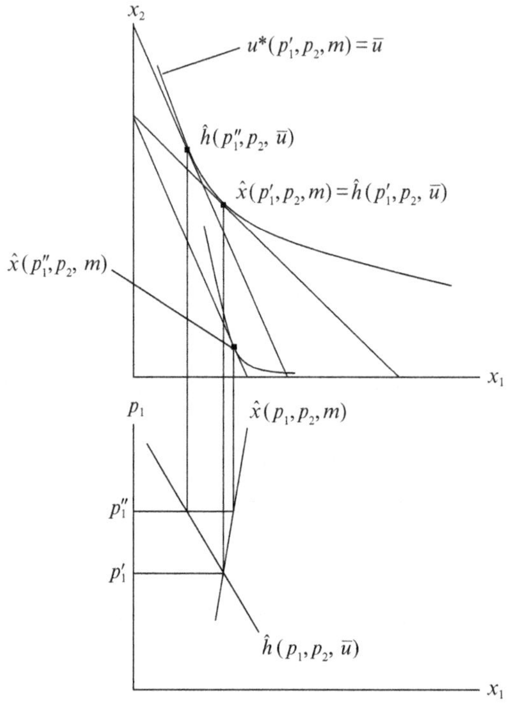

Fig. 10.6 Hicksian and Marshallian demands for a Giffen good.

demand slopes upward, and we say x_i is a *Giffen good*. A Giffen good is illustrated in Fig. 10.6.

It is *not* possible in general to classify goods as substitutes or complements based on Marshallian demands. Due to income effects, which need not be symmetric between two goods, the price derivatives of Marshallian demands are not symmetric. Hence it is possible that $\frac{\partial \hat{x}_i}{\partial p_j} > 0$ while $\frac{\partial \hat{x}_j}{\partial p_i} < 0$, in which case any classification is arbitrary. As the Hicksian demand slopes *are* symmetric, it is possible as noted in Chapter 9 to classify substitutes and complements based on Hicksian demands (or equivalently based on the Hicks-Slutsky matrix, which is observable). Note, however, that homotheticity resolves the ambiguity associated with classifying goods as substitutes or complements based on Marshallian demands (see Exercise 15).

10.6 NOTES

Marshallian demand is from [2, Book III, Chapter III]. Walras [3, Part II] developed utility-maximizing demand curves before Marshall, leading some to use the term "Walrasian" demand rather than "Marshallian" demand. Walras' Law is from [3, Section 123]. The Slutsky Decomposition derives its name from [4] although there were elements of it in [2]. The exposition of income and substitution effects in [5, Chapter 2] is exceptionally clear and evidently derived independently from Slutsky; leading to the label "Hicks-Slutsky Decomposition." The Giffen case is mentioned in [2, p. 132]. The label "indirect utility function" is due to [6, p. 157], where some properties of the utility maximum and its relationship to the expenditure minimum are derived, but the concept appeared in earlier papers by Houthakker and in [7, 8]; Roy's Identity appears on p. 214 of the latter.

The elasticity identities appear in [9, p. 105] and [10, pp. 338–341].

10.7 EXERCISES

1. For the utility function defined in part (d) of Exercise 14 in Chapter 8:
   a. Assume $p_1 = 2$, $p_2 = 1$, and $m = 4$, where p_i is the price of commodity i and m is the consumer's money endowment. How much of each good will the consumer choose?
   b. Assume $p_1 = 2$, $p_2 = 1$, and $m = 2.5$. How much of each good will the consumer choose?
2. Find the optimal consumption for the consumer in part (c) of Exercise 14 in Chapter 8 when prices are $p_1 = p_2 = 1$ and income is $m = 10$.
3. For each of the following utility functions defined on $\mathbb{R}^2_+$, find the Marshallian demand correspondence and indirect utility function for a price-taking consumer with given money income.
   a. $u(x_1, x_2) = x_2(x_1 + 1)$.
   b. $u(x_1, x_2) = x_2 + \sqrt{x_1}$.
   c. $u(x_1, x_2) = \sqrt{x_1 + 4} + x_2$ (first carefully draw a typical indifference curve for utility level $\bar{u} \geq 2$ (since $u(0) = 2$)).
   d. The utility functions in Exercises 1–3 of Chapter 9.
4. Assume a consumer's utility function is $u(x_0, x_1) = x_0 x_1$, where x_0 is spending for consumption in the present time period, period 0, and x_1 is spending for consumption one time period later. The consumer will have an income of \$1000 in time period 1 but has no income

in period 0. The consumer can borrow any amount of money up to \$1000 in period 0 at an interest rate of 10% but must pay back the loan in period 1. Do the utility maximizing choices of x_0 and x_1 involve borrowing? If yes, how much?

5. Suppose a consumer has utility function $u(x_1, x_2) = x_2/(x_1 + 1)$ on $\mathbb{R}^2_+$. Draw a few representative indifference curves. Derive the Marshallian and Hicksian demands, and indirect utility and expenditure functions.
6. Here is a Marshallian demand for a price-taking consumer of two goods, in standard notation:
$$\hat{x}(p_1, p_2, m)^{\perp} = \left(\frac{m}{4p_1}, \frac{3m}{4p_2}\right).$$
Here is an indirect utility function for a price-taking consumer of two goods, also in standard notation:
$$u^*(p_1, p_2, m) = \frac{m^3}{p_1 p_2^2}.$$
Is it possible that the given Marshallian demands are for the same consumer (i.e., same preferences) as the given indirect utility function? Explain why or why not.
7. Use comparative statics methodology to find expressions for $\frac{\partial \hat{\lambda}}{\partial p_i}$ and $\frac{\partial \hat{\lambda}}{\partial m}$ in the utility maximization problem, where $\hat{\lambda}$ is the Lagrange multiplier. Can either of these be signed? Why/why not? Give an economic interpretation of $\frac{\partial \hat{\lambda}}{\partial m}$.
8. Assume the consumption set is $\mathbb{R}^3_+$ and the preferences of a consumer are as follows: The utility received from consumption of x_1 units of commodity 1 is x_1, irrespective of the amounts consumed of commodities x_2 and x_3; the utility received from consumption of x_2 units of commodity 2 is $\sqrt{x_2}$, irrespective of the amounts consumed of commodities x_1 and x_3; and the utility received from consumption of x_3 units of commodity 3 is $-x_3$, irrespective of the amounts consumed of commodities x_1 and x_2.
    a. Explain whether the preferences are complete, transitive, continuous, locally nonsatiable, convex, and monotonic.
    b. Find the Marshallian demand correspondence and indirect utility function.
9. A price-taking consumer has utility function $u = x_1 + x_2$ on $\mathbb{R}^2_+$. The price of good 2 is p_2, but good 1 can only be purchased if the consumer

first pays \$10 to join a club. After paying the \$10 membership fee, the consumer can purchase good 1 at price p_1 per unit.

a. Draw the budget constraint.

b. Find the Marshallian demand correspondence.

10. A graduate student consumes only two goods, books (B) and cups of coffee (C), and has utility function $u = BC + B$ for $(B, C) \in \mathbb{R}^2_+$. The student has income of \$100 per month. The price of books is \$50 per book and the price of coffee is \$1 per cup. Both goods are divisible.

a. What is the constrained utility-maximizing consumption of books and coffee for this student?

b. What is the marginal utility of income for this student?

11. Suppose a consumer has income \$$m$ and has two goods, food and cigarettes, on which to spend it. Let p_f be the price of food and p_c be the price of cigarettes. Suppose further that this consumer receives \$50 in food stamps, which can only be spent on food.

a. Draw the budget set of this consumer.

b. Must this consumer's Marshallian demand be homogeneous of degree zero in prices and income? Why/why not?

12. Alan has a monthly income consisting of \$400 earnings and \$150 provided by the government in the form of food stamps. If we create a composite good food, which we label X_F, and a composite good of all other things, which we label X_O, his preferences can be represented by the utility function $U_A = X_F^{1/2} X_O^{1/2}$ on $\mathbb{R}^2_+$. Assume the price of X_F and X_O are both 1. Assume that food stamps can be used to buy food at a dollar-for-dollar rate but that they cannot be used to buy other things. However, food stamps can be traded for cash on a black market, where \$1 in cash is received for every \$2 in food stamps.

a. Draw Alan's effective budget constraint in (X_F, X_O) space, taking explicit account of how food stamps differ from cash. Be sure to label all critical points and slopes.

b. What will Alan's monthly expenditures on food and other goods be, and what is the face value of the food stamps he sells on the black market?

c. Betty has the same budget constraint as Alan but has utility function $U_B = X_F^{1/4} X_O^{3/4}$. What are Betty's monthly expenditures on food and other goods, and the face value of the food stamps she sells on the black market?

d. Carla has utility function $U_C = X_F^2 + \frac{X_O^3}{300}$. What are Carla's monthly expenditures on food and other goods, and the face value of the food stamps she sells on the black market?

13. Each evening, J. P. enjoys consumption of cigars (C) and glasses of brandy (B) according to the utility function:

$$U(C, B) = 20C - C^2 + 18B - 3B^2.$$

Suppose C and B each cost \$1 and J. P. may spend up to \$20 each evening.

a. How many cigars and glasses of brandy does J. P. consume each evening?

b. Now suppose J. P. is advised by his doctors that he must limit the sum of glasses of brandy and cigars consumed to no more than 5 each evening. If J. P. follows this advice, how many glasses of brandy and cigars will he consume each evening?

c. What standard properties are either satisfied or violated by J. P.'s preferences? Explain why.

14. Consider a price-taking consumer whose preferences are represented by $u(x)$ for $x \in \mathbb{R}^n_+$. Let the corresponding vector of prices be p, income be m, and assume the marginal utility of income is positive.

Suppose the government places an *ad valorem* tax on good 1 at a rate of t, so that the consumer pays price $p_1(1 + t)$ (assume prices do not respond to the tax), and then rebates back to the consumer the revenue that the tax would generate if the consumer stayed at the pre-tax consumption level. Show, *using the "Envelope Theorem,"* that the consumer benefits from an increase in the tax rate if and only if the government is incurring a deficit on this consumer.

15. A consumer's preferences on $\mathbb{R}^n_+$ are called *homothetic* if the preferences are represented by a utility function that is a monotonic transformation of a function that is homogeneous of degree $r > 0$ (i.e., $u(x) = f(g(x))$, where $f : \mathbb{R}^1 \to \mathbb{R}^1$ is strictly increasing and $g : \mathbb{R}^n_+ \to \mathbb{R}^1$ is homogeneous of degree r).

a. Show there is no loss of generality in just assuming the consumer's utility function is homogeneous of degree 1. Assume this henceforth.

b. Assume local nonsatiation and unique interior optima that are differentiable as needed. Show that $MRS_{ij}(x)$ is homogeneous of degree zero. Use this to show that the Marshallian demand is homogeneous of degree one in income: $\hat{x}(p, \alpha m) = \alpha\hat{x}(p, m)$. Comment on classifying commodities as normal or inferior when preferences are homothetic.

c. Now show $u^*(p, m) = \hat{\lambda}(p, m)m$ using Euler's Theorem, where $\hat{\lambda}(p, m)$ is the Lagrange multiplier for the utility maximization problem.

d. Differentiate to show that $\frac{\partial \hat{\lambda}}{\partial p_i} = -\frac{\hat{\lambda}\hat{x}_i}{m}$.

e. Now use part (c) and the usual approach to deriving symmetry results to show that the matrix of price derivatives of the Marshallian demand is symmetric when preferences are homothetic (even though it is not symmetric in general).

f. Comment on classifying commodities as Marshallian substitutes or complements when preferences are homothetic.

16. For the utility function in part (c) of Exercise 3 in Chapter 9, suppose income is $m = 5$ and the price of x_2 is $p_2 = 1$. Carefully draw a graph illustrating the substitution and income effects on x_1 of a decrease in the price of x_1 from $p_1 = 9$ to $p_1 = 1$. Calculate the substitution and income effects on the quantity demanded of x_1.

17. For the utility function in part (d) of Exercise 3 in Chapter 9, suppose $p_2 = 1$. Carefully draw a graph that illustrates the substitution and income effects on x_1 of a change in p_1 from $p_1^0 = \frac{1}{2}$ to $p_1^1 = 2$.

18. A consumer's preferences $(\mathbb{R}^2_+, \succsim)$ are represented by the function $u(x_1, x_2) = x_1^{1/2} + x_2^{1/2}$.

a. Derive the Marshallian and Hicksian demands.

b. What are the quantities demanded when the prices are $(p_1, p_2) = (4, 1)$ and the monetary resource is $m = 80$?

c. Derive the substitution and income effects on x_1 when p_1 increases to $p_1 = 8$ (and p_2 and m remain at 1 and 80, respectively). Illustrate these effects on a carefully drawn and labeled indifference/budget graph.

19. Consider a price-taking consumer with locally nonsatiable preferences over $\mathbb{R}^{10}_+$. Suppose all prices are 1 and the income effects for goods 2 through 10 are 0.05. Show that good 1 is normal.

20. Let $\hat{x}_i(p, m)$ be a differentiable Marshallian demand for good i. Fix prices p at $p^0 \gg 0$. Suppose Mr. Giffen makes the following claim:

> *"There must exist an income level $m^0 > 0$ such that $\hat{x}_i$ is not upward-sloping in p_i at (p^0, m^0)."*

Is Mr. Giffen right or wrong? Explain why.

21. Suppose income is fixed. Can a Marshallian demand look like this?

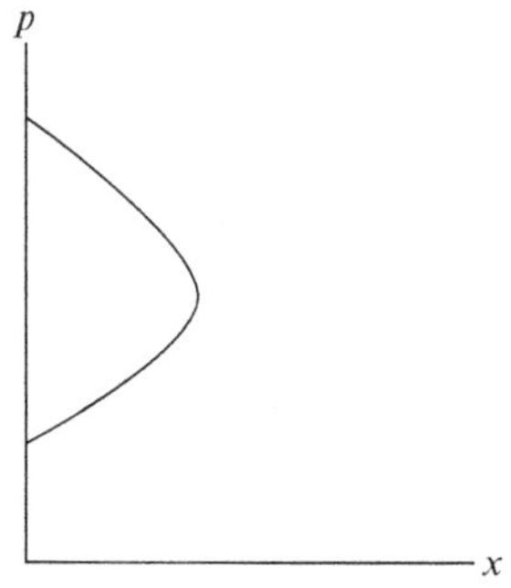

Explain why/why not.

22. Consider a consumer whose utility function is additively separable:

$$u(x_1, \ldots, x_n) = f_1(x_1) + f_2(x_2) + \cdots + f_n(x_n),$$

where each f_i is an increasing, concave function. Show that the Marshallian demands are downward-sloping. (Hint: determine whether each good is normal.)

23. Find the Marshallian demand correspondence for Mr. Aristotle, introduced in Exercise 25 of Chapter 8. Then draw a price change on an indifference graph and identify the income and substitution effects of the price change.

24. Consider a price-taking consumer with utility function $u(x, L)$, where x is a nonnegative vector of quantities and L is the quantity (number of hours) of leisure consumed. Let $p \gg 0$ be the price of x and $w > 0$ be the price of leisure (i.e., the wage rate). Let $m \geq 0$ be the consumer's non-wage income and $\bar{L} > 0$ be the consumer's endowment of hours that can be devoted to either labor or leisure.

a. Write the consumer's budget constraint. What are the price and income arguments of the leisure demand function?

b. Define the supply of labor to be the difference between the time endowment and the demand for leisure. Write the own-price slope of the labor supply curve in terms of leisure demand slopes.

c. Now use the Hicks-Slutsky Decomposition to write the labor supply slope in terms of a Hicksian demand for leisure slope and the effect of income on leisure.

d. What happens when leisure is an inferior good? What might happen if leisure is a normal good?

25. A consumer has utility function on $\mathbb{R}^2_+$ given by:

$$u(x_1, x_2) = \begin{cases} 3(x_1 + x_2), & \text{for } x_2 \geq 2x_1 \\ x_1 + 4x_2, & \text{for } x_2 \leq 2x_1 \end{cases}.$$

a. Find the Marshallian demand correspondence and indirect utility function.
b. Find the expenditure function.
c. Assume $p_1 > p_2$. Find the Hicksian demand correspondence for this range of prices.

26. Here is a utility function on $\mathbb{R}^2_+$:

$$u(x_1, x_2) = \begin{cases} 3x_1 + x_2, & \text{if } x_1 < x_2 \\ 2(x_1 + x_2), & \text{if } x_1 \geq x_2 \end{cases}.$$

a. Carefully graph a typical indifference curve.
b. Derive the Marshallian demand correspondence and the indirect utility function.

27. Consider a price taking consumer of two commodities, $(x_1, x_2) \in \mathbb{R}^2_+$, with utility function:

$$u(x_1, x_2) = \begin{cases} \min\{3x_1, x_2\} & \text{if } x_2 \geq x_1 \\ \min\{x_1, 3x_2\} & \text{if } x_2 \leq x_1 \end{cases}.$$

a. Carefully draw a typical indifference curve.
b. List standard properties of preferences and describe whether this consumer's preferences have each property.
c. Denote the price of commodity i by p_i and money income by m. Derive the Marshallian demand.
d. Derive the indirect utility function and the expenditure function.
e. Derive the substitution and income effects on consumption of x_1 from a change in p_2 when $p_1 > p_2$. Do the same for the change in consumption of x_2 from a change in p_1. Use your results to confirm that the matrix of $\frac{\partial \hat{x}_i}{\partial p_j} + \hat{x}_j \frac{\partial \hat{x}_i}{\partial m}$ terms is symmetric when $p_1 > p_2$.

28. Suppose a consumer's Hicksian demand for a good is $\hat{h} = \frac{100}{p}$ when utility is u^0, where p is the price of the good and all other prices are fixed at some unspecified levels. Suppose further that indirect utility is u^0 when $p = 2$, income $m = 133$, and all other prices are fixed

at the same unspecified levels. What is the value of this consumer's Marshallian demand for this good at $p = 2$, when $m = 133$ and all other prices are fixed at the same unspecified levels?

29. A consumer of three goods has complete, transitive, continuous, and locally nonsatiated preferences on $\mathbb{R}^3_+$. At prices $p_1 = 1$, $p_2 = 2$, and $p_3 = 5$ the Marshallian quantities demanded are $x_1 = 450$, $x_2 = 150$, and $x_3 = 30$. At these same prices, the first two income derivatives are $\frac{\partial \hat{x}_1}{\partial m} = \frac{1}{2}$ and $\frac{\partial \hat{x}_2}{\partial m} = \frac{1}{6}$, and the matrix of Marshallian price derivatives is:

$$\begin{bmatrix} -450 & s_{12} & s_{13} \\ s_{21} & -75 & s_{23} \\ s_{31} & s_{32} & -6 \end{bmatrix}.$$

Fill in the values of the s_{ij} terms in this matrix. Show and explain very carefully how you obtain each value.

30. Given the indirect utility function $u^*(p_1, p_2, m) = \left(\frac{m^2}{p_1 p_2}\right)^{1/4}$ in standard notation, find the:

a. Expenditure function.

b. Hicksian demand correspondence.

c. Marshallian demand correspondence.

31. Suppose a consumer has expenditure function $e^*(p_1, p_2, \bar{u}) = \bar{u}\sqrt{p_1 p_2}$. Find the Marshallian demand correspondence.

32. Consider a price-taking consumer whose preferences on $\mathbb{R}^3_+$ satisfy completeness, transitivity, continuity, and local nonsatiation. Here is some information about this consumer's demand behavior at prices $p_1 = 1$, $p_2 = 2$, $p_3 = 6$ and income $m = 10$:

$$\frac{\partial \hat{x}_1}{\partial p_2} = -5, \quad \frac{\partial \hat{x}_1}{\partial p_3} = 2, \quad \frac{\partial \hat{h}_1}{\partial p_1} = -10.$$

Suppose further that the income effects on the Marshallian demand for commodities 2 and 3 are zero at these prices and income level. What is the Marshallian quantity demanded of commodity 1 at these prices and income level?

33. Suppose a price-taking consumer of two goods, x_1 and x_2, has utility function $u(x_1, x_2) = x_2 - \frac{1}{x_1}$. Note that u can be negative at positive values of x_1 and x_2.

a. Draw a typical indifference curve for a utility level $\bar{u}$ that is nonnegative.

b. Find the Hicksian demand correspondence for values of $\bar{u}$ that are nonnegative.

c. Use your answer to part (b) to find the indirect utility function for values of income m and prices p_1 and p_2 that satisfy a particular condition. What is the condition?

d. Use your answer to part (c) to find the Marshallian demand correspondence for values of income and prices that satisfy your condition.

34. Suppose a consumer has Hicksian demand as defined in Exercise 3a of Chapter 11. The government is considering the following two taxes for this consumer. Tax A charges $t\%$ on the amount spent on good 1. That is, if the price received by the seller is p_1 then the price paid by the consumer is $(1+t)p_1$. Tax B reduces the consumer's income by an amount T. That is, if income is m before paying the tax then income is $m-T$ after paying the tax. Suppose prices p_1 and p_2 are not affected by these taxes, and that the government calculates T so that the consumer is indifferent between Tax A and Tax B.

a. Derive an expression for the government's revenue from Tax A in terms of income m, prices p_1 and p_2, and the tax rate t.

b. Derive an expression for the government's revenue from Tax B in terms of income m, prices p_1 and p_2, and the tax rate t.

c. Show which tax collects more revenue for the government.

35. Assume $\hat{x}(p, m)$ is the Marshallian demand for a price-taking consumer with complete, transitive, continuous and locally nonsatiated preferences on the consumption set $\mathbb{R}^2_+$ (assume the Marshallian demand is single-valued on the entire price/income space $(p, m) \in \mathbb{R}^2_{++} \times \mathbb{R}^1_+$).

The government wants to raise money revenue $\bar{R} \in (0, m)$ by imposing excise taxes on this consumer in a way that is least damaging to the consumer's utility. Denote the excise tax rate on commodity i by t_i, making the tax rate vector $t^{\perp} = (t_1, t_2)$. Excise taxes are levied per unit of consumption, not on the cost of the purchase (the taxes on gasoline and cigarettes in the US are examples of excise taxes), so imposition of the excise taxes changes the price vector paid by the consumer to $p + t$. Assume throughout that the government's actions do not affect the market price vector p.

a. Write an expression for the government's revenue, $R(t)$, as a function of the tax rates. Write the government's optimization problem and give an argument that the constraint binds at the optimum.

b. Assume henceforth that the consumer's preferences are homothetic. Give a geometric argument that the government's optimal tax rates do not change the slope of the consumer's budget line (that is, $\frac{p_1+t_1}{p_2+t_2} = \frac{p_1}{p_2}$).

c. Let $\alpha = \frac{\hat{x}_2(p,m)}{\hat{x}_1(p,m)}$ be the consumption ratio before the taxes are implemented. Derive $\hat{x}(p+t,m)$ in terms of α and the revenue target $\bar{R}$ (as well as (p,m)).

d. Solve for the government's optimal tax rates.

36. Consider a price-taking consumer with utility function $u(x_1, x_2, x_3) = x_1 x_2 + x_3$. Assume a fixed amount of good 3 is given to the consumer by the government at no charge, and the consumer cannot buy or sell good 3 at any price. Also assume that prices p_1 and p_2 are fixed, and money income is fixed at m.

a. Suppose the government gift is $x_3 = 0$. Find the Marshallian demand for x_1 and x_2.

b. Use your result from part (a) to obtain the Marshallian demand when $x_3 > 0$. Be sure your solution method plainly relies on your solution to part (a) and is not obtained by simply resolving the problem.

c. Find the indirect utility function for a fixed arbitrary level of x_3.

d. Use your result for part (c) to obtain the expenditure function. Again, do not simply resolve the problem.

e. Suppose income is $m = 10$, both prices are $p_1 = p_2 = 1$, and the amount of good 3 provided by the government is $x_3 = 11$. If the government wants to eliminate the gift of x_3 and give income instead, how much income must the government transfer to the consumer in order to leave utility unchanged?

REFERENCES

[1] Apostol TM. Mathematical analysis. 2nd ed. Reading, MA: Addison-Wesley; 1974.

[2] Marshall A. Principles of economics. 9th variorum ed. London: MacMillian; 1961 [first ed. 1890].

[3] Walras L. Éléments D'Économie Politique Pure. Paris: L. Corbaz & Co.; 1874. English translation: Elements of Pure Economics by W. Jaffé. London: George Allen and Unwin; 1954.

[4] Slutsky E. Sulla Teoria del Bilancio del Consumatore. Giornale degli Economisti 1915; English reprint "On the theory of the budget of the consumer" by O. Ragusa. In: Stigler GJ, Boulding KE, editors. A.E.A. Readings in price theory VI. Homewood, IL: Irwin; 1952.

[5] Hicks JR. Value and capital. 2nd ed. Oxford: Oxford University Press; 1946 [first ed. 1939].
[6] Houthakker H. Compensated changes in quantities and qualities consumed. Rev Econ Stud 1952–1953;19:155–64.
[7] Roy R. De l'Utilité: Contribution à la Théorie des Choix. Paris: Hermann; 1942.
[8] Roy R. La Distribution du Revenu entre les divers Biens. Econometrica 1947;15: 205–25.
[9] Samuelson PA. Foundations of economic analysis. Cambridge, MA: Harvard University Press; 1947.
[10] Silberberg E. The structure of economics: a mathematical analysis. 2nd ed. New York: McGraw-Hill; 1990.

CHAPTER 11

Duality of the Utility Maximum

Chapter Outline

11.1 DUALITY OF THE INDIRECT UTILITY FUNCTION

Theorem 10.1 establishes that an indirect utility function *necessarily* has the basic properties of homogeneity, quasiconvexity, monotonicity, and continuity; and that the income image of an indirect utility function is the same interval in $\mathbb{R}^1$ for every positive price vector, and this interval contains its infimum. These basic properties rely only on existence of a continuous utility function on $\mathbb{R}^n_+$, so aside from assuming preferences are complete, transitive and continuous these properties are pure consequences of the price-taking utility maximization behavioral postulate.

As with the other optimization problems studied herein, a natural question to ask now is whether these properties are *sufficient* for an indirect utility function. That is, given an arbitrary function Φ possessing these properties but that is not known *a priori* to be the supremum of some $u(x)$ function over a budget set $x \in B(p, m)$, is that function indeed an indirect utility function for some price-taking consumer? If so, any function with these properties can be used in an econometric or applied theory investigation with the knowledge that the function is a complete representation of utility-maximizing behavior.

Again because the objective is not a monetary value function and the constraint is active with respect to price the approach to this question is somewhat different than for other optimization problems studied herein.

However, we can use the fact that a utility maximum is an expenditure minimum, and then use duality of the expenditure function. This approach entails an extra restriction because the equivalence between utility maximization and expenditure minimization requires that the indirect utility function be strictly increasing (local nonsatiation is sufficient but not necessary). Recall also that monotonicity in prices is a redundant property of expenditure functions. Hence the following theorem is stated with these modified monotonicity properties, and the proof relies on duality of the expenditure function.

Theorem 11.1 (Duality of the Indirect Utility Function). *Assume $\Phi : \mathbb{R}^n_{++} \times \mathbb{R}^1_+ \to \mathbb{R}^1$ is a homogeneous of degree zero, quasiconvex and continuous function that is strictly increasing in its last argument. Assume further that $\Phi(p, \mathbb{R}^1_+)$ is the same interval U for every $p \in \mathbb{R}^n_{++}$, and U contains its infimum $\underline{u}$. Then there exists a continuous, nondecreasing and quasiconcave utility function $u_\Phi : \mathbb{R}^n_+ \to \mathbb{R}^1$ such that $\Phi(p, m) = u^*_\Phi(p, m)$ for every $(p, m) \in \mathbb{R}^n_{++} \times \mathbb{R}^1_+$, where $u^*_\Phi(p, m) = \sup\{u_\Phi(x) : x \in B(p, m)\}$. That is, there exists a continuous, nondecreasing and quasiconcave utility function for which Φ is the indirect utility function.*

Proof. As Φ is strictly increasing in its last argument, it has an inverse function (for given p). Moreover, the domain of that inverse function is U for every $p \in \mathbb{R}^n_{++}$ because this interval is the image of Φ for every p. Let $\phi : \mathbb{R}^n_{++} \times U \to \mathbb{R}^1$ be this inverse function, defined by:

$$\Phi(p, \phi(p, \bar{u})) = \bar{u}.$$

Note that ϕ is strictly increasing in its last argument. Note also that $\Phi(p, 0) = \underline{u}$ for every $p \in \mathbb{R}^n_{++}$ because Φ is defined at $(p, 0)$, $\underline{u}$ is the minimum of the image of Φ for every p, and Φ is strictly increasing in its last argument. That is, $\phi(p, \underline{u}) = 0$ for every $p \in \mathbb{R}^n_{++}$.

We now show $\phi(p, \bar{u})$ is homogeneous of degree one in p. Evaluating the definition of ϕ at αp for some $\alpha > 0$ yields $\Phi(\alpha p, \phi(\alpha p, \bar{u})) = \bar{u}$. By homogeneity of Φ, this is:

$$\Phi\left(p, \frac{\phi(\alpha p, \bar{u})}{\alpha}\right) = \bar{u} = \Phi(p, \phi(p, \bar{u})).$$

As Φ is strictly increasing in its last argument, this implies $\frac{\phi(\alpha p, \bar{u})}{\alpha} = \phi(p, \bar{u})$.

Next we show $\phi(p, \bar{u})$ is concave in p. Fix $p^0, p^1 \in \mathbb{R}^n_{++}$ and $\bar{u} \in U$. As Φ is quasiconvex:

$$\begin{aligned}&\Phi(\alpha p^0 + (1-\alpha)p^1, \alpha\phi(p^0, \bar{u}) + (1-\alpha)\phi(p^1, \bar{u})) \\ &\quad \leq \max\{\Phi(p^0, \phi(p^0, \bar{u})), \Phi(p^1, \phi(p^1, \bar{u}))\}\end{aligned}$$

for every $\alpha \in (0,1)$. From the definition of ϕ:

$$\max\{\Phi(p^0, \phi(p^0, \bar{u})), \Phi(p^1, \phi(p^1, \bar{u}))\} = \bar{u}$$
$$= \Phi(\alpha p^0 + (1-\alpha)p^1, \phi(\alpha p^0 + (1-\alpha)p^1, \bar{u})).$$

Hence:

$$\Phi(\alpha p^0 + (1-\alpha)p^1, \alpha\phi(p^0, \bar{u}) + (1-\alpha)\phi(p^1, \bar{u}))$$
$$\leq \Phi(\alpha p^0 + (1-\alpha)p^1, \phi(\alpha p^0 + (1-\alpha)p^1, \bar{u})).$$

As Φ is strictly increasing in its last argument, this implies:

$$\alpha\phi(p^0, \bar{u}) + (1-\alpha)\phi(p^1, \bar{u}) \leq \phi(\alpha p^0 + (1-\alpha)p^1, \bar{u}).$$

These observations establish that ϕ satisfies the assumptions of Theorem 9.4. That is, ϕ has properties sufficient to ensure it is an expenditure function on $P = \mathbb{R}^n_{++}$ for some collection of preferred sets $V_\phi(\bar{u})$ defined on U. Note further that, for given $p \in \mathbb{R}^n_{++}$, $\phi(p, \bar{u})$ takes on every value in $\mathbb{R}^1_+$ as $\bar{u}$ varies over U because U is the image of $\Phi(p, m)$ on $m \in \mathbb{R}^1_+$. In particular, $\phi(p, \bar{u})$ is unbounded on $\bar{u} \in U$ for every $p \in \mathbb{R}^n_{++}$. And $\phi(p, \bar{u})$ is continuous because it is the inverse of the continuous function Φ. Therefore, from the comments following Theorem 9.4, there exists a continuous, nondecreasing and quasiconcave utility function $u_\phi : \mathbb{R}^n_+ \to U$ for which ϕ is the expenditure function. From strict monotonicity of $\phi(p, \bar{u})$ on $\bar{u} \in U$ and the definition of the expenditure minimum, $u_\phi(\mathbb{R}^n_+) = U$ (i.e., the image of u_ϕ is the same as the image of $\Phi(p, \cdot)$ for every p). As ϕ is derived from Φ, it is perhaps better to denote this utility function u_Φ.

Finally, an indirect utility function $u^*_\Phi : \mathbb{R}^n_{++} \times \mathbb{R}^1_+ \to U$ exists since u_Φ is a continuous utility function. By Theorem 10.4:

$$u^*_\Phi(p, \phi(p, \bar{u})) = \bar{u}.$$

From the definition of ϕ:

$$\Phi(p, \phi(p, \bar{u})) = \bar{u}.$$

Hence $u^*_\Phi(p, \phi(p, \bar{u})) = \Phi(p, \phi(p, \bar{u}))$ for every $p \in \mathbb{R}^n_{++}$ and $\bar{u} \in U$ (using the fact that $u_\Phi(\mathbb{R}^n_+)$, and hence $u^*_\Phi(p, \mathbb{R}^1_+)$ from item 7 of Theorem 10.1, are both U). As $\Phi(p, m)$ is strictly increasing on $m \in \mathbb{R}^1_+$ and $\phi(p, \bar{u})$ is strictly increasing on $\bar{u} \in U$, equality of u^*_Φ and Φ for every $\bar{u}$ implies $u^*_\Phi(p, m)$ is strictly increasing on $m \in \mathbb{R}^1_+$. Hence $u^*_\Phi(p, m) = \Phi(p, m)$ for every $(p, m) \in \mathbb{R}^n_{++} \times \mathbb{R}^1_+$. □

In short, Φ is indeed the indirect utility function for the utility function $u_\Phi(x)$ derived from the function Φ. *The homogeneity, quasiconvexity, continuity, strict monotonicity in income, and income image properties are sufficient as well as necessary for a function $\Phi : \mathbb{R}^n_{++} \times \mathbb{R}^1_+ \to \mathbb{R}^1$ to be the maximum of a continuous, nondecreasing and quasiconcave utility function over a standard budget set that has a strictly increasing maximal value in income.* Hence we can use **any** function satisfying these properties as an indirect utility function without actually deriving it from some underlying utility function. This also shows V_ϕ is the utility-relevant preferred set correspondence for a consumer with indirect utility function Φ, and the utility-relevant preferences **always** have the continuity, free disposal, and convexity properties.

11.2 REVEALED PREFERENCE

Theorem 10.1 tells us that any correspondence $\eta : \mathbb{R}^n_{++} \times \mathbb{R}^1_+ \to 2^{\mathbb{R}^n_+}$; if it is to arise as an optimal choice correspondence from maximization of a continuous utility function $u(x)$ over a standard budget set $x \in B(p, m)$; must be homogeneous of degree zero and upper hemicontinuous. Of course any candidate Marshallian demand correspondence must also be nonempty at every (p, m) because a utility maximum always exists; and must honor feasibility ($\eta(p, m) \subset B(p, m)$). Is this enough to ensure η is the Marshallian demand for *some* continuous utility function? The answer is "no," because these properties do not address optimality of the elements of $\eta(p, m)$.

Homogeneity can be used to reduce the dimensionality of the problem. Note first that the feasibility and existence requirements evaluated at $m = 0$ yield $\eta(p, 0) = \{0\}$ for every $p \in \mathbb{R}^n_{++}$. Once this is verified for a candidate Marshallian demand, we can assume $m > 0$ and normalize on m to obtain $\eta(p/m, 1) = \eta(p, m)$. Then it suffices to examine $\eta(p, 1)$ for $p \in \mathbb{R}^n_{++}$. For the remainder of this discussion the income argument in η and B is suppressed and feasibility is imposed on η by requiring $\eta(p) \subset B(p)$ for every $p \in \mathbb{R}^n_{++}$.

Now consider optimality of the elements of $\eta(p)$ for each $p \in \mathbb{R}^n_{++}$, which relies on the concept of *revealed preference*. Consider two distinct consumption bundles $x^0, x^r \in \mathbb{R}^n_+$. If we witness a consumer purchasing x^r when x^0 could have been purchased under the same budget constraint, we say x^r is *directly revealed preferred* to x^0 (weakly) for that consumer. Put in terms of a candidate Marshallian demand correspondence η, x^r is directly revealed preferred to x^0 by η if, at some price $p \in \mathbb{R}^n_{++}$, we have $x^r \in \eta(p)$ and $x^0 \in B(p)$.

It is possible for a consumer to (weakly) prefer x^r to x^0 without this preference being directly revealed by the Marshallian demand. If x^r is not optimal at any price then it cannot be directly revealed preferred to anything. For example, the only optimal points for a consumer with symmetric Leontief preferences on $\mathbb{R}^2_+$ are on the line $x_2 = x_1$, so no other points in $\mathbb{R}^2_+$ can be directly revealed preferred to anything by a Leontief Marshallian demand correspondence.

Another possibility is that x^r is optimal at some price(s) but x^0 is not feasible at any of those prices. For example, if x^r is the Marshallian demand point at some price for a consumer with Cobb-Douglas preferences and x^0 lies between the budget line and the indifference curve through x^r, then x^r is strictly preferred to x^0 but this preference is not directly revealed by the Cobb-Douglas Marshallian demand. Still it might be possible to infer from the Marshallian demand that x^r is preferred to x^0 via a finite chain of pairwise comparisons, using transitivity. That is, suppose x^i is directly revealed preferred to x^{i-1} for $i = 1, \ldots, r$. Then transitivity requires that x^r be preferred to x^0. When this happens we say x^r is (indirectly; unless $r = 1$) *revealed preferred* to x^0 (weakly) for the consumer. In terms of a candidate Marshallian demand correspondence η, x^r is revealed preferred to x^0 by η if there is a finite collection of consumption bundles $x^1, \ldots, x^{r-1}$; and corresponding prices $p^1, \ldots, p^r$; such that $x^i \in \eta(p^i)$ and $x^{i-1} \in B(p^i)$ for $i = 1, \ldots, r$. Fig. 11.1 illustrates this.

Now return to a candidate Marshallian demand correspondence η. By feasibility every element of $\eta(p)$ is (directly) revealed preferred by η to

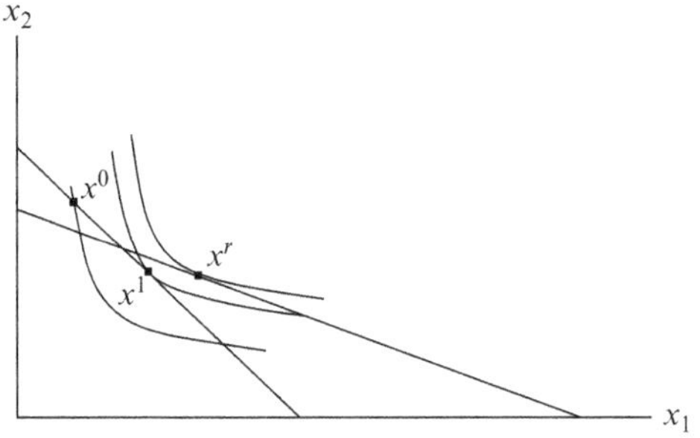

Fig. 11.1 Indirect revealed preference. x^r is strictly preferred to x^0 with the Cobb-Douglas indifference curves shown here. But this is not directly revealed by the Marshallian demand because, when price is such that x^r is optimal, x^0 is not feasible. However, x^1 is feasible at that price and is optimal at a price for which x^0 is feasible. Hence the Marshallian demand directly reveals that x^r is preferred to x^1 and x^1 is preferred to x^0, leading to the indirect conclusion that x^r is preferred to x^0.

every element of $B(p)$, but without restrictions on η the converse might fail: There may be elements of $B(p)$ that are revealed preferred by η to every element of $B(p)$ (by prices different from p) but that are not elements of $\eta(p)$. This would be an inconsistency in the alleged optimality of the choices defined by η; hence the key optimality condition for η to be a Marshallian demand is that η not display this inconsistency. That is, $\eta(p)$ must be *exactly* those elements of $B(p)$ that are revealed preferred by η to every element of $B(p)$. This leads us to the following duality theorem for Marshallian demand, which we state without proof.

Theorem 11.2 (Duality of the Marshallian Demand Correspondence via Revealed Preference). *Assume $\eta : \mathbb{R}^n_{++} \to 2^{\mathbb{R}^n_+}$ is upper hemicontinuous, nonempty at every point in its domain, and satisfies:*

$$\eta(p) = \{x^r \in B(p) : x^r \textit{ is revealed preferred by } \eta \textit{ to every } x^0 \in B(p)\} \quad \textit{for every } p \in \mathbb{R}^n_{++}.$$

Assume further that the image $\eta(\mathbb{R}^n_{++})$ is a convex set. Then there exists a function $u : \mathbb{R}^n_+ \to \mathbb{R}^1_+$ such that:

$$\eta(p) = \{x \in B(p) : u(x) \geq u(x')\ \forall x' \in B(p)\} \textit{ for every } p \in \mathbb{R}^n_{++}.$$

That is, η is the Marshallian demand correspondence for the utility function u.

Note that feasibility is implied by the definition of η and homogeneity is implicit from the normalization $m = 1$. The additional assumption of convexity is restrictive. It is easy to draw indifference curves that lead to a Marshallian demand whose image is not convex (for example, part (c) of Exercise 3 in Chapter 9).

11.3 INTEGRABILITY

A second method for determining whether a given correspondence is a Marshallian demand is called *integrability*. This approach begins with Theorems 10.4 and 10.5, and Shephard's Lemma, to write:

$$\hat{x}(p, e^*(p, \bar{u}))^\perp = \hat{h}(p, \bar{u})^\perp = \mathbf{D}_p e^*(p, \bar{u}).$$

That is, a Marshallian demand function forms a system of partial differential equations of the expenditure function (involving both e^* and $\mathbf{D}_p e^*$). The expenditure function is found by solving this system, whence the term "integrability," after which the methods discussed following Theorem 9.4 can be used to find an expenditure-relevant utility function. The key condition for this system to have a solution is that the matrix of derivatives

$\mathbf{D}_p\hat{x}(p,m)+\mathbf{D}_m\hat{x}(p,m)\hat{x}(p,m)^{\perp}$ be symmetric at every $(p,m) \in \mathbb{R}^n_{++} \times \mathbb{R}^1_+$. This is the Hicks-Slutsky substitution matrix, which is symmetric when the demand derivatives are continuous and must also be negative semidefinite to ensure concavity of the implied expenditure function.

This discussion suggests a candidate Marshallian demand function $\hat{\eta} : \mathbb{R}^n_{++} \times \mathbb{R}^1_+ \to \mathbb{R}^n_+$ with the necessary properties from Theorems 10.1 and 10.2 that underlie the Hicks-Slutsky Decomposition (homogeneity, continuity, and Walras' Law); and that has a symmetric and negative semidefinite Hicks-Slutsky matrix $\mathbf{D}_p\hat{\eta}(p,m) + \mathbf{D}_m\hat{\eta}(p,m)\hat{\eta}(p,m)^{\perp}$; is indeed the optimal choice function for some underlying utility function. Establishing this formally begins with the main integrability result.

Lemma 11.1. *[1, Lemma 1 (p. 124)] Suppose* $\hat{\eta} : \mathbb{R}^n_{++} \times \mathbb{R}^1_+ \to \mathbb{R}^n$ *satisfies:*

1. $\hat{\eta}(p,m)$ *is differentiable on its entire domain (one-sided with respect to m at* $m = 0$*).*
2. $\mathbf{D}_m\hat{\eta}(p,m)$ *is bounded on* $A \times \mathbb{R}^n_+$*, where A is any compact subset of* $\mathbb{R}^n_{++}$*.*
3. *The matrix of derivatives* $\mathbf{D}_p\hat{\eta}(p,m) + \mathbf{D}_m\hat{\eta}(p,m)\hat{\eta}(p,m)^{\perp}$ *is symmetric at every* (p,m) *in the domain.*

Then, for each (p^0, m^0) *in the domain, there exists a unique continuous function* $g(p; p^0, m^0)$ *such that:*

$$\hat{\eta}(p, g(p; p^0, m^0))^{\perp} = \mathbf{D}_p g(p; p^0, m^0) \ \forall p \gg 0, \ \text{and}$$
$$g(p^0; p^0, m^0) = m^0.$$

This result, stated here without proof, is a variant of Frobenius' Theorem for this particular set of partial differential equations. The variant here gives a *unique global* solution to the system of partial differential equations. The condition $g(p^0; p^0, m^0) = m^0$ is the "initial condition" for the system.

An important property of the solution g is:

Lemma 11.2. *[1, Lemma 3 (p. 125)] Let* $(p^0, m^0), (p^1, m^1) \in \mathbb{R}^n_{++} \times \mathbb{R}^1_+$ *be two initial conditions. If* $g(p^2; p^0, m^0) < g(p^2; p^1, m^1)$ *for some* $p^2 \gg 0$*, then:*

$$g(p; p^0, m^0) < g(p; p^1, m^1) \ \forall p \gg 0.$$

Proof. Suppose not, so there exists $p^3 \gg 0$ such that $g(p^3; p^0, m^0) \geq g(p^3; p^1, m^1)$. Then, by continuity of g (follows from differentiability), there exists p^4 between p^2 and p^3 such that:

$$g(p^4; p^0, m^0) = g(p^4; p^1, m^1).$$

As g is a unique solution to the system of partial differential equations (Lemma 11.1), we then have $g(p; p^0, m^0) = g(p; p^1, m^1)$ for all $p \gg 0$ (i.e., the two solutions $g(p; p^0, m^0)$ and $g(p; p^1, m^1)$ to the system are equal at a point p^4, and their values as we depart from that point are determined by the derivatives, which are the same at all points, so the "two" solutions must be the same). This contradicts $g(p^2; p^0, m^0) < g(p^2; p^1, m^1)$. □

Lemmas 11.1 and 11.2 are the backbone of a duality theorem for Marshallian demand.

Theorem 11.3 (Duality of the Marshallian Demand Function via Integrability). *Assume $\hat{\eta} : \mathbb{R}^n_{++} \times \mathbb{R}^1_+ \to \mathbb{R}^n_+$ has the following properties at every $(p, m) \in \mathbb{R}^n_{++} \times \mathbb{R}^1_+$:*

1. *Walras' Law ($p^\perp \hat{\eta}(p, m) = m$).*
2. *Differentiable (one-sided with respect to m at $m = 0$).*
3. *The income Jacobian $\mathbf{D}_m \hat{\eta}(p, m)$ is bounded on $A \times \mathbb{R}^n_+$, for every compact subset A of $\mathbb{R}^n_{++}$.*
4. *The Hicks-Slutsky matrix $\mathbf{D}_p \hat{\eta}(p, m) + \mathbf{D}_m \hat{\eta}(p, m) \hat{\eta}(p, m)^\perp$ is symmetric and negative semidefinite.*

Then $\hat{\eta}$ is the Marshallian demand for some consumer with complete, transitive, continuous, convex, and weakly monotone preferences on $\mathbb{R}^n_+$.

Proof. Use $(p^0, 0)$ as the initial condition in Lemma 11.1 for any arbitrary $p^0 \gg 0$ and define a candidate expenditure function by $\phi(p, \bar{u}) \equiv g(p; p^0, \bar{u})$ on $(p, \bar{u}) \in \mathbb{R}^n_{++} \times \mathbb{R}^1_+$ (p^0 is suppressed in ϕ for convenience). Consider the sufficient conditions for ϕ to be an expenditure function from Theorem 9.4:

1. The specified domain of ϕ, $P \times U = \mathbb{R}^n_{++} \times \mathbb{R}^1_+$, has all required properties. Given this domain, the range is $\mathbb{R}^1_+$. Otherwise there exists $p \gg 0$ and $\bar{u} \geq 0$ such that $\phi(p, \bar{u}) < 0$. Select $\alpha > 0$ such that $\alpha p > p^0$. Then, from the definition of ϕ and the initial condition defining g, and using the monotonicity (because $\mathbf{D}_p \phi = \hat{\eta}^\perp \geq 0$) and homogeneity of ϕ (below), we have:

$$0 \leq \bar{u} = \phi(p^0, \bar{u}) \leq \phi(\alpha p, \bar{u}) = \alpha \phi(p, \bar{u}) < 0,$$

   a contradiction.
2. $\phi(p, \bar{u})$ is concave in p because the Hessian $\mathbf{D}^2_p \phi$ is the Hicks-Slutsky matrix, which is negative semidefinite.
3. $\phi(p, \bar{u})$ is homogeneous of degree one in p. Walras' Law is $p^\perp \hat{\eta}(p, \phi(p, \bar{u})) = \phi(p, \bar{u})$. Substituting from the partial differential equations that define ϕ, this is $\mathbf{D}_p \phi(p, \bar{u}) p = \phi(p, \bar{u})$. Euler's Theorem (Theorem 1.16) then establishes ϕ is homogeneous of degree one in p.

4. $\phi(p, \bar{u})$ is strictly increasing in $\bar{u}$. Consider $\bar{u}^0 < \bar{u}^1$ and note that, from the initial condition defining g:

$$\phi(p^0, \bar{u}^0) = g(p^0; p^0, \bar{u}^0) = \bar{u}^0 < \bar{u}^1 = g(p^0; p^0, \bar{u}^1) = \phi(p^0, \bar{u}^1).$$

By Lemma 11.2, this holds at every $p \gg 0$. That is, $\phi(p, \bar{u}^0) < \phi(p, \bar{u}^1)$.

5. $\phi(p, 0) = 0 \; \forall p \gg 0$. Suppose otherwise. As $\phi \geq 0$, there exists $p^1 \gg 0$ such that $\phi(p^1, 0) = g(p^1; p^0, 0) > 0$. Taking $(p^1, 0)$ as the initial condition defining g then yields $g(p^1; p^1, 0) = 0 < g(p^1; p^0, 0)$, so by Lemma 11.2 we have $g(p; p^1, 0) < g(p; p^0, 0)$ for every $p \gg 0$. But, again using the initial condition, this implies $g(p^0; p^1, 0) < g(p^0; p^0, 0) = 0$, a contradiction to $\phi \geq 0$ (p^0 is arbitrary, so the demonstration that $\phi \geq 0$ therefore holds for the $(p^1, 0)$ initial condition).

Theorem 9.4 therefore ensures ϕ is an expenditure function for some consumer with complete, transitive, continuous, convex, and weakly monotone preferences on $\mathbb{R}^n_+$. Shephard's Lemma then shows the corresponding Hicksian demand is $\hat{h}(p, \bar{u}) = \mathbf{D}_p\phi(p, \bar{u})$.

Moreover, $\phi(p, \bar{u})$ is a continuous and unbounded function of $\bar{u} \in \mathbb{R}^1_+$ for every $p \in \mathbb{R}^n_{++}$. Continuity is from Lemma 11.1. For unboundedness, suppose there were $p^1 \in \mathbb{R}^n_{++}$ and a bound $B \geq 0$ such that $\phi(p^1, \bar{u}) < B$ for every $\bar{u} \in \mathbb{R}^1_+$. That is, $g(p^1; p^0, \bar{u}) < B$ for every $\bar{u} \in \mathbb{R}^1_+$. Taking $(p^1, \bar{u})$ as the initial condition defining g then yields $g(p^1; p^0, \bar{u}) < B = g(p^1; p^1, B)$ for every $\bar{u} \in \mathbb{R}^1_+$, so by Lemma 11.2 we have $g(p; p^0, \bar{u}) < g(p; p^1, B)$ for every $(p, \bar{u}) \in \mathbb{R}^n_{++} \times \mathbb{R}^1_+$. Evaluating at $p = p^0$ yields $g(p^0; p^0, \bar{u}) = \bar{u} < g(p^0; p^1, B)$ for every $\bar{u} \in \mathbb{R}^1_+$. Let $\bar{u} \to \infty$ for the contradiction.

Thus, from Theorem 10.5, the indirect utility function $u^*(p, m)$ corresponding to $\phi(p, \bar{u})$ is strictly increasing in m and satisfies $\phi(p, u^*(p, m)) = m$, and the corresponding Marshallian demand is $\hat{x}(p, m) = \hat{h}(p, u^*(p, m))$. From Shephard's Lemma and the definition of ϕ, this Marshallian demand is:

$$\begin{aligned}\hat{x}(p, m) &= \hat{h}(p, u^*(p, m)) = \mathbf{D}_p\phi(p, \bar{u})|_{\bar{u}=u^*(p,m)} \\ &= \hat{\eta}(p, \phi(p, u^*(p, m))) = \hat{\eta}(p, m).\end{aligned}$$

□

Some readers may wonder why homogeneity of $\hat{\eta}$ (or that the Hicks-Slutsky matrix is singular) is not assumed in the statement of this theorem, recognizing that homogeneity is a necessary property of Marshallian demand. The answer is that $\hat{\eta}$ satisfying the conditions for the system of partial differential equations with the given initial condition to have a solution, and also Walras' Law, together imply homogeneity of the expenditure function (see the proof of item 3 above), which in turn is equivalent to homogeneity of the associated indirect utility function and Marshallian demand. In short, homogeneity is a redundant property when a candidate Marshallian demand satisfies Walras' Law and the system of partial differential equations has a solution.

The theorem shows $\hat{\eta}$ *is indeed a Marshallian demand for some underlying preference relation. The properties of a Marshallian demand (including Walras' Law), along with uniqueness and the differentiability assumptions 1 and 2 of Lemma 11.1, are sufficient for* $\hat{\eta}$ *to be a Marshallian demand for some well-behaved underlying preference relation on* $\mathbb{R}^n_+$. This theorem is restrictive in that it applies only to singleton-valued demands that are differentiable and have bounded income derivatives, but it is constructive in that, in principle, it gives an algorithm to derive an underlying demand-relevant (direct) utility function. We say "in principle" here because actually finding the solution g to the system of partial differential equations can be quite tedious and perhaps possible only via numerical methods. The choice $\bar{u} = m^0$ in this theorem is a convenient choice but we actually only need a differentiable, strictly increasing and unbounded mapping $\bar{u}(m^0)$ of income values m^0 into utility values $\bar{u}$; different mappings correspond to different utility representations of the same preferences.

11.4 NOTES

The concept of revealed preference is due to Samuelson [2] and Houthakker [3]. The duality theorem for Marshallian demand via revealed preference stated herein is a minor modification of Richter [4, Theorem 2] and [5, Theorem 14]. The integrability approach originated with Antonelli [6]. The version presented here is from Hurwicz and Uzawa [1]. Hurwicz [7] provides an overview.

11.5 EXERCISES

1. Assume $(p_1, p_2) \in \mathbb{R}^2_{++}$ and $m \in \mathbb{R}^1_+$. Are each of the following Marshallian demands for a consumer with complete, transitive, and continuous preferences over $\mathbb{R}^2_+$?

   a.

$$\hat{x}(p_1, p_2, m)^\perp = \left(\frac{2m}{3p_1}, \frac{m}{3p_2}\right).$$

b.

$$\hat{x}(p_1, p_2, m)^{\perp} = \left(1 + \frac{p_2 + m}{p_1}, 1 + \frac{p_1 + m}{p_2}\right).$$

c.

$$\hat{x}(p_1, p_2, m)^{\perp} = \begin{cases} \left(\frac{m^2}{p_1 p_2}, \frac{m}{p_2}\left[1 - \frac{m}{p_2}\right]\right) & \text{if } m \leq p_2 \\ \left(\frac{m}{p_1}, 0\right) & \text{if } m > p_2 \end{cases}.$$

d.

$$\hat{x}(p_1, p_2, m)^{\perp} = \left(\frac{p_2 m}{p_1(p_1 + p_2)}, \frac{p_1 m}{p_2(p_1 + p_2)}\right).$$

2. Does the consumer in part (d) of Exercise 1 have the same preferences as the consumer in part (a) of Exercise 7 in Chapter 9? Why?
3. Assume $(p_1, p_2) \in \mathbb{R}^2_{++}$ and $\bar{u} \in \mathbb{R}^1$. For each of the following equations, verify that $\hat{\eta}$ is a Hicksian demand for a price-taking consumer with preferences over $\mathbb{R}^2_+$ and $\bar{u}$ in some set you specify. Then find corresponding expenditure, indirect utility, and Marshallian demand functions. Finally, find a relevant (direct) utility function.

a.

$$\hat{\eta}(p_1, p_2, \bar{u})^{\perp} = \bar{u}\left(\left(\frac{p_2}{p_1}\right)^{1/2}, \left(\frac{p_1}{p_2}\right)^{1/2}\right).$$

b.

$$\hat{\eta}(p_1, p_2, \bar{u})^{\perp} = \left(1 - \frac{1}{\bar{u}}\right)\left(\left[\left(\frac{p_2}{p_1}\right)^{1/2} + 1\right], \left[\left(\frac{p_1}{p_2}\right)^{1/2} + 1\right]\right).$$

c.

$$\hat{\eta}(p_1, p_2, \bar{u})^{\perp} = \sqrt{\bar{u}}\left(\sqrt{\frac{p_2}{p_1}}, \sqrt{\frac{p_1}{p_2}}\right).$$

4. Suppose $u^* = \frac{m(p_1 + p_2)}{p_1 p_2}$ is an indirect utility function for a price-taking consumer, in standard notation.
   - **a.** Derive the Marshallian demands.
   - **b.** Derive the expenditure function.
   - **c.** Derive the Hicksian demands.
   - **d.** Find a (direct) utility function $u(x_1, x_2)$ such that u^* is the maximum of $u(x_1, x_2)$ over $x_1, x_2 \in \mathbb{R}^2_+$, subject to $p_1 x_1 + p_2 x_2 \leq m$.

5. Here is an indirect utility function for a consumer of two commodities with prices p_1 and p_2, and money income m: $u^*(p_1, p_2, m) = \frac{m}{p_1+p_2}$.

a. Verify that u^* has the properties required of an indirect utility function.

b. DERIVE a (direct) utility function for which u^* is the indirect utility function. Note the emphasis on the word "DERIVE;" show the derivation.

6. Consider the function:

$$\hat{x}^{\perp} = \left(\frac{m}{ap_1}, \frac{m}{bp_2} \right)$$

defined for $(p_1, p_2) \in \mathbb{R}^2_{++}$ and $m \in \mathbb{R}^1_{+}$. For what value(s) of the parameters a and b is this a Marshallian demand for some consumer with complete, transitive, continuous, and locally nonsatiated preferences over $\mathbb{R}^2_{+}$?

7. A price-taking consumer has indirect utility function $u^*(p_1, p_2, m) = \frac{p_2}{p_1} + \frac{m}{p_2}$ when $\frac{m}{p_2} > \frac{p_2}{p_1}$ and the prices are positive, where p_i is the price of good i and m is money income.

a. Verify that this is indeed an indirect utility function on the part of the price/income space satisfying $\frac{m}{p_2} > \frac{p_2}{p_1}$.

b. Find a (direct) utility function that represents this consumer's preferences.

8. Consider the following correspondence:

$$\eta^*(p_1, p_2, \bar{u}) = \begin{cases} \left\{ \left(\frac{\bar{u}}{2}, 0 \right) \right\} & \text{if } \frac{p_1}{p_2} < 2 \\ \left\{ \left(\frac{\bar{u}}{2}, 0 \right), (0, \bar{u}) \right\} & \text{if } \frac{p_1}{p_2} = 2 \\ \{ (0, \bar{u}) \} & \text{if } \frac{p_1}{p_2} > 2 \end{cases}.$$

a. Verify that this is a Hicksian demand.

b. Find the corresponding Marshallian demand.

c. Verify the Hicks-Slutsky Decomposition for $\hat{x}_1$ in response to a change in p_1.

9. Consider the following function:

$$\hat{\eta}(p_1, p_2, \bar{u})^{\perp} = \bar{u} \left(b_{11} + b_{12} \left(\frac{p_2}{p_1} \right)^{1/2}, b_{22} + b_{21} \left(\frac{p_1}{p_2} \right)^{1/2} \right).$$

a. Verify that this is a Hicksian demand if the b_{ij} parameters satisfy particular restrictions. What are the restrictions?

b. Find the Marshallian demand.

10. Can the proposed Marshallian demand given in Exercise 1a be for the same consumer as the proposed Hicksian demand given in Exercise 3a? Explain why.

11. Here are two equations in notation typical for a Hicksian demand system of a price-taking consumer:

$$\hat{h}_i(p_1, p_2, \bar{u}) = \left[\frac{\bar{u} p_j^{1/3}}{4(p_1^{1/3} + p_2^{1/3})} \right]^4 \quad \text{for } i, j = 1, 2 \ (i \neq j),$$

where $\bar{u} \in \mathbb{R}^1_+$ and $(p_1, p_2) \in \mathbb{R}^2_{++}$.

a. Confirm that this is indeed a Hicksian demand.

b. Derive the expenditure function.

c. Derive the indirect utility function.

d. Derive the Marshallian demand function.

e. Derive a (direct) utility function that represents this consumer's preferences on the consumption set $\mathbb{R}^2_+$.

12. Assume $u^*(p, m)$ is an indirect utility function for complete, transitive, continuous, and locally non-satiated preferences on the consumption set $\mathbb{R}^n_+$. Here, $p \in \mathbb{R}^n_{++}$ is the price vector and $m \in \mathbb{R}^1_+$ is the consumer's monetary resources. Let $e^*(p, \bar{u})$ be the corresponding expenditure function. Taking the standard monotonicity properties of u^* and e^* and the identities between these functions as known, formally prove that u^* is quasiconvex if and only if e^* is concave in prices.

13. A line in the proof of Theorem 11.1 states: "... $\phi(p, \bar{u})$ is continuous because it is the inverse of the continuous function Φ." Prove this: If X is an interval in $\mathbb{R}^1$, $Y \subset \mathbb{R}^n$, and $f : X \times Y \to \mathbb{R}^1$ is continuous, strictly increasing on X (for every $y \in Y$), and has the same image $f(X, y) = Z$ for every $y \in Y$; then the inverse function $g(x, z)$ defined by $f(x, g(x, z)) = z$ is continuous.

REFERENCES

[1] Hurwicz L, Uzawa H. On the integrability of demand functions. In: Chipman JS, Hurwicz L, Richter MK, Sonnenschein HF, editors. Preferences, utility, and demand. New York: Harcourt Brace Jovanovich; 1971.

[2] Samuelson PA. A note on the pure theory of consumer's behaviour. Economica 1938;5:61–71.

[3] Houthakker HS. Revealed preference and the utility function. Economica 1950;17: 159–74.

[4] Richter MK. Revealed preference theory. Econometrica 1966;34:635–45.

[5] Richter MK. Rational choice. In: Chipman JS, Hurwicz L, Richter MK, Sonnenschein HF, editors. Preferences, utility, and demand. New York: Harcourt Brace Jovanovich; 1971.
[6] Antonelli GB. Sulla Teoria Matematica della Economia Politica. In: Nella Tipogrofia del Folchetto. Pisa; 1886. English reprint: "On the mathematical theory of political economy" by Chipman JS, Kirman AP. In: Chipman JS, Hurwicz L, Richter MK, Sonnenschein HF, editors. Preferences, utility, and demand. New York: Harcourt Brace Jovanovich; 1971.
[7] Hurwicz L. On the problem of integrability of demand functions. In: Chipman JS, Hurwicz L, Richter MK, Sonnenschein HF, editors. Preferences, utility, and demand. New York: Harcourt Brace Jovanovich; 1971.

CHAPTER 12

Consumer Welfare

Chapter Outline

Assume a consumer's preferences are complete, transitive, continuous, and locally nonsatiable on the consumption set $\mathbb{R}^n_+$. Then the consumer's welfare as a function of prices and income is measured by an indirect utility function. But this welfare measure is merely a utility index, stated in arbitrary units depending on the particular utility representation used for the consumer's preferences. It is convenient for many purposes to obtain a monetary measure of welfare. Such a measure allows calculation of the fixed-amount (lump-sum) tax or subsidy that must be imposed on a consumer to achieve a particular welfare goal. The most pressing need for such calculations is to evaluate the welfare consequences of price changes.

12.1 COMPENSATING AND EQUIVALENT VARIATIONS

Consider Fig. 12.1, which illustrates an increase in the price of a normal good with singleton-valued demand (good 1) from p_1^0 to p_1^1. Quantity demanded drops from $\hat{x}_1(p^0, m)$ to $\hat{x}_1(p^1, m)$ and indirect utility drops from $u^*(p^0, m)$ to $u^*(p^1, m)$. Thus, in utility terms, the damage to consumer welfare from the price increase is $u^*(p^1, m) - u^*(p^0, m) < 0$. One way to state in monetary units this change in utility is to ask:

> *"By how much would the consumer's income have to be reduced,* rather than *increasing the price, in order to impose the same welfare loss as the price increase imposes?"*

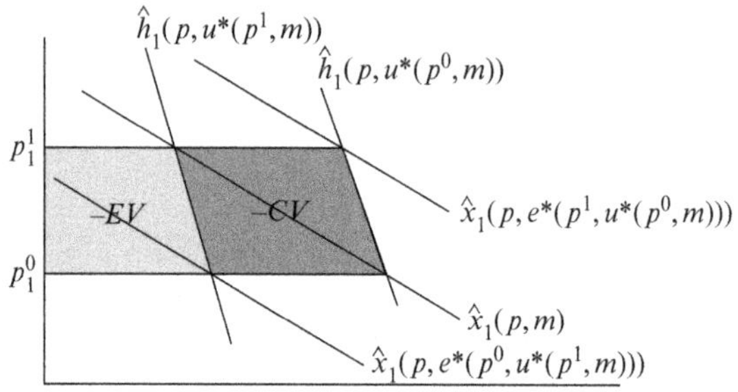

Fig. 12.1 Equivalent and compensating variations from a price increase: EV is the (negative) lightly shaded area. CV is both the lightly and darkly shaded areas.

On the graph, the lower utility $u^*(p^1, m)$ places the consumer on the lower Hicksian demand $\hat{h}_1(p, u^*(p^1, m))$. Utility is constant at the new lower level all along this Hicksian demand, so the new income level must shift the Marshallian demand at the old price p^0 leftward to this lower Hicksian demand. The income level that accomplishes this is $e^*(p^0, u^*(p^1, m))$, so the reduction in the consumer's income that is *equivalent* in welfare terms to the price increase is $e^*(p^0, u^*(p^1, m)) - m$. As $m = e^*(p^1, u^*(p^1, m))$, when the expenditure function is differentiable this change is:

$$\begin{aligned} EV &\equiv e^*(p^0, u^*(p^1, m)) - e^*(p^1, u^*(p^1, m)) \\ &= \int_{p_1^1}^{p_1^0} \frac{\partial e^*(p, u^*(p^1, m))}{\partial p_1} \, dp_1 \\ &= -\int_{p_1^0}^{p_1^1} \hat{h}_1(p, u^*(p^1, m)) \, dp_1 . \end{aligned}$$

This shows that the change in income that is *equivalent* in welfare terms to the price increase is the (negative of the) area to the left of the Hicksian demand for the new utility level $u^*(p^1, m)$. This area gives a monetary equivalent to the price increase, so it is called the *equivalent variation* (EV) of the price increase.

Another way to state in monetary units the change in utility from the price increase is to ask:

> *"By how much would the consumer's income have to increase,* after the price increase, *in order to neutralize the welfare effect of the price increase?"*

On the graph, this means the consumer must be given income that returns utility to $u^*(p^0, m)$ despite the fact that the price has risen to p^1, so the consumer must be placed on the original Hicksian demand $\hat{h}_1(p, u^*(p^0, m))$ at price p^1. Thus the new income level must shift the Marshallian demand at p_1^1 rightward to the original Hicksian demand. The income level that accomplishes this is $e^*(p^1, u^*(p^0, m))$, so the increase in the consumer's income that *compensates* in welfare terms for the price increase is $e^*(p^1, u^*(p^0, m)) - m$. The convention is to measure income variations with the same sign as the welfare change that would occur in their absence. Therefore, using $m = e^*(p^0, u^*(p^0, m))$, when the expenditure function is differentiable the income change is:

$$\begin{aligned} CV &\equiv e^*(p^0, u^*(p^0, m)) - e^*(p^1, u^*(p^0, m)) \\ &= -\int_{p_1^0}^{p_1^1} \frac{\partial e^*(p, u^*(p^0, m))}{\partial p_1} \, dp_1 \\ &= -\int_{p_1^0}^{p_1^1} \hat{h}_1(p, u^*(p^0, m)) \, dp_1. \end{aligned}$$

This shows that the change in income that *compensates* in welfare terms for the price increase is the (negative of the) area to the left of the Hicksian demand for the original utility level $u^*(p^0, m)$. This area gives a monetary compensation for the price increase, so it is called the *compensating variation* (CV) of the price increase.

For a price increase, the CV is larger in absolute value than the EV.

Both the equivalent and compensating variations give theoretically correct monetary comparisons of the welfare levels at the two prices. The expenditure changes:

$$\begin{aligned} EV &= e^*(p^0, u^*(p^1, m)) - e^*(p^1, u^*(p^1, m)) \text{ and} \\ CV &= e^*(p^0, u^*(p^0, m)) - e^*(p^1, u^*(p^0, m)) \end{aligned}$$

do not depend on whether one or more prices are changing, or on whether the expenditure function is differentiable over the range of prices. These two measures differ in the utility levels they use as the basis for comparison. The equivalent variation uses as a basis the utility level that would occur if the price change were imposed, while the compensating variation uses as a basis the utility level that occurs with no price change. The former corresponds to using the new price as the base and the latter corresponds to using the original price as the base. There are, in principle, many other monetary measures that could be proposed, each using a different price for the base and therefore a different base utility level. EV and CV simply use the most natural bases, since they are the bases actually under consideration.

Notice, however, that the area to the left of the Marshallian demand does *not* generally give a theoretically correct monetary comparison of the two welfare levels. This is because welfare varies along the Marshallian demand as the consumer continuously shifts across Hicksian demands, each one corresponding to a different utility level. In other words, the welfare basis is constantly changing along a Marshallian demand. This is unfortunate, as the Marshallian demand is the observable component here. It would be very convenient if the area to the left of a Marshallian demand delivered a monetary measure of a welfare change. Indeed, there is a long tradition in economics of studying *consumer's surplus*, which is usually defined to be exactly the area to the left of a Marshallian demand.

The fact that consumer's surplus measures the wrong area is not an insurmountable problem. There are several ways to overcome this. First, note that consumer's surplus is bounded above and below by the EV and CV. Thus, consumer's surplus is between two theoretically correct measures. It is possible to state bounds on the size of the error committed when consumer's surplus is used in lieu of either the EV or CV, and thus to state upper and lower bounds on a theoretically correct monetary measure.

Second, the relationships between utility maximization and expenditure minimization from Theorems 10.4 and 10.5 can be used to derive the EV and CV from a known Marshallian demand. Doing this uses the integrability result to derive the expenditure function from the Marshallian demand, and then find the difference between the two relevant expenditure levels.

Third, a condition can be identified under which consumer's surplus coincides with the EV or CV, or is at least very close to these correct measures. Then, assuming this condition holds, consumer's surplus is indeed a theoretically correct measure. As the problem here arises because the Marshallian and Hicksian demands do not coincide over the entire price range, the needed condition is that the source of difference between Marshallian and Hicksian demands be zero. From the Hicks-Slutsky Decomposition, the difference between these two demands is the income effect. The two demands coincide at the original utility level and price, and the Hicks-Slutsky Decomposition tells us they have the same slope moving away from this point whenever the income effect is zero, in which case the two demands must coincide over the entire range of prices at which the income effect is zero. Thus, *if there is no income effect on the good(s) under study over the range of prices and incomes under study, then consumer's surplus is an exact monetary measure of the welfare consequences of a price change.* Moreover, if the income effect is "small" over this range, then consumer's surplus is an approximate monetary measure of the welfare change.

The preference structure that results in zero income effects is the *quasilinear* form $u(x) = x_i + g(x_{-i})$ for some commodity x_i and some continuous function g. That is, if the utility function is additively separable into two terms, one of which is linear in one commodity (the ith), then the income effect on all other commodities is zero (assuming the optimal choice of x_i is positive). This is illustrated in Fig. 12.2. See Exercise 9.

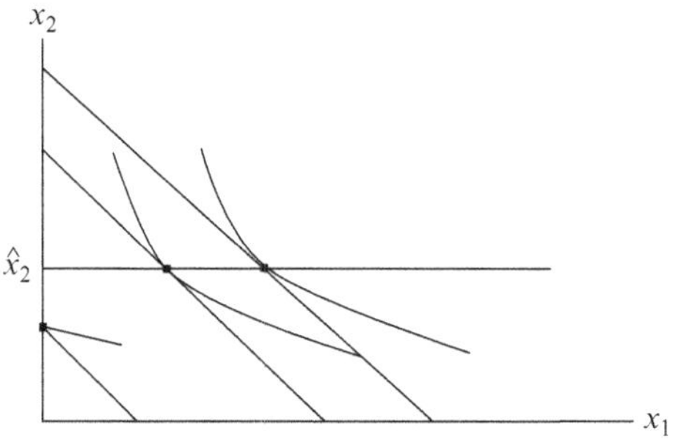

Fig. 12.2 Quaslinear utility $u(x_1, x_2) = x_1 + g(x_2)$. Note that $MRS_{21} = 1/g'(x_2)$, which is constant along horizontal lines. That is, the indifference curves are parallel along horizontal lines. Hence the income expansion paths are horizontal lines, with the optimal value of x_2 not changing in response to parallel shifts of the budget line. However, if the horizontal line along which MRS equals the price ratio is above the budget line, then the optimal choice is a corner with $x_1 = 0$. This is illustrated at the lowest budget line in the graph. In this case, there are income effects on x_2 because the optimum is not described by a tangency. As income increases from the lowest budget line in the graph, x_2 increases along its axis until x_2 reaches $\hat{x}_2$.

12.2 DEADWEIGHT LOSS

These area-based measures of welfare lead to area-based measures of the so-called "deadweight loss" associated with a price change. Consider Fig. 12.3. If the price increase is forgone and instead an equivalent variation is imposed on the consumer, the area EV on the graph is taken from the consumer. On the other hand, if the price is allowed to increase then consumption drops from the original level to $\hat{x}_1(p^1, m)$, and so the extra take from the consumer is only the extra revenue from these sales at the higher price p_1^1. That is, the take from the consumer is just $(p_1^1 - p_1^0)\hat{x}_1(p^1, m)$. Because the Hicksian demand is downward-sloping, new revenue from the consumer is

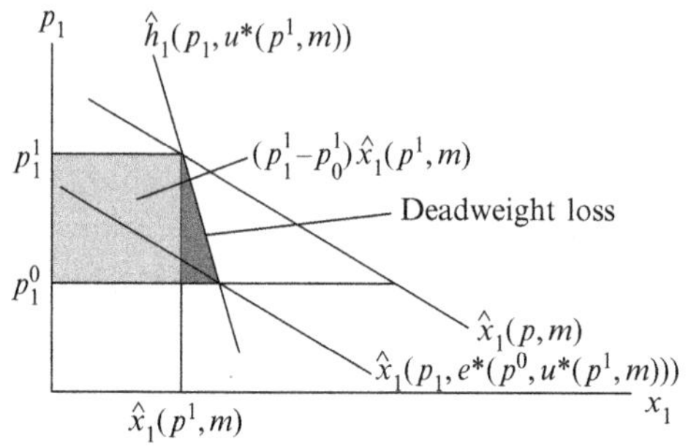

Fig. 12.3 Deadweight loss from a price increase based on the EV: EV is both the (negative) light and dark shaded areas. Revenue from the price increase is only the light shaded area. Hence the deadweight loss of the price increase is the dark shaded area.

necessarily larger when an equivalent variation is imposed than when the price is increased, even though the consumer is left with the same utility in either case. In other words, the EV is a more efficient way to impose the utility decrease on the consumer. The difference between the two areas is the dark shaded triangle on the graph, and this triangle is called the *deadweight loss* of the price increase.

Deadweight loss can be illustrated in terms of the CV as well, as in Fig. 12.4. If the price is increased and then the consumer is compensated for the price increase, consumption still drops to $\hat{x}_1(p^1, e^*(p^1, u^*(p^0, m)))$ due to the negative slope of the Hicksian demand. Extra revenue of $(p_1^1 - p_1^0)\hat{x}_1((p^1, e^*(p^1, u^*(p^0, m)))$ is collected from the consumer, but the compensation to the consumer costs the area CV. So a net amount is paid

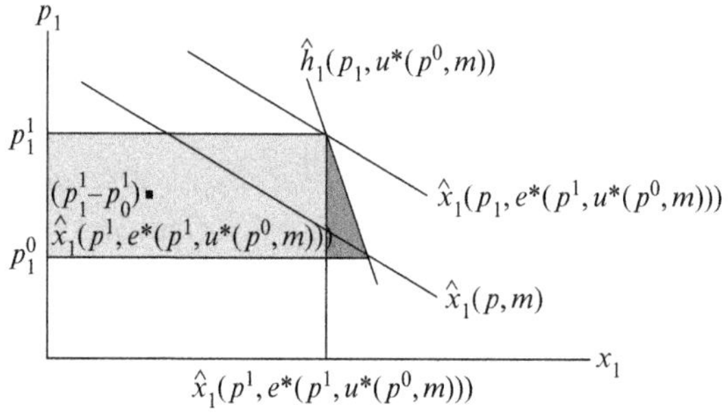

Fig. 12.4 Deadweight loss from a price increase based on the CV: CV is both the (negative) light and dark shaded areas. Revenue from the price increase is only the light shaded area. Hence the deadweight loss of the price increase is the dark shaded area.

equal to the difference between the two areas, illustrated as the dark shaded triangle on the graph, even though the consumer's utility is unchanged. This dark shaded area is once again the *deadweight loss* of the price increase.

These deadweight losses may or may not be offset by other savings, for example cost savings from lower production. If such savings exceed the deadweight loss then the price increase may be beneficial overall.

The welfare analysis of a price decrease is not substantially different. But, as utility increases with a price decrease, and EV is based on the new utility level while CV is based on the original utility level, the two measures switch positions on the graph when the price change is a decrease rather than an increase. In this case EV is larger than CV and both are positive. See Exercise 1.

The welfare analysis of an inferior good is also not substantially different but the relative positions of the two Hicksian demands switch because they are less steeply sloped than the Marshallian demand. For a price increase, the EV is larger than the CV. See Exercise 2.

12.3 AGGREGATE DEMAND

Consider $k \geq 1$ price-taking consumers; each with complete, transitive and continuous preferences on the consumption set $\mathbb{R}^n_+$. Consumer j's Marshallian demand is $x^{j*}(p, m_j)$. The *aggregate Marshallian demand* of these k consumers is a correspondence $D : \mathbb{R}^n_{++} \times \mathbb{R}^k_+ \rightarrow 2^{\mathbb{R}^n_+}$ defined by:

$$D(p, m) = \{x^1 + \cdots + x^k : x^j \in x^{j*}(p, m_j) \text{ for } j = 1, \ldots, k\}.$$

Here, $m = (m_1, \ldots, m_k) \in \mathbb{R}^k_+$ is a vector of consumer incomes. This aggregation is illustrated in Fig. 12.5 for one good with individual demands

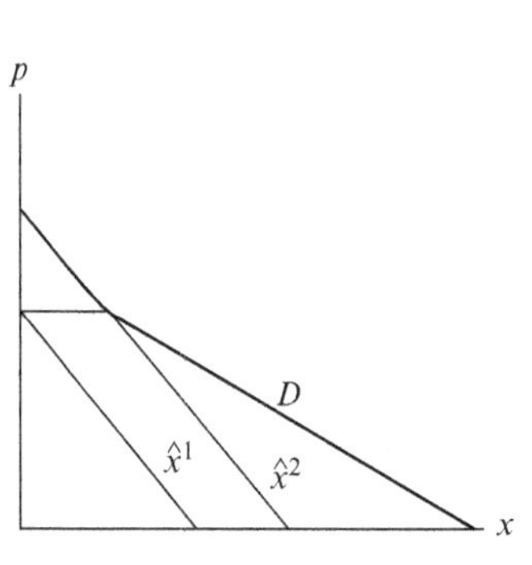

Fig. 12.5 Aggregate demand. The summation is horizontal. Algebraically, this means individual demand functions *must* be solved for quantity, not price, before they are summed.

that are singleton-valued. Note that aggregate demand is a *horizontal* sum in a conventional supply/demand graph. That is, quantities are added at a given price, *not* prices at a given quantity.

Recall that the Marshallian demand correspondence of consumer j, $x^{j*}(p, m_j)$ for $(p, m_j) \in \mathbb{R}^n_{++} \times \mathbb{R}^1_+$, is:

1. Nonempty.
2. Homogeneous of degree zero by Theorem 10.1.
3. Upper hemicontinuous by Theorem 10.1.
4. A subset of the budget line (i.e., $p^{\perp}\hat{x}^j(p, m_j) = m_j$), and therefore equal to the Hicksian demand $h^{j*}(p, u^*(p, m_j))$, when consumer j's preferences have the local nonsatiation property, by Theorems 10.2, 10.4, and 10.5.
5. Convex-valued when consumer j's preferences are convex, by Theorem 10.2.
6. Uniformly bounded on $\{(p, m_j) : p \geq p^0 \text{ and } m_j \leq m_j^0\}$, for any $(p^0, m_j^0) \in \mathbb{R}^n_{++} \times \mathbb{R}^1_+$. This is because Marshallian demand points cannot lie above the budget line. Formally, every coordinate of a Marshallian demand point is no greater than $\frac{m_j^0}{\min\{p_1^0, \ldots, p_n^0\}}$, for every $p \geq p^0$ and $m_j \leq m_j^0$.

Aggregate Marshallian demand inherits properties 1–6 from the individual Marshallian demands.

Theorem 12.1 (Properties of Aggregate Demand). *$D(p, m)$ for $(p, m) \in \mathbb{R}^n_{++} \times \mathbb{R}^k_+$ is:*

1. *Nonempty,*
2. *Homogeneous of degree zero,*
3. *Upper hemicontinuous,*
4. *A subset of the aggregate budget line (i.e., $p^{\perp}\hat{D}(p, m) = \sum_{j=1}^k m_j$) when all consumers' preferences have the local nonsatiation property,*
5. *Convex-valued when all consumers' preferences are convex, and*
6. *Uniformly bounded on $\{(p, m) : p \geq p^0$ and $m \leq m^0\}$, for any $(p^0, m^0) \in \mathbb{R}^n_{++} \times \mathbb{R}^k_+$.*

Proof. Items 1, 2, 4, and 6 are immediate from the corresponding properties of individual demands.

For item 3, consider convergent sequences $(p^i, m^i) \to (p^0, m^0)$ and $x^i \to x^0$, with $(p^i, m^i) \in \mathbb{R}^n_{++} \times \mathbb{R}^k_+$ and $x^i \in D(p^i, m^i)$ for $i = 1, 2, \ldots$ (and $p^0 \in \mathbb{R}^n_{++}$). We must show $x^0 \in D(p^0, m^0)$. Write $x^i = x^{i,1} + \cdots + x^{i,k}$, where $x^{i,j} \in x^{j*}(p^i, m_j^i)$. As (p^i, m_1^i) is arbitrarily close to (p^0, m_1^0) for i large, item 6 (above) implies $x^{i,1}$ is a bounded sequence. It therefore has a convergent subsequence $x^{\ell_{i1},1}$. Similarly, $x^{\ell_{i1},2}$ is a bounded sequence and therefore has a convergent subsequence $x^{\ell_{i2},2}$. Continuing sequentially, we obtain a convergent subsequence $x^{\ell_{ik},k}$ and, by construction, $(x^{\ell_{ik},1}, \ldots, x^{\ell_{ik},k})$ is convergent. Thus $x^{\ell_{ik},1} + \cdots + x^{\ell_{ik},k} \to x^{0,1} + \cdots + x^{0,k} = x^0$. Upper hemicontinuity of the individual Marshallian demands implies $x^{0,j} \in x^{j*}(p^0, m_j^0)$. Therefore $x^0 \in D(p^0, m^0)$.

For item 5, consider x^0 and x^1, both elements of $D(p, m)$. Write $x^i = x^{i,1} + \cdots + x^{i,k}$ for $i = 0, 1$, where $x^{i,j} \in x^{j*}(p, m_j)$. For $\alpha \in (0, 1)$ we have:

$$\alpha x^0 + (1-\alpha)x^1 = \alpha \sum_{j=1}^{k} x^{0,j} + (1-\alpha) \sum_{j=1}^{k} x^{1,j} = \sum_{j=1}^{k} (\alpha x^{0,j} + (1-\alpha)x^{1,j}).$$

Convexity of each individual $x^{j*}(p, m_j)$ implies $\alpha x^{0,j} + (1 - \alpha)x^{1,j} \in x^{j*}(p, m_j)$. Therefore $\alpha x^0 + (1 - \alpha)x^1 \in D(p, m)$. □

Note that items 3 and 6 imply aggregate Marshallian demand is a continuous function at positive prices when it is singleton-valued, by Theorem 1.9.

It is straightforward to define aggregate Hicksian demand analogous to $D(p, m)$, as a function of the price vector and a vector of individual consumers' utility levels. The analysis of Figs. 12.1–12.4 applies without modification using these aggregate Marshallian and Hicksian demands because the income changes (integrals, in the differentiable case) are additive across consumers. Aggregate EV or CV calculated in this manner must be correctly apportioned to the individual consumers to achieve the desired equivalency or compensation.

It is often useful to express aggregate Marshallian demand in the form of prices as a function of quantities. Doing so depends on strict monotonicity so that the inverse exists. Although an aggregate Giffen good is a theoretical possibility (when the good is Giffen for one or more individual consumers, and the aggregate nonnegative own-price slope for those consumers is sufficiently steep to offset the negative own-price slope for all other consumers), it is usually reasonable to assume $D(p, m)$ is decreasing in prices on the set of prices where $D(p, m)$ is strictly positive (if any), in the sense that $(p^1 - p^0)^{\perp}(\hat{D}(p^1, m) - \hat{D}(p^0, m)) < 0$. When this holds and $D(p, m)$ is singleton-valued the function can be inverted to express the price vector as a function of the quantity vector. This inverse function is called the *inverse demand*.

12.4 NOTES

The concept of consumer's surplus is due to Dupuit [1] but the important role of the income effect was not recognized until Marshall [2, Book 3,

Chapter VI]. Marshall essentially renders the income effect irrelevant by assuming constant marginal utility of income (i.e., effectively, quasilinear utility). Hicks [3, p. 40, p. 331] recognizes the importance of Marshall's assumption and presents the compensating and equivalent variations. Willig [4] derives bounds on consumer's surplus using the compensating and equivalent variations, however it is worth noting that bounds on consumer's surplus are not bounds on deadweight loss and the latter may be the most salient for welfare analysis, as pointed out by Hausman [5]. Hausman [5] shows how to use integrability to calculate exact deadweight loss with the relevant Hicksian demands.

12.5 EXERCISES

1. Carefully graph the EV and CV for a price decrease of a normal good. Place the Marshallian demands after both variations on your graph. Illustrate the deadweight losses based on both the EV and CV.
2. Carefully graph the EV and CV for a price increase of an inferior good. Place the Marshallian demands after both variations on your graph. Illustrate the deadweight losses based on both the EV and CV.
3. A consumer has expenditure function $e^* = \sqrt{p_1}$ for some particular level of utility. The price p_1 increases from 1 to 100. What is the compensating variation of this price change? Why?
4. Using ϕ from Exercise 7a of Chapter 9, what is the compensating variation of an increase in p_1 from p_1^0 to p_1^1, for given m and p_2?
5. A consumer has continuous, complete, and transitive preferences on $\mathbb{R}_+^2$ with indifference curves that appear as follows:

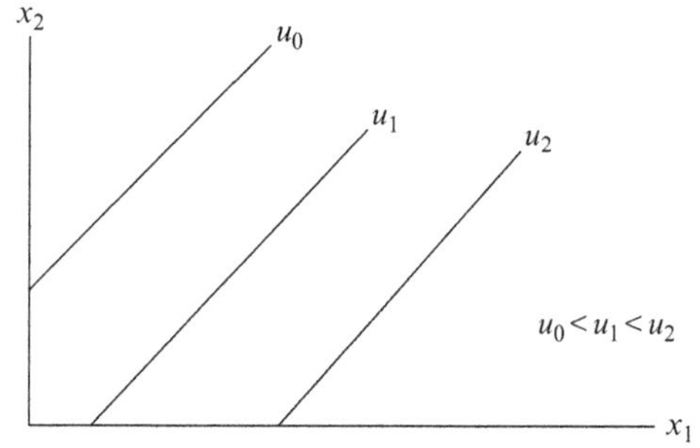

Graph and describe the deadweight loss caused by an increase in the price of x_1.

6. Here is a utility function on $\mathbb{R}^2_+$: $u(x_1, x_2) = x_1x_2 + x_1$. Let p_i denote the price of commodity i and m denote money income. Assume $p_1 = 1$ and $m = 50$. Find the deadweight loss in consumer welfare due to an increase in p_2 from $\hat{p}_2 = 2$ to $\tilde{p}_2 = 4$.
7. Suppose the Hicksian demand $\hat{h}^{\perp} = \bar{u}\left(\frac{p_2}{p_1}, \frac{p_1}{p_2}\right)$ has been econometrically estimated. Based on this estimate, what is the equivalent variation of a change in p_1 from $p_1 = 1$ to $p_1 = 31$ when income is $m = 160$ and $p_2 = 1$?
8. A consumer has Hicksian demand $\hat{h}^{\perp} = \left(e^{\bar{u}}\right)^{1/2}\left(\left(\frac{p_2}{p_1}\right)^{1/2}, \left(\frac{p_1}{p_2}\right)^{1/2}\right)$.

   Suppose $p_2 = 1$ and money income is $m = 8$. Consider a change in p_1 from $p_1^0 = 1$ to $p_1^1 = 2$. Calculate the percent error if the change in Marshallian surplus is used to measure the welfare change rather than the compensating variation (surplus and CV both on commodity 1).
9. A consumer receives utility $u = \sqrt{x} + y$ from consuming quantity x of one good and quantity y of a second good (x and y both in $\mathbb{R}^1_+$). This consumer has income $m = 10$ to spend. Let p denote the relative price per unit of x (the price of y is normalized to one).
   a. Calculate the error if we use the change in Marshallian surplus for good x as a measure of the utility gain due to a price decrease from $p = .04$ to $p = .03$.
   b. What happens if the price change under consideration is from $p = .03$ to $p = .02$?
10. A consumer has the following utility function on $\mathbb{R}^3_+$: $u = x_1x_2e^{x_3}$. Let m, p_1, and p_2 denote money income and the prices of commodities x_1 and x_2, respectively, *relative* to the price of commodity x_3.
    a. Find the Marshallian demand correspondence in terms of m, p_1, and p_2. Hint: Be careful to distinguish between the $\hat{x}_3 = 0$ and $\hat{x}_3 > 0$ cases.
    b. Find the indirect utility function in terms of m, p_1, and p_2.
    c. Find the expenditure function in terms of $\bar{u}$ (the utility level), p_1, and p_2.
    d. Suppose $p_2 = m = 1$. Find the compensating variation of an increase in p_1 from 1 to 4. Draw a graph of Marshallian and Hicksian demands that illustrates your answer.
    e. Now suppose $m = 4$. How does your answer to part (d) change? Add the demand information to your graph from part (d) that clearly illustrates the difference between the $m = 1$ case and the $m = 4$ case.

11. Consider a consumer of three goods in $\mathbb{R}^3_+$ with prices p_1, p_2, and p_3. Let m denote the endowed money income of this consumer. This consumer's indirect utility function is:

$$u^*(p_1, p_2, p_3, m) = \frac{m}{p_1 + p_2 + p_3}$$

for positive prices and non-negative incomes.

a. Find the Marshallian demand correspondence.

b. Verify that your answer to part (a) satisfies the necessary and sufficient conditions for the Marshallian demand of a consumer with locally nonsatiated preferences.

c. Suppose $m = 100$, $p_2 = 1$, and $p_3 = 2$. Find the compensating and equivalent variations for a change in p_1 from $p_1 = 1$ to $p_1 = 7$.

d. Find a (direct) utility function for which u^* is the indirect utility function.

e. Are this consumer's preferences complete, transitive, and continuous on $\mathbb{R}^3_+$? Why?

12. Suppose indirect utility is:

$$u^*(p_1, p_2, p_3, m) = \frac{m}{p_1^{1/2} p_2^{1/4} p_3^{1/4}}.$$

a. Verify that the u^* function satisfies the sufficient conditions to be an indirect utility function.

b. Derive the expenditure function.

c. Calculate the equivalent variation of a price increase from $p_3 = 16$ to $p_3 = 81$ when $p_1 = 9$, $p_2 = 16$, and $m = 36$.

d. Derive the Hicksian demand for commodity 3. What are the (Hicksian) quantities demanded for commodity 3 at the two price vectors under consideration in part (c) and utility level $u^*(9, 16, 81, 36)$?

e. Calculate the true deadweight loss of the price increase in part (c) at utility $u^*(9, 16, 81, 36)$.

f. Derive the Marshallian demand for commodity 3. What are the (Marshallian) quantities demanded for commodity 3 at the two price/income vectors under consideration in part (c)?

g. Calculate the deadweight loss of the price increase in part (c) based on the Marshallian demand for commodity 3 (Note: Use $\ln(3/2) \approx 0.4$).

h. Compare the true deadweight loss in part (e) with the Marshallian deadweight loss in part (g). How large is the error in the Marshallian measure as a percent of the true deadweight loss?

i. Verify that the Hicks-Slutsky Decomposition holds for a change in the demand for commodity 3 with respect to the price of commodity 3.

REFERENCES

[1] Dupuit J. De la Mesure de l'Utilité des Travaux Publics. Annales des Ponts et Chaussées 1844;8(second series). English reprint "On the measurement of the utility of public works" by Barback RH. In: Arrow KJ, Scitovsky T, editors. A.E.A. Readings in welfare economics XII. Homewood, IL: Irwin; 1969.
[2] Marshall A. Principles of economics. 9th variorum ed. London: MacMillan; 1920 [First ed. 1890].
[3] Hicks JR. Value and capital. 2nd ed. Oxford: Oxford University Press; 1946 [First ed. 1939].
[4] Willig RD. Consumer's surplus without apology. Am Econ Rev 1976;66:589–97.
[5] Hausman JA. Exact consumer's surplus and deadweight loss. Am Econ Rev 1981;71:662–76.

Part 4

Partial Equilibrium

Parts 2 and 3 explore optimal behavior of individual economic agents. Part 4 places these economic agents together in a market system and studies equilibrium that results from their interactions. There are two broad types of equilibria studied for market systems. *General equilibrium* refers to a simultaneous equilibrium in all markets for all commodities, while *partial equilibrium* refers to equilibrium in the market for only one (or perhaps a small subset of) commodity, assuming the parameters and choices in other markets are fixed. Buyers and sellers in one market are in general affected by the parameters and choices in other markets, so general equilibrium is the only true equilibrium. However in many cases the most salient features are captured by considering one market, or a small subset of markets. Most of Part 4 studies the simpler partial equilibrium settings, although parts of Chapter 13 consider general equilibrium. The commodities under study are final products in the partial equilibrium settings, making the buyers consumers and the sellers firms. Even in these settings there must be at least two goods for there to be meaningful choices, so $n \geq 2$ always, and when only one commodity is under study it is often arbitrarily labeled good 1. Throughout this Part there are $\ell \geq 1$ firms and the profit of firm i is denoted π^{i*}. π^{i*} is a profit function in the sense described in Chapter 4 (i.e., a function of price) only when firm i is a price-taker.

Also throughout this part there are $k \geq 1$ price-taking consumers expressing demand for the n commodities; each with complete, transitive, and continuous preferences on the consumption set $\mathbb{R}^n_+$. Consumer j's preferences are represented by the continuous utility function u^j. Local nonsatiation is often assumed as well. A consumption bundle for consumer j is denoted $x^j \in \mathbb{R}^n_+$, yielding utility $u^j(x^j)$. All resources are ultimately owned by consumers in a private-ownership economy, and this ownership forms the basis for each consumer's monetary resource. Consumer j is assumed to be endowed with a vector of commodities $\bar{x}^j \in \mathbb{R}^n_+$ and a vector of ownership shares $\alpha^j \in \mathbb{R}^\ell_+$ in each of the ℓ firms. $\bar{x}^j_i = 0$ is permitted, so there is no assumption that each consumer has an endowment of every commodity. Often we think of one commodity as labor and assume each consumer has an endowment of labor but, perhaps, nothing else. Indeed, even $\bar{x}^j = 0$ is possible. The aggregate endowment of the economy is $\bar{x} = \sum_{j=1}^k \bar{x}^j$. The vectors α^j determine the distribution of profits to consumers. The firms are wholly-owned, so $\sum_{j=1}^k \alpha^j_i = 1$ for $i = 1, \ldots, \ell$ (implying $\alpha^j_i \leq 1$). The monetary resource of consumer j at price $p \in \mathbb{R}^n_+$ is therefore $m_j = p^\perp \bar{x}^j + \sum_{i=1}^\ell \alpha^j_i \pi^{i*}$. Note that the behavioral postulates assume consumers and firms are distinct economic actors, whence consumer j takes the choices underlying π^{i*} as fixed when making consumption choices. These consumers have individual Marshallian demands $x^{j*}(p, m_j)$ and aggregate Marshallian demand $D(p, m)$ as described in Section 12.3. This aggregate demand is sometimes assumed to be singleton-valued and strictly decreasing in prices whenever it is positive, in which case an inverse aggregate demand function $p(x)$ exists for $x \geq 0$ (if $D(p, m)$ drops to zero at a finite price $\bar{p}$, define $p(0) = \bar{p}$).

The chapters in Part 4 consider equilibria under different behavioral postulates for firms. Chapter 13 begins with price-taking firms. Chapter 14 considers monopoly behavior. Chapter 15 considers various forms of oligopoly behavior.

Partial equilibrium analysis often makes the simplifying assumption that consumers' monetary resources do not vary with prices. This can be implemented by assuming consumers of the commodity under study have no endowment of that commodity and no ownership shares in the producers of that commodity. We adopt this assumption in Chapters 14 and 15. However this assumption cannot be used when studying the efficiency of a general equilibrium as in Chapter 13 because assessing efficiency requires that all resources be counted.

CHAPTER 13

Perfect Competition

Chapter Outline

This chapter studies equilibrium when $\ell \geq 1$ firms engage in price-taking behavior. Throughout, firm i has nonempty production set Z^i, (possibly infinite) profit function $\pi^{i*}(p)$ and (possibly empty) net supply/demand correspondence $z^{i*}(p)$.

13.1 AGGREGATE SUPPLY

The *aggregate supply/demand correspondence* is obtained by summing individual firms' choices in the same way individual consumer demands are summed to obtain aggregate Marshallian demand:

$$S(p) \equiv \{z^1 + \cdots + z^\ell : z^i \in z^{i*}(p) \text{ for } i = 1, \ldots, \ell\}.$$

This aggregation is illustrated in Fig. 13.1 for one good with individual supplies that are singleton-valued. As with aggregate demand, aggregate supply is a *horizontal* sum in a conventional supply/demand graph. That is, quantities are added at a given price, *not* prices at a given quantity. We shall call $S(p)$ "aggregate supply" for brevity and to avoid confusion with $D(p, m)$ but this label must not be interpreted to mean $S(p)$ has only nonnegative elements.

Although an aggregate supply vector is a sum of individually optimal production plans, that sum also maximizes *aggregate* profit among

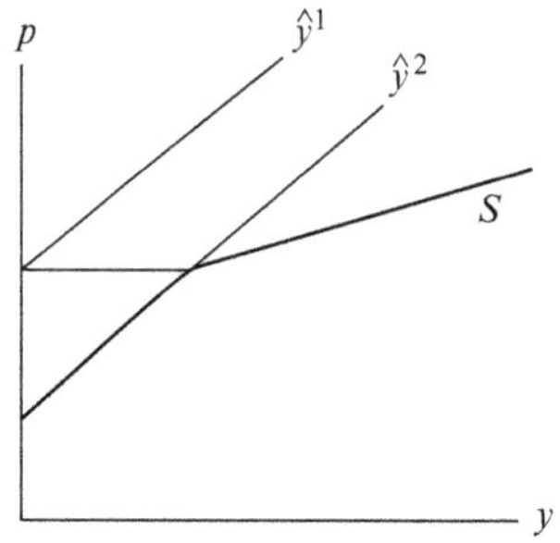

Fig. 13.1 Aggregate supply. The summation is horizontal. Algebraically, this means individual supply functions *must* be solved for quantity, not price, before they are summed.

production plans that are aggregations of individually feasible production plans. The set of all such aggregations is the *aggregate production set*:

$$Z \equiv \{z^1 + \cdots + z^\ell : z^i \in Z^i \text{ for } i = 1, \ldots, \ell\}.$$

The aggregate profit function is then:

$$\pi^*(p) = \sup\{p^\perp z : z \in Z\},$$

defined (although possibly infinite) for price vectors $p \in \mathbb{R}^n_+$.

Lemma 13.1 (Aggregate Supply Maximizes Aggregate Profit).

$$S(p) = \{z \in Z : p^\perp z = \pi^*(p)\}.$$

Proof. Suppose first that $(\hat{z}^1 + \cdots + \hat{z}^\ell) \in S(p)$. Then $\hat{z}^i \in z^{i*}(p)$ for each i, whence $\hat{z}^i \in Z^i$ and $p^\perp \hat{z}^i \geq p^\perp z^i$ for every $z^i \in Z^i$. Thus $p^\perp(\hat{z}^1 + \cdots + \hat{z}^\ell) \geq p^\perp(z^1 + \cdots + z^\ell)$ for every $(z^1 + \cdots + z^\ell) \in Z$. Conversely, if $(\hat{z}^1 + \cdots + \hat{z}^\ell) \in Z$ and $p^\perp(\hat{z}^1 + \cdots + \hat{z}^\ell) \geq p^\perp(z^1 + \cdots + z^\ell)$ for every $(z^1 + \cdots + z^\ell) \in Z$, then $\hat{z}^i \in Z^i$ and $p^\perp \hat{z}^i \geq p^\perp z^i$ for every $z^i \in Z^i$, for each i (otherwise aggregate profit could be increased by holding $\hat{z}^h$ fixed for $h \neq i$ and choosing $z^i \in Z^i$ to improve upon $p^\perp \hat{z}^i$; and the resulting sum of production plans is an element of Z). Hence $\hat{z}^i \in z^{i*}(p)$ for every i. That is, $(\hat{z}^1 + \cdots + \hat{z}^\ell) \in S(p)$. □

The aggregate supply correspondence inherits other properties from individual supply/demand correspondences. Recall that $z^{i*}(p)$ is:

1. Nonempty on a cone of the price space that includes zero, and homogeneous of degree zero, by Theorem 4.1,
2. Nondecreasing, in the sense that $(p^1 - p^0)^\perp(\hat{z}^i(p^1) - \hat{z}^i(p^0)) \geq 0$, by Theorem 4.1,

3. Convex-valued when firm i's production set is convex, by Theorem 4.4, and
4. Upper hemicontinuous when firm i's production set is closed, by Theorem 4.4.

Properties 1–3 easily pass to aggregate supply, but a complication arises with property 4 because the aggregate production set may not be closed even when individual production sets are all closed (see Exercise 5). This complication arises because of the potential for unbounded individual supply/demand choices that aggregate in an offsetting way, thereby leaving the corresponding aggregate production plans bounded. This possibility is not a mere curiosity, as individual supply/demand choices are unbounded in the important special case of constant returns. Yet continuity of aggregate supply is a property of fundamental importance. The standard solution is to add an assumption that aggregate production is *irreversible*, meaning that a nonzero production plan and its negative are not both feasible. Irreversibility is a somewhat blunt assumption. It is easy to draw production sets that violate irreversibility and yet have continuous aggregate supply. Irreversibility holds if, for example, there is a natural input (i.e., labor) that must be present for a feasible production plan to have a positive (net output) component. In any case, the important property for continuity of the aggregate supply correspondence is that there be no price near which an unbounded input demand by one producer is satisfied by an unbounded supply from another producer. The next theorem imposes this assumption directly.

Theorem 13.1 (Properties of Aggregate Supply). *$S(p)$ is:*

1. *Nonempty on a cone of the price space that includes zero, and homogeneous of degree zero,*
2. *Nondecreasing, in the sense that $(p^1 - p^0)^{\perp}(\hat{S}(p^1) - \hat{S}(p^0)) \geq 0$,*
3. *Convex-valued when every firm's production set is convex, and*
4. *Upper hemicontinuous when every firm's production set is closed; provided $z_h^{q*}(p)$ has a uniform lower bound in a neighborhood of p for every $q = 1, \ldots, \ell$ whenever $z_h^{i*}(p)$ does not have a uniform upper bound in a neighborhood of p for some i (for each $h = 1, \ldots, n$).*

Proof. Items 1 and 2 are immediate from the corresponding properties of individual supply/demands. The proof of item 3 is identical to the proof of convexity of aggregate Marshallian demand in Theorem 12.1. For item 4, consider sequences $p^j \to p^0$ (all in the cone) and $z^j \to z^0$ with $z^j \in S(p^j)$ for $j = 1, 2, \ldots$. We must show $z^0 \in S(p^0)$. Write $z^j = z^{j,1} + \cdots + z^{j,\ell}$ with $z^{j,i} \in Z^i$ for $i = 1, \ldots, \ell$. First we establish that each $z^{j,i}$ is bounded as $j \to \infty$. Suppose $z_h^{j,q}$ has a subsequence approaching ∞ as $j \to \infty$ for some $h \in \{1, \ldots, n\}$. Then, because $z_h^j = z_h^{j,1} + \cdots + z_h^{j,\ell}$ converges, there is an i such that the corresponding subsequence of $z_h^{j,i}$ approaches $-\infty$. This contradicts the boundedness assumption in a neighborhood of p^0. If $z_h^{j,q} \to -\infty$ then the corresponding subsequence of $z_h^{j,i}$ approaches ∞, again contradicting the boundedness assumption in a neighborhood of p^0. Hence each $z^{j,i}$ is bounded as $j \to \infty$, and therefore each has a convergent subsequence. Label the limit points $z^{0,i}$ for $i = 1, \ldots, \ell$ and note that $z^{0,i} \in Z^i$ because each Z^i is closed. Hence $z^0 = z^{0,1} + \cdots + z^{0,\ell} \in Z$. Moreover, by Lemma 13.1 the elements of $S(p^j)$ maximize aggregate profit over Z:

$$(p^j)^{\perp} z^j \geq (p^j)^{\perp}(\tilde{z}^1 + \cdots + \tilde{z}^{\ell}) \text{ for every } (\tilde{z}^1 + \cdots + \tilde{z}^{\ell}) \in Z.$$

For a given $(\tilde{z}^1 + \cdots + \tilde{z}^{\ell}) \in Z$, letting $j \to \infty$ yields $(p^0)^{\perp} z^0 \geq (p^0)^{\perp}(\tilde{z}^1 + \cdots + \tilde{z}^{\ell})$. As this holds for every $(\tilde{z}^1 + \cdots + \tilde{z}^{\ell}) \in Z$, and $z^0 \in Z$, we have $z^0 \in S(p^0)$. □

It is possible that the price cones where each firm's optimal production plans exist are disjoint (except for the zero price). Thus there is no assurance that the cone referred to in item 1 has any nonzero elements, even when each firm has well-defined supply choices at some nonzero prices. It is also possible to have free lunches in the aggregate production set even when all individual production sets have the no free lunch property (see Exercise 5). These seemingly strange properties arise when the rate at which one firm can convert one commodity into another exceeds, at least over some ranges, the rate at which some other firm can convert the second commodity into the first.

13.2 EXCESS DEMAND

Consumer j's monetary resource when the firms are price-takers is:

$$m_j(p) = p^{\perp}\bar{x}^j + \sum_{i=1}^{\ell} \alpha_i^j \pi^{i*}(p).$$

If all production sets have the possibility of inaction then each consumer's monetary resource is nonnegative at all prices in the convex cone where every profit is finite because profits are nonnegative (Theorem 4.4). Profits $\pi^{i*}(p)$ are homogeneous of degree one on this convex cone and continuous on its interior by Theorem 4.1. Therefore $m_j(p)$ is homogeneous of degree one and continuous, as is the price-dependent vector of consumers' monetary resources $m(p)$. This homogeneity yields $D(\alpha p, m(\alpha p)) = D(\alpha p, \alpha m(p)) = D(p, m(p))$ for every $\alpha > 0$ by Theorem 12.1, whence aggregate demand is homogeneous of degree zero in p once the dependence of consumers' monetary resources on price is considered. Continuity of $m(p)$ ensures aggregate demand remains upper hemicontinuous on the interior of the convex price cone despite the dependence of m on p. Aggregate demand is denoted $D(p)$ rather than $D(p, m(p))$ hereinafter, for brevity, as there is no dependence of D on m distinct from p in a private-ownership economy composed of price-takers. It must be understood, however, that when p changes there is an income effect on $D(p)$ arising from a change in consumers' monetary resources. This income effect is distinct from the usual implicit income effect that arises from a price change when consumers' monetary resources are fixed. $D(p)$ is homogeneous of degree zero on the convex cone where every profit is finite, and upper hemicontinuous on the interior of this convex cone.

Equilibrium in an economy of price-taking economic actors occurs when a price balances aggregate demand and aggregate supply. This balance must recognize that the aggregate endowment $\bar{x}$ is available for consumption or use in production and therefore must be counted as part of supply. Hence we define the extent of imbalance as the difference between aggregate demand and the sum of aggregate supply and the aggregate endowment. This difference is called the *aggregate excess demand correspondence* $\Gamma : \mathbb{R}^n_+ \to 2^{\mathbb{R}^n}$:

$$\Gamma(p) \equiv \{x - z - \bar{x} : x \in D(p) \text{ and } z \in S(p)\}.$$

Excess demand inherits properties from aggregate demand and aggregate supply.

Theorem 13.2 (Properties of Aggregate Excess Demand). *On the cone of the price space where $S(p)$ is nonempty, $\Gamma(p)$ is:*

1. *Homogeneous of degree zero,*
2. *Nonincreasing, in the sense that $(p^1 - p^0)^{\perp}(\hat{\Gamma}(p^1) - \hat{\Gamma}(p^0)) \leq 0$, when $D(p)$ has this same property,*
3. *Convex-valued when all consumers' preferences are convex and all firms' production sets are convex,*
4. *Upper hemicontinuous on the interior of the convex cone where every profit is finite when every firms' production set is closed; provided $z_h^{q*}(p)$ has a uniform lower bound in a neighborhood of p for every $q = 1, \ldots, \ell$ whenever $z_h^{i*}(p)$ does not have a uniform upper bound in a neighborhood of p for some i (for each $h = 1, \ldots, n$),*

5. *Of zero value (i.e., $p^\perp \hat{\Gamma}(p) = 0$) when all consumers' preferences have local nonsatiation (Aggregate Walras' Law).*

Proof.

1. Immediate from homogeneity of $S(p)$ (Theorem 13.1) and of $D(p)$.
2. Immediate from $S(p)$ nondecreasing (Theorem 13.1) and the assumption on $D(p)$.
3. The proof is identical to the proof of convexity of aggregate Marshallian demand in Theorem 12.1, using convexity of $S(p)$ (Theorem 13.1) and convexity of $D(p)$.
4. Consider sequences $p^h \to p^0$ (all in the interior of the convex cone) and $\gamma^h \to \gamma^0$ with $\gamma^h \in \Gamma(p^h)$. We must show $\gamma^0 \in \Gamma(p^0)$. Write $\gamma^h = x^h - z^h - \bar{x}$ with $x^h \in D(p^h)$ and $z^h \in S(p^h)$. Theorem 12.1 ensures $D(p^h)$ is bounded as $h \to \infty$. Therefore x^h has a convergent subsequence; label the limit point x^0 and note that $x^0 \in D(p^0)$ due to upper hemicontinuity of D. Then:

$$\lim_{h\to\infty} z^h = \lim_{h\to\infty} (x^h - \gamma^h) - \bar{x} = x^0 - \gamma^0 - \bar{x}.$$

Label this limit z^0 and note that $z^0 \in S(p^0)$ due to upper hemicontinuity of S (Theorem 13.1). Therefore $\gamma^0 = x^0 - z^0 - \bar{x} \in \Gamma(p^0)$.

5. Write $\hat{\Gamma}(p) = x - z - \bar{x}$ for $x \in D(p)$ and $z \in S(p)$. By Theorem 12.1 and the definition of consumer j's monetary resource:

$$p^\perp x = \sum_{j=1}^{k} m_j(p) = \sum_{j=1}^{k} p^\perp \bar{x}^j + \sum_{j=1}^{k}\sum_{i=1}^{\ell} \alpha_i^j \pi^{i*}(p).$$

Use the definition of the aggregate endowment $\bar{x} = \sum_{j=1}^{k} \bar{x}^j$, and reverse the order of summation for the last term and use $\sum_{j=1}^{k} \alpha_i^j = 1$, to obtain:

$$p^\perp x = p^\perp \bar{x} + \sum_{i=1}^{\ell} \pi^{i*}(p).$$

Now substitute the definition of profit $\pi^{i*}(p) = p^\perp \hat{z}^i(p)$ and the definition of aggregate supply $z = \sum_{i=1}^{\ell} \hat{z}^i(p)$ to obtain:

$$p^\perp x = p^\perp \bar{x} + p^\perp z. \qquad \square$$

Item 5 is sometimes summarized by saying *the value of aggregate excess demand is zero at every price (where it is defined) when consumers' preferences have local nonsatiation*. As mentioned in Chapter 10, this observation is known as Walras' Law.

13.3 EQUILIBRIUM

A price at which aggregate supply equals aggregate demand is the basic notion of equilibrium in an economy composed of price-taking economic actors.

Definition 13.1. A *perfectly competitive equilibrium* is a price $p^e \in \mathbb{R}^n_+$ such that $0 \in \Gamma(p^e)$.

If p^e is an equilibrium then αp^e is also an equilibrium for every $\alpha > 0$ because $\Gamma(p)$ is homogeneous of degree zero. If we arbitrarily single out one commodity, say commodity 1, Walras' Law can be rewritten:

$$p_1 \hat{\Gamma}_1(p) = -\sum_{h=2}^{n} p_h \hat{\Gamma}_h(p).$$

Thus, if the markets for commodities $2, \ldots, h$ are in equilibrium at price p and $p_1 > 0$ then the market for commodity 1 is in equilibrium as well. This is sometimes summarized by saying that *when consumers' preferences have local nonsatiation and $n - 1$ markets are in equilibrium at a strictly positive price then the remaining market is in equilibrium as well.* This makes it possible to ignore one of the commodities when deriving an equilibrium price.

Two issues that immediately arise are whether an equilibrium price exists, and if so whether it is unique. It is easy to construct examples in which there are multiple equilibrium prices. A very simple example is an economy in which every consumer has Leontief preferences $u^j(x) = \min\{x_1, \ldots, x_n\}$, each consumer's endowment is $\bar{x}^j = (\alpha, \ldots, \alpha)$, and no firm has an ability to produce positive output ($Z^i = \mathbb{R}^n_-$ for $i = 1, \ldots, \ell$). Then $S(p) = \{0\}$ for all $p \gg 0$ and every consumer demands her endowment point $\bar{x}^j$ at every $p \gg 0$. Hence every strictly positive price is an equilibrium. Note that this setting satisfies all standard assumptions: Preferences are complete, transitive, continuous, locally nonsatiable, weakly monotone, and convex; while production sets are nonempty, closed, convex, and have the possibility of inaction, no free lunch and free disposal. Stronger assumptions, that production sets and preferences are all strictly convex, are typically employed to demonstrate uniqueness.

Existence of an equilibrium price is of more importance. Existence theorems for a general equilibrium are beyond the partial equilibrium scope of this book, although it is worth mentioning that aggregate excess demand for a commodity can be negative even when the price of that commodity is zero. Local nonsatiation of all preferences does not preclude this possibility because local nonsatiation does not ensure unbounded demand for *individual* commodities as price approaches zero. Thus a general equilibrium price is usually defined as a price at which aggregate excess demand is nonnegative and, if some component is negative, then the corresponding price is zero. The definition given above that requires zero aggregate excess demand is in accord with typical partial equilibrium settings in which the market is of interest only if it is "economic," in the sense that trades occur between buyers and sellers at positive marginal values. Meeting this standard, however, requires assumptions to ensure, for the commodity under study, that aggregate supply exists and is positive at sufficiently high prices while aggregate demand is near zero at such prices; and aggregate supply exists and is near zero (or negative) at sufficiently low prices while aggregate demand is large enough to exceed the endowment at such prices. It is also typical in partial equilibrium settings to assume aggregate demand is nonincreasing. That is, any implicit and explicit income effects are not sufficiently strong to offset the substitution effects. These assumptions are nonstandard in general equilibrium settings but are common, although sometimes only implied, in partial equilibrium analyses. Importantly, these assumptions do not preclude the possibility of either local or global constant returns to scale but it is, of course, required that aggregate supply exist on an appropriate subset of the price space. If not, the price-taking behavioral postulate for firms is probably inappropriate given the production possibilities and demand, and we should instead be studying suppliers who recognize some effect on price from their actions.

Assume therefore that there are $n = 2$ commodities and commodity 1 is under study. If there is a price vector at which aggregate supply is defined with $p_2 > 0$ then homogeneity of aggregate excess demand can be used to normalize the price of commodity 2 to unity, and Walras' Law ensures commodity 2 is in equilibrium whenever commodity 1 is in equilibrium. Suppress the commodity subscript for the remainder of this existence discussion, so that $S(p)$, $D(p)$ and $\Gamma(p)$ denote the aggregate supply, demand and excess demand of commodity 1 considered as correspondences of the price p of commodity 1; and $\bar{x}$ denotes the aggregate endowment of commodity 1.

Theorem 13.3 (Existence of a Partial Equilibrium Price). *Assume every consumer's preferences have local nonsatiation and $p_2 = 1$ so that commodity 2* *can be ignored via Walras' Law. Let* $P \equiv \{p \in \mathbb{R}^1_{++} : S(p) \neq \emptyset\}$ *denote the subset of the price space on which aggregate supply and demand both exist. Assume further that:*

1. *There exists* $\bar{p} \in P$ *at which supply is no smaller than demand: There is* $(z, x) \in S(\bar{p}) \times D(\bar{p})$ *such that* $z \geq x$.
2. *There exists* $\underline{p} \in P$ *at which the endowment plus supply is no larger than demand: There is* $(z, x) \in S(\underline{p}) \times D(\underline{p})$ *such that* $z + \bar{x} \leq x$.
3. *Every firm's production set has the possibility of inaction.*
4. $D(p)$ *is nonincreasing on* P.
5. *All firms' production sets and consumers' preferences are convex.*
6. *Every firms' production set is closed; and* $z_h^{q*}(p)$ *has a uniform lower bound in a neighborhood of* p *for every* $q = 1, \ldots, \ell$ *whenever* $z_h^{i*}(p)$ *does not have a uniform upper bound in a neighborhood of* p *for some* i *(for each* $h = 1, \ldots, n$*).*

Then there exists an equilibrium price p^e.

Proof. We begin by showing that P is an interval. Consider an arbitrary firm i and let $P^i = \{p \in \mathbb{R}^1_+ : z^{i*}(p) \neq \emptyset\}$ denote the subset of the price space on which firm i's supply exists. Then $P = \cap_{i=1}^{\ell} P^i$ and P is an interval if each P^i is an interval, so it suffices to show P^i is an interval. By assumption, each P^i is nonempty. For notational ease, suppress the superscript i for the remainder of this discussion.

By Theorem 4.1, $\hat{z}_1(p)$ is nondecreasing on P. With only one other commodity, $\hat{z}_2(p)$ is nonincreasing. To see why, consider $p^0, p^1 \in P$ with $p^0 < p^1$. Then:

$$p^0\hat{z}_1(p^0) + \hat{z}_2(p^0) \geq p^0\hat{z}_1(p^1) + \hat{z}_2(p^1).$$

Rearranging this inequality and using monotonicity of $\hat{z}_1(p)$ yields $\hat{z}_2(p^0) \geq \hat{z}_2(p^1)$.

Now let $\underline{p} = \inf P$ and $\bar{p} = \sup P$. If $\underline{p} = \bar{p}$ then P is trivially an interval, so consider $p \in (\underline{p}, \bar{p})$. We must show $p \in P$. By definition of the infimum and supremum, there exists $p^0, p^1 \in P$ with $p^0 < p < p^1$. Hence $\hat{z}_1(p^0) \leq \hat{z}_1(p^1)$ and $\hat{z}_2(p^0) \geq \hat{z}_2(p^1)$. Now consider any $z = (z_1, z_2) \in Z$. If $z < \hat{z}(p^j)$ for either $j = 0$ or $j = 1$ then z is irrelevant for optimization. $z > \hat{z}(p^j)$ for either $j = 0$ or $j = 1$ contradicts optimality of $\hat{z}(p^j)$. Thus, for the purpose of maximizing $pz_1 + z_2$, we may confine attention to $(z_1, z_2) \in Z$ satisfying one of the following for $j = 0, 1$:

1. $z_1 \leq \hat{z}_1(p^j)$ and $z_2 \geq \hat{z}_2(p^j)$, or
2. $z_1 \geq \hat{z}_1(p^j)$ and $z_2 \leq \hat{z}_2(p^j)$.

Suppose item 1 holds for $j = 0$. Using $p^0\hat{z}_1(p^0) + \hat{z}_2(p^0) \geq p^0 z_1 + z_2$, if $pz_1 + z_2 > p\hat{z}_1(p^0) + \hat{z}_2(p^0)$ then adding the two inequalities and rearranging yields $(p - p^0)(z_1 - \hat{z}_1(p^0)) > 0$, a contradiction. Therefore it is not possible to improve upon $\hat{z}(p^0)$ when maximizing $pz_1 + z_2$ by using z that satisfies item 1. A similar argument shows it is not possible to improve upon $\hat{z}(p^1)$ when maximizing $pz_1 + z_2$ by using z that satisfies item 2. Hence:

$$\pi^*(p) = \sup\{(z_1, z_2) \in Z : \hat{z}_1(p^0) \leq z_1 \leq \hat{z}_1(p^1) \text{ and } \hat{z}_2(p^1) \leq z_2 \leq \hat{z}_2(p^0)\}.$$

This set is an intersection of two closed sets, and is therefore closed. It is also bounded and nonempty. Thus the maximum is attained on this set: $z^*(p) \neq \emptyset$, or $p \in P$.

Now return to the main argument. $\Gamma(\bar{p}) \cap \mathbb{R}^1_-$ and $\Gamma(\underline{p}) \cap \mathbb{R}^1_+$ are both nonempty, by assumptions 1 and 2, respectively. If 0 is an element of either $\Gamma(\bar{p})$ or $\Gamma(\underline{p})$ then we have an equilibrium price, so assume $\Gamma(\bar{p}) \subset \mathbb{R}^1_{--}$ and $\Gamma(\underline{p}) \subset \mathbb{R}^1_{++}$. This implies $\underline{p} < \bar{p}$ by monotonicity of Γ (Theorem 13.2). Hence $[\underline{p}, \bar{p}]$ is a nondegenerate interval in $\mathbb{R}^1_{++}$ and $S(p)$ is nonempty on this interval. $D(p)$ is also nonempty on this interval by Theorem 10.1, using possibility of inaction to ensure each consumer's monetary resource is nonnegative. Thus $\Gamma(p)$ is nonempty on this interval. Now define:

$$\bar{p}^* \equiv \inf\{p \in P : \Gamma(p) \subset \mathbb{R}^1_{--}\}$$
$$\underline{p}^* \equiv \sup\{p \in P : \Gamma(p) \subset \mathbb{R}^1_{++}\}.$$

From above, each of these sets is nonempty. Moreover, again using monotonicity of Γ, the first set is bounded below by $\underline{p}$ and the second set is bounded above by $\bar{p}$. Hence both $\bar{p}^*$ and $\underline{p}^*$ are finite, and $\underline{p}^* \leq \bar{p}^*$. By definition of the infimum there exists a sequence $p^i \downarrow \bar{p}^*$ with $\Gamma(p^i) \subset \mathbb{R}^1_{--}$. Monotonicity of Γ then yields a corresponding nondecreasing sequence $\gamma^i \in \Gamma(p^i)$. The latter is bounded above by zero and therefore has a finite limit $\bar{\gamma} \leq 0$. Similarly, there exists a sequence $\tilde{p}^i \uparrow \underline{p}^*$ with $\Gamma(\tilde{p}^i) \subset \mathbb{R}^1_{++}$ and a corresponding sequence $\tilde{\gamma}^i \downarrow \underline{\gamma} \geq 0$. $\bar{\gamma} \in \Gamma(\bar{p}^*)$ and $\underline{\gamma} \in \Gamma(\underline{p}^*)$ by upper hemicontinuity of Γ (Theorem 13.2). If $\underline{p}^* = \bar{p}^*$ then there exists $\alpha \in (0,1)$ such that $\alpha\bar{\gamma} + (1-\alpha)\underline{\gamma} = 0$, and $\alpha\bar{\gamma} + (1-\alpha)\underline{\gamma} \in \Gamma(\bar{p}^*)$ because Γ is convex-valued (Theorem 13.2). Then $p^e = \underline{p}^* = \bar{p}^*$. If $\underline{p}^* < \bar{p}^*$ then select any $p \in (\underline{p}^*, \bar{p}^*)$ and note that $\Gamma(p)$ has both a nonpositive and a nonnegative element, by definition of $\underline{p}^*$ and $\bar{p}^*$. Convexity of $\Gamma(p)$ then yields $p^e = p$. □

13.4 PARETO EFFICIENCY

An important property of a perfectly competitive equilibrium with locally nonsatiated consumers is that resources cannot be reallocated in a way that improves the welfare of one economic agent without harming the welfare of another agent. This is called *Pareto Efficiency*. To demonstrate that competitive equilibria are Pareto Efficient, we must formalize the concepts of an *allocation* and what it means for an allocation to be Pareto Efficient.

Definition 13.2. An *allocation* (x, z) is an assignment of quantity bundles to each consumer and firm:

$$x = (x^1, \ldots, x^k) \quad z = (z^1, \ldots, z^\ell);$$

where $x^j \in \mathbb{R}^n_+$ for $j = 1, \ldots, k$ and $z^i \in \mathbb{R}^n$ for $i = 1, \ldots, \ell$. An allocation (x, z) is *feasible* if it satisfies the resource constraints:

$$\sum_{j=1}^{k} x^j \leq \sum_{i=1}^{\ell} z^i + \bar{x}, \quad \text{and } z^i \in Z^i \text{ for } i = 1, \ldots, \ell.$$

If aggregate supply exists at a price $p \gg 0$ then there are allocations in which each agent receives an optimal quantity choice for this price. Denote these individually optimal allocations by:

$$(\hat{x}(p), \hat{z}(p)) = ((\hat{x}^1(p), \ldots, \hat{x}^k(p)), (\hat{z}^1(p), \ldots, \hat{z}^\ell(p))).$$

Note that the monetary resources of consumers are suppressed in this notation, in accord with the discussion above that these resources are continuous and homogenous functions of price in a private-ownership economy composed of price-taking actors. If p^e is an equilibrium price then, by definition, there is an individually optimal allocation $(\hat{x}(p^e), \hat{z}(p^e))$ such that:

$$\sum_{j=1}^{k} \hat{x}^j(p^e) = \sum_{i=1}^{\ell} \hat{z}^i(p^e) + \bar{x}.$$

Such an allocation is called a *competitive equilibrium allocation*. As $\hat{z}^i(p^e) \in Z^i$, also by definition, it is immediate that every competitive equilibrium allocation is feasible.

Definition 13.3. An allocation (x, z) is *Pareto Efficient* if:

1. (x, z) is feasible, and
2. For any other feasible allocation $(\tilde{x}, \tilde{z})$, if there exists a consumer i such that $u^i(\tilde{x}^i) > u^i(x^i)$ then there exists a consumer j such that $u^j(\tilde{x}^j) < u^j(x^j)$.

Note that Pareto Efficiency is purely an efficiency concept; there is no notion of equity here. A Pareto Efficient allocation can be derived by choosing an allocation to maximize the utility of one consumer subject to the feasibility constraints and that the utility of every other consumer j satisfies $u^j(x^j) \geq \bar{u}^j$ for arbitrary feasible utility levels $\bar{u}^j$. The collection of Pareto Efficient allocations, called the *Pareto Set*, is found by varying the $\bar{u}^j$'s over mutually feasible values.

Consumers always benefit from greater monetary resources when preferences have local nonsatiation. In other words, there is no opportunity for individual consumption decisions to waste resources. This property ensures a competitive equilibrium allocation is Pareto Efficient. The intuition for this result can be displayed for an economy with $n = 2$ commodities and $k = 2$ consumers using a graph known as an *Edgeworth Box*.

Quantities of each commodity are measured on the axes in Fig. 13.2. One commodity pair is the aggregate initial endowment $\bar{x}$. It is always possible for aggregate supply inclusive of the endowment to be this point if firms all have the possibility of inaction. Indeed, as mentioned previously, it may be possible for firms to generate an aggregate free lunch. Hence the boundary of the aggregate production set, including the endowment (i.e., the set $\{z + \bar{x} : z \in Z\}$), passes through or above the endowment point. An equilibrium must exist to meaningfully assess its efficiency, so for illustrative purposes the boundary shown is for a closed and strictly convex aggregate production set. For any given price ratio p_1/p_2, firms collectively choose a production plan $S(p) + \bar{x}$ on the highest feasible aggregate isoprofit

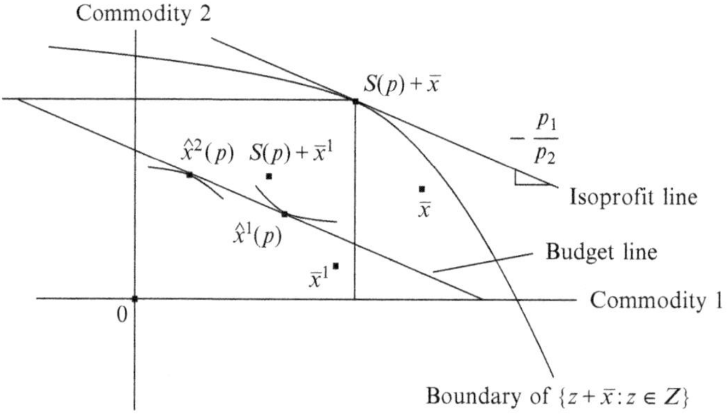

Fig. 13.2 Edgeworth box.

line (Lemma 13.1), as illustrated. This choice establishes the dimensions of the "economic pie." That is, the quantity of each commodity available for consumption. Any quantity pair within the illustrated box can be collectively consumed.

Now place the two consumers in this economy. If consumer 1's consumption is measured from the origin then consumer 2's consumption is measured in the negative direction starting from the aggregate supply point $S(p) + \bar{x}$. The budget line has the same slope as the isoprofit and passes above consumer 1's endowment point $\bar{x}^1$ (measured from the origin) because at any price, if consumer 1 consumes exactly her endowment, she has monetary resources leftover equal to her share of aggregate profit. The budget line also passes below $S(p) + \bar{x}^1$ for the same reason—consumer 2's origin is $S(p) + \bar{x}$ and his consumption point is $S(p) + \bar{x} - \bar{x}^2 = S(p) + \bar{x}^1$ if he consumes exactly his endowment, leaving him with monetary resources equal to his share of aggregate profit. Consumer j chooses a point $\hat{x}^j(p)$ on the highest indifference curve that is on or below the budget line (measured from that consumer's origin). The behavioral postulate is price-taking, so neither consumer considers the boundaries of the box as binding constraints even though points outside the box cannot be collectively consumed given the aggregate production choice. Consumers simply maximize given the position of the budget line. The case illustrated has each consumer's choice within the box but their choices do not equate demand and supply. There is excess demand for good 1 because $\hat{x}_1^1(p) + \hat{x}_1^2(p)$ exceeds the horizontal dimension of the box, and excess supply of good 2 because $\hat{x}_2^1(p) + \hat{x}_2^2(p)$ is less than the vertical dimension of the box.

Equilibrium requires a higher price ratio so that the aggregate production choice moves along the production boundary to the southeast and consumers collectively substitute commodity 2 for commodity 1. Fig. 13.3 shows an equilibrium. Note that the consumers' preferred sets lie on opposite sides of the budget line at the equilibrium consumption point. Hence any consumption point that respects the size of the economic pie and strictly improves utility of one consumer strictly diminishes utility of the other consumer. This would not necessarily be true if either consumer had an optimal consumption point below his budget line. This is the essence of the efficiency property for competitive equilibria. When consumers' optima must be on their budget lines (i.e., when there is local nonsatiation) every competitive equilibrium allocation is Pareto Efficient.

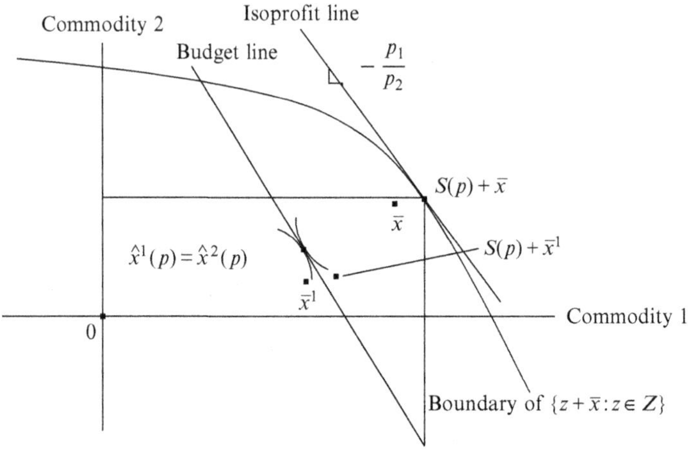

Fig. 13.3 Edgeworth box in equilibrium.

Theorem 13.4 (First Fundamental Theorem of Welfare Economics). *Assume all consumers' preferences are locally nonsatiated. Then every competitive equilibrium allocation is Pareto Efficient.*

Proof. Let p^e be an equilibrium price and $(\hat{x}(p^e), \hat{z}(p^e))$ be the corresponding competitive equilibrium allocation. Suppose $(\tilde{x}, \tilde{z})$ is another feasible allocation satisfying $u^j(\tilde{x}^j) \geq u^j(\hat{x}^j(p^e))$ for $j = 1, \ldots, k$ with strict inequality for at least one consumer, which we arbitrarily label consumer 1. We will show that the existence of such an allocation leads to a contradiction.

Feasibility of $(\tilde{x}, \tilde{z})$ implies:

$$\sum_{j=1}^{k} \tilde{x}^j \leq \sum_{i=1}^{\ell} \tilde{z}^i + \bar{x}.$$

Subtract the equilibrium condition to obtain:

$$\sum_{j=1}^{k} (\tilde{x}^j - \hat{x}^j(p^e)) \leq \sum_{i=1}^{\ell} (\tilde{z}^i - \hat{z}^i(p^e)). \tag{13.1}$$

By local nonsatiation, Walras' Law holds for each consumer in the competitive equilibrium allocation:

$$(p^e)^{\perp} \hat{x}^j(p^e) = m^j(p^e) \text{ for } j = 1, \ldots, k.$$

Using $u^j(\tilde{x}^j) \geq u^j(\hat{x}^j(p^e))$, local nonsatiation also implies:

$$(p^e)^{\perp} \tilde{x}^j \geq m^j(p^e) \text{ for } j = 1, \ldots, k,$$

with strict inequality for $j = 1$. Subtract the former from the latter and sum over $j = 1, \ldots, k$ to obtain:

$$0 < (p^e)^{\perp} \sum_{j=1}^{k} (\tilde{x}^j - \hat{x}^j(p^e)).$$

Multiplying Eq. (13.1) by $(p^e)^{\perp}$, this implies:

$$0 < (p^e)^{\perp} \sum_{i=1}^{\ell} (\tilde{z}^i - \hat{z}^i(p^e)).$$

Feasibility implies $\tilde{z}^i \in Z^i$, so optimality implies $(p^e)^{\perp}(\tilde{z}^i - \hat{z}^i(p^e)) \leq 0$ for $i = 1, \ldots, \ell$. Sum over $i = 1, \ldots, \ell$ to obtain a contradiction. □

Note that this theorem does not rely on there being only $n = 2$ commodities. Of course, the theorem is vacuous if an equilibrium does not exist and we have proven existence only for the partial equilibrium case of $n = 2$. General equilibrium presentations address the existence issue for $n > 2$.

13.5 LONG-RUN EQUILIBRIUM

The perfectly competitive equilibria discussed so far are for a fixed number ℓ of firms. These equilibria can be thought of as "short-run" equilibria, pertaining to a time period during which entry into and exit from the market do not occur. Now we turn to the "long-run," which is *defined* to be a time period during which all firms (both actual and potential) have the largest existing production set and that set has the possibility of inaction, making entry and exit costless (i.e., there are no sunk costs). The long run may be very long indeed for some commodities; for example those whose production requires large, specialized initial investments; or that utilize complicated production processes; or for which some firm has patent protection on its technology. The effects of such complications are studied in courses on industrial organization. For present purposes we simply avoid these issues and study a time period sufficiently long to overcome such rigidities.

In this long-run scenario, potential firms enter the market if their optimal profit at the prevailing price will be positive, and existing firms exit the market if their optimal profit at the prevailing price is negative (recall that all opportunity costs are counted in Z^i, including the opportunity cost of capital and the owners' efforts, so the entry/exit criterion here is based on *economic* profit). Note that the firms, including the entrants, are still presumed to be price-takers. Hence we are still studying pure perfect competition. This means, in particular, that $z^i = 0$ is an optimal choice at the equilibrium price if i is a potential firm. Thus, the number of firms producing positive output in equilibrium is endogenous here, determined by market demand and the technology, rather than being fixed as in the previous section. Indeed, in the welfare theorem above the set of economic agents under consideration was fixed. Once entry is allowed it may be possible to obtain a Pareto improvement compared to an equilibrium with a fixed number of firms (unless there is a firm among the fixed ℓ whose equilibrium allocation is zero).

Consider again the partial equilibrium setting with commodity 1 under study and its subscript suppressed for brevity. There are substantial nonexistence problems for perfectly competitive long-run equilibrium prices. Begin by assuming the technology is globally increasing returns to scale. Then the average cost curve is downward-sloping, with some asymptote at price p^0, as in Fig. 13.4. At any price $p > p^0$, all price-taking firms perceive that infinite profit can be earned by simply producing an arbitrarily large level of output. Thus, aggregate supply is infinite at all such prices. At any price $p \leq p^0$, all price-taking firms perceive that negative profit will be earned at any positive output. Thus, aggregate supply is zero at all such prices, and we see that there is no price at which aggregate demand equals long-run aggregate supply. Aggregate supply has a discontinuity here at p^0, where it jumps from zero to infinity.

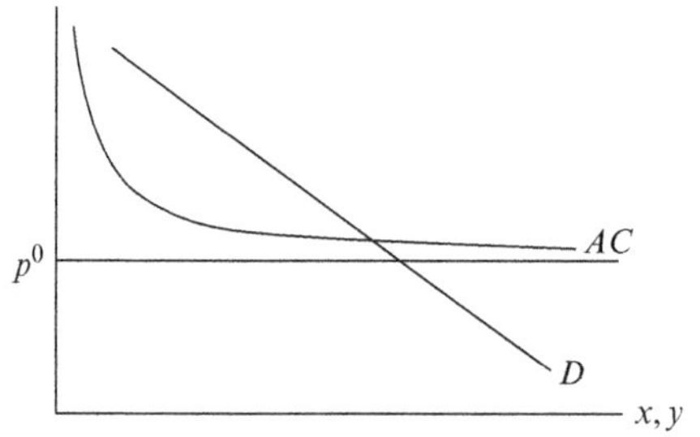

Fig. 13.4 Existence failure for long-run perfectly competitive equilibrium when there is increasing returns.

This outcome may seem nonsensical. After all, shouldn't firms perceive that, by supplying infinite output, they will drive the price that consumers are willing to pay down below average cost? Certainly in any realistic setting firms would indeed know that an arbitrarily large output cannot be sold at any profitable price. However, this is a description of firms that are not price-takers. Firms that incorporate the knowledge that their actions may affect price are behaving according to a different behavioral postulate than the price-taking (perfectly competitive) postulate. Thus, the real lesson here is that the perfectly competitive behavioral postulate is inconsistent with an increasing returns technology as a reasonable description of how a market functions in the long-run.

Now suppose the technology is globally decreasing returns to scale. Then the average cost curve is upward-sloping, with some nonnegative intercept at price p^0, as in Fig. 13.5. At any price $p > p^0$, for example p^1 on the graph, all price taking firms perceive that positive profit can be earned by simply producing a level of output below y^0. Thus, unabated entry occurs, driving aggregate supply above y^1. At any price $p \leq p^0$, all price-taking firms perceive that negative profit will be earned at any positive output. Thus, aggregate supply is zero at all such prices, and we see once again that there is no price at which aggregate demand equals long-run aggregate supply. Aggregate supply still has a discontinuity at p^0, where it jumps from zero to infinity.

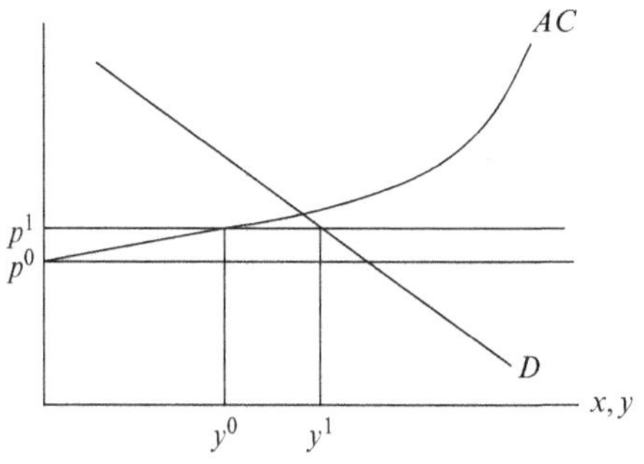

Fig. 13.5 Existence failure for long-run perfectly competitive equilibrium when there is decreasing returns.

Finally, consider the case of globally constant returns to scale. Then the average cost curve is horizontal at some price, say p^0, as in Fig. 13.6. At any price $p > p^0$, all price-taking firms perceive that infinite profit can be earned by producing an arbitrarily large level of output. Thus, aggregate supply is infinite at all such prices. At any price $p < p^0$, all price-taking firms perceive that negative profit will be earned at any positive output. Thus, aggregate supply is zero at all such prices. However, at $p = p^0$ all levels of output produce the same profit (zero), so all firms are indifferent to the amount produced when price is p^0. Thus aggregate supply is horizontal at p^0, and p^0 is the only equilibrium price. The number of active firms and the amount produced by each firm is indeterminate in this equilibrium, however. Any combination of firms and individual output levels that sum to y^0 is equilibrium. Thus, although equilibrium exists in this case, the model makes no predictions about individual firm behavior.

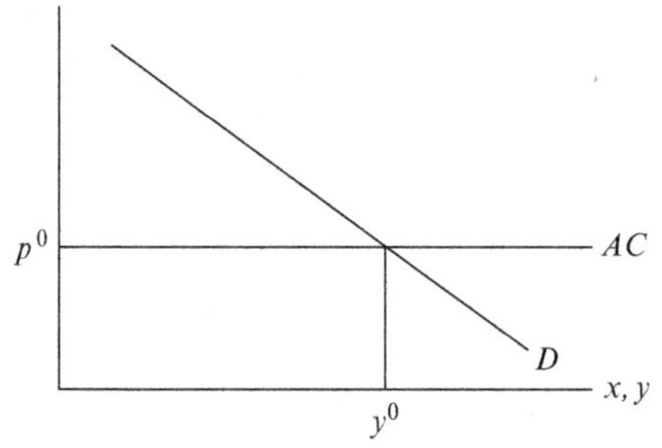

Fig. 13.6 Long-run perfectly competitive equilibrium when there is constant returns.

These existence and indeterminacy problems can be substantially ameliorated if the technology has locally increasing returns at low output levels and then locally constant or decreasing returns at higher output levels. In this case the average cost curve falls at first, then reaches a minimum, and then eventually rises whenever a point of decreasing returns is achieved. This case is illustrated in Fig. 13.7. The quantities at which average cost reaches its minimum are called *efficient scales* of operation. In the graph, all quantities in $[\underline{y}, \bar{y}]$ are efficient scales, and of course $\underline{y}$ is the MES.

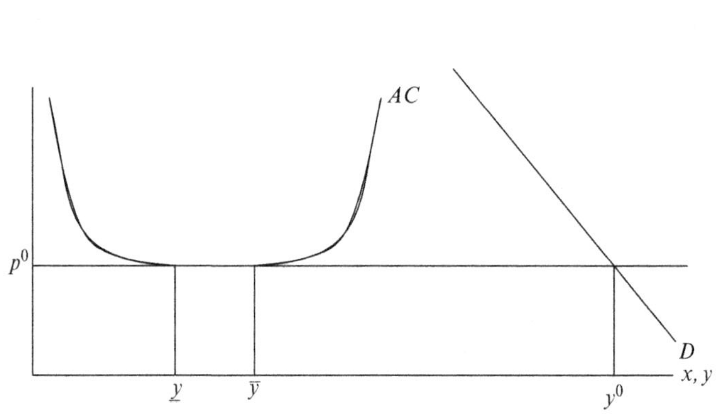

Fig. 13.7 Initially increasing but eventually decreasing returns.

Interesting possibilities arise for long-run perfectly equilibrium when the technology is like Fig. 13.7. It is clear that the only possible equilibrium price is p^0, because at any price above p^0 all firms perceive that positive profit can be earned by choosing a quantity between $\underline{y}$ and $\bar{y}$, so aggregate supply is infinite, while at any price below p^0 all firms perceive that profit will be negative at any positive output, so aggregate supply is zero. At price p^0, an equilibrium is possible but not guaranteed. Equilibrium exists at this price if some combination of firms, each producing an efficient scale of output, can produce aggregate quantity y^0. The aggregate supply curve here consists of horizontal segments and thus equilibrium exists if one of these segments includes output level y^0. Otherwise there is no equilibrium price. Note that in any such equilibrium every firm *must* produce at an efficient scale. This property is called *productive efficiency*, as it says all production takes place at the lowest cost per unit that is possible using the most efficient technology. The discussion here makes it clear that this is a general property of long-run perfectly competitive equilibrium.

Theorem 13.5. *Long-run perfectly competitive equilibria always achieve productive efficiency.*

If there is an equilibrium in Fig. 13.7, it is likely to be much more determinate than the constant returns case, depending on the width of the interval of efficient scales. When the interval is small, we have relatively accurate information on how much each firm must produce and on how many firms will participate in equilibrium. In the limit, when the interval is a single point, the only possible equilibrium is $\ell = y^0/\text{MES}$ firms, each producing the MES. As the interval grows, in the limit approaching the constant returns case, the possibilities for equilibrium become progressively less determinate.

A sufficient condition can be formulated for existence of an equilibrium when the technology is like Fig. 13.7. If one firm produces positive output, aggregate supply at p^0 is the horizontal segment $[\underline{y}, \bar{y}]$. If two firms produce positive output, aggregate supply is the segment $[2\underline{y}, 2\bar{y}]$. Continuing, if ℓ firms produce positive output, aggregate supply is the segment $[\ell\underline{y}, \ell\bar{y}]$. As ℓ grows, the width of the aggregate supply segment grows. Eventually, the segment overlaps the segment for one fewer producing firms. That is, for ℓ large enough we have $(\ell - 1)\bar{y} \geq \ell\underline{y}$. Once ℓ reaches this level, all subsequent intervals overlap and thus aggregate supply is horizontal. Here, ℓ "large enough" means ℓ at least as large as the smallest value of ℓ that satisfies the inequality $(\ell - 1)\bar{y} \geq \ell\underline{y}$. That is, aggregate supply is horizontal at p^0 for $y \geq (\ell^* - 1)\underline{y}$, where:

$$\ell^* \equiv \min\left\{\ell : \ell \geq \frac{\bar{y}}{\bar{y} - \underline{y}}\right\}. \quad (13.2)$$

Note that ℓ^* exists and is at least 1 when $\bar{y} > \underline{y}$; since $\frac{\bar{y}}{\bar{y}-\underline{y}} \geq 1$, so the set here is bounded below by 1; and $\frac{\bar{y}}{\bar{y}-\underline{y}}$ is finite, so the set here is nonempty. However, if there is only one efficient scale then the set here is empty and then ℓ^* does not exist. In this case we adopt the convention $\ell^* = \infty$. Thus, we have:

Lemma 13.2. *Let $[\underline{y}, \bar{y}]$ be the interval of efficient scales for the most efficient technology, $p^0 = ac(\bar{y})$ be average cost at these efficient scales, and $D(p)$ be aggregate demand. A long-run perfectly competitive equilibrium exists if:*

$$D(p^0) \geq (\ell^* - 1)\underline{y},$$

where ℓ^* is defined by Eq. (13.2).

Note that this condition is sufficient but not necessary for existence of an equilibrium. If the condition fails, one of the aggregate supply segments for $\ell < \ell^* - 1$ can still include y^0, in which case an equilibrium exists. This is the only possibility for equilibrium when $\bar{y} = \underline{y}$, in which case the segments are single points, and so equilibrium exists in this case if and only if y^0 is (coincidently) an integer multiple of the MES.

13.6 NOTES

Marshall [1, Book V] is generally credited with the full exposition of price-taking partial equilibrium. The distinction between the short-run and long-run is contrasted in [1, Book V, Chapter III] versus [1, Book V, Chapters V and XII]. Walras [2] also developed price-taking equilibrium but the focus was on general equilibrium treating consumers and producers separately. The mathematical tools to formally prove existence of a general equilibrium (i.e., Brouwer's fixed point theorem) did not exist in Walras' lifetime. I am grateful to Jonathan Hamilton for helpful discussions concerning the role of irreversibility.

Smith [3, Book IV, Chapter II, p. 423] is the originator of the idea that a competitive equilibrium is efficient, through his famous mention of the "invisible hand." Generally, Smith assumed constant returns without explicitly recognizing the importance of the assumption. Marshall [1, Book

V, Chapter XIII] examines the "doctrine of maximal satisfaction" (i.e., efficiency) but largely dismisses it as ignoring distributional issues (i.e., equity). Edgeworth [4] is credited with the diagrammatic exposition but the formal definition and demonstration that a price-taking equilibrium is efficient is due to Pareto [5, especially the Appendix beginning at Section 89], who also converted Edgeworth's diagrams into the box diagram (which was later popularized by Bowley [6]).

The role played by "flat spots" on the bottom of the average cost curve in existence of long-run price-taking equilibrium is due to [7, p. 33].

13.7 EXERCISES

1. Consider the following economy. There are two commodities, x_1 and x_2. Let p denote the price of x_1 and assume the price of x_2 is normalized to one. There is one firm with production function $x_1 = 2\sqrt{x_2}$ for $x_2 \geq 0$. There is one consumer with utility function $u = \left[x_1^{2/3} + x_2^{2/3}\right]^{3/2}$. This consumer is endowed with $\bar{x}_2 = 3$ units of good x_2. This consumer is also the sole owner of the firm. Suppose the firm and the consumer each acts (separately) as a price-taker. Find the equilibrium value of p.
2. Suppose there are k identical price-taking consumers, each with income m and utility function $u(x, y) = \ln x + \ln y$. Let p denote the price of x and assume the price of y has been normalized to one. Suppose also there are ℓ identical producers of x, each with constant marginal cost $c > 0$ and no fixed costs.
   a. Derive the aggregate demand for x. If the firm(s) behave as price takers, what are the equilibrium price and quantity of x?
   b. Suppose the firms do not behave as price-takers, and that the end result of their behavior is an equilibrium price $p = \frac{c\ell}{\ell - 1}$. Derive an expression for the deadweight loss that is incurred if the government compensates consumers for the higher price caused by the non-price-taking behavior of the firms.
   c. Suppose there are $k = 1$ million consumers who each have income of $m = \$30$ thousand, and the firms are sufficiently competitive to make the price no more than 10% above the perfectly competitive price. How large is the deadweight loss?
3. Consider an economy with one firm and one consumer. The consumer's welfare is accurately measured by the Marshallian surplus for

good 1. The only endowment is $\bar{x}_2 = \$m$, possessed by the consumer. The firm produces good 1 from good 2. The consumer's Marshallian demand and the firm's costs are:

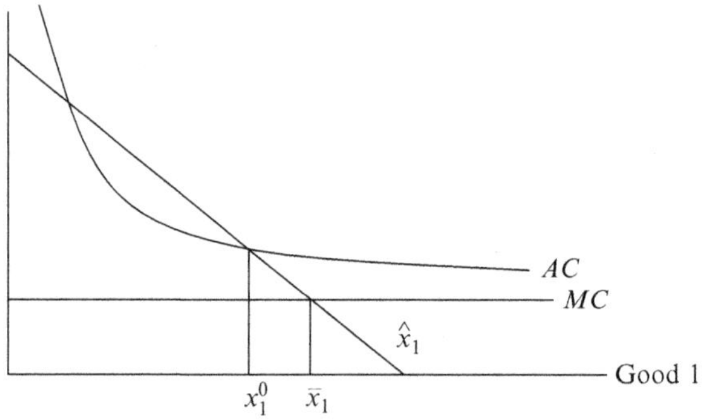

a. Is the allocation $(x_1^0, m - AC(x_1^0))$ for the consumer and $(x_1^0, AC(x_1^0))$ for the firm feasible? Why?

b. Is the allocation in part (a) Pareto Efficient? Why?

c. Is the allocation in part (a) a (competitive) equilibrium allocation? Why?

d. Is the allocation $(\bar{x}_1, m)$ for the consumer and $(\bar{x}_1, 0)$ for the firm feasible? Why?

e. Is the allocation in part (d) Pareto Efficient? Why?

f. Is the allocation in part (d) a (competitive) equilibrium allocation? Why?

g. Relate your answers to parts (b),(c) and parts (e),(f) to the First Fundamental Theorem of Welfare Economics.

4. Suppose all buyers and sellers in a private-ownership economy have "well-behaved" production sets and preferences, except that there is a consumer whose preferences do not satisfy local nonsatiation.

a. Is it possible that a competitive equilibrium allocation is Pareto Efficient? If so, give an example of a Pareto Efficient competitive equilibrium (a graph will suffice). If not, explain why not.

b. Is it possible that a competitive equilibrium allocation is not Pareto Efficient? If so, give an example of a competitive equilibrium that is not Pareto Efficient (a graph will suffice). If not, explain why not.

5. Suppose two individual production sets are:

$$Z^1 = \{(z_1, z_2) \in \mathbb{R}^2 : z_2 \leq \min\{0, -2z_1\}\}$$

$$Z^2 = \left\{(z_1, z_2) \in \mathbb{R}^2 : z_1 \leq 0 \text{ and } z_2 \leq 1 - 2z_1 + \frac{1}{z_1 - 1}\right\}.$$

   a. Very carefully draw each production set.
   b. Based on your graph, does each production set have the following properties: Closed, convex, possibility of inaction, free disposal and no free lunch?
   c. Consider now the aggregate production set:

$$Z = \{z^1 + z^2 : z^1 \in Z^1 \text{ and } z^2 \in Z^2\}.$$

   Can the aggregate production point $z^0 = (1, -1)$ be produced by either firm acting alone (i.e., when the other firm's production plan is zero)? What about if one firm's production plan is negative?
   d. For any given $z_1^1 \geq 0$, what is the largest z_2 value from Z^1? For any given $z_1^2 \leq 0$, what is the largest z_2 value from Z^2? Use these observations to state an upper bound on z_2 as a function of $z_1^2 \leq 0$ when $(1, z_2) \in Z$.
   e. Is z^0 an element of Z? Is there a sequence in Z that approaches z^0? What do you conclude about whether Z is closed?
   f. What is the supply correspondence of each firm? What is the aggregate supply correspondence?
   g. Does Z have the no free lunch property?

6. Suppose there are a large number k of buyers of a final product. The buyers each buy at most one unit and are each willing to pay up to \$$A$ for that one unit (A is the same for all k buyers).
   a. Draw the aggregate demand curve for the final product.
   b. Assume sellers are price-takers who all have constant marginal cost $c < A$ and no other cost. Is there a competitive equilibrium in this market? Why? If so, what is it?

7. Consider an agricultural industry facing the demand curve $Y = 2800 - 100p$ for $0 \leq p \leq 28$. p is the price of the industry's product and Y is the aggregate industry quantity demanded. The industry has 100 firms. Each firm perceives itself to be a perfect competitor. All firms in the industry produce the same product with the same technology and

inputs, and so have the same total cost function, $c(y) = 100 + y + \frac{y^2}{4}$. y is an individual firm's output.

a. What is the current market equilibrium price for this industry?

b. Is this industry in long-run equilibrium? Why or why not?

c. The firms in the industry vote to form an agricultural marketing board. This is a legal cartel that acts as a single seller. Each firm shares equally in the industry's output. What will be the cartel's price, output, and profit per firm?

8. Consider a market with aggregate demand $D(p) = 10 - p$ for $0 \leq p \leq 10$, where p is the per-unit price. The production technology for this good is summarized by the cost function $c(y) = F + y^2/F$, where y is the output of one supplier and $c(y)$ is that supplier's total cost of producing y units. F is an investment in the scale of the production process. $F > 0$ can be chosen by each supplier before production takes place. When a supplier chooses investment level F, variable cost is y^2/F and the amount invested (i.e., F) becomes sunk.

a. Carefully draw the average and marginal cost curves for a supplier who has sunk $F = 1$. Carefully draw the same curves for a supplier who has sunk $F = 2$. Finally, carefully draw the curves for arbitrary F. What are the long-run (i.e., when F is variable) average and marginal cost curves?

b. Suppose there is a monopolist who chooses F first and then chooses output in the standard monopoly way. What values of F, output, and price will the monopolist choose? Illustrate the monopolist's choice on a graph of demand, marginal revenue, and the cost curves. Comment on the monopolist's efficiency.

c. Suppose there are ℓ suppliers with this production technology who have each chosen investment levels $F > 0$. Assume the suppliers are price-takers. Find the equilibrium price and aggregate quantity. Illustrate this equilibrium on a graph of demand, the cost curves of one supplier, and the aggregate supply curve of all ℓ suppliers. Comment on the equilibrium.

9. Consider a market with inverse demand $p = 100 - y$, where y is market output, and a large number of potential firms who all behave as price takers and who all have cost function $c(y_i) = 1 + y_i^2$, where y_i is the output of firm i.

a. If there is a long-run equilibrium, what is the price?

b. Is there a long-run equilibrium? If so, find it.

10. Suppose the most efficient technology looks like this:

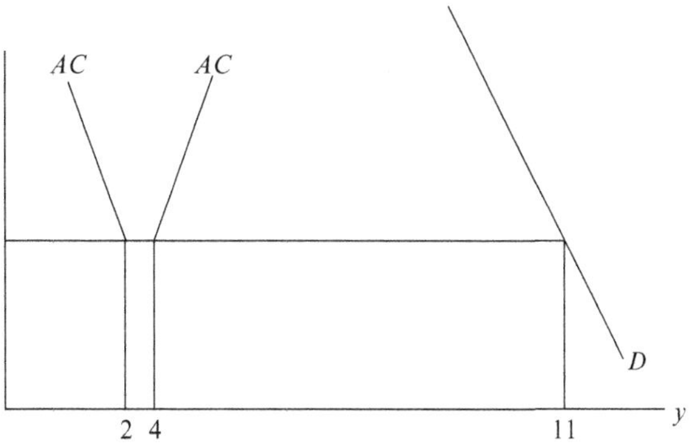

a. Is there a long-run perfectly competitive equilibrium? Why?

b. What is the maximum number of firms that can produce positive output in a long-run perfectly competitive equilibrium? What is the minimum number?

11. Suppose we have a perfectly competitive market and that all firms are identical with average cost:

$$AC(y) = \begin{cases} 10 - y, & 0 < y \leq 5 \\ 5, & 5 \leq y \leq 6 \\ y - 1, & 6 \leq y, \end{cases}$$

where y is the output of an individual firm. The market inverse demand is $p(Y) = a - Y$ for $0 \leq Y \leq a$, where Y is market quantity.

a. If there is a long-run equilibrium, what must the price be?

b. How large must a be in order to guarantee that there is a long-run equilibrium?

12. There are 50 perfectly competitive firms producing a homogeneous product. Market inverse demand is $p = 102 - y$ for $0 \leq y \leq 102$, where p is the market price and y is market quantity. Firm i has cost function $c_i^* = F_i + c_i y_i^2$, where y_i is the output of firm i. The technology is such that firm i can choose the amount of fixed cost F_i to invest. Firm i's marginal cost is inversely related to the amount firm i invests. Assume the relationship between F_i and c_i is $c_i = \frac{1}{F_i}$.

a. Find a long-run perfectly competitive equilibrium price, market quantity, and quantity for each firm. Is there more than one equilibrium? If so, describe them.

b. Assume these firms use only one input and are price-takers in the market for that input, with input price w. Describe the long-run technology of these firms.

13. Consider a market with inverse demand $p(Y) = 600 - Y$ for $0 \leq Y \leq 600$, where Y is market output, and 10 identical price-taking firms, each of which has cost function:

$$c(y) = \begin{cases} 1 + y^2, & y > 0 \\ 0, & y = 0 \end{cases},$$

where y is individual firm output.

a. Find the equilibrium price, market output, individual firm output, and individual firm profit if there is no entry into this market.

b. Strictly speaking, is there a perfectly competitive equilibrium in this market when there is free entry? If not, explain why. If so, derive the equilibrium price and outputs.

14. One way the problems with potential nonexistence of long-run price-taking equilibrium might be ameliorated is if the sellers' collective use of scarce inputs drives up the price of those inputs. This increases all costs as the size of the industry grows, and thereby limits the size of the industry. To model this, suppose there are many identical potential sellers with cost function $c(y) = \left[F + \frac{1}{2}y^2\right]\ell$, where y is the output of one seller and ℓ is the number of sellers who are producing positive quantity.

a. Carefully draw the AC and MC curves when there is one active producer.

b. Carefully draw the AC and MC curves when there are two active producers. What is the long-run supply of two producers?

c. What is the long-run supply curve of the industry, and how does it differ from the long-run industry supply that we would have if cost did not depend on ℓ?

d. Suppose market inverse demand is $p(Y) = \alpha - Y$, where Y is aggregate industry output. For what values of α is there a perfectly competitive equilibrium? How does this differ from the values of α for which there would be a perfectly competitive equilibrium if cost did not depend on ℓ?

15. The state of California has found that an electric utility is facing the demand curve $y = 20 - p$ for $0 \leq p \leq 20$, where p is the unit price of electricity and y is the quantity demanded. The state has also estimated that the marginal cost function of the utility is $MC = 2 + y$. California has decided to set a single regulated price for electricity.

a. What price should the state set if the objective is to eliminate all (Marshallian) deadweight loss?

b. How much deadweight loss is eliminated using the price in part (a) relative to allowing the firm to set its own (unregulated monopoly) price?

16. The Stanley Paper Company produces newsprint which they sell in a perfectly competitive market. They have just built a new plant in which the marginal cost (in dollars) of additional newsprint is $MC_n(y) = 5y$, where y denotes tons of newsprint produced. They have also retained their old plant in which the marginal cost of producing additional newsprint is $MC_o(y) = 10y + 10$.

a. If the competitive market price of newsprint is \$25 per ton, will they use both plants or only the new one? If they use both plants, how much newsprint will they produce in each? If they use only the new plant, how much newsprint will they produce?

b. How does your answer to (a) change if the newsprint price falls to \$5 per ton?

17. Consider a perfectly competitive industry in which all firms possess the technology summarized by the average cost function:

$$AC(y) = \begin{cases} y + \frac{1}{y}, & 0 < y < 1 \\ 2, & 1 \leq y \leq 2 \\ (y-1) + \frac{1}{y-1}, & 2 < y \end{cases}.$$

a. Sketch this average cost curve.

b. If there is a long-run equilibrium price p^e, what is it?

c. How large must market demand be at price p^e in order to guarantee there is a long-run equilibrium?

d. Give a production function and input price for which the average cost function is that given above.

18. Assume market aggregate inverse demand is $p = 10 - 2Y$ for $0 \leq Y \leq 5$, where p is market price and Y is market quantity. Assume further that all firms produce a homogeneous product and are identical with cost function:

$$c(y) = \begin{cases} 6y - y^2, & 0 \leq y \leq 2 \\ 4 + 2y, & 2 \leq y \end{cases},$$

where y is the output of one firm and c is the total cost of one firm.

a. Carefully draw the demand, marginal cost, and (market) marginal revenue curves on one graph. Label the intercepts, slopes, and points where the curves cross.

b. Is there a pure price-taking equilibrium in this market? If so, what is it?

c. What is the monopoly output and price?

d. Assume consumer welfare is accurately measured by Marshallian consumer surplus. What is the socially efficient output level?

e. Compare your answers to parts (b) and (d). Explain why your answers are consistent with the First Theorem of Welfare Economics.

f. Calculate the (Marshallian) deadweight loss in the monopoly outcome.

19. Consider a perfectly competitive market with demand curve $D(p)$ and an arbitrarily large number of actual and potential firms who all have average cost curve:

$$AC(y) = \begin{cases} 11 - y, & 0 < y \leq 10 \\ 1, & 10 \leq y \leq 11 \\ y - 10, & 11 \leq y \end{cases}.$$

Suppose also that $c(0) = 0$ (i.e., their technologies have the possibility of inaction). Give a lower bound on demand that ensures existence of a long-run perfectly competitive equilibrium with free entry and exit.

20. Consider a market with 10 identical sellers, each of which has cost function $c(y) = y^2$, where y is the quantity produced by one seller. Market demand is $Y = 780 - p$ for $0 \leq p \leq 780$, where Y is aggregate quantity and p is price per unit. Derive the market equilibrium price and quantity when each seller behaves as a price-taker. What will happen in this market if there is free entry and a large number of identical potential entrants?

21. Consider a price-taking firm with short-run cost function $c_{SR}(y) = y^2 + 4$.

a. Find the short-run supply function for this firm.

b. If there are ℓ price-taking firms with this identical short-run cost function, what is the short-run market supply function?

c. If the market demand function is $y = 100 - 2p$ for $0 \leq p \leq 50$, find the short-run equilibrium price when there are ℓ firms in the market.

d. Now suppose this firm has the same cost function in the long-run, except that the fixed cost can be avoided by choosing to produce zero output. That is:

$$c_{LR}(y) = \begin{cases} y^2 + 4 & \text{if } y > 0 \\ 0 & \text{if } y = 0 \end{cases}.$$

Find the long-run supply function for a price-taking firm with this cost function.

e. If there are ℓ price-taking firms with this identical long-run cost function, what is the long-run market supply function?

f. With the market demand curve given in (c), find the long-run equilibrium price when there are ℓ firms in the market.

g. With the market demand curve given in (c) and free entry, how many price-taking firms will exist in this market in long-run equilibrium? What is the long-run equilibrium price when there is free entry? What is the long-run equilibrium quantity when there is free entry? How much of this does each firm produce? What is the long-run profit of each firm when there is free entry?

22. Consider an economy with two price-taking consumers who have quasilinear utility functions $u^1(x_1^1, x_2^1; x_1^2) + x_3^1$ and $u^2(x_1^2, x_2^2) + x_3^2$ that are twice continuously differentiable (superscripts denote consumers 1 and 2; subscripts denote commodities 1, 2, and 3). Note that consumer 1 is unusual in that her utility is affected by the quantity of commodity 1 consumed by consumer 2. Assume this externality is negative: $\frac{\partial u^1}{\partial x_1^2} \leq 0$. Let m^1 and m^2 denote the monetary resources of the consumers and p_1 and p_2 denote the prices (p_3 is normalized to one). Assume all three commodities are supplied perfectly elastically at these prices by price-taking (zero profit) constant returns industries.

The government imposes an excise tax t per unit of good 1 on consumers and also gives lump-sum subsidies s^1 and s^2. This means the effective price of good 1 for consumers is $p_1 + t$ and the effective monetary resource of consumer i is $m^i + s^i$.

a. Write the consumers' optimization problems, taking account of the quasilinear functional forms.

b. Denote consumers' optimal values with hats and assume throughout that $\hat{x}_3^i > 0$ for both consumers. Use the Envelope Theorem to write the effect of a change in the tax rate on each consumer's optimal utility. Take care with consumer 1.

c. Now suppose the government sets each lump-sum payment equal to the tax paid by that consumer (but consumers regard the lump-sum payments as fixed). Use the Envelope Theorem to write the effect of a change in the tax rate on each consumer's optimal utility, accounting for the implied changes in lump-sum payments.

d. The government wants to design a tax/subsidy system to maximize the sum of the consumers' utilities. Continuing to assume the subsidies are lump-sum rebates of the taxes paid by each consumer, what should the government do? Explain. Is the government policy a Pareto improvement? Compare your answer to the First Theorem of Welfare Economics.

REFERENCES

[1] Marshall A. Principles of economics. 9th variorum ed. London: MacMillan; 1920 [First ed. 1890].
[2] Walras L. Éléments D'Économie Politique Pure. Paris: L. Corbaz & Co.; 1874. English translation: "Elements of pure economics" by Jaffé W. London: George Allen and Unwin; 1954.
[3] Smith A. An inquiry into the nature and causes of the wealth of nations. New York: Random House; 1937 [First ed. 1776].
[4] Edgeworth FY. Mathematical psychics: an essay on the application of mathematics to the moral sciences. London: C.K. Ball; 1881.
[5] Pareto V. Manual of political economy (Manuale d'economia politica) [Schwier AS, Trans.]. New York: Kelley; 1971 [First ed. 1905].
[6] Bowley AL. The mathematical groundwork of economics. Oxford: The Clarendon Press; 1924.
[7] Baumol WJ, Panzar JC, Willig RD. Contestable markets and the theory of industry structure. New York: Harcourt Brace Jovanovich; 1982.

CHAPTER 14

Monopoly

Chapter Outline

Perfect competition is one extreme on a continuum of competition intensities. The other extreme is *monopoly*. The dictionary definition of monopoly is a market in which there is only one seller. Although this definition is sometimes used casually in economics, it is not the definition of monopoly *behavior*. Monopoly behavior occurs when the single seller recognizes the aggregate demand relationship between price and quantity, and chooses quantity (or price) to maximize profit in full recognition of this relationship. In contrast, it is sometimes conceptually useful to study a market with only one seller when that seller behaves as a price-taker. This is a monopoly but is not monopoly behavior.

14.1 BASIC OPTIMIZATION POSTULATE

We continue to focus on partial equilibrium in a final product market. Therefore, the sole firm's production possibilities are summarized by a single-output cost function $c : Y \to \mathbb{R}^1_+$ (with input prices suppressed), where Y is the set of feasible output levels from the underlying production set. The simplest monopoly model assumes buyers are price-taking consumers whose choice behavior for the good under study is summarized by a strictly decreasing aggregate demand function $D(p)$. Typically the potential for changes in p to affect consumers' monetary resources is ignored (see the Introduction to Part 4). An inverse demand function $p(y)$ therefore exists and the revenue function of the monopolist, expressed as a function of quantity, is $R(y) = p(y)y$. The monopoly behavioral postulate is to choose quantity y to maximize the profit objective $\pi(y) = R(y) - c(y)$. The outcomes from this behavior are an optimal profit level and set of optimal production levels:

$$\pi^* = \sup\{p(y)y - c(y) : y \in Y\}$$
$$y^* = \{y \in Y : \pi(y) = \pi^*\}.$$

Note that these outcomes do not depend on price. This lack of dependence is the consequence of the behavioral postulate that the aggregate demand relationship between price and quantity is recognized when making optimizing choices, whence price is not an exogenous parameter to a firm engaged in monopoly behavior. Profit π^* is an extended real number rather than a function and supply y^* is one subset of Y rather than a correspondence. The implied set of optimal prices is $p^* = p(y^*)$. Indeed, as demand is a one-to-one relationship between price and quantity, this behavior can be equivalently expressed, when convenient, as choosing price p to maximize $\pi(p) = pD(p) - c(D(p))$. The outcomes π^*, p^*, and $y^* = D(p^*)$ are unaffected by whether the behavior is expressed as a quantity or price choice.

Existence of a monopoly profit maximum is typically addressed as follows. Suppose there is a price $\bar{p} \in (0, \infty)$ at which $D(p)$ drops to zero (so $D(p)$ is identically zero at $p \geq \bar{p}$), $D(0)$ is finite (i.e., there is aggregate satiation of the good under study), and $c(y)$ is nondecreasing (i.e., the production set has free disposal—item 5 of Theorem 6.5). Then the feasible set can be confined to $[0, D(0)]$ without loss of generality because $\pi(0) = -c(0)$ is finite and $\pi(y) = -c(y) \leq -c(D(0)) \leq -c(0)$ for $y > D(0)$ (so $y > D(0)$ is not optimal[1]). The feasible set is effectively nonempty, closed and bounded under these assumptions. If, in addition, inverse demand is upper semicontinuous and cost is lower semicontinuous (i.e., $-c(y)$ is upper semicontinuous) then by Theorem 1.2 a profit maximum exists

[1]Technically, these assumptions admit the possibility that $\pi(y)$ is constant on $y \in [0, \bar{y})$ for some $\bar{y} > D(0)$, in which case $y \in (D(0), \bar{y})$ is optimal. We take it as a maintained assumption that the profit objective is not so meaningless.

(y^* is nonempty and π^* is finite). Theorem 12.1 establishes that demand is continuous at positive prices (when it is singleton-valued), so the only additional property imposed on demand by the continuity assumption is that continuity persists at the boundary $p = 0$. Theorem 1.2 assures $-c(y)$ is upper semicontinuous on the feasible output set Y when the input requirement correspondence $V(y)$ is upper hemicontinuous (recall that $V(y)$ is effectively bounded at positive input prices). As discussed in Section 4.5, upper hemicontinuity of the input requirement correspondence is, in turn, equivalent to upper semicontinuity of the production function when the production function exists and there is free disposal; and existence of the production function can be assured via various assumptions on the production set while upper semicontinuity is obtained from Theorem 1.3 via those same assumptions on the production set.

If, in addition, $\pi(y)$ is strictly concave then the profit maximum is unique (y^* is a singleton; see Exercise 1 of Chapter 3). Although $\pi(y)$ is strictly concave for many standard demand and cost functions, a common situation in which it is not concave arises when there is a fixed cost (non-sunk or only partially sunk), in which case the corner must be studied even when there is a local interior maximum to see if the global maximum occurs at $y = 0$.

If demand and cost are differentiable the necessary first order condition for an interior maximum is:

$$[p'(y)y + p(y)] = c'(y),$$

which is the familiar requirement that output be chosen to equate marginal revenue and marginal cost (note that the term in brackets is marginal revenue, the derivative of $R(y)$). It is useful to contrast this condition with the optimality condition $p = c'(y)$ for a price-taker. The difference between the two conditions is the term $p'(y)y$, which is the effect on profit of the decrease in price that must accompany an increase in quantity when aggregate demand responds negatively to price changes. The difference between the monopoly and price-taking marginal revenues is illustrated in Fig. 14.1. If y is increased by Δy, the monopolist's price drops by Δp. Thus the firm loses Δp on every unit of output sold, for a total of $(\Delta p)y$, which is the lightly shaded area. The monopolist gains revenue of $(p - \Delta p)\Delta y$ from new sales, which is the dark shaded area. A price-taker acts as if price does not change, and thus sees only the gain, which is $p\Delta y$ at the original price. Hence the monopolist's marginal revenue at output level y, $p(y) + p'(y)y$, is $p'(y)y$ lower than a price-taker's perceived marginal revenue of $p(y)$ (recall that $p'(y)$ is negative). Thus the monopolist's marginal revenue is below its

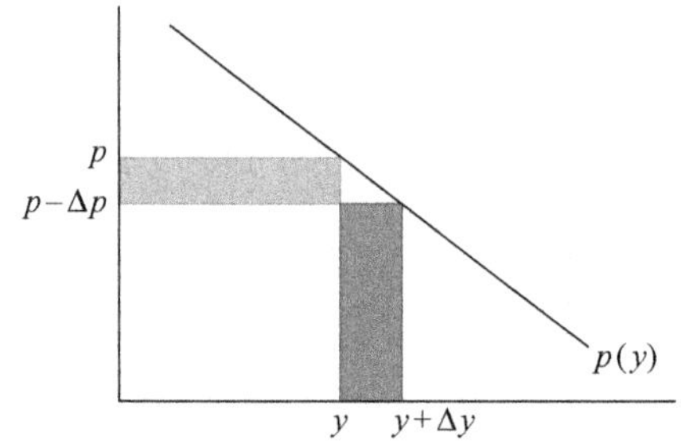

Fig. 14.1 Monopoly marginal revenue.

price at every output level. Marginal revenue $MR(y)$ as a function of output on a graph like Fig. 14.1 lies everywhere below inverse demand $p(y)$.

If demand and cost are twice differentiable the necessary second order condition for an interior maximum is:

$$p''(y)y + 2p'(y) - c''(y) \leq 0.$$

This requires that the marginal cost curve cross the marginal revenue curve from below at the optimum. It does *not* require that marginal cost be upward-sloping, but merely that marginal cost have a less severe negative slope if both marginal cost and marginal revenue are downward-sloping.

The conventional case of a monopolist's maximum is illustrated in Fig. 14.2. The optimal output $\hat{y}$ is determined by the intersection of marginal revenue and marginal cost. As marginal cost crosses marginal revenue from below in the graph, the case illustrated is indeed a maximum. If there is no fixed cost, then total cost is the integral of marginal cost up to $\hat{y}$. Total revenue is $p(\hat{y})\hat{y}$, so the difference between total revenue and total cost is the shaded area, and this is the monopolist's optimal profit π^*. If

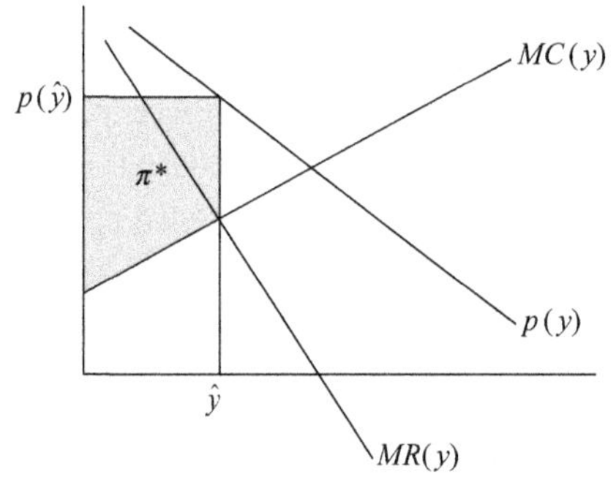

Fig. 14.2 Monopoly optimum.

there is a fixed cost, profit is the shaded area less the fixed cost. If the non-sunk part of fixed cost exceeds this area then the firm is better off choosing the corner $\hat{y} = 0$. The illustrated $\hat{y}$ is a local maximum in this case, but it is not the global maximum because the fixed cost creates a non-concavity in the profit objective.

The first order condition that determines $\hat{y}$ (assuming an interior solution) is expressed in a variety of ways for different purposes. Factoring out $p(\hat{y})$ yields:

$$\left[\frac{p'(\hat{y})\hat{y}}{p(\hat{y})} + 1\right] p(\hat{y}) = c'(\hat{y}).$$

The price elasticity of market demand at quantity y is $\epsilon(y) \equiv \frac{p(y)}{p'(y)y} < 0$, so the first order condition says that $\hat{y}$ is determined by:

$$\left[\frac{1}{\epsilon(\hat{y})} + 1\right] p(\hat{y}) = c'(\hat{y}).$$

This indicates $-\epsilon(\hat{y}) > 1$ because price and marginal cost are both positive. That is, *a monopolist chooses an interior output level at which market demand is elastic*. This is because marginal revenue is zero at quantities where demand is unit elastic, positive at quantities where demand is elastic, and negative at quantities where demand is inelastic. Hence the monopolist can equate marginal revenue with positive marginal cost only at a point of elastic demand.

Another version of the monopolist's first order condition is:

$$\frac{p(\hat{y}) - c'(\hat{y})}{p(\hat{y})} = \frac{1}{-\epsilon(\hat{y})}.$$

The left side of this expression is the firm's *price/cost margin*, also known as the *Lerner Index*. This index measures how far the firm optimally raises price above marginal cost, in percentage terms. Thus it is a measure of the degree of *market power* possessed by the monopolist. If demand is very elastic, then the monopolist cannot raise price much above the price-taking level (i.e., marginal cost) because doing so entails a large reduction in quantity. Hence, even though the firm is the only seller, it does not possess much power to exercise its monopoly position. Note that the price-taking behavioral postulate is the extreme version of this, in that the demand perceived *by the individual firm* (not necessarily the market demand) is infinitely elastic (horizontal) when a firm is a price-taker. Conversely, if a monopolist perceives very inelastic aggregate demand then the monopolist can raise price substantially with little loss of quantity, and thus the firm possess formidable market power. A rule like this for determining price (or, equivalently, output) is called an *inverse elasticity rule.* The Lerner Index is used in antitrust and merger analysis as one way to measure whether a firm is behaving anticompetitively, or whether a merger would damage welfare. But its use is problematic for various reasons, the most outstanding of which is that it requires an accurate measurement of marginal cost, which is rarely available in a contested legal setting.

There are a few standard comparative statics results for the monopoly outcomes. Assume α is a parameter that shifts marginal cost upward. Letting $F \geq 0$ be fixed cost, write cost as $c(y;\alpha) = F + \int_0^y MC(x;\alpha)dx$ with $\frac{\partial MC}{\partial \alpha} > 0$. Then, from the envelope theorem:

$$\frac{\partial \pi^*}{\partial \alpha} = -\int_0^{\hat{y}(\alpha)} \frac{\partial MC(x;\alpha)}{\partial \alpha} < 0.$$

Thus anything that increases marginal cost decreases profit. Similarly, anything that shifts demand outward increases profit. Moreover, from the standard comparative statics methodology:

$$\frac{\partial \hat{y}}{\partial \alpha} = -\left.\frac{\frac{\partial^2 \pi(y;\alpha)}{\partial y \partial \alpha}}{\frac{\partial^2 \pi(y;\alpha)}{\partial^2 y}}\right|_{y=\hat{y}(\alpha)} = \left.\frac{\frac{\partial MC(\hat{y}(\alpha);\alpha)}{\partial \alpha}}{\frac{\partial^2 \pi(y;\alpha)}{\partial^2 y}}\right|_{y=\hat{y}(\alpha)}.$$

The denominator is negative by the necessary second order condition (assuming the implicit function theorem can be applied here), so the entire expression is negative. Thus anything that increases marginal cost decreases output and, therefore, increases price.

14.2 WELFARE

It is immediately apparent from Fig. 14.2 that monopoly behavior produces less output and charges a higher price than would occur with a price-taking firm that has the same cost function (assuming both firms' optimal output choices are positive). This means consumers receive less welfare from a monopoly seller than from a price-taking seller because indirect utilities are decreasing in prices. But the monopoly firm receives more profit than a price-taking firm, so the observation that consumer welfare is harmed is not sufficient to conclude that the monopoly equilibrium is less efficient than a price-taking equilibrium.

Fig. 14.3 illustrates the true damage inflicted by monopoly behavior. If the firm were a price-taker, output would be y^c and price would be p^c.

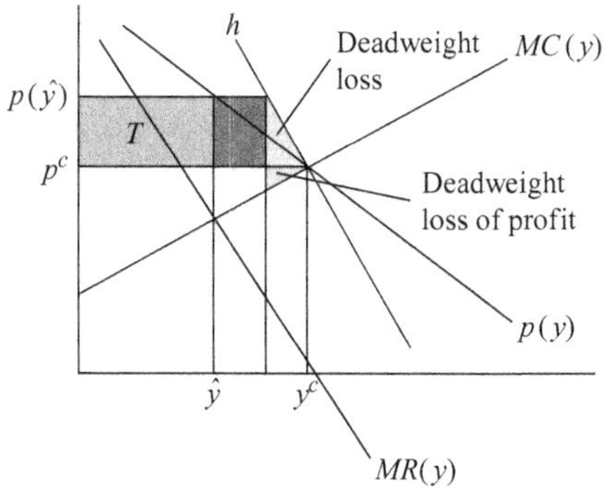

Fig. 14.3 The inefficiency of monopoly.

Theorem 13.4 establishes that this allocation is Pareto Efficient. At the monopoly output level $\hat{y}$, welfare in monetary terms equal to the shaded area T is transferred from consumers to the firm in the form of a higher price. This price increase decreases indirect utilities, and to compensate for these lost utilities consumers collectively would have to receive $-CV$. This compensation would shift Marshallian demand outward (the graph assumes the good under study is normal), making the transfer to the firm larger by the dark shaded area. Still the amount $-CV$ paid to consumers exceeds the transfer to the firm. Thus there is the familiar deadweight loss of consumer welfare from the price increase, indicated by the shaded triangle (h is the aggregate Hicksian demand when the distribution of utilities is that obtained at price p^c).

Although there are cost savings when output is lower, there is also a loss of revenue beyond the transfer/compensation just discussed, equal to p^c multiplied by the units of lost output. The net effect of these cost savings and revenue losses is the area between the MC curve and p^c, from the post-compensation output level to y^c. If MC is upward-sloping, as in the graph, this is an additional loss, beyond the deadweight loss from $-CV$. This additional loss is called the *deadweight loss of producer's surplus (or of profit)*. If MC is horizontal at p^c there is no additional loss. If MC is (locally) downward-sloping these effects might appear to generate a net gain of profit, but y^c would not be the price-taking output choice in such a case (the price-taker's necessary second order condition requires that MC be nondecreasing at the optimum). Thus, the monopoly equilibrium is not Pareto Efficient. Consumers would be more than willing to compensate the firm for the profit it would lose by choosing the quantity where marginal cost crosses demand rather than engaging in monopoly behavior.

The inefficiency of monopoly is the economic rationale for using government authority to regulate, prevent, and/or dismantle monopolies. The Sherman Antitrust Act and Clayton (anti-merger) Act are the major federal legislation in the U.S. for fighting the exercise of market power. Other countries have similar legislation. Under the Sherman Act, it is not illegal to be a monopolist. Rather, the *exercise of market power* is the target of this legislation (i.e., engaging in monopoly *behavior* by pricing above marginal cost). In other words, a firm can be a monopoly provided it doesn't act like one (or, at least, doesn't act enough like one to have it proven in court).

14.3 REGULATION

Sometimes it is considered desirable to preserve a monopoly. For example, if there is strict subadditivity of cost over the relevant range of output then the monopolist will produce at lower cost than any combination of two or more firms. As discussed in Chapter 7, when total output is produced at lowest-cost by one firm the market structure is called a natural monopoly. The problem in such cases lies in inducing the monopolist to behave more like a price-taker. This is usually done through regulation in the U.S., and traditionally has been accomplished through government ownership of particular enterprises in many other parts of the world (although the U.S. has used government ownership as well, such as municipal water and sewer utilities or the federal postal service).

Although rarely done, it is often possible at least in principle to eliminate the deadweight loss created by monopoly behavior using an excise subsidy s to the firm. The purpose of the subsidy is to increase the effective price received by the firm at output level y from $p(y)$ to $p(y) + s$. This induces a higher output choice by the monopolist. Fig. 14.4 illustrates this policy. When consumers pay $p(y)$, the firm receives $p(y) + s$. Thus the firm's "effective" inverse demand curve is $p(y) + s$ with corresponding "effective" marginal revenue curve $MR(y) + s$. If s is chosen to shift the effective marginal revenue curve so that it passes through the efficient consumption point (y^c, p^c) then this policy induces the monopolist to select that point. The policy costs the government sy^c, which could be collected from the firm as a non-distorting lump-sum tax, thereby leaving the firm with the competitive profit level $\pi^* = (p^c + s)y^c - c(y^c) - sy^c = p^c y^c - c(y^c)$. More importantly, the deadweight loss triangle is eliminated.

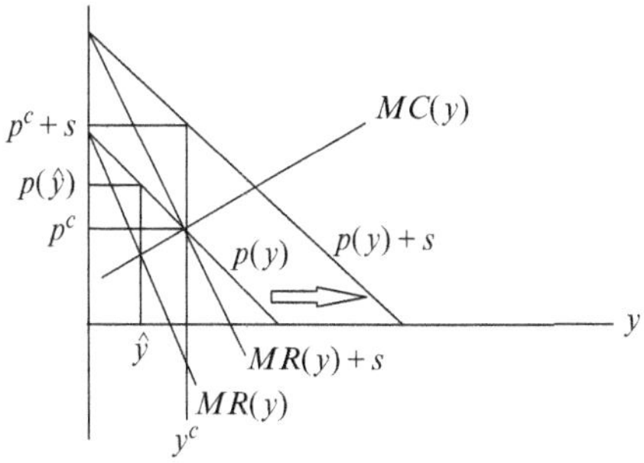

Fig. 14.4 Eliminating monopoly deadweight loss with an excise subsidy.

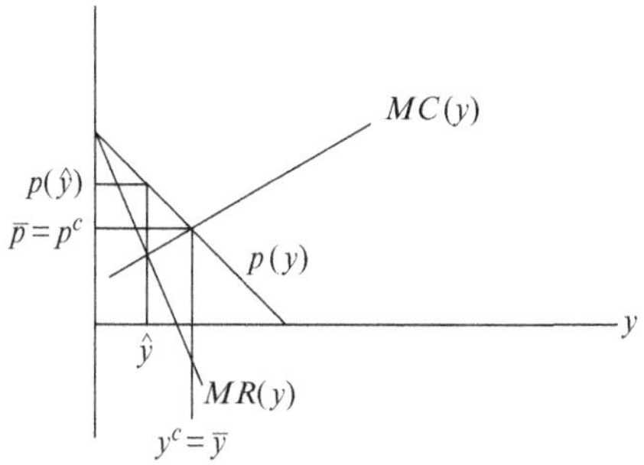

Fig. 14.5 Eliminating monopoly deadweight loss with a price cap.

A more realistic and widely used form of regulation is called a *price cap*. Under this form of regulation, the government announces that the monopolist is not permitted to charge a price above some cap $\bar{p}$ but is free to charge any price at or below $\bar{p}$. This regulation changes the shape of the monopolist's "effective" demand and marginal revenue curves. As illustrated in Fig. 14.5, the effective demand curve is horizontal at price $\bar{p}$ up to output level $\bar{y}$, and follows the ordinary demand curve for prices below $\bar{p}$ and output levels above $\bar{y}$. As price received is constant at output levels below $\bar{y}$, the effective marginal revenue curve is horizontal at $\bar{p}$ up to output level $\bar{y}$, and then has a downward discontinuity to the original MR curve, which is effective marginal revenue at output levels above $\bar{y}$. The discontinuity occurs because the revenue function has a kink at $\bar{y}$, so technically marginal revenue is not defined at $\bar{y}$. If the price cap is chosen to be $\bar{p} = p^c$, as illustrated, marginal cost is below effective marginal revenue left of y^c, while marginal cost is above effective marginal revenue right of y^c (assuming MC is not downward-sloping). So this regulation induces the monopolist to optimally choose the competitive output level y^c and charge the competitive price p^c. This type of regulation is studied more in Exercises 9–11.

Both price caps and excise subsidies work by inducing the monopolist to increase output, thereby reducing or eliminating deadweight loss. A significant problem with both of these policies is that implementation requires accurate knowledge of both marginal cost and demand. Excise subsidy regulation is also politically unpopular.

Depending on the market, deadweight loss can either understate or overstate the inefficiency caused by monopoly behavior. The potential for super-normal profits induces actual and potential suppliers to expend resources in pursuit of those profits. Monopoly or partial-monopoly markets are often fertile territory for excessive lobbying, advertising, and research and development; all targeted toward erecting or maintaining entry barriers to other suppliers. Monopoly costs might also be excessive due to a lack of market discipline that makes it difficult for owners to judge whether managers are operating efficiently. Offsetting these concerns are potentially significant limits on monopoly behavior. Monopolists that sell a durable good must contend with the competition created by resale of their own products or by consumer anticipation of future price cuts. In the extreme, the latter can reduce monopoly profit to zero, a result known as the *Coase Conjecture.*

14.4 PRICE DISCRIMINATION

We now consider the possibility that a monopolist charges different consumers different prices. Sometimes consumers pay different prices because consumers cost different amounts to serve, in which case even a perfectly competitive equilibrium would have consumers paying different prices. Therefore *price discrimination* is defined to mean that the *difference* between price and per-unit cost varies across consumers. This definition is narrow in that it presumes the commodities sold to different consumers are homogeneous, and that the per-unit cost of serving an *individual* consumer can be identified (e.g., how are fixed costs allocated across consumers?). These restrictions are not addressed herein.

A firm with knowledge of the aggregate demand relationship between price and quantity might also have some knowledge of individual consumers' demands. If not, the firm cannot tailor prices to individuals, and therefore is limited to charging all consumers the same price per unit, as in Fig. 14.2. The analysis of monopoly behavior in Fig. 14.2

essentially begins with an implicit assumption that the monopolist must charge all consumers the same price per unit. Thus the extent and type of possible price discrimination is determined partly by what the firm knows about individual consumers. The potential for price discrimination is also affected by how costly it is for consumers or a third party to evade discriminatory prices by, for example, taking advantage of a discount for large purchases by redistributing one large purchase among multiple consumers. There are three main categories of price discrimination; known as first, second, and third degree discrimination; roughly corresponding to decreasing knowledge possessed by the firm about individual consumers and increasing opportunity for consumers to evade discriminatory prices.

The remainder of this section assumes consumer welfare is accurately measured by Marshallian surplus. That is, income effects are negligible for the good under study over the range of charges discussed.

14.4.1 First Degree

As a benchmark, consider a monopolist that knows each consumer's entire individual demand curve. Such a firm could calculate the marginal revenue curve for each individual consumer and charge that consumer a price consistent with equating that consumer's marginal revenue with that consumer's marginal cost. This would be a disaggregated version of Fig. 14.2. Doing so, however, would underutilize the monopolist's information. A more profitable strategy is to set a consumer's price at the efficient level where individual marginal cost crosses individual demand, thereby inducing the consumer to purchase a Pareto Efficient allocation, and then charge the consumer a lump-sum amount for the privilege of being allowed to purchase the product. The profit-maximizing lump-sum charge is the value of the purchase to the consumer at the stated price, which is the entire Marshallian surplus area above the efficient price.

This strategy has two parts: First generate the maximal welfare from the individual consumer by inducing an efficient consumption level via a carefully chosen per-unit price; then transfer all of that maximal welfare to the firm via a lump-sum. Such a price is called a *two-part tariff*. It consists of, essentially, a membership fee that is unrelated to the amount purchased and a constant price per unit. In the particular implementation described here each consumer is charged a two-part tariff customized to that consumer's individual demand. Pricing that transfers all possible surplus to the firm, based on complete knowledge of disaggregated demands, is called *first degree*, or *perfect*, price discrimination. An omniscient firm can accomplish first degree discrimination without even bothering to design two part tariffs. The firm simply announces to each consumer that the only purchase she can make is a package containing the efficient allocation for that consumer, for a total charge equal to the Marshallian surplus (entire area under the demand curve up to the stated quantity) that consumer receives from that quantity. Note that this requires knowledge of the identity of each individual consumer. A perfectly discriminating firm does not announce a menu of packages from which each consumer can choose. Rather, such a firm offers *one* individually tailored package to each consumer, and can enforce the offering because the firm knows the identity of each consumer. Such knowledge is unrealistic but serves as a useful benchmark.

Note that a perfectly discriminating monopolist eliminates the deadweight loss associated with nondiscriminatory monopoly behavior. A perfectly discriminating monopolist has sufficient information to do so, and incentive to do so because the firm can appropriate whatever surplus is generated. Thus aggregate welfare is maximized by a perfectly discriminating monopolist but the distribution of welfare is entirely to the firm.

14.4.2 Third Degree

Consider now a more realistic knowledge base for the monopolist. Specifically, suppose the monopolist can segment consumers into groups based on observable characteristics such as gender, age, geographic location, or income. The firm knows, or has good estimates of, aggregate demand for each group but has no knowledge of individual demands within each group. Thus the firm can charge only one price per unit to each group but is not constrained to charge each group the same price.[2] Pricing that segments consumers by group and charges all members of each group the same per-unit price, but charges different groups different per-unit prices, is called *third degree* price discrimination.

Suppose the monopolist can segment aggregate demand into r groups of consumers and denote the inverse demand of group i by $p_i(y_i)$. Then the third-degree price discriminating behavioral postulate is that the monopolist chooses an output vector $(y_1, \ldots, y_r)$ from within the feasible output set $\left(\sum_{i=1}^{r} y_i \in Y\right)$ to maximize aggregate profit from all groups:

[2]The monopolist could consider charging the same two-part tariff, or some other scheme, to all members of a group, but doing so risks foreclosing some members of the group because the monopolist is assumed to have little knowledge of individual demands within each group.

$$\pi(y_1, \ldots, y_r) = \sum_{i=1}^{r} p_i(y_i)y_i - c\left(\sum_{i=1}^{r} y_i\right).$$

The necessary first order condition for an interior maximum is:

$$p_j'(y_j)y_j + p_j(y_j) = c'\left(\sum_{i=1}^{r} y_i\right) \text{ for } j = 1, \ldots, r.$$

This condition has two interesting interpretations.

First, note that the left side is marginal revenue from group j, and *every* group's marginal revenue is equated to the common marginal cost. Hence, for whatever aggregate output the firm chooses, that aggregate is allocated across groups by equating marginal revenues across groups. This is a standard marginal allocation principle and it would be the allocation rule even if the firm's aggregate output were predetermined (if, for example, allocation across groups were a relatively short-run choice made after a longer-run aggregate production decision had been made). Optimal allocation must obey this principle; otherwise the firm could move some quantity from a market in which marginal revenue is relatively low to a market in which marginal revenue is relatively high, thereby improving revenue, without changing aggregate quantity and thus without changing cost.

Second, the same manipulations used for the non-discriminating monopolist show that the optimal quantity vector $(\hat{y}_1, \ldots, \hat{y}_r)$ is chosen to satisfy an inverse elasticity rule for *each* group:

$$\frac{p_j(\hat{y}_j) - c'\left(\sum_{i=1}^{r} \hat{y}_i\right)}{p_j(\hat{y}_j)} = \frac{1}{-\epsilon_j(\hat{y}_j)} \text{ for } j = 1, \ldots, r,$$

where $\epsilon_j(y_j) \equiv \frac{p_j(y_j)}{p_j'(y_j)y_j}$ is the price elasticity of group j's demand. The inverse elasticity rule is more informative in this multiproduct setting. It says that *optimal quantities are chosen to create relatively high markups in markets where demand is relatively inelastic, and relatively low markups in markets where demand is relatively elastic.* Allocation according to this principle arises in many settings, notably in designing optimal tax rates, and is known as a *Ramsey Rule.* The concept is that less deadweight loss is created when prices are far above marginal cost along a relatively inelastic demand curve because the quantity distortion is relatively small.

Having the knowledge to engage in third degree price discrimination cannot harm the monopolist's profit relative to the non-discriminating case because it expands the monopolist's feasible set. The option of choosing quantities so that prices are equal across the groups remains available, if doing so coincidentally happens to be profit-maximizing.

The welfare effects on consumers are less clear. Consumers in groups with relatively inelastic demand are usually harmed by third degree discrimination because they pay higher prices, and consumers in groups with relatively elastic demand correspondingly benefit. Thus the effect on consumer surplus involves comparing surplus across groups. An exception occurs when there are two groups and the group with relatively elastic demand is foreclosed in the absence of discrimination because the monopolist's non-discriminatory price is too high for those consumers. In this case the non-discriminatory price is the monopoly price for the relatively inelastic group, and is the same as the discriminatory price for that group. But the optimal discriminatory price for the elastic group might be low enough to induce some sales to that group. If so, third degree discrimination enables a Pareto improvement: The firm and elastic demand group are better off, and the inelastic demand group is unaffected.

If the assumption that Marshallian surplus accurately measures welfare is taken literally, surplus comparisons can be made across consumer groups because welfare is measured in monetary units and can therefore be conceptually transferred across groups. When the monopolist has constant returns, a necessary condition for aggregate consumer surplus to be higher with third degree price discrimination is that aggregate quantity be higher (relative to no discrimination).

Usually the boundaries among consumer groups are not as rigid as the discussion here suggests. It is not worth the cost, for example, to drive 200 miles to the next sizable community to buy a car for $100 less. But the potential for consumers to move across groups in response to price differences limits the extent of third degree discrimination. Formally such possibilities make the demand elasticities of the groups more similar because consumers can migrate from the relatively inelastic group to the relatively elastic group if price differences exceed the cost of such migration.

14.4.3 Second Degree

An intermediate case arises when a monopolist has knowledge about the distribution of individual consumers' demands but does not know the identity of individual consumers. In this case the monopoly behavioral postulate is that the firm uses the distributional information to charge different prices to different consumers, in pursuit of profit, but in doing so must recognize that discriminatory prices cannot be enforced on individual consumers and therefore must be designed so that each consumer voluntarily chooses the package intended for him from the menu of options offered by the firm. In other words, the options offered by the monopolist must be *incentive compatible* for consumers, also described as honoring the "self-selection" constraints. Prices can be designed for individual consumers rather than groups in this setting because of the firm's knowledge about the distribution of individual demands. But such prices cannot be *imposed* on individuals because individuals' identities are not known by the firm.

The monopoly behavioral postulate is formalized in this setting with a model of the firm's knowledge about individual consumer demands. The firm has knowledge of a cumulative distribution F of consumer "types" indexed by parameter $\theta \in [\underline{\theta}, \bar{\theta}] \subset \mathbb{R}^1$. Inverse demand for the good under study by a consumer of type θ is $p(y, \theta)$, where p is decreasing in quantity y. Continuing with the assumption that utility is measured by Marshallian surplus, gross utility for a consumer of type θ from consumption of quantity y is the area under the Marshallian demand up to the quantity consumed:

$$u(y, \theta) \equiv \int_0^y p(x, \theta) dx.$$

Without loss of generality, assume consumer "types" are labeled in a natural way so that u is increasing in θ. Consumer type θ's net utility from consumption of quantity y is $u(y, \theta)$ less whatever the monopolist charges for quantity y.

The monopolist offers an *outlay function*, or *tariff*, $T(y)$ to the entire distribution of consumers. T specifies the total charge a consumer must pay for quantity y. For example, $T(y) = py$ is a constant price p per unit, whereas:

$$T(y) = \begin{cases} 0 & y = 0 \\ E + py & y > 0 \end{cases}$$

is a single two-part tariff offered to all consumers with membership fee E and constant price p per unit for consumers who pay the membership fee. More generally, $T : \mathbb{R}^1_+ \to \mathbb{R}^1_+$ could be any function satisfying $T(0) = 0$ (we presume the firm cannot impose charges on consumers who do not consume anything). Profit maximization implies attention can be limited to increasing outlay functions.

If T is concave the tariff entails quantity discounts for consumers because the charge for the next increment of consumption decreases as a consumer's total consumption increases. The two-part tariff is an example of quantity discounts because the membership fee is spread over more units as y increases. Quantity discounts create an incentive for consumers to pool together and make group purchases, or for a middleman to do it for them. Thus the extent of quantity discounting the monopolist can offer is limited by the costs, including inconvenience and coordination, of arranging group purchases. Similarly, a convex tariff means the firm charges a premium as a consumer's total consumption increases. Quantity premia can be charged only to the extent it is costly for a consumer to make multiple small purchases rather than one large purchase. Typically it is assumed for the purpose of deriving second degree discriminating monopoly behavior that costs of resale and repeat purchasing are high enough to render these limits on tariff design non-binding constraints. Second degree discriminating monopolists often erect barriers to increase the costs of these activities, such as nontransferable warranties or requiring that photo identification be presented when making a purchase.

For any given T, a price-taking (i.e., tariff-taking) consumer of type θ chooses a quantity that maximizes net surplus:

$$u^*(T(\cdot),\theta) = \sup\{u(y,\theta) - T(y) : y \geq 0\}$$
$$y^*(T(\cdot),\theta) = \{y \geq 0 : u(y,\theta) - T(y) = u^*(T(\cdot),\theta)\}.$$

This specification of how consumers' choices respond to different tariffs T is the incentive compatibility constraint from the firm's perspective. Assuming each consumer's optimal choice is a singleton $\hat{y}(T(\cdot),\theta)$, profit from the tariff T is:

$$\pi(T(\cdot)) = \int_{\underline{\theta}}^{\bar{\theta}} T(\hat{y}(T(\cdot),\theta))dF(\theta) - c\left(\int_{\underline{\theta}}^{\bar{\theta}} \hat{y}(T(\cdot),\theta)dF(\theta)\right).$$

The monopoly behavioral postulate under the second degree price discrimination assumption about the firm's knowledge of consumers is that the monopolist chooses a tariff $T : \mathbb{R}^1_+ \to \mathbb{R}^1_+$ satisfying $T(0) = 0$ to maximize this objective.

A limiting case arises when all consumers are identical. Formally, this means the cumulative distribution F has a mass of one at one particular value of θ, say θ^0. Then the firm can implement first degree price discrimination because the firm's knowledge of individual consumer demand is perfect, and can do so with a single two-part tariff targeted at the "representative" consumer whose inverse demand is $p(y,\theta^0)$. The firm's optimum is to set a per-unit price $\hat{p}$ where aggregate demand crosses marginal cost, calculate the individual quantity $\hat{y}$ satisfying $p(\hat{y}, \theta^0) = \hat{p}$ each price-taking consumer will choose based on $\hat{p}$, and set the membership fee E to appropriate the entire remaining surplus of the representative consumer: $E = u(\hat{y}, \theta^0) - \hat{p}\hat{y}$. A variant of this tariff, in which the membership fee is set to recover a fixed cost rather than to maximize profit, is known as the *Coase two-part tariff*. Either way, Pareto Efficiency is achieved. The only difference is how aggregate welfare is shared between consumers and the monopolist. Pareto Efficiency from such a tariff requires, at least, that no consumer be foreclosed by the entry fee. The case of identical consumers is an extreme version of non-foreclosure.

More generally, the choice "variable" for the second degree discriminating monopolist is an entire function T, so characterizing the monopoly behavior requires assumptions that the objective is "well-behaved" and use of variational or optimal control techniques. One important assumption is the so-called "single crossing" property that individual consumer demands shift outward as θ increases ($p(y, \theta)$ is increasing in θ for every y). Assuming necessary first order conditions characterize both the consumer and firm choices, and suppressing T in consumers' optimal choices for notational ease, consumer type θ chooses $\hat{y}(\theta)$ to satisfy $p(\hat{y}(\theta), \theta) = T'(\hat{y}(\theta))$. Standard comparative statics is that $\hat{y}'(\theta)$ has the same sign as $p_2(\hat{y}(\theta), \theta)$, which is positive due to the single crossing property. This means $\hat{y}(\theta)$ is strictly increasing and can therefore be inverted to yield $\hat{\theta}(y)$, which is the *marginal consumer type* at consumption level y (the consumer type that is just willing to purchase y, but no more, given the tariff T). $\hat{\theta}(y)$ satisfies the consumers' first order condition $p(y, \hat{\theta}(y)) = T'(y)$, so the tariff is related to the consumers' optimal choices by:

$$T(y) = T(\hat{y}(\underline{\theta})) + \int_{\hat{y}(\underline{\theta})}^{y} p(x, \hat{\theta}(x))\,dx.$$

This equation is, in essence, a version of the incentive compatibility constraint. Consumers' choices are related to the tariff chosen by the firm according to this equation.

Characterizing the monopolist's behavior requires that this constraint be incorporated into the monopolist's objective so that the entire objective is expressed in terms of *one* choice function. Toward this end, we perform a change of variable designed to eliminate $\hat{\theta}$. Let $x = \hat{y}(t)$. Then $dx = \hat{y}'(t)dt$ and the constraint becomes:

$$T(y) = T(\hat{y}(\underline{\theta})) + \int_{\underline{\theta}}^{\hat{\theta}(y)} p(\hat{y}(t), t)\hat{y}'(t)\,dt.$$

Note that $\frac{d}{dt}u(\hat{y}(t),t) = p(\hat{y}(t),t)\hat{y}'(t) + u_2(\hat{y}(t),t)$. So, using the fundamental theorem of calculus:

$$u(\hat{y}(\theta),\theta) = u(\hat{y}(\underline{\theta}),\underline{\theta}) + \int_{\underline{\theta}}^{\theta} \left[p(\hat{y}(t),t)\hat{y}'(t) + u_2(\hat{y}(t),t)\right] dt.$$

Evaluating the incentive compatibility constraint at $y = \hat{y}(\theta)$ therefore gives:

$$T(\hat{y}(\theta)) = T(\hat{y}(\underline{\theta})) + u(\hat{y}(\theta),\theta) - u(\hat{y}(\underline{\theta}),\underline{\theta}) - \int_{\underline{\theta}}^{\theta} u_2(\hat{y}(t),t)dt.$$

This equation is expressed exclusively in terms of the function $\hat{y}(\cdot)$. It can be used to write the firm's objective exclusively in terms of this function.

The firm can modify any given T by imposing a membership fee, and doing so does not change the marginal choices of consumers but strictly increases profit provided that doing so does not foreclose any consumers. Recall that we assumed θ "orders" consumers: $u(y,\theta)$ is increasing in θ. This implies no consumer is foreclosed provided the smallest consumer $\underline{\theta}$ is not foreclosed. Thus the profit-maximizing tariff must satisfy $u(\hat{y}(\underline{\theta}),\underline{\theta}) = T(\hat{y}(\underline{\theta}))$. This is the "participation constraint" and it eliminates two terms in the incentive compatibility constraint. Substituting the re-written incentive compatibility constraint into the monopolist's profit expression yields a restatement of the firm's objective:

$$\max_{\{\hat{y}(\cdot)\}} \pi = \int_{\underline{\theta}}^{\bar{\theta}} \left[u(\hat{y}(\theta),\theta) - \int_{\underline{\theta}}^{\theta} u_2(\hat{y}(t),t)dt\right] f(\theta)d\theta - c\left(\int_{\underline{\theta}}^{\bar{\theta}} \hat{y}(\theta)f(\theta)d\theta\right),$$

where we have assumed the distribution of consumer types is continuous with density function $f(\theta)$. Integrate the double integral by parts, using $u = \int_{\underline{\theta}}^{\theta} u_2(\hat{y}(t),t)dt$ and $dv = f(\theta)d\theta$, to obtain:

$$\int_{\underline{\theta}}^{\bar{\theta}} \int_{\underline{\theta}}^{\theta} u_2(\hat{y}(t),t)dtf(\theta)d\theta = \int_{\underline{\theta}}^{\bar{\theta}} [1 - F(\theta)]u_2(\hat{y}(\theta),\theta)d\theta.$$

Then the profit objective becomes:

$$\max_{\{\hat{y}(\cdot)\}} \pi = \int_{\underline{\theta}}^{\bar{\theta}} \Big[u(\hat{y}(\theta),\theta)f(\theta) - [1 - F(\theta)]u_2(\hat{y}(\theta),\theta)\Big] d\theta - c\left(\int_{\underline{\theta}}^{\bar{\theta}} \hat{y}(\theta)f(\theta)d\theta\right).$$

Now we have a standard optimal control problem, except for the unspecified structure of the cost function. Assuming constant marginal cost ($c(y) = F + cy$) yields:

$$\max_{\{\hat{y}(\cdot)\}} \pi = \int_{\underline{\theta}}^{\bar{\theta}} \left[u(\hat{y}(\theta), \theta) f(\theta) - [1 - F(\theta)] u_2(\hat{y}(\theta), \theta) - c\hat{y}(\theta) f(\theta) \right] d\theta.$$

The integrand in this objective involves $\hat{y}(\theta)$ and θ but does not involve $\hat{y}'(\theta)$. So the objective is optimized by choosing $\hat{y}$ pointwise for each value of θ. Differentiating the integrand with respect to $\hat{y}$ and setting the derivative to zero yields:

$$p(\hat{y}(\theta), \theta) = c + \frac{1 - F(\theta)}{f(\theta)} p_2(\hat{y}(\theta), \theta).$$

This characterizes second degree discriminatory monopoly behavior. Recalling that F is strictly increasing with $F(\bar{\theta}) = 1$ and that $p_2 > 0$ due to the single-crossing assumption, the behavior sets the price paid by consumer type θ for that consumer's last increment of consumption (and for all inframarginal units $y < \hat{y}(\theta)$) above marginal cost, $p(\hat{y}(\theta), \theta) > c$, except when $\theta = \bar{\theta}$. Second degree discriminatory monopoly behavior distorts all but the largest consumer away from the Pareto Efficient allocation, forcing smaller consumers to buy less than the efficient amount, to maintain incentive compatibility.

Using $p(\hat{y}(\theta), \theta) = T'(\hat{y}(\theta))$, the characterization of second degree discriminatory monopoly behavior can be written:

$$\frac{T'(\hat{y}(\theta)) - c}{T'(\hat{y}(\theta))} = \frac{1 - F(\theta)}{f(\theta)} \frac{p_2(\hat{y}(\theta), \theta)}{p(\hat{y}(\theta), \theta)}.$$

The left side of this equation is the (marginal) price/cost margin, analogous to the fraction $\frac{p-c}{p}$ that appears in the inverse elasticity rule for a nondiscriminating monopolist, and the equation indeed has in inverse elasticity rule interpretation.[3] Consider the market for an additional increment dy of output at some given output y. The price of this increment is $T'(y)$. The consumer's optimality condition can be written in terms of the consumer

[3]In general, we cannot say whether the price/cost margin is increasing or decreasing in θ. Some presentations of second degree discrimination assume a more specialized structure for utility that has $\theta p_2 = p$, which leads to the conclusion that T' is decreasing (i.e., T is concave), in which case T can be regarded as the lower envelope of a continuum of optional two-part tariffs.

type $\hat{\theta}(y)$ who is indifferent between buying and not buying increment dy at price $T'(y)$: $p(y, \hat{\theta}(y)) = T'(y)$. All consumer types $\theta > \hat{\theta}(y)$ buy dy at price $T'(y)$ because of the single crossing assumption $p_2 > 0$, so the quantity demanded of dy increments at price $T'(y)$ is $1 - F(\hat{\theta}(y))$. Thus, the price elasticity of demand for increment dy at y is:

$$\epsilon(y) = -f(\hat{\theta}(y))\frac{\partial\hat{\theta}(y)}{\partial(T'(y))}\frac{T'(y)}{1 - F(\hat{\theta}(y))}.$$

Now differentiate $p(y, \hat{\theta}(y)) = T'(y)$ to obtain $\frac{\partial\hat{\theta}(y)}{\partial(T'(y))} = \frac{1}{p_2(y,\hat{\theta}(y))}$, and use $(y, \hat{\theta}(y)) = (\hat{y}(\theta), \theta)$ by definition at $y = \hat{y}(\theta)$, and $T'(y) = p(y, \hat{\theta}(y))$ again, to write the expression for ϵ as:

$$\frac{1}{-\epsilon(\hat{y}(\theta))} = \frac{1 - F(\theta)}{f(\theta)}\frac{p_2(\hat{y}(\theta), \theta)}{p(\hat{y}(\theta), \theta)}.$$

Hence the characterization of second degree discriminatory monopoly behavior is that the price/cost margin for an increment dy at each $\hat{y}(\theta)$ equals the inverse of the (negative) demand elasticity for dy. That is, second degree discriminatory monopoly behavior is formally equivalent to setting marginal prices $T'(y)$ according to an inverse elasticity rule in each of a continuum of markets for increments dy.

14.5 NOTES

Almost any modern microeconomics text provides the basics of monopoly behavior. The particular presentation herein relies somewhat on Tirole [1, Chapter 1]. Cournot [2, Chapter III] gives a very early complete treatment of the first and second order conditions for maximization of monopoly profit, and also derives the comparative statics of a change in marginal cost (Cournot also notes in Chapter II that monopoly revenue maximization occurs where demand is unit elastic, although he does not use the term "elasticity"). The Lerner Index is due to [3]. Dupuit's [4] analysis of the deadweight loss caused by an excise tax to finance a government-owned enterprise is essentially the same as the deadweight loss caused by private monopoly behavior (particularly if the tax is set to maximize government revenue). Posner [5] provides a broad discussion of the inefficiency caused by monopoly behavior. Price cap regulation was popularized in regulatory circles by Littlechild [6, Section 13] but the basic graph presented herein is due to Ferguson and Gould [7, p. 305]. I am grateful to Richard Kihlstrom and David Sappington for pointing out these references. The Coase Conjecture is due to [8]. The three degrees of price discrimination were originally described by Pigou [9], shortly after which Ramsey [10] originated the notion of Ramsey Pricing. The observation that aggregate quantity must increase under third degree discrimination if it is to improve aggregate consumer surplus is due to Varian [11]. The Coase two-part tariff is from [12]. The "increment markets" interpretation of second degree price discrimination is due to [13].

14.6 EXERCISES

1. Consider a monopolist with inverse demand $p(y) = 7 - \frac{y}{2}$ for $0 \leq y \leq 14$ and cost function:
$$c(y) = \begin{cases} 10y - y^2, & 0 \leq y \leq 5 \\ \infty, & 5 < y. \end{cases}$$
Find the optimal output level and price for this monopolist.
2. Consider a monopolist facing inverse demand $p(y) = 100 - y$ for $0 \leq y \leq 100$ with cost function:
$$c(y) = \begin{cases} 0, & y = 0 \\ 500 + y^2, & y > 0 \end{cases}.$$
Find the optimal output level and price for this monopolist. How much profit will it earn?
3. Suppose market demand is $y = 780 - p$ for $0 \leq p \leq 780$ and cost is as given in Exercise 2. What price and quantity will the seller choose? What is the price elasticity of demand at the seller's choice? Based on the elasticity, what is the seller's percent markup (Lerner Index)?
4. Suppose there is a monopolist with average cost given in Exercise 17 of Chapter 13 and market inverse demand is $p = 4 - y$ for $0 \leq y \leq 4$. How much (Marshallian) surplus is lost due to the monopoly behavior of this firm?
5. A monopolist produces output y with constant marginal cost $c \geq 0$. The inverse demand for y is $p = \alpha - \beta y$ for $0 \leq y \leq \frac{\alpha}{\beta}$, where $\alpha > c$ and $\beta > 0$. Find the monopoly output, price, and profit. Also find the deadweight loss caused by the monopoly under the assumption that there are no income effects on this good.
6. Consider a monopolist producing output y. Assume a unique interior solution that is characterized by standard calculus conditions. Suppose

this monopolist must pay an excise tax of \$$t$ per unit sold. Use the Envelope Theorem to show that profit is a decreasing function of the tax rate t (there are other ways to show this; the point of the exercise is to use the Envelope Theorem).

7. Consider the model of Exercise 6 in Chapter 13.

a. If one of the sellers described is a monopolist, what will the monopolist do?

b. Compare and contrast the efficiency (Marshallian consumer surplus plus profit) of the monopoly and price-taking equilibria.

8. A monopolist producing output y has cost function $c(y)$ and faces market inverse demand $p(y) = Ay^{-1/\epsilon}$ for $y > 0$. Assume c is strictly increasing and $A, \epsilon > 0$.

a. Interpret the demand parameter ϵ.

b. Derive an expression for this monopolist's marginal revenue. What happens to MR when $\epsilon < 1$? When $\epsilon = 1$? Explain. What is the monopolist's optimal behavior in these cases?

c. Suppose MC is constant and $\epsilon > 1$. Derive the optimal quantity. Substitute to obtain the optimal price and profit. Use the optimal price to write an expression for $\frac{p-MC}{MC}$.

d. Still assuming MC is constant, what happens to price as $\epsilon \to \infty$? What happens to quantity? What happens to profit?

9. Suppose electric power is provided by one firm whose average cost curve is $AC(y) = 10 + 5y$ and whose demand curve is the market demand curve, which is $y = 25 - p/4$ for $0 \leq p \leq 100$.

a. Is this firm a natural monopolist? Why?

b. Show graphically and algebraically the price and quantity this firm would choose. Also graph and calculate the profit this firm would make.

c. Suppose there is a Public Utilities Commission which is responsible for regulating the power company. The Public Utilities Commission imposes a price cap for electric power, and they choose this price to be where marginal cost crosses market demand since this is what happens in a competitive market. Call this price $\bar{p}$.

i. What price does the Public Utilities Commission choose?

ii. Set up the revenue function for this regulated firm. Using this function find the marginal revenue function and draw this function.

iii. Indicate on your graph the output this firm will produce and the price it will charge. Calculate the output and price algebraically as well. Is marginal cost equal to marginal revenue at this price-output choice? Explain why profit is maximized when the regulated monopolist makes this decision but not when the firm makes any other price-output choice. Calculate the profit of this regulated firm.

iv. How is the price charged by the regulated monopolist related to the price charged by the unregulated monopolist? How is the output produced by the regulated monopolist related to the output produced by the unregulated monopolist?

v. Does the regulated monopolist supply all demands made at the price it charges?

vi. How do your answers to (ii)–(v) change if the price cap is above $\bar{p}$? What if the price cap is below $\bar{p}$? What if the price cap is above the price charged by the unregulated monopolist? In answering this question remember that the "effective demand curve" is different if the maximum price imposed by the commission is different from $\bar{p}$.

vii. Assume that the firm behaves like a price-taker even though it is the only firm in the industry. In this single-firm "competitive market," what price equates market supply and demand? What is the corresponding equilibrium output? Compare the price and output levels chosen by this "competitive" monopolist to those chosen by the unregulated monopolist, the regulated monopolist when the maximum price is $\bar{p}$, and the regulated monopolist when the maximum price differs from $\bar{p}$. Does the price cap of $\bar{p}$ accomplish the Public Utilities Commission's goal of making the price and output of the company the same as if the industry were competitive?

10. Consider a monopolist producing output y with cost function $c(y) = 400 + y^2$ and facing the demand curve $y = 340 - p$ for $0 \leq p \leq 340$.

a. What is the profit-maximizing level of output and price for the monopolist?

b. If the government can set a maximum price (i.e., prohibit the monopolist from selling above a specified price), what will it set to minimize deadweight loss? Is this also the price that maximizes consumer surplus? If not, indicate a price level that produces a higher consumer surplus. If the government is able to impose a lump sum tax on the firm and distribute this amount to consumers, does this alter your answer?

c. If the government can allow new entries into the industry as well as specifying the price, what price level and number of firms will minimize deadweight loss?
d. Explain why this industry is not a natural monopoly. Specify an alternative demand so that it would be a natural monopoly (for simplicity, assume demand is linear, so that your task is to specify A and B in the demand $y = A - Bp$). Explain the logic of your alternative.

11. Consider a monopolist whose average cost curve is $AC(y) = 170 - y$ (for $0 \leq y \leq 85$) and whose demand curve is the market demand curve, given by $y = (230 - p)/4$ for $0 \leq p \leq 230$.
   a. Is this firm a natural monopolist? Why?
   b. Show graphically and algebraically the price and quantity this firm would choose. Also graph and calculate the profit this firm would make.
   c. Now consider regulating this firm. Suppose the Public Utilities Commission decides to set $\bar{p}$ where marginal cost crosses demand, as in Exercise 9.
      i. What price does the Public Utilities Commission choose?
      ii. How much profit will this regulated firm make? Compare this to the profit made under the regulation in Exercise 9. Explain why there is a difference.
      iii. Instead of setting $\bar{p}$ where marginal cost crosses demand, suppose the Public Utilities Commission sets $\bar{p}$ where average cost crosses demand. What is the new regulated price and output? How does this regulation affect the profit of the firm? How is this new regulation justified?
      iv. Explain the difference between the two regulations. Which one is preferable? Defend your answer.

12. Consider a non-discriminating monopolist facing aggregate inverse demand $p(y) = \alpha - y$ for $y \leq \alpha$ and who has two production facilities with cost functions:

$$c_1(y_1) = y_1 + \frac{y_1^2}{2}$$
$$c_2(y_2) = 2y_2 + y_2^2.$$

   a. Suppose $\alpha = 12$. How much should the monopolist produce in each plant to maximize profit? Explain.
   b. Suppose $\alpha = 2.5$. Now how much should the monopolist produce in each plant to maximize profit? Explain.

13. Suppose a monopolist sells the same product in two distinct markets with inverse demands:

$$p_a = 50 - \frac{y_a}{2}$$

$$p_b = 10 - \frac{y_b}{2}$$

(where they are positive).

a. Draw side-by-side graphs for each market, with each graph showing the inverse demand and marginal revenue curve for that market. Take care to draw them roughly to scale and to label the intercepts on both axes and the slopes.

b. Suppose the monopolist has a total of 48 units to allocate across the two markets. What price should the monopolist charge in each market in order to maximize revenue? Calculate and compare the price elasticities of demand in the two markets at the chosen prices.

c. What is the marginal revenue in market a when $y_a = 40$? Based on this, what should the monopolist do to maximize revenue if the monopolist has fewer than 40 units to allocate across the two markets? Why?

d. What should the monopolist do to maximize revenue if the monopolist has more than 60 units to allocate across the two markets? Why?

14. A monopolist faces 10 identical buyers, each of whom has individual demand $y = 10 - p$ for $p \leq 10$.

a. What is the aggregate demand curve for all 10 buyers?

b. If the monopolist can charge only a constant price per unit, what price should be charged to maximize revenue? How much revenue is obtained?

c. Assume resale is prohibitively expensive. Can the monopolist get more revenue using a two-part tariff? If so, how? If not, why not?

d. Could the monopolist do just as well in part (c) if resale were not prohibitively expense? If so, how? If not, why not?

15. A monopolist faces 3 buyers: Small, Medium, and Large. The monopolist knows that Small is willing to pay \$5 for one unit and does not want more than one unit; Medium is willing to pay \$8 for one unit, \$4 for a second unit, and does not want more than two units; and Large is willing to pay \$10 for one unit, \$6 for a second unit, \$2 for a third unit, and does not want more than three units.

a. Assume the monopolist knows exactly which buyer is Small, which is Medium, and which is Large. What pricing policies will maximize the monopolist's revenue? Why?

b. Now assume the monopolist cannot distinguish which buyer is Small, which is Medium, and which is Large; and also cannot prevent one buyer from making more than one purchase; but the nature of the product is such that resale is not possible. Now what pricing policies will maximize the monopolist's revenue? Be careful to explain why your proposed policy is better than alternatives.

c. What is the revenue-maximizing two-part tariff? Compare your answer with your answer to part (b) and explain the relationship between the two pricing policies.

16. Suppose a monopolist serves two types of buyers and cannot separate them (so all price offerings will be available to both types). Assume resale is prohibitively expensive. Buyer type "Big" will pay up to \$5 for the first unit of the monopolist's product, up to \$1 for a second unit, and does not want more than two units. Buyer type "Small" will pay up to \$2 for the first unit and does not want more than one unit.

a. Suppose at least half of all buyers are type "Big." How should the monopolist price its product to maximize revenue?

b. Now suppose there are more "Small" buyers than "Big" buyers. Might this change your answer? If so, what would your alternative price(s) be?

17. Suppose a monopolist faces 3 buyers: Sally, Mary and Larry. The monopolist knows the following willingness to pay values: Sally is willing to pay \$6 for one unit and does not want more than one unit; Mary is willing to pay \$9 for one unit, \$5 for a second unit, and does not want more than two units; Larry is willing to pay \$10 for one unit and does not want more than one unit. Assume the seller cannot distinguish which buyer is Sally, which is Mary, and which is Larry; and also cannot prevent one buyer from making more than one purchase.

a. Assume the nature of the product is such that resale is not possible. What pricing options maximize the monopolist's revenue? Explain why your proposed policy is better than the alternatives.

b. What is the revenue-maximizing two-part tariff? Explain why.

c. Now suppose it is costless for the buyers to resell the product to each other (but there are no middlemen). What, if anything, would happen under the policy you proposed in part (a) of this question?

18. Suppose there are two consumers with inverse demands:

$$p = 20 - y_1$$
$$p = 30 - y_2$$

(where they are positive) and a monopolist whose only cost is $MC = 5$. Assume that resale and repeat purchases are not possible.

a. Find p^m, the nondiscriminatory monopoly price.

b. Suppose the monopolist cannot identify the individual consumers, and decides to offer a second degree discriminatory price by continuing to offer p^m but also offering a price $p^a \leq p^m$ that applies to quantities larger than some threshold y^a. What (p^a, y^a) should the monopolist offer? This type of tariff was studied by R. Willig (Pareto superior nonlinear outlay schedules. Bell J Econ 1978;9: 56–69) and is a Pareto improvement relative to the nondiscriminatory monopoly price.

c. Is the tariff you found in part (b) the best second-degree discriminatory tariff for the monopolist? If not, what is?

d. What would a perfectly discriminating monopolist charge?

REFERENCES

[1] Tirole J. The theory of industrial organization. Cambridge, MA: MIT Press; 1988.
[2] Cournot A. Recherches sur les Principes Mathématiques de la Théorie des Richesses. Paris: Hachette; 1838. English translation: "Researches into the mathematical principles of the theory of wealth" by Bacon N. New York: MacMillan; 1897.
[3] Lerner A. The concept of monopoly and the measurement of monopoly power. Rev Econ Stud 1934;1:157–75.
[4] Dupuit J. De la Mesure de l'Utilité des Travaux Publics. Annales des Ponts et Chaussées 1844;8(second series). English reprint "On the measurement of the utility of public works" by Barback RH. In: Arrow KJ, Scitovsky T, editors. A.E.A. Readings in welfare economics XII. Homewood, IL: Irwin; 1969.
[5] Posner R. The social costs of monopoly and regulation. J Polit Econ 1975;83:807–27.
[6] Littlechild S. Regulation of British Telecommunications' Profitability: report to the Secretary of State. London: UK Department of Industry; 1983.
[7] Ferguson CE, Gould JP. Microeconomic theory. Homewood, IL: Irwin; 1975.
[8] Coase R. Durability and monopoly. J Law Econ 1972;15:143–9.
[9] Pigou AC. The economics of welfare. London: Macmillan; 1920.
[10] Ramsey FP. A contribution to the theory of taxation. Econ J 1927;37:47–61.
[11] Varian H. Price discrimination and social welfare. Am Econ Rev 1985;75:870–5.
[12] Coase R. The problem of social cost. J Law Econ 1960;3:1–44.
[13] Goldman M, Leland H, Sibley D. Optimal nonuniform pricing. Rev Econ Stud 1984;51:305–20.

CHAPTER 15
Oligopoly

Chapter Outline

Oligopoly is often defined as a market in which there are a few sellers. However, as with monopoly, this is not a definition of oligopoly *behavior*. It is, rather, a statement of the circumstances that might lead to oligopoly behavior. Oligopoly *behavior* postulates that each seller makes choices to maximize profit recognizing that those choices may affect price, as with monopoly behavior, but also recognizing the presence of competitors whose choices may affect its profit opportunities. Hence sellers engaged in oligopoly behavior *strategically interact*, each recognizing that its welfare is affected by the behavior of the others and its behavior affects the welfare of the others. There are many possible forms of strategic interaction. As with monopoly behavior, sellers do not regard price as a parameter so there is no supply curve in an oligopoly market. Instead, sellers select particular responses to rivals that, depending on the form of the interaction, aggregate in some way to produce aggregate supply point(s). Oligopoly behavior typically lies between price-taking and monopoly behavior on a spectrum of competition intensities.

We continue to study partial equilibrium in a final product market. Analogous with our study of monopoly, firm i's production possibilities are summarized by a single-output lower semicontinuous and nondecreasing cost function $c_i : Y_i \to \mathbb{R}^1_+$ for $i = 1, \ldots, \ell$ (with input prices suppressed), where Y_i is the feasible output set of firm i and there are $\ell > 1$ firms. The output of firm i is denoted $y_i \in Y_i$. Note that, because we are focused on single-output technologies, the notation has switched to using the subscript of a firm's output to denote that individual firm rather than using a superscript to denote an individual firm.

The simplest oligopoly models assume buyers are price-taking consumers whose choice behavior for the good under study is summarized by an aggregate demand function $D(p)$. As in our study of monopoly, it is assumed throughout that D is upper semicontinuous, there is a price $\bar{p} \in (0, \infty)$ such that $D(p) = 0$ for $p \geq \bar{p}$, $D(0)$ is finite, and D is strictly decreasing on $p \in [0, \bar{p}]$. Typically the potential for changes in p to affect consumers' monetary resources is ignored (see the Introduction to Part 4). An inverse demand function $p(Y)$ therefore exists, where $Y = \sum_{i=1}^{\ell} y_i$ is aggregate output. We begin with these assumptions but must consider multiple products and specification of consumers' preferences for them in the sections on product differentiation.

15.1 ELEMENTS OF GAME THEORY

Game Theory is used to predict outcomes when actors are postulated to strategically interact. Only enough game theory is introduced here to enable a brief introduction to oligopoly behavior. A *game* (of complete information) is defined by a set of players $\{1, 2, \ldots, \ell\}$ who each know the entire game specification, a set S_i of possible strategies for each player $i = 1, \ldots, \ell$ (called the *strategy space* of the player), and a payoff function $\pi_i : S_i \times S_{-i} \to \mathbb{R}^1$ for each player $i = 1, \ldots, \ell$. The subscript $-i$ is notation commonly used in game theory to denote all players except player i. So S_{-i} is the Cartesian product of all other players' strategy spaces:

$$S_{-i} = S_1 \times \cdots \times S_{i-1} \times S_{i+1} \times \cdots \times S_\ell,$$

and s_{-i} is an element of S_{-i}. As we are interested in games with economic meaning, it is generally assumed without comment that each S_i is nonempty. In a *noncooperative* game, the behavioral postulate is that each player i chooses a strategy s_i from its strategy space S_i to maximize its payoff $\pi_i(s_i; s_{-i})$, *without regard for the effects of this choice on other players' payoffs.* In other words, each player acts exclusively and unilaterally in its own self-interest, leading to an optimal value function and optimal choice correspondence for each player:

$$\pi_i^*(s_{-i}) = \sup\{\pi_i(s_i; s_{-i}) : s_i \in S_i\}$$
$$s_i^*(s_{-i}) = \{s_i \in S_i : \pi_i(s_i; s_{-i}) = \pi_i^*(s_{-i})\},$$

both defined on $s_{-i} \in S_{-i}$. The relationship $s_i^* : S_{-i} \to 2^{S_i}$ is called the *best response* correspondence of player i, as it gives the feasible strategies that are unilaterally best for player i in response to a given specification s_{-i} of feasible strategies for all other players. s_i^* is alternatively called player i's *reaction* correspondence.

When S_i is a subset of a Euclidean space the standard discussion of existence and uniqueness of maxima applies to s_i^*. Sufficient conditions for existence are that S_i is closed and bounded (in addition to nonempty) and that π_i is an upper semicontinuous function of s_i (Theorem 1.2), but none of these conditions is necessary (except S_i nonempty). Given existence, sufficient conditions for uniqueness are that S_i is a convex set and π_i is a strictly concave function of s_i (Exercise 1 of Chapter 3). However, it is common in oligopoly games for strategy spaces to not be subsets of Euclidean spaces, in which case existence and uniqueness of best responses must either be established on a case-by-case basis or studied as a general matter in non-Euclidean spaces.

The most basic concept of equilibrium for a noncooperative game is known as *Nash Equilibrium.* Generally, equilibrium in an economic model is an internal consistency condition. The price-taking behavior of Chapter 13, for example, was defined to be in equilibrium when all buyers and sellers could simultaneously execute their optimal choices. The monopoly behavior of Chapter 14 honored internal consistency automatically because the monopolist made choices consistent with the assumed price-taking demand behavior. The Nash Equilibrium concept requires this same internal consistency among actors whose behavior is noncooperative strategic interaction. Specifically, the collective behavior is a Nash Equilibrium when it entails simultaneous optimal choices for all players.

Definition 15.1 (Nash Equilibrium)**.** Let $S = S_1 \times \cdots \times S_\ell$ denote the Cartesian product of all ℓ players' strategy spaces. An element $s = (s_1, \ldots, s_\ell)$ of S therefore specifies one feasible strategy for each player and is called a *strategy profile.* A strategy profile $\tilde{s} \in S$ is a *Nash Equilibrium* if $\tilde{s}_i \in s_i^*(\tilde{s}_{-i})$ for $i = 1, \ldots, \ell$.

In other words, a strategy profile is a Nash Equilibrium if it specifies optimal behavior for player i given the behavior of all other players, for every player $i = 1, \dots, \ell$. An equivalent definition is often given in terms of the payoff functions rather than the best response correspondences by saying $\tilde{s} \in S$ is a Nash Equilibrium if:

$$\pi_i(\tilde{s}_i; \tilde{s}_{-i}) \geq \pi_i(s_i; \tilde{s}_{-i}) \ \forall s_i \in S_i,$$

for every $i = 1, \dots, \ell$.

Nash's famous theorem [1] establishes conditions on the strategy spaces and payoff functions sufficient for existence of a Nash Equilibrium strategy profile. This generally requires strategy spaces that are probability distributions of possible underlying choices. Those underlying choices are called *pure strategies* and the distributions are known as *mixed strategies*. Hence a formal general treatment of existence requires non-Euclidean strategy spaces and is therefore beyond the scope of the present discussion, but Nash's core sufficient conditions are familiar: Best response correspondences that are nonempty, upper hemicontinuous and convex-valued. For example, if each S_i is a nonempty, closed and bounded subset of a Euclidean space (i.e., a compact pure strategy space) and each $\pi_i(s_i; s_{-i})$ is continuous then Theorem 1.2 ensures each $s_i^*(s_{-i})$ is nonempty for every s_{-i} and the Maximum Theorem (Theorem 1.5) ensures s_i^* is upper hemicontinuous (note that player i's feasible set S_i does not depend on that player's optimization "parameter" s_{-i}—this is an important aspect of the definition of a game and is sometimes overlooked in applications). If, in addition, each S_i is a convex set and each $\pi_i(s_i; s_{-i})$ is a quasiconcave function of s_i then $s_i^*(s_{-i})$ is a convex set for every $s_{-i} \in S_{-i}$ (Exercise 11 of Chapter 3). Most of the discussion herein is confined to such settings and attention is restricted to pure strategy Nash equilibria. However there are some basic oligopoly models that have discontinuous payoff functions, making some case-by-case considerations of existence (in pure strategies) unavoidable.

These concepts are evident in a simple example of strategic interaction between two players who each must choose one of two strategies. Suppose the set of players is $\{1, 2\}$, their strategy spaces are $S_1 = S_2 = \{A, B\}$, and their payoff functions for $i, j \in \{1, 2\}$ $(i \neq j)$ are:

$$\pi_i(s_i; s_j) = \begin{cases} a & \text{if } (s_i, s_j) = (A, A) \\ b_i & \text{if } (s_i, s_j) = (B, A) \\ c_i & \text{if } (s_i, s_j) = (A, B) \\ d & \text{if } (s_i, s_j) = (B, B) \end{cases},$$

where a, b_i, c_i, and d are real numbers.

A game like this with two players who each have finite strategy spaces is often presented in a table with one row for each strategy of player 1, one column for each strategy of player 2, and the corresponding payoff pairs π_1, π_2 displayed as the table entries. Fig. 15.1 gives the tabular form.

		S_2: A	S_2: B
S_1	A	a, a	c_1, b_2
	B	b_1, c_2	d, d

Fig. 15.1 A 2 × 2 noncooperative game.

Suppose to begin that $b_1 = b_2 = b$ and $c_1 = c_2 = c$, in which case the players are symmetric. If $a > b$ and $c > d$ then neither player is unilaterally maximized at (B, B): Player 1 receives the higher payoff $c > d$ by unilaterally switching to row A and player 2 receives the higher payoff $c > d$ by unilaterally switching to column A. Hence (B, B) is not a Nash Equilibrium. At (B, A), player 1 is not unilaterally maximized because 1 receives the higher payoff $a > b$ by unilaterally switching to row A. Similarly, player 2 is not unilaterally maximized at (A, B) because 2 receives the higher payoff $a > b$ by unilaterally switching to column A. Therefore neither (B, A) nor (A, B) is a Nash Equilibrium. (A, A) is a unique Nash Equilibrium in this case: A unilateral switch from (A, A) by either player causes that player's payoff to decrease from a to b. Note that the strategy profile (A, A) is the Nash Equilibrium, *not* the payoff pair a, a. The latter is called a *Nash Equilibrium payoff vector*.

It is easy to repeat this analysis when $a > b$ and $d > c$, with the conclusion that (A, A) and (B, B) are both Nash Equilibria. Thus there is no assurance even in a very simple game that a Nash Equilibrium, if it exists, is unique. Finally, relax the symmetry and suppose $b_2 < a < b_1$ and $c_2 < d < c_1$. Then at least one player has a unilateral incentive to depart from each of the four cells. Thus it is quite easy to construct a case with no Nash Equilibrium, even in a very simple game. In terms of the sufficient conditions for existence, the failure in this case occurs because the strategy spaces are not convex sets.

Sometimes a player's strategies have multiple parts. This does not change analysis of Nash Equilibrium provided care is exercised to correctly define that player's strategy space. Consider, for example, the game in Fig. 15.1

with one change: Player 2 learns, before selecting either A or B, the selection player 1 has made from $S_1 = \{A, B\}$. Then player 2 can entertain the possibility of *contingent plans* by conditioning whether A or B is selected on what is observed about player 1's selection. Hence player 2's strategies are *pairs* (s_2^A, s_2^B), where the first entry specifies what player 2 chooses when a choice of A by player 1 is observed and the second entry specifies what player 2 chooses when a choice of B by player 1 is observed. This seemingly small change in the game is formally presented as a change in player 2's strategy space to $S_2 = \{(A, A), (A, B), (B, A), (B, B)\}$ and a change in the tabular presentation to Fig. 15.2. Every element of the restated strategy space is a *complete contingent plan*, meaning that every strategy must specify what player 2 does in every possible contingency.

		S_2			
		(A, A)	(A, B)	(B, A)	(B, B)
S_1	A	a, a	a, a	c_1, b_2	c_1, b_2
	B	b_1, c_2	d, d	b_1, c_2	d, d

Fig. 15.2 A 2 × 2 noncooperative game with sequential play.

Now suppose $a < b_1 < d < c_1$ and $a < c_2 < d < b_2$, and consider the strategy profile $(A, (B, A))$. b_2 is the largest possible payoff for player 2, so player 2 has no unilateral incentive to change. Player 1 also has no unilateral incentive to change because doing so would decrease player 1's payoff from c_1 to b_1. Hence $(A, (B, A))$ is a Nash Equilibrium. But this profile does not "seem" like equilibrium behavior because player 2 has a unilateral incentive to renege on the claim that A will be chosen following an observed choice of B by player 1. If player 2 actually observed a choice of B by player 1 then player 2 could obtain the higher payoff $d > c_2$ by selecting B. Knowing this, player 1 ought to present player 2 with a *fait accompli* of B, thereby daring player 2 to carry out the threat of playing A. It is reasonable to expect in the game of Fig. 15.2 that player 2 would indeed relent and select B. One is tempted to argue that player 2 must carry out the threat to maintain credibility. However, that argument presumes there is a future in which player 2's credibility matters. No such future exists in the simple game of Fig. 15.2, although we could certainly specify a game with future interaction and study the conditions under which it is unilaterally optimal for player 2 to carry out the threat after observing a choice of B by player 1. Within the context of the game we have specified, however, a choice of A by player 2 following a choice of B by player 1 is called a *noncredible threat*. The profile $(A, (B, A))$ is a Nash Equilibrium only because of this noncredible threat. This suggests that Nash Equilibrium is, perhaps, not the most salient equilibrium concept when players' strategy spaces include contingent plans.

A *refinement* of the Nash Equilibrium concept known as *subgame perfect equilibrium* is used to eliminate from consideration seemingly nonsensical equilibria like $(A, (B, A))$ in Fig. 15.2. To do so we must define, at least loosely, the concept of a *subgame* of a given game. There are two defining properties. First, the initial choice(s) in a subgame are made by player(s) who know everything that happened leading to those initial choices. For example, player 2 in the example is the initial decision-maker following a choice of either A or B by player 1, and player 2 knows which has been chosen by player 1. Second, any choice situation in the game that can occur after the initial choice(s) in a subgame can *only* occur after those initial choice(s). In other words, a subgame is "self-contained." Player 2 in the example has the choice between A and B *only* after knowing whether player 1 has chosen A or B. Hence, there are two subgames of the game in Fig. 15.2 (in addition to the entire game, which is itself a subgame): Player 2's choice following a choice of A by player 1, and player 2's choice following a choice of B by player 1. If there were an "ignorance" path to player 2's choice between A and B then neither of these would be subgames. It is not required that there be only one player making an initial choice in a subgame. For example, both players choose at the start of the game in Fig. 15.1, but both know that nothing has happened prior to that initial choice and there is no other way to that initial choice. Note that a subgame is itself a game: Because there is no ambiguity about what has transpired prior to the initial choice(s) and no alternative paths into the subgame, we can unambiguously define from the original game the set of (completely informed) players in the subgame, their (remaining, restricted) strategy spaces, and the payoffs of the players as functions on these strategy spaces.

Definition 15.2. A *subgame perfect equilibrium* for a game (of complete information) is a strategy profile that is a Nash Equilibrium for each of its subgames.

The strategy profile $(A, (B, A))$ is not a subgame perfect equilibrium of the game presented in Fig. 15.2 because player 2 is not optimized in the subgame that begins following a choice of B by player 1. The most common approach to deriving subgame perfect equilibria is to begin at the end: First identify the optimal choice(s) for the player(s) who choose at each possible final choice of the game, then presuming this is what will happen in those subgames identify the optimal choice(s) for the player(s) who choose at each possible penultimate choice of the game, and so on until the initial choice(s) in the original game are considered. This procedure is called *backward induction*. In Fig. 15.2, this procedure identifies B as the Nash Equilibrium in the subgame that begins following a choice of A by player 1; and B as the Nash Equilibrium in the subgame that begins following a choice of B by player 1. In other words, the requirement of Nash Equilibrium in the two final subgames dictates that player 2's strategy is (B, B). Knowing this, the only profiles player 1 considers at the first decision are $(A, (B, B))$ and $(B, (B, B))$, leading player 1 to choose A. The unique subgame perfect equilibrium in Fig. 15.2 is $(A, (B, B))$. The "nonsensical" Nash Equilibrium $(A, (B, A))$ is excluded by the requirement of optimality in each subgame.

15.2 COURNOT OLIGOPOLY

Our first economic application of Nash Equilibrium is the *Cournot Duopoly*. In this oligopoly model the players are two firms, their strategy spaces are $S_1 = S_2 = [0, D(0)]$, and their payoff functions for $i, j = 1, 2$ $(i \neq j)$ are:

$$\pi_i(y_i; y_j) = p(y_1 + y_2)y_i - c_i(y_i).$$

The behavioral postulate is that firm i chooses an output level y_i from the interval $[0, D(0)]$ of economically relevant output levels to unilaterally maximize π_i, taking as fixed an economically relevant output level y_j for the other firm. y_i is used rather than s_i to denote player i's strategy in this game because the strategy has an economic interpretation as an output level. The economic interpretation of the payoff is that $p(y_1 + y_2)$ is the price at which consumers demand the aggregate output of *both* firms, so $p(y_1 + y_2)y_i$ is revenue firm i receives from selling y_i units at that price; and $c_i(y_i)$ is cost incurred by firm i to produce those y_i units. Thus firm i's payoff function in this game is firm i's profit as a function of its quantity *assuming the price at which its sales are made equates a given aggregate demand to the aggregate of its own output and an assumed output of the other firm*. This recognition by each player that price depends on both its own quantity choice and the quantity choice of the other player is what endows the game with meaningful strategic interaction. The Cournot Duopoly game is completely defined by the set of two players, their strategy spaces as (economically relevant) output levels, their payoff functions as stated above, and the informational assumption that both players know all of this.

It is worth pausing to clarify a common misuse of terminology. The game specified in the previous paragraph is called a "Cournot" Duopoly in deference to A. Cournot [2, Chapter VII], who analyzed the interaction long before formal development of game theory. Nash Equilibrium is sometimes mistakenly called "Cournot-Nash Equilibrium" in reference to the Nash Equilibrium concept used in a Cournot Duopoly game. This is a natural abuse of terminology because the Cournot Duopoly is often the first formal application of Nash Equilibrium encountered by economics students. But it is poor terminology. The Nash Equilibrium concept can be applied to *any* noncooperative game of complete information, whether an economic game of firms choosing quantities or otherwise. The moniker "Cournot" signifies, specifically, that the players are firms who unilaterally choose quantities to maximize profit under the presumption that the price received equates aggregate supply to aggregate demand.

The presence of y_j in the inverse demand of firm i's profit function has the geometric effect of shifting the aggregate inverse demand y_j units leftward, as illustrated in Fig. 15.3. Demand remaining net of rivals' choices is generally called a firm's *residual demand*. Residual demand is an exogenously given demand curve from the perspective of the individual firm, and under the Cournot behavioral postulate residual demand resembles aggregate demand because they differ only by a fixed horizontal shift. Thus it can be useful under the Cournot behavioral postulate to view firm i as engaging in monopoly behavior along its residual demand. But the resulting choice(s) are not part of a Nash Equilibrium profile for the game unless the leftward shift of the aggregate demand is optimal for firm j given the choice firm i makes along this residual demand. Nash Equilibrium requires *simultaneous* unilateral optimality. It should be carefully noted that, although each firm in a Cournot Duopoly can be viewed as engaging in monopoly

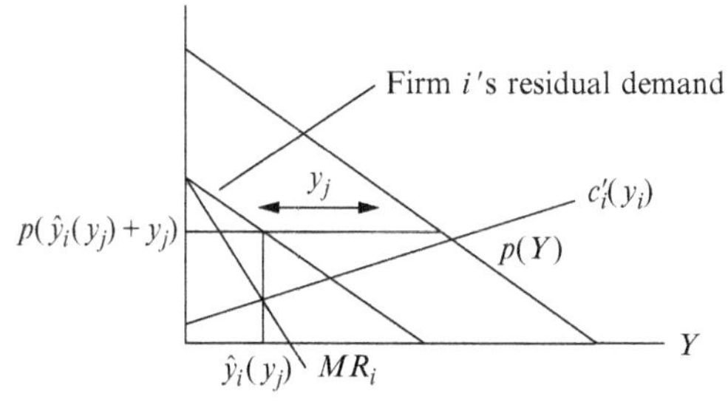

Fig. 15.3 Cournot residual demand and optimal choice.

behavior, that monopoly behavior is conditional on a conjectured *quantity* produced and sold by the rival. We will see in subsequent sections that a Nash Equilibrium of the entire duopoly game can be dramatically different if the behavioral postulate for firms is different; for example, duopolists who conjecture that a rival's *price* is fixed. Both conjectures have each firm choosing point(s) on a given (residual) demand to maximize profit; but the form of the residual demand is significantly different with the price conjecture than it is with the quantity conjecture.

Viewing a Cournot duopolist as engaged in monopoly behavior along the left-shifted residual demand, the discussion in Chapter 14 about existence and uniqueness of an optimal choice applies (for each fixed strategy of the other firm). In particular, if aggregate demand and firm i's cost are differentiable the necessary first order condition for an interior maximum is:

$$[p'(y_1 + y_2)y_i + p(y_1 + y_2)] = c_i'(y_i),$$

which again is the familiar condition that firm i choose output to equate marginal revenue and marginal cost, but in this case the term in brackets is the marginal revenue (MR_i) derived from firm i's residual demand. As with a pure monopolist, if aggregate demand and cost are twice differentiable the necessary second order condition is that the slope of marginal cost be no less than the slope of this residual marginal revenue at the optimum:

$$\frac{\partial^2 \pi_i}{\partial y_i^2} = 2p'(y_1 + y_2) + p''(y_1 + y_2)y_i - c_i''(y_i) \leq 0.$$

This is illustrated in Fig. 15.3. At each possible quantity for firm i, the leftward shift of the residual demand makes price lower compared to aggregate demand, and thus tends to drive down the individually optimal output choices compared with a monopolist who faces the entire market inverse demand $p(Y)$.

If the conditions of the implicit function theorem apply to the first order condition then that condition implicitly defines a differentiable function $\hat{y}_i(y_j)$ that is the best response function of firm i. Standard comparative statics then yields:

$$\hat{y}_i'(y_j) = -\frac{\frac{\partial^2 \pi_i}{\partial y_i \partial y_j}}{\frac{\partial^2 \pi_i}{\partial y_i^2}} \stackrel{s}{=} \frac{\partial^2 \pi_i(\hat{y}_i(y_j); y_j)}{\partial y_i \partial y_j} = p''(\hat{y}_i(y_j) + y_j)\hat{y}_i(y_j) + p'(\hat{y}_i(y_j) + y_j).$$

Hence concave inverse demand is a sufficient condition for the (interior) best response function to be downward-sloping. Note that $\frac{\partial^2 \pi_i}{\partial y_i^2} < \frac{\partial^2 \pi_i}{\partial y_i \partial y_j}$ at a positive quantity when cost is convex, so the second order condition is implied when $\frac{\partial^2 \pi_i}{\partial y_i \partial y_j}$ is nonpositive and cost is convex. Downward-sloping best responses is considered the usual case for Cournot competitors, although it is not assured by the optimization behavioral postulate because even with constant marginal cost the necessary second order condition requires only that $p''\hat{y}_i + 2p'$ be nonpositive (i.e., MR_i is not upward-sloping), which can hold when $\hat{y}_i'(y_j)$ above is positive if demand is convex. When the best response is downward-sloping and cost is convex, the relationship $\frac{\partial^2 \pi_i}{\partial y_i^2} < \frac{\partial^2 \pi_i}{\partial y_i \partial y_j}$ implies the slope of the best response is greater than -1.

Both firms must be simultaneously optimized in a Nash Equilibrium, so the best response by firm 1 must be consistent with the choice actually made by firm 2 and vice-versa. Therefore a Nash Equilibrium is a (y_1, y_2) point at which the best response curves cross. As mentioned in the previous section, given existence of best responses sufficient conditions for existence of an intersection are that the best responses be upper hemicontinuous and convex-valued on compact strategy spaces. The standard case is illustrated in Fig. 15.4. Note that the best response curve of firm i follows the $y_i = 0$ axis beyond the intercept (each firm chooses an output of zero if the competitor's output is large enough), and the quantity where firm i's best response intersects the $y_j = 0$ axis is the monopoly quantity for firm i (firm i chooses along the aggregate demand curve when firm j produces nothing). Algebraically, an (interior) equilibrium strategy profile is found by simultaneously solving the two first order conditions for the two unknowns (y_1, y_2). This point is labeled (y_1^e, y_2^e) on the graph. Then the market equilibrium price is found by substituting the sum of the equilibrium quantities into the inverse demand, and from this the equilibrium profit for each firm can be calculated. When the slopes of the best responses exceed -1 there cannot be more than one interior point where they cross, so in this "standard" situation an interior equilibrium, if it exists, is unique. The optimal isoprofit lines in equilibrium are labeled on the graph as π_1^* and π_2^*. An increase in y_2, for example, shifts firm 1's residual demand leftward and therefore decreases firm 1's profit at each value of y_1. Hence firm 1 seeks the lowest isoprofit curve subject to staying on the horizontal line dictated by firm 2's choice y_2^e, so a maximum along this line must occur where a concave isoprofit is tangent to the line. Firm 1's optimal isoprofit for each possible value of y_2 is therefore horizontal where that value of y_2 crosses firm 1's best response. Similarly, firm 2's isoprofits are vertical where they cross firm 2's best response.

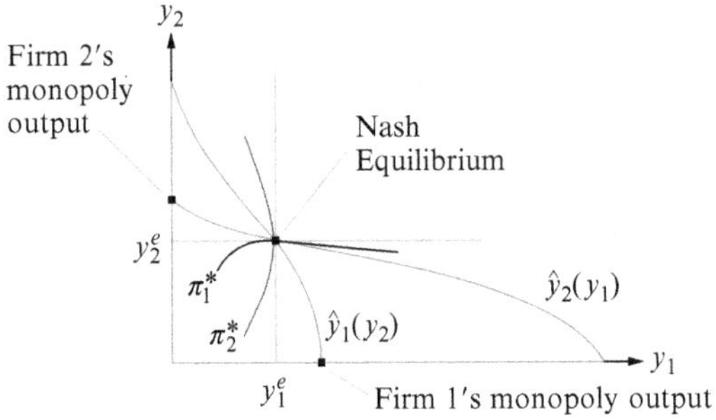

Fig. 15.4 Nash Equilibrium (y_1^e, y_2^e) in the Cournot Duopoly.

If the firms have identical cost functions then their optimization problems are identical. The best response curves are therefore identical and the duopoly is called *symmetric*. One firm's best response curve can be found from the other firm's best response curve by simply interchanging the roles of y_1 and y_2 in the function. If the firms were symmetric in Fig. 15.4 then firm 2's best response curve would be a reflection across the 45-degree line of firm 1's best response curve. Then the two curves would cross on the 45-degree line (assuming continuity), and a Nash Equilibrium could be found by simultaneously solving either of the first order conditions along with the condition $y_1 = y_2$. There can be more than one Nash Equilibrium, but if the reaction curves are downward-sloping there can be only one point where they cross the 45-degree line, so this equilibrium is called the *symmetric* Nash Equilibrium.

As firm *i*'s first order condition includes the monopoly-like term $p'(y_1 + y_2)y_i < 0$, an equilibrium price is greater than marginal cost. Hence the Cournot Duopoly prices above the perfectly competitive level and produces less output than price-takers would produce. We can also compare the Cournot Duopoly equilibrium with monopoly behavior. Adding the first order conditions yields:

$$p'(Y)Y + 2p(Y) = c_1'(y_1) + c_2'(y_2),$$

where Y is market output. If the firms are symmetric with common cost function c, then in the symmetric equilibrium this condition is:

$$\frac{1}{2}p'(Y)Y + p(Y) = c'\left(\frac{Y}{2}\right).$$

Let Y^m be the monopoly output. If marginal cost is nondecreasing, then:

$$\frac{1}{2}p'(Y^m)Y^m + p(Y^m) > p'(Y^m)Y^m + p(Y^m) = c'(Y^m) \geq c'\left(\frac{Y^m}{2}\right).$$

So the monopolist's price is too high to satisfy the duopoly optimality conditions. That is, with reasonably well-behaved functions, the symmetric Cournot Duopoly prices below the monopoly level and produces greater aggregate output than a monopolist would produce. "Reasonably well-behaved functions" here rules out the case of decreasing marginal cost, which is an important instance in which monopoly behavior may produce more output than a Cournot Duopoly. From the analysis of monopoly deadweight loss in Chapter 14, we can immediately conclude that the Cournot Duopoly is not Pareto Efficient (consumers are more than willing to compensate the duopolists for the profit they would forego if they behaved as price-takers), but is likely to be more efficient than monopoly behavior (i.e., Cournot Duopoly probably generates less deadweight loss than monopoly). Thus we see that Cournot competition restrains the exercise of market power, but not as severely as perfect competition.

The Cournot Duopoly model easily generalizes to a Cournot oligopoly with an arbitrary number ℓ of firms. Then the objective of the ith firm is:

$$\max_{\{y_i \in [0, D(0)]\}} \pi_i(y_i; y_{-i}) = p\left(\sum_{j=1}^{\ell} y_j\right) y_i - c_i(y_i),$$

so the first order condition for an interior maximum is:

$$p'\left(\sum_{j=1}^{\ell} y_j\right) y_i + p\left(\sum_{j=1}^{\ell} y_j\right) = c_i'(y_i).$$

There are ℓ first order conditions like this; one for each $i = 1, \ldots, \ell$; that must be solved simultaneously for the ℓ unknowns $(y_1, \ldots, y_\ell)$ to find an interior equilibrium output profile. If the oligopoly is symmetric with common cost function c and we focus on the symmetric equilibrium, the solution is much simpler. In this case we can set all y_i's to the common equilibrium value, say y, in the first order condition for one firm and then solve for y. Note that the objective *must* be differentiated *before* setting all firm's outputs equal, since the behavioral postulate is that all rivals' outputs are fixed as each firm chooses its own output. Setting all y_i's equal to y in π *before* differentiating with respect to y is a different (incorrect) objective from the Cournot objective. So, in the symmetric case with ℓ firms the symmetric interior equilibrium output for one firm is the value of y that solves:

$$p'(\ell y)y + p(\ell y) = c'(y).$$

Denote the solution by $y^e(\ell)$. Market output is then $\ell y^e(\ell)$, and the equilibrium price is $p(\ell y^e(\ell))$.

When $\ell = 1$ this gives the standard monopoly equilibrium. On the other hand, we can use this condition to show that the oligopoly equilibrium approaches the long-run price-taking equilibrium as $\ell \to \infty$. Keeping in mind the potential for existence problems with a long-run price-taking equilibrium, as discussed in Chapter 13, the most sensible (simple) technology for studying this result is constant returns to scale. Assume marginal cost is a constant value c', and let Y^* be the long-run perfectly competitive aggregate output, defined by $p(Y^*) = c'$. For any ℓ, the symmetric Cournot competitors must earn nonnegative profit in equilibrium, implying $p(\ell y^e(\ell)) \geq c'$, so $\ell y^e(\ell) \leq Y^*$. That is, $\ell y^e(\ell)$ is bounded as $\ell \to \infty$. As demand is assumed to be nicely behaved (in particular, assume inverse demand has a bounded derivative), this implies $p'(\ell y^e(\ell))\frac{\ell y^e(\ell)}{\ell}$ approaches zero as $\ell \to \infty$. From the condition defining $y^e(\ell)$, this means $p(\ell y^e(\ell)) \to c'$ as $\ell \to \infty$. That is, the equilibrium Cournot price converges to the long-run perfectly competitive price as the number of Cournot competitors increases.

15.3 BERTRAND DUOPOLY

The Cournot oligopoly is only one of many possible oligopoly models. Although the predictions of the Cournot model seem plausible, there is a troubling inconsistency with the Cournot behavioral postulate. Each firm recognizes that its quantity choice affects price, yet behaves as if the price that equates supply and demand will arise automatically via some unspecified mechanism. In other words, price-setting is not explained by the Cournot model. Price-taking behavior also does not explain price-setting, but price-takers are consistent in their view that whatever determines prices is outside of their influence.

The *Bertrand Duopoly* differs from the Cournot model in that the firms' strategies are assumed to be prices rather than quantities. The set of players remains $\{1, 2\}$. We continue to assume there is an aggregate demand function $D(p)$ that is finite at $p = 0$, zero for $p \geq \bar{p}$, downward-sloping on $p \in [0, \bar{p}]$, and upper semicontinuous; and that firm i has a lower semicontinuous cost function c_i. The strategy spaces are economically relevant prices $S_1 = S_2 = [0, \bar{p}]$, and firm i's payoff function is:

$$\pi_i(p_i; p_j) = p_i D(p_i; p_j) - c_i(D(p_i; p_j)),$$

where $D(p_i; p_j)$ is firm i's residual demand. A key part of the Bertrand behavioral postulate is specification of the residual demand. All completely informed consumers who regard the firms' products as homogeneous (and whose indirect utilities are strictly decreasing in price) strictly prefer a lower price. Therefore each firm's residual demand curve under the Bertrand behavioral postulate is the market demand when it charges the low price and is zero when it charges the high price. When the two prices are equal, some assumption is required about how the indifferent consumers behave. Usually we just assume each firm receives half of the demand. Thus, firm i's residual demand is:

$$D(p_i; p_j) = \begin{cases} D(p_i), & \text{for } p_i < p_j \\ \frac{D(p_i)}{2}, & \text{for } p_i = p_j \\ 0, & \text{for } p_i > p_j \end{cases}.$$

Notice that this demand is discontinuous as a function of firm i's choice variable p_i, at $p_i = p_j$. It is illustrated in Fig. 15.5. Thus the payoff function of firm i is also discontinuous.

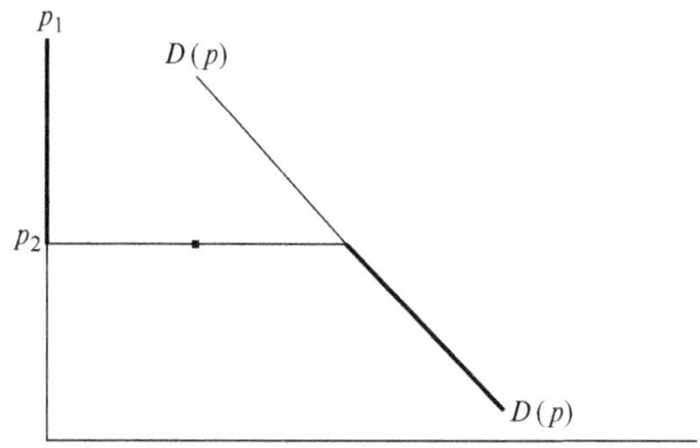

Fig. 15.5 Residual demand function for a Bertrand duopolist. The dark line is the residual demand faced by firm 1 when firm 2's price is p_2.

This discontinuity in the objective creates substantial existence problems for a Nash Equilibrium price profile. If firm 1 charges a price slightly below p_2 (this strategy is called *Bertrand undercutting*) then it receives much larger revenue than if it prices at or above firm 2's price. Thus, whenever p_2 is above firm 1's marginal cost across all relevant quantities and below firm 1's monopoly price, the optimal strategy for firm 1 is to slightly undercut firm 2 (if p_2 is above firm 1's monopoly price the optimal strategy for firm 1 is its monopoly price), thereby leaving firm 2 with zero profit. Firm 2 has the same incentive, so a price pair cannot be simultaneously optimal unless some type of cost constraint binds. The simplest case is when both firms have the same constant marginal cost. In this case a Nash Equilibrium exists but the only Nash Equilibrium price pair is both prices equal to the common marginal cost. This is because Bertrand undercutting is optimal for at least one firm if either price is above marginal cost. Note that *both* firms must charge price equal to marginal cost in equilibrium because, if one price were above marginal cost, the low-price firm would have incentive to increase its price at least a small amount. Thus, prices equal the perfectly competitive equilibrium price, firms make zero profit, and a Pareto Efficient allocation occurs in equilibrium. While this equilibrium seems desirable from a welfare perspective, it is widely regarded as highly implausible and empirically invalid. The notion that only two firms compete intensely enough to eliminate all profit is unrealistic in most settings. Consequently, the zero-profit property of the Bertrand equilibrium is known as the *Bertrand Paradox*.

The paradoxical nature of this equilibrium is unfortunate because the Bertrand model has the nice feature that it endogenizes price-setting. In contrast, the Cournot model does not provide an explanation for how the firms' quantity choices are combined to generate the price $p(y_1 + y_2)$, since no economic agent actually chooses the price. Rather, the Cournot behavioral postulate simply assumes this price arises through some unmodeled process for any (y_1, y_2) pair the firms choose. A much nicer model would endogenize price-setting while also producing a more plausible equilibrium. This can be accomplished by introducing strategic precommitment, repeated play, entry and exit decisions, product differentiation, or incomplete information into the Bertrand model.

15.4 STACKELBERG LEADERSHIP

A well-known variant of the Cournot Duopoly arises when firms choose quantities but do so sequentially rather than simultaneously. "Simultaneously" in the context of a complete information game should not be taken too literally. It merely means players choose strategies in ignorance of the choice(s) made by other players. In contrast, "sequentially" in the present context means the *leader's* quantity choice is observed by the *follower* before the latter chooses its quantity, and both firms know this. Formally, this model differs from the Cournot Duopoly in that the follower's pure strategy space is not merely quantities but is, rather, the *set of complete contingent quantity plans in which the contingency is the leader's quantity choice.* Arbitrarily denoting the leader as firm 1, the strategy spaces are $S_1 = [0, D(0)]$ and:

$$S_2 = \{\hat{y}_2 : S_1 \to [0, D(0)]\}.$$

That is, the follower's strategy space is the set of functions that map a quantity choice by the leader to an economically relevant output level. Each such function specifies a complete contingent quantity plan. The payoff functions are then:

$$\pi_1(y_1; \hat{y}_2(\cdot)) = p(y_1 + \hat{y}_2(y_1))y_1 - c_1(y_1)$$
$$\pi_2(\hat{y}_2(\cdot); y_1) = p(y_1 + \hat{y}_2(y_1))\hat{y}_2(y_1) - c_2(\hat{y}_2(y_1)).$$

The set of 2 players, these strategy spaces and payoff functions, and the informational assumption that both players know all of this completely specifies the game. This game is known as the *Stackelberg Quantity Leadership Duopoly*. It is our first economic model that involves one player learning something after another player has taken an action but before making some choice. Attention is usually confined to subgame perfect equilibria in this game, whence we utilize backward induction.

Note that the follower's quantity choice, contingent on a particular quantity y_1 chosen by the leader, and the subsequent payoffs, are indeed a subgame. The follower knows y_1 has been chosen at this decision point and there is no other sequence of choices yielding the payoffs that result from the follower's choices. Hence a Nash Equilibrium in the subgame is a choice of y_2 that maximizes π_2 contingent on y_1. That is, a Nash Equilibrium in the subgame solves:

$$\max_{y_2 \in [0, D(0)]} p(y_1 + y_2)y_2 - c_2(y_2).$$

This is the choice problem for a Cournot duopolist. Under the assumptions stated for the Cournot model, there is a solution $\hat{y}_2(y_1)$ that gives the follower's best response to each contingency the follower might encounter following a choice by the leader. Hence equilibrium in the subgame is simply the Cournot best response of the follower to the contingency presented by the leader. The follower's subgame perfect equilibrium complete contingent plan is therefore the Cournot best response *function* of the follower. The leader ignores all other possible contingent plans by the follower in a subgame perfect equilibrium, so the leader's strategy in such an equilibrium solves:

$$\max_{y_1 \in [0, D(0)]} p(y_1 + \hat{y}_2(y_1))y_1 - c_1(y_1).$$

This behavior differs from Cournot behavior because the *leader chooses output anticipating the follower's Cournot best response to that choice, rather than making a fixed conjecture about the follower's output level.* The first order condition for the leader's optimization is:

$$p(y_1 + \hat{y}_2(y_1)) + p'(y_1 + \hat{y}_2(y_1))[1 + \hat{y}_2'(y_1)]y_1 = c_1'(y_1).$$

This differs from the Cournot first order condition by the term $p'(y_1 + \hat{y}_2(y_1))\hat{y}_2'(y_1)y_1$, which is the effect of a change in y_1 on price through the follower's best response of y_2. Solving this first order condition for y_1 gives the optimal choice $\hat{y}_1$ for the leader (assuming an interior optimum). Substituting that choice into $\hat{y}_2(y_1)$ gives the equilibrium output of the follower. The Nash equilibrium profile is $(\hat{y}_1, \hat{y}_2(\cdot))$. The pair $(\hat{y}_1, \hat{y}_2(\hat{y}_1))$ is sometimes mistakenly called the Nash Equilibrium of the Stackelberg game. This is natural but careless terminology because the follower's strategies are entire functions, so the follower's entry in a Nash Equilibrium profile must be an entire function (i.e., a complete contingent plan). The *value* $\hat{y}_2(\hat{y}_1)$ is the particular part of the follower's equilibrium complete contingent plan that the follower carries out in equilibrium.

The leader in a Stackelberg duopoly earns at least as much profit as it would in a Cournot duopoly. This is because the leader selects its optimal point on the follower's best response curve, whereas a Cournot competitor simply accepts the point where the two best response curves cross. This is illustrated in Fig. 15.6. Whether the leader makes more or less profit than the follower is more difficult, but if the best response curves have the traditional shape then it is better to be the leader in a Stackelberg duopoly.

While it may seem intuitive that the leader earns more profit, this outcome does not always generalize to other models in which one firm is a leader and the other is a follower. There are (plausible) settings in which it is preferable to be the follower. One such setting is known as *price leadership*. There are several versions of price leadership models. If

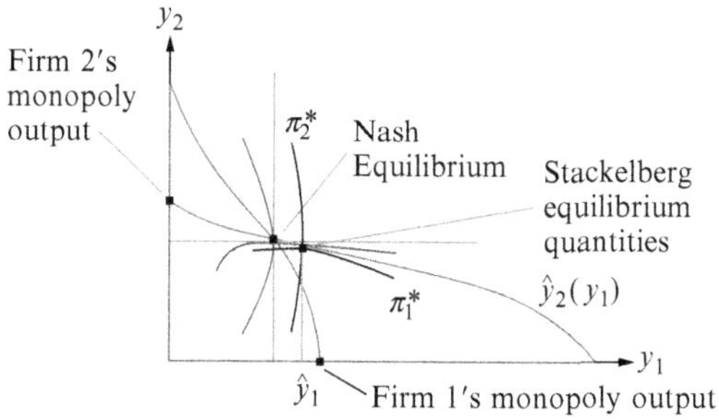

Fig. 15.6 Subgame perfect equilibrium in the Stackelberg duopoly. The Cournot equilibrium is reproduced from Fig. 15.4 for reference. The Stackelberg leader (firm 1) seeks its lowest (best) isoprofit subject to the follower's entire Cournot best response curve $\hat{y}_2(\cdot)$. This causes the leader to move down the follower's best response curve, choosing a larger quantity and thereby decreasing the equilibrium quantity of the follower.

the products are differentiated, then we can construct a model in which both the leader and follower choose price and make sales in equilibrium. But with a homogeneous product this type of model degenerates to the Bertrand situation, since the follower wants to undercut and, anticipating this, the leader does not care about price (because the leader makes no sales except, possibly, at zero profit). This version of the story assumes nonincreasing marginal cost, and is a dramatic example of followership being preferred to leadership.

15.5 DOMINANT FIRM WITH A COMPETITIVE FRINGE

Another version of price leadership is known as the *dominant firm* model. Here, the strategy space of the leader (firm 1) is economically relevant prices $S_1 = [0, \bar{p}]$. The follower observes the leader's price choice and then makes a quantity choice. Hence the follower behaves as a price-taker, taking as given whatever price the leader chooses. Formally, the follower's strategy space is again a set of complete contingent quantity plans, but the contingency is the leader's price choice:

$$S_2 = \{\hat{y}_2 : S_1 \rightarrow [0, D(0)]\}.$$

Usually this model is studied in the context of a large firm with scale economies that endow it with relatively low marginal cost, who sets a price adhered to by multiple relatively small followers with relatively high marginal costs. These followers are collectively referred to as the *competitive fringe*. A fringe composed of a large number of small firms makes the price-taking assumption for the followers more plausible but the salient features of the model are displayed even if the market is a duopoly.

Once again attention is confined to subgame perfect equilibria. After firm 1 selects price p, the best response of a price-taking firm 2 in its choice subgame is to choose a quantity that equates this price with marginal cost. Thus, the strategy of firm 2 in a subgame perfect equilibrium strategy profile is (the inverse of) its marginal cost curve. That is, the equilibrium $\hat{y}_2(p)$ is defined by:

$$p \equiv c_2'(\hat{y}_2(p)).$$

This assumes firm 2's optimum is interior and unique. When the follower offers $\hat{y}_2(p)$ for sale at price p, the leader can sell only $D_1(p; \hat{y}_2(\cdot)) = \max\{D(p) - \hat{y}_2(p), 0\}$ at the stated price. This difference is the leader's residual demand. Hence, when the leader confines attention to a contingent plan that is optimal for the follower, the leader chooses p to:

$$\max_{p \in [0\,\bar{p}]} \pi(p; \hat{y}_2(p)) = pD_1(p; \hat{y}_2(\cdot)) - c_1(D_1(p; \hat{y}_2(\cdot))).$$

If there is more than one follower then the leader substitutes the aggregate supply of the competitive fringe in place of $\hat{y}_2(p)$ when forming the residual demand. As always, the residual demand is fixed from the leader's perspective, whence the leader's choice can be viewed as a monopolist's quantity choice on this residual demand. An interior optimum for the leader is therefore a point on the residual demand at a quantity that equates the leader's residual marginal revenue (MR_1) with the leader's marginal cost.

This is illustrated in Fig. 15.7. Aggregate demand $D(p)$, its associated marginal revenue MR, and the leader's and follower's marginal costs c_1' and c_2', respectively, are shown. The leader's residual demand $D_1(p; \hat{y}_2(\cdot))$ is the dark kinked curve obtained by horizontally subtracting the follower's marginal cost c_2' from aggregate demand. It is zero above the price where c_2' crosses $D(p)$ and coincides with aggregate demand at prices below the vertical intercept of c_2'. Residual demand implies residual marginal revenue MR_1, the discontinuous dark curve that coincides with aggregate marginal revenue at quantities greater than the kink in the residual demand. The leader chooses quantity $\hat{y}_1$ (i.e., price p^e) where its marginal cost c_1' crosses residual marginal revenue. The follower then executes contingent plan $\hat{y}_2(p^e)$. The subgame perfect equilibrium strategy profile is $(p^e, \hat{y}_2(\cdot))$. Residual demand is shifted left from aggregate demand and is more price elastic, which induces the leader to set a price lower than a pure monopoly price p^m (assuming the follower(s) produce positive output at that pure monopoly price), thereby leading to equilibrium output $\hat{y}_1 + \hat{y}_2(p^e)$ above the pure monopoly level y^m. However, the price leader, being a type of monopolist, still prices above the competitive level where c_1' crosses demand (unless the price leader has substantially higher marginal cost than the follower(s), which would be a puzzling attribute for a dominant firm).

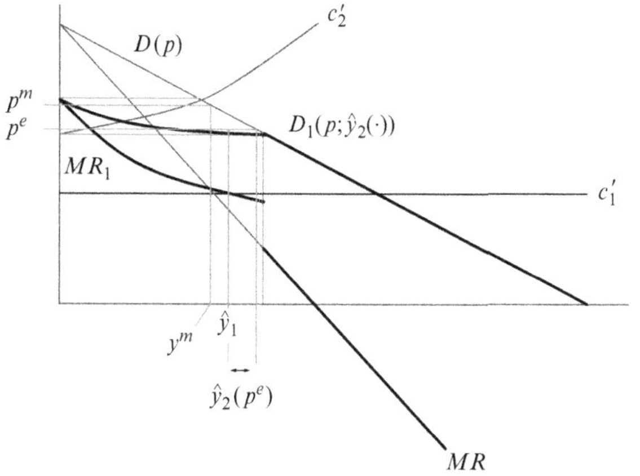

Fig. 15.7 Subgame perfect equilibrium in the dominant firm duopoly.

15.6 HORIZONTAL DIFFERENTIATION

All of the oligopoly models presented above assume the commodity under study is homogeneous from consumers' perspectives. All sales occur at *one* price because no completely informed consumer (with indirect utility strictly decreasing in price) will pay more than the lowest price for available quantity of a product the consumer regards as identical to some other quantity offered at a higher price.

Horizontal differentiation occurs when different firms' products are close substitutes but not identical from consumers' perspectives and no product is considered better than the alternatives by all consumers. Available quantities of the different products may be traded at different prices although the firms may still be in close competition. Horizontal differentiation concerns consumers' preferences, and is therefore modeled with relatively simple demand specifications that capture the main feature of two or more products regarded as close but imperfect substitutes. The two main types of demand specification used for this purpose are the *representative consumer* and *location (spatial)* models. The simplest versions of these models assume a duopoly, although there are many variants that consider entry and exit of firms and how firms might make choices about product variety.

15.6.1 Representative Consumer Horizontal Duopoly

Consider a consumer of closely related goods 1 and 2, and a third good representing an index of all other commodities not under immediate study and in which utility is quasilinear:

$$u(x_1, x_2, x_3) = \tilde{u}(x_1, x_2) + x_3.$$

If the two goods under study are a relatively small portion of the consumer's budget then we may presume $x_3 > 0$ at any optimum under study, in which case $\tilde{u}(x_1, x_2)$ is the gross Marshallian surplus from consumption of the quantities x_1 and x_2. Normalizing the price of x_3 to unity and substituting x_3 from the budget line leaves the consumer's optimization problem as:

$$\max_{(x_1,x_2)\in\mathbb{R}^2_+} \tilde{u}(x_1, x_2) - p_1x_1 - p_2x_2,$$

with first order condition $\mathbf{D}\tilde{u}(x_1, x_2) = (p_1, p_2)$ for an interior solution (the consumer's monetary resource is omitted because it has no effect on the optimum when $x_3 > 0$; $\tilde{u}$ is usually assumed to be concave).

Typically this type of model is used as a framework in which to study some aspects of a concentrated industry, so the simplest demand structure consistent with horizontal differentiation is often specified. For example, suppose the Marshallian surplus function is quadratic:

$$\tilde{u}(x_1, x_2) = \alpha_1x_1 + \alpha_2x_2 - \frac{1}{2}\left[\beta_1x_1^2 + 2\gamma x_1x_2 + \beta_2x_2^2\right],$$

where $\alpha_i, \beta_i > 0$ and $|\gamma| < \beta_i$ are preference parameters. Then the first order condition is $p_i = \alpha_i - \beta_ix_i - \gamma x_j$ for $i, j = 1, 2$ $(i \neq j)$. Hence this utility specification is a system of two linear inverse demand curves at an interior solution for the quantities (and nonnegative prices). Both inverse demands are downward-sloping. The assumption $|\gamma| < \beta_i$ ensures the impact of a change in x_i on its price p_i is of larger magnitude than a change in the other quantity. Inverting the system yields the Marshallian demands:

$$\hat{x}_i(p_i, p_j) = \frac{\beta_j(\alpha_i - p_i) - \gamma(\alpha_j - p_j)}{\beta_1\beta_2 - \gamma^2}$$

(when they are nonnegative). If $\gamma < 0$ the goods are complements because the demand for good i decreases when the price of good j increases. If

$\gamma > 0$ the goods are substitutes. The goods are unrelated to each other from a preference (demand) perspective if $\gamma = 0$.

If the equation above yields $\hat{x}_i < 0$ then the Marshallian demand for x_i is zero at the prices under consideration and the demand for x_j must be recalculated using $\hat{x}_i = 0$ to obtain $\hat{x}_j = \frac{1}{\beta_j}[\alpha_j - p_j]$. If $p_i > \alpha_i$ for $i = 1, 2$ then both optimal quantities are zero. The full Marshallian demand $(\hat{x}_1(p_1, p_2), \hat{x}_2(p_2, p_1))$ is therefore the equation above with these modifications for corner solutions.

Now consider a duopoly in which firm 1 sells good 1, firm 2 sells good 2, there are k consumers each of whom has the "representative" demand structure presented above, and the goods are substitutes ($\gamma > 0$) so that the firms are in competition with each other. Then firm i's demand is $D_i(p_i; p_j) = k\hat{x}_i(p_i, p_j)$. Note that demand for *both* commodities derives from *each* representative consumer. Individual consumers in this model are not sorting across firms with some consumers buying from firm 1 and other consumers buying from firm 2. Rather, every consumer buys from both firms (at an interior equilibrium). Nothing is gained nor lost by presuming there are $k > 1$ consumers, each with the quadratic utility function specified above. Thus we typically assume $k = 1$.

Depending on the industry under study, the duopoly could be specified as either Cournot-style (strategies are quantities) or Bertrand-style (strategies are prices). Consider first price competition. Then the strategy spaces are economically relevant prices $S_i = [0, \alpha_i]$ and the payoff functions are:

$$\pi_i(p_i; p_j) = p_i D_i(p_i; p_j) - c_i(D_i(p_i; p_j)).$$

For example, if marginal cost $c_i' \in [0, \alpha_i]$ is constant then setting $\frac{\partial \pi_i}{\partial p_i}$ to zero and solving for p_i yields (interior) best response function:

$$\hat{p}_i(p_j) = \frac{\beta_j(\alpha_i + c_i') - \gamma(\alpha_j - p_j)}{2\beta_j}.$$

Solving the two best responses simultaneously yields the Nash equilibrium:

$$p_i^e = \frac{2\beta_1\beta_2(\alpha_i + c_i') - \beta_i\gamma(\alpha_j - c_j') - \gamma^2\alpha_i}{4\beta_1\beta_2 - \gamma^2},$$

provided these prices are both positive and the quantities are both positive at these prices.

Note that the Bertrand-style best response function is upward-sloping, in contrast to the "standard" Cournot best response function shown in Fig. 15.4. This is a fundamental difference between quantity and price competition: Best responses are typically upward-sloping when firms' strategies are prices and typically downward-sloping when firms' strategies are quantities. The former is described by saying the strategies are *strategic complements* and the latter is described by saying the strategies are *strategic substitutes*. Price competition is often considered more intense than quantity competition because of strategic complementarity. When one firm cuts price to take more demand the other firm responds aggressively by cutting price as well, thereby taking back some of the lost demand. In contrast, when one firm increases quantity in Cournot competition the other firm responds passively by decreasing its own quantity, thereby dampening the impact on price of the rival's quantity increase.

Note also that firm i's equilibrium price typically exceeds marginal cost at an interior equilibrium. For example, if the firms are identical with $\beta_1 = \beta_2 = \beta$, $\alpha_1 = \alpha_2 = \alpha$, and $c_i' = c_j' = c'$ then the equilibrium price/cost margins are both:

$$p^e - c' = \frac{(2\beta^2 - \beta\gamma - \gamma^2)(\alpha - c')}{4\beta^2 - \gamma^2} > 0.$$

The Bertrand Paradox disappears when there is representative horizontal differentiation. This is because firms do not have discontinuous residual demands and therefore do not unilaterally benefit from the extreme price war characterized by Bertrand undercutting. Residual demands are continuous because consumers' preferences make good i desirable even when its price exceeds the price of good j. Note that $p^e - c'$ approaches zero as γ approaches β. That is, the equilibrium approaches the Bertrand Paradox as consumers regard the goods offered by two identical firms as nearly identical.

The Bertrand equilibrium prices are both increasing in marginal costs, as illustrated in Fig. 15.8. This occurs for two reasons. First, an increase in firm i's marginal cost shifts firm i's best response curve upward. Second, the slope of firm i's best response is:

$$\hat{p}_i'(p_j) = \frac{\gamma}{2\beta_j} < 1,$$

analogous to the Cournot best response slopes in Fig. 15.4 being greater than -1. The fact that firm 2's best response function is flatter than firm 1's best response in Fig. 15.8 is important in determining comparative static effects. An increase in marginal cost would *decrease* equilibrium prices if the best response curves crossed the other way. The relative slope configuration in Fig. 15.8 is sometimes called "stability" of the equilibrium, in reference to the following thought experiment: If $p_1 < p_1^e$ then firm 2's best response is below p_2^e, to which firm 1's best response is above the original p_1 and closer to p_1^e. Hence an infinite sequence of best responses would move prices toward the equilibrium (and similarly for any initial price), whereas the same infinite sequence of best responses would move prices away from the equilibrium if the best response curves crossed the other way. This is an intuitive thought experiment, but it is important to not take the story literally. The Nash Equilibrium in Fig. 15.8 is a purely static concept. There are no dynamics underlying the definition of the equilibrium. Hence the notion of "stability" is heuristic, at best. Note finally that if "stability" occurs because the slopes of the best responses are less than unity then there can be, at most, only one interior equilibrium; and the effect of an increase in c_i' is larger on p_i^e than on p_j^e.

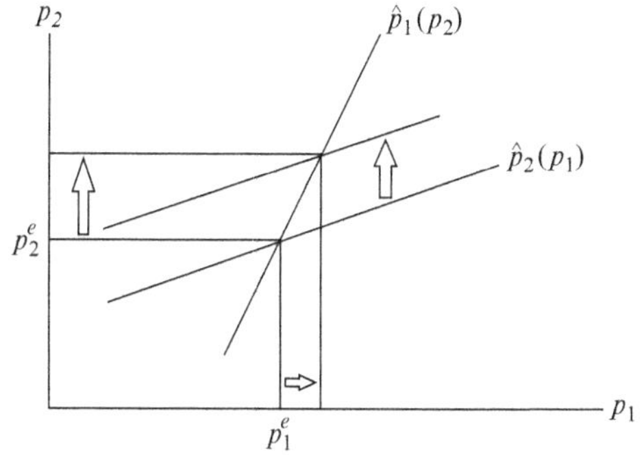

Fig. 15.8 Nash Equilibrium in the representative consumer differentiated Bertrand Duopoly. Arrows indicate the effects of an increase in firm 2's marginal cost.

The quantity competition version of the representative consumer differentiated duopoly specifies strategy spaces of economically relevant quantities $S_i = [0, \alpha_i/\beta_i]$ and payoff functions:

$$\pi_i(y_i; y_j) = p_i(y_i; y_j)y_i - c_i(y_i),$$

where $p_i(y_i; y_j)$ for $i, j = 1, 2$ $(i \neq j)$ are the inverses of the demand functions D_i, given by $p_i = \alpha_i - \beta_i y_i - \gamma y_j$ when $k = 1$, as described above (when the result is nonnegative). If marginal costs are constant it is again straightforward to derive the (interior) best response functions:

$$\hat{y}_i(y_j) = \frac{\alpha_i - c_i' - \gamma y_j}{2\beta_i}.$$

The Cournot best response functions retain their slope between −1 and 0 in the differentiated products version. Solving these best responses simultaneously yields the Nash Equilibrium when the solution is at positive quantities:

$$y_i^e = \frac{2\beta_j(\alpha_i - c_i') - \gamma(\alpha_j - c_j')}{4\beta_i\beta_j - \gamma^2}.$$

An increase in firm *i*'s marginal cost decreases firm *i*'s equilibrium quantity and increases firm *j*'s equilibrium quantity. This is illustrated in Fig. 15.9. Note that the conclusion depends on both the fact that the cost increase shifts firm *i*'s best response downward and that the best responses cross in a "stable" manner. Again stability occurs because the best response slopes are less than unity in magnitude, so there is, at most, one interior equilibrium and the effect of an increase in c_i' is larger in magnitude on y_i^e than on y_j^e.

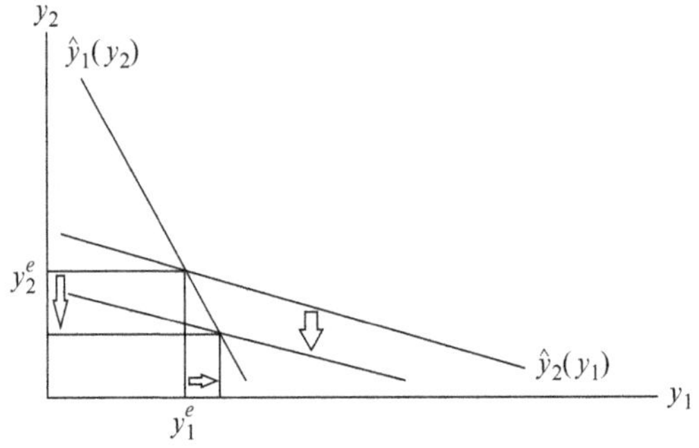

Fig. 15.9 Nash Equilibrium in the representative consumer differentiated Cournot Duopoly. Arrows indicate the effects of an increase in firm 2's marginal cost.

15.6.2 Spatial Horizontal Duopoly

One characteristic of the representative consumer horizontal duopoly is that each consumer buys both products in (an interior) equilibrium, an outcome innate to specification of a "representative" consumer. In contrast, differentiated demand could arise from consumers who have heterogeneous preferences for the two goods rather than from "representative" consumer(s). Preferences that are heterogenous may cause consumers to sort across firms, with some consumers buying from one firm while other consumers buy from the other firm in equilibrium. This comports with the empirical fact that for some types of goods consumers tend to buy from one favorite supplier, and firms in those industries seek to build their customer bases.

A heterogeneous consumer demand specification therefore begins with products that have idiosyncratic characteristics appealing to different consumers. Each firm produces a version of the product with a particular set of characteristics and this product appeals most to those consumers who like its particular characteristics. This is called a "location" or "spatial" model because we can think of the structure as consumers and firms located in some "space" of possible product characteristics. If prices of all products are equal, each consumer buys from the firm that is closest in the space of product characteristics. This gives firms some market power, as each firm can raise its price slightly above the level all other firms are charging and drive away only those consumers who are just far enough away in the product space to be indifferent between their current purchase and a purchase of some other firm's idiosyncratic product. Hence the residual demand discontinuity characteristic of homogeneous price competition need not arise. The Bertrand Paradox is ameliorated because heterogeneous consumers might not react as a herd to arbitrarily small price differences.

A spatial demand specification is formalized with the following utility structure. Each consumer receives quasilinear utility from consumption of three goods:

$$u(x_1, x_2, x_3) = \tilde{u}(x_1 + x_2) + x_3,$$

just as in the representative consumer model except that x_1 and x_2 enter $\tilde{u}$ as a sum and are therefore perfect substitutes (indifference curves in (x_1, x_2) space are linear with slope -1). The assumption $x_3 > 0$ at all outcomes under study is maintained, so each consumer seeks to maximize net Marshallian surplus:

$$\tilde{u}(x_1 + x_2) - p_1 x_1 - p_2 x_2,$$

again just as in the representative consumer model. The maximum involves consumption of only the low-price good because the goods are perfect substitutes (unless the prices are equal). Let $u^*(p)$ denote indirect utility received from consumption of one of the two goods at price p. Then the consumer buys exclusively from firm 1 if $u^*(p_1) > u^*(p_2)$ (i.e., if $p_1 < p_2$), and exclusively from firm 2 if $u^*(p_1) < u^*(p_2)$ (i.e., if $p_1 > p_2$). So far, this specification is exactly the homogeneous products Bertrand model.

Horizontal differentiation is introduced as follows. Each consumer is endowed with a "type" θ that represents the consumer's location in a one-dimensional product space. The length of the product space is arbitrary and unimportant, and is usually assumed to be one. Firms are also located in the product space, so there is a "distance" $d_i(\theta)$ between firm i and a consumer of type θ. This distance represents the extent of mismatch between the product offered by firm i and the consumer's ideal product (which would be of type θ). The mismatch imposes a cost on the consumer, typically represented as $td_i(\theta)$, making the parameter $t > 0$ the consumer cost per unit of mismatch distance. Consumer type θ's net Marshallian surplus is reduced by the mismatch cost $td_i(\theta)$ when the consumer buys from firm i. Therefore a consumer of type θ receives net surplus $u^*(p_i) - td_i(\theta)$ when buying from firm i. No consumer optimally buys from both firms, even when prices are equal, because doing so would incur *both* mismatch costs $td_1(\theta)$ and $td_2(\theta)$. When prices are equal the consumer could obtain the same utility from consumption without the redundant mismatch costs by making all purchases at one firm, because the products are perfect substitutes except for the mismatch costs. This structure is sometimes called a "shopping cost" model because of this feature—the mismatch costs are incurred per place of consumption, not per unit of consumption, as if there is a cost of traveling to a shopping place but once there the available products are identical to products available at the other shopping place.

By Roy's Identity, each consumer's Marshallian demand is $\hat{x}(p) = -u^{*\prime}(p)$ (the marginal utility of income is unity due to quasilinear utility). Firm i sells $\hat{x}(p_i)$ to each consumer of type θ satisfying:

$$u^*(p_i) - td_i(\theta) > \max\{u^*(p_j) - td_j(\theta), 0\}$$

(ties do not affect firms' profits unless there is a mass of consumer types who are indifferent). The aggregate of $\hat{x}(p_i)$ over all such consumers is decreasing in p_i and increasing in p_j, and is firm i's demand curve.

One version of the product space is the line segment $[0, 1]$, usually called the *linear city* because it can be interpreted as firms and consumers located throughout a line-segment city. In some urban economics models locations are thought of as literal geographic locations, but in general they can be any product characteristic and it is important to keep in mind that differences in locations are merely convenient metaphors for the extent of mismatch between a product offered for sale and a consumer's "ideal" product.

The simplest linear city has firm 1 located at 0 and firm 2 located at 1, consumer types uniformly distributed on the segment, and distance measured as the simple difference between a consumer's location and a firm's location. Then $d_1(\theta) = \theta$ and $d_2(\theta) = 1 - \theta$, and the consumer type $\hat{\theta}_i(p_i)$ who is just indifferent between buying from firm i and not buying is defined by:

$$u^*(p_1) - t\hat{\theta}_1(p_1) = 0, \quad u^*(p_2) - t(1 - \hat{\theta}_2(p_2)) = 0,$$

provided these values are in $[0, 1]$. Hence $\hat{\theta}_1(p_1) = \min\{u^*(p_1)/t, 1\}$ and $1 - \hat{\theta}_2(p_2) = \min\{u^*(p_2)/t, 1\}$. Similarly, the consumer type $\hat{\theta}(p_1, p_2)$ who is just indifferent between the two firms is defined by:

$$u^*(p_1) - t\hat{\theta}(p_1, p_2) = u^*(p_2) - t(1 - \hat{\theta}(p_1, p_2)), \text{ or:}$$

$$\hat{\theta}(p_1, p_2) = \frac{1}{2} + \frac{u^*(p_1) - u^*(p_2)}{2t}.$$

The firms' demands are then:

$$D_1(p_1; p_2) = \hat{x}(p_1) \min\{\hat{\theta}_1(p_1), \hat{\theta}(p_1, p_2)\}$$
$$D_2(p_2; p_1) = \hat{x}(p_2)(1 - \max\{\hat{\theta}_2(p_2), \hat{\theta}(p_1, p_2)\}).$$

This is illustrated in Fig. 15.10. As $\hat{\theta}(p_1, p_2) \leq \hat{\theta}_1(p_1)$ if and only if $\hat{\theta}(p_1, p_2) \geq \hat{\theta}_2(p_2)$, when the extent of firm i's consumers is given by $\hat{\theta}_i(p_i)$ the situation is called "local monopolies" because there is a group

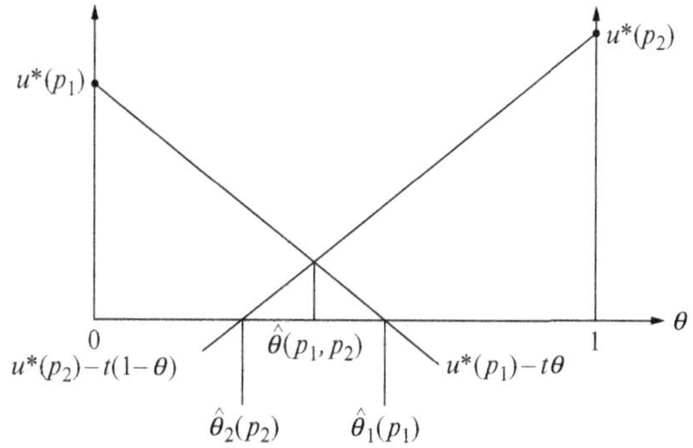

Fig. 15.10 Welfare possibilities in the linear city with linear distance measure. Firm 1 is located at the left end of the city. The axis there measures the indirect utility a consumer located at θ receives when a purchase is made from firm 1. Firm 2 is located at the right end of the city. The axis there measures the indirect utility a consumer located at θ receives when a purchase is made from firm 2. Each welfare line decreases with slope $-t$ as the consumer's location becomes more distant from the firm. Full coverage is illustrated, but higher prices would shift each welfare line downward, eventually creating local monopolies with $\hat{\theta}_1(p_1) < \hat{\theta}(p_1, p_2) < \hat{\theta}_2(p_2)$.

of consumers in the middle of the city who chose to not buy, so a small change in p_i has no effect on firm j's demand. When $\hat{\theta}(p_1, p_2)$ measures the extent of both firms' consumers the situation is called "full coverage" because every consumer in the city buys from one firm or the other, and the firms are competing even over small changes in prices. There is little reason to specify a duopoly model that does not entail competition between the firms, so a common assumption is that u^* is large enough at all prices under consideration to ensure full coverage.

An aspect of the linear city is that firms' locations can materially affect the nature of competition. Suppose firm 1 were located at $L \in (0, 1)$ instead of at 0 and there is full coverage. Then consumers left of L would have to travel past firm 1 to make a purchase from firm 2. With distance measured as a simple difference, if it is beneficial for one such consumer to do so then it is beneficial for all such consumers to do so. This recreates the problem of discontinuous residual demand because there is a mass of consumers who are indifferent between the firms at some price pairs. For a given value of p_1, firm 2's residual demand jumps at the value of p_2 that makes consumers left of firm 1 just indifferent between buying from firm 1 or passing firm 1 to buy from firm 2. There is a jump because the entire segment $[0, L]$ of consumer types make the same decision at every price pair—they all either buy from firm 1 or bypass firm 1 to buy from firm 2. These discontinuities create existence problems for pure strategy equilibria, especially in two stage games that have firms making location decisions before engaging in price competition. One way to address such problems is to assume distance is measured as the square (or some other strictly convex function) of the difference between the consumers' and firms' locations. The mismatch cost is, after all, a rather arbitrary specification merely intended as a simple parameterization of consumer heterogeneity.

Another way to address the problem is to consider a product space that does not have edges, such as a circle. A *circular city* may be more appropriate when a change in product characteristics that makes one firm's product less similar to another firm's product in some ways makes the two products more similar in other ways. Like the linear city, the standard circular city has length (circumference) arbitrarily set to unity, consumers uniformly distributed on the circle, and mismatch cost $td_i(\theta)$ for a consumer of type θ who buys from firm i; with $d_i(\theta)$ the simple difference between the consumer's location and firm i's location (along the circle). Suppose location 0 is arbitrarily placed at the top of the circle and distance is measured clockwise. Equally arbitrarily, assume firm 1 is located at position 0 and let L

denote the location of firm 2. Under full coverage, there are two consumer types who are just indifferent between the two firms—one between 0 and L and one between L and 1 (location 1 is back at the top of the circle). The consumer type $\hat{\theta}_1(p_1, p_2)$ between 0 and L who is just indifferent between the two firms is defined by:

$$u^*(p_1) - t\hat{\theta}_1(p_1, p_2) = u^*(p_2) - t(L - \hat{\theta}_1(p_1, p_2)), \text{ or:}$$

$$\hat{\theta}_1(p_1, p_2) = \frac{u^*(p_1) - u^*(p_2)}{2t} + \frac{L}{2}.$$

Similarly, the consumer type $\hat{\theta}_2(p_1, p_2)$ between L and 1 who is just indifferent between the two firms is defined by:

$$u^*(p_1) - t(1 - \hat{\theta}_2(p_1, p_2)) = u^*(p_2) - t(\hat{\theta}_2(p_1, p_2) - L), \text{ or:}$$

$$\hat{\theta}_2(p_1, p_2) = \frac{u^*(p_2) - u^*(p_1)}{2t} + \frac{1 + L}{2}.$$

Firm 1 sells $\hat{x}(p_1)$ to each consumer between 0 and $\hat{\theta}_1(p_1, p_2)$ and each consumer between $\hat{\theta}_2(p_1, p_2)$ and 1. Therefore firm 1's demand is:

$$\begin{aligned} D_1(p_1; p_2) &= \hat{x}(p_1)[\hat{\theta}_1(p_1, p_2) + (1 - \hat{\theta}_2(p_1, p_2))] \\ &= \hat{x}(p_1)\left[\frac{1}{2} + \frac{u^*(p_1) - u^*(p_2)}{t}\right]. \end{aligned}$$

Similarly, firm 2 sells $\hat{x}(p_2)$ to each consumer between $\hat{\theta}_1(p_1, p_2)$ and L and each consumer between L and $\hat{\theta}_2(p_1, p_2)$, so firm 2's demand is:

$$\begin{aligned} D_2(p_2; p_1) &= \hat{x}(p_2)[\hat{\theta}_2(p_1, p_2) - \hat{\theta}_1(p_1, p_2)] \\ &= \hat{x}(p_2)\left[\frac{1}{2} + \frac{u^*(p_2) - u^*(p_1)}{t}\right]. \end{aligned}$$

This is illustrated in Fig. 15.11.

Note that firms' demands in the circular city are identical to firms' demands in the linear city with firms located at the endpoints, except that t replaces $2t$ in the denominator of the former. This is because there are two margins of consumer response in the circular city, and is of no consequence because the parameter t is arbitrary. Hence analysis of (full coverage) equilibrium does not depend on which representation of the product space is utilized.

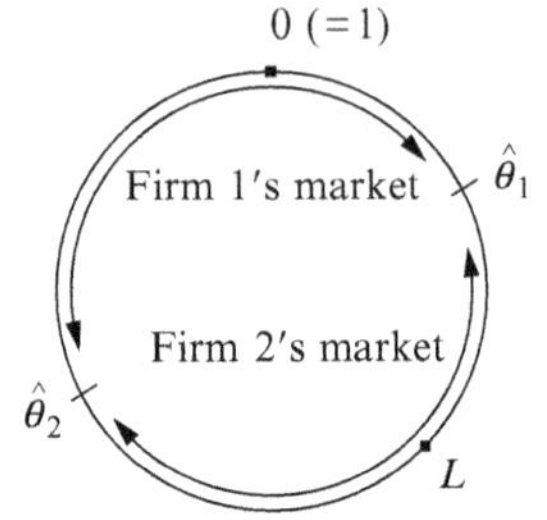

Fig. 15.11 Market division in the circular city with linear distance measure and full coverage. The figure assumes $p_1 = p_2$. Both marginal consumers move toward firm i's location as p_i increases relative to p_j.

A standard simplifying assumption is that gross Marshallian surplus has the discrete form:

$$\tilde{u}(x_1 + x_2) = \begin{cases} R & \text{if } x_1 + x_2 \geq 1 \\ 0 & \text{otherwise} \end{cases}.$$

Here, $R > 0$ is called the consumers' *reservation value.* Each consumer buys one and only one unit of the product at prices below this reservation value and buys nothing at prices above this reservation value (usually we break ties by assuming consumers buy one unit when price equals the reservation value). This means indirect utility is $u^*(p) = \max\{R - p, 0\}$, individual consumer demand is $\hat{x}(p) = 1$ if $p \leq R$ and $\hat{x}(p) = 0$ if $p > R$, $\hat{\theta}(p_1, p_2) = \frac{1}{2} + \frac{p_2 - p_1}{2t}$, and the firms' demands take the particularly simple form:

$$D_i(p_i; p_j) = \frac{1}{2} + \frac{p_j - p_i}{2t}$$

at prices low enough to ensure full coverage. This "unit demand" specification of utility is useful for studying many aspects of competition when there is horizontal differentiation because the firms' demands are so simple, but it should be used with caution. It can be misleading, for example, to use this specification in welfare analyses because the perfectly inelastic consumer demands at prices below R preclude the possibility of Marshallian deadweight loss when prices exceed marginal costs but full coverage is maintained. There can be inefficient welfare outcomes with this demand specification due to mismatch costs, but not due to high (full coverage) prices.

A full derivation of equilibrium in the linear city is straightforward with the unit demand specification. We have:

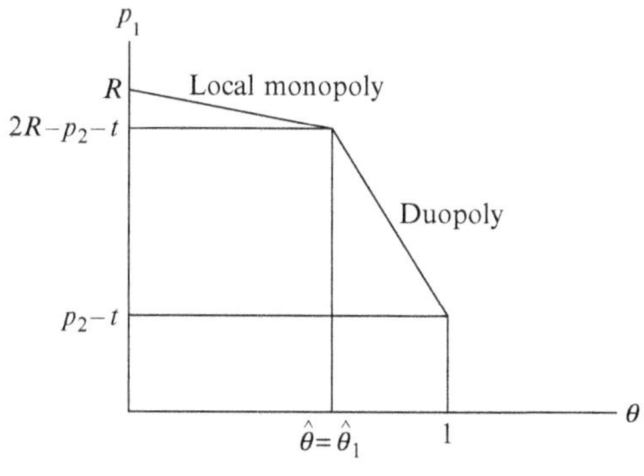

Fig. 15.12 Linear city demand for firm 1.

$$\hat{\theta}_1(p_1) = \frac{R-p_1}{t} \quad \text{and} \quad \hat{\theta}_2(p_2) = 1 - \frac{R-p_2}{t}.$$

Thus, the firms' demand curves are:

$$D_1(p_1; p_2) = \begin{cases} 1, & p_1 \le p_2 - t \\ \hat{\theta}(p_1, p_2), & p_2 - t < p_1 < 2R - p_2 - t \\ \hat{\theta}_1(p_1), & 2R - p_2 - t \le p_1 < R \\ 0, & R \le p_1, \end{cases}$$

$$D_2(p_2; p_1) = \begin{cases} 1, & p_2 \le p_1 - t \\ 1 - \hat{\theta}(p_1, p_2), & p_1 - t < p_2 < 2R - p_1 - t \\ 1 - \hat{\theta}_2(p_2), & 2R - p_1 - t \le p_2 < R \\ 0, & R \le p_2 \end{cases}.$$

Firm 1's demand is illustrated in Fig. 15.12. When p_1 is high, demand is $\hat{\theta}_1$ and firm 1 is a "local monopolist" because there is a buffer of consumers in the middle of the city who are not purchasing, so a small decrease in p_2 merely attracts some of those unserved consumers to firm 2. When p_1 is lower, the duopolists are competing with each other in the sense that a price decrease by either firm decreases the demand of the other firm. Finally, when p_1 is very low, firm 1 has captured the entire market and so demand is 1. It is clear that firm 1 will never charge less than $p_2 - t$, since no additional demand is generated at prices lower than this.

Now suppose the firms are symmetric with constant marginal cost. Nothing is lost by assuming marginal cost is zero, in which case the firms choose prices to maximize revenue. That is, firm 1 seeks to:

$$\max_{\{p_1 \in [0,R]\}} \pi_1(p_1; p_2) = p_1 D_1(p_1; p_2),$$

and firm 2 seeks to maximize an analogous objective. The derivative of firm 1's profit is:

$$\frac{\partial \pi_1}{\partial p_1} = \begin{cases} \frac{p_2 - 2p_1 + t}{2t}, & p_2 - t < p_1 < 2R - p_2 - t \\ \frac{R - 2p_1}{t}, & 2R - p_2 - t < p_1 < R \end{cases}.$$

Since the firms are symmetric, we can look for a symmetric Nash Equilibrium in the prices. Setting $p_1 = p_2$ in this derivative yields:

$$\frac{\partial \pi_1}{\partial p_1} = \begin{cases} \frac{t - p_1}{2t}, & p_2 - t < p_1 < 2R - p_2 - t \\ \frac{R - 2p_1}{t}, & 2R - p_2 - t < p_1 < R \end{cases}.$$

At the kink in firm 1's demand curve, $p_1 = p_2 = R - \frac{t}{2}$, in which case:

$$\frac{\partial \pi_1}{\partial p_1} = \begin{cases} \frac{\frac{3}{2}t - R}{2t}, & \text{for price decreases} \\ \frac{t - R}{t}, & \text{for price increases.} \end{cases}$$

Thus, if $1 \leq \frac{R}{t} \leq \frac{3}{2}$ then a symmetric equilibrium occurs at the kink in the demand curve and $p_1 = p_2 = R - \frac{t}{2}$ are the equilibrium prices. If $\frac{R}{t} < 1$ then firm 1's optimum occurs along the monopoly portion of the demand curve and the symmetric equilibrium prices are found by setting the derivative there to zero, which yields $p_1 = p_2 = \frac{R}{2}$. In this case $\hat{\theta}_1 = \frac{R}{2t} < \frac{1}{2}$ in equilibrium and $\hat{\theta}_2 > \frac{1}{2}$, so the symmetric Nash Equilibrium involves two local monopolies. If $\frac{R}{t} > \frac{3}{2}$ then firm 1's optimum occurs along the duopoly portion of the demand curve and the symmetric equilibrium prices are found by setting the derivative there to zero, which yields $p_1 = p_2 = t$. In this case $\hat{\theta} = \frac{1}{2}$ and the Nash Equilibrium involves competition between the duopolists.

Note that this last case applies as $t \to 0$, and the equilibrium prices approach zero along with t. This is because the mismatch cost t is the only feature that differentiates the products in this model. As t approaches zero, the duopolists' products begin to look identical to all consumers, and so the model is approaching the homogeneous-products price competition model (i.e., pure Bertrand competition). Accordingly, the equilibrium prices approach the Bertrand equilibrium prices, which are equal to marginal cost (zero in the model specified here). Thus we see that *more substantial product differentiation softens price competition and allows firms to extract positive profit.* Marshallian deadweight loss from this market power occurs in this model if the "local monopoly" equilibrium occurs (when mismatch costs are high relative to the consumption value of the good), since at least some of the consumers in the middle of the city would consume a unit of the good if the prices were zero, but not if the monopoly equilibrium occurs.

There are many variations on the linear city model useful for studying different phenomena. A quadratic distance measure makes distant purchases relatively more costly and can be used to smooth consumer responses to price differences. The interpretation is that product differentiation becomes more severe as a product's characteristics depart from a consumer's ideal characteristics. An initial stage can be added in which firms choose their locations in the city. This leads to two conflicting effects in firms' location decisions. First, firms want to locate as far as possible from each other to soften the ensuing price competition as much as possible. This phenomena is known as *the principle of maximal differentiation*, and leads firms to locate at the ends of the city as in the simple model studied here. However, locations like this cause some consumers to travel farther than necessary to obtain the good. Clearly aggregate mismatch costs would be minimized if the firms located at $\frac{1}{4}$ and $\frac{3}{4}$ rather than at the ends of the city. Excessive mismatch cost is deadweight loss that some firm may be able to capture by changing its location. In some types of models, the benefits of attracting more consumers by moving closer to a competitor in the characteristics space outweigh the benefits of softened price competition obtained by moving as far as possible from competitors. In such cases, differentiation may still occur but it will not be maximal. Moreover, the main motive for maximal differentiation is to soften price competition. When there is no price competition, the *principle of minimal differentiation* arises. This principle says that, when firms can only compete on characteristics, they move as close together as possible since they are only competing over the consumers who are located between them. This may explain why political candidates sometimes take positions that are not very different from each other (in the political context, we say that candidates may target the median voter and therefore call such a model the *median voter model*). Other variants of the linear city study mismatch costs that are incurred per unit of consumption rather than per place of consumption, or prices that vary by consumer type.

15.7 VERTICAL DIFFERENTIATION

Product differentiation occurs when different firms' products are close substitutes but not identical from consumers' perspectives. The differentiation studied in the previous section is called horizontal because no product is considered better than the alternatives by all consumers. In contrast, *vertical differentiation* occurs when all consumers share the same ordering of relative desirability among the products. Relatively high desirability is usually labeled high "quality." Available quantities of different products must be traded at different prices although the firms may still be in close competition, because if prices are equal then all consumers will buy the highest quality product. Like horizontal differentiation, vertical differentiation concerns consumers' preferences and is therefore modeled with relatively simple demand specifications that capture the main feature of two or more products regarded as close but imperfect substitutes with a clear quality ranking.

Consider again the quasilinear utility specification with perfect substitutes given by $u(x_1, x_2, x_3) = \tilde{u}(x_1 + x_2) + x_3$. Vertical differentiation can be introduced by designating $\Delta > 0$ as the quality advantage of good 1 relative to good 2 and consumer types θ who differ in the strength of their preference for high quality. $\Delta\theta$ then measures the additional (money-valued) utility a consumer of type $\theta > 0$ receives from consuming a unit of the high-quality product. If the prices are p_1 and p_2 the net surplus consumer type θ receives from the bundle (x_1, x_2) is:

$$\tilde{u}(x_1 + x_2) + \Delta\theta x_1 - p_1 x_1 - p_2 x_2.$$

The quality advantage plays the role of a price reduction in this specification. Consumer type θ pays "effective" prices $(p_1 - \Delta\theta)$ for good 1 and p_2 for good 2. As the goods are otherwise perfect substitutes, consumer type θ buys good 1 exclusively when the effective price ratio $\frac{p_1 - \Delta\theta}{p_2}$ is less than one and buys good 2 exclusively when the effective price ratio exceeds one. The consumer type who is indifferent between the two goods is therefore:

$$\hat{\theta}(p_1, p_2) = \frac{p_1 - p_2}{\Delta}.$$

Consumer types $\theta > \hat{\theta}$ purchase the high quality good 1 and consumer types $\theta < \hat{\theta}$ purchase the low quality good 2. Still letting $u^*(p)$ denote the indirect utility received from consumption of one of the two goods at effective price p, each consumer's (interior) demand is again $\hat{x}(p) = -u^{*\prime}(p)$ by Roy's Identity. Assuming θ is uniformly distributed on an interval of positive values $[\underline{\theta}, \bar{\theta}]$, the firms' demands are therefore:

$$D_1(p_1; p_2) = \int_{\hat{\theta}(p_1, p_2)}^{\bar{\theta}} \hat{x}(p_1 - \Delta\theta)\, d\theta$$

$$D_2(p_2; p_1) = \hat{x}(p_2)[\hat{\theta}(p_1, p_2) - \underline{\theta}].$$

This specification assumes $\hat{\theta}(p_1, p_2) \in [\underline{\theta}, \bar{\theta}]$, so that neither firm is foreclosed, and that the consumers of low quality receive positive surplus ($u^*(p_2) \geq 0$, where u^* is indirect utility). Performing the change of variable $v = p_1 - \Delta\theta$ in D_1 and using Roy's Identity (i.e., $u^{*\prime}(p) = -\hat{x}(p)$) yields:

$$D_1(p_1; p_2) = \frac{u^*(p_1 - \Delta\bar{\theta}) - u^*(p_2)}{\Delta}.$$

That is, demand for the high quality good is the additional net surplus per unit of quality the most quality-loving consumer receives by consuming the high-quality product.

If firm i has constant marginal cost c_i' then profits are:

$$\pi_1(p_1; p_2) = (p_1 - c_1')\frac{u^*(p_1 - \Delta\bar{\theta}) - u^*(p_2)}{\Delta}$$
$$\pi_2(p_2; p_1) = (p_2 - c_2')\hat{x}(p_2)[\hat{\theta}(p_1, p_2) - \underline{\theta}].$$

Vertically differentiated price competition is then modeled as a Nash Equilibrium between duopolists with payoff functions π_i defined on strategy spaces of economically relevant prices $S_1 = [0, u^{*-1}(0) + \Delta\bar{\theta}]$ and $S_2 = [0, u^{*-1}(0)]$. The first order conditions for an interior equilibrium are:

$$\frac{\partial \pi_1}{\partial p_1} = \frac{1}{\Delta}[u^*(p_1 - \Delta\bar{\theta}) - u^*(p_2) - (p_1 - c_1')\hat{x}(p_1 - \Delta\bar{\theta})] = 0$$
$$\frac{\partial \pi_2}{\partial p_2} = \frac{1}{\Delta}\left[\hat{x}(p_2)[(p_1 - \Delta\underline{\theta}) - p_2] + (p_2 - c_2')[\hat{x}'(p_2)[(p_1 - \Delta\underline{\theta}) - p_2] - \hat{x}(p_2)]\right] = 0.$$

We must have $\frac{\partial^2 \pi_i}{\partial p_i^2} \leq 0$ at such an equilibrium. Assume these second order conditions hold strictly so standard comparative statics methodology can be applied to the first order conditions. Then the best response slopes are:

$$\hat{p}_i'(p_j) = \frac{\frac{\partial^2 \pi_i}{\partial p_i \partial p_j}}{-\frac{\partial^2 \pi_i}{\partial p_i^2}} \stackrel{s}{=} \frac{\partial^2 \pi_i}{\partial p_i \partial p_j}$$
$$= \begin{cases} \frac{\hat{x}(p_2)}{\Delta} > 0, & \text{if } i = 1,\ j = 2 \\ \frac{1}{\Delta}[\hat{x}(p_2) + (p_2 - c_2')\hat{x}'(p_2)] > 0, & \text{if } i = 2,\ j = 1 \end{cases}$$

(the sign of $\hat{p}_2'(p_1)$ is implied by firm 2's first order condition). Hence we once again have strategic complementarity when suppliers of substitute products engage in price competition. Also, as is typical under price competition, a cost increase shifts that firm's best response curve upward:

$$\frac{\partial \hat{p}_i(p_j)}{\partial c_i'} = \frac{\frac{\partial^2 \pi_i}{\partial p_i \partial c_i'}}{-\frac{\partial^2 \pi_i}{\partial p_i^2}} \overset{s}{=} \frac{\partial^2 \pi_i}{\partial p_i \partial c_i'}$$

$$= \begin{cases} \frac{\hat{x}(p_1 - \Delta\bar{\theta})}{\Delta} > 0 & \text{if } i = 1,\ j = 2 \\ \frac{1}{\Delta}[\hat{x}(p_2) - \hat{x}'(p_2)[(p_1 - \Delta\underline{\theta}) - p_2]] > 0 & \text{if } i = 2,\ j = 1 \end{cases}.$$

Hence a cost increase causes both equilibrium prices to increase if the equilibrium is "stable" (see Fig. 15.8). The standard sufficient condition for stability is that each best response slope be less than unity. That is, $\frac{\partial^2 \pi_i}{\partial p_i \partial p_j} < -\frac{\partial^2 \pi_i}{\partial p_i^2}$ for $i, j = 1, 2$ $(i \neq j)$.

Interesting predictions from this model include (1) whether the high-quality firm earns more profit than the low-quality firm, (2) whether profits increase as the quality differential Δ increases so that firms have incentives to differentiate their qualities, (3) what happens when a firm is foreclosed (i.e., when $\hat{\theta}$ falls outside the support $[\underline{\theta}, \bar{\theta}]$), and (4) what happens as consumers' preferences about quality become more disparate. Definitive answers to most of these questions require simplifying assumptions but a few observations can be made about the general case.

Let (p_1^e, p_2^e) denote a simultaneous solution to the first order conditions (i.e., an interior equilibrium price pair) and (π_1^e, π_2^e) denote the corresponding equilibrium profits. Using the tangency property of the Envelope Theorem:

$$\frac{d\pi_i^e}{d\Delta} = \frac{\partial \pi_i}{\partial \Delta} + \frac{\partial \pi_i}{\partial p_j}\frac{\partial p_j^e}{\partial \Delta}$$

$$= \begin{cases} (p_1^e - c_1')\left[\frac{-1}{\Delta^2}[u^*(p_1^e - \Delta\bar{\theta}) - u^*(p_2^e) - \hat{x}(p_1^e - \Delta\bar{\theta})\Delta\bar{\theta}] + \frac{\hat{x}(p_2^e)}{\Delta}\frac{\partial p_2^e}{\partial \Delta}\right], & i = 1 \\ (p_2^e - c_2')\frac{\hat{x}(p_2^e)}{\Delta^2}\left[-(p_1^e - p_2^e) + \Delta\frac{\partial p_1^e}{\partial \Delta}\right], & i = 2 \end{cases}.$$

Using Roy's Identity, the mean-value theorem can be used to show $\frac{\partial \pi_1}{\partial \Delta} > 0$. And $\frac{\partial \pi_2}{\partial \Delta} \overset{s}{=} p_2^e - p_1^e < 0$. Hence we have the following conclusions: An increase in the quality differential increases profit of the high-quality firm provided the low-quality firm does not cut its price "too much;" and decreases profit of the low-quality firm provided the high-quality firm does not raise its price "too much." Unfortunately, the price effects are ambiguous at this level of generality but these conclusions can be tightened in the important special case of unit demands (considered below).

Similarly,

$$\frac{d\pi_i^e}{d\bar{\theta}} = \frac{\partial \pi_i}{\partial \bar{\theta}} + \frac{\partial \pi_i}{\partial p_j}\frac{\partial p_j^e}{\partial \bar{\theta}} = (p_i^e - c_i')\frac{\partial D_i}{\partial p_j}\frac{\partial p_j^e}{\partial \bar{\theta}} + \begin{cases} (p_1^e - c_1')\hat{x}(p_1^e - \Delta\bar{\theta}), & i = 1 \\ 0, & i = 2 \end{cases}$$

$$\frac{d\pi_i^e}{d\underline{\theta}} = \frac{\partial \pi_i}{\partial \underline{\theta}} + \frac{\partial \pi_i}{\partial p_j}\frac{\partial p_j^e}{\partial \underline{\theta}} = (p_i^e - c_i')\frac{\partial D_i}{\partial p_j}\frac{\partial p_j^e}{\partial \underline{\theta}} + \begin{cases} 0, & i = 1 \\ -(p_2^e - c_2')\hat{x}(p_2^e), & i = 2 \end{cases}.$$

Hence an increase in the spread of consumer types (higher $\bar{\theta}$ and/or lower $\underline{\theta}$) increases the profit of both firms provided equilibrium prices increase when $\bar{\theta}$ increases and/or $\underline{\theta}$ decreases. The interpretation is that a wider spread of consumer preferences gives each firm a market niche and thereby softens competition. The price effects of more consumer disparity are "almost" determinate. Differentiating the system of first order conditions with respect to the supports of the distribution yields the standard comparative statics equation:

$$\begin{bmatrix} \frac{\partial^2 \pi_1}{\partial p_1^2} & \frac{\partial^2 \pi_1}{\partial p_1 \partial p_2} \\ \frac{\partial^2 \pi_2}{\partial p_2 \partial p_1} & \frac{\partial^2 \pi_2}{\partial p_2^2} \end{bmatrix} \begin{bmatrix} \frac{\partial p_1^e}{\partial \underline{\theta}} & \frac{\partial p_1^e}{\partial \bar{\theta}} \\ \frac{\partial p_2^e}{\partial \underline{\theta}} & \frac{\partial p_2^e}{\partial \bar{\theta}} \end{bmatrix} = - \begin{bmatrix} \frac{\partial^2 \pi_1}{\partial p_1 \partial \underline{\theta}} & \frac{\partial^2 \pi_1}{\partial p_1 \partial \bar{\theta}} \\ \frac{\partial^2 \pi_2}{\partial p_2 \partial \underline{\theta}} & \frac{\partial^2 \pi_2}{\partial p_2 \partial \bar{\theta}} \end{bmatrix}.$$

The first matrix is the Jacobian J of the system of first order conditions with respect to prices and its determinant is:

$$|J| = \frac{\partial^2 \pi_1}{\partial p_1^2}\frac{\partial^2 \pi_2}{\partial p_2^2} - \frac{\partial^2 \pi_1}{\partial p_1 \partial p_2}\frac{\partial^2 \pi_2}{\partial p_2 \partial p_1}.$$

Assume the equilibrium is "stable" so that $|J| > 0$. The matrix on the right side is:

$$\begin{bmatrix} 0 & -[\hat{x}(p_1^e - \Delta\bar{\theta}) + (p_1^e - c_1')\hat{x}'(p_1^e - \Delta\bar{\theta})] \\ \hat{x}(p_2^e) + (p_2^e - c_2')\hat{x}'(p_2^e) & 0 \end{bmatrix}.$$

Firm 2's first order condition implies the $(2, 1)$ element is positive. The $(1, 2)$ element is the marginal profit firm 1 earns from the most quality-loving consumer. Concave individual consumer demand implies this is positive at an interior optimum (this demand property is consistent with firm 1's second order condition). Assuming so, standard applications of

Cramer's Rule yield $\frac{\partial p_i^e}{\partial \underline{\theta}} < 0$ and $\frac{\partial p_i^e}{\partial \bar{\theta}} > 0$ for $i = 1, 2$. That is, increases in the spread of consumer preferences benefit both firms.

As in the spatial horizontal duopoly, a standard simplifying assumption in vertical differentiation models is that gross Marshallian surplus has the discrete form:

$$\tilde{u}(x_1 + x_2) = \begin{cases} R & \text{if } x_1 + x_2 \geq 1 \\ 0 & \text{otherwise} \end{cases}.$$

If the quality premium for consumer type θ is also changed to the discrete form $\Delta\theta$ when $x_1 \geq 1$ (and zero otherwise) then unit demands are generated:

$$\hat{x}(p) = \begin{cases} 1, & \text{if } R \geq p \\ 0, & \text{if } R < p \end{cases}$$

and indirect utility is $u^*(p) = R - p$, where p is the "effective" (quality-adjusted) price. Again it is important to recognize that the unit demand specification can be misleading for welfare analyses because there is no potential for Marshallian deadweight loss when individual demands are perfectly inelastic and there is full coverage.

The profit objectives in the unit demand case are:

$$\pi_1(p_1; p_2) = \frac{p_1 - c_1'}{\Delta}[p_2 - (p_1 - \Delta\bar{\theta})]$$

$$\pi_2(p_2; p_1) = \frac{p_2 - c_2'}{\Delta}[(p_1 - \Delta\underline{\theta}) - p_2],$$

which lead to best responses:

$$\hat{p}_1(p_2) = \frac{p_2 + c_1' + \Delta\bar{\theta}}{2}$$

$$\hat{p}_2(p_1) = \frac{p_1 + c_2' - \Delta\underline{\theta}}{2}.$$

Note that their slopes are $1/2$, so an interior equilibrium is indeed stable with unit demands. The best responses intersect at interior equilibrium prices:

$$p_1^e = \frac{2c_1' + c_2' + \Delta(2\bar{\theta} - \underline{\theta})}{3}$$

$$p_2^e = \frac{2c_2' + c_1' + \Delta(\bar{\theta} - 2\underline{\theta})}{3}.$$

The full coverage condition $u^*(p_2^e) \geq 0$ is $R \geq [2c_2' + c_1' + \Delta(\bar{\theta} - 2\underline{\theta})]$ in the unit demand case. This is satisfied provided consumers' reservation value R is sufficiently high. The interiority condition $\underline{\theta} \leq \hat{\theta}(p_1^e, p_2^e) \leq \bar{\theta}$ is:

$$\Delta(2\underline{\theta} - \bar{\theta}) \leq c_1' - c_2' \leq \Delta(2\bar{\theta} - \underline{\theta}).$$

We might expect that quality is costly, in which case $c_1' \geq c_2'$. The left side of the interiority condition then requires that the spread of consumers' quality preferences be large relative to the cost of quality. Otherwise, the low-quality firm is foreclosed in equilibrium because the high quality firm does not lose much by cutting price enough to attract all consumers to the high-quality option. The right side of the interiority condition requires that quality not cost too much relative to the spread of consumers' quality preferences. Otherwise, the high-quality firm is foreclosed in equilibrium because quality is too costly.

Assuming the full coverage and interiority conditions are satisfied, the equilibrium price responses to changes in the quality differential are:

$$\frac{\partial p_1^e}{\partial \Delta} = \frac{2\bar{\theta} - \underline{\theta}}{3} > 0$$
$$\frac{\partial p_2^e}{\partial \Delta} = \frac{\bar{\theta} - 2\underline{\theta}}{3}.$$

The latter is nonnegative from the interiority condition when $c_1' = c_2'$ but can be negative at an interior equilibrium when quality is costly. These price responses leave open the question of whether an increase in the quality differential increases firms' profits. It is straightforward to substitute the equilibrium prices into the profit expressions to obtain:

$$\pi_1^e = \frac{1}{9\Delta}[\Delta(2\bar{\theta} - \underline{\theta}) - (c_1' - c_2')]^2$$
$$\pi_2^e = \frac{1}{9\Delta}[(c_1' - c_2') - \Delta(2\underline{\theta} - \bar{\theta})]^2.$$

Thus:

$$\frac{d\pi_1^e}{d\Delta} = \frac{1}{9\Delta^2}[\Delta(2\bar{\theta} - \underline{\theta}) - (c_1' - c_2')][(c_1' - c_2') - \Delta(\underline{\theta} - 2\bar{\theta})] > 0$$
$$\frac{d\pi_2^e}{d\Delta} = \frac{1}{9\Delta^2}[(c_1' - c_2') + \Delta(\bar{\theta} - 2\underline{\theta})][\Delta(\bar{\theta} - 2\underline{\theta}) - (c_1' - c_2')].$$

Hence the potential cut in firm 2's price in response to an increase in the quality differential is not strong enough to offset the direct benefit to the high-quality firm. However, although the first bracketed term of $\frac{d\pi_2^e}{d\Delta}$ is positive at an interior equilibrium, the second bracketed term can be negative when quality is costly. In this case it is possible that the low-quality firm's profit decreases when the quality differential increases. This can occur when the appeal of quality to the consumer with the least preference for quality increases faster than the high-quality firm's price.

It is straightforward to confirm that both firms indeed benefit from an increase in the spread of consumer types when there are unit demands.

If quality is not too costly then the high-quality firm earns more profit in equilibrium:

$$\pi_1^e - \pi_2^e = \frac{1}{9\Delta}\left[[\Delta(2\bar{\theta} - \underline{\theta}) - (c_1' - c_2')]^2 - [(c_1' - c_2') - \Delta(2\underline{\theta} - \bar{\theta})]^2\right].$$

This is positive at an interior equilibrium when $c_1' = c_2'$, but the first term approaches zero as $(c_1' - c_2')$ approaches $\Delta(2\bar{\theta} - \underline{\theta})$ from below, in which case firm 2 earns higher profit. This is unsurprising: It can be worse to be the high quality firm when quality is sufficiently costly.

15.8 NOTES

Existence of an equilibrium profile for a noncooperative game of complete information is due to Nash [1]. Selten [3] formalized the subgame perfection concept.

Cournot [2] is the first mathematical treatment of duopoly, a very early presentation of the now famous Cournot duopoly in virtually the same form used today. Almost 50 years would pass before Bertrand's [4] price competition version of duopoly, which brought into doubt whether duopoly equilibria are "stable." Edgeworth [5] extended Bertrand's work and introduced capacity constraints. The stability debate led to Hotelling's Linear City [6]. The circular version was introduced by Salop [7]. d'Aspremont et al. [8] establish that a pure strategy Nash Equilibrium does not exist for some firm locations in the linear city when distance is measured as a simple difference, but that maximal differentiation occurs in equilibrium when distance is measured as the square of the location difference.

Stackelberg leadership is due to von Stackelberg [9]. Origins of the dominant firm/competitive fringe model are vague but an early presentation is in Nichol [10]. The representative consumer model with linear demands originated with Dixit [11] and was fully analyzed by Singh and

Vives [12]. The section on vertical differentiation is a generalization of Shaked and Sutton [13] and relies heavily on Tirole's [14, pp. 296–298] interpretation. I am grateful to Jonathan Hamilton for many comments on this chapter.

15.9 EXERCISES

1. Suppose two firms compete as homogeneous products Cournot duopolists. Aggregate inverse demand is $p = 12 - y$ for $0 \le y \le 12$. Firm one has constant marginal cost of 4 and firm two has constant marginal cost of 10. There are no fixed costs.
   - **a.** Find the Nash Equilibrium quantities and market price.
   - **b.** Suppose firm one is a monopolist. Find the quantity and price for this monopolist.
   - **c.** Compare your answers to parts (a) and (b), and explain the relationship.
2. Suppose two firms compete as homogeneous products Bertrand duopolists. Aggregate demand is $y = 100 - p$ for $0 \le p \le 100$. Firm one has constant marginal cost of 30 and firm two has constant marginal cost of 40. These are the only costs. Find the Nash Equilibrium prices. Explain why your prices are equilibrium. How much does each firm sell in equilibrium?
3. Carefully draw a graph of the best response functions for identical homogeneous products Cournot duopolists when demand and marginal cost are linear (and there are no fixed costs). Include on your graph the equilibrium isoprofit curve of each duopolist. Also include the equilibrium isoprofit curve for one of the duopolists when that firm is a Stackleberg leader rather than a Cournot competitor. Explain the slope and curvature of the isoprofit curves.
4. Consider a homogeneous products Cournot duopoly with aggregate inverse demand $p = 10 - y$ for $0 \le y \le 10$. Firm i has constant unit cost of production c_i for $i = 1, 2$.
   - **a.** Find the Nash Equilibrium quantities assuming $0 < c_i < 5$ for $i = 1, 2$.
   - **b.** What are the Nash Equilibrium quantities if $c_1 < c_2 < 10$ but $c_1 + 10 < 2c_2$?
5. Two homogeneous products Bertrand duopolists each have constant marginal cost $c = 4$ and compete for aggregate demand $y = 20 - p$ for $0 \le p \le 20$. These two sellers choose prices noncooperatively and

simultaneously (they split the market if they charge the same price). However, the only possible prices they can choose are either $p = 10$ or $p = 6$ (i.e., each seller's strategy space is the doubleton $\{10, 6\}$).

a. Describe Nash Equilibrium in this model.

b. What, if anything, about equilibrium changes if the two possible prices are $p = 10$ and $p = 7$? Why?

c. Now suppose the players move sequentially, with one of them (the leader) credibly committing to a price that is observed before the other (the follower) makes a price choice. Describe subgame perfect equilibrium if the only possible prices are $p = 10$ and $p = 6$. Describe subgame perfect equilibrium if the only possible prices are $p = 10$ and $p = 7$.

6. Suppose individual-firm average cost is $AC(y) = y + \frac{1}{y}$ and aggregate demand is $y = 100 - p$ for $0 \leq p \leq 100$.

a. Determine the optimal price and quantity for a monopolist. How much profit does the monopolist earn?

b. Determine the equilibrium price and quantities produced by two firms who behave as price-takers. How much profit does each firm earn?

c. Determine the equilibrium price and quantities produced by two firms who behave as Cournot competitors. How much profit does each firm earn?

d. Compare your answers to parts (a)–(c). Give *verbal intuition* for the results.

7. Suppose there are two identical firms each with average cost $AC(y) = \frac{1}{y} + y$, and aggregate inverse demand given in Exercise 4 in Chapter 14. How much (Marshallian) consumer surplus plus profit is lost if these firms engage in Cournot behavior rather than price-taking behavior?

8. Consider a market with two sellers. Market inverse demand for their homogenous product is $p = a - y$ for $0 \leq y \leq a$, where $y = y_1 + y_2$. Firm i's cost function is $c(y_i) = c_i y_i$, with $0 \leq c_1 < c_2 < a$.

a. Suppose the firms simultaneously and noncooperatively choose quantities. Find their Nash Equilibrium quantities.

b. Suppose firm 1 chooses its quantity first and firm 2 chooses its quantity after observing firm 1's choice. Find their subgame perfect equilibrium quantities.

c. Suppose the firms simultaneously and noncooperatively choose prices. Find their Nash Equilibrium prices.

9. Suppose we have a symmetric homogeneous products Cournot duopoly with aggregate inverse demand $p = 100 - y$ for $0 \leq y \leq 100$, where $y = y_1 + y_2$, and cost:

$$c(y_i) = \begin{cases} 0, & y_i = 0 \\ 1200 + y_i, & y_i > 0 \end{cases} \quad \text{for } i = 1, 2.$$

a. Derive the best response curves for these duopolists, and graph them.

b. What do you notice about Nash Equilibrium?

10. Suppose two firms compete as homogeneous products Cournot duopolists with aggregate inverse demand $p = 150 - y$ for $0 \le y \le 150$. Firm 1 has a non-sunk fixed cost of 1600 and a constant marginal cost of 10. Firm 2 has a non-sunk fixed cost of 900 and a constant marginal cost of 20.

a. Derive the best response curves of the two firms. Graph them, labeling slopes and all critical points.

b. Find all Nash Equilibria.

c. Suppose all consumers' income effects are zero for this good.

i. Which of the Nash Equilibria from part (a) delivers the highest aggregate welfare? Why?

ii. Can the outcome you identified in part (i) be assured by enacting a law that makes it illegal for one of the firms to produce, but does nothing else to regulate the firms? Why?

iii. Is the outcome you identified in part (i) Pareto Efficient? Why?

iv. Discuss equilibrium if the firms were to behave as price-takers.

11. Consider a market with 10 identical sellers, each of which has cost function $c(y) = y^2$, where y is the quantity produced by one seller. Aggregate demand is $Y = 780 - p$ for $0 \le p \le 780$, where Y is aggregate quantity and p is price per unit.

a. Derive the market equilibrium price and quantity when each seller behaves as a price-taker.

b. Derive the market equilibrium price and quantity when each seller behaves as a Cournot competitor.

c. How much (Marshallian, for consumers) deadweight loss is created by Cournot behavior?

d. What will happen in this market if there is free entry and a large number of identical potential entrants?

e. Suppose additional sellers with identical cost function can enter this market except that each entrant incurs a \$1000 sunk cost of entry. Each potential entrant anticipates before entry that, after entry, Cournot equilibrium will occur among the firms that have entered. How many firms will be in the market in a subgame perfect equilibrium?

12. A market has aggregate inverse demand $p = 11 - y$ for $0 \leq y \leq 11$, where p is price per unit (in dollars) and y is aggregate quantity. There is an integer number $\ell \geq 1$ of identical potential suppliers. The suppliers engage in a two-stage game: First they simultaneously and noncooperatively decide whether to pay a fixed cost of \$1 to enter the market. Those who do not pay the fixed cost cannot produce anything in the second stage. Those who pay the fixed cost compete as Cournot competitors in the second stage. The Cournot competitors have no costs in the second stage.
   a. Find the subgame perfect equilibrium quantities and price as functions of the number of potential suppliers ℓ (assume firms always choose to enter the market if their profit from entering and not entering is the same).
   b. Now find equilibrium welfare (defined as the aggregate of industry profit and Marshallian consumer surplus) as a function of ℓ.
   c. Show whether welfare with a large number of potential suppliers is above or below welfare under monopoly.
   d. Suppose the government can regulate the number of potential suppliers. How many potential suppliers should the government choose to maximize welfare? Why?
13. Suppose there are k identical price-taking consumers, each with monetary resources m and utility function $u(x, x_2) = \ln x + \ln x_2$. Let p denote the price of x and assume the price of x_2 has been normalized to one. Suppose also there are ℓ identical producers of x, each with constant marginal cost $c > 0$ and no fixed costs.
   a. Derive the aggregate demand for x.
   b. Write the revenue function for the monopolist when $\ell = 1$. What is unusual about this revenue function? What does this imply about the monopolist's optimal behavior?
   c. If the firm(s) behave as price-takers, what is the equilibrium price of x?
   d. Suppose for the remainder of this problem that $\ell \geq 2$. Derive the Cournot equilibrium price of x as a function of the number of firms ℓ. How many firms are required to drive the Cournot equilibrium price down to within 10% of the perfectly competitive price?
   e. Derive an expression for the deadweight loss that is incurred if the government compensates consumers for the higher price caused by the non-price-taking behavior of the Cournot oligopolists. (Hint: From your calculations in part (a), find the indirect utility function for one consumer and invert it to obtain the expenditure

function. Evaluate the expenditure function at arbitrary p and at the optimal utility level for the perfectly competitive price, and then multiply by k to obtain the aggregate expenditure function for the perfectly competitive utility level. Use this to derive deadweight loss.) Suppose there are $k = 1$ million consumers who each have monetary resources of $m = \$30$ thousand, and there are enough firms to make the Cournot equilibrium price no more than 10% above the perfectly competitive price. How large is the deadweight loss?

14. Suppose two firms compete as Stackelberg duopolists. Label the leader ℓ and the follower f. Each firm has constant marginal cost of 10. This marginal cost is the only cost for the leader. The follower, however, has an avoidable fixed cost of $F > 0$. Aggregate inverse demand is $p = 100 - y$ for $0 \leq y \leq 100$, where p is price per unit and y is aggregate quantity.

a. Derive and graph the follower's best response curve for an arbitrary value of F, labeling the slope, intercepts and any other important points. Illustrate how the best response curve changes as F increases from zero to an arbitrarily large number.

b. Illustrate some typical isoprofit lines for the leader on your graph from part (a), indicating the direction of increasing profit.

c. Now adopt the following terminology to describe possible subgame perfect equilibrium behavior by the leader: (1) The leader *accommodates entry* if the follower produces positive output in equilibrium; (2) The leader *deters entry* if the follower produces zero output in equilibrium but the leader's output choice is affected by the presence of the follower; and (3) The leader *blockades entry* if the follower produces zero output in equilibrium and the leader's output choice is unaffected by the presence of the follower. Draw three graphs, each with the follower's best response curve and the leader's optimal isoprofit line for that best response curve. The graphs should differ in the level of F illustrated. One graph should illustrate *entry accommodation*, one should illustrate *entry deterrence*, and one should illustrate *entry blockade*.

d. What is the critical value of F at which the equilibrium switches between entry accommodation and entry deterrence? Illustrate this value of F on a best response curve/isoprofit graph.

e. What is the critical value of F at which the equilibrium switches between entry deterrence and entry blockade? Illustrate this value of F on a best response curve/isoprofit graph.

15. Consider the model of Exercise 6 in Chapter 13.

a. Assume there are two sellers who compete by choosing quantities simultaneously and noncooperatively. Seller 1 has constant marginal cost c_1 and seller 2 has constant marginal cost c_2. Assume $c_1 < c_2 < A$, there are no other costs, and both sellers know all these parameters. Find all Nash Equilibria and explain why they are equilibria.

b. Now assume the duopolists described in item (a) compete by choosing prices simultaneously and noncooperatively rather than quantities. Find all Nash Equilibria, and explain why they are equilibria.

c. Now assume seller 1 described in item (a) is a Stackelberg leader and seller 2 is a Stackelberg follower. Find all subgame perfect equilibria. What happens if the roles of leader and follower are reversed?

d. Compare and contrast the efficiency (Marshallian consumer surplus plus profit) of the equilibria in items (a)–(c).

16. Suppose aggregate demand is $y = 100 - p$ for $0 \leq p \leq 100$, where p is the price per unit and y is the number of units sold. Assume there are two firms whose only costs are the constant marginal costs c_1 and c_2.

a. If firm 1 is a monopoly, how much does it produce? What price does it charge? How much profit does it earn?

b. If the two firms compete as Cournot duopolists, how much does each firm produce at an interior equilibrium? What is the aggregate quantity? What is the equilibrium price? How much profit does each firm earn?

c. Denote by p_1 the monopoly price charged by firm 1 in part (a). How much does firm 2 produce in the Cournot equilibrium if $c_2 = p_1$? Assume the area under the Marshallian demand measures consumer welfare. What happens to aggregate welfare (sum of consumer surplus and profit) in the Cournot equilibrium when there is a small decrease in c_2 from the level $c_2 = p_1$? Does the introduction of Cournot competition benefit society (compared with monopoly) when the new firm has marginal cost near the existing monopoly price? Why? What if the new firm has marginal cost near the marginal cost of the existing monopolist? Why?

d. If the two firms compete as Bertrand duopolists, what price does each firm charge in equilibrium? How much does each firm produce? What is the aggregate quantity?

e. Is society better off under Bertrand competition than under monopoly? Why? Is the conclusion different from when the duopolists compete in quantities? Why?

17. Assume we are studying a market with aggregate inverse demand $p = 10 - 2Y$ for $0 \leq Y \leq 5$, where p is market price and Y is market quantity; and all firms produce homogeneous products and are identical with individual cost functions:

$$c(y) = \begin{cases} 6y - y^2, & 0 \leq y \leq 2 \\ 4 + 2y, & 2 \leq y \end{cases},$$

where y is the output of one firm and c is the cost of one firm. Also assume consumer welfare can be measured by Marshallian consumer surplus.

a. Carefully draw the market demand, individual marginal cost, and market marginal revenue curves on one graph. Label the intercepts, slopes, and points where the curves cross.

b. Is there a price-taking equilibrium in this market with only one firm? If so, what is it?

c. What is the monopoly output and price?

d. What is the socially efficient output level?

e. Compare your answers to items (b) and (d). Explain why your answers are consistent with the First Theorem of Welfare Economics.

f. Calculate the deadweight loss in the monopoly outcome.

g. Find the Cournot duopoly symmetric Nash Equilibrium output of each firm, and the equilibrium price.

h. Calculate the deadweight loss in the symmetric Cournot duopoly Nash Equilibrium (be careful!).

i. Compare your answers to items (f) and (h), and give an economic explanation.

j. At what price does a single seller make zero profit?

k. Is the price you found in item (j) a Nash Equilibrium price in a Bertrand Duopoly? Explain why or why not.

l. Suppose firm 1 is the leader and firm 2 is the follower in a Stackelberg duopoly. Find the subgame perfect Nash Equilibrium strategy profile (state the equilibrium strategies carefully!).

18. Assume aggregate inverse demand is $p = 100 - y$ for $0 \leq p \leq 100$. Assume also there are two firms whose only costs are the constant marginal costs $c_1 = 50$ and $c_2 = 72$.

a. Suppose the two firms compete as Cournot duopolists. Carefully draw the best response curves, labeling slopes, intercepts, and the equilibrium values. What is the aggregate quantity in equilibrium? What is the equilibrium price? How much profit does each firm earn in equilibrium?

b. If firm 1 is a monopoly, how much does it produce? What price does it charge? How much profit does it earn?

c. Carefully draw a graph of market demand. Mark the prices and aggregate quantities from parts (a) and (b) on your graph.

d. Assume consumers' income effects are zero at all prices under consideration. On your graph from part (c), shade the equivalent variation when the market moves from the monopoly in part (b) to the duopoly in part (a). Calculate this equivalent variation. Does the Cournot competition in part (a) improve social welfare relative to the monopoly situation in part (b)? Explain why or why not.

e. If the two firms compete as Bertrand duopolists, what price does each firm charge in equilibrium? How much does each firm produce? What is the aggregate quantity?

f. Put the price and aggregate quantity from part (e) on your graph from part (c). Continuing to assume consumers' income effects are zero, is society better off under Bertrand competition than under the monopoly in part (b)? Why? Contrast your answer with your answer about social welfare from part (d).

g. Suppose the two firms find a way to collude. How much should each firm produce in order to maximize collusive profit? Suppose each firm believes they will end up in the Cournot equilibrium if they don't collude. How should the collusive profit be divided in order to enforce collusion?

h. Suppose the two firms compete as Stackelberg duopolists with firm 1 the leader and firm 2 the follower. Find the subgame perfect equilibrium. Use isoprofit lines to illustrate this equilibrium on your graph from part (a). What is the equilibrium price? How much profit does each firm earn in equilibrium? Still assuming consumers' income effects are zero, is society better off under this Stackelberg competition than under the monopoly situation in part (b)? Explain why. Contrast your answer with your answer about social welfare from part (d).

i. Suppose the two firms are each price-takers. What are the equilibrium price and market quantity? How much does each firm produce in equilibrium?

j. Now change the assumption that income effects are zero. In particular, suppose the good is normal. Does this change your answer from part (d) about whether society is better off under Cournot competition than the monopoly in part (b)? Does it change your answer from part (f) about social welfare? Does it change your answer from part (h) about social welfare? Draw graphs to illustrate and explain your answers.

19. Consider a duopoly with aggregate inverse demand $p = a - by$ for $0 \leq y \leq a/b$. Firm $i = 1, 2$ has cost function $C(y_i) = cy_i$, where y_i is the output of firm i (so $y = y_1 + y_2$). Assume $a > c > 0$ and $b > 0$. Suppose the firms each choose their outputs simultaneously and noncooperatively to maximize a weighted sum of their own profit and own revenue. Each firm puts the same weight of α $(0 < \alpha < 1)$ on profit and $(1 - \alpha)$ on revenue.

a. Find the Nash Equilibrium quantities.

b. Compare the Nash Equilibrium quantities in part (a) with the Nash Equilibrium quantities when the firms maximize profit.

c. Solve for the Stackelberg equilibrium quantities, assuming firm 1 is the leader and each firm maximizes its weighted average of profit and revenue.

20. Suppose a small city sells licenses to taxi drivers. A taxi cannot operate in the city without a license. The licensed taxis compete as identical Cournot competitors with aggregate inverse demand $p = \alpha - \frac{y}{10}$ for $0 \leq y \leq 10\alpha$, where y is the quantity of taxi services consumed. Each taxi has total cost $c(y_i) = y_i^2$, where y_i is the output of taxi i. Suppose the city wants to maximize its revenue from license sales. How many licenses should the city sell?

21. Suppose the city of New York requires that each taxicab have a license. Aggregate inverse demand for taxi service is $p = 510 - Y$ for $0 \leq Y \leq 510$, where Y is the quantity of taxi services consumed. Each taxi has cost $c = 1 + y^2$ where y is the quantity supplied by the individual taxi, not including the cost of the license, and each taxi behaves as a price-taker. There is a large number of potential sellers of taxi services.

a. If the city auctions 100 licenses and the auction result is all licenses sold at their profit potential, what will the auction price of the licenses be? How much revenue does the city receive?

b. If the city issues a license to anybody that wants one, how many licenses will be issued?

c. How much Marshallian consumer surplus is lost due to the supply restriction of only 100 licenses?

d. Suppose the city gives all of the revenue from selling the 100 licenses to consumers, in a way that does not depend on the quantity of taxi services consumed. Can the city fully reimburse consumers for their lost Marshallian surplus? If not, how much surplus is still lost after the rebate?

e. Now suppose the city wants to maximize revenue from auctioning the licenses (with the auction result again that all licenses are sold at their profit potential). Let ℓ be the number of licenses offered for sale, so that the city's problem is to choose the optimal ℓ. For an individual supplier of taxi services, the price depends on ℓ and so the optimal profit of each supplier depends on ℓ. Denote this by $\pi^*(\ell)$. In this notation, what is the city's revenue from offering ℓ licenses for sale? (Note: do not attempt to find $\pi^*(\ell)$). Explain how you would use the Envelope Theorem in finding the optimal number of licenses for the city (but do not actually try to find the optimal ℓ).

22. Suppose the city of New York requires that each taxicab have a license. Aggregate inverse demand for taxi service is $p = 1011 - Y$ for $0 \leq Y \leq 1011$, where Y is the market quantity of taxi services consumed. There is a large number of potential sellers of taxi services, each with cost $c = 100 + y$ for $y > 0$ (not including the cost of the license), where y is the quantity of taxi services produced by the individual taxi. Suppose each licensed taxi behaves as a Cournot competitor, and that the equilibrium is symmetric.

a. If the city sells 9 licenses, what is the maximum price the city can charge per license? How much total revenue would the city receive?

b. If the city issues a free license to any seller of taxi services that wants a license, how many licenses will be issued?

c. How much Marshallian consumer surplus is lost due to the supply restriction of only nine licenses?

d. Suppose the city gives to consumers all of the revenue from selling nine licenses at the maximum possible price. Are consumers better or worse off than in the case where licenses are distributed for free? Explain.

e. Can you think of a way that the city council might be able to improve consumer welfare relative to the identified approaches? Assume the city has full information on firms' cost functions.

23. Suppose there are ℓ identical Cournot competitors, each of which has constant marginal cost of 1 and no other costs. Aggregate inverse demand is $p = 10-2y$ for $y \in [0, 5]$. The United States Department of Justice considers any firm whose price exceeds marginal cost by more than 5% to have market power. How many firms must exist in this market in order for the US Department of Justice to judge that the firms do not have market power? Explain.

24. Suppose ℓ identical firms compete by simultaneously and noncooperatively choosing quantities of their homogeneous products. Aggregate inverse demand is $p = 100 - y$ for $0 \le y \le 100$ and the only non-sunk cost is constant marginal cost equal to 20.

a. How large must ℓ be to assure that the Nash Equilibrium price-cost margin satisfies the Justice Department's guideline of being no larger than 5%? Show why.

b. Suppose $\ell = 2$ and there is no possibility of entry by additional firms. How much is one of the firms willing to pay to acquire the other firm before the quantity-setting occurs? Assume there are no income effects. How much Marshallian deadweight loss would be created by an acquisition like this?

c. Now suppose, in addition to the ℓ firms described in part (a), there is an additional firm (label it firm 0). This firm has marginal cost of 20 like all of the other firms, but selects its quantity before the other ℓ firms. In other words, this firm behaves as a Stackelberg leader and the other ℓ firms behave as simultaneous followers.

i. Let $\pi_0^*(\ell)$ be the equilibrium profit of firm 0. Use the envelope theorem to show that $\frac{\partial \pi_0^*}{\partial \ell} = -(\ell + 1)^{-1}\pi_0^*(\ell)$ (ignore the integer constraint on ℓ when doing this).

ii. How much does firm 0 produce in equilibrium?

25. The *Herfindahl Index* is a measure of industry concentration sometimes used in antitrust analyses. It is defined as the sum of squares of each firm's quantity as a proportion of industry quantity. With ℓ firms:

$$H = \sum_{i=1}^{\ell} \left(\frac{y_i}{Y}\right)^2,$$

where y_i is the quantity sold by firm i and $Y = \sum_{j=1}^{\ell} y_j$ is aggregate quantity. Thus, if only one firm has positive output the index is one, while if the firms are equally sized the index is $\frac{1}{\ell}$. A higher index indicates a more concentrated industry.

Consider now the market of Exercise 19, except there are ℓ firms and each has its own constant marginal cost c_i and no other costs (so the firms are not symmetric), and the firms maximize profit (i.e., act as homogeneous products Cournot competitors). Assume a unique interior Cournot equilibrium $(y_1^e, \ldots, y_\ell^e)$.

a. Show that firm i's equilibrium profit is $\pi_i^e = b(y_i^e)^2$.

b. Sum to obtain equilibrium industry profit Π^e, and divide the result by equilibrium industry revenue $R^e = p^e Y^e$.

c. Write an expression for the price elasticity of demand at the equilibrium in terms of industry revenue and industry output.

d. Multiply the result from (b) by the result from (c) to obtain H. This shows that the Herfindahl Index can be motivated as industry profits as a percent of industry revenue, scaled by the demand elasticity, in a Cournot equilibrium (when all firms have constant returns).

26. Suppose aggregate demand is $y = 100 - p$ for $0 \leq p \leq 100$. Assume there is a dominant firm with cost function $c_d(y_d) = y_d$ and a competitive fringe with ℓ identical firms, each of which has cost function $c_f(y_f) = 10y_f + 10y_f^2$, where y_d is the output of the dominant firm and y_f is the output of a typical fringe firm (so $y = y_d + \ell y_f$).

a. Assume $\ell < 180$. How much does the dominant firm produce, and what price does it charge?

b. What happens to the output of the dominant firm in part (a) if ℓ increases? Give a graphical and verbal explanation for this.

c. How much does the dominant firm produce and what price does it charge if $\ell > 180$?

27. Consider a homogeneous-products Cournot oligopoly with inverse market demand $p(Y)$, where Y is aggregate output, and ℓ identical competitors each with cost function $c(y)$ (y is individual-firm output). Assume there is a symmetric interior equilibrium, and assume for this equilibrium that individual-firm output decreases as ℓ increases while aggregate output increases as ℓ increases. Use the Envelope Theorem to determine whether individual-firm equilibrium profit increases or decreases as ℓ increases.

28. Consider the following duopoly. There is a leader who chooses an output level. The follower observes the leader's output choice and then chooses the market price, under the assumption that the leader's output will be sold at that price and the follower can then sell output equal to the remaining demand at that price. Compare this model to the Stackelberg duopoly.

29. Consider a market with aggregate demand $D(p) = 10 - p$ for $0 \leq p \leq 10$. The production technology for this good is summarized by the cost function $c(y) = F + y^2/F$, where y is the output of one supplier and $c(y)$ is that supplier's total cost of producing y units. F is an investment in the scale of the production process. $F > 0$ can be chosen by each supplier before production takes place. When a supplier chooses investment level F, variable cost is y^2/F and the amount invested (i.e., F) becomes sunk.

a. Carefully draw the average and marginal cost curves for a supplier who has sunk $F = 1$. Carefully draw the same curves for a supplier who has sunk $F = 2$. Finally, carefully draw the curves for arbitrary F. What are the long-run (i.e., when F is variable) average and marginal cost curves?

b. Suppose there is a monopolist who chooses F first and then chooses output in the standard monopoly way. What values of F, output, and price will the monopolist choose? Illustrate the monopolist's choice on a graph of demand, marginal revenue, and the cost curves. Comment on the monopolist's efficiency.

c. Suppose there are ℓ suppliers with this production technology. They compete in two stages. In the first stage, the suppliers simultaneously and noncooperatively choose investment levels $F_1, \ldots, F_\ell$. After these investment levels are sunk and observed by all ℓ suppliers, the suppliers simultaneously and noncooperatively choose quantities. The suppliers are price-takers in BOTH stages. That is, they assume their choice of production level does not affect price in the second stage, and assume their choice of investment level in the first stage does not affect the equilibrium price that will ultimately occur in the second stage. Find the (symmetric) subgame perfect equilibrium price, aggregate quantity, and investment level of each supplier. Illustrate this equilibrium on a graph of demand, the cost curves of one supplier, and the aggregate second-stage supply curve of all suppliers. Comment on the equilibrium.

30. Consider an oligopoly with three firms producing homogeneous products and aggregate inverse demand $p = 80 - y$ for $0 \leq y \leq 80$. The three firms have constant marginal costs of $MC_1 = 10$, $MC_2 = 20$, and $MC_3 = 30$; and no other costs. Suppose firm 1 behaves as a Stackelberg leader, and firms 2 and 3 behave as (simultaneous with each other) Stackelberg followers. Find the equilibrium quantities, price, and profits. Do all firms produce positive output in equilibrium?

31. Two sellers compete in a duopoly market by simultaneously and non-cooperatively choosing prices. Seller one has demand $y_1 = \max\{0, 10-2p_1 + p_2\}$ and seller 2 has demand $y_2 = \max\{0, 10 - 4p_2 + p_1\}$ (y_i is the quantity for seller i and p_i is the price for seller i). Marginal costs are constant at $MC_1 = 5$ and $MC_2 = 4$, and these are the only costs. Find the best response functions of the sellers and carefully graph them. Then find the Nash Equilibrium.

32. Suppose there is one seller located in the middle of a Hotelling linear city. That is, the city is the interval $[0, 1]$; consumers all have unit demands with reservation price R and are uniformly distributed in the city; and the sole seller has zero cost and is located at $1/2$. Assume further that each consumer incurs "transport cost" equal to t times the *square* of the distance between the consumer's location and the seller's location. Derive the optimal price, quantity, and profit for the seller. How does the optimum depend on the ratio R/t? Interpret your conclusion.

33. Suppose an economic actor's objective is to choose a variable y to maximize an objective $f(y; \theta)$, where θ is a parameter that the actor takes as given when making the choice of y. Assume there is a unique choice of y that is characterized by standard calculus conditions.

a. What is the critical feature of the objective function f that determines whether the actor's choice of y will increase or decrease when θ increases?

b. Suppose the actor is a profit-maximizing firm with cost function $c(y)$ (y is output here) that is a price-taker in its output market. What does your answer to part (a) say about how supply will respond to an increase in fixed cost? Be sure to relate your answer to part (a).

c. Suppose the actor is a differentiated Bertrand duopolist who takes the rival's price as fixed, with demand $D(p; p^r)$ and constant marginal cost c, where p is the own-price and p^r is the rival's price. Based on your answer to part (a), is substitute products sufficient for an increase in the rival's price to cause an increase in this duopolist's price choice? If not, give a graphical and intuitive explanation why. Be sure to relate your answer to part (a).

d. Suppose the actor is a homogeneous Cournot duopolist with market inverse demand $p(y + y^r)$ and constant marginal cost c, where y is the own-quantity and y^r the rival's quantity. Based on your answer to part (a), what does an increase in this duopolist's marginal cost do to its best response curve? Assuming the duopolists' best response curves are downward sloping and yield a unique and stable equilibrium, what does an increase in marginal cost do to the Cournot equilibrium? Again, be sure to relate your answer to part (a).

34. Suppose aggregate demand is the continuous function $D(p)$ and there are three homogeneous products Bertrand competitors whose only costs are constant marginal costs c_i for $i = 1, 2, 3$, all below the low-cost firm's monopoly price. Assume $c_2 = c_3$. What is the Nash Equilibrium if $c_1 < c_2$? What is the Nash Equilibrium if $c_1 \geq c_2$? Comment.

35. Consider duopolists with zero cost in Hotelling's linear city. Assume consumers all have reservation price R, are uniformly distributed in the city, and have transport cost t per unit of linear distance. The firms compete in two stages. In the first stage they simultaneously and noncooperatively choose locations ℓ_1 and ℓ_2. In the second stage both firms observe ℓ_1 and ℓ_2; and then simultaneously and noncooperatively choose prices p_1 and p_2. Assume transport cost is high relative to reservation prices, so that $\frac{R}{t} \leq \frac{1}{2}$. Find a subgame perfect equilibrium. Is it unique?

36. Here is a two-stage duopoly game. In stage 1, firm 1 chooses a level of advertising $A \geq 0$ at cost $g(A)$. In stage 2, firm 2 observes A, decides whether to enter, and if entry occurs competes simultaneously and noncooperatively with firm 1. The entry cost for firm 2 is $F \geq 0$ (and is sunk for firm 1 before stage 1). We are interested in subgame perfect equilibria.

a. Suppose the second stage consists of differentiated products price competition with demands:

$$y_1 = 1 + A - p_1 + bp_2$$
$$y_2 = 1 - p_2 + bp_1,$$

where $b \in (0, 1)$. Use the Envelope Theorem to write a *symbolic* expression for the effect of firm 1's advertising on firm 2's second stage equilibrium profit (assuming firm 2 entered at stage 1). Because g is not specified, you cannot do this by solving for the downstream equilibrium—do it by exploring how the best response curves shift and then stating the effect of the resulting change on firm 2's profit.

b. Perform the same analysis when the second stage consists of differentiated products quantity competition with inverse demands:

$$p_1 = 1 + A - y_1 + by_2$$
$$p_2 = 1 - y_2 + by_1$$

where, again, $b \in (0, 1)$. What do you notice about the answers to parts (a) and (b)? What is "unusual" about the demands in part (b)?

c. Now suppose $g(A) = A^2$ and $F = 0$. Solve for the subgame perfect equilibrium when second stage competition is in quantities. Does firm 1 blockade, deter, or accommodate (see Exercise 14)?

37. Consider duopolists with zero cost located at the endpoints of Hotelling's linear city. Assume consumers all have reservation price R that is sufficiently large to ensure full coverage, are uniformly distributed in the city, and have transport cost t per *squared* unit of linear distance. Find the Nash Equilibrium prices.

REFERENCES

[1] Nash JF. Equilibrium points in N-person games. Proc Natl Acad Sci 1950;46:48–9.
[2] Cournot A. Recherches sur les Principes Mathématiques de la Théorie des Richesses. Paris: Hachette; 1838. English translation: "Researches into the mathematical principles of the theory of wealth" by Bacon N. New York: MacMillan; 1897.
[3] Selten R. Spieltheoretische Behandlung eines Oligopolmodells mit Nachfragetragheit. Zeitschrift fur die gesamte Staatswissenschaft 1965;121:301–24.
[4] Bertrand J. Théorie Mathématique de la Richesse Sociale. J Savants 1883;499–508.
[5] Edgeworth FY. Teoria Pura del Monopolio. Giornale degli Economisti 1897. English translation: Papers relating to political economy, vol. I. London: MacMillan; 1925. p. 116–26.
[6] Hotelling H. Stability in competition. Econ J 1929;39:41–57.
[7] Salop S. Monopolistic competition with outside goods. Bell J Econ 1979;10:141–56.
[8] d'Aspremont C, Gabszewicz J, Thisse JF. On Hotelling's stability in competition. Econometrica 1979;17:1145–51.
[9] von Stackelberg H. Marktform und Gleichgewicht. Vienna: Julius Springer; 1934. English translation: "Market structure and equilibrium" by Bazin D, Urch L, Hill R. Berlin: Springer-Verlag; 2011.
[10] Nichol AJ. Partial monopoly and price leadership: a study in economic theory. Philadelphia: Smith-Edwards; 1930.
[11] Dixit A. A model of duopoly suggesting a theory of entry barriers. Bell J Econ 1979;10:20–32.
[12] Singh N, Vives X. Price and quantity competition in a differentiated duopoly. RAND J Econ 1984;15:546–54.
[13] Shaked A, Sutton J. Relaxing price competition through product differentiation. Rev Econ Stud 1982;49:3–13.
[14] Tirole J. The theory of industrial organization. Cambridge, MA: MIT Press; 1988.

INDEX

Note: Page numbers followed by *f* indicate figures and *np* indicate footnotes.

D

N

O

Q

R

Printed in the United States
By Bookmasters